This modern text is designed to prepare you for your future professional career. While theories, ideas, techniques, and data are dynamic, the information contained in this volume will provide you a quick and useful reference as well as a guide for future learning for many years to come. Your familiarity with the contents of this book will make it an important volume in your professional library.

EX LIBRIS

Operations Management

Productivity and quality

Operations Management

Productivity and quality

Richard J. Schonberger
College of Business Administration
University of Nebraska

1985   Second Edition

BUSINESS PUBLICATIONS, INC.
Plano, Texas   75075

ISBN 0-256-03074-X

Library of Congress Catalog Card No. 83–62733

Printed in the United States of America

1 2 3 4 5 6 7 8 9 0 K 2 1 0 9 8 7 6 5

Preface

The current era in production/operations management is one of profound changes in concepts and techniques. The changes were triggered by growing awareness in North America of industrial complacency and malaise. The first reactions were hand-wringing, blaming, and finger-pointing. But these have given ground to reflecting on our wasteful ways and setting forth on a course of improvement. Operations management instruction cannot stand still and silently observe (or ignore) the changes that are under way in industry. This edition of *Operations Management* is a significant revision, which I believe is necessitated by the course of events.

Productivity and Quality

Throughout the industrially developed world the typical long-term rate of productivity improvement of labor is around two or three percent per year. We thought a company was doing well when, through good management, the rate of improvement could be nudged upward to four or five percent per year. But companies able to achieve the higher rates found they were still losing ground in global competition. One reason: In the 1960s and 1970s the rate of productivity improvement in Japan was eight or nine percent—about double that of the good Western companies (and over three times higher than the U.S. average).

The first significant revelation was finding out that the Japanese have been using quality control practices far more rigorous than our own. Many of their *techniques* of quality control originated in the United States, although the Japanese developed a few new techniques and also refined some of the overriding concepts of quality assurance. Perhaps more important than the techniques and concepts is the positioning of *quality,* center stage in the competitive strategy of the organization.

The believers in quality as a strategic weapon base those beliefs not only on the appeal of quality itself in the marketplace but also in cost savings, that is, the avoidance of the costly waste of making defective products. Cost savings and productivity improvement come from a variety of other factors as well, especially from rigorous attention to preventing and solving problems: keeping machines from breaking down or malfunctioning, keeping tools sharp and gauges calibrated, making sure that materials and other resources arrive on time, figuring out how to change quickly from one product model to another and from one design to another, and creating a climate for all employees to solve problems instead of trying to live with them.

Problem Solving

Trying to live with problems or plan around them can be a fatal error. The problems covered up are contributors to poor quality, high cost, and loss of markets. Making a transition to problem *solving* requires phasing out wasteful backup options: Reshape the work environment so that people cannot easily get by without making improvements.

An analogy may be helpful: We all know of somebody's son or daughter who moved out of the family home into an apartment, taking along dishes and other cooking supplies. The cooking commences. Dishes get dirty and fill up the kitchen sink. Soon the clean ones are gone. Time to wash dishes? No! Go back to mother's and get another box of dishes. Or just go out to a restaurant and let someone else take care of problems like dirty dishes.

This scenario is not unlike conditions in many of our factories, offices, and other work places. Employees come to depend on having storehouses full of extra parts—safety stock, we call it—to smooth out problems. It is like having cabinets full of clean dishes so that there is no need to wash the dirty ones. And our production employees rely on outside experts to change light bulbs, clean typewriters, fix machines, move materials, sort out defective parts, plan and control the work flow, and so forth. This is rather like going to restaurants so those who do the eating do not have to plan menus, buy groceries, cook, or clean up.

Remove the excess stock and cut back on the number of outside experts. The effect on the worker is profound: It becomes hard to meet a schedule without making adjustments and solving problems as they occur. The operator's job is not just to produce, but also to apply experience and good sense to diagnosing and perhaps solving the problems that occur at that operator's work site. For example, in the case of dishes to do all the time and no one to do them for you, you might be able to suggest (or invent) a type of self-cleaning dish or a dish that rejects contaminants, which would permanently remove the aggravation.

Merger of Old and New

The details of how to stimulate problem solving are contained in the chapters—amidst a good deal of other material. My goal in writing this second edition was to effect a merger: Take the best of the old materials and combine them with the new materials on harnessing frugality and simplicity to stimulate quality and productivity. There are grounds for thinking that a more satisfying work life for both operators and professionals is a part of the package of benefits that should come from the improved operations management practices of the new era.

There are a few wholly new chapters in this edition. Most of the rest have been modified a good deal. A new emphasis on strategy and effects on people is found in most chapters. Major changes in techniques and tools are found in just a few chapters, which minimizes the difficulties for instructors in making the transition from the first to the second edition.

Integrating the Professions

A goal of the first edition was to prepare college students for what they will find in business and industry and also to help with the continuing education of people already employed in operations management positions. For example, the first edition included extensive materials useful in studying for the certification examinations of the American Production and Inventory Control Society (APICS). Those materials are preserved and strengthened. Now APICS has launched a new campaign for the 1980s—the "zero inventory" or "just-in-time" production crusade, which is based on Japanese techniques. This edition fully incorporates materials that are emphasized in the new APICS crusade.

Even more importantly, the second edition attempts to *integrate* the concerns of APICS with those of other top professional societies in operations management, for example, the American Society for Quality Control, the National Association for Purchasing Management, and the Institute of Industrial Engineers. These and other societies ought to be preaching the same message. Part of the message is for professionals to stay out of the operators' and supervisors' hair and let them solve as many problems as they can—using their superior experience and perspective; respond to calls for help; and, in pursuing overall strategy, play a statesman's role, rather than just the limited role of practicing one's own narrow specialty.

Those Who Helped

Professors Edward Knod, Dennis McLeavey, and Ralph Hocking reviewed early drafts of this edition. I am grateful for their insightful suggestions—roughly reflecting three different kinds of concerns. Practicality, teachability, and rigor are what those fine reviewers sought in the new edition, and my challenge was to try to achieve all three.

Later materials were reviewed by Professors Edward Thode, Joseph Biggs, and Daniel McNamara. These levelheaded gentlemen reined me in a bit. I had been infected by the zeal for change that I have been witnessing in some of the better-known North American companies, and the original draft of the manuscript was aimed too much in that direction; I hope that the final version is evenhanded and relevant also for organizations that are slow or cautious about adopting new ideas.

The death of my editor, Donald A. Kolbe, Jr., near the end of the writing process was a setback. Don had encouraged me to go ahead with my notions about trying to help usher in a new approach to instruction in operations management. His appreciation for what I had in mind was inspirational. I hope that the end product would have pleased him.

Richard J. Schonberger

Contents

Operations Management

Productivity and quality

Part One

Introduction to Operations Management

The operating end of the business is where the goods are made and services provided, and it is where most of the money is spent and people are employed. How are operations managed? That is the question that this book addresses. Part One breaks that grand question into detailed issues.

The first chapter in Part One introduces the reader to the functions of operations management. It also provides background and sorts out the different kinds of operating environments. Chapter 2 presents operations strategy, which ties the operations themselves to the goals of the whole organization.

CHAPTER 1
Looking at Operations
  Management

CHAPTER 2
Operations Strategy

CASE STUDY
Automated Parking Systems, Inc.

Chapter 1

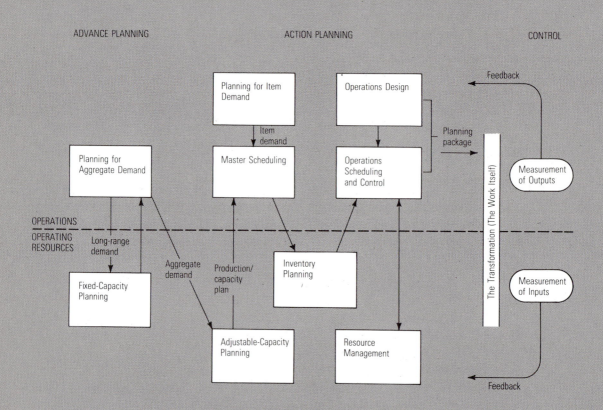

ADVANCE PLANNING

ACTION PLANNING

CONTROL

Planning for Item Demand

Operations Design

Feedback

Planning for Aggregate Demand

Item demand

Master Scheduling

Operations Scheduling and Control

Planning package

The Transformation (The Work Itself)

Measurement of Outputs

OPERATIONS

OPERATING RESOURCES

Long-range demand

Fixed-Capacity Planning

Aggregate demand

Production/ capacity plan

Inventory Planning

Measurement of Inputs

Adjustable-Capacity Planning

Resource Management

Feedback

Looking at Operations Management

This is a book about managing ends and means. Productive **operations,** resulting in goods and services, are the ends, and **operating resources** are the means. Providing goods and services is a group effort. Designers design the goods and services, operators produce them, and support people keep the operators supplied with the right resources. The manager tries to coordinate all of these people and their activities. This book concerns the coordination, or management, role.

Management of operations and operating resources is a matter of planning, supervision, and control. Supervision is not included in this book, because it is a *general* function, not one that is unique to operating personnel. Furthermore, we shall not concern ourselves with work activities themselves but rather with the planning and control of the work.

PLANNING AND CONTROL: TOOLS AND MODELS

The modern course in production/operations management (POM) includes a large variety of planning and control tools. POM studies are less theoretical and more application oriented than are most management studies. Emphasis is on techniques—graphic, mathematical, and procedural—and on ways to get the POM functions to run smoothly as a system.

Scientific Management and Operations Research

The graphic tools are the heritage of the pioneers of **scientific management,** whose work began around the turn of the century. They used numbers for measurement but did not rely much on mathematical approaches. Work sequence charts are one example of a graphic tool. A general example is shown in Figure 1–1. The arrows and circles (or other geometric figures) in a work sequence chart go by many names, including flowchart, block diagram, network, lead-time chart, gozinto chart, and assembly diagram.

Some mathematical and statistical tools were pulled together during World War II as the foundation for **operations research,** also called **management science** (which is quite different from scientific management). Queuing models and statistical probability distributions are examples with which some readers may be familiar. Operations research provides tools for complex decisions involving costly resources, which certainly include the operating resources that are of concern in this book. We shall draw on some of the operations research tools in our discussions of operating resource management.

The graphic and mathematical tools are often called **models.** The idea is that the operations manager creates a model or likeness of the reality: the flows of work through an office, the costs that are likely to arise if a certain action is taken, the resources that are required as a result of a demand forecast, and so forth.

Mental processes in decision making may also be thought of as modeling. Relying on mental models is sometimes referred to as the "fire-fighting" approach—in contrast to the planning approach to operations management. If you are, by nature, more of a fire fighter than a planner, do not feel that you are out of place in operations management. The practice of POM has by no means been reduced to graphics, numbers, and plans that work. Nor will it be in the foreseeable future. Actually there is not a wide gulf between the planning and the fire-fighting approach, because good planning narrows the margins of error so that fire fighting can be more effective.

FIGURE 1–1

A Graphic Tool: The Work Sequence Chart

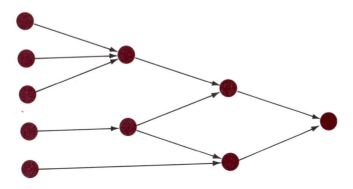

Standard Operating Procedures

One way that margins of error are reduced is by adopting standard operating procedures, the third kind of POM tool. Actions of a fire-fighting nature are taken under certain conditions (like running out of raw materials), which are spelled out in the procedures.

Procedural techniques have been a prime focus for operations management since antiquity. Major works such as building the pyramids surely owe much of their success to clever people who developed standard procedures for providing resources and getting work done.

The standard operating procedures, sometimes called SOPs, are step-by-step rules or routines that govern recurring decision activities. Computer programmers refer to them as algorithms. Indeed as we automate recurring operations, the first step is to define the operations in plain English as SOPs; tighten the logic, and you have decision rules; structure the decision rules, and you have algorithms; finally, in a few cases, the algorithm may be programmed in a computer language for automated decision making. An example of the latter is automated ordering in a grocery store when sales data on a given item (automatically recorded through bar-code reading) shows that the store is low on that item.

Some general POM procedures are usable in a wide variety of work situations. Demand forecasting procedures, inventory procedures, and quality control procedures are good examples. Often the general procedure is custom-tailored to fit a given environment.

One approach to custom-tailoring is to try out a set of procedures using numbers to represent work activities and resources. The procedures may be changed and tried again on the same stream of numbers to see what procedural set works best. This way of testing procedures is known as **simulation,** and when many numbers are needed to simulate properly, computer-assisted simulation may be used.

Decision models and procedures serve to simplify or "routinize" operations management. Demands on higher-level operations managers are overwhelming unless decision making can be made somewhat routine. Application of many of the routines—graphs, math models, procedures—may be assigned to lower-level employees. These include lower-paid managers, staff professionals, technicians, clerks, and operators. The goal is better management at lower cost.

FUNCTIONS OF THE ORGANIZATION

It is common to look at organizations—any organizations—as having three basic functions that must be managed. As is shown in Figure 1–2, these are money, demand, and operations. These are said to be **line** functions. They tend to be the first departments that form when an organization grows large enough to create departments. These departments may be known as finance, marketing, and production. Other departments that form later are called **staff** departments. They provide advice and support for the line departments. Typical staff departments are personnel, quality control, engineering, purchasing, production control, and information systems.

Why should money, demand, and operations be basic but not, say, personnel or engineering? Consider this illustration. Suppose you buttonholed an employee at random coming out of a place of business and asked, "What is the purpose of this business?" The reply might well be, "To make a profit." Or it might be, "To satisfy a customer demand." Or it might be, "To produce products or services." These replies relate to money, demand, and operations. It is far less likely that the reply would be, "To employ people"—a personnel function—or, "To design products and services"—the engineering function. The latter may reasonably be considered as supportive—hence staff rather than line.

Figure 1–3 shows the three basic functions as pieces of the total management pie. A gray area shows where managing operations overlaps with managing money on the one hand and managing demand on the other.

Finance and accounting concern managing money. This includes assessing proposals to invest money in operating resources. A goal is to fund proposals that maximize return on investment or net dollar benefits. Managers of operating resources must

FIGURE 1–2

Basic or Generic (Line) Departments

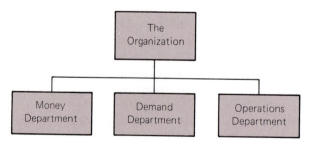

FIGURE 1–3

The Total Management Pie

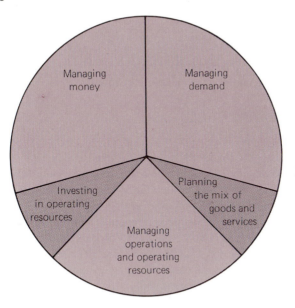

assess the same investment proposals, but from another angle. They deal with productive capacity and capability, with efficiency of the asset, and with cost minimization. The focus in this book will be more on those factors and less on profitability for the organization as a whole. This serves to minimize duplications with studies in finance and accounting.

The marketing function involves managing demand. This includes planning the mix of goods and services: which products, how many of each, and when they are to be available. The same questions face operations managers but with a difference. In the marketing view the question is, "What products will the customer want?" From the operations standpoint the question is, "What customer demands are within our capacity to produce?"

Managing the gray areas (shaded) in Figure 1–3 is a special problem. The problem is made worse by excessive specialization in large organizations. That is, marketing managers pursue their own objectives, operations managers pursue their own but different objectives, and the same tendencies hold true for finance and accounting managers. William Ouchi, in his book, *Theory Z,* argues that the specialization problem is acute in U.S. industry. Ouchi states: "In the United States we conduct our careers between organizations but within a single specialty. In Japan people conduct careers between specialties but within a single organization."[1] The pros and cons of specializa-

---

[1] William Ouchi, *Theory Z: How American Business Can Meet the Japanese Challenge* (Reading, Mass.: Addison-Wesley Publishing, 1981), p. 83 (HD70.J3088).

tion are not at issue here. But the potential for misunderstanding between operations and other specialties is. Ways of coping with such misunderstanding are presented in several chapters. (It is worth noting that accredited schools of business in the United States and some in Canada require all students to learn about all of the pieces in the pie, Figure 1–3, regardless of whether they intend to specialize in one discipline or piece of the pie.)

OPERATIONS AND OPERATING RESOURCES MANAGEMENT FUNCTIONS

Twenty-five years ago predecessors to this kind of textbook had titles like *Industrial Management* and *Manufacturing Management.* Later the term **production management** became more common. And now **production/operations management** (POM) or just plain **operations management** are popular terms.

One reason for the shifting terms is concepts and techniques for managing production in factories have been found to be useful in government and services as well. A journal article, "Production-Line Approach to Service," discusses an example.[2] The author describes the thorough use of planning and control techniques in producing McDonald's hamburgers. Today there is wide recognition that operations management concepts and techniques are applicable in services and government, and discussion of such applications is found in all the chapters.

There is a reason for keeping in mind the distinction between operations (ends) and operating resources (means). A brief story may help to illustrate. The author worked for a time in various planning and analysis jobs for the U.S. Navy. The jobs sometimes included interviews with managers of shore-based commands. These meetings generally began with a commanding officer or department head stating the mission of the command, which was always, "Support the fleet." Placards on their desks or walls proclaimed the same simple message. Keeping this message in prominent view helped avoid mixing up priorities in the vast bureaucratic organization that is the U.S. Navy. The thousands of people in these shore-based commands were to understand that they serve the fleet, not the other way around. They serve the fleet largely by helping to provide operating resources, but the operating resources people are the first to go if there is a budget cut or if they serve poorly.

When the distinction between operating resources and the operations themselves is widely understood, there are likely to be more harmonious working relationships among operations management people. It becomes less likely that a foreman will say to a plant engineer or buyer: "Wait a minute. Aren't you supposed to be helping me?"

---

[2] Theodore Leavitt, "Production-Line Approach to Service," *Harvard Business Review,* September–October 1972, pp. 45–52.

Functional Model

Operations management activities are diverse: Plant maintenance, demand forecasting, job scheduling, purchasing, and planning labor needs are just a few of the POM subfunctions. They may seem not to be closely related. They are. All of the functions examined in this book are concerned either with managing the operations themselves or with managing the resources directly used in operations.

Figure 1–4 shows how the POM functions are related. The figure is a functional model of operations and operating resources management. (It is not a model of a *system* of management; in later chapters we consider several actual systems that will work—systems with names like critical path method and material requirements planning.) In the figure, the functions concerned with the operations themselves are *above* the dashed line; those concerned with operating resources are *below* the line.

The functions, in blocks, are connected by arrows, which stand for certain key information flows. Not shown in Figure 1–4 are informational links with other major functions, such as marketing and finance. To show them would require a complicated grand model of information linkages. Ties to other sectors are discussed in appropriate places in the book.

Vertically the functions group into zones of **advance planning, action planning,** and **control.** Advance planning is longer range and strategic. Action planning is shorter range and tactical. Control involves keeping track of how well the operations are conforming to the plans—once the work begins.

Advance planning concerns strategic planning of the product line and fixed resources. These strategic plans are approved infrequently, and their implementation often takes years. They are not directly related to flows of goods and services, but they set limits on the kinds of goods and services the organization may provide for months or years to come.

The control zone at the extreme right in Figure 1–4 includes measurement of outputs and measurement of inputs. These measurements provide data for comparing actual outputs and resource usage with planned outputs and inputs. Measurement data are fed back to the planners, who may decide to adjust the plans. Since measurement is closely related to planning, measurement and control are included in the relevant planning chapters (Chapters 9–12).

In the center zone of Figure 1–4 are the functions that are most directly involved with the flow of goods and services. The planning becomes more detailed and complete as action planning functions take place, in the general sequence shown by the arrows. Some of the center functions in the chart are covered early in the book as Part Two, Translating Demand into Planned Orders (Chapters 3–8). After planned orders comes scheduling and quality assurance, which are covered in Chapters 9–12; these chapters comprise Part Three, Translating Planned Orders into Operations.

All remaining chapters, 13–18, are in Part Four, Operations Support. The support consists of process and product design, plus planning and caring for operating resources. Product and process designs may be developed upon acceptance of customer orders. They may also be developed in advance and filed away for future use, which improves service to customers by cutting out design time before production can begin.

FIGURE 1-4

Operations/Operating Resources Management—Functional Model

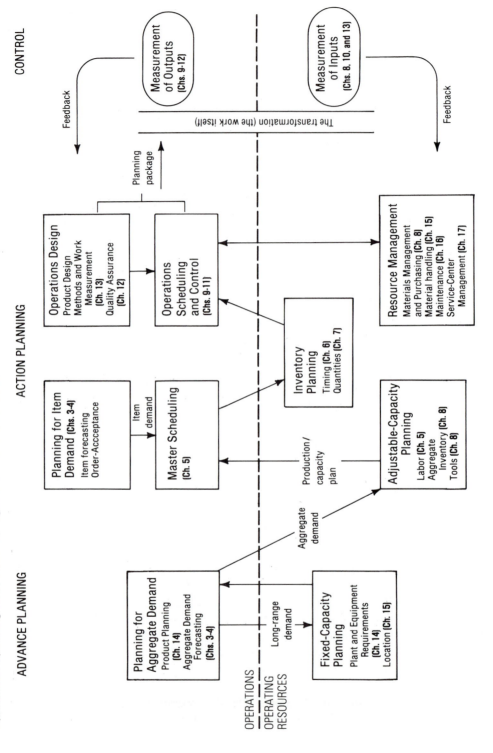

Descriptions of Functions

Each of the blocks in the functional model is considered separately below. A number of terms and concepts are briefly introduced. The terms, the concepts, and the functional model may be a lot to absorb at this point. Comprehension will improve as the topics are reintroduced one at a time in later chapters.

Planning for Aggregate Demand.   Planning for aggregate demand, in the upper left of the functional model, sets operations management in motion. Planning consists of developing a line of goods and services for which there is or will be sufficient demand. **Product planning** specifies types of goods and services, and **aggregate demand forecasting** predicts quantities.

Fixed-Capacity Planning.   The downward arrow between the leftmost blocks in Figure 1–4 indicates that **long-range demand** triggers fixed-capacity planning. The logic is simple: There is no sense in laying out capital for plant and equipment without customer demand for the goods and services that those fixed resources might produce. But the arrow is two-headed. An existing organization already has its plant and equipment. The organization seeks a volume of business that will pay for (amortize) those fixed resources. Thus, the upward-pointing arrowhead tells us that the firm should develop products and generate demand to suit the existing plant and equipment.

Adjustable-Capacity Planning.   **Aggregate demand** refers to demand for a group of products that share a block of capacity, such as a machine shop. The adjustable resources (e.g., **labor, materials,** and **tools**) in the block of capacity may be planned for on the basis of an aggregate demand forecast, usually for a period of a few months. (While labor, materials, and tools may be built up or depleted within a few months, fixed resources—plant and equipment—often take years to place in service.) The adjustable-capacity plan may specify how many shifts or days per week the plant will operate. The plan can be expressed as a percent of maximum (fixed) capacity. For example, a capacity plan may call for the plant to operate two shifts, seven days a week, which is 67 percent of maximum—three-shift—capacity. Convert the capacity plan to units, and you have what is called the **production plan.**

One part of production/capacity planning is assuring that production allows for medium-range swings in demand. Seasonal demand is common. Planning options may include seasonal hiring, part time, shift work, overtime, layoffs, cross-training, reassignments, subcontracting, inventory buildup, backordering, and so forth. A goal is to come up with a production/capacity plan that minimizes total capacity costs.

Inventory is shown in two places in Figure 1–4. It is shown as a resource planned for in the aggregate—part of the organization's capacity plan. Inventory is also planned in detail to provide the materials needed to make the items in the master production (or services) schedule.

Planning for Item Demand.   Detailed operations planning cannot go far without some planning for **item demand,** i.e., specific models, styles, and sizes of goods and services. Item demand consists of customer orders and a forecast of customer orders. Operations managers have to accept, modify, or deny customer orders in the light of other orders already stacked up; this is the **order-acceptance** part of planning for item demand. And goods may be produced in advance of customer orders; anticipating customer orders is the purpose of **item forecasting.**

Master Scheduling. The **master schedule** shows the plan for timed completions of end products or services or major modules. In Figure 1–4 item demand is shown as a necessary input to master scheduling. The production/capacity plan, another input, is the upper limit on the master schedule.

Inventory Planning. For human services operations there is usually little inventory to plan. But for some goods producers, inventory planning is a major activity. The end products or major product modules found on the master schedule divide into subassemblies and parts, which must be planned to be available at the right times **(timing)** and in the right amounts **(quantities).**

Operations Scheduling and Control. Every part, subassembly, and assembly is a separately planned order. The orders may be scheduled and controlled as jobs, lots, batches, project events, or repetitive production runs. The model of Figure 1–4 shows three inputs into operations scheduling and control: the inventory plans for the items, an indication (from resource management) of availability of resources, and operations design information.

Operations Design. The **operations** designers determine how to produce the product and how to assure product quality. **Product** design is largely an engineering function or its counterpart in services (such as a dietitian in food service). For our purposes, engineering design is not separately discussed but is assumed as an external input to operations planning.

Figure 1–4 shows that operations design information and schedules comprise a **planning package.** The planning package is dispatched to the work force, and **transformation** of inputs into outputs begins. As the work proceeds, it is measured (see the two measurement blocks at the right in the model) and compared with the plan. These are the control functions. When plans go awry, revised plans must be issued or supervisors must employ motivational techniques to get back on course. This may be called a control cycle, with plans fed forward and progress information fed back so that revised plans may be fed forward and progress information fed back, and so forth, until the work is completed.

The lower loop in Figure 1–4 represents **feedback** on usage of **inputs** or resources. For example, there might be feedback on waste and idleness. This is a big worry if the resource is costly (e.g., platinum material or a computer-controlled machine tool). We should keep in mind that the upper feedback loop, which refers to operations **outputs,** is more vital, because ends—on-time production with good quality—take precedence over means.

Resource Management.   Operating resources—plant, equipment, tools, labor, and ma-terials—have a life cycle. They are acquired, deployed, maintained (or simply stored), and eventually disposed of. (In the case of labor, the terms are *hiring, assigning, training,* and *releasing.* A diagram of the life cycle is shown below.

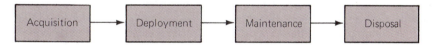

The life-cycle stages are referred to in Figure 1–4 as resource management. There is a two-headed arrow between resource management and scheduling. This signifies the need for resource deliveries to dovetail with operations schedules. Included in upcoming discussions of resource management are **materials management and purchasing; material handling; maintenance** of equipment; and **management of service centers,** such as tool rooms, libraries, motor pools, duplicating services, and cafeterias.

The functional model of Figure 1–4 is general enough to apply in any operations management environment, though not always in the same way. Types of environments are examined next.

OPERATIONS MANAGEMENT ENVIRONMENTS

Operations management is common in our society. It is found at different organizational levels and for different types of operations, and different types of people are involved. These three aspects of the operations management environment—levels, operations, and people—are considered next.

Levels

Organizations usually have several levels—subunits within organizational units. Every unit and subunit has its own operations to perform and its own particular operating resources to manage. A personnel department, for example, has a line of services that it offers. Personnel services should be properly planned and forecast in the aggregate and by type of service—hiring, training, determining pay, and so forth. Resources—from personnel specialists to file cabinets—are carefully planned and managed. Operating procedures, time standards, and schedules for personnel services are developed. And systematic feedback on quantity and quality of each personnel service and resource usage may be provided. The same goes for a marketing department, an engineering department, or any other department.

Operations

While the functional model is general, the decision models and analysis techniques of operations management are not. They depend on types of operations. For example, certain models and techniques apply to **continuous** or **repetitive** production. Much of goods manufacturing is of this type. At the opposite extreme are the fine arts and crafts. The artist and the craftsman do nicely without the aid of operations management models and analytical techniques.

A builder is neither a repetitive producer nor an artist, although we often desire that our buildings include some artful or unique features. There is a need for better management of such partly unique endeavors. Large-scale endeavors of this type are known as **projects;** for example, construction projects and research and development (R&D) projects. If small-scale, they are known as **jobs;** for example, painting a room or performing surgery on a patient.

Besides the three basic types of production—continuous or repetitive, project, and job—there are two notable hybrids: One is what some refer to as **job-lot** production, a hybrid of job and repetitive operations that is important in both consumer and industrial products manufacturing. The second is what we shall call (for lack of a simpler term) **limited-quantity large-scale** production, a hybrid of project and repetitive operations. The three basic and two hybrid types of operation are diagramed, with examples, in Figure 1–5. In the following discussion of the figure a few other terms are introduced. The terms distinguish among the great diversity of processes and operations, products and services, and firms and industries.

Continuous and Repetitive.   Three examples of continuous or repetitive operations are given in Figure 1–5: refineries, egg hatcheries, and insurance home offices. Processing one type of insurance policy application or claim form can be a repetitive operation, and the insurance example is listed in order to show that services providers as well as goods producers may be classed as repetitive. But repetitive production of goods is far more common. An enormous variety of goods are repetitively produced. If produced in high volume, the popular term is **mass production,** a term that is less useful to us in operations management than the terms, continuous and repetitive.

Refineries and egg hatcheries differ in an important way. Refining deals with a material that pours. Egg hatcheries have procedures to assure that the material does not pour! In statistics studies there are terms to describe things that do or don't pour. Things that pour are said to be **continuous** variables, and they may be counted in fractional parts. Things that do not pour are said to be **discrete** variables, and they are counted only in whole units.

Firms that process materials that pour are often referred to simply as the **process industry**—short for continuous-flow process. Liquids, gases, grains, flakes, and pellets are made by the industry. Makers of nails, toothpicks, pens, and even flashlight batteries sometimes consider themselves part of the process industry. Such products may be planned, scheduled, counted, and controlled by volume rather than by unit or piece. The process industry tends to be highly capital intensive. Refineries and chemical plants, for example, run with few workers. Labor is a small portion of product cost; plant and equipment (capital) is a large portion of cost. There are relatively few day-to-day production control problems, but advance planning of fixed resources is extensive.

Repetitive production of discrete items is planned, scheduled, counted, and con-

FIGURE 1–5

Five Types of Operations

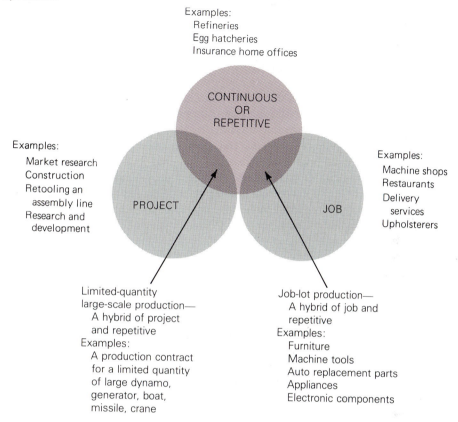

Examples:
  Refineries
  Egg hatcheries
  Insurance home offices

Examples:
  Market research
  Construction
  Retooling an
    assembly line
  Research and
    development

Examples:
  Machine shops
  Restaurants
  Delivery
    services
  Upholsterers

CONTINUOUS OR REPETITIVE

PROJECT

JOB

Limited-quantity
large-scale production—
  A hybrid of project
  and repetitive
Examples:
  A production contract
  for a limited quantity
  of large dynamo,
  generator, boat,
  missile, crane

Job-lot production—
  A hybrid of job and
  repetitive
Examples:
  Furniture
  Machine tools
  Auto replacement parts
  Appliances
  Electronic components

trolled by natural unit or piece. A wide variety of products are of this type. Some, like eggs, require much handling but little processing. Others, like chairs and circuit breakers, require extensive parts fabrication followed by assembly into finished goods (the **fabrication/assembly** industry.) Discrete production operations tend to require more human assistance and to be less automated than continuous operations. Many products, like spaghetti and noodles, are in an early state of continuous flow but later are chopped or formed into pieces and packaged in discrete units.

The method of counting or measuring materials—continuously or discretely—is of importance in a few spots in this book. But continuous and repetitive are put together in one circle in Figure 1–5, because both have lack of variety as their main feature. Job operations, considered next, are characterized by great variety.

Job. Examples of job operations in Figure 1–5 are machine shops, restaurants, delivery services, and upholsterers. It is appropriate to include three services providers among the four examples, because the services sector is mostly job oriented. Repetitive processing of insurance forms, discussed earlier, is an uncommon service-industry exception. Job shops are also plentiful in the goods manufacturing sector. Some industrial job shops make special parts in small volumes for assembly into final products. Other industrial job shops repair equipment and make tooling. While standardization (to the point of automation) is an aim in repetitive operations management, flexibility is essential in job operations management, because the mix of jobs is always changing.

Project.   Projects are large scale: A single project typically takes months or years to complete. Repetitive production of a product may also run for months or years, but each unit is completed in minutes, hours, or days. Both job and project operations are low-volume endeavors (a project is usually unique—a unit of one), but projects are large, whereas jobs are small.

Examples of projects in Figure 1–5 are a market-research project, a construction project, a project to retool an assembly line, and a research and development (R&D) project. In the project environment, the total number of projects is usually small, but each is composed of a large, diverse mix of small jobs or activities to be planned and controlled.

Limited-Quantity Large-Scale.   The shaded zone of intersection between repetitive and project in Figure 1–5 represents the hybrid, limited-quantity large-scale operations. The listed examples are production contracts for a limited quantity of large dynamo, generator, boat, missile, or crane. Since multiple units are produced, this is not the same as project production. The quantity is not large enough to settle into a standardized routine, as in repetitive production.

Job-Lot.   The interface between repetitive and job is an extra-special case. It is job-lot (or batch) production. Most goods-producing firms fall into that zone of overlap. Within the important zone are three kinds of goods producers:

1. Those that make to stock intermittently. Intermittent means off and on. Each successive lot may be for a different product or a different model, style, or size. Lots or batches of each product can be planned and scheduled, perhaps in rotation, based on rates of depletion of the firm's *stock* of each item. Some appliance manufacturers make their own brand-name goods in this manner.

2. Those that make to order, in quantity. Quantities of a given item are rather large, but who knows when there will be another order for the same item? Planning and scheduling may not be done very far in advance since the producer depends on an uncertain flow of customer *orders,* as in job operations. Some electronic component producers operate in this environment.

3. Those that make parts to stock and assemble to order. Furniture and machine-tool manufacturers are good examples. They usually stock frames and subassemblies, which are assembled in various styles based on customer preference when orders are booked.

Combinations of the above three environments are common. For example auto-replacement parts producers usually make their own brand-name goods to stock and also bid on large orders in which another supplier's brand name will be used. (A strategy is to bid low when outside orders are needed and to bid high or not bid otherwise.)

Planning and Control Requirements. The five types of operations that have been described differ mainly in *variety* of models processed and *size* of the operation to produce the unit or units. The variety/size combinations are important for our purposes, because each of the five resulting types of operation calls for a different set of planning and control techniques. The specific techniques are taken up throughout the book. A few summary remarks about them follow.

1. Continuous and repetitive operations require elaborate advance planning but are comparatively easy to control. Simple, inflexible rules and rather rigid standards of performance will suffice. The advantages of this type of production are many, and it is natural for any company to want either to become more continuous or repetitive, or else to streamline their operations in order to enjoy some of the advantages of continuous operations.
2. Job-oriented operations are variable from job to job. Waiting lines are common, and priority-ordering schemes are needed. Excess resources must be on hand to handle short-run changes.
3. Project-oriented operations change as the project progresses, and large numbers of operations are in progress at any given time. Planning and control of sequence of operations are critical.
4. Limited-quantity large-scale production requires controls to keep track of the progress of units in various stages of completion. Scheduling should allow for learning improvements from one unit to the next.
5. Job-lot operations involve standard component parts, which are steadily monitored. Periodic shifts from one end product to another related end product call for careful planning to translate end products into exact needs for components.

People

In very small organizations a single operating manager may direct virtually all of the functions in Figure 1–4. At the other extreme, in very large organizations, especially goods producers, the operating manager may have responsibility for the transformation and virtually nothing else. What happens to all of the functions? They are gradually "staffed off." That is, staff specialists are hired to help plan and control operations and operating resources.

The staff specialists start out working for the line manager; as staff specialists become more numerous, they cluster into new staff (advisory) departments of their own. Figure 1–6 describes some common tendencies to staff off most of the operations management responsibilities. Production control, engineering, and quality assurance departments may inherit operations planning and progress monitoring duties. A master scheduling group may take over scheduling end products and services. Purchasing,

FIGURE 1–6

Diffusion of Line Responsibilities ("Staffing off") as Organization Grows

Function	Responsibility
The transformation	Direct responsibility of the line (e.g., manufacturing or operating managers)
Planning operations and monitoring progress	Often staffed off wholly or partly to production control, engineering, and quality assurance groups
Scheduling end products and services	Usually staffed off to a master production scheduling group (which might include representatives of manufacturing, production control, marketing, and finance)
Planning and controlling adjustable capacity (labor, materials, and tools)	Usually staffed off to an executive group for aggregate planning and to staff specialists (e.g., purchasing, personnel, and maintenance) for execution and control of plans
Planning fixed capacity (plant and equipment)	Usually staffed off to high-level finance/executive committee for decisions and to facilities planning/capital budgeting specialists for detailed planning
Demand planning	Usually staffed off to high-level executive committee for planning and to product development, marketing, and forecasting groups for execution of plans

personnel, maintenance, and other special departments form to execute plans for adjustable capacity, based on aggregate planning decisions by an executive group. Facilities planning and capital budgeting groups perform detailed planning for fixed capacity, based on finance and executive committee decisions. And product development, marketing, and forecasting groups perform detailed demand planning, based on executive committee guidance.

Staffing off can be carried too far. As noted earlier, the Japanese get by without much staff specialization; Western companies wonder if they should not follow suit.

In the next section, the clustering of responsibilities into staff departments is examined further, with specific examples.

ORGANIZATION STRUCTURES FOR OPERATIONS MANAGEMENT

It would make things simple if one could point to a certain block on the organization chart and say, "That's why you find the management of operations and operating resources." No such luck. Operations management functions are scattered about the organization chart. (Similarly, the management of people is scattered about the chart and is in no way limited to a personnel department.)

The Industrial Organization

Figure 1–7 illustrates the degree of scatter of the functions. Operations management functions and activities are at the bottom. At the top is a typical organization chart

FIGURE 1–7

Operations Management Model and Sample Organization Chart

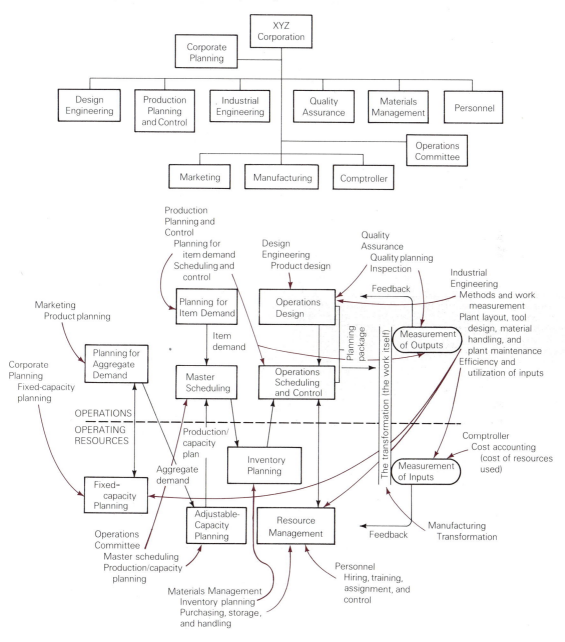

for a goods manufacturer. (It may be a bit presumptuous to say "typical," because organization charts vary a good deal.) The departments from the organization chart are repeated around the perimeter of the operations management model. Relevant department activities are also listed, and arrows point to allied functions within the model in the lower part of the chart.

Certain organizational tendencies deserve comment. The three line departments—marketing, manufacturing, and comptroller—are shown on the lower row of the organization chart. The main role of marketing is to assess demand and to help plan the line of products and services; the comptroller's main concern is with cost of resources; and the manufacturing superintendent's role is to implement operating plans. These three line managers comprise the operations committee. Production/capacity planning and master scheduling require cooperative decision making by this committee.

A high-level corporate planning group has final responsibility for planning fixed capacity, since plant and equipment have long-range effects on the corporation as a whole.

Six staff advisory departments are shown on the middle row of the organization chart. Design engineering is totally committed to design of products; quality assurance is concerned with quality planning and control, including inspection. Personnel has responsibilities in human resource dynamics: hiring, training, assigning, and controlling the work force—topics that are generally beyond the scope of this book.

Industrial engineering (IE) has major roles in managing facilities and tools and in measuring the efficiency and utilization of operating resources. Efficiency of human resources is based on methods and time standards (work measurement) determined by IEs.

The other two departments, production planning and control (PP&C) and materials management, are wholly devoted to operations management. PP&C performs planning for item demand and operations scheduling and control; materials management handles inventory planning and inventory purchasing, storage, handling, and disposal. In some firms materials management is included in the PP&C department. (For brevity it is often named production control instead of production planning and control.) The two together make up a sizable department. Its function centers on day-to-day production and inventory scheduling.

We see, in general, that PP&C has central responsibility for short-range management of ends (outputs) and IE has central responsibility for medium-range management of means (resource inputs). But for the organization providing services instead of manufacturing goods, this does not hold true. Since service providers are not "industrial" and do not "produce," there may be no industrial engineering department and no production control department.

The Service Organization

Operations management is scattered even more widely about the organization chart for services than for goods organizations. A chart like that for an industrial organization (Figure 1–7) will not be presented for a services example. Service enterprises are too diverse for there to be an organization that could in any sense be considered as typical. Two particular characteristics of operations management in service organizations deserve comment.

One is that the line department providing the service may be commonly found as a staff department in a manufacturing organization. Examples are firms that provide engineering, accounting, employment, and maintenance services. Each of these is a staff speciality that contributes product design and operating resources services in a manufacturing organization. They are line departments performing primary operations when they exist as services firms.

The second characteristic is that some functions that are separate specialties in manufacturing become the combined responsibility of a person or a small group in a services organization. Part of the reason is simply that services organizations are often too small for much specialization. Chefs and physicians tend to take responsibility not only for service operations themselves but also for product design, methods and processes, and quality assurance. In large services organizations operations management takes on more of a manufacturing flavor. Large banks, insurance companies, fast-food chains, and postal services hire industrial engineers and management analysts to design layouts, study methods and processes, set time standards, and compute efficiency and utilization of resources. Large data-processing shops sometimes have both a production-control and a quality-control department.

Organization Structure: A Compromise

Some conclusions may be drawn from the above discussions of organization structures. One conclusion is operating organizations are not structured to suit the operations management function. Nor should they be. Organizations are designed so that resources cluster together around common objectives, one of which is the production or operations objective. But some resources needed in operations—space, supplies, forecasting experts, operations researchers, the maintenance work force—may also serve marketing, the comptroller, personnel, and so forth. The organization is not put together by simple and obvious associations. The organization structure is a compromise.

Another conclusion is that an operations management cluster is more likely to stand out in the organization chart of a goods than a services producer. This is reasonable: In goods manufacturing there is a lot of attention to planning and controlling the output and also the productive resources. While there is growing emphasis on these factors in service organizations, services do not have a full range of raw-material, work-in-process, and finished-goods inventories to be concerned with; catering to the customer's immediate need is dominant, and this is likely to shape organization structures in service enterprises.

A final conclusion is that organization structure is not a "given." It should be planned with care, just as operations and operating resources should be. Technologies are subject to change—sometimes rapid change, as with information processing technology. Usually, changing technology means changing responsibilities. Responsibility clusters—that is, organizational units—should therefore evolve. The tie between technology and organization structure is explored further in selected future chapters.

SYSTEMS IN OPERATIONS MANAGEMENT

At one time, operations management books (and their predecessors) paid much attention to tools, little to systems. In other words, each technique or tool was discussed separately from each other technique or tool. It tended to stand alone. One reason for separate treatments is that there are many tools, many kinds of organization, and many options. A few industries have managed to chain together some of the tools to form cohesive, efficient systems. But there is not enough room in a general textbook to present industry-specific operations management systems.

Over the years it has become increasingly possible to treat some of the subject matter of operations management in terms of integrated systems. A computer-based project planning and control approach, known as the program evaluation and review technique (PERT) or the critical path method (CPM) was developed in the 1950s. While PERT/CPM is not a fully integrated system of operations management, it is a step in that direction—for project operations.

An even more comprehensive systems approach has been developed for the production and inventory control area in job-lot operations. These developments began moving forward in the 1960s. A high point was the formation of the American Production and Inventory Control Society (APICS). Joseph Orlicky, Oliver Wight, and George W. Plossl, whose works are referenced in several places in this book, were instrumental in developing new computer-based technologies in production and inventory control; APICS has served as the torchbearer to spread their message throughout industry.

The term **system** has been around far longer than digital computers have been in use, and many fine management systems do not involve computers. For example, while U.S. industry was caught up in the APICS "MRP Crusade" of the 1970s, Japanese industry was honing a noncomputer-based approach to repetitive production known as the just-in-time (JIT) system. Japan's rapid ascendancy as one of the world's premier producers has kindled outside interest in JIT and related methods, including total quality control (TQC). JIT and TQC are closely examined in Parts Two and Three.

Methods related to MRP and to JIT/TQC serve to join together some of the POM functions; they extend farther to forge badly needed links to the marketing and finance functions and materials suppliers. These new systems make it possible for medium and large producers to enjoy the kind of coordination that used to be possible only in smaller firms.

SUMMARY

The management of operations and operating resources supports the producing end of the business. It is one of three basic functions of any organization; the other two are marketing (or demand) management and money management. Managing operations involves planning, control, and supervision.

In this book the emphasis is on planning and control tools. These include graphic and mathematical models for decision making and procedural techniques for recurring operations. Choice of the correct tool depends partly on type of operation: continuous or repetitive, job, project, or a hybrid type of operation.

A distinction may be made between managing operations and managing operating resources. Operations are central, and providers of operating resources may be hired as specialists whose purpose is to help those in operations.

Operations management includes a number of functions. The triggering function is advance planning of aggregate demand for a line of goods and services. Advance planning of fixed capacity is a closely related function.

Action planning begins with two functions: (1) planning for item demand and (2) planning production rate and adjustable capacity level, that is, labor, aggregate inventory, and tools. A master schedule of completions of end items may be developed from item-demand projections and the production/capacity plan. Master scheduling is followed by inventory planning, the function that determines the need for parts to go into the end items. The next function is operations scheduling and control of parts orders. Two functions that support operations scheduling and control are operations design and resource management. Operations design provides for design of product, method and time, and quality control procedures. Resource management assures the right operating resources at the right time.

The control functions proceed after the planning package (operations design and schedule data) has been forwarded to the work force and the work has begun. Measurement of outputs and resource usage (inputs) is compared with plans and standards, and corrective action may be taken when there are variances.

It is unlikely that operations management will take shape as one or two self-contained blocks of related functions on an organization chart. Organization structure is a compromise, and resources serving operations management may also serve marketing, finance, personnel, or another function. Therefore, operations management functions tend to be scattered about the organization chart to some extent.

A recent integrating influence has been the development of operations management systems, which are most advanced in job-lot and repetitive manufacturing. The job-lot systems center on computerized material requirements planning and also extend into new methods for planning and controlling capacity and schedules. The repetitive systems, perfected in Japan, rely on simpler noncomputer approaches.

This book is organized around four parts, the first of which consists of this introductory chapter and a second chapter on operations strategy. Part Two consists of six of the action-planning chapters, from demand management, forecasting, and capacity planning through inventory management. Part Three includes Chapters 9–11 on operations scheduling and control, plus quality assurance. Part Four includes six chapters on operations support, ranging from process and product design to fixed capacity management to service-center management.

REFERENCES

A Reference list appears at the end of each chapter. The lists provide limited help for further research. The book lists are intended to lead you to the various parts of the library that hold material on a given topic. Thus a list might include one book with a management (HD) Library of Congress call number, one with an industrial engineering (T or TA) number, one with a management accounting (HF) number, and so forth. That will help you to the right shelf, where there are likely to be other books on the same topic. Also included are lists of magazines, journals, and professional societies that are useful for people who have operations management interests.

For more recent books, Library of Congress call numbers are given. *These may or may not be valid for your library.* There has been a nationally organized effort to standardize Library of Congress call numbers in university and college libraries, but it has not been in operation long.

Books

Anderson, E. J., and G. T. Schwenning. *The Science of Production Organization.* New York: John Wiley & Sons, 1938.

Buffa, Elwood S., and Richard G. Newman. *PLAID Series Programmed Learning Aid for Production and Operations Management.* Rev. ed. Homewood, Ill.: Dow Jones-Irwin, 1981.

Carson, Gordon B.; Harold A. Bolz; and Hewill H. Young. *Production Handbook.* New York: Ronald Press, 1972 (TS155.P747).

Daniells, Lorna M. *Business Information Sources.* Berkeley: University of California Press, 1976 (HF5351.D375X).

Greene, James, H., ed. *Production and Inventory Control Handbook.* New York: McGraw-Hill, 1974 (TS155.P74).

Lindemann, A. J.; Earl F. Lundgren; and H. K. von Kaas. *Encyclopaedic Dictionary of Management and Manufacturing Terms.* 2d ed. Dubuque, Iowa: Kendall/Hunt Publishing, 1974 (HD19.L5).

Wallace, Thomas A., ed. *APICS Dictionary.* 5th ed. Falls Church, Va.: American Production and Inventory Control Society, 1984.

Periodicals (societies)

Business Periodicals Index, an index of articles published in a limited number of business magazines and journals.

Engineering Index, an index of articles published on engineering, including production engineering, in a large number of periodicals.

Interfaces (Institute for Management Science), a journal aimed at the interface between management scientist and practitioner.

Journal of Operations Management (Operations Management Society), a practitioner and academic journal.

Production and Inventory Management (American Production and Inventory Control Society), a practitioner's journal.

Technical Book Review Index.

REVIEW QUESTIONS

1. Explain the difference between operations and operating resources.

2. Management science and scientific management sound alike but are *quite* different. One dates back about 40 years, the other about 80 years. One is procedural and the other mathematical. Explain which is which, giving some details.

3. What is a "fire-fighting" type of manager?

4. What are standard operating procedures (SOPs)?

5. What are the advantages of "routinizing" operations management?

6. Why are operations, sales, and finance *line* functions, as opposed to staff functions?

7. How does the *overspecialization* problem affect operations management?

8. How do action-planning functions differ from advance-planning functions?

9. In Figure 1–4 why does an arrow go upward from "fixed-capacity planning" to "planning for aggregate demand"?

10. What is the role of the *planning package?*

11. Which is more important: feedback on outputs? or on inputs? Explain.

12. How does master scheduling differ from operations scheduling?

13. How does fixed-capacity planning differ from adjustable-capacity planning?

14. Does every manager have a set of operations management duties to perform? Explain.

15. Explain the main differences between the three main types of operations in Figure 1–5.

16. Why are the "hybrids" in Figure 1–5 notable?

17. What do we mean by "staffing off"?

18. Is it easy to find the operations management functions on organization charts? Why or why not?

19. To what extent are proven *systems* of operations management available for use in any company?

PROBLEMS

Note: **Some problems in this book have answers that are based almost solely on text materials. Others require thought and judgment that go beyond the book, and in those cases you should include discussion of reasons, assumptions, and outside sources of information.**

1. All of us use technology to "routinize" life's daily tasks: feeding, transportation, buying, bill-paying, and so on. Try to think of ways in which the *management* of those tasks

may be routinized. Think in terms of models, information, and organization for planning and control. The disorganized person who doesn't plan and doesn't control is like what type of manager?

2. Consolidated Enterprises has three main manufacturing "businesses": (1) a fiberglass business in which products are made to customers' specifications, usually in small quantities; (2) a snowblower and lawnmower business in which several models of each product are made, a business in which Consolidated is one of the industry leaders; and (3) a man-made fiber business in which tuberous plants are converted into thread.

    What type of production (continuous, job, etc.) would apply to each business? Explain.

3. Listed below are various types of organizations. For each one, try to decide what its main kind of operation is: repetitive or continuous, job, project, limited-quantity large-scale, or job-lot. Discuss each.

Medical clinic	Cafeteria	Commercial fishing
Crane manufacturing	Book printing	Grocery checkout
Auditing	Petroleum refining	Farming
Architecture	Purchasing	Mowing grass on campus
Shoe repair	Bottling	Law practice
Radio manufacturing	Construction	Welding shop

4. Why does operations management tend to be more highly developed in repetitive than in job or project operations?

5. As organizations grow, their productive character may change, for example, from job-shop (custom) to repetitive or job-lot or from project to repetitive. Describe how this might happen for a type of organization of your own choosing. Also describe the accompanying changes in the management of operations; that is, why would different kinds of planning and control models be called for?

6. What kinds of organization/industry have a need for extremely long-range demand forecasting? Why? What kinds have a need for extremely short-range forecasting? Why?

7. Do you put planning packages together for your own life's activities (trips, school assignments, meals, dates, etc.)? Describe each element of the planning package in terms of one of your own activities.

8. News stories about businesses sometimes include statements such as, "The firm is operating at 80 percent of capacity." What kind of planning results in the rate of capacity use? How may the rate be measured? Find a news story that discusses rate of capacity use, and summarize what you learn (or surmise) about this kind of planning. (Or, alternatively, telephone a local manufacturing firm to learn what you can about how that firm sets its capacity use rate.)

9. In Japan, business colleges are rare, and the M.B.A. degree does not exist. How is this characteristic of Japan's educational system related to the specialization issue?

10. What kinds of feedback is the very small business most interested in? That is, what *results* are of special interest? What kinds of feedback information are common in larger firms but not in small firms? Illustrate by referring to a particular very small firm you know of.

11. How does competition affect operations management? Consider, for example, some of the most successful firms in the highly competitive fast-food, lodging, and grocery industries. What do the successful firms do in operations management that their less successful competitors (maybe some that went under!) do not do?

12. Think of five diverse examples of nonprofit organizations. For each, describe what its three line management functions (money, demand, and operations management) would consist of.

13. Obtain an organization chart that shows enough detail to identify the operations management functions. Identify those functions and explain your reasoning in a way similar to the way in which this was done in the chapter discussion of organization structures. Do you believe the organization structure properly provides for clustering of common operations management responsibilities? Why or why not?

14. Think of cases in which you were given exaggerated delivery promises on goods you had ordered. Why is it so common for the seller to be unable to say with reasonable accuracy when the goods will arrive? Think especially of reasons pertaining to the operating resources management function.

15. W. Edwards Deming, America's famous quality control expert, who is in his 80s and still going strong, says that the manager's job is to *design systems*. If that is so, why not just use "canned" systems and not even hire lower and middle managers?

16. A partial organization chart for a company that provides services (instead of goods) is shown in Figure 1–8. The organization chart is for a hypothetical firm called ABC Power Company, a provider of electric power and allied services. (The chart is similar to one obtained from a real power company.) On separate paper, develop a chart similar to the chart of Figure 1–6 for a goods producer. Your task is to relate blocks on the organization chart to blocks on the functional model of operations/operating resources management (Figure 1–4). Explain your reasoning.

FIGURE 1–8

Partial Organization Chart, ABC Power Company

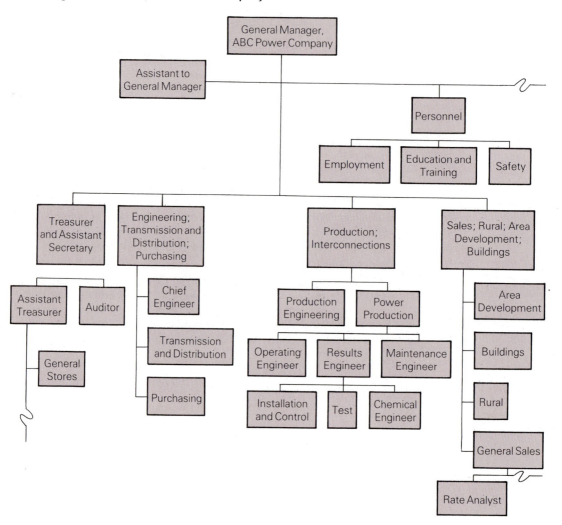

Chapter 2

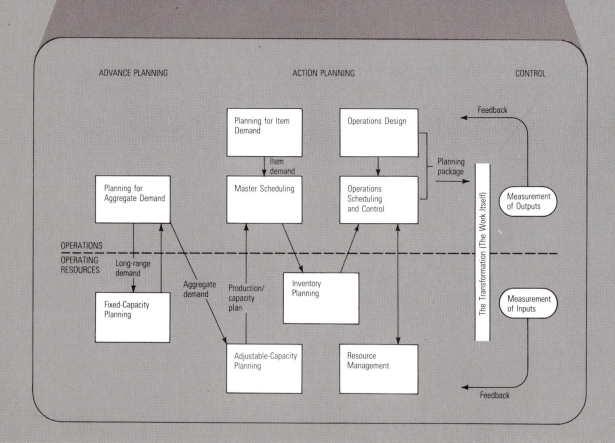

ENVIRONMENTAL
INFLUENCES
GLOBAL
REGIONAL
LOCAL

STRATEGIES
ORGANIZATIONAL
OPERATIONAL

ADVANCE PLANNING   ACTION PLANNING   CONTROL

Planning for Item Demand

Operations Design

Feedback

Planning for Aggregate Demand

Master Scheduling

Operations Scheduling and Control

Planning package

Measurement of Outputs

Item demand

OPERATIONS
OPERATING RESOURCES

Long-range demand

Aggregate demand

Production/ capacity plan

Inventory Planning

The Transformation (The Work Itself)

Measurement of Inputs

Fixed-Capacity Planning

Adjustable-Capacity Planning

Resource Management

Feedback

Operations Strategy

The average citizen in a town with, say, three hospitals, may not see much difference between them. "A hospital is a hospital," might be the citizen's opinion. But ask the administrator or a board member at one of the hospitals whether theirs is different, and the responder is likely to bristle with indignation that you didn't know. "We are the only hospital in town—in the region for that matter—with a fully equipped trauma center," you might be told. Or, "For one thing, we have the only neonatal care unit in the region. For another. . . ."

DISTINCTIVE COMPETENCE

What a hospital does—and what almost any enterprise does—is attempt to develop **distinctive competencies** which set it apart from its competitors. When a company is unable to sustain any distinctive competencies, the company goes under; Minnie Pearl chicken, a now defunct fast-food chain, comes to mind. On the other hand, when a company can be distinctively competent in several ways, it wows the world. IBM, Delta Airlines, McDonald's, and Toyota are examples. All four have dependably high quality. Delta, McDonald's, and Toyota have very low production costs. IBM, Delta, and Toyota have fanatically dedicated employees. IBM and Delta offer customer service unparalleled in their industries. Toyota and McDonald's have spectacular process efficiency and control, which leads to product uniformity. McDonald's provides extremely fast response to customer orders.

All of these competencies—quality, cost, employee dedication, customer service, process efficiency and control, and response time—are closely related to the POM strategies of the companies. The ultimate goal of POM is to strategically guide the operations and operating resources toward achievement of these sorts of competencies for the company as a whole. We admire the few companies able to demonstrate high success in this endeavor. We worry about a "productivity crisis" when there seem to be all too many companies whose competencies have slipped badly, especially in comparison to foreign competitors. The path toward competency of some kind is partly good strategic management and partly fate, luck, and environmental forces. Luck and fate do not warrant much comment. But environmental forces and strategic management do.

STRATEGIES SHAPED BY GLOBAL ENVIRONMENT

There are global, regional, and local environmental forces that shape the strategies of the firm and of the production/operations management function within the firm. The great depression that began in 1929 is one example of a global environmental factor. A relatively recent global shaper of strategies was the "oil crisis," in which crude oil prices rose more than fivefold in the first few years of the 1970s. Industries all over the world are still scrambling to adjust product designs, process technologies, plant configurations and locations, sources of supply, and numerous other operating factors.

World War II had an even more powerful global influence on industrial strategies. Industry was mobilized to produce for the war effort, and production of many consumer goods—home appliances, rubber tires, and automobiles, for example—ground to a halt. Companies that had been innovation oriented became production oriented. Companies that had been customer-service or advertising oriented became production oriented. American industry became production oriented. Production engineers and manufacturing managers were the "glamour boys" of industry.

The productivity emphasis continued after the war for a few years, until the consumer pipelines were full again. At that point, the productivity era ended for many industrial companies. The new problem was too much capacity, and marketing strategies—how to gain market share at the expense of one's competitors—became dominant in many companies. Business colleges expanded marketing curricula, and marketing careers became important paths to advancement.

Intensive competition in the 1950s and 1960s produced winners and losers. The winners found themselves with a surfeit of cash to invest, and the losers were ready targets for takeover by the cash holders. The era of merger and the conglomerates was launched. But let us call it the financial-legal era, because financial analysts and accountants were the new wizards who sought out financially attractive marriage partners, and legal experts were needed to tie the knots. The business schools responded with expanded finance and accounting curricula, and the law schools turned out increasing numbers of corporate lawyers.

The trouble is, when mergers are arranged for financial reasons, operational compatibility may be neglected. James Ling parlayed a $4,000 stake in the late 1950s into the giant LTV conglomerate that at one time included such dissimilar subsidiaries as Wilson foods, Wilson sporting goods, Braniff Airline, Jones and Laughlin Steel, Allied Radio, National Car Rental, Vought Helicopter, LTV Aerospace, Computer Technology, and many more. In 1970, Ling's LTV empire was collapsing, as were a number of other conglomerates. Many of the companies that were acquired in the 1960s had to be sold in the 1970s to avoid total ruin.

Why were so many conglomerates assembled with so little regard for operational compatibility? One reason was the lack of top corporate officers who had operating experience. Corporate suites that were deep in production people in the productivity era of the 1940s and early 1950s were dominated by financial-legal people in the 1970s. A good understanding of POM competencies—quality, productivity, on-time performance, innovativeness, responsiveness—was lacking. The balance sheets of, say, Burger King and Lum's, might have looked good together, and analysts might have assumed that there was an operational fit as well. There wasn't. Burger King's distinctive operational competencies lie in the areas of fast response, plus process efficiency and control over a narrow product line; Lum's (which avoided ruin by being acquired in 1978 by a German restaurant chain) nurtured a semispecialty product image: a place to go for a stein of beer, a German-style Lumburger or frankfurter, and a variety of other easy-to-prepare foods served to sit-down patrons. The expertise of Burger King management in achieving very fast response times for a narrow line of fast foods to stand-up patrons would not have cured Lum's ills; indeed it might have hastened the destruction of Lum's product image and the pace of restaurant closings. (This is a fictitious example; Burger King and Lum's may never have been analyzed seriously as merger partners.)

In some respects, Lum's was operationally about as similar to Emery Air Freight as to Burger King. Emery Air Freight handles things that can be transported economically by air and gives overnight service; Lum's offered an economical (e.g., $5) meal from a moderately differentiated menu and offered semifast service. If you want faster air freight, you charter a plane; if you want faster food service, you go to Burger King.

The point of this example is that in the financial-legal era strategic decisions were

FIGURE 2-1

Cycle of Strategy Changes

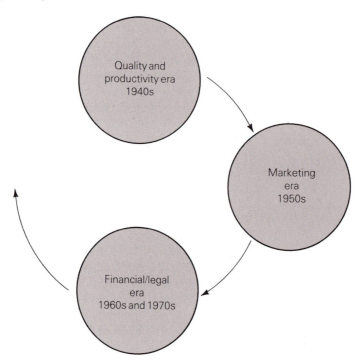

often made without a close look at all the strategic factors. Strategic financial factors, yes. Strategic marketing factors, maybe or sometimes. Strategic operating factors, often not.

As Robert Reich puts it, our managerial innovations in recent years "have been based on accounting, tax avoidance, financial management, mergers, acquisitions, and litigation. They have been innovations on paper. Gradually, over the past 15 years, America's professional managers have become paper entrepreneurs."[1]

It is no wonder that the news media began to proclaim in the late 1970s that North America was in the throes of an industrial crisis. The years of neglect of the operating end of the business had taken their toll, and our industrial corporations were sending study teams by the planeload to Japan in an effort to "meet the Japanese challenge." There is renewed industrywide, indeed worldwide, interest in industrial productivity, quality, product design, customer service, and other operational matters. As Figure 2-1 suggests, we have come full circle, back to recognition of the importance of operations; but this time, having seen the folly of overemphasizing a particular

---

[1] Robert B. Reich, *The Next American Frontier* (New York: Times Books, 1983), pp. 140–41 (JK467.R45).

function, our corporate leaders may see fit to base future corporate strategies on a blend of POM, financial, and marketing considerations.

STRATEGIES SHAPED BY REGIONAL ENVIRONMENT

World War II, of course, affected industry in the rest of the world as well as in North America. The productive capacity of Europe and Japan was devastated. The immediate industrial strategy was to rebuild capacity. Beyond that, regional and local environmental forces shaped strategies. Of the regional forces, one set affected Japan, another set affected Europe, and still another set affected the United States and Canada.

Japan

Among industrialized countries and regions, Japan was in some ways the worst off. Japan is small, crowded, and resource poor. It faced not only the need to rebuild but also had to face up to a worldwide prewar reputation as an exporter of shoddy products, or junk. There was an industrywide consensus that quality improvement should be a high-priority strategy. The strategy was translated into a management training effort unprecedented before or since in any country: Japanese managers from top to bottom learned Western quality control concepts and techniques, and Japan turned itself into the nation with perhaps the best rather than the worst reputation for quality. Japanese industry's *operating* strategy of quality improvement has been central to a *national* strategy of rapid growth in exports (there was no other way to finance the rebuilding of Japan) and *corporate* strategies of rapid growth in market share. A bonus of high quality is avoidance of costly scrap, rework, and customer returns. Avoiding those costs improves productivity, which stimulates exports and market-share growth still more.

Japan's overcrowding and lack of natural resources led to a second important operating strategy: avoidance of waste or idleness of material resources. The just-in-time production system and Toyota's ingeniously simple **kanban** (card) system of inventory control were perfected in response to this material-control operating strategy. This kind of resourcefulness improves productivity by reducing the material input component of product cost, and it sets off a chain reaction of problem solving to improve productivity and quality still more.

Europe

Europe did not have Japan's quality image problem nor its severe lack of natural resources. Instead, Europe's postwar industrial strategies were constrained by shortages of plant and skilled labor, combined with small fractionated markets and little labor mobility. Much of Europe's capacity was rebuilt to serve relatively small national markets, and industrial strategies were shaped by the widespread public desire for stability and preservation of community and national traditions. Operationally, this translates into strategies favoring flexible plants that can keep going even as consumer demands change; such plants are known as job shops. The typical strategy also calls for running plants close to full capacity. European inventories tend to be high, but companies stay put and jobs are protected.[2]

United States and Canada

The United States and Canada did not need to rebuild. The transition from wartime production to peacetime competition was relatively swift. Competition for market share led to a proliferation of options: models, styles, colors, sizes. The auto industry is the most visible example. As *The Wall Street Journal* put it, "For years, marketing departments in auto companies have demanded numerous options and different trim packages so that customers can practically design their own cars. Manufacturing executives usually agreed to the idea of options because it didn't add much to the amount of labor that went into a car."[3] While the options may not add a lot of labor cost, they add a great deal of inventory cost, because every option must be kept in stock. Furthermore, there are significant extra costs for tooling (dies, fixtures, etc.) and setup time to change machines from one option to another. The very idea of "mass production," which the United States was at one time famous for, is eroded when scores of options are allowed. (Henry Ford: "They can have any color they want, so long as it's black.") The Japanese had higher priorities that kept them from getting caught up in the options game. By pursuing its quality and productivity strategy for gaining market share and export business, Japan assumed world leadership in high-volume repetitive (mass) production.

There are many other regional environmental factors that shape corporate and operations strategies. National laws, policies, and regulations are especially influential: minimum wage, labor, immigration, tax, antitrust, liability, tariff, and patent laws; private versus public ownership; regulation of rates, routes, leases, and building permits; health, safety, and physical environmental protection laws; and economic policies to stimulate business activity.

Each of these factors is potent enough that whole books are written about it. Take immigration, for example. U.S. immigration laws and policies result in nearly half a million legal immigrants and at least that many illegal immigrants per year. But the immigrant "problem" is used (legally or illegally) in support of a labor-cost-saving strategy in many U.S. companies—from high-fashion clothing manufacturing in New York, to restaurants in Chicago, to construction in Texas, to auto refurbishing in California. Some labor economists feel that the United States will enjoy a

---

[2] Robert E. Fox, "Keys to Successful Materials Management Systems: A Contrast Between Japan, Europe and the U.S.," *1981 Conference Proceedings, American Production and Inventory Control Society,* Boston, 1981, pp. 322–26.

[3] "U.S. Auto Makers Are Having Trouble Adopting 'Kanban'," *The Wall Street Journal,* April 7, 1982, pp. 1, 32.

significant labor cost advantage in the next decade because of the likely continual influx of immigrant labor, whose willingness to work at entry-level wages and to perform less desirable tasks serves to hold down the entire wage structure. By contrast, Japan's low birth rate and low immigration portend long-run labor shortages and wage escalation as the work force ages. A POM strategy, already undertaken by many Japanese manufacturers, is to circumvent the labor-supply and wage-escalation problems by using robots. In the United States, robots perhaps are needed less for growth and productivity improvement than for quality reasons.

STRATEGIES SHAPED BY LOCAL ENVIRONMENT

Regional factors affect whole countries or continents. What is left are local environmental influences, that is, factors that shape the strategies of particular industries, companies, or organizations. Figure 2–2 shows four kinds of local factors within the center circle, along with previously discussed regional and global factors in the outer circles.

One kind of local environmental influence is community and supplier inputs. Community factors include labor supply and prevailing wages, tax rates, availability of utilities and transportation, and quality of life. Supplier factors concern materials, equipment, and services. The inputs that the community and suppliers are able to provide help shape strategic operating decisions, such as extent of vertical integration; plant size and location; and overall policies on subcontracting, shift work, and aggregate inventories.

Going clockwise in Figure 2–2, the next local influence is nature of the products that the organization is in business to provide. The organization's line of goods and services is distinguishable by product technology, process technology, and stage in the product life cycle (introduction, growth, maturity, decline). High-technology products require a research and development (R&D) strategy that assures a source of new product designs. Hard-to-make products require a strategy of high investing in process engineering. Both product and process design strategies are changeable as the product line ages.

The third local influence is demand. Demands for an organization's goods and services are generated by market forces and constrained by extent of the competition. Demand factors are critical in the shaping of four key operating strategies, i.e., strategies for design responsiveness, delivery responsiveness, quality, and productivity. Most other POM strategies—plant location, aggregate inventories, R&D, and so forth—are also affected somewhat by demand factors.

The last local influence in Figure 2–2 is present capabilities. The operational capabilities of the work force and plant may be very limited, or may be quite flexible. In the Japanese system, workers are quite flexible. This flexibility permits a low-inventory operating strategy, because flexible workers are moved around to make whatever items are currently needed. Existing management capabilities also affect operational strategies. In the early 1970s, large supermarket chains such as A&P and Kroger were considering adopting optical scanning for grocery checkout. None decided to proceed with this far-reaching strategic change until the late 1970s. While immediate

FIGURE 2–2

Environmental Influences on Organizational and Operational Strategies

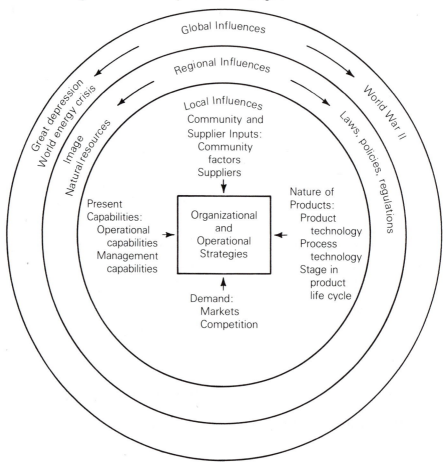

adoption was technologically feasible, the grocery industry had little experience in managing technological change, and caution was probably correct.

POSITIONING STRATEGIES

Organizational success—survival, growth, profitability, esteem—is attainable in various ways. The paths to success seem to reduce neatly to a few basic "positioning strategies," as we call them in POM. Positioning strategy refers to the organization's overall plan for fitting (or positioning) itself among its competitors in order to carve out a share of the market. In the case of nonprofit organizations, such as a government agency, the plan is to position the organization among competitors for public esteem—and budgets.

Western Viewpoint

A currently popular Western view poses three basic positioning strategies: (1) **cost leadership,** (2) **differentiation,** and (3) **focus.**[4]

A positioning strategy of cost leadership may be pursued via one or more of the following kinds of operating strategies: intensive process engineering, plant location in low-wage areas, economies of scale (large plants), becoming a "focused factory," and so forth. A focused factory tries to do less, but do it better.[5] For example, in the competitive microcomputer market, one of the upstarts was the Osborne 1, which entered the market as a price leader. The company's low-cost strategy was based on buying rather than making the components. The focused factory making the Osborne 1 was strictly an assembly plant, which was efficient enough that "it takes precisely 40 screws and 68 minutes" to assemble one.[6] (Osborne did not stay competitive. The company was forced to file for bankruptcy. But now their concept of the focused assembly plant is widely followed in the companies that are still in the small-computer industry—for example, IBM, Apple, Hewlett-Packard, and Commodore. And today many of the assembly lines require virtually *no* screws.)

Differentiation means product uniqueness. That is, your products or services are thought to be different from those of your competitors. Among color TV makers, Sony and Curtis Mathes are perceived to have superior quality, which is a particularly effective differentiation strategy. Bayer cultivates a similar image among aspirin companies. In consumer electronics Casio has pursued a differentiation strategy by releasing a continual series of new products: calculators with clocks, alarms, musical memory and playback, and so forth. The state of Kentucky has been projecting itself as the state most favorable to business. Chicago is said to be "a city that works." States and cities sometimes adopt differentiation strategies in order to gain industry and convention and tourist dollars.

In the process industries, companies tend not to pursue a differentiation strategy. One company's coal, lumber, pork bellies, or soda ash look about the same as those of the next company. They all process the commodities to meet about the same standards. Thus, the process industries tend to strive for cost leadership or for focus, considered next.

The third positioning strategy is focus, which means aiming at only a segment of the market. (Note: Focus as an overall corporate positioning strategy should not be confused with the focused-factory operating strategy.) Focus may be attained by either low costs or differentiation or both. While the focused company is not a leader

---

[4] Porter refers to them as "competitive strategies": Michael E. Porter, *Competitive Strategy: Techniques for Analyzing Industries and Competitors* (New York: Free Press, 1980), pp. 34–46 (HD41.P67).

[5] Wickham Skinner, "The Focused Factory," *Harvard Business Review,* May–June 1974, pp. 113–21.

[6] Bro Uttal, "A Computer Gadfly's Triumph," *Fortune,* March 1, 1982, pp. 74–76.

industrywide, it may do the best job for its own geographical area, for a nearby plant that it sells to, for serious hobbyists but not general consumers, or for some other specialized market segment. In Winnipeg, there are about 70 janitorial services listed in the yellow pages of the phone directory. One of them, let us call it Bright Way, has the focused strategy of cleaning only nice places, like carpeted office buildings. Bright Way charges more but does a better cleaning job, because it hires better people, trains them better, pays them better, and keeps them longer than most of the other janitorial services.

Each of the three positioning strategies is thought to require a different set of management and worker skills, types of plant and equipment, and operating systems. It seems unlikely that a single organization can succeed without a well-developed strategy in at least one of the three positions. Porter says that firms "stuck in the middle" of the three strategies are "almost guaranteed low profitability," and he cites Clark Equipment, Chrysler, British Leyland, and Fiat as examples.[7] The three-positioning-strategy theory does allow for the possibility of a company being so good that it is recognized both for cost leadership and for differentiation, but it is not easy to think of many examples in Western industry.

Japanese Strategies

While we can't think of many Western companies that are cost leaders and also differentiated or unique in the consumer's eye, we *can* come up with quite a few Japanese companies of that kind: Toyota, Nippon Steel, Yamaha, Matsushita Electric, Fujitsu, Hitachi, Bridgestone, and a large number of less well-known producers of machine tools, industrial sewing machines, communication equipment, vaccines, and so on. These are *low-cost* producers that at the same time have fine worldwide reputations for quality—which is a common form of differentiation among Japanese manufacturers. (Differentiation is usually associated with unique product designs, but uniquely excellent quality can set a company apart just as surely as product designs can.)

It was once presumed that high quality had its price. A few of our Western quality control experts—especially Joseph Juran, W. Edwards Deming, and A. V. Feigenbaum—tried for years to tell us that good quality actually lowers cost, but we didn't listen. The Japanese did listen. Deming and Juran have been trekking to Japan for more than 30 years telling about quality control—to very receptive ears.

What the Japanese seem to have demonstrated is the concept of *two* rather than three basic positioning strategies: One strategy is a market position as *cost/quality* leader. The second is a *focused* position. The companies listed above—Toyota, Nippon Steel, Yamaha, and so forth—are cost/quality leaders. Sony and Seiko are examples of focused companies; their focus is on the high-quality segment of the market. A more typical focus is that of thousands of small supplier plants in Japan. They have the single mission of providing parts, often to just one parent company, and the

---

[7] Porter, *Competitive Strategy,* pp. 41–44 (HD41.P67).

suppliers go so far as to locate their plants within a few miles of the parent plant in order to become so responsive as to be virtually indispensable.

STRATEGY AND TECHNIQUE

The central message of this chapter is that there are critical operating strategies that have tended to be neglected in Western industry for the past two decades. The discussion has been brief, but most of the points made in this chapter are reintroduced in more detail in later chapters.

While the forthcoming chapters mostly concern POM techniques, there is some discussion in every chapter of how the techniques affect strategies. For example, in the Chapter 8 discussion of the make-or-buy decision, analysis techniques are discussed. But companies have make-or-buy *strategies* that guide make-or-buy analysis in a particular case. For example, as has been mentioned, the manufacturer of the Osborne 1 microcomputer had a strategy of buying just about everything. As we shall see in the continuing discussion in Chapter 8, many Japanese companies have the same strategy, and in 1981 the U.S. auto industry began moving toward a buy and away from a make strategy.

Other seemingly narrow issues that have fascinating strategic ramifications include the following:

Quality (Chapter 12)—may be central to fast growth.

Repetitive production (Chapter 9)—may be the basis of cost leadership.

Production line balancing (Chapter 16)—important to high capacity utilization.

Capacity planning (Chapter 5)—the basis for planning labor requirements.

Inventory control (Chapter 8)—shown by the Japanese to affect cost, quality, need for fixed capacity, even worker behaviors.

Plant maintenance (Chapter 17)—affects quality and capital investment.

The chapters present many techniques, and the chapters are also spiced up a bit with commentary on issues that are strongly affecting the success and survival of companies that once seemed virtually immune from competitive, technological, or other types of risk.

Our profit-making companies *need help* from people who have not only intelligence but also knowledge and experience in operations. Our nonprofit sector needs the same sort of help in order to demonstrate ability to provide high-quality public service at reasonable cost—and thereby avert the budget cutters' axes. Your interest in operations management may be kindled enough by your POM studies to take advanced POM courses, to incorporate time and space in your career for gaining POM experience, or to make POM your chosen career. As the Uncle Sam-like cartoon character says, Operations needs *you!* And you need at least *some* operations experience—if you are to become a capable and contributing member of your organizational community.

OPERATIONS NEEDS YOU!

And you need at least some operations experience.

SUMMARY

Most organizations try to cultivate a public image of having certain *distinctive competencies* that set them apart from competitors. Examples are low costs, dedicated employees, superb customer service, product uniformity, and fast response. Operations management strategies are aimed at these kinds of competencies.

World War II was the major shaper of corporate and operations management strategies in the modern era. The war triggered a resource mobilization and productivity era. Then a postwar marketing era was spawned to sell excess capacity built up during the war. A financial-legal era arose in the 1960s and 1970s to assist in mergers between winners and losers from the marketing era. Finally, we are in the current era of productivity crisis, because buying other companies has taken managerial attention away from internal quality and productivity matters. Perhaps the influence of the war has run its course, and productivity will be emphasized with equal measures of the rest.

Aside from the war's global influence, it affected regional strategies differently. Japan was devastated and had to rebuild. Also, it had to overcome an image of shoddy export goods. The Japanese environment of overcrowdedness and lack of resources encouraged an operating strategy of waste avoidance, including the waste of bad-quality goods, idle inventories, and inefficiency. These operating strategies resulted in high-quality, low-cost goods, which met the national and corporate strategies of rapid export growth.

Europe also had to rebuild but did not have Japan's bad-quality image or lack of natural resources. So Europe rebuilt its traditional industrial base composed of smaller, more regional (less international) companies.

The United States and Canada did not have to rebuild and so were able to convert to peacetime competition swiftly. Proliferation of models and growth of inventory were corporate strategies for gaining a competitive edge.

There are many other regional influences on corporate and operations strategies—national laws and regulations, for example. U.S. immigration policies are not tough enough to stem the tide of illegal immigrants, but the immigrants provide cheap labor, which can be an asset to industry. Japan, on the other hand, faces future labor shortages and wage growth. One effect is that robots are strategically more vital for Japan than for most other countries.

Local influences on strategy include community and supplier factors, the nature of a company's own product line, the competitive climate, and present capacity and capability to produce. These factors shape a company's strategies for plant location, R&D, competitive response, technology, and so forth.

A company responds to its environment by developing positioning strategies for carving out a market. One theory recognizes three basic positioning strategies: cost leadership, differentiation, and focus. Western companies tend to aim at one of the three. If they don't, poor performance is likely. Some Japanese manufacturers have been able to achieve in two of the three areas at the same time. Well-known companies like Toyota and Bridgestone Tire achieve both cost leadership and products differentiated from those of their competitors by high quality. Thousands of smaller supplier companies have focus as their strategy, i.e., focus on supplying to only one or a few buying companies rather than selling in the whole world market.

This book is technique oriented, but in nearly every chapter, points are made about how techniques are shaped by strategies and vice versa.

REFERENCES

Books

Peters, Thomas J., and Robert H. Waterman, Jr.   *In Search of Excellence.* New York: Harper & Row, 1982 (HD70.U5.P424).

Porter, Michael E.   *Competitive Strategy: Techniques for Analyzing Industries and Competitors.* New York: Free Press, 1980 (HD41.P67).

Reich, Robert B.   *The Next American Frontier.* New York: Times Books, 1983 (JK467.R45).

Skinner, Wickam.   *Manufacturing in the Corporate Strategy.* New York: John Wiley & Sons, 1978 (TS155.S55).

REVIEW QUESTIONS

1. What is the likely fate of an organization that has no distinctive competencies? Why?

2. What are the two major *global* environmental shapers of organizational strategies (in the modern age)? Explain.

3. Why did the productivity emphasis of World War II dissolve after the war?

4. Why did many of the conglomerates, put together in the 1960s, begin to crumble in the 1970s?

5. What differences are there in how World War II affected Japanese and European versus North American industrial strategies?

6. Why did North American industry adopt a post-World War II corporate and operations strategy of proliferation of models?

7. What are likely future effects on industry of labor supply in the United States versus Japan?

8. Distinguish between product technology and process technology.

9. What are four major types of *local influences* on industrial strategies?

10. How does the *focus* positioning strategy differ from the *cost leadership* and *differentiation* strategies?

11. Is a *quality* strategy one of *focus, cost leadership,* or *differentiation?* Explain.

12. What positioning strategies have been particularly effective among leading Japanese manufacturers, and why?

PROBLEMS

1. Do the following organizations appear to have a strong differentiation strategy? Explain.
   a. Pizza Hut.
   b. E. I. duPont de Nemours & Co.
   c. The U.S. Army.
   d. Timex Corp.

2. What is the *basic positioning strategy* of each of the following? Discuss.
   a. United Parcel Service.
   b. Your local gas company.
   c. Mayo Clinic.
   d. Manufacturers and distributors of no-label foods, cigarettes, and beer.

3. What are the dominant elements of operations strategy in each of the following organizations? Discuss.
   a. Holiday Inn.
   b. U.S. Marines.
   c. Boeing.
   d. Procter and Gamble.

4. The Great Depression, World War II, and the Oil Shock of 1973 are cited in this chapter as being global shapers of corporate strategy. There are other lesser factors that have had effects on strategies. Four are listed below. Discuss each one separately. Is it a global, regional, or local factor? What has been its impact on strategy?
   a. Pollution control legislation.
   b. The Korean Conflict.
   c. Desegregation laws.
   d. The Viet Nam War.

5. What are the key local environmental influences on each of the following? Discuss.
   a. The typical department store.
   b. The typical commercial bus line.
   c. The typical lawn service.
   d. Your phone company.

6. What are two examples of non-Japanese companies that have been generally successful in achieving both cost leadership and quality leadership? Discuss.

7. What are two examples of prominent organizations or industries whose positioning strategy has drastically changed in your lifetime? Explain.

8. What are two examples of prominent organizations or industries whose positioning strategies have remained stable for many years? Explain.

PART ONE CASE STUDY: AUTOMATED PARKING SYSTEMS, INCORPORATED*

Automated Parking Systems was formed to build automated parking structures. Principal stockholders were a mechanical engineer and a building contractor who had jointly developed what they felt was a unique and technologically advanced parking concept. The plan was to construct standardized, modular structures for organizations needing concentrated parking facilities such as banks, hospitals, department stores, hotels, restaurants, and parking lot operators. Automated Parking would build the structures for their clients, who would then own and operate the facilities.

PARKING SYSTEM

As shown in Exhibit 1, the structures were of circular, concrete design, 20 levels high, and approximately 70 feet in diameter. Each level could hold 10 vehicles and was serviced by a computer control system, vertical hoist, turntable, and transfer mechanism capable of automatically parking or retrieving one vehicle each minute.

Except for support columns and exterior wall panels, each level was open space. Floors sloped toward an exterior drain trough that received dripping water or melting snow carried in on vehicles. A stairway, used only for maintenance and emergencies, serviced each level; a lock and access alarm at ground level limited entrance to authorized persons.

Safety barriers at the ground level, together with remote TV surveillance by a cashier-operator, minimized the possibility of accidents to customers. Ingress and egress ramps could be designed to be compatible with any site configuration and traffic flow pattern. The cashier's office and control room occupied the space of a ground-level parking stall or could be in a separate building. A single cashier-operator was expected to be able to handle the complete operation, exclusive of maintenance, of from one to three 200-car structures.

The vehicle hoist was an open-frame platform capable of vertical travel up to 400 feet per minute. The hoist shaft was 26 feet in diameter with guide rails to assure platform stability and alignment. Hoist drive was a 75-hp DC motor that operated through a speed-reducing mechanism. Power was provided by a 50-Kw motor generator set operated from the incoming AC line power. The hoist drive motor provided dynamic braking. Also, the hoist drive assembly had an electromechanical brake.

A rotary turntable, as shown in Exhibit 2, was mounted on the hoist platform to position the vehicle transfer device to any of 10 positions. The transfer device, which was mounted on the platform, was approximately 24 feet long. The transfer device raised the vehicle, moved it onto the hoist, and moved it off of the hoist into the parking stall.

---

* Adapted from Robert C. Meier, Richard A. Johnson, William T. Newell, and Albert N. Schrieber, *Cases in Production and Operations Management,* © 1982, pp. 13–18. Reprinted by permission of Prentice-Hall, Inc., Englewood Cliffs, N.J.

EXHIBIT 1

Automated Parking Structure

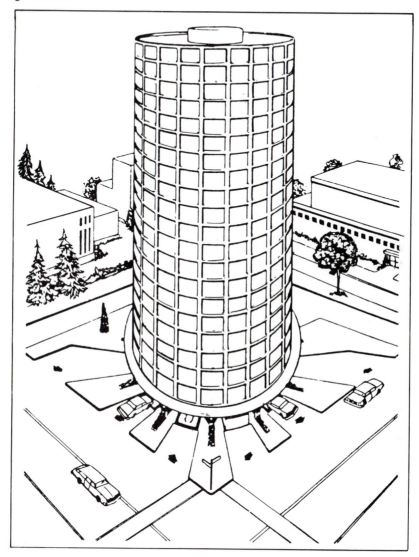

EXHIBIT 2

Vehicle Transfer Device

OPERATION OF THE SYSTEM

Vehicle parking was under the control of a small computer system. Normal system operation was completely automatic, although the cashier-operator could elect semiautomatic operation and control each operating step through the computer console. A complete manual control station located on the hoist platform could bypass the computer system in an emergency or service situation.

The computer system stored information about each vehicle parked. Vehicle identification code and entry time were contained on the customer's parking ticket. When the ticket was read by a system ticket reader, the computer initiated vehicle retrieval and calculated parking charges. These were displayed for the cashier-operator and recorded on tape for management and accounting reports. The operator console allowed manual vehicle retrieval in case of a lost or mutilated parking ticket.

In a typical case, a customer would enter an ingress stall, park, lock, and leave the vehicle. At departure the customer would activate a ticket dispenser. This would start the computer park cycle and code the time on a claim check. Prominent signs would provide instructions and remind the customer to take the claim check from the dispenser. The vehicle would then be automatically parked in the nearest available stall. The vehicle would not be moved until the ingress stall was clear and a protective barrier was in place.

Upon returning, the customer would present the claim check to the cashier. The claim check would be inserted in a reader to permit the computer to compute the parking fee and retrieve the vehicle. The customer would be directed to an egress stall to wait. A barrier would protect the customer while the vehicle was being delivered to the egress stall.

COSTS

Major operating costs were salaries and fringe benefits for the cashier-operators and costs of maintenance, utilities, taxes, and insurance. These costs would, of course, vary depending on the city and specific site. However, the developers estimated that the single cashier-operator would cost approximately $9.25 per hour, including fringe benefits, and that maintenance, utilities, taxes, and insurance might run about $475 per stall per year.

COMPETITIVE ADVANTAGES

The developers believed that the following were the most important features in competing with other parking systems:

1. **Speed of operation.** Automated parking structures could pick up one car or deliver one car in an average time of 60 seconds and could provide multiple entrances and exits for every 200 cars parked.
2. **Productivity.** An automated parking structure could provide a land use-productivity ratio of 10:1 on average with substantial savings in land and related costs. Twenty-two automobiles parked on the ground required roughly 6,500 square feet whereas an automated parking structure could park 200 automobiles in the same area.
3. **Price.** Estimates showed that an automated parking structure could be sold for the same price per stall as any competing indoor parking system.
4. **Operating economics.** Estimated operating costs were less than those for other parking systems due to fewer operating personnel and a smaller area to be cleared, lighted, and controlled for security.
5. **Computerized operations.** Traffic counts and tabulation of revenues were handled automatically by the computer, which was impervious to tampering by employees. The computer could provide centralized accounting records and reports via telephone interface, if desired.
6. **Adaptability.** The client could use one structure or as many as needed to meet any parking requirements.
7. **Protection.** A structure could be closed in for protection from the elements, thieves, and muggers. Cars would be protected from dents, scratches, and pilferage, as no person other than the customer would drive them.
8. **Air pollution.** No carbon monoxide or nitrogen oxide would be generated inside, because the car motor would be turned off on entry and not started again until after the customer entered the car to drive it away.

Small scale models and prototypes of portions of the automated parking structure and equipment had been built by the developers, but no complete system had been built or tested. However, the developers were confident that the design concept was sound and that the systems were simple enough that there would be little difficulty in actually building a structure. In addition, detailed specification and engineering drawings had been prepared for the concrete structure and equipment.

Using engineering drawings, architectural sketches, and other promotional literature, representatives of Automated Parking Systems engaged in a sales campaign in San Francisco and in several cities in Nevada. After six months, 10 prospects had indicated an interest, and contract negotiations were in progress for building a total of 33 structures with an estimated cost of $34,308,000. Details of the proposed projects are shown in Exhibit 3.

EXHIBIT 3

Automated Parking Systems Projects in Contract Negotiation

Project	Number of structures	Number of spaces	Approximate in-place cost*
San Francisco			
1. Bay Medical Center	1	200	$ 1,045,000
2. Golden State Bank	1	200	1,188,000
3. Main police station	3	600	3,000,000
4. Toyota dealer	3	600	3,000,000
5. Chang property	4	800	4,000,000
Nevada			
6. Casino A	5	1,000	4,875,000
7. Casino B	3	600	3,000,000
8. Casino C	6	1,200	7,200,000
9. Casino D	4	800	4,000,000
10. Casino E	3	600	3,000,000
			$34,308,000

* Cost of structure alone; does *not* include land.

DISCUSSION QUESTIONS

1. What is the "product" of this company? Discuss.

2. What type of operations (continuous, repetitive, job, etc.) applies in an automated parking system? Explain.

3. What *positioning strategy* does Automated Parking Systems appear to be striving for? Explain.

4. Is the automated parking structure concept competitively sound? What "distinctive competencies," if any, is the company trying to develop? Discuss fully.

Translating Demand into Planned Orders

An employee looking outward sees customer demand. But looking inward, the employee sees *orders*. In Part Two we see how demand is translated into orders. First, there is the demand itself; Chapters 3 and 4 explain the demand management function and demand forecasting techniques. Next comes capacity planning and master scheduling in Chapter 5. The rest of Part Two—Chapters 6–8—tells about breaking down the master schedule into plans for component inventory items and the management of materials.

Chapter 3

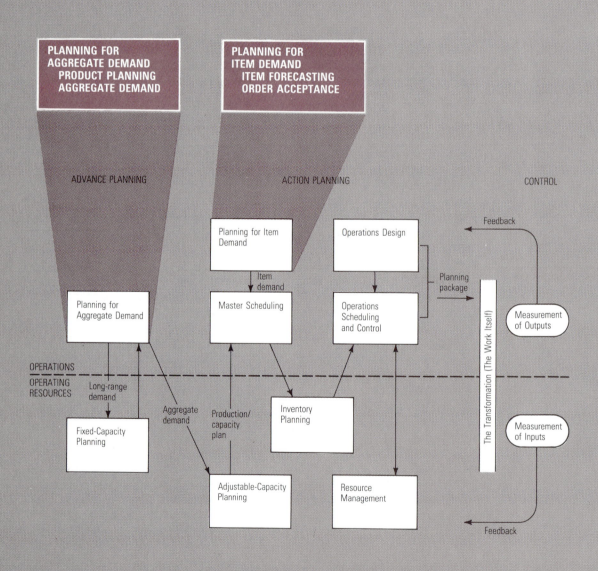

PLANNING FOR AGGREGATE DEMAND PRODUCT PLANNING AGGREGATE DEMAND

PLANNING FOR ITEM DEMAND ITEM FORECASTING ORDER ACCEPTANCE

ADVANCE PLANNING

ACTION PLANNING

CONTROL

Planning for Item Demand

Operations Design

Feedback

Item demand

Planning for Aggregate Demand

Master Scheduling

Operations Scheduling and Control

Planning package

The Transformation (The Work Itself)

Measurement of Outputs

OPERATIONS
OPERATING RESOURCES

Long-range demand

Aggregate demand

Fixed-Capacity Planning

Production/ capacity plan

Inventory Planning

Measurement of Inputs

Adjustable-Capacity Planning

Resource Management

Feedback

Demand Management and Product Planning

One reason for the existence of an enterprise is the customers who could use the goods and services of that enterprise. Who is it that is supposed to plan for meeting those customers' needs? Clearly, marketing has part of that planning responsibility. Just as clearly, operations has another part of it. Coordinated planning by these two parties is known as **demand management.**

Product planning is closely related to demand management. As demand for one product or service fades late in its life cycle, new ones must be phased in. The timing of product introduction is indicated by demand projections for current items. The discussion of demand management flows naturally into subsequent discussion of product planning.

DEMAND MANAGEMENT

Demand management encompasses actual customer orders, forecasts of orders, service (replacement) parts, interplant orders, branch warehouse demands, and international requirements.[1] Although the demand management concept was spawned in manufacturing, it fits well in services also. Insurance companies, government agencies, laundries, trucking, and schools also have coordination problems between those who sell and promote and those who provide the services and plan for the resources. Demand management in services is somewhat simpler since services do not involve external demands for service parts, nor interplant, branch warehouse, and international requirements for inventoriable products.

Greater difficulties are in manufacturing. Many manufacturers find it helpful to assign the coordination of demand management to a **master scheduler.** There may also be a master scheduling committee. One role of the master scheduler is to act as coordinator between production and marketing. Relationships between production and marketing generally involve too many surprises and not enough accurate information flow in either direction. A strong master scheduler can help.

While the master scheduler position is pivotal, there are others with key roles in demand management. Sales forces book orders, order entry clerks (or an order entry computer routine) process orders further, product managers (or a computer) forecast demand for orders not yet received, warehouses confirm or deny material availability, and traffic checks delivery dates against shipping capabilities. On the other side— the internal side—there are people who determine capacity, financial, and other limits on what is to be produced and delivered. But that is another story—to be taken up in Chapter 5.

PURPOSES OF DEMAND MANAGEMENT

There are short-term, medium-term, and long-term purposes of demand management. The short-term question concerns **item demand.** That is, the organization needs to know what demands there are in the near future for its mix of goods and services— the items it produces. The medium term covers about 6–18 months in manufacturing, but often much less in the service sector. The medium-term purpose of demand management is to project aggregate demands for capacity groups (product families)

---

[1] *APICS Dictionary,* 5th ed., Thomas F. Wallace (Falls Church, Va.: American Production and Inventory Control Society, 1984).

so that productive capacity can be adjusted properly. In the medium term the adjustments apply especially to labor, machine usage, and aggregate inventory; planning for these resources is called adjustable-capacity planning, or, for short, **capacity planning.** Long-term demand projections are needed for planning facilities—buildings, utilities, and equipment—rather than other more adjustable elements of capacity. Long-term demand management also concerns the introduction of new products and phasing out of old ones: **product planning.** Medium- and long-term demand management involve decisions that are made infrequently. The short-term product mix activities, by contrast, keep a good many employees busy all of the time—handling orders, and guessing about orders not yet formally booked. Order-processing activities are examined next.

ORDER PROCESSING

When things are going well, operations is able to produce and deliver what marketing sells. To keep things going well, operations management must play an active role in customer ordering. In most cases it is poor policy for the operating department to simply put into backlog any orders that sales is able to "scare up." Instead, there should be a well-devised order-processing system, which includes **order promise.** In the case of services, the order promise is known as an appointment.

Order promise by operations management serves as its commitment in the close partnership that marketing and operations should have. Speedy notice of this commitment can provide salespeople with sound information to use in making sales and delivery agreements. In return, the sales force may be able to gear its selling activities more toward operating capacity. That is, salespeople may push sales of items that help to keep slack shops busy and ease off on items that would strain other shop capacities.

The only situation in which operations does not have an order promise function is the pure make-to-stock company: Goods are made to a forecast and placed in distribution centers, and customer order processing is up to the marketing arm of the business. But few companies are strictly make-to-stock. Special large orders, orders for service parts, and so forth may be accepted. In that case there should be a formal order promise procedure so that sales can give the customer some assurance that production has a commitment to meet the agreed-upon delivery date.

The sequence of order processing is shown in Figure 3–1. The first step is **order booking.** That is, an order is booked by sales. The second step is **order entry,** in which the order is entered into the organization's order-processing system. Order entry may include credit checking, documenting pertinent customer data, determining if the order may be filled from stock, and assigning an internal order number.

The next seven steps are operations functions. Step 3 is to determine **total requirements.** When there are orders by multiple customers for the same product (or service), the orders must be totaled. Also, there may be a need to translate sales catalog terminology into part numbers and names used by production. In some companies, there are as many as three sets of part numbers, which associate with three different

FIGURE 3–1

The Order-Processing Sequence

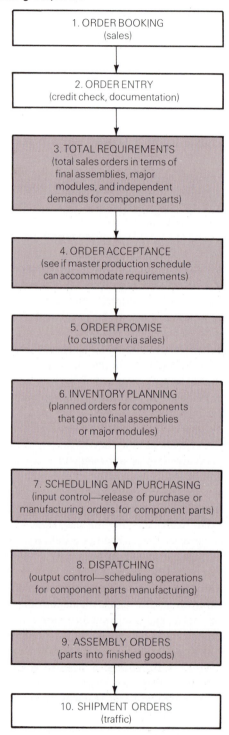

Note: Shading indicates operations management responsibilities.

scheduling procedures: (1) the final assembly schedule—for assembly of finished end products, (2) the master production schedule—for production of major modules, like frames and engines, and (3) a schedule for the manufacture of service parts, interplant transfer parts, customer optional parts, and so forth.

Step 4, **order acceptance,** is a check to see if present schedules may accommodate new requirements. If the customer is willing to wait, that customer's order may be accepted and placed at the tail end of the backlog of orders. The preferred procedure in competitive industries is to make, or partially make, the goods, based on a forecast. Thus, parts, major modules, and final assemblies are scheduled in advance, and it is these schedules that are checked to see if they will result in the goods requested by a given customer at the desired future date.

Step 5 is the culmination of step 4. If the schedule can meet the customer order, an order promise notice goes to the customer via sales. In client-oriented services, the order promise is known as an appointment. The order is not a legal promise. It just means that production schedules have been checked, and, barring problems, the customer order should be done on time. But all parties realize that problems do occur and some orders are going to be late.

In steps 6–8 customer identification is lost, and these steps are generally out of the realm of demand management. In the sixth step, **inventory planning,** accepted orders are divided into requirements for component parts. Where the parts are not on hand, this results in manufacture and purchase orders for parts. The component parts orders do not easily tie to a given customer, because common parts go into various end items ordered by various customers. **Scheduling,** at a detailed level, and **purchasing,** are the seventh step: Schedulers release the parts manufacturing orders with care so as not to overload the shop; buyers release the purchase orders. **Dispatching** is the eighth step: Dispatchers control the priorities of parts orders as they queue up in the work centers to have certain operations done.

Finally, in the ninth step, **assembly orders,** the customer order reemerges as the basis for orders for the final assembly of end items (and accessories) into finished goods or end products. **Shipment orders,** geographically consolidated, constitute the 10th and last step in Figure 3–1.

It is clear from Figure 3–1 that order processing is complex. It will take the next nine chapters to fully explain all the steps and the techniques used to achieve good results—which means on-time completions with good quality at reasonable cost, and responsiveness to new customer orders or changes in present orders. In complex cases, the very word, *order,* has multiple meanings. For example, as we have seen, there can be a sales order, a consolidation of sales orders into a few order batches (total requirements), scheduled production orders for major modules, planned orders for component parts from inventory planning, shop orders and purchase orders for component parts and raw materials, separate operations (with their own operation numbers) for each shop order, final assembly orders, and shipment orders. Each type of order can have its own set of order numbers and documents. Clearly, in a manufacturing company, you will not necessarily get the response you are looking for if you say, "Where's my order?"

Even in the services sector the customer order may explode into several subtypes.

For example, at a medical clinic, you, the patient, are an order; when you go to X-ray, an X-ray order number is assigned; when you go to the lab, several lab test orders are created; finally, when you are finished, there will be a billing number for total services rendered.

DEMAND FORECASTING

Actual customer orders are nice, but many a company has made its mark serving phantom customers, that is, customers that do not order until the goods already have been made. Such make-to-stock companies produce to a demand forecast. It could be said that a demand forecast differs from actual orders only in that actual orders are more certain. Forecasts are unlikely to be correct, but actual orders are uncertain, too, because they may be cancelled or changed. Thus, the order-processing steps explained above take place whether production is triggered by orders or by a forecast. Demand forecasting is a vital demand management activity, aside from the rest of the order processing steps, and it warrants a good deal of discussion. General discussion continues here, and the techniques of demand forecasting are presented in detail in the next chapter.

Types of Demand Forecasting

The purposes of demand forecasting are the same as the three for demand management: determine items to be produced, plan for adjustable capacity, and plan for facilities. Item forecasts must express demand in natural item units. Examples are tons of steel and gallons of diesel fuel in the process industries and clients, light bulbs, paper tablets, trucks, and so forth in discrete production industries. The forecast is expressed in those terms, and so is the schedule. Item forecasts are short term, from a few minutes for some fast foods to many months for some long lead time, heavy industrial products.

Adjustable-capacity planning concerns labor, equipment, and aggregate inventory, and it calls for medium-term forecasts. Medium term could be just a few days for a firm that uses untrained workers, and hires and lays off based on a few days' notice as demand rises and falls. Most firms adjust the labor force less often, because of the cost of training labor. In that case, the medium-term forecast would extend several months or quarters into the future. Medium-term forecasts are often expressed in labor-hours' or machine-hours' worth of demand. Other units of measure, including dollars, are workable, since they may be converted to labor, machine usage, and aggregate inventory.

Long-term forecasts for facilities—plant and equipment—may go 10–20 years in the future for plants that require extensive hearings, licenses, debate, and approvals. Nuclear power plants are one example. At the other extreme, the long-term forecast may need to project demand only a couple of years out for a restaurant. Dollars are the preferred measure of long-term demand, but it may be useful to subdivide the total dollars into forecasts by type of product to indicate how the plant should be equipped—that is, how much should be spent for equipment in each product area.

Forecasting in Selected Industries

Competition affects the kind of forecast required. In some industries there are competitive pressures to meet customer demand immediately from stock. Examples are auto replacement parts, consumer goods, and cafeteria foods. These are make-to-stock/ship-to-order businesses. They require that everything from raw materials to finished goods be based on demand forecasts.

At the other extreme are industries that have very long manufacturing lead times, such as ships, locomotives, missiles, and heavy construction. These heavy-capital-goods firms are project oriented, and they make to order. Such firms may maintain no inventories, not even raw materials. They need only long- and medium-term forecasting—as the basis for capacity and facilities planning. Purchase of raw materials and production of goods are based on firm contracts rather than on forecasts.

Figure 3–2 illustrates the two extreme types of industry plus two in between. As is shown, it is customer lead time that dictates how much forecasting is required.

FIGURE 3–2

Demand Lead Times and Forecasts Required

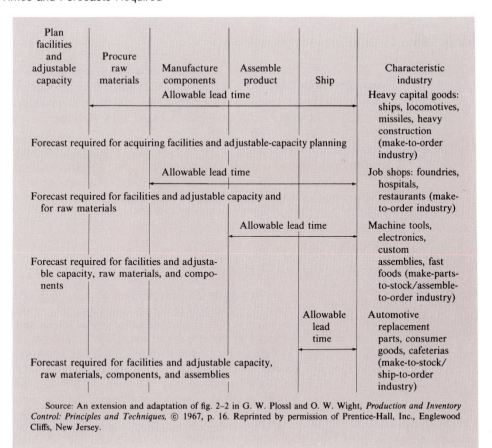

Source: An extension and adaptation of fig. 2–2 in G. W. Plossl and O. W. Wight, *Production and Inventory Control: Principles and Techniques,* © 1967, p. 16. Reprinted by permission of Prentice-Hall, Inc., Englewood Cliffs, New Jersey.

The first of the in-between industries is the class referred to as the job shop. Job shops, including foundries, hospitals, and restaurants, forecast for facilities and adjustable-capacity planning and for raw materials. These firms make to order but from materials on hand.

The other in-between type of industry is that which produces components and plans facilities, adjustable capacity, raw materials, and fixed capacity based on forecasts. But assembly and shipment await firm customer ordering. Examples are machine tools, electronics, custom assemblies, and fast foods. (Fast-food restaurants often precook or preassemble ingredients based on forecasts.) These are assemble-to-order firms.

The figure may give the impression that in a given firm up to five different types of forecasts could be required: one for facilities, one for adjustable capacity, one for raw materials, one for components, and one for product assembly. Modern production and inventory control, based on time-phased material planning, is able to cut this to two or three forecasts: a long-term and a medium-term forecast for facilities and adjustable capacity and a shorter-term forecast that links materials to components and perhaps to product assembly.

Forecasting in Support Organizations

The common view seems to be that forecasting should be done by those with responsibility for basic products/services. This would limit forecasting to items earning revenue. Or for nonrevenue-producing organizations, forecasting would be restricted to major-mission items; for example, in social work, forecast the number of eligible clients.

That view of forecasting is too narrow. *All* managers should forecast. Putting it another way, all staff services and nonrevenue items should be forecast—in addition to forecasting for revenue and major-mission items. An example may help to show why forecasting is necessary in support departments.

EXAMPLE 3–1

Apex Steel Cabinet Company

O. R. Guy is the new president of Apex. One of his first acts is to create the department of management science and to assign corporate forecasting to it. Corporate forecasting applies to the firm's revenue-earning products: its line of steel cabinets.

Management science department analysts arrive at a forecast of a 10 percent increase in total steel cabinet sales for next year. Mr. Guy informs key department heads that they may consider 10 percent increases their targets for planning departmental budgets. Protests come at Mr. Guy from several directions. Most notable are the following three:

1. Engineering chief: "Mr. Guy, I hate to protest any budget increase.

But I'd rather wait until I need it. The engineering workload often goes down when cabinet sales go up. That's because marketing pressures us less for new product designs when sales are good. But then in some years of good sales we have a lot of new design and design modification work. This happens when several key products are in the decline phase of their life cycles. So you can see that our budget should not depend strictly on corporate sales."

2. Personnel chief: "We are the same way, Mr. Guy. The personnel workload depends more on things like whether the labor contract is up for renewal. Sure, we need to do more interviewing and training when corporate sales go up. But we have bigger problems when they go down. Layoffs and reassignments are tougher. Also, when sales go down, we may get more grievances."

3. Marketing chief: "Well, I hate to be the crybaby. But it's marketing that bears most of the load in meeting that 10 percent forecast sales increase. I was going to ask for a 20 percent budget increase—mainly for a stepped-up advertising campaign. I don't dispute the management science projection of a 10 percent sales increase. The market is there; we just need to spend more to tap it."

Based on these three comments, Mr. Guy rescinds his note about a 10 percent targeted budget increase. He then informs managers at all levels in the firm that they are expected to formally forecast their key workloads. This becomes the basis for their plans and budgets. The management science department is assigned to serve as adviser for those managers requesting help.

To explain what is meant by key workloads, Mr. Guy provides each manager with a simple forecasting plan developed by the chief of personnel. This plan is shown in Figure 3–3.

The plan in Figure 3–3 provides for forecasting *in units of demand* as much as possible. The alternative is to skip this step and directly plan for staff, equipment, and other resources. This is the approach taken for item 7 in Figure 3–3, miscellaneous workloads. Some of the same methods—trend projection and judgment—may be used in this approach. But it is not demand forecasting; it is supply, or resource capacity, planning.

Planning resources directly rather than translating from a forecast of workload units is the easy way. It is also less precise. The precise approach is to forecast demand in units. The standard time to produce one unit may be determined—very precisely if the product is a key one. Then the unit forecast may be multiplied by the standard time to give staffing needs. And the unit forecast may be multiplied by material factors, space factors, and so on, to give the projected needs for other resources. The cost of all these resources then becomes the budget.

In the example, Mr. Guy is following a rational approach in requesting demand forecasts of all managers. It would be a mistake, however, to expect every manager to use extensive—and expensive—record keeping and historical data analysis. For lesser demands, a less formal approach should be satisfactory.

FIGURE 3–3

Forecasting Plan—Personnel Department, Apex Company

	Workloads	Forecast basis
1.	Hiring/interviewing	Number of job openings—based on data from other departments Number of job applicants—based on trend projection and judgment
2.	Layoffs and reassignments	Number of employees—based on data from other departments
3.	Grievances	Number of stage 1, 2, and 3 grievances, estimated separately—based on trend projection and judgment
4.	Training	Number of classroom hours Number of OJT hours Both based on data from other departments
5.	Payroll actions	Number of payroll actions—based on number of employees and judgment on impact of major changes
6.	Union contract negotiations	Number of key issues—based on judgment
7.	Miscellaneous—all other workloads	Not forecast in units; instead resource needs are estimated directly based on trends and judgment

Forecast Error—Item versus Aggregate

The nature of forecasting is such that we expect demand forecasts to be wrong. If our average forecast error is high, we end up with too many of the items or resources that are overforecast and too few of the items or resources that are underforecast.

A normal part of demand forecasting is finding a pattern in past demand data and then calculating the error in that pattern. There are a number of ways to arrive at a pattern. The forecast errors of each pattern may then be compared to see which one seems to explain changes in demand the best.

Happily, the average error is likely to be far less for a group of items than for the average item within a group. This is seen in Figure 3–4, which shows six items in a small group. Third-quarter actual demand and third-quarter forecasts are given for each item. The error is the difference between actual and forecast amounts. The percent error is the absolute error (no minus signs) divided by actual demand. The average of the percent errors for the six items is 18.1 percent. But the average error for the items as a group is only 6.6 percent.

The result of forecasting for whole product or capacity groups is the aggregate demand forecast, which could be measured in pieces, pounds, and so on, or converted to capacity units like labor-hours or machine-hours. Aggregate demand forecasts

FIGURE 3-4

Item-Forecast versus Group-Forecast Accuracy

Item	(1) Third-quarter actual	(2) Third-quarter forecast	(3) Error (column 1 − column 2)	(4) Percent error (column 3/ column 1)
Bracket	1,600	1,280	+320	20.0
Doorknob	23,200	20,300	+2,900	12.5
Hinge	18,660	15,120	+3,540	19.0
Vise	22,210	32,010	−9,800	44.1
Tool case	7,960	7,880	+80	1.0
Grate	36,920	41,290	−4,370	11.8
Average item forecast error				18.1
Group totals	110,550	117,880	−7,330	6.6

are useful in planning for adjustable capacity, such as work force and inventories. (See the chart on the chapter title page.) The purpose is to adjust capacity to fit forecast aggregate demand. Matching capacity to aggregate demand works well only if groupings are set wisely; this is explained in a later chapter. The point here is simply that it *is* possible to avoid large overcommitment or undercommitment of resources; the way to avoid such costly errors is to rely on the lower error rates of group forecasts.

Note: Figure 3-4 may give the impression that a group forecast is the sum of the forecasts of items in the group. That is *not* the best way. It is better to develop the forecast by examining trends, seasonality, and so forth for the *group as a whole*. This is not only easy; it is likely to be more accurate than the sum of several item forecasts, because of the possibility of leaving out some items produced within the capacity group. Figure 3-4's purpose is just to show the differences in accuracy of an item versus a group forecast.

Item forecasts have a different purpose. Item forecasts are an input into product scheduling. The high level of inaccuracy of the item forecast is a challenge that the master scheduler must live with, because production scheduling is by item, not by groups.

Forecast Error in Out-Periods

Forecasts are more accurate for shorter periods of time. This makes intuitive sense, and it can be shown by an example, Figure 3-5. The demand forecast is set at 500 per week (column 2). Only a sample of weeks is included for illustration: weeks 2, 5, 10, 15, 20, and 25. Cumulative demand forecast (column 3) is simply number of weeks times the weekly forecast of 500. That is, column 3 = (column 1) × (column

FIGURE 3–5

Cumulative Forecast Error, Picture Frames

(1) Week number	(2) Weekly demand forecast	(3) Cumulative demand forecast (column 1 × column 2)	(4) Cumulative actual demand	(5) Cumulative absolute error (column 4 − column 3)	(6) Cumulative error as a multiple of weekly forecast (column 5/ column 2)
2	500	1,000	1,162	162	0.3
5	500	2,500	2,716	216	0.4
10	500	5,000	5,488	488	1.0
15	500	7,500	8,110	610	1.2
20	500	10,000	11,250	1,250	2.5
25	500	12,500	14,010	1,510	3.0

2). Cumulative actual demand figures (column 4) were made up but are realistic. Cumulative absolute error (column 5) is actual (column 4) minus forecast (column 3). The error as a multiple of the weekly forecast is the error in column 5 divided by the forecast, 500. The result is a pattern of rising error as the forecast takes in more weeks of demand.

Knowing this does not mean that longer-term forecasting is futile. There must be such forecasts for capacity planning purposes. They must project as far into the future as the planning lead time for the given resource or unit of capacity.

Two useful principles follow from the knowledge that shorter forecasts are more accurate:

1. As time passes, forecasts should be refined by interjecting newer data and rolling the forecast over.
2. The planning and control systems that are sustained by the forecast should be segmented, if possible, according to the need for forecast accuracy.

As an example of both points, some goods producers master-schedule product modules and component parts based on projections of 52 weeks; the master schedule is refined every month based on latest revised forecasts plus actual orders. Final assembly of end products is based on shorter-term projections, maybe for only a few days or weeks.

Since schedules for product modules and component parts are based on longer-range forecasts, they are subject to large errors. But modules and parts are not so costly as end products, and there is some flexibility as to what end products the modules and parts may be assembled into. Since the more costly and inflexible end products are assembled based on short-term assembly schedules, the end-product error is small.

Final-Consumer Demand Data

Layers of middlemen in the product distribution system can hide some truths about real demand for one's products. If a forecast is based on recent sales to distribution centers, wholesalers, or retailers, a phony picture may be painted. Real demand is what final consumers are buying. All else is pipeline filling. A system of gathering recent data on sales to final consumers can greatly improve the forecast.

Wight notes that the main purpose of warranty cards enclosed with consumer products is not to validate the product guarantee.[2] The guarantee is valid regardless. The main value of the cards is to provide the company with fast feedback, a direct tap on the pulse of the marketplace. The cards go right to the manufacturer without interference or delay by middlemen.

THE PRODUCT LINE

Planning new products and services involves high-risk strategic decisions. They put into motion plans for facilities (fixed capacity)—plans that can be set aside only at great expense. Because facilities are so costly to change, they, in turn, influence the development of the product line. Thus, the diagram introducing this chapter shows arrows going both ways between planning for aggregate demand and facilities planning.

Product Development—Strategic Factors

The primary trigger for new product development is *strategic need for new products.* As Figure 3–6 indicates, there are two key strategic factors. One is the organization's **growth strategy.** A fast-growth strategy generally requires the introduction of one product after another. The second factor concerns **capacity utilization.** In order to pay for (amortize) fixed capacity and retain talented workers, new products must be phased in as old ones are phased out.

Once the strategic needs for new products have been determined, **product development options**—next in Figure 3–6—may be considered. First of all, there are various **research strategies** to be considered. These range from little research, to relying on outside research and development (R&D), to extensive in-house R&D capabilities. Specific research options may be revealed by **technological forecasting.** The idea is to try to predict the next product or process breakthrough. Research and development efforts may then be directed toward a predicted breakthrough—to fulfill one's own prophesy! Research strategies and technological forecasting are discussed in greater detail in the next section.

Having established a need for new products and having considered the R&D options, the organization's **plan for new products and services** is ready to go. Carrying

---

[2] Oliver W. Wight, *MRP II: Unlocking America's Productivity Potential* (Williston, Vt.: Oliver Wight Limited Publications, 1981), pp. 187–88 (TS161.Wrx).

FIGURE 3–6

New Product Planning

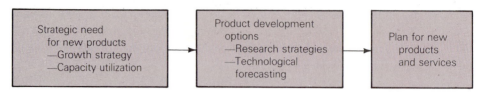

out the plan is a scientific and an engineering function, beyond the scope of this book. However, the management of R&D projects is an operations management topic, which is taken up in Chapter 14. The problem of translating an engineering design into a process plan—how to make the item—is discussed next.

Producibility

Is the engineer's design (or the dietician's menu or the teacher's syllabus) "doable"? That is, can the design reasonably be executed? The organization should make sure that it can.

There are quite a few ways of trying to make sure that a design is producible. Some companies put manufacturing engineers on temporary assignment in design engineering; the idea is to have the manufacturing engineers on hand to check the designs for producibility. Another approach is to send engineers' designs through one or more reviews; these **design reviews** are checks to make sure that the product meets the customer's requirements and can be made. (A special type of review known as value analysis or value engineering has cost minimization as its purpose. Value analysis is discussed in Chapter 8 in connection with purchasing.)

There are three major problems inherent in the business of translating designs into products. One is organizational. Our design engineers are in their own department apart from the production or manufacturing engineering department.

The second problem is related to the first. It is the problem, mentioned in Chapter 2, of overspecialization. Our design engineers (or dieticians or teachers) may spend their whole careers in a single specialty. If so, they may become isolated. They develop myopic vision. They "suboptimize," as the management scientists would put it.

The third problem is also related. In the product design profession it has become customary for designers to take professional pride in developing a design so complete, so fully specified and annotated, that the receiver of the blueprints (or equivalent) can find scarcely anything to question. While this type of professional dedication seems admirable, it works against the cause of producibility. Why? Because the designer can scarcely have full knowledge of productive capabilities, and therefore the design is likely to have features that are difficult, costly, or impossible to make. What can be done?

For one thing, the company may simply set forth a policy that designers will specify only critical product features and leave noncritical features to be determined at the time of production. One company that follows this policy is Deere & Company. At Deere, design engineers put circles next to dimensions on the design drawing. A full circle means the dimension is critical, a half circle means the dimension may be changed with design approval, and an empty circle means change it as you please.

This kind of policy keeps design engineers from falling into the trap of believing that their best effort is the one that raises the fewest questions. In fact the policy encourages questions. The questions, in turn, often call for designers to come out onto the production floor to discuss and help resolve the issues. Thus, the policy of specifying only critical dimensions helps break down organizational barriers.

Some Japanese manufacturing companies practice "minimum dimensioning" or "minimal specifications" policies extensively—to the point where design engineers spend much of their time on the shop floor with sleeves rolled up, or in suppliers' plants in the case of bought parts. These policies are less common in North America right now. But as our companies adopt Japanese techniques like just-in-time production, changes in design engineering practices, including minimal specifications, will probably also be adopted. The reasons why just-in-time production tends to trigger changes in engineering design will be made clear in later chapters.

Research Strategies

Research strategies have to do with the extent of research, the type of research, and the source of research expertise. Commitment to product research ranges from massive for a corporation like Du Pont to meager for, say, the cemetery business. The amount depends more on the dynamics and competition in the industry than on the size of the organization. It also depends on the character and image of the given organization.

Surveys have been done to show how much different organizations spend on research. More data are available for manufacturing industries than for service industries. Table 3–1 gives the results of a survey of R&D expenditures as a percentage of sales in large manufacturing firms. As might be expected, the semiconductor and computer industries rank highest. Firms in these industries spend about 10 times more than the percentage that the food, beverage, textile, and apparel industries spend.

In both manufacturing and services, research expenditures wax and wane. Much of this change is reaction to competitive pressures. A prominent example is the U.S. government's reaction to the missile crisis of the 1960s. Congress was prompted to appropriate huge amounts of research money to close the Soviet-U.S. missile gap. Later, with the gap closed, Congress saw fit to cut way back on research support.[3]

---

[3] "From 1961 to 1967 government-funded R&D increased 5.6 percent a year. . . . But from 1967 to 1975 the government R&D shrank 3 percent a year." Reported in "The Silent Crisis in R&D," *Business Week,* March 8, 1976, p. 90.

TABLE 3–1

Percentage of Sales Spent on Company-Financed R&D

Industry	Percent of annual sales spent on company-financed R&D
Semiconductors	7.8%
Computers	6.8
Instruments	5.2
Aerospace	5.1
Automotive	4.0
Electronics	3.8
Chemicals	2.9
Electrical	2.8
Machine tools	2.6
Food and beverage	0.7
Textiles, apparel	0.6

Source: "R&D Scoreboard, 1982," *Business Week,* June 20, 1983, pp. 122–52. The survey included 776 larger firms and more industries than the 11 shown in this table.

Commitment to research should depend primarily on conditions. Figure 3–7 shows how the organization's research strategy might be roughly related to various uncertainty conditions. The question in column 1—Can we design it?—is the one most germane to this discussion. But that question is best viewed in context with these equally important questions: Can we make it well? Can we sell it? Yeses to all three questions are needed before the product or service is added to the line. Where the answer is uncertain, research may be called for. For example, product design research is called for in the last four cases, where there is uncertainty about designing the product or service. That research should be intensive if management believes that the product can easily be made and marketed (case 5). The research should be exploratory where uncertainty surrounds all three questions (case 8).

While product research has most of the glamour and gets most of the publicity, **process** research can be every bit as valuable strategically. The Japanese have been notably adept at process research. In the remaining chapter discussion, process research is considered as being supportive of product research—since processes concern how to produce certain products. Process planning, including process research, is a basic operations management topic. It is discussed in more detail in later chapters dealing with work methods, quality control, plant layout, material handling, and so forth.

Commitment to research is secondarily a matter of organizational character. There is room for both leaders and followers in most industries. The leaders may adopt aggressive or **offensive** product design strategies; the followers may adopt **defensive** strategies; and those in between may make moderate commitments by **contracting** research or by **licensing** other people's product designs as necessary.

The offensive strategy is to commit a lot of money to building a research team.

FIGURE 3–7

Research Strategies for Coping with Uncertainties

	Uncertainties			
Case	Can we design it?	Can we make it well?*	Can we sell it?†	Research strategies
1	Easily	Easily	Easily	Little research except for pilot testing and trial marketing
2	Easily	Easily	Uncertain	Intensive market research
3	Easily	Uncertain	Uncertain	Market research and process/plant studies
4	Easily	Uncertain	Easily	Intensive production process and plant design study
5	Uncertain	Easily	Easily	Intensive product design research using parallel approaches
6	Uncertain	Easily	Uncertain	Product design research and market research
7	Uncertain	Uncertain	Easily	Product design research and process study
8	Uncertain	Uncertain	Uncertain	Exploratory product design, process, and market research

* Uncertainty about "making it" calls for process research; see process planning in Chapter 13.
† Uncertainty about "selling it" calls for marketing research, which is not discussed in this book.
Source: Adapted from *Innovation: The Management Connection* by Robert O. Burns (Lexington, Mass.: Lexington Books, D. C. Heath and Company, Copyright 1975, D. C. Heath and Company).

The objective of such a strategy is to design and market products while competition is light or nonexistent. An organization may also assume an offensive strategy for a short-run reason, such as product diversification. Large firms are better able to afford the risks of an offensive strategy, but many small firms have grown large by taking such risks. Xerox, Polaroid, and Texas Instruments are examples. In some industries—the aerospace and electronics industries, for instance—nearly every firm sees the need for an offensive strategy. Other industries, such as railroads, seem to have a defensive research strategy.

An offensive **product** research strategy generally costs a lot of money for building a research team. Process research can also be costly, but money may be saved by harnessing the common sense and experience of the workers who produce the goods and provide the services. Western employee suggestion and work simplification programs attempt to do just that. Japanese manufacturers get workers involved in a never-ending succession of work improvement projects—sometimes formally designated as quality control circles. These matters are discussed further in later chapters.

With the organization's research strategy as a foundation, the concern shifts to the question of what research projects to pursue. Technological forecasting sometimes provides guidance.

Technological Forecasting

Technological forecasting might be thought of as systematic crystal ball gazing. It predates but fits in with the field of study known as futurology.[4] Some colleges now offer courses and even degrees in futurology.

Much of the emphasis in futures studies concerns broad socioeconomic matters: food and energy supplies, automation, leisure, lifestyles, population, and so forth. Technological forecasting, however, is generally directed toward specific organizations or industries.

The major techniques of technological forecasting include the following:

Predictive techniques
    Trend extrapolation
    Enveloping
    "Involvement" (or gaming) techniques
Normative (advocacy) techniques
    Morphological analysis
    Relevance trees

Many of these techniques have been developed in so-called think tanks. These include RAND Corporation, the Hudson Institute, and the Institute for the Future. Contributions have also been made by a few consulting and research groups, including Battelle Memorial Institute, Stanford Research Institute, and Arthur D. Little. The Department of Defense, NASA, and the aerospace and electronics industries have provided much of the backing.

The predictive techniques are best known. These include trend extrapolation methods as well as various methods of active involvement, such as role playing, scenario writing, brainstorming, and Delphi.

Trend Extrapolation. Everyone who is old enough or is knowledgeable enough about history tries his hand at trend extrapolation. Some are doomsayers and see trends leading to flood, famine, and war. Others extrapolate hopeful trends and forecast peace, plenty, and happiness.

Scientific extrapolation aims at avoiding optimism or pessimism. It involves plotting points on graph paper, fitting curves to the points, and projecting into the future.

One step in graphic trend extrapolation is to establish the past rate of technological

---

[4] A World Futures Society was formed in 1966.

improvement in some technological area, for example, coal-mining output per miner or the density of information bits in computer memory. The rate of improvement may then be projected any number of years into the future. The projected improvement may show when present items in the product line are likely to become obsolete. The projection may also show where new products or processes need to be introduced. For example, a company making coal-drilling equipment may project when its current line of drills will be obsolescent. This projection enables it to put a research and development team to work at roughly the right time to have an advanced type of drill developed when it will be needed.

Figure 3–8 shows examples of graphic projection. Figure 3–8A plots hypothetical outputs of mine-drilling equipment. A curve is drawn through the plotted points and extended by "eyeball" into the future. The projection may be analyzed for product development opportunities, as was discussed above.

Figure 3–8B plots hypothetical densities of information bits in computer memory. In this case the plotted points are fitted to a curve that follows a particular mathematical formula. In the example the general formula $Y = ab^x$ is shown—for illustrative purposes only. (The parameters, a and b, would have to be determined to actually plot or describe the curve.) $Y = ab^x$ is the general form of what is known as an exponential curve. Some experts feel that technological advances of many kinds have tended to follow an exponential pattern.[5]

There are statistical curve-fitting techniques for finding out the type of mathematical formula (such as exponential or straight line) and the formula parameters that best fit a group of plotted points. The techniques are beyond the scope of this book but are widely available in statistics and operations research books.

The advantage of finding a mathematical formula is that this permits turning over to a computer much of the work of projecting technological advances. Extrapolating technological advances by computer is worthwhile if there are a good many extrapolations to perform.

Enveloping.   Trend extrapolation may be improved by the construction of "envelopes." Real trends do not often follow a clear mathematically projectable pattern such as those shown in Figure 3–8. Instead, there is often a series of curves, each curve representing a technological forward leap. Such a series may be plotted on a graph—usually over a very long period so as to include several major technological changes. Then the small curves may be connected by a larger curve, which may be projected into the future. Connecting up the smaller curves is called enveloping. *Envelop* means to wrap or surround, which, in a way, is what is done in connecting the smaller curves.

Since enveloping must usually cover a long period, it is not suitable for products as narrow and recent as coal-drilling equipment or computer memory. Instead, enve-

---

[5] But other experts are not so sure. A logarithmic curve plots as a straight line on a special type of graph paper known as semilog paper, and Lenz charges "semilogarithmic paper with . . . occult powers which distort data and extort false forecasts." Ralph C. Lenz, Jr., "Forecasts of Exploding Technologies by Trend Extrapolation," in *Technological Forecasting for Industry and Government,* ed. James R. Bright (Englewood Cliffs, N.J.: Prentice-Hall, 1968), p. 58 (T174.T4).

FIGURE 3–8

Examples of Trend Extrapolations

A. Output of coal mine drilling equipment

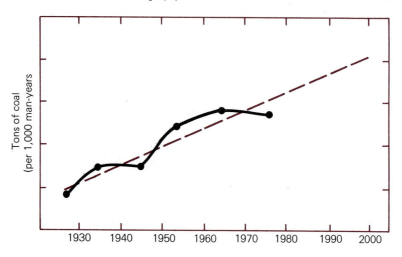

B. Exponential curve projecting bit density in computer memory

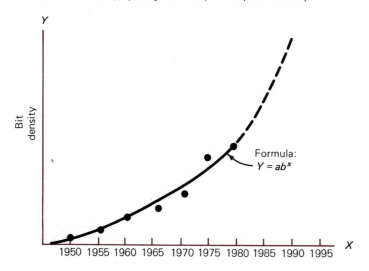

FIGURE 3–9

Velocity Trends

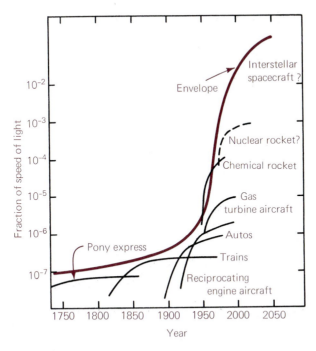

Source: D. G. Samaras, USAF, as cited by Robert U. Ayres, *Technological Forecasting and Long-Range Planning* (New York: McGraw-Hill, 1969), p. 21 (T174.A9). Used with permission.

loping is applied to broad *classes* of devices—such as cooking devices. (But a particular device like a waffle iron would be too recent, and a class of devices like appliances would not be specific enough to measure.)

Figure 3–9 is an example of an enveloping projection. It shows that the trend in vehicle velocity yields an envelope that extrapolates toward the speed of light. The curve suggests that a vehicle for interstellar travel will be developed. In the enveloping method there is no suggestion as to *how*. Predicting how is a possible aim in other methods of technological forecasting.

Involvement (or gaming) Methods.   Involvement methods are governed more by principles (heuristics) or trial and error than by mathematics and graphs. These methods involve people in a **gaming** mode. (Gaming refers to a type of training or education in which participants make decisions or interact in a simulated situation.) **Role playing** is a gaming technique that has been used mainly in human relations training; a trainee acts out an assigned role to gain insights into the role. This approach has been extended to generating possible futures, including futures in which technological changes have taken place. For example, two teams could be formed, one representing the firm and the other representing a major competitor. The teams could then interact in role-playing sessions to generate scenarios of plausible future actions and reactions.

The dictionary defines a scenario as an outline of a dramatic performance. As used here, the term *scenario* refers to an outline of an imagined set of future conditions: possible outcomes of battles, political campaigns, and in our case, product or process development.

Besides being used in role playing, **scenario writing** is a gaming technique in itself. The environmental impact statement is a special type of scenario used for forecasting. For example, an environmental impact statement for building a power plant in Western coalfields (filed for approval with the Environmental Protection Agency) might forecast a scenario in which strip-mined lands are restored to bloom with native grasses.

Another involvement technique is **brainstorming.** In brainstorming a group meets to generate ideas, perhaps on new products or future predictions. Uninhibited thinking is encouraged. A wild idea may trigger a good idea. A brainstorming session at one company is described as follows: "The staff bats around ideas, and scrawls them down on scraps of paper, which are tossed into a huge fishbowl. . . . Any idea goes in if it has aroused even a glimmer of response from the group. Later on, a two-man team—always one engineer and one industrial designer—cull out the most promising candidates."[6]

Still another involvement technique is the **Delphi** process, named after the Greek oracle at Delphi. The technique obtains a consensus among experts through an anonymous process. Delphi avoids some of the shortcomings of typical face-to-face committees, such as dominance by a vigorous member, majority pressures, and pressures to adjourn.

The Delphi process is led by a coordinator, who sends written questions to a selected group of experts who may be unaware of one another's participation. The experts' written predictions are pooled statistically, and such data as the mean prediction, the interquartile range, and pertinent supporting comments are sent out again to the same group. Each participant learns what the others are predicting and why, and then the participants submit new, perhaps modified, predictions. These steps are repeated, usually for two to four rounds, with some degree of consensus the usual end result.[7]

Delphi is frequently used to project a date for a particular technological event. For example, a maker of cough medicines might conduct a Delphi poll to determine in what year the protein interferon will be in widespread use for killing the viruses that cause the common cold. The panel of experts might include molecular biologists engaged in basic interferon research, developmental biochemists, research managers, and public health specialists. First-round replies to the question "What year?" might range from "Never" to "Well into the 21st century." The coordinator might express the replies as a mean and as an interquartile range. (The interquartile range is the

---

[6] *Business Week,* July 2, 1966, p. 54.

[7] Teachers sometimes try out Delphi on their students for instructional purposes. This is really just opinion polling, not Delphi—unless the topic is one on which the students are truly experts.

highest year minus the lowest year, but only for the middle 50 percent of the predictions.) If an expert has a good argument for saying "Never" or "The year 2030," the coordinator summarizes the argument and passes it on to the panel for the second round. When the polling ceases, the consensus should be valuable in indicating to the manufacturer how urgent it is, if at all, to move out of the cough-medicine business.

Normative Techniques.   Normative techniques try to determine what the future should be and then to make this happen. These are searching techniques; they involve looking for technological gaps that might be exploited.

Morphological analysis is one such technique. Morphology is a commonly used term in such sciences as biology, physical geography, and linguistics. It means the study of forms and structures. When morphological analysis is applied to technological forecasting, diagrams, lists, tables, and so forth, are used to show the structures of given technology areas. The completeness of the structures may suggest a few options that had not been given serious consideration previously.[8]

Relevance-tree analysis is also a type of morphological approach. The form and structure (morphology) of a productive objective are expressed as a "tree" that looks somewhat like an organization chart. The first "branches" are major modules that are necessary to achieve the productive objective, which is usually to provide a good or a service. Second branches drop from the first ones, third branches from the second, and so forth, until an entire structure of the relevant parts of the objective has been displayed—as a relevance tree.

The relevance tree aids in planning a complex future set of events. For example, a relevance tree might be helpful in planning a governmental program. A governmental manpower program might be displayed in a relevance tree like the one in Figure 3–10. The tree shows what is relevant in planning for the program. The program should provide for the high school dropout, the illiterate, the physically handicapped, the technologically displaced, and the returnee to the labor market. Training the high school dropout is shown broken down into a third level of relevant needs, which break down into fourth-level needs, and so on.

There is no more to relevance-tree analysis than constructing the tree. The relevance tree does nothing more than show—*clearly*—what factors are relevant in planning for future events. But this information can be valuable. The tree in Figure 3–10 shows areas into which governmental agencies might expand their line of services, and it sets the stage for further analysis of demand, capacity needs, costs, feasibility, and so forth.

Frame of Mind.   Formal technological forecasting, using the kinds of models discussed above, is still not widely practiced, although informal reflections on the future

---

[8] For examples of morphological analysis, see Joseph P. Martino, *Technological Forecasting for Decision Making* (New York: Elsevier-North Holland Publishing, 1972).

FIGURE 3–10

Relevance Tree

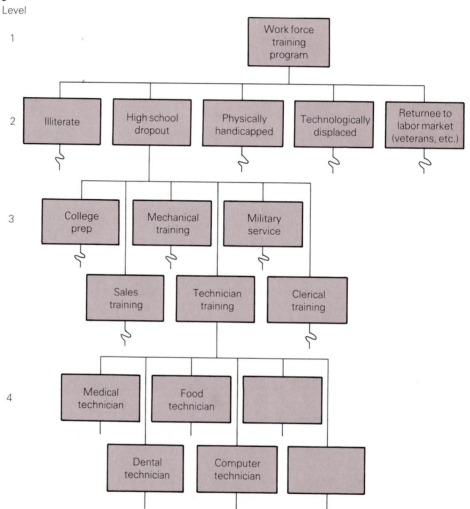

Source: Adapted from Fred Luthans, *Introduction to Management: A Contingency Approach* (Richard J. Schonberger, contributing author) (New York: McGraw-Hill, 1976), p. 88 (HD31.L86). Used with permission.

probably are common in industry. Skepticism about the ability to forecast technology is widespread, and justifiably so. But even if the formal techniques do not often result in accurate predictions, they at least coax managers into thinking about the future, which is the right frame of mind to have when planning for research.

The forecasting discussion continues in the next chapter, but the topic is techniques of demand forecasting, which is in far wider use than technological forecasting.

SUMMARY

Demand management responds to customer orders, forecasts, and other external demands. The master scheduler plays the key role of keeping marketing plans and production schedules in step. The short-, medium-, and long-term purposes of demand management are to know what items are to be produced and what adjustable capacity (labor and aggregate inventory) and facilities (plant and equipment) are needed to meet future demand.

Present and future demands are expressed as orders. A 10-step order processing sequence consists of (1) order booking, (2) order entry, (3) order consolidation into total requirements, (4) order acceptance, (5) order promise, (6) component inventory planning, (7) scheduling and purchasing, (8) dispatching, (9) assembly orders, and (10) shipment orders. Customer identification is lost at the component part level, steps 6–8, but reemerges with assembly and shipment orders. The order promise (or appointment, in human services) is an assurance to the salesperson and customer that the order has been successfully fitted in (or covered by) the schedule.

Medium- and long-term demand forecasts are vital for planning adjustable capacity and facilities. Short-term item demand forecasts, expressed in units of assembled end products, major product modules, and externally demanded components, are needed for scheduling the product mix.

The needs for forecasts vary depending on the environment. All organizations need medium- and long-term forecasts for facilities and capacity planning. Short-term forecasts are needed: *(a)* for scheduling material purchases, component parts production, and final assemblies in the make-to-stock, ship-to-order industries, *(b)* for materials and component parts in the make-parts-to-stock, assemble-to-order industries, *(c)* for materials only in make-to-order job shops, and *(d)* not at all in make-to-order heavy capital good manufacturing.

Forecasting is not only for the income-producing end of the business. *All* managers have resources to plan for, and the rational approach is to base the resource plans on forecasted workloads.

Item forecasting is prone to high error, but aggregate forecasts (groups of items) are more accurate. Thus, adjustable-capacity plans based on aggregate forecasts can be relatively valid. The farther out the forecast, the more error. Therefore, it is best to commit production to demand that is forecast only slightly out into the future. If competition requires it, parts and even major modules, which may assemble into a variety of end products, may be made to a forecast of demand weeks or months into the future; then final assemblies can be scheduled to a very short-term forecast or to actual orders.

In order to sustain cash inflows and pay for existing capacity, new products must be planned to dovetail with declines in demand for old products. Product plans also depend on the need for new products to support the organization's growth strategy.

Product development may be pursued via a number of research options. Leaders tend to adopt offensive strategies—to beat the competition to the market place, to control patents for possible licensing to other firms, and so forth. Followers tend to adopt the defensive strategy of letting others do the research and development. Research strategies may focus on new and improved processes, as the Japanese have done so successfully. Product research tends to be more expensive than process research, since highly paid scientists and engineers are usually engaged as researchers.

Some firms, especially in high-technology industries, conduct technological forecasting to try to predict research opportunities. Trend extrapolation and enveloping trend projection are aimed at predicting when the next breakthrough might occur in a given technology. Role playing, scenario writing, brainstorming, and the Delphi technique try to tap people's minds and expertise to predict technological change. Morphological analysis and relevance trees systematically search for untried patterns and combinations. None of these technological forecasting techniques is likely to predict accurately, but they help get managers thinking about what they should be doing in R&D to assure that the line of goods and services stays healthy.

Discussion of forecasting continues in Chapter 4, which gives detailed explanation of demand forecasting techniques.

REFERENCES

Books

Ayres, Robert U. *Technological Forecasting and Long-Range Planning.* New York: McGraw-Hill, 1969 (T174.A9).

Berry, William L.; Thomas E. Vollmann; and D. Clay Whybark. *Master Production Scheduling.* American Production and Inventory Control Society, 1979.

Bright, James R., ed. *Technological Forecasting for Industry and Government.* Englewood Cliffs, N.J.: Prentice-Hall, 1968 (T174.T4).

Burns, Robert O. *Innovation: The Management Connection.* Lexington, Mass.: D. C. Heath, 1975 (HD20.R564).

Gerstenfeld, Arthur. *Effective Management of Research and Development.* Reading, Mass.: Addison-Wesley Publishing, 1970. (T175.5.T94).

Heyal, Carl, ed. *Handbook of Industrial Research Management.* 2d ed. New York: Van Nostrand Reinhold, 1968 (T175.5.H4).

Martino, Joseph P. *Technological Forecasting for Decision Making.* New York: Elsevier-North Holland Publishing, 1972.

Periodicals (societies)

The Futurist (World Futures Society).

IEEE Transactions on Engineering Management (Institute of Electrical and Electronics Engineers).

Long Range Planning—British.

R&D Management—British.

R&D Management—digest.

Research Management—international.

Research Policy—international.

Technological Forecasting and Social Change—international.

REVIEW QUESTIONS

1. Why is demand management more involved for goods producers than for services providers?

2. Why does the term *order* have different meanings to different people in a producing organization?

3. Regarding the order promise, who promises what to whom? How firm is the promise?

4. Forecasting is done for short-, medium-, and long-term planning. Why is it not so simple to say exactly how far into the future each of these three terms goes?

5. What is the relationship between lead time to provide a product and requirements for demand forecasts?

6. If a manager told you that "I don't need to do demand forecasting," what arguments could you come up with to counter that statement?

7. What is the role of forecast error analysis in demand forecasting?

8. Why is group forecast error less than item forecast error? Why is it useful to understand this basic difference in forecast error?

9. Since forecast error is worse for out-periods than for the near term, is it prudent *only* to forecast for the near term? Explain.

10. To what extent can technological change be predicted? Why try to predict it?

11. What problems can a policy of "minimal specifications" cope with, and why?

12. What types of companies are most likely to pursue an offensive research strategy, and why?

13. Distinguish between product and process research.

14. Compare predictive with normative technological forecasting.

15. Describe a good method for assessing experts on future technological developments.

PROBLEMS

1. Think back on your experiences with appointments to see a physician and select the appointment system that worked the best. What demand management activities must be taking place among the staff that served you in order for the system to work well? Explain.

2. Describe the order-processing sequence for a real organization that you are familiar with, or visit an organization to collect the necessary data. You may wish to supplement your description with a flowchart of some kind.

3. Below is a list of a variety of organization types. Figure 3–2 shows that forecasts may be required for planning (1) facilities and adjustable capacity, (2) raw materials, (3) components, and (4) assemblies. Refer to the concepts presented in the figure in order to match

up the types of organizations listed below with the four purposes. Briefly explain your match-ups.

Furniture manufacturing	Roller-skating rink
Clothing manufacturing	Natural gas distributor
Air conditioning/heating contractor	Orthodontist
Highway construction	A church parish
Airframe manufacturing	Sound system manufacturing
Commercial printing	Small appliance manufacturing
Tractor manufacturing	Toy manufacturing

4. At Apex Steel Cabinet Company, Personnel was the first department to separately forecast its key workloads—see Example 3–1 in the chapter. Mr. Guy, the president, wants key workload forecasting extended to other departments. Your assignment is to prepare logical workload lists and forecast bases, similar to Figure 3–3 in the chapter, for the following departments or sections: Public Relations, Advertising, and Data Processing.

5. Planners at the county hospital are preparing a staffing plan and budget for next quarter. The listing below is computer data on labor-hours in various departments for last quarter. The trouble is, the average forecast error looks very high. Is the forecast error too high, or could next quarter's computer forecast be useful as the basis for a quarterly staffing plan? Perform any necessary calculations, and discuss.

Class	Last-quarter labor-hour forecast	Last-quarter labor-hour actual
Anesthesia	130	208
Cardiopulmonary	210	175
Emergency	650	589
Obstetrics	380	391
Pathology	90	68
Physical therapy	110	71
Radiology	200	277
Surgery	810	950

6. At Henry, Henry, and Henry, Public Accountants, the administrative vice president has the responsibility of forecasting demand for professional accounting services. The forecast for the preceding six-month period (made six months ago) was 120 client-days of work per month. Actual demand turned out to be 130, 100, 150, 150, 90, and 80.

    Calculate the monthly error as a multiple of the monthly forecast. Is the pattern of forecast error about what you would expect? Why or why not?

7. Metro Auto Sales forecasts new-car demand 12 months into the future. The forecast is updated every month. Metro's supplier, a large U.S. automaker, requires a 12-month forecast of total number of cars of all types, so that it may plan equipment, space, labor, etc., in its manufacturing plants. It also requires a two-month forecast of numbers of each model. Internally Metro finds the forecast useful for staffing (new-car salespeople) and for seeing that it has the correct amount of lot space on lease.

    Clearly Metro and its new-car supplier are practicing a number of the concepts and principles of demand forecasting that were discussed in the chapter. Your assignment is to discuss the principles and concepts that apply to this situation—as many as you can come up with.

8. NOK, Inc., is a Japanese-owned company with a plant in Georgia making oil seals for engines. Top managers at the plant are Japanese. One American middle manager in the company states that he is particularly struck by the Japanese managers' insistence on "*very* accurate demand forecasts and not just a projection of past demands." The American marketing people who turn in a forecast are asked penetrating questions, such as: What customers? How much is each customer's share of the forecast-amounts? Did you check thoroughly with all of those customers to see how sure they are about what they intend to buy from us? How do our customers estimate their buys from us? Have you established trusting relationships with our customers so they will give you these kinds of information? And so forth.

   Does the approach of the Japanese managers appear to deal effectively with the problem of unreliable forecasts? Discuss.

9. A study of forecast accuracy, over a recent past time period, for five products, A, B, C, D, and E, reveals the following:

Product	Forecast error	Percent error
A	−20	10%
B	−10	5
C	+20	8
D	−30	15
E	+40	12

   Calculate the average percent error, first by item, and second for the five items as a group. (Note: You will be able to make these calculations even without being given the raw data on forecast and actual demands.) Explain the resulting percent error for the group. Comment on why the item and group errors are so different.

10. When Mazda first came out with a rotary (Wankel) engine, there were serious performance problems. The public virtually quit buying the car, and Mazda's existence was threatened. Survival measures included sending design engineers all over Japan to sell cars. Besides cutting costs, what design engineering problem would this practice help deal with?

11. Tokyo Seating Company operates TRI-CON, a subsidiary manufacturing division, in the United States. Some years ago TRI-CON asked an American metal products company to bid on a contract to provide TRI-CON with metal seat pans for motorcycle seats. TRI-CON's "request for proposal" specified the gauge of steel and little else. The American firm was uncomfortable with TRI-CON's "minimal specifications" and refused to bid. Why would TRI-CON say so little about what kind of seat pan it wanted?

12. What kind of research strategy do you think has been followed in each of the industries listed below in the past decade or two? Discuss tendencies in both product and process research.

Major appliances	Banking
Supermarkets	Home construction

13. The following is a list of possible uses of the Delphi technique for gaining consensus. Which is a good use of Delphi, and which is a poor use? Explain.

    Polling consumers on which cola they prefer.

    Polling defense scientists on when they believe laser weapons will become a reality for combat use.

    Polling physicians on whether or not to proceed with surgery.

14. According to one business news story, 5 and 10 year plans, based partly on forecasts, were instituted in many a firm in the early 1960s, but many were abandoned or neglected in the early 1970s. Some executives stated that the plans simply were not used.

    Can any of this disillusionment be explained based on forecast error tendencies? Explain.

15. Assume that you are an analyst for Kitchen Technology, Inc. Develop an enveloping projection for predicting technological advances in the cooking of food. Technological developments in the past would range from cooking on an open fire to cooking in microwave ovens. Your task is to fill in with intervening developments and to project into the future. You will need to select a suitable unit of measure as the vertical scale on the graph.

16. Assume that you are an analyst in the planning department of North American Electric Corp. Develop an enveloping projection for predicting technological advances in street lighting. Past technologies include oil lamps (with lamplighters), incandescent lamps, mercury vapor lamps, and sodium vapor lamps. Your task is to fill in with other technologies, if any, and to project into the future. You will need to select a suitable unit of measure as the vertical scale on the graph.

Chapter 4

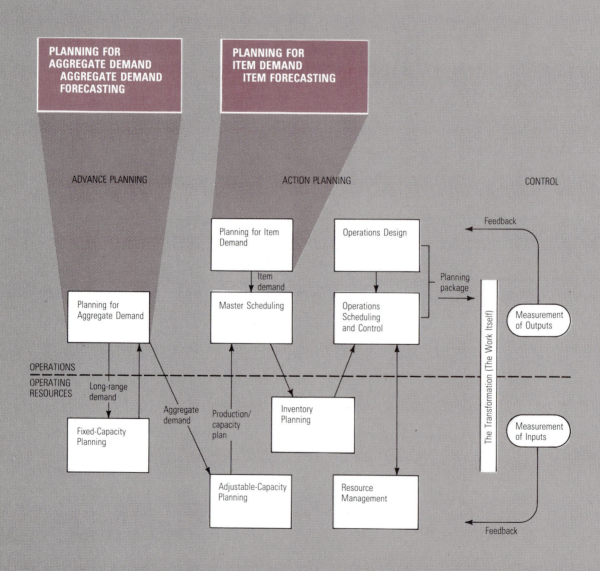

PLANNING FOR
AGGREGATE DEMAND
AGGREGATE DEMAND
FORECASTING

PLANNING FOR
ITEM DEMAND
ITEM FORECASTING

ADVANCE PLANNING

ACTION PLANNING

CONTROL

Planning for Item
Demand

Operations Design

Feedback

Item
demand

Planning for
Aggregate Demand

Master Scheduling

Operations
Scheduling
and Control

Planning
package

Measurement
of Outputs

OPERATIONS

OPERATING
RESOURCES

Long-range
demand

Aggregate
demand

Production/
capacity
plan

Inventory
Planning

The Transformation (The Work Itself)

Measurement
of Inputs

Fixed-Capacity
Planning

Adjustable-Capacity
Planning

Resource
Management

Feedback

Demand Forecasting Techniques

The nature of demand forecasting was examined in Chapter 3. This chapter continues the discussion by looking closely at the prominent demand forecasting techniques and their uses.

DEMAND FORECASTING

Demand forecasting is easily confused with other popular—and specialized—uses of the general term *forecasting*. Some of the various meanings of forecasting are explained below.

If you should ask a librarian for reading materials on forecasting, you should expect to receive lore on *weather forecasting*. That is the popular meaning of forecasting.

If you look up forecasting in the subject card catalog in a library, you will find mostly readings on *economic forecasting*, for example, readings on the forecasting of gross national product and disposable personal income. Economic forecasting is a second meaning of forecasting, and it has some bearing on the topic of this chapter.

A third meaning of forecasting is *demand forecasting*. That is the topic of concern here.

A fourth meaning is *technological forecasting*, which means predicting process and product breakthroughs. That is of some interest to us.

A fifth meaning is *sales forecasting*. This has somewhat the same meaning as demand forecasting except that the word *sales* implies private enterprise; the word *demand* is better for our purposes, since it would also apply to the public services sector. Also, marketing managers and operations managers have different outlooks: The marketing outlook is one of *sales to the customer;* the operations outlook is one of *demands for production* and for the *operating resources to produce.* (Subject card catalogs in libraries tend to include more under the sales-forecasting than the demand-forecasting designation.)

A sixth, less common use of the term *forecasting* is in phrases such as "personnel forecast," "materials forecast," and "tool forecast." Those uses concern resources or means, as opposed to products and services or ends. While direct forecasting of resources may be done, an often better approach is to translate a product demand forecast into resource needs using conversion factors or standards.

Still other terms associated with forecasting include *time-series analysis, econometrics,* and *trend projection.* These are a few of the methods of forecasting, and they are discussed in the next chapter.

DEMAND FORECASTING SOURCES

In large national corporations demand forecasting is often a three-pronged process, perhaps coordinated by a corporate planning department. This is shown in Figure 4–1. Marketing produces one set of forecasting figures. Economists look at how the economy is likely to affect the organization's demand, which gives another set of figures. And statisticians or computerized statistical routines project past demand trends, thus giving a third set of figures. Then top management may review all three

FIGURE 4–1

Three Determinants of Demand Forecast

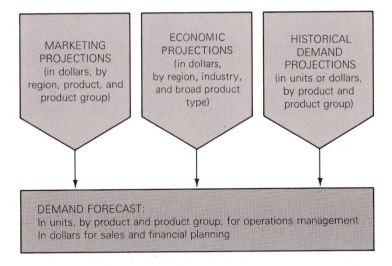

sets and the "jury of executive opinion" may overrule them all. Executives may prefer to trust their own experience and judgment. Even so, the three sets of figures would surely have helped to sharpen judgments about future demands.

The three major sources of demand projection data involve different techniques and have different uses. Figure 4–2 illustrates.

Marketing Projections

Marketing departments assemble demand projections, in dollars, based on sales projections, sales force estimates, test market results, and market research. A sales promotion has a major impact on short-term demand. Moving excessive inventory is one purpose of a sales promotion. Simply increasing cash inflow—in the absence of excess—is another purpose. Clearly the latter financial purpose can wreak havoc with production schedules. It is important that promotions of products not yet produced be closely coordinated with production scheduling. One of the duties of a master scheduler is to interact closely with marketing and finance on such matters. Sales promotions usually do not extend beyond the near future. Therefore, as Figure 4–2 indicates, sales promotions generally do not affect medium- and long-term demand forecasting, nor capacity planning.

Salespeople may be required to submit periodic estimates of sales for their product lines and districts. The estimates are consolidated to yield product forecasts for the whole company. While sales force estimates are not likely to be very accurate on the whole, they are valued in particular cases because salespeople are able to find

FIGURE 4–2

Techniques of Demand Forecasting

		Forecast horizon		
Forecast basis	Unit of measure	Short term	Medium term	Long term
Marketing projections	$			
Sales promotions		Yes	No	No
Sales force estimates		Yes	Somewhat	No
Consumer surveys and test marketing		No	Yes	Yes
Economic projections	$	No	Yes	Yes
Historical demand projection	Items or $			
Multiperiod pattern projection (Mean, trend, seasonal)		Yes	Yes	Yes
Single-period patternless projection (Moving average, exponential smoothing, and simulation)		Yes	No	No
Associative projection (Leading indicator and correlation)		Yes	Yes	Yes
		↑ Product scheduling	↑ Adjustable-capacity planning	↑ Facilities planning
			Forecast purposes	

out early about major orders for a given product. Such information contributes especially to short-term forecasting, but sometimes salespeople also glean demand data helpful for medium-term forecasting and adjustable-capacity planning.

Consumer surveys and test marketing are helpful in finding out customers' future buying plans or reactions to a new product or a product idea. Future, in this case, generally means next year or beyond, which affects medium- and long-term forecasts and adjustable-capacity and facilities planning.

Economic Projections

Economic projections, shown next in Figure 4–2, are useful for medium- and long-term purposes. As an example, any firm offering goods and services related to homemaking surely is interested in national economic projections for housing starts in the next few years. Economic projections range from educated guesses of an economist or a panel of economists to computer projections based on mathematical equations. Economic forecasting based on sets of mathematical equations processed by computers is a field known as econometrics.

The econometrician builds forecasting models by such methods as statistical regression analysis. A simple approach is to use a single regression equation. For example, suppose that farm machinery demand is to be forecast. The econometrician tries out various possible causes of change in farm machinery expenditures. Past data on different sets of causal factors are put into a computer for regression tests. The set of causal factors that works best on past data may be used to forecast future demand. The forecast equation would have the causal variables (e.g., good crops, machinery prices, advertising) on the right side of the equation and the demand projection (the dependent variable) on the left side.

A single regression equation may not be accurate enough, because causes of demand may be complicated by interrelationships. For example, demand for machinery may indeed be affected by price and advertising, but price probably goes up when there are more advertising expenses. It may be prudent to set up and test factors that affect price, which results in a second regression equation. Perhaps a third regression equation should be set up to test causal factors affecting advertising. A system of simultaneous regression equations may emerge. A forecast of farm machinery is based on solving the simultaneous equations.

Historical Demand Projections

The final basis of forecasting shown in Figure 4–2 is historical demand projection. Eight techniques grouped into three categories are listed, and each of these is fully discussed in this chapter. All of the techniques rely on historical demand data, and for operations management uses they express the forecast in units (or dollars converted to units).

Three of the techniques—mean, trend, and seasonal—search for a pattern that can be projected as many periods into the future as is desirable (but with decreasing accuracy). Hence they are referred to as multiperiod pattern projection techniques. They are useful for product scheduling, adjustable-capacity planning, and facilities planning.

The next three techniques, moving average, exponential smoothing, and simulation, do not seek to discover a pattern (except in advanced models). They merely react to recent demand changes. Thus, they are referred to as single-period patternless techniques and are used for short-term product scheduling but generally not for longer-term purposes.

The last two techniques are leading indicator and correlation. These techniques attempt to discover an association between demand and some other known factors. The time horizon may be short, medium, or long term (but with poor accuracy in the long term), and the technique may be usable for product scheduling or, in some cases, adjustable-capacity and facilities planning.

All of the historical demand projection techniques rely on demand records. Larger firms that keep careful records are likely to have profuse data on past demands for goods and services, but in other organizations recorded data on past demands may be nil. Minimal records are most likely in small organizations or in small departments within larger organizations.

Where records are nil, historical demand projections are still made, but they are totally judgmental: The manager or department head reflects on his past experience and comes to a decision on what future demands to expect. This is likely to result in rough forecasts. Lack of accuracy in the demand forecast will surely mean idle resources at some times and failure to meet customer demands at other times. The failure of many small businessmen to keep even minimal demand records may be a key reason for business failure. The small firm, often poorly financed, can ill afford to badly misjudge demand.

If demand records are kept, statistical analysis may be used. The object is to find and to project into the future underlying patterns of demand for each product or service. This is a bit like a search for the Holy Grail. You won't find it. But in searching for it, you may expect to gain insights. In demand forecasting, this means making smaller prediction errors than would have been made without the search.

The forecasting methods discussed in this chapter are proven and widely used. It will be seen, however, that computers and statistical forecasting routines are only tools. Judgment is still the more important element. Judgment is needed to access the situation, to select the proper analysis methods, to test the reasonableness of the results, and to revise and reanalyze when necessary. This is not just a platitude that applies equally to all topics in the book. Examples and cautionary remarks throughout this chapter reemphasize the key role that judgment plays in forecasting.

COMPONENTS OF DEMAND

In most of the techniques of historical projection, demand is examined on a time scale. These are often called *time-series analysis* techniques, and different techniques are aimed at isolating different *components of demand.*

Four general components of demand are mentioned in Figure 4–3. These components are a long-term demand pattern, a medium-term pattern, a short-term pattern, and what may be called noise. As the figure shows, there is an underlying long-term demand pattern, a slowly changing function. Segments of the long-term pattern split off into medium-term segments, which may be divided further into short-term ups and downs. The other demand component is unpredictable noise. The analyst would not try to predict or dissect it—just as the physicist would not try to predict or dissect electronic white noise that is everywhere in space.

Actual demand is related to forecast demand as follows:

Actual demand = Long-term forecast + Long-term forecast error
+ Medium-term forecast + Medium-term forecast error
+ Short-term forecast + Short-term forecast error
+ Noise

FIGURE 4–3

Four Components of Demand

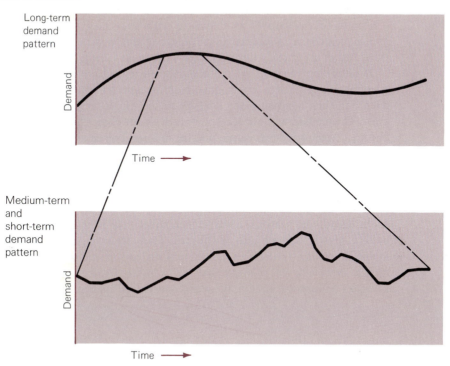

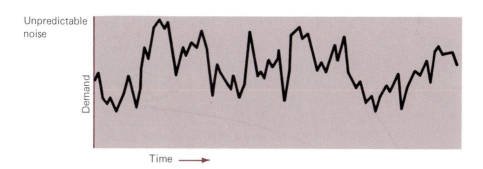

The forecaster attempts to cut down the forecast errors. One way is by using good analysis methods. Another is by gathering together a good data base. A third is by exhaustive processing of the data, using the analysis methods. All cost money. A firm acquires good analysis methods by hiring well-trained analysts. The data base requires a costly information system. And the processing cost, by computer or calculator, increases with thoroughness. It is easy to see that cost puts a limit on forecast accuracy. Even if there weren't these costs, there would still be forecast inaccuracy due to noise.[1]

A number of forecasting methods reduce forecast error. Each method results in a forecast that is smooth as compared with the erratic actual demand pattern. The idea is to arrive at a forecast that rounds off the "spikes" in actual demand, because those spikes are mostly unpredictable—the noise factor.

In addition to forecasting methods, there are routines for analyzing forecast error. A common approach is to try out several forecasting methods, using historical demand data, and then conduct error analysis to see which method yields the least forecast error. The method with the least error is the likely choice for projecting future demand. Forecast error analysis is woven into the following discussion of forecasting techniques.

MULTIPERIOD PATTERN PROJECTION

Mean, trend, and seasonal analysis techniques may be used to project a past demand pattern several periods into the future. They are often used in the **rolling-forecast** mode. A rolling forecast is one that is redone or rolled over at intervals—every month, every quarter, or every year, for example. The forecast horizon may be limited to weeks or months, or it may extend years into the future.

Mean

The simplest time series is the arithmetic mean. Where demand is steady and not inherently seasonal, the simple mean may be suitable for forecasting. Consider the example below.

EXAMPLE 4–1

Data Services and the Mean

Data Services, Inc., offers computer programming commercially. Figure 4–4 shows three years of past quarterly demand, in hours of programmer time. No strong trend or seasonal pattern is evident from the graph. If first-quarter demand is high one year, it looks as likely to be low the next. The same goes for the other quarters. The up-and-down movement seems random. And one would not reason that programming should be a service having some sort of seasonal demand pattern. What should the forecast be for upcoming quarters in 1985? Perhaps it should be the mean, 437.

---

[1] Maybe the truth is that so-called noise represents our ignorance. Even so, it is probably composed of so large a number of causal variables that we had best treat it with benign neglect.

FIGURE 4–4

Demand Forecast by Arithmetic Mean—Data Services, Inc.

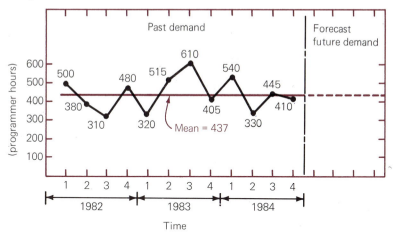

Note: Do *not* assume that this forecast method is a good one for Data Services. There may be better ones.

That may be the best way to minimize forecast error for so nondescript a demand.

Trend

Some would look at Figure 4–4 and see something other than the mean as the forecast basis. For example, in the last seven quarters the trend is downward. Perhaps that 7-quarter downward trend is more logical as a forecast basis than the 12-quarter mean. Perhaps the Data Services example ought to be reconsidered.

EXAMPLE 4–2

Data Services and "Eyeball" Trends

Figure 4–5 is an "eyeball" projection of the seven-quarter trend for Data Services. The trend line is moving Data Services toward out-of-business status. The trend downward may be reasonable for the first quarter of 1985. But surely, *if* Data Services is a sound enterprise, business will turn upward. *This* trend line may be invalid for forecasting several periods into the future.

For a better forecast, better demand data would be helpful. Let us assume that 20 instead of 12 quarters of past demand data are available. The demand history is displayed in Figure 4–6.

Quite a different pattern emerges. The long-run trend is definitely upward. With a straightedge, the eyeballed upward trend line is drawn and projected two years (eight quarters) into the future. The 1985 quarterly forecasts are

FIGURE 4–5

Seven-Quarter "Eyeball" Trend—Data Services, Inc.

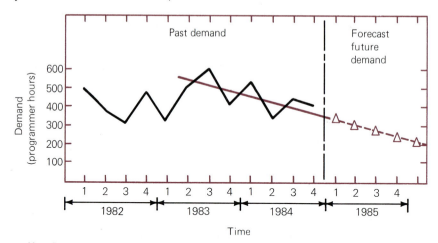

Note: Do *not* assume that this forecast method is a good one for Data Services. There may be much better ones.

FIGURE 4–6

Twenty-Quarter "Eyeball" Trend—Data Services, Inc.

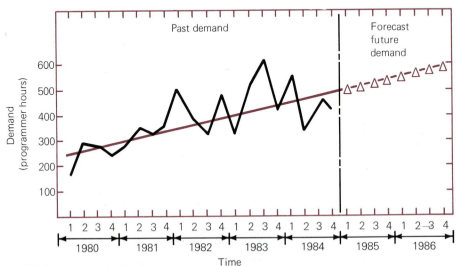

Note: Do *not* assume that this forecast method is a good one for Data Services. There may be better ones.

FIGURE 4–7

Twenty-Quarter "eyeball" Curve—Data Services, Inc.

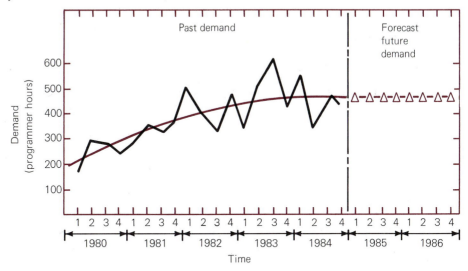

Note: Do *not* assume that this forecast method is a good one for Data Services. There may be better ones.

now in the range of 500 programmer-hours instead of the 300 range resulting from only a seven-quarter trend projection (in Figure 4–5).

Another interpretation of the 20 quarters of demand data is that they describe a slow curve. Figure 4–7 shows such a curve projected by the eyeball method through 1986. The 1985–86 forecast is now between the two previous straight-line forecasts. This projection is for a leveling-off at about 450.

The curving projection looks valid. In other cases a straight-line projection may look valid. In any case the managers may use the graphic projection only to sharpen their own judgment. For example, the managers of Data Services, Inc., may have other information about their customers that leads them to a more optimistic forecast than the projected 450. Even where such outside information seems to overrule historical projection, the projection is worth doing. It is quick and simple.

Now let us turn to a method that is less quick, less simple. The reader who has studied statistics may have wondered about the crudity of the eyeball method. The precise way is to project mathematically, using regression analysis. The least-squares technique of regression analysis (see chapter supplement) results in the formula for the straight line of best fit. (The least-squares method may also be modified so that it yields a formula for a curving line of projection instead of a straight line.)

While the least-squares method is more accurate than the eyeball method, it is sometimes unnecessary. Some rules of thumb on which method to use are:

1. Use the eyeball method if only one or a small number of products/services are to be forecast.
2. Use least squares—run on a calculator or a computer—if many products/services are to be forecast.

The eyeball method is generally accurate enough for something so speculative as forecasting. But drawing graphs for eyeball projections is time-consuming. The eyeball method would take many hand-drawn graphs if there were a large number of products. Least squares takes time to set up, but after that it goes fast, especially with a programmable calculator or computer. Computer-based forecasting routines have some extra benefits: They are generally able to print out mathematical formulas as approximations of the demand pattern, graphic projections, and tabular listings. Thus, least-squares regression is valued not for its forecasting accuracy but because it aids in routinizing some of the steps in forecasting.

Seasonal

A seasonal index is the ratio of the demand for a particular season to the demand for an average season. Thus, if demand is for 100 units in an average season and demand for the summer season is 80, the summer-season index is 80/100 = 0.8. Some sort of averaging process is used to arrive at the 100 per season figure. The term *season* should not be limited to spring, summer, fall, and winter. The forecaster looking for seasonality may wish to consider a rainy season, a holiday season, a hunting season, or any other period that comes once a year.

Seasonal Index Calculations.   Seasonal analysis is explained in Example 4–3 for a moving company, Metro Movers. The example seems apt since the moving industry is known to be highly seasonal. Metro Movers' seasonal demand pattern is examined below for the four seasons, spring, summer, fall and winter. This is not quite the same as the four quarters. The first fiscal quarter is January–February–March; by contrast, the winter season is usually December–January–February. For a mover it makes more sense to use seasons than quarters because of the heavy surge in demand in June–July–August—during school vacations.

EXAMPLE 4–3

Metro Movers and Seasonal Indices

There is no need to look at actual demand data to know that a moving company has a seasonal demand. It is common sense. Even so, a good starting point in seasonal analysis is scrutiny of the demand graph.

The graph of past quarterly demand for Metro Movers is shown in Figure 4–8. It is clear that summer demands are by far the highest in every year.

FIGURE 4–8

Seasonal Demand History—Metro Movers

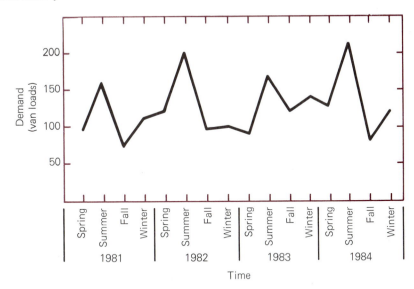

Also, fall demands are generally the lowest. The seasonal index measures how much higher and how much lower. Figure 4–9 shows calculations of seasonal indices for the 16 available past demands. (Note: Besides seasonality, it looks as though there is a slight upward trend over the 16 quarters. We shall ignore the trend for now.)

These seasonal indices are rearranged by year and season in Figure 4–10. The three values for each season need somehow to be reduced to a single index. The index for fall is steadily rising, from 0.61 to 0.73 to 0.96; that is not sufficient reason to expect it to continue to rise, especially since the other seasons do not show trends. Thus, the projections of the seasonal indices for 1985 are the means of each column.

Seasonally Adjusted Trends. Metro Movers may now use the seasonal indices in fine-tuning its forecasts of demand for each coming season. For example, suppose that Metro Movers expects to move 480 vans of goods next year, based on projection of the mean of past years' demands. It would be naive to divide 480 by 4 and project 120 vans in each season. Instead,

Divide 480 by 4 $= 120$ vans in an average season.

$120 \times 0.85 = 102$ vans forecast for spring 1985.
$120 \times 1.46 = 175$ vans forecast for summer 1985.
$120 \times 0.76 = 91$ vans forecast for fall 1985.
$120 \times 0.93 = \underline{112}$ vans forecast for winter 1985–86.
Yearly total $= 480$

FIGURE 4–9

Seasonal Index Calculations—Metro Movers

(1) Time	(2) Actual demand	(3) Mean seasonal demand (basis: four-period moving average)*	(4) Seasonal index (column 2/column 3)
Spring 1981	90		
Summer 1981	160		
Fall 1981	70	115	0.61
Winter 1981	120	125	0.96
Spring 1982	130	132	0.98
Summer 1982	200	132	1.52
Fall 1982	90	124	0.73
Winter 1982	100	114	0.88
Spring 1983	80	115	0.70
Summer 1983	170	125	1.36
Fall 1983	130	136	0.96
Winter 1983	140	147	0.95
Spring 1984	130	146	0.89
Summer 1984	210	138	1.52
Fall 1984	80		
Winter 1984	120		

* This four-period moving average is centered on the middle of a given season, that is, $1\frac{1}{2}$ months into the season. It includes demands going back six months and forward six months from that point. Thus, the first figure in column 3 is based on demands for the last $1\frac{1}{2}$ months of spring 1981; all of summer, fall, and winter 1981; and the first $1\frac{1}{2}$ months of spring 1982. So,

$$\frac{(90/2 + 160 + 70 + 120 + 130/2)}{4} = 115$$

This is a bit cumbersome, but it assures that no one season is weighted more heavily than any other. (There is another way to get the same figures: Calculate ordinary four-period moving averages; then average each successive pair of those figures. This process is demonstrated in some other textbooks, usually under the heading "centered moving average.")

Note: Do *not* assume that this forecast method is a good one for Metro Movers. There may be better ones.

FIGURE 4–10

Summary and Projection of Seasonal Indices—Metro Movers

		Spring	Summer	Fall	Winter	
Past	1981			0.61	0.96	
	1982	0.98	1.52	0.73	0.88	
	1983	0.70	1.36	0.96	0.95	
	1984	0.89	1.52			
Future	1985	0.85	1.46	0.76	0.93	←—Mean of each column

It takes a few more steps if the basic demand projection is an up or down trend instead of a level line. For example, assume that Metro Movers again projects 1985 demand at 480 vans; this time it is based on historical projection of an upward trend of about 2.5 percent per quarter. The 480 is the sum of four quarterly demands, at a 2.5 percent upward slope:

$$
\begin{array}{l}
116\text{—spring 1985} \\
119\text{—summer 1985} \\
121\text{—fall 1985} \\
\underline{124}\text{—winter 1985–86} \\
480
\end{array}
$$

Basis: 480/4 = 120, the average seasonal value, applicable to mid-year. 1.25 percent less = 119, the projection for mid-summer; and 2.5 percent less than 119 = 116, the projection for mid-spring. Fall and winter are calculated similarly.

Now the seasonal adjustments are:

$$
\begin{array}{l}
116 \times 0.85 = 99 \text{ vans forecast for spring 1985} \\
119 \times 1.46 = 174 \text{ vans forecast for summer 1985} \\
121 \times 0.76 = 92 \text{ vans forecast for fall 1985} \\
124 \times 0.93 = 115 \text{ vans forecast for winter 1985–86}
\end{array}
$$

A comparison of the last two cases, without trend and with trend, is shown in Figure 4–11. The figure shows what might be expected: Trend effects, which are so important in the long run, tend to be overshadowed in the short run by seasonal (or other) influences.

Seasonality and "Pipeline Filling." Goods that are new or back in the market after interruption generally should not be forecast based on seasonality logic. The reason is the "pipeline" phenomenon: When the product hits the market, its demand may rise slowly and then become very heavy until the wholesale/retail pipeline is filled; then demand may go slack for a time until consumers become fully aware of and respond to the product. A simple moving average (to be covered in the next section), unadjusted for seasonality, may be the best forecasting method during this transitional period. Later, when product demand reaches a steadier state, seasonal indexing refinements may be added.

SINGLE-PERIOD PATTERNLESS PROJECTION

The patternless projection techniques do not make inferences about past demand data but merely react to the most recent demands. These techniques, the moving average, exponential smoothing, and simulation, project just one period into the future. But in practice, the projection for next period is sometimes used as the projection for several more periods. In that case the forecast rolls over each period: The previous projection is dropped, and the newly computed forecast becomes the new projection for the periods included in the new forecast horizon. It is like driving at night with

FIGURE 4–11

Seasonal Adjustment of Level and Upward Projection—Metro Movers

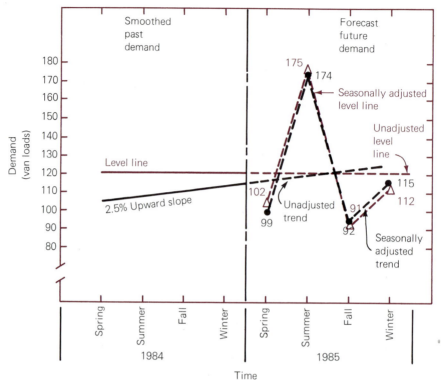

Note: Do *not* assume that these forecast methods are good ones for Metro Movers. There may be better ones.

headlights aimed 300 feet out, always reaching out another 300 feet as the car rolls over the nearest feet of pavement. These techniques are best suited to short-term forecasting for scheduling the product mix. The forecast period is typically a week, a month, or a quarter (and the forecast horizon may include just one, or several, periods).

Moving Average

The moving average, which became popular in the 1950s and 1960s, is simply the mean of a given number of the most recent actual demands. The given number may be called the time span of the moving average. Like other time-series methods, the moving average smooths the actual historical demand fluctuations by reducing variation of forecast error.

Time Span. The proper time span for forecasting a certain item by moving average may be determined by analysis. The following example shows how.

EXAMPLE 4–4

Metro Movers and Moving Average

Metro Movers has good records on the number of van loads it has moved per week. A part-time student employee (S.E., for short) offers to analyze the data in order to develop a moving-average forecasting system. The manager accepts his offer.

Demand data for the last 16 weeks are shown on the left in Figure 4–12, where −1 means one week ago, −2 means two weeks ago, and so forth. On the right in Figure 4–12 is S.E.'s calculation of three-week moving averages. A sample calculation for week −15 is shown below the figure.

Next, S.E. calculates the forecast error that would have resulted if this moving average forecast had been used in the past. See Figure 4–13. It can be seen that the three-week moving average for weeks −16, −15, and −14 becomes the forecast for week −13. Actual demand in week −13 turns out to be 11, so the forecast error is 11 − 9 = 2. That is a shortage or underestimate of two vans for that week. Then the moving average for weeks −15, −14, and −13 becomes the forecast for week −12. The forecast error is 11 − 10.7 = 0.3. The process continues, the average moving (or rolling over) each week, dropping off the oldest week and adding the newest; hence, a moving average.

FIGURE 4–12

Demand Data and Moving Average—Metro Movers

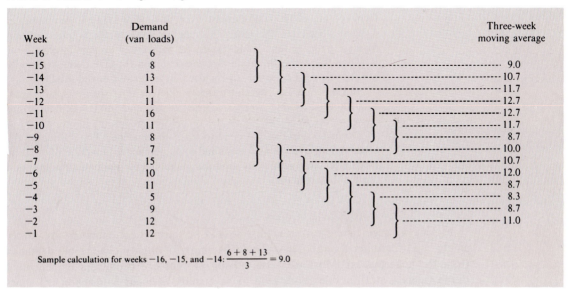

Week	Demand (van loads)	Three-week moving average
−16	6	
−15	8	9.0
−14	13	10.7
−13	11	11.7
−12	11	12.7
−11	16	12.7
−10	11	11.7
−9	8	8.7
−8	7	10.0
−7	15	10.7
−6	10	12.0
−5	11	8.7
−4	5	8.3
−3	9	8.7
−2	12	11.0
−1	12	

Sample calculation for weeks −16, −15, and −14: $\dfrac{6+8+13}{3} = 9.0$

FIGURE 4–13

Three-Week Moving Average and MAD—Metro Movers

(1) Week	(2) Actual demand	(3) Forecast demand (three-week moving average)	(4) Forecast error (column 2 − column 3)	(5) Absolute sum of forecast errors*
−16	6			
−15	8			
−14	13			
−13	11	9.0	2.0	2.0
−12	11	10.7	0.3	2.3
−11	16	11.7	4.3	6.6
−10	11	12.7	−1.7	8.3
−9	8	12.7	−4.7	13.0
−8	7	11.7	−4.7	17.7
−7	15	8.7	6.3	24.0
−6	10	10.0	0.0	24.0
−5	11	10.7	0.3	24.3
−4	5	12.0	−7.0	31.3
−3	9	8.7	0.3	31.6
−2	12	8.3	3.7	35.3
−1	12	8.7	3.3	38.6

$$\text{MAD} = \frac{38.6}{13} = 3.0 \text{ vans per week}$$

* *Absolute sum* means the sum of the digits only, ignoring whether they are plus or minus.

Note: Do *not* assume that this forecast method is a good one for Metro Movers. There may be better ones.

Column 5 cumulatively sums the absolute values of the forecast errors from column 4. The total forecast error, 38.6, is divided by the number of forecast weeks, 13. The result, 3.0 vans per week, is the average or mean forecast error. In forecasting circles this measure of average forecast error is widely known as the mean absolute deviation (MAD). Some companies use the standard deviation, or standard error, instead of the MAD.

Suppose that S.E. decides to try a different time span, say six weeks. The six-week moving average, forecast errors, and MAD calculations are shown in Figure 4–14.

The mean error of 2.4 is better than the previous 3.0. S.E. could try other moving average time spans and could perhaps reduce the error further. In a larger firm with many products, searching for the best time span is a job for the computer.

Moving average time spans generally should be long where demands are rather stable (e.g., for toilet tissue). They should be short for highly changeable demands (e.g., for houseplants). Most users of moving average are producers or sellers of durable goods, and durable goods tend to have stable demand patterns in the short run. Therefore, longer time spans, say 6–12 periods, are common.

FIGURE 4–14

Six-week Moving Average and MAD—Metro Movers

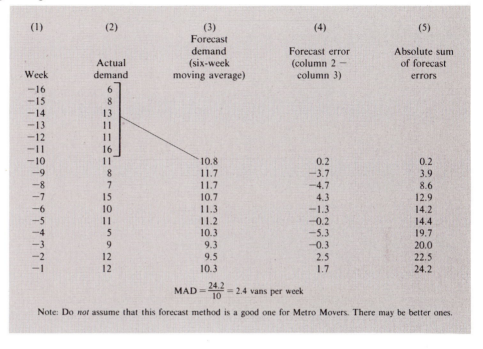

(1) Week	(2) Actual demand	(3) Forecast demand (six-week moving average)	(4) Forecast error (column 2 − column 3)	(5) Absolute sum of forecast errors
−16	6			
−15	8			
−14	13			
−13	11			
−12	11			
−11	16			
−10	11	10.8	0.2	0.2
−9	8	11.7	−3.7	3.9
−8	7	11.7	−4.7	8.6
−7	15	10.7	4.3	12.9
−6	10	11.3	−1.3	14.2
−5	11	11.2	−0.2	14.4
−4	5	10.3	−5.3	19.7
−3	9	9.3	−0.3	20.0
−2	12	9.5	2.5	22.5
−1	12	10.3	1.7	24.2

$$MAD = \frac{24.2}{10} = 2.4 \text{ vans per week}$$

Note: Do *not* assume that this forecast method is a good one for Metro Movers. There may be better ones.

The time span that results in the lowest MAD would be the best choice for actual use in forecasting future demands. But keep in mind that we prove it based on past data. As long as we think that the future will be similar to the past, this is fine. If we are quite sure that the future will be different, then there is little point in expending much time analyzing past demands.

Smoothing Effects. History-based forecasting analysis methods like moving average attempt to wash out some of the forecast error from historical demand data. The effect is to produce a series of forecast values that are smoother—less variable— than the historical time series. These smoothing effects are illustrated in Figure 4–15 for the three-week and six-week data in the moving average example. The actual demand pattern, taken from Figure 4–12, exhibits some extreme high and low spikes. The three-week moving average data pattern, taken from Figure 4–13, has spikes that are much less pronounced. And the six-week moving average data pattern, taken from Figure 4–14, is smoothed to look like gently rolling hills. Taken to the extreme, the 12 weeks of actual data would be smoothed to a single flat prediction line—no peaks or valleys—which is the mean (discussed earlier). The "correct" amount of smoothing—the correct moving average time span—is that which results in the least error (smallest MAD).

A weakness of the simple moving average is that it puts as much weight on the

FIGURE 4–15

Smoothing Effects of the Moving Average

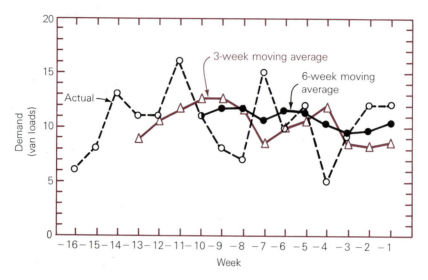

oldest as on the most recent demands. An extension known as the weighted moving average deals with the weakness by placing extra weight on more recent actual demands in the time span. We may safely omit further discussion of weighted moving average, because there is a simpler technique that gives about the same forecast results: exponential smoothing.

Exponential Smoothing

Many firms that adopted the moving average technique in the 1950s saw fit to change to exponential smoothing in the 1960s or 1970s. In exponential smoothing the forecast for next period equals the forecast for last period plus a portion (alpha, or α) of last period's forecast error:[2]

$$F_N = F_{N-1} + \alpha(D_{N-1} - F_{N-1})$$

Next forecast = Last forecast + α(Last demand − Last forecast)

For example, assume that the last forecast was for 100 units but that only 90 were demanded. If α is set at 0.2, then the exponential smoothing forecast is:

$$
\begin{aligned}
\text{Next forecast} &= 100 + 0.2(90 - 100) \\
&= 100 + 0.2(-10) \\
&= 100 - 2 \\
&= 98
\end{aligned}
$$

---

[2] Some people prefer to transform it into this equivalent form:

Next forecast = α(Last demand) + $(1 - \alpha)$(Last forecast)

Exponential smoothing example. This forecast of two units less than last period makes sense because the last period was overestimated. Thus, exponential smoothing results in lower forecasts where you have recently overestimated, and it results in higher forecasts where you have underestimated. This is shown for the Metro Movers data in the example below.

EXAMPLE 4–5

Metro Movers and Exponential Smoothing

Exponential smoothing, where $\alpha = 0.2$, is shown in Figure 4–16. Data from Metro Movers, Example 4–4, are used. In exponential smoothing there must be a start-up forecast. In this case it is 10.6 for week −5. Following the suggestions of Brown,[3] the start-up value here is the simple mean of past demand data. The past demand data, for weeks −16 through −6, are taken from Figure 4–12.

FIGURE 4–16

Exponentially Smoothed Demand Forecasts—Metro Movers

(1) Week	(2) Actual demand	(3) Forecast	(4) Forecast error (column 2 − column 3)	(5) Smoothing adjustment [(0.2) (column 4)]	(6) Exponentially smoothed forecast (column 3 + column 5)	(7) Absolute sum of forecast errors in column 4	
−5	11	10.6	0.4	0.1	10.7		Start-up phase
−4	5	10.7	−5.7	−1.1	9.6	5.7	Forecasting phase
−3	9	9.6	−0.6	−0.1	9.5	6.3	
−2	12	9.5	2.5	0.5	10.0	8.8	
−1	12	10.0	2.0			10.8	

$$\text{MAD} = \frac{10.8}{4} = 2.7 \text{ vans per week}$$

Note: Do *not* assume that this forecast method is a good one for Metro Movers. There may be better ones.

The underestimate for start-up week −5 was slight, only 0.4 unit. Multiplying that 0.4 by the 0.2 smoothing constant yields an adjustment of 0.1, rounded off. Adding that 0.1 to the old forecast of 10.6 yields 10.7 as the forecast for the next week, week −4.

In week −4 the 10.7 forecast exceeds actual demand of 5; the error is −5.7. That times 0.2 gives an adjustment of −1.1. Thus, the next forecast, for week −3, is cut back by −1.1 to 9.6. And so on.

---

[3] Robert Goodell Brown, *Smoothing, Forecasting, and Prediction of Discrete Time Series* (Englewood Cliffs, N.J.: (Prentice-Hall, 1963), p. 102 (TA168.B68).

Figure 4–16 results may be compared with the three-month moving average results in Figure 4–13. Moving average forecast errors for the last four weeks from Figure 4–13 sum to 14.3 (7.0 + 0.3 + 3.7 + 3.3). Exponential smoothing forecast errors in Figure 4–16 are better at 10.8 (week −5 is not counted). This is by no means a fair comparison since the number of demand weeks is so small and since exponential smoothing has not run long enough for the artificial start-up forecast to be "washed out." Yet it is indicative of the tendency for exponential smoothing to be more accurate than moving average forecasts.

In testing for the proper value of α, the mean absolute deviation is again helpful. Using past demand data, the MAD could be calculated for $\alpha = 0.1, 0.2, \ldots 0.9$. The α yielding the lowest MAD could then be adopted. It is common to use an α in the range of 0.1 to 0.3. The reason is the same as that mentioned earlier for using longer moving average time spans: Most larger firms using exponential smoothing are manufacturers or sellers of durable goods having rather stable short-run demand patterns. A small α, such as 0.2, fits this situation well. A small α means a small adjustment for forecast error, and this keeps each successive forecast close to its predecessor. A large α, say 0.7, would result in new forecasts that follow even large up-and-down swings of actual demand. This would be suitable for the less stable demand pattern of a luxury good or service.

Exponential Smoothing Compared with Moving Average. It may appear that the next exponential smoothing forecast is always based solely on what happened last period with no regard for all preceding demand periods. Not so. Metaphorically, if the forecast for next period, F_N, is the son, then the father is F_{N-1}, the grandfather is F_{N-2}, the great-grandfather is F_{N-3}, and so forth. The current sibling, F_N, has inherited a portion, α, of the error attributable to the father, F_{N-1}; a smaller portion of the error attributable to the grandfather; and so forth.

This creates a mathematical series. It could be shown that the series takes a form that would have the following results: In the case where $\alpha = 0.2$,

0.2 is the weight assigned to the F_{N-1} error;
$(0.2)(0.8)$ is the weight assigned to the F_{N-2} error;
$(0.2)(0.8)^2$ is the weight assigned to the F_{N-3} error;
$(0.2)(0.8)^3$ is the weight assigned to the F_{N-4} error;
or, in general, $(\alpha)(1 - \alpha)^{t-1}$ is the weight assigned to the F_{N-1} error.

The pattern of decreasing weights for $\alpha = 0.2$ is plotted on the chart in Figure 4–17. Also plotted are the calculated weights for $\alpha = 0.5$. The exponential smoothing weights extend back into the past indefinitely.

It is possible to construct a weighted moving average that closely approximates exponential smoothing. But why bother? The word *exponential* and the symbol α may tend to frighten off those who "don't speak mathematics." But exponential smoothing is actually simpler and less expensive to perform than any moving average process. Exponential smoothing involves one small formula, while moving average requires adding all the past demands in the time span. A greater advantage of exponential smoothing as compared with moving average is in data storage. Only the latest

FIGURE 4–17

Weights for Moving Average and for Exponential Smoothing

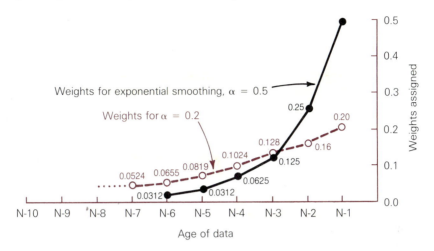

Age of data

exponential smoothing forecast need be saved; by contrast, all the data in the most recent time span must be saved for moving average forecasting.

The main strengths of both exponential smoothing and moving average are that they are simple and automatic. Thus, they are suitable for computer programming. Simplicity and automaticity are also weaknesses. That is, the methods are sometimes too simple—or crude; and they are sometimes too automatic—or inflexible. A cafeteria chain might be willing to turn over the demand forecasting for bread, salad, and desserts to a computer using a moving-average method. But for expensive meat entrées, it might prefer to project demand by combining analysis techniques with a strong dose of judgment and experience. A business can afford to devote more time and study to its costliest product.

Another weakness of exponential smoothing and moving average lies in the underlying assumption that the recent past is the best indicator of the future. This is often true. But sometimes the very fact that a product or service was just demanded in large quantities might mean that less is likely to be demanded in the near future. That is, buyers may become partly sated after a period of high demand; they may hold off for awhile, thereby resulting in a period of low demand.

Double Exponential Smoothing and Other Advanced Methods

The exponential smoothing method explained above is known as single-order exponential smoothing. Single-order exponential smoothing does not keep up with trends. For example, if there is a general upward trend in demand, the single-order exponential smoothing forecast will be consistently too low. Double exponential smoothing, which is a bit more complicated, includes an adjustment feature to bring the forecast up (or down) to the trend line. (A further adjustment that we shall not cover allows for seasonality.) The double exponential smoothing calculation method has the following formula:

$$D_t = 2S_{t-1} - F_{t-2}$$

where

D_t = Double exponential smoothing forecast for next period, t
S_{t-1} = Single-order exponential smoothing forecast for last period, $t - 1$
F_{t-2} = Double exponential smoothing function for period before last, $t - 2$

The value of the S and F functions are obtained by:

$$S_t = S_{t-1} + \alpha(A_{t-1} - S_{t-1})$$
$$F_t = \alpha S_t + (1 - \alpha)F_{t-1}$$

where

α = Smoothing constant
A = Actual demand

EXAMPLE 4–6

Data Services and Double Exponential Smoothing

The actual demands for programmer-hours at Data Services for third quarter, 1983, through fourth quarter, 1984, are: 610, 405, 540, 330, 445,

FIGURE 4–18

Double Exponentially Smoothed Demand Forecasts—Data Services

(1) Period t	(2) A	(3) S $(S_{t-1} +$ col. 5)	(4) Single exponential smoothing error (col. 2-) col. 3	(5) Smoothing adjustment (0.3)(col. 4)	(6) F $[(0.3)(S)+$ $(0.7)(F_{t-1})]$	(7) D $(2S_{t-1}-$ $F_{t-2})$	(8) Double exponential smoothing error (col. 2- col. 7)
1	—		Assumed		565		
2	—	580			560		
3*	610	530	80	+24	551	595	15
4	405	554	−149	−45	552	500	−95
5	540	509	+31	+9	532	557	−17
6	330	518	−188	−56	528	466	−136
7	445	462	−17	−5	508	504	−59
8	410	457	−47	−14	493	396	14
	Absolute error		512				336

*Corresponds to 3rd quarter, 1983.

and 410. For these six quarters, single-order exponential smoothing and double exponential smoothing calculations, and their errors, are shown in Figure 4–18. So that the double exponential smoothing forecast may be determined for third quarter, 1983, assumed S and F factors are given for the two preceding quarters. A smoothing constant, α, of 0.3 is used. The total absolute forecast error is 512 using single-order smoothing. The error is 336 for double exponential smoothing. Double exponential smoothing performs better, as it should, because there is a clear trend downward in actual demand over the six quarters.

Double exponential smoothing may be demonstrated using data from the last seven quarters for the Data Services example (presented earlier in the chapter).

A **tracking signal** routine may be added to an exponential smoothing process (it would also work for a moving-average process). A tracking signal is a continuous check on the *direction* of the forecast error, i.e., positive or negative deviation. The formula is:

$$\text{Tracking signal} = \frac{\text{Cumulative deviation}}{\text{Mean absolute deviation}}$$

where the cumulative deviation may be positive or negative (not the absolute deviation). The tracking signal may be a part of a procedure for changing the smoothing constant when the error is too negative or positive. A helpful rule of thumb is: Consider changing the smoothing constant when the tracking signal exceeds 4 for high-value items, or 8 for low-value items. For example, if the cumulative deviation is 850 and the MAD is 100, then the signal is 850/100 = 8.5, which is above the maximum. Forecast error is overly positive, i.e., forecasts are too low. Other α-values should be tested on recent data to see if the error may be reduced.

Forecasting by Simulation

Trend and seasonal analysis, moving average, and exponential smoothing are standard forecasting tools, especially for durable goods manufacturers. The techniques do not require a computer, but most firms have computerized the techniques for efficiency reasons. The modern computer, however, provides the firm with computational power to run *forecasting simulations* involving several techniques. Forecasting simulation has the potential to surpass, in accuracy, any of the individual forecasting techniques.

In each simulated trial, the forecast values are subtracted from a set of actual demands from the recent past, giving simulated forecast error. The forecast method yielding least error is selected by the computer. The simulations are run every forecasting period, and the best method is recommended only for that forecast. For each successive forecast a new simulation is done, and a new technique may be its basis. (By contrast, the search for a time span or a smoothing constant—for a moving average or exponential smoothing—is performed as an occasional review rather than every forecasting period.)

One ardent advocate of forecasting simulation is Bernard T. Smith, inventory manager at American Hardware Supply.[4] Smith devised a forecast simulation system that applied to 100,000 hardware products. In Smith's system, each product is simulated every month for the next three months, and seven forecast techniques are tested. Each of the seven is simple for buyers and other inventory people in the company to understand. For example, one of the seven forecast techniques is a simple three-month sum (which is not quite the same as a three-month moving average). The simulation for that method uses historical demand data for only the past six months, which is grouped into two three-month demand periods. To illustrate the simulation, let us assume that demand for giant-size trash bags was 500 in the last three-month period and 400 in the period before that. In a three-month-sum forecast method, the latest three-month sum is the forecast for the next period. Therefore the computer simulation treats 400 as the forecast for the three-month period in which actual demand was 500. The simulated forecast error is $500 - 400 = 100$ trash bags. That forecast error is converted to a percent error so that it may be compared with six other computer-simulated methods for forecasting trash bags. The percent error is $1 - (400/500) = 0.20$, or 20 percent.

Six other simple, easy-to-understand methods (including simple trend and simple seasonal) are simulated to see what percent error results. If the three-month-sum method turns out to have a lower percent error than the other six simulated methods, then the computer uses the three-month-sum method to make the next forecast. The forecast would be 500 for the next three months, and for each of the next three months the forecast is simply $500/3 = 167$ trash bags. The forecast rolls over (is recomputed) each month. The computer prints out the forecast for each of the 100,000 items, but buyers may overrule the printed forecast if they do not believe it.

On Forecast Error

As we have seen, history-based forecasting involves (1) analysis of historical demand data by some method and (2) analysis of error by that method. We have focused on the mean absolute deviation (MAD) as the measure of error. But some companies (and some books) use other equally valid measures of error. Let us briefly look at some of the most common other measures of error. Three are considered: the standard deviation, mean squared error, and mean absolute percent error.

The three are compared with the MAD in Figure 4–19. The figure first presents some demand data for comparison. Eight periods of past actual historical demand data and a level forecast for the same eight periods are given.

Below the demand data, in the middle of Figure 4–19, are working figures needed to calculate the MAD and the other three measures of forecast error. The first row of working figures is simply the forecast error for each period. The second row is

---

[4] See Bernard T. Smith, *Focus Forecasting: Computer Techniques for Inventory Control* (Boston: CBI Publishing, 1978) (HD55.S48).

FIGURE 4–19

Measures of Forecast Error

				Period				
	−8	−7	−6	−5	−4	−3	−2	−1
Actual historical demand	10	8	13	5	9	8	11	12
Forecast demand	10	10	10	10	10	10	10	10
Working figures:								
Error (Actual − Forecast)	0	−2	3	−5	−1	−2	1	2
Absolute sum of error	$= 0 + 2 + 3 + 5 + 1 + 2 + 1 + 2 = 16$							
Error squared	0	4	9	25	1	4	1	4
Sum of error squared	$= 0 + 4 + 9 + 25 + 1 + 4 + 1 + 4 = 48$							
Error-to-actual ratio	0/10	−2/8	3/13	−5/5	−1/9	−2/8	1/11	2/12
Error-to-actual percent	0%	−25%	23%	−100%	−11%	−25%	9%	17%
Absolute percent error	0%	25%	23%	100%	11%	25%	9%	17%
Sum of absolute percent error	$= 0 + 25 + 23 + 100 + 11 + 25 + 9 + 17 = 210\%$							

Measures of forecast error:

$$\text{Mean absolute deviation (MAD)} = \frac{\text{Absolute sum of error}}{\text{Periods}} = \frac{16}{8} = 2.0$$

$$\text{Standard deviation} = \sqrt{\frac{\text{Sum of error squared}}{\text{Periods} - 1}} = \sqrt{\frac{48}{7}} = 2.62$$

$$\text{Mean square error} = \frac{\text{Sum of error squared}}{\text{Periods}} = \frac{48}{8} = 6.0$$

$$\text{Mean absolute percent error} = \frac{\text{Sum of absolute \% error}}{\text{Periods}} = \frac{210}{8}$$
$$= 26.25\%$$

the absolute sum (signs ignored) of the error for the eight periods. Next is the error (from the first row) squared. Then the sum of the error squared is computed. The error-to-actual forecast ratio for the eight periods is given next, followed by that ratio expressed as a percentage, and then expressed as an absolute percentage. Finally, the sum of the absolute percent error is given.

The bottom part of the figure gives the formulas and computes the four measures of forecast error. First is the MAD. It divides the absolute sum of error, 16 (from the working figures) by 8, which is the number of periods of demand data. The result is 2.0.

Next is the standard deviation, which uses the sum of error squared, 48 (from the working figures) as the numerator. The denominator is the number of periods, 8, minus 1. (The denominator would be "periods − 2″ if the forecast were an upward or downward trend instead of a level line.) The square root of the dividend is the answer, 2.62.

The mean squared error, the third measure, uses the same numerator, 48, as the standard deviation. The denominator is the number of periods, 8. The result is 6.0.

The last measure is the mean absolute percent error. The sum of absolute percent error goes in the numerator. From the working figures, the entry is 210 percent. It is divided by the number of periods, 8, to give 26.25 percent as the answer. (Note: The mean absolute percent error was introduced in Chapter 3 discussion of item versus group forecasting error.)

Why have four measures of error? No reason. In practice it is best to pick the one you prefer and stay with it. Or it may be that the forecaster is using a computer program that automatically prints out more than one of the measures of error each time historical demand is analyzed. In that case the forecaster may have a choice.

One more point needs to be made about these measures of error: They do not apply to the associative forecasting techniques, which are considered next. The associative techniques are judged in other ways, not based on error.

ASSOCIATIVE PROJECTION

In all of the preceding techniques, demand is tracked over *time*. In associative projection, demand is tracked not against time but against some other known variable, perhaps student enrollment or inches of precipitation. The associative techniques are the leading indicator and correlation.

Leading Indicator

A superior kind of forecasting tool is the leading indicator. Changes in demand may be preceded by changes in some other variable. If so, the other variable is a leading indicator. The leading indicator is helpful if the patterns of change in the two variables are similar (i.e., they correlate) and if the lead time is long enough for action to be taken before the demand change occurs.

Few firms are able to discover a variable of this type—one that changes with demand but leads it significantly. The reason is probably that demand for a given good or service usually depends on (is led by) a number of variables rather than one dominant variable. The search for such a variable can be costly and futile. Therefore most of the work with leading indicators has centered on national economic forecasting instead of local demand forecasting. Nevertheless, the leading indicator should be part of the demand forecaster's tool kit, since it is a valued predictor in those cases where it can be isolated.

One story about leading indicators has been widely circulated. It is said that the Rothschild family reaped a fortune by having advance news of Napoleon's defeat at Waterloo. Nathan, the Rothschild brother who was located in England, is said to have received the news via carrier pigeon. On that basis he supposedly bought depressed war-effort securities and sold them at a huge profit after the news reached England.[5]

The leading indicator in this case was news of the war, and it led prices of securities. The Rothschilds' astuteness was not in realizing this, for it was common knowledge; rather it was in their development of an information network to capitalize on the knowledge. A costly information system like that set up by the Rothschilds can provide highly accurate information fast. By contrast, personal judgment as a basis for action is cheap but tends to be less accurate and to be hindsight rather than foresight. That is, our personal judgment often does not lead events.

In sum, leading indicators should have long lead times as well as accuracy. This requires good information systems. The following example demonstrates this.

EXAMPLE 4–6

State Jobs Service and Leading Indicators

Mr. H. Hand, manager of the Metro City office of the State Jobs Service, sees the need for better demand forecasting. The problem has been that surges in clients tend to catch the office off guard. Advance warning of demand is needed in order to plan for staff, desks, phones, forms, and even space.

One element of demand is well known: Many of the job seekers are there as a result of being laid off by Acme Industries. Acme is by far the largest employer in Metro City. Mr. Hand is able to obtain Acme records on layoffs over the past year. The layoff data are plotted on a time chart along with the Jobs Service office's data on job applicants. The chart is shown in Figure 4–20. The chart shows job applicants ranging from a high of 145 (in period 8) to a low of 45 (in period 20). Layoffs at Acme range from a high of 60 (in periods 6 and 7) to a low of zero (in several periods).

Plotting the points seems well worth the effort, because Mr. Hand notes a striking similarity in the shapes of the two plots. Furthermore, the layoffs plot seems to lead the applicants plot. For example, the high of 145 applicants occurred two weeks after the high of 60 layoffs; and the low of 45 applicants occurred two weeks after layoffs spiked downward to zero. Weeks 1, 3, 17, 21, and 22 are other places on the layoff plot where a two-week lead appears; and the lead is close to two weeks in weeks 11–15.

Does a two-week lead make sense? Or could it be coincidence? Mr. Hand feels that it makes sense. He bases this on the impression that laid-off Acme people tend to live off their severance pay for a time—two weeks seems reasonable—before actively seeking another job.

Mr. Hand therefore takes the final steps: (1) He establishes an information

---

[5] One historian disputes the stories, asserting that the Rothschilds made more money during the war than at its end and that the news was forwarded by a courier in a Rothschild ship, not a carrier pigeon. Virginia Cowles, *The Rothschilds: A Family of Fortune* (New York: Alfred A. Knopf, 1973), pp. 47–50 (HG 1552.R8C66).

FIGURE 4–20

Layoffs at Acme and Job Applicants at Jobs Service—With Time Scale

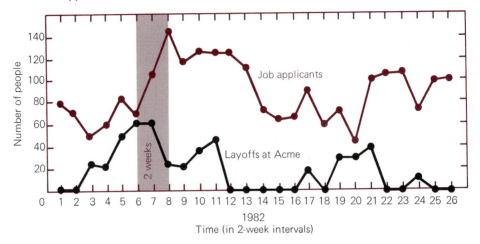

system. It is simply an agreement that every two weeks Acme will release the number of its laid-off employees to the Jobs Service office. (2) He establishes a forecasting procedure based on that layoff information and the two-week lead pattern of Figure 4–20.

In establishing a forecasting procedure, Mr. Hand regraphs the data

FIGURE 4–21

Correlation of Layoffs at Acme (N − 2) with Demand at Jobs Service (N)

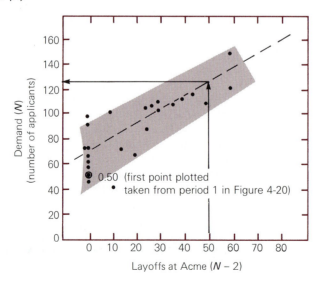

from Figure 4–20 into the form shown in Figure 4–21 (a scatter diagram). That is, layoffs at Acme for period $N - 2$ matched with applicants at the Jobs Service office for period N constitute points that are plotted as the two axes of the graph. For example, the first point plotted is (0,50), which is taken from Figure 4–20, where for period 1, layoffs are 0 and two weeks later applicants are 50. Each other point is plotted in the same way. The points tend to go upward left to right clustering around the dashed line (an "eyeball" regression line) shown in the future.

The dashed line is used for forecasting purposes. Suppose, for example, that Mr. Hand learns today that Acme is laying off 50 people this week. In Figure 4–21 a solid vertical line extending from 50 to the dashed line and leftward yields a forecast demand of about 125. Thus, the procedure tells Mr. Hand to expect 125 applicants in two weeks.

Correlation

How good is Mr. Hand's leading indicator? (1) By one measure, the supporting information system, it is very good! Getting the layoff data from Acme is cheap and highly accurate. (2) In terms of lead time, it is not so good. Two weeks' notice is not much for the purpose of adjusting resources on hand. (3) In terms of validity, the leading indicator *seems* good, but how may we measure "good"? One answer is: Measure it by the correlation coefficient. That is the next topic.

Correlation means degree of association. The **correlation coefficient,** r, is a measure of degree of association. The value of r ranges from 1.0 for perfect correlation to 0.0 for no correlation at all to -1.0 for perfect negative correlation. In positive correlation a rise in one attribute occurs along with a rise in the other; in negative correlation a rise in one occurs along with a fall in the other. To calculate r a number of pairs of values are needed. The chapter supplement provides a formula and sample calculations.

For the Jobs Service example the correlation coefficient is quite good, about $+0.78$ (calculations not given). A good correlation could be expected by looking at Figure 4–21. The points tend to cluster along the broad shaded band running upward at about a 45-degree angle. This is the pattern of a positive correlation. (Negative correlations go downward left to right.)

In the Jobs Service example the amount of lead was determined visually. The two variables were plotted on the time scale in Figure 4–20, and brief inspection showed that the two curves were generally two weeks apart. Sometimes the amount of lead is hard to see; and where there are many potential leading indicators to check out, manual plotting and visual inspection become tedious. In such cases computers may take over. It is simple for the computer to calculate r for a number of different lead periods. The one with the best r may then be selected.

What about a lead period of zero? That would exist where a pair of events occur at the same time.[6] Even if the correlation is perfect ($r = 1.0$), it *appears* that it is

---

[6] The introductory statistics course usually focuses on this type of simple correlation—with no lead time.

of no help in forecasting: No lead time means no forewarning and therefore, it might seem, no *fore*casting. This impression is not correct. Correlation with no lead *can* be valuable *if* the indicator (independent variable) is more predictable than demand is.

As an example, a phone company in a large city may know that new residential phone orders correlate nearly perfectly with new arrivals in the city—with no lead time. There is probably value in knowing this, because in most large cities careful studies are done to project population increases. Fairly reliable projections of new residences may be available. The phone company need not spend a lot of money projecting residential telephone installations; instead, the city's data on new residences may be used. For these reasons most large firms are indeed interested in establishing good correlations, even without lead time.

Multiple regression/correlation is an extension of simple regression and correlation. In this method, multiple causal variables may be analyzed. The result is a formula with demand on the left side of the equal sign and each of the causal variables, properly weighted, on the right. For example, the phone company may look for other predictors besides new residences. Level of savings in local thrift institutions and amount of phone advertising are possibilities. A multiple regression equation might be put together with three causal variables in it: new residences *(N)*, savings *(S)*, and advertising *(A)*. Then computer processing using past data would yield the parameters for each of the three causal variables. As an example, the equation to forecast next month's demand *(D)* for phone installations might be:

$$D = 0.36N + 2.81S + 0.89A$$

Since advertising effects may take awhile, advertising perhaps should be analyzed as a leading indicator. Perhaps it could be shown that advertising leads demand by one month. The revised multiple regression equation might appear as:

$$D = 0.41N + 2.70S + 0.88A_{n-1}$$

Much more has been done with multiple regression/correlation in economic forecasting than in demand forecasting. The method, which is complex and requires a computer, is beyond the scope of this book. The approach has often proven futile at the level of the firm; however, multiple regression has frequently been used for large utilities or large public agencies whose demand is likely to be affected by a number of broad socioeconomic variables.

For example, a news story about power rates includes a statement that "an econometric approach . . . which most utilities use, involves multiple regression analysis to determine the sensitivity of electricity demand to such variables as economic growth and inflation."[7] The gist of the story is that the utilities have a preference for the econometric approach because it tends to show a high demand growth rate, which helps justify rate boosts. A simpler trend analysis approach, recommended by a consulting group to the Illinois Commerce Commission, tends to show lower demand

---

[7] "Why It's Tougher to Justify Rate Boosts," *Business Week,* November 7, 1977, p. 56.

rate increase. In the article the consultants' approach is called an "engineering approach" in which "categories of residential electricity users are multiplied by expected use of air conditioners, refrigerators, and other appliances."

SUMMARY

The demand forecast, in units (not dollars), triggers many of the other activities in managing operations and operating resources. The forecast provides advance notice so that changes may be planned.

National economic projections may serve as one input into a company's demand forecast. Marketing projections, including information on sales promotions and major shifts in customer buying intentions, provide another input. Historical analysis of demand patterns is a third basis for demand forecasts.

Tools of historical demand analysis include the simple mean, trend, and seasonal analysis. These are multiperiod pattern projection techniques, and they are useful in short-, medium-, and long-term projection. The least-squares technique of trend projection may be used where precision is desired or where there are many products/ services to be forecast. Calculators or computers are helpful in routinizing the calculation process. Seasonal indices may be combined with trend projection to produce improved forecasts sensitive to seasonal influences.

Single-period patternless projection tools include moving average, exponential smoothing, and simulation. These are useful for short-term projection. Moving average is a simple mean of recent past demands in a given time span. The moving average forecast is recomputed—rolled over—every forecast period. Exponential smoothing adds a portion *(alpha)* of last period's forecast error to the last forecast to yield a new forecast. Double exponential smoothing does the same thing, but also adds a trend adjustment. A tracking signal may keep tabs on positive and negative error tendencies so that *alpha* may be adjusted.

The mean absolute deviation (MAD) is a common measure of forecast accuracy, and the MAD may also serve as a test of what moving average time span or exponential smoothing *alpha* value is best. Another test of accuracy is percent error, which is used in one approach to forecasting by computer simulation. The simulation tests several forecasting methods and automatically selects the one yielding the least percent error. The simulation is repeated every forecast period for every item being forecast.

The leading indicator and correlation are associative projection techniques. They attempt to isolate an association (correlation) between one known variable and demand. A correlation is most useful if a predictor variable, *X*, can be shown to lead demand, *Y*. This is the leading indicator technique, and the longer the lead and the higher the correlation, the better the forecast. Correlation without lead may be valuable if the independent variable is more predictable than your own demand is. Multiple regression/correlation admits more than one independent variable.

While all of the historical techniques are potentially useful, demand forecasting is inherently inexact. No amount of statistical analysis can change that fact.

REFERENCES

Books

Box, G. E. P., and G. M. Jenkins.   *Time Series Analysis, Forecasting, and Control.* San Francisco: Holden-Day, 1970 (QA280.B67).

Brown, R. G.   *Smoothing, Forecasting, and Prediction of Discrete Time Series.* Englewood Cliffs, N.J.: Prentice-Hall, 1963 (TA168.B68).

Butler, William F.; Robert A. Kavesh; and Robert B. Platt, eds.   *Methods and Techniques of Business Forecasting.* Englewood Cliffs, N.J.: Prentice-Hall, 1974 (HB3730.M42).

Chambers, J. C.; S. K. Mullick; and D. D. Smith.   *An Executive's Guide to Forecasting.* New York: John Wiley & Sons, 1974 (HF5415.2.C38).

Forecasting.   2d ed. American Production and Inventory Control Society, 1979.

Gross, Charles W., and Robin T. Peterson.   *Business Forecasting.* Boston: Houghton Mifflin, 1976.

Wheelwright, S. C., and S. Makridakis.   *Forecasting Methods for Management.* John Wiley & Sons, 1973 (HD69.F58W5).

REVIEW QUESTIONS

1. Why are demand forecasts in *dollars* not adequate in operations management?

2. Marketing projection and economic projections are both done in dollars. How, then, do the two differ?

3. What are the consequences for organizations that don't keep demand records?

4. What is *noise* in forecasting, and what should be done about it?

5. When would a trend forecast be preferable over the mean?

6. Why is it sometimes difficult to decide whether to use the mean, straight-line trend, or curving trend as your forecast basis?

7. Is *accuracy* the main reason why computers are used in demand forecasting? Discuss.

8. How can you make a preliminary judgment—without calculations—as to whether demand for a product is seasonal?

9. What do you *do* with seasonal indices?

10. Explain the differences between the pattern-projection and the patternless forecasting techniques.

11. If a product is a stable necessity (rather than a faddish item), will the moving average time span be large or small? How about the exponential smoothing constant? Explain.

12. Why did companies switch from moving average to exponential smoothing?

13. What forecasting techniques have smoothing effects? Explain.

14. Why does forecasting by simulation take so much computing?

15. What is the purpose of forecast-error analysis?

16. A leading indicator is a great demand forecasting technique but isn't used much. Explain.

17. How may the value of a leading indicator be assessed?

18. If you have a good correlation but no lead, can it be at all valuable for demand forecasting? Explain.

PROBLEMS

1. Huckleberry Farms, Inc., has three years of monthly demand data for its biggest seller, Huckleberry Jam. The planning director aims to use the data, given below, for demand forecasting.

| | Cases of Huckleberry Jam | | |
	Three years ago	Two years ago	Last year
January	530	535	578
February	436	477	507
March	522	530	562
April	448	482	533
May	422	498	516
June	499	563	580
July	478	488	537
August	400	428	440
September	444	430	511
October	486	486	480
November	437	502	499
December	501	547	542

a. Calculate a six-month moving-average *forecast*. What time period in the future is this forecast applicable to?

b. Which of the following moving average time spans is best: three months, six months, or nine months? Prove your answer by calculating mean absolute deviations (MAD), using data *for the last 12 months only*. (If suitable computer facilities and software are available to you, use the full 36 months' data.)

c. If the most recent forecast—for December of last year—was 495, what is the next exponential smoothing forecast? Use $\alpha = 0.3$. What time period in the future is this forecast applicable to?

d. Which of the following alphas is best for exponential smoothing forecasting: 0.1, 0.3, or 0.5? Prove your answer by calculating MADs, using monthly data *for the last three months only*. In each case, assume that 570 was the exponentially smoothed forecast for September of last year.

e. Although the given data are monthly, Huckleberry also needs a forecast for next quarter and next year. Manipulate the monthly data (create new tables of data) so that they are useful for a quarterly and an annual forecast. Now compute a quarterly and an annual moving average forecast, using a three-period (*not* three months in this case!) time span. And compute a quarterly and an annual exponential smoothing forecast, using $\alpha = 0.3$ and assuming that the last period forecast was (1) 1,596 for quarterly and (2) 5,990 for annual.

f. Plot the data on a scatter diagram, with time as the horizontal axis (use graph paper, or else take some care in creating a substitute on ordinary lined paper). Now use the eyeball trend projection method to produce a forecast (not adjusted for seasonality) for Huckleberry Jam for the next 12 months. Either a straight or curving line may be used—whichever fits best. Write down each of the 12 forecast values. (If suitable computer facilities and software are available to you, verify your plotted trend line by processing the data on the computer.)

g. Most consumer products show some degree of demand seasonality. What kind of seasonality pattern would you expect for Huckleberry Jam? Why? *After responding to the preceding question,* examine the three years history to see if the data tend to follow your reasoning. You may find it helpful to plot the three sets of 12-month data "on top of each other" on a graph to see if there is a pattern of seasonality. Now comment further on Huckleberry's demand patterns.

h. Select any 3 of the 12 months, and calculate seasonal indices for those 3 months for each year. Follow the method of Figure 4–9, modified so that the basis is a 12-month moving average. Now develop projected (next-year) seasonal indices for each of the three months. (If suitable computer facilities and software are available to you, develop seasonal indices for the full 12 months.)

i. Combine your results from g and h, that is, your trend projection with your seasonal indices. What are your seasonally adjusted trend forecasts for next year?

2. Seal-Fine Sash Company has three years of quarterly demand data for its standard "bedroom" window unit. The production control manager uses the data, given below, for demand forecasting.

	Number of window units		
	Three years ago	Two years ago	Last year
Winter	190	215	401
Spring	147	210	510
Summer	494	755	925
Fall	773	1,088	1,482

a. Calculate the three-quarter moving-average *forecast.* What time period in the future is this moving average for?

b. Which of the following moving-average time spans is best: three quarters or four quarters? Prove your answer by calculating mean absolute deviations (MAD), using all 12 quarters of data. (If suitable computer facilities and software are available to you, process the data by computer rather than manually.) Do the MAD values seem to show that moving average is a suitable method for the quarterly forecasting of Seal-Fine's window units? Explain.

c. If the most recent forecast—for fall of last year—was 1,550, what is the next exponential smoothing forecast? Use $\alpha = 0.2$. What time period in the future is the forecast applicable to?

d. Which of the following alphas is best for exponential smoothing forecasting: 0.1, 0.3, or 0.5? Prove your answer by calculating MADs, using quarterly data *for the last three quarters only*. In each case, assume that 540 was the exponentially smoothed forecast for winter of last year. Do the MAD values seem to show that exponential smoothing is a suitable method for quarterly forecasting of Seal-Fine's window units? Explain.

e. Plot the data on a scatter diagram, with time as the horizontal axis (use graph paper, or else take some care in creating a substitute on ordinary lined paper). Use the eyeball trend projection method to produce a forecast (not adjusted for seasonality) for the window units for the next four quarters. Now combine the data in such a way as to yield yearly forecasts for the next three years. Either a straight or curving line may be used—whichever fits best. Write down each of the forecast values. (If suitable computer facilities and software are available to you, verify your plotted trend line by processing the data by computer.)

f. What kind of seasonal demand pattern would you expect for Seal-Fine's product line? Explain. *After responding to the preceding question,* examine the three years history to see if the data tend to follow your reasoning. You may find it helpful to plot the three sets of quarterly data "on top of each other" on a graph to see if there is a pattern of seasonality. Now comment further on Seal-Fine's demand patterns.

g. Select any two of the four quarters, and calculate seasonal indices for those two quarters for each year. Follow the method of Figure 4–9. Now develop projected (next-year) seasonal indices for each of the two quarters. (If suitable computer facilities and software are available to you, develop seasonal indices for all four quarters.)

h. Combine your four-quarter trend projection from *e* with your seasonal indices from *g*. What are your seasonally adjusted trend forecasts for next year?

3. Anderson Theaters owns a chain of movie theaters. In one city, a college town, there are several Anderson Theaters. There is interest in finding out exactly what influence the college student population has on movie attendance. Student population figures have been obtained from local colleges. These, along with movie attendance figures for the past 12 months, are given below:

	Month											
	1	*2*	*3*	*4*	*5*	*6*	*7*	*8*	*9*	*10*	*11*	*12*
Students*	8	18	18	18	15	9	11	6	17	19	19	13
Attendance*	14	15	16	12	10	8	9	7	11	13	14	17

* In thousands. The student figures are monthly averages.

a. What is the correlation coefficient?

b. Is this correlation analysis useful for Anderson Theaters? Discuss fully.

4. Computer Media, Inc., sells floppy disks, print paper, and other such computer media, which it reorders based on monthly exponential smoothing demand forecasts. Recent actual demand data, single-order exponential smoothing forecasts, and double exponential smoothing functions are given below.

Month	Actual demand	Single-order exponential smoothing forecast	Double exponential smoothing function
January	—	—	150
February	140	164	
March	166		

a. If the smoothing constant is 0.3, what is the double exponential smoothing forecast for March: What are the forecast errors for third quarter, first for single-order exponential smoothing and then for double exponential smoothing? What is the double exponential smoothing forecast for April?

b. What would the double exponential smoothing forecast for April be if the smoothing constant were 0.1 instead of 0.3?

c. Comparing your April results in parts a and b, would you say that the choice of a smoothing constant makes much difference?

5. The stockroom manager at Citrus Life and Casualty Co. forecasts use of office supplies by exponential smoothing, $\alpha = 0.3$. Three weeks ago demand for letterhead envelopes was 12 boxes and the forecast was also 12. Actual demands since then were 18 and 5 boxes. What is the forecast for next week?

6. Ohio Rubber Co. sells tires to original equipment manufacturers (e.g., the auto companies) and also to the aftermarket (replacement tires). Aftermarket demand is forecast using single-order exponential smoothing with $\alpha = 0.2$. For one tire model, a BR78-14 whitewall, June demand was 70 truckloads, and the forecast was 80 truckloads. Actual demand was 73 truckloads in July. What was the July forecast and forecast error?

7. Bayou Airways, a small commuter line, is investigating single-order exponential smoothing as a basis for forecasting passengers. The following is a table showing recent passenger data and ES calculations using $\alpha = 0.2$, 0.4 and 0.6. Which α is best based on this admittedly small sample of data?

Week	Actual passengers	Exponentially-smoothed forecasts		
		$\alpha = 0.2$	$\alpha = 0.4$	$\alpha = 0.6$
−5	3,600	2,940	3,000	3,040
−4	3,100	3,072	3,240	3,376
−3	4,200	3,078	3,184	3,210
−2	4,900	3,302	3,590	3,804
−1	3,500	3,622	4,114	4,462

8. B. C. Electric Products, Ltd., manufactures small electric motors and allied products, and forecasts end product demand based on a weekly exponential smoothing forecast.

BC planners are considering use of double exponential smoothing as a replacement for the presently used single-order exponential smoothing method. As a test, past demand data for one model of motor, a ¼ HP model used in kitchen sink disposers and in many other products, are used to compare the exponential smoothing methods. The past six weeks' demand data are:

Week	−6	−5	−4	−3	−2	−1
Demand	32	39	38	38	43	47

  a. Compute the forecast errors, in mean absolute deviation, using single-order and double exponential smoothing. But use *only* the errors for weeks −3, −2, and −1. (Weeks −6, −5, and −4 will use assumed start-up values and therefore will yield artificial forecast errors.) As start-up data, assume that the single-order exponential smoothing value for week −6 was 33 and that the double exponential smoothing functions for weeks −6 and −5 were 30 and 33 respectively. Use 0.2 as the smoothing constant.
  b. Does double exponential smoothing seem to be a *good* forecasting technique for this application? Explain.

9. Service-part demands for lawn mower blades at Lawngirl Manufacturing Co. are shown below, along with three-week and nine-week moving average data.

								Week								
	−16	−15	−14	−13	−12	−11	−10	−9	−8	−7	−6	−5	−4	−3	−2	−1
Demand	800	460	630	880	510	910	420	740	790	700	840	600	930	680	900	800
Three-week moving average			630	657	673	767	613	690	650	743	777	713	790	737	837	793
Nine-week moving average						682	671	713	710	716	734	733	776			

  a. For weeks −12 through −5, plot the raw demand data, the three-week moving average data, and the nine-week moving average data on one graph. Comment on the smoothing effects of the different time spans (note that the raw data constitute a one-week moving average).
  b. Assuming a nonseasonal demand, what is the forecast for next week if a one-week moving average is used? If a three-week moving average is used? If a nine-week moving average is used?
  c. Consider your answer from part *b* and the nature of the product, lawn mower blades. Which moving-average time span seems best?

10. Recent monthly caseload in a public defender's office is shown below.

January	February	March	April	May	June	July	August	September	October	November	December
180	100	90	110	110	120	140	170	150	160	160	170

a. Graph the demands as a two-month moving average and as a six-month moving average. What do the graphs show about the smoothing effects of different moving-average time spans?

b. Calculate a five-month moving average centered on June. Now use that value to calculate a seasonal index for June.

c. What factors would determine the usefulness of the seasonal index of part *b?*

11. Demand data and 7-month moving average data are given below.

		Month										
	−12	*−11*	*−10*	*−9*	*−8*	*−7*	*−6*	*−5*	*−4*	*−3*	*−2*	*−1*
Actual demand	130	160	80	130	100	40	150	160	210	200	150	170
7-month moving average	133	121	107	113	117	124	141	144	154			

a. Compute a seasonal index applicable to next month.

b. If the trend projection, not adjusted for seasonality, is 168, what is the seasonally adjusted forecast for next month? Use the seasonal index from part *a* in your calculation.

c. If the product is *not* seasonal but the seven-month moving average time span is optimal, what should the forecast be for next month?

12. Demand data and a four-quarter moving average are shown below.

Time	Actual demand	Four-quarter moving average
1st quarter, 1983	20	
2d quarter, 1983	16	19.8
3d quarter, 1983	21	19.0
4th quarter, 1983	18	
1st quarter, 1984	22	

a. If the forecaster finds that the product is *not* seasonal but that four quarters *is* the best moving-average time span, what should the forecast be for second quarter, 1984?

b. If the unadjusted trend projection for second quarter, 1983, is 21, what should the *seasonally adjusted* forecast be for that quarter?

13. Below are recent actual demands and forecast demands for a particular low-value service part.

	Time				
	−5	*−4*	*−3*	*−2*	*−1*
Actual demand	9	10	17	25	27
Forecast	10	12	15	19	25

a. What is the mean absolute deviation of forecast error?
b. What is the latest tracking signal? Is it acceptable?

14. Below are the last four months of demand data and exponential smoothing forecasts for the custom drapery department at a local department store. The data are in number of customer orders.

Month	Actual demand	Forecast
−4	18	20
−3	6	18
−2	12	16
−1	9	15

a. Determine the mean absolute deviation of forecast error.
b. Calculate the tracking signal as of today. What does it suggest?

15. Q. R. Smith, owner-manager of Smith's Kitchens, Inc., sees some evidence that demand for kitchen cabinets is related to local tax mill rates, which are adjusted twice yearly. The following are recent data that Smith has collected.

	Half-year period									
	−10	−9	−8	−7	−6	−5	−4	−3	−2	−1
Cabinet demand	55	70	75	70	80	85	90	80	70	75
Mill rate	110	125	135	145	140	140	160	150	150	140

a. Develop a graph (scatter diagram) in which cabinet demands (Y_t) are on the vertical axis and mill rates three periods earlier (X_{t-3}) are on the horizontal axis. Plot each combination of demand and mill rate three periods earlier (i.e., Y_t and X_{t-3}) on the graph. For example the first point would be the demand, 70, for period −7 and the rate, 110, for period −10. Examine your graph. Is there enough association between demand and mill rates three periods (one-and-a-half years) earlier to be useful for forecasting? Explain.
b. Calculate the formula for the straight line of best fit for the data in part a. Using your formula along with the appropriate mill rate, what is the forecast of cabinet demand for the next six-month period?
c. Calculate the coefficient of correlation. Is your impression from part a confirmed?

16. The chief of planning at North American Hotels, Inc., suspects that convention business may be associated with productivity indices and that tourist business may be associated with weather. The graphs below show two of the chief's attempts to make these associations.

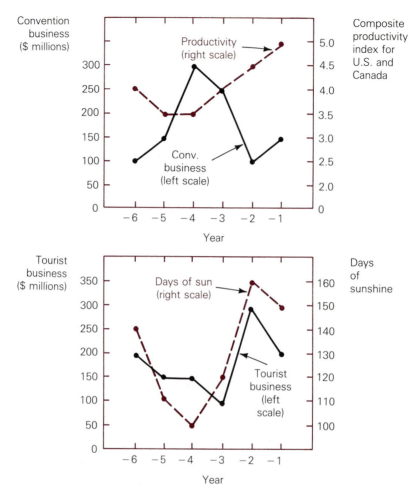

a. Based on your visual inspection of the productivity-convention business graph, what should the chief of planning conclude? Comment on the usefulness of the analysis for the hotel.

b. Based on your visual inspection of the sunshine-tourist business graph, what should the chief of planning conclude? Comment on the usefulness of the analysis for the hotel.

17. The safety division at Acme Manufacturing Co. has written the following numbers of safety citations in the past seven months:

	Month						
	−7	−6	−5	−4	−3	−2	−1
Citations	71	63	60	58	61	40	42

a. Plot the data and project the number of citations that might be expected next month. Use the eyeball method.

b. The chief safety inspector suspects that safety citations are related to number of new hires. She has collected the following data on new hires for the same seven months:

	Month						
	−7	−6	−5	−4	−3	−2	−1
New hires	40	31	27	33	10	25	25

Conduct an analysis of the association between new hires and citations. Look for a leading indicator.

c. Calculate the formula for the straight line of best fit (line of regression) for the last seven months of citations. Use the formula to calculate the projected demand for the next two months.

d. Calculate the coefficient of correlation between new hires and citations. Make the same calculation but with new hires leading citations by one month. (Base the calculations on citations for months −6 to −1 and new hires for months −7 to −2.) Comment on the difference—and on the type of associative forecast that is appropriate.

18. The captain of the *Pescado Grande,* a sportfishing boat that docks at Ensenada, Mexico, is trying to develop a plan for crew needs by days of the week. The basis is number of paying customers per day. The following are data for the last three weeks.

	Day of the week						
	Monday	Tuesday	Wednesday	Thursday	Friday	Saturday	Sunday
Week −3	12	6	10	12	18	30	26
Week −2	9	4	5	8	22	32	34
Week −1	3	10	8	7	14	27	31

a. Calculate "seasonal" (daily) indices for Sunday and for Monday. Base the calculations on the appropriate seven-day average demand. What index should be used for planning the crew on Sunday and Monday this week? Explain.

b. If the *average* number of paying customers per day next week is expected to be 16, how many should be forecast for Monday?

19. In a certain time-sharing computer system the quarterly number of "connects" or "logons" is one useful indicator of demand. Recent data are as follows:

	Quarter							
	−8	−7	−6	−5	−4	−3	−2	−1
Number of connects (in thousands)	8	9	11	10	11	13	16	12

What is your forecast for next quarter? Look for seasonality and trend. Explain.

Supplement to Chapter 4
Least Squares and Correlation
Coefficients

In this supplement two related techniques are examined. Both concern the straight line that most closely fits a set of plotted data points:

1. The least-squares technique, considered first, is a method of developing the equation for the straight line of best fit (line of regression).
2. The correlation coefficient, considered last, measures how well a given straight line or line of regression fits a set of plotted data points.

Least Squares

The general formula for a straight line is:

$$Y = a + bX$$

For any set of plotted data points, the least-squares method may be used to determine values for a and b in the formula that best fits the data points; a is the Y-intercept, and b is the slope. Least-squares formulas for a and b follow, first in the general form and then in a simpler form for a special case.

General form:

$$a = \frac{\Sigma Y}{N} - b\left(\frac{\Sigma X}{N}\right)$$

$$b = \frac{N\Sigma XY - \Sigma X\Sigma Y}{N\Sigma X^2 - (\Sigma X)^2}$$

Special form (when $\Sigma X = 0$):

$$a = \frac{\Sigma Y}{N} \text{ and } b = \frac{\Sigma XY}{\Sigma^2},$$

where

$\Sigma Y = $ Sum of the Y-values for all plotted points
$N = $ Total number of plotted points

$\Sigma XY=$ Sum of the product of X-value times Y-value for all plotted points

$\Sigma X^2=$ Sum of squares of X-values for all plotted points

$\Sigma X=$ Sum of the X-values for all plotted points

The least-squares technique is shown in a forecasting example using the special form of the equations, as follows:

EXAMPLE S4–1

Least-Squares Trend Line, Data Services

In the last seven quarters, demand, in programmer-hours, was as follows at Data Services, Inc.:

510   600   400   520   340   440   420

What is the trend line?

Solution:

A table simplifies computation of a and b values. In the table the fourth quarter, in which 520 was the demand, is treated as the base period. It is numbered as period 0. The three previous periods are numbered -1, -2, and -3; the three succeeding periods are numbered $+1$, $+2$, and $+3$. The small numbers simplify calculations, and since their sum is zero, i.e., $\Sigma X = 0$, the simpler least-squares equations apply. The Y-values are the seven demand figures. The table is given below.

	Y	X	X^2	XY	
	510	-3	9	$-1,530$	
	600	-2	4	$-1,200$	
	400	-1	1	-400	
	520	0	0	0	← Base period
	340	$+1$	1	$+340$	
	440	$+2$	4	$+880$	
	420	$+3$	9	$+1,260$	
Sums	3,230	0	28	-650	

Since

$$a=\frac{\Sigma Y}{N} \text{ and } b=\frac{\Sigma XY}{\Sigma X^2}$$

$$a=\frac{3,230}{7}=461$$

$$b=\frac{-650}{28}=-23.2$$

The formula for the line of best fit is:

$$Y=461-23.2X$$

The formula may be used to forecast, say, the next quarter. With the base or centermost period numbered 0, the next quarter is numbered $+4$. Then,

$$Y = 461 - 23.2 \ (+4)$$
$$= 461 - 93$$
$$= 368 \text{ programmer-hours}$$

Figure S4–1 summarizes the results of the least-squares computations and the forecast for next quarter. Dates are put on the figure to make it agree with the dates for Figure 4–5 in the chapter. It may be seen that the least-squares trend is very nearly the same as the eyeball trend of Figure 4–5.

FIGURE S4–1

Seven-Quarter Least-Squares Trend—Data Services, Inc.

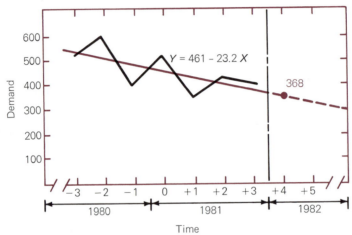

Correlation Coefficients

The coefficient of correlation, *r*, ranges from ±1.0 for perfect correlation to 0.0 for no correlation at all. An *r* of ±1.0 applies to the case where all plotted points are on the straight line of best fit.

A widely used formula for *r* is:

$$r = \frac{\Sigma XY - \Sigma X \Sigma Y / N}{\sqrt{[\Sigma X^2 - (\Sigma X)^2 / N]\,[\Sigma Y^2 - (\Sigma Y)^2 / N]}}$$

An extension of Example 4–6 in the chapter serves to demonstrate the formula.

EXAMPLE S4–2

Correlation Coefficient, Jobs Service

In Example 4–6 layoffs at Acme two weeks earlier are plotted against job applicants at the Jobs Service office. Figure 4–21 shows the correlation visually. What is the calculated coefficient of correlation, *r*?

Solution:

A table simplifies the computations. Figure S4–2 provides the necessary totals to solve for *r*. All *X* and *Y* values are taken from Example 4–6. Since there are 24 data items, $N = 24$. Calculation of *r* is shown below:

$$r = \frac{\Sigma XY - \Sigma X \Sigma Y/N}{\sqrt{[\Sigma X^2 - (\Sigma X)^2/N][\Sigma Y^2 - (\Sigma Y)^2/N]}}$$

$$= \frac{51,825 - (2,130)(470)/24}{\sqrt{(18,900 - (470)^2/24)(206,350 - (2,130)^2/24)}}$$

$$= 0.78$$

FIGURE S4–2

Working Figures for Computing *r*, Jobs Service

	Number of applicants Y	Layoffs at Acme (N − 2) X	Y²	X²	XY
	50	0	2,500	0	0
	60	0	3,600	0	0
	80	25	6,400	625	2,000
	65	20	4,225	400	1,300
	110	50	12,100	2,500	5,500
	145	60	21,025	3,600	8,700
	115	60	13,225	3,600	6,900
	125	25	15,625	625	3,125
	120	20	14,400	400	2,400
	120	35	14,400	1,225	4,200
	110	45	12,100	2,025	4,950
	70	0	4,900	0	0
	60	0	3,600	0	0
	65	0	4,225	0	0
	90	0	8,100	0	0
	55	0	3,025	0	0
	70	20	4,900	400	1,400
	45	0	2,025	0	0
	100	30	10,000	900	3,000
	105	30	11,025	900	3,150
	105	40	11,025	1,600	4,200
	70	0	4,900	0	0
	95	0	9,025	0	0
	100	10	10,000	100	1,000
Sums	2,130	470	206,350	18,900	51,825

An *r* of 0.78 is rather high. Layoffs at Acme may be considered a good leading indicator.

Chapter 5

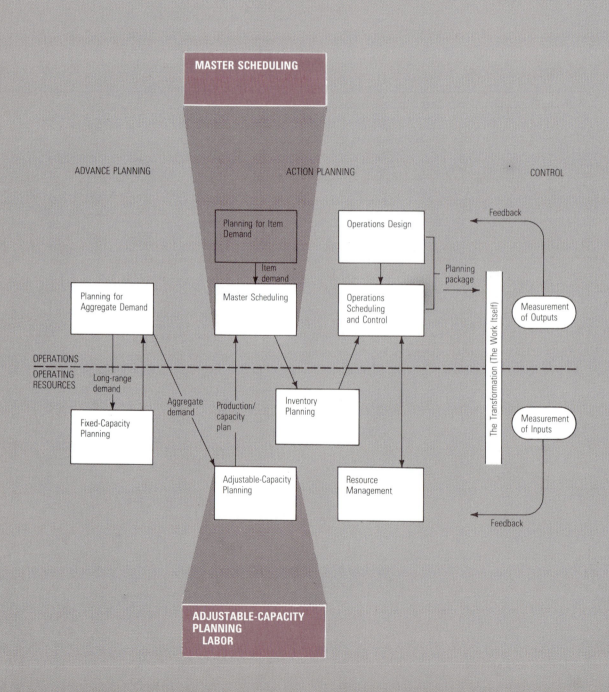

Capacity Planning and Master Scheduling

What capacity plan will meet aggregate demand? This is the question in capacity planning. Can unit ("disaggregated") demand be met by planned capacity? This is a central issue in master scheduling. Capacity planning and master scheduling are a closely related pair. They involve medium- and upper-level managers and medium-term planning.

PURPOSE OF CAPACITY PLANNING AND MASTER SCHEDULING

Two main objectives of capacity planning and master scheduling are meeting demand and utilizing capacity. The master schedule is a key part of the plan for meeting item demand. Capacity planning has the goal of keeping overall capacity utilization at a high level.

Capacity utilization may be expressed as a percent of available hours that facilities (fixed capacity) are in productive use. Available hours may be single shift or multiple shift, and may refer to labor-hours, machine-hours, tool-hours or other special categories like passenger-seat-hours on a bus. Capacity utilization is a critical concern because of the cost of idleness of the resources in the given unit of capacity. Formal measurement of capacity is discussed in more depth in Chapters 10 and 13.

Medium-Term Planning

A company's medium-term **business plan** generally is a month-by-month or quarter-by-quarter plan for sales, production, shipment, research and development, and cash flow. The planning horizon is typically 6 to 18 months. Our interest is in the **production planning** segment of the business plan.

The production plan states the quantity of output in broad terms and by product family. In a consumer electronics company, TV sets might be one family and tape decks another. The quantity may be stated in units or dollars' worth in the electronics company, tons in a steel company, and gallons in a refinery.

The production plan acts as a regulator.[1] It regulates the production, inventories or backlogs, and expenses for purchasing and manufacturing. Levels of inventories and backlogs in turn determine customer service, and production expenses determine cash outflow. Thus, the production plan is critical for translating the business plan into action. (Note: Product planning, discussed in Chapter 3, refers to what is in the product line; the production plan refers to how many of each are to be made.)

The business plan may specify expected sales and shipments, by product family, and also specify inventory (or backlog) levels. For example, the business plan may call for shipment of 12,000 television sets next quarter and a reduction of the finished goods inventory by 2,000 sets, yielding a net production plan of 10,000 televisions next quarter. The inventory reduction could be dictated by financial need. Or perhaps a change in the market or in distribution channels makes it possible to cut inventory and still meet customer demand quickly.

For most operations management purposes, it is a bit more useful to plan in units of capacity (inputs) than in units of production (outputs). Thus, a production plan for 10,000 televisions next quarter, might be translated into a **capacity plan** for, say, 5,000 labor-hours of TV assembly, 10,000 labor-hours of TV component subassembly, and so forth.

---

[1] Oliver W. Wight, *MRP II: Unlocking America's Productivity Potential* (Williston, Vt.: Oliver Wight Limited Publications, Inc., 1981), p. 149 (TS161.W5x).

Sometimes machine capacity, in addition to labor capacity, is of interest. For example, 10,000 molded plastic cabinets for a portable TV might be expressed as 2,500 machine cycles for an injection molding machine in which four cabinets are molded per cycle. Labor, machine cycles, and level of inventory are adjustable from month to month and quarter to quarter. Therefore, this type of medium-term planning is adjustable-capacity planning, usually known simply as **capacity planning.** Plant facilities—buildings (space) and equipment—are also frequently referred to as capacity; to avoid confusion, we will use the term **facilities** when referring to buildings and equipment. Note that machines are acquired based on long-term forecasts; but the **intensity of use** of the machines is an element in medium-range adjustable-capacity planning.

Popular press and even business uses of the term *capacity* are not always precise. For example, a newspaper story saying that a local plant is running at 70 percent of capacity, often refers to intensity of use of total plant facilities, though we are not always sure whether the basis is a maximum of one, two, or three shifts.

Production/Capacity Planning

Another term that we shall use, especially in this chapter, is **production/capacity planning,** which is short for production planning and/or adjustable-capacity planning. The shortened term conveys meaning. It reminds us that we are referring to a plan that may be expressed in output terms (production plan) or in input terms (adjustable capacity). Some of these terms and a few more are included in a special glossary at the end of the chapter.

Production/capacity planning is fed by an aggregate demand forecast. The production/capacity plan, in turn, sets limits on *master scheduling,* which is the medium-term plan for production of each major product model. In manufacturing it is often called the master production schedule, or "build" schedule. The master schedule specifies how much and in what future periods each major product is to be completed. In the services sector, such as, in a dentist's office, the master schedule may consist of an appointment book. While the production/capacity plan sets an upper limit on the master schedule, item forecasts and actual orders determine the composition (product mix) of the master schedule. These twin forces—production/capacity plan and item forecasts/actual orders—must be in balance as much as possible. Methods of achieving good balance are examined later, after production/capacity planning has been more carefully explained.

PLANNING FOR AGGREGATE DEMAND

The production/capacity plan is governed by the company's business plan and capacity strategies and policies on one hand and by aggregate demand on the other hand. The diagram on page 140 illustrates.

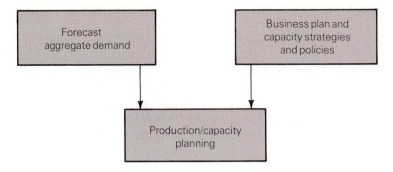

Capacity Strategies

One element of operations strategy is capacity strategy, which depends a good deal on type of industry. The process industries tend to be capital intensive and thus are intent on achieving high utilization of machine capacity.[2] For example, petrochemical plants and steel mills run day and night if demand is sufficient.

Many other industries, especially in the services sector, tend to be labor intensive, so that capacity strategy centers on labor. If a company in these industries has a positioning strategy (see Chapter 2) of cost leadership, its labor-capacity strategy may then be to maintain only enough labor to meet current demand. This "bare-bones" labor-capacity strategy is known as **chase demand:** Hire when demand is good; lay off when demand is poor.

An alternate labor strategy is known as **level capacity:** Try to retain the workers through thick and thin. The lifetime (or career-time) employment policies of government agencies, large Japanese companies, and some American firms like IBM are examples. Level capacity is favored in labor-intensive operations when a quality positioning strategy is pursued. This is especially true if workers' skill qualifications are high or the skills are scarce.

The level-capacity strategy sometimes governs materials and backlogs as well as labor. For a firm that makes to stock (an inventoriable product), when demand dips, inventory may be allowed to grow in order to keep capacity (labor) level. In the make-to-order firm, by contrast, it is backlogs of orders (instead of inventory) that may grow to keep capacity level.

Policies

Policies translate strategies into directions for action. Some examples follow.

A municipal power company may have a strategy of providing employee security in order to gain a stable work force (low turnover). This might translate into

---

[2] Sam G. Taylor, Samuel M. Seward, and Steven F. Bolander, "Why the Process Industries Are Different," *Production and Inventory Management,* Fourth Quarter, 1981, pp. 9–24.

policies to absorb surges in demand without much short-term hiring and layoffs. For example, one policy could be to maintain excess work force, especially linesmen and installers. Another policy might be to subcontract extraordinary maintenance, such as repairing downed lines.

A bowling proprietor may have a strategy of high capacity utilization. A supportive policy is lower prices for daytime bowling.

A food wholesaler may have a strategy of very fast service to retail grocers. Supportive policies might include the use of shift work, weekend hours, overtime, and cross-trained workers for interdepartmental worker loans. A supportive inventory policy would be to maintain large inventories.

Any kind of organization might adopt the strategy of keeping a tight rein on internal service costs. One policy for this would be to use service pools: typing pools, motor pools, and labor pools, for example. These are usually less costly than assigning the service units to individual departments—but service quality and response time may suffer.

The examples point out common kinds of capacity policies. The following is a more complete list:

Hiring and layoffs	Maintenance work as a filler
Overtime and extra shifts	Use of marginal facilities
Part-time and temporary labor	Renting space or tools
Cross-training and transfers (of people or work) between departments	Subcontracting
Labor pools	Refusing, backordering, or postponing work
Motor pools	Building inventories
	Peak/off-peak price differences

Capacity policies (as well as underlying strategies) are set by top officers. These include high-level managers in operations, such as the plant manager or plant superintendent, chief production controller, and materials manager.

Capacity policies may be expressed generally, such as "Avoid overtime and keep inventories low." Or they may be expressed quantitatively, with minimums, maximums, or ranges, and may be priority ordered. For example, a set of priority-ordered policies aimed at maintaining a level permanent work force might be:

For insufficient demand

1. Keep workers busy by building inventory—maximum of 10 percent buildup above predicted demand.
2. Lay off workers only after a 10 percent excess inventory is on hand.

For excess demand

1. Use temporary labor for first 5 percent of excess demand.
2. Use overtime for next 5 percent.
3. Reduce customer service beyond that (refuse or postpone orders, offer partial shipments, etc.).

With such specific policies, production/capacity planning is straightforward. Managers just follow the policies.

Usually, however, a company will not hem itself in with policies quite so specific. For example, the famous "lifetime employment policy" of Japanese companies is really not an explicit policy in Japanese companies. The Japanese employee tends to have a lifetime (or career-time) commitment to a single company, but the company may or may not be able to retain the employee that long. Japan has a highly competitive economy, and each year many companies go under, putting their employees out of work. More successful Japanese companies are often able to claim with pride that they have never had to lay off employees, just as is true of IBM and a surprising number of other companies in the United States. But Japanese companies do tend to work very hard at avoiding layoffs, as is demonstrated by the example of a subsidiary motorcycle plant of Kawasaki in Lincoln, Nebraska.

In spring of 1981, Kawasaki built up a surplus of labor, largely because of productivity improvements. Later in the year, the recession cut motorcycle demand a great deal and entirely killed off Kawasaki's snowmobile product line. The actions taken, in chronological order, were:

1. Assign excess direct laborers to essential support tasks including modifying, moving, and installing equipment.
2. Assign excess to maintenance work such as painting, caulking, and minor remodeling.
3. In fall of 1981, Kawasaki lent 11 of its excess employees to the City of Lincoln, where they worked for several months with Kawasaki paying wages and benefits.
4. The first layoffs, 24 white-collar workers, occurred in October.
5. In November, 16 blue-collar workers voluntarily took a six-month furlough with call-back rights.
6. In February, 1982, 98 production workers were terminated.
7. In October, 1982, the plant went to a four-day work week to preserve jobs for the remaining work force.

These actions were not governed by policy, other than the general one of seeking to avoid layoffs in the face of insufficient demand. Actions of this kind tend to *look* as if they were policy based to the outside observer using hindsight. (Such is probably the case with much of what is referred to as policy.)

Forecasting Aggregate Demand

In Chapter 3 a distinction was made between item forecasting and aggregate forecasting. The reasons for this split may now be more fully explained. Forecasting demand, by item, is needed for planning specific components and end products or services. Forecasting aggregate demand, by capacity (product) groups, has the broader purpose of setting production rates and adjustable capacity.

We know from Chapter 3 that forecasting by capacity groups can be more accurate than item forecasting. The challenge is to form meaningful groups. Normally it is best to group by common **labor skills,** common **machine types,** or dominant **routings.** These groups make up units of capacity that can be separately staffed, subcontracted, set up, inventoried, and so forth.

The forecast for a capacity group should account for seasonal and promotional surges and extend across several time periods. A forecast for a few weeks into the future may be enough in services. This is especially true in services that use mostly unskilled labor; such labor is usually plentiful and therefore adjustable over a short time horizon. A forecast for several months or quarters into the future is needed where skilled labor is used or for goods producers. Goods make a difference, since they may be inventoried.

The forecast of aggregate demand provides data for production/capacity planning, considered next.

PRODUCTION/CAPACITY PLANNING

The production/capacity plan sets forth planned rates of production and of capacity utilization. The plan considers aggregate demand and:

1. Maximum plant facilities and present labor.
2. Planned inventory levels.
3. Planned backlogs.

If orders are processed on demand, there can be no backlogs, and number 3 would not apply. For services providers and make-to-order goods producers, the output is not inventoriable, so number 2 would not apply. But number 1, facilities and present labor, is always of concern.

In very small firms or firms with a single, narrow product line, a single production/capacity plan may be sufficient. For example, a company that makes unfinished furniture may have laborers who are cross-trained to run any woodworking machine or tool. The aggregate forecast might be translated first into labor hours and then into number of workers needed. Since workers are cross-trained, there is no need to subdivide the plan into capacity groups.

In most firms, two or more logical capacity groups may be identified for aggregate capacity planning. In a firm making *finished* furniture, woodworkers might form one logical group, wood finishers a second group, and upholsterers a third. The forecast should show how much aggregate demand there is for woodworking, for wood finishing, and for upholstering. Then the right amount of aggregate labor can be planned in each of the three capacity groupings.

Our discussion of production/capacity planning includes five topics:

1. Chase-demand versus level-capacity plans.
2. Learning-curve planning.
3. The quarterly ordering system.
4. Group-forecasting-based approaches.
5. Capacity planning for just-in-time production.

The first topic concerns basic *policy* for handling variability of demand. The other four are practical and usable tools for planning. (Other capacity-planning techniques that are not covered in this chapter are the linear decision rule and the transportation method. They are useful for showing basic cost-quantity relationships but are too restrictive for ready application. The linear decision rule is reserved for more advanced studies; a use of the transportation method other than in capacity planning is covered later in the book.)

Chase-Demand versus Level-Capacity Plans

Capacity planning is not so hard to do if demand is fairly steady. What if it isn't? Then the firm must set a capacity-planning strategy for responding to swings in demand. At one extreme the strategy is called *level capacity;* at the other it is called *chase demand.*

Consider, for example, the ABC brokerage company on Wall Street.[3] ABC handles transactions coming in from branch offices around the country, and SEC regulations say that all transactions must be settled within five days. The five days give ABC managers time to smooth out the daily volume fluctuations—so that transaction-handling capacity will not be strained one day and underused the next. But stock market volume can swing dramatically overnight. For example, a rumor about a SALT agreement might cause the volume to soar. This can tax capacity for processors of stock transactions. How would ABC cope with such sudden changes? Here are what two different ABC managers might propose:

Manager A: Our capacity should be set at 12,000 transactions per day. This will allow us to meet demand most days. Last year we had a few hot periods when demand ran at 14,000–15,000 per day, and we probably will this year, too. We can handle those problems by overtime for a few days—until new clerks can be hired. Our labor turnover rate is high, so when transaction volume drops we can ease capacity down by not filling vacancies.

Manager B: I think we should keep capacity right at 17,000 transactions per day. That will be enough to handle the spurts in volume, which are very hard to predict.

Who is right? In this case both are right, because each is managing a different end of the business of handling the stock transactions. Manager A is in charge of cashiering: processing certificates, cash, and checks. Clerks and messengers with uncomplicated tasks are the work force.

Manager B, on the other hand, runs order processing. The work force has higher skills: key punch, EDP specialists, programmers, and information analysts. Equipment is expensive, and lead times to change data-processing procedures are long.

Manager A is advocating a chase-demand strategy, which seems rational for his department. Manager B prefers a level-capacity strategy, which is rational for her department. Since low-skill labor from A's department cannot handle the work in

---

[3] This example is adapted from W. Earl Sasser, R. Paul Olsen, and D. Daryl Wychoff, *Management of Service Operations* (Boston: Allyn & Bacon, 1978), pp. 303–5 (HD9981.5.S87).

FIGURE 5–1

Comparison of Chase-Demand and Level-Capacity Strategies

	Chase demand	Level capacity
Labor skill level	Low	High
Wage rate	Low	High
Working conditions	Sweatshop	Pleasant
Training required per employee	Low	High
Labor turnover	High	Low
Hire-fire costs	High	Low
Error rate	High	Low
Type of budgeting and forecasting required	Short term	Long term

B's department, each manager should have a separate capacity plan—rather than one plan covering the whole transaction-processing operation—and each may be governed by a different capacity strategy.

Figure 5–1 outlines the two strategies. The chase strategy tends to be followed when there are low-skill people doing jobs at low pay in a less-than-pleasant work environment. With low skill levels, training costs are low per employee, but they could be high per year since turnover tends to be high. Turnover also means high hire-fire costs, and, along with low skills, would contribute to high error rates. Forecasting and budgeting may be short term since lead times to add to or cut the work force are short.

The level strategy has opposite features. Higher skills have to be attracted, so pay and working conditions need to be better. High skills need to be honed to suit the demanding jobs, so training costs per employee are high. The attractions of the job are meant to keep turnover and hire-fire costs low, and high labor skills hold down error rates. Forecasting and budgeting must be long term since hiring and training skilled people takes a long time.

The level strategy seems best from the outlook of the employee. But many businesses cannot compete that way. Thus, there are some industrial companies and lots of service industries—fast food, hotels, amusement parks, etc.—that pay minimum wages and have most of the other characteristics of the chase strategy as well.

Chase demand fits nicely with a quick-response positioning strategy (discussed in Chapter 2). On the other hand, level capacity goes well with a high-quality positioning strategy. There may be a competitive niche for both strategies in a given locale.

Learning-Curve Planning

As people learn, their time to do a given task decreases. In industry this is known as the learning-curve phenomenon, and it applies not only to direct labor but also to those who support the direct-labor effort. Where the learning-curve effect is signifi-

FIGURE 5–2

Eighty Percent Learning Curve

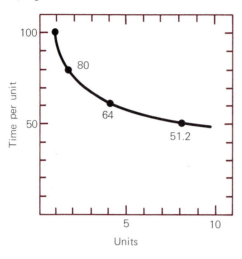

cant, planning production rates and capacity should allow for it. With learning effects, production rates may increase over time with no change in capacity level, or capacity levels may be cut over time without reducing production rates.

The learning-curve phenomenon was observed in airframe manufacturing as far back as 1925.[4] In later years, aircraft manufacturers found a dominant learning pattern, the 80 percent learning curve: The 2d plane required 80 percent as much direct labor as the 1st; the 4th required 80 percent as much as the 2d; the 10th, 80 percent as much as the 5th; and so forth. The rate of learning to assemble aircraft was 20 percent between doubled quantities.

Graphically an 80 percent learning curve appears in Figure 5–2. Mathematically, the learning curve follows the general formula

$$Y = aX^b$$

where

Y = Labor-hours per unit
X = Unit number
a = Labor-hours for first unit
$b = \dfrac{\text{Logarithm of learning-curve rate}}{\text{Logarithm of 2}}$

---

[4] The commander of Wright-Patterson Air Force Base was reported to have observed it in 1925: Winfred B. Hirshmann, "Profit from the Learning Curve," *Harvard Business Review*, January–February 1964, p. 125.

In production/capacity planning by the learning curve, labor requirements over time are calculated. An example follows.

EXAMPLE 5–1

Learning-Curve Planning, Bellweather Electric, Inc.

Bellweather has a contract for 60 portable electric generators. The labor-hour requirement to manufacture the first unit is 100 hours. With that as a given, Bellweather planners develop an aggregate capacity plan, using learning-curve calculations. A 90 percent learning curve is used, based on previous experience on generator contracts.

Using the general formula, the labor requirement for the second generator is:

$$Y = aX^b$$

$$Y = (100)(2)^{\left(\frac{\log 0.9}{\log 2.0}\right)}$$

$$= (100)(2)^{\left(\frac{-0.0457}{0.3010}\right)}$$

$$= (100)(2)^{-0.152}$$

$$= (100)(0.9)$$

$$= 90 \text{ hours}$$

There was no need to go through the calculations for the second unit, since, for a 90 percent learning curve, there is 10 percent learning between doubled quantities.

For the fourth unit,

$$Y = aX^b = 100(4)^{-0.152} = (100)(0.81) = 81$$

This result may be obtained more simply by

$$(100)(0.9)^2 = (100)(0.9)(0.9) = (100)(0.81) = 81$$

For the eighth unit,

$$Y = aX^b = 100(8)^{-0.152} = (100)(0.729) = 72.9$$

This result is also obtained by

$$(100)(0.9)^3 = (100)(0.9)(0.9)(0.9) = (100)(0.729) = 72.9$$

This way of avoiding logarithms works for the 16th, 32d, 64th, etc., units—for any unit that is a power of 2; but for the 3d, 5th, 6th, 7th, 9th, etc., units, the logarithmic calculation is necessary.

Figure 5–3 displays some of the results of the learning-curve calculations. With these figures, Bellweather may assign labor based on the decreasing per unit labor-hour requirements. For example, the 60th generator requires only 53.7 labor-hours, which is only about half of the labor required for the first unit. Completion of finished generators can be master-scheduled to increase at the 90 percent learning-curve rate.

FIGURE 5–3

Labor-Hour Requirements for Generator Manufacturing, Bellweather
Electric

Generator number	Labor-hours required	Cumulative labor-hours required
1	100	100.0
2	90	190.0
3	84.6	274.6
10	70.5	799.4
20	63.4	1,460.8
30	59.6	2,072.7
40	57.1	2,654.3
50	55.2	3,214.2
60	53.7	3,757.4

Learning Curve and Productivity Improvement

Learning-curve planning is most closely associated with limited-quantity, large-scale production: airplanes, earthmovers, and so on. At first everyone is unfamiliar with the work, and the production system needs to be debugged. As units are produced improvements are natural. The learning curve may also be used in repetitive manufacturing—if the work climate is favorable for productivity improvement. In all too many companies, it is not. The labor union may resist a productivity enhancing idea, derogatorily calling it "speedup." If there is no union, then workers may resist changes in less vocal ways. In an entertaining book about his working life, Robert Schrank explains how workers tend to set their own informal output norms or "bogeys" and enforce them through peer pressure.[5] Thus, the system is not allowed to learn. It is easy to blame the worker or the union. But when we consider the many companies that do have a climate for productivity improvement, that explanation looks weak.

North American repetitive-oriented industries that are receptive to steady learning-curve improvements in productivity include electronics, fast food, agriculture, air freight, and perhaps even the revitalized shoe manufacturing industry. Japan goes much farther. Production systems have been devised to make productivity improvement part of the Japanese worker's job, and productivity improvement rates are spectacular in many Japanese companies. Indeed, it is popular for Japanese industrial people to speak in terms of a 67 percent learning curve, which is exceedingly high:

---

[5] Robert Schrank, *Ten Thousand Working Days* (Cambridge, Mass.: MIT Press, 1978), (HD8073.S34A37).

33 percent between doubled quantities, as compared with usual Western rates of 5 to 20 percent. A popular Japanese expression of the 67 percent rate is:

$$2V = 2/3 \ C$$

where

$V =$ Volume, or unit number
$C =$ Cost per unit

The expression is not mathematically correct but is intuitively intended to mean: Doubling the volume results in two-thirds of the unit cost.

Of course, nearly all companies enjoy some rate of productivity improvement, which may suggest that companies could use the learning curve for labor-capacity planning, costing, budgeting, pricing, and so forth. But the learning curve is no good as a planning aid unless the productivity improvements are measurable over each planning increment, e.g., each month or quarter. The companies performing poorly tend to get measurable productivity improvements at model changeover time, when advanced equipment is bought, and when plant expansion is undertaken. In between, the climate for improvement may be so poor that none takes place. How production systems may be designed so as to achieve *steady* productivity improvement is a central issue in this book and is treated in most of the chapters. For now, let us return to capacity planning and examine techniques besides the learning curve.

Quarterly Ordering and Group-Forecasting-Based Approaches

Following World War II, consumer waiting lists for refrigerators, washing machines, rubber tires, and so forth, were often a year or two long. For the manufacturer, such order backlogs provided long planning lead times. The *quarterly ordering system* came into use. The firm merely decided what items and components it would produce next quarter, and resource needs were thoroughly planned to fit that production.

While the quarterly ordering system directly concerns ordering of parts and raw materials, it also yields capacity plans. And the planners need not settle for aggregate capacity plans; it is possible to convert "sure-thing" orders into highly detailed capacity plans—down to the number of labor-hours on a given machine. For example, if it took 15 minutes to spray paint one electric range and the quarterly orders for ranges totaled 4,000, the number of paint spraying hours for the quarter is:

4,000 ranges $\times$ 15 minutes/range $\times$ 1 hour/60 minutes = 1,000 hours

At 40 hours per week, or 520 hours per 13-week quarter per worker, 1,000 hours equals 1.9 workers (1,000/520) to run the paint sprayers. All other elements of adjustable capacity may be determined the same way, and hiring, training, etc., may be planned accordingly.

The quarterly ordering system began to lose its effectiveness as postwar backlogs were whittled down and the consumer pipeline gradually filled up with goods. In the late 1950s and early 1960s a new era of short backlogs and stiff competition emerged. Without the luxury of long backlogs, manufacturers had to turn to demand forecasting by capacity group.

One method of grouping is product families—families having production, not marketing commonality. For example, a sales catalog might have aluminum and wood doors and windows grouped as a product family. But for capacity planning, it makes more sense to group all aluminum items separately from all wood items. In repetitive production, all the products going through one production line may be considered as a capacity group. Such a group can account for a large block of capacity, which is desirable in view of the forecast-error reductions gained by larger forecasting groups.

In less repetitive production (job shops), it is harder to develop families or capacity groups. But some companies are able to find common flow paths or *routings* through the factory that account for large quantities of products. A later example of capacity planning in a make-to-stock plant demonstrates this idea.

Where dominant routings do not exist, it is best to group by common skills. For example, paint spraying, riveting, brazing, and a variety of other semiskilled jobs could be treated as a capacity group, which makes sense since a riveter may be able to learn to handle a sprayer in a short time. Trend projection, seasonal analysis, and other methods (see Chapter 4) could then be used to forecast demand for this capacity group. If the forecast were for 11,440 labor-hours of work next quarter, that translates into a capacity plan for 22 semiskilled fabrication workers (11,440 labor-hours per quarter divided by 520 labor-hours per worker per quarter). A second capacity plan could be prepared for machining and a third for final assembly and packaging.

Capacity planning based on group forecasting need not be specific with regard to what machines the workers work on. That can be determined later in the scheduling and dispatching phase. The purpose of group-forecasting-based capacity planning is to have the right amount of labor on hand *in the aggregate*. The result can be surprisingly accurate, since, as we learned in Chapter 3, group forecasting error is low, at least as compared with item forecast error. Capacity plans based on group forecasts cannot, however, compare with the accuracy of the quarterly ordering-based method.

Capacity Groups in a Make-to-Order Plant

We shall look at two examples of group-forecasting-based approaches. One is for make-to-order plants, and the other is for make-to-stock plants.

The following example of production/capacity planning in a make-to-order plant focuses on order backlogs and lead times. The method follows a two-step process:

1. Identify broad capacity groups or similar processes—following the principle that forecasts are more accurate for larger groupings.
2. Develop a production/capacity plan based on projecting recent total demands into the future and on backlog and lead-time policies.

EXAMPLE 5–2

Production/Capacity Planning, Tail and Exhaust Pipe Plant

Hot Pipes Division of International Industries makes tail pipes and exhaust pipes for the aftermarket. (That means replacement parts.) Orders are rather small and diverse, and Hot Pipes does not retail its own brand name. Therefore, it is strictly a make-to-order plant.

An aggregate capacity plan, to cover a number of weeks, is needed. Fine-tuning is possible on a day-to-day basis; that is, Hot Pipes can do a limited amount of overtime work and labor borrowing on a daily basis. But the regular work force must be hired and trained in advance—and planned for, using production planning methods.

Make-to-order planning is difficult in view of lack of order lead time. Still, a quick and simple projection of recent data into the future is helpful.

Step 1. Step 1 is to identify broad capacity groupings. Tail pipes and exhaust pipes seem to be the two key groups that are logical for separate capacity plans: They are built in separate areas of the factory with different equipment and different worker skills. Capacity may be measured in *pieces* for both groupings.

Step 2. In step 2, demands for recent past periods are totaled and capacity (piece) requirements are developed, based on projecting the demand pattern into the future.

Figure 5–4 shows past demands for tail pipes on the left and two capacity options on the right. Option 1 provides for 1,800 pieces per week—100 less than the mean demand for the past eight weeks. The deviations range from +700 to −1,400 pieces per week. Option 2 provides for 300 less pieces per week than option 1. The deviations range from +100 to −3,500 pieces per week. (Note: At Hot Pipes the positive deviations, e.g., +700, do *not*

FIGURE 5–4

Capacity/Backlog Options for Tail Pipes

Week	Recent weekly demands Pieces	Cumulative pieces	Option 1: 1,800 pieces per week Cumulative	Deviation	Option 2: 1,500 pieces per week Cumulative	Deviation
1	1,800	1,800	1,800	0	1,500	−300
2	1,100	2,900	3,600	+700	3,000	+100
3	1,800	4,700	5,400	+700	4,500	−200
4	1,950	6,650	7,200	+550	6,000	−650
5	2,300	8,950	9,000	+50	7,500	−1,450
6	2,800	11,750	10,800	−950	9,000	−2,750
7	2,250	14,000	12,600	−1,400	10,500	−3,500
8	1,200	15,200	14,400	−800	12,000	−3,200

$$\text{Mean demand} = \frac{15,200}{8} = 1,900 \text{ pieces per week}$$

represent idle excess capacity. In such weeks of insufficient demand, the work force could be kept busy making standard lengths of pipe, and so forth.)

The first option results in excess capacity in four of the eight weeks: weeks 2–5. The second results in excess capacity in only one of the weeks: week 2.

Projected backlogs are the opposite: For option 1, the backlog reaches 1,400 pieces in the seventh week. That is nearly a one-week backlog at the planned production rate of 1,800 pieces per week. For option 2, the backlog reaches 3,500 pieces in the seventh week. That is over two weeks' backlog: 3,500 pieces/1,500 pieces per week = 2.3 weeks.

A backlog exceeding two weeks means a lead time greater than two weeks for Hot Pipes's customers. For its rather competitive industry, that may be unacceptable. Thus, Hot Pipes may decide to pay for the excess capacity of option 1 in order to keep planned backlogs and lead times down to within a week.

Planners at Hot Pipes are quite aware that projecting future backlogs based on the past is fraught with error. The total pieces in the next eight weeks may be fairly close to the total (15,200 pieces) for the past eight weeks. But the week-by-week demand pattern is sure to be quite different, so that the maximum backlogs can be much more or less than projected. Still, this single method is helpful in planning, and there is some flexibility (overtime, job transfers, etc.) in the short term to correct for planning errors.

In the preceding simplified example we did not consider options such as extra shifts and subcontracting. Overtime, labor borrowing, and similar very short-range adjustments normally should *not* be considered in the production/capacity-planning stage; those are measures to be taken when all other capacity planning fails.

For this method, the assumption is that orders may be backlogged and worked off in later periods. Note that backlogs are carried forward by the cumulative totals.

In some firms an unmet order is a lost order; backlogs are not carryable. This tends to be the case in transportation, restaurants, lodging, and similar fast-reaction-oriented industries. Such industries also may base their production/capacity planning on recent demands. But the demands would not be cumulative; therefore, negative deviations are lost sales, not backlogs.

Capacity Groups in a Make-to-Stock Plant

Production/capacity planning in a make-to-stock plant begins with the same two steps as in the make-to-order case: Identify capacity groups and develop production rates to fit projected group demands. That may complete the plan, but more often the firm will add a third step: Refine the production rates to provide for desired inventory levels. Occasionally there is a fourth step: Refining the plan by examining how production loads onto individual shops or departments. All four steps are presented in the following example.

EXAMPLE 5–3

Production/Capacity Planning, Electronics Plant

Step 1. For production/capacity-planning purposes, Quark Electronics divides its productive processes into three product families or groups. These are identified simply as groups 1, 2, and 3. Each group covers a large number of produced items, including end products, subassemblies, and parts.

The reason for the division into three groups is seen in Figure 5–5. There are three dominant process-flow paths, or routings. The three routings wind through the four shop areas and include 13 of the 16 work centers in the four shops. A number of products do not exactly fit any of the three routings. But enough do to provide a solid basis for production/capacity planning, i.e, groups large enough for decent forecast accuracy.

Next, Quark forecasts aggregate demand for each product group identified; then both labor-hour and machine-hour requirements are roughly matched against product demand.

Step 2. In the next step Quark develops a production/capacity plan

FIGURE 5–5

Common Routings, Quark Electronics

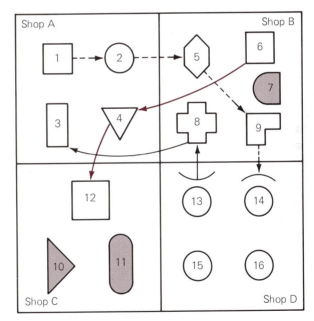

Key: Product group 1:   ------▸
      Product group 2: ▬▬▬▬▸
      Product group 3: ▬▬▬▬▸
      Work centers not included in common routings: ▭
Note: Machines 13, 14, 15, and 16 are identical.

based on desired labor utilization. Figure 5–6 shows a forecast and a trial production plan for product group 1. The plan provides for an even 10,200-piece-per-week production rate for the four weeks covered by the forecast. All different kinds of pieces are counted. Still, Quark planners feel that pieces are a meaningful measure for producing a production/capacity plan. Product groups 2 and 3 should be similarly planned.

The plan appears to provide a good balance between forecast demand and planned production. They are equal at 40,800 cumulative pieces.

Step 3. In the third step Quark refines the production/capacity plan to provide for desired inventory levels. As Figure 5–6 shows, the beginning inventory is 14,000 pieces and the ending inventory (week 4) is also 14,000 pieces. Sometimes a change in inventory level is desired. For example, the firm may desire an inventory buildup, perhaps in anticipation of a seasonal or promotional surge in demand. If so, increase the planned production rate above the 10,200 pieces per week shown in the trial production plan. Decrease the planned rate to work off some inventory.

Quark planners would also examine inventory levels for product groups 2 and 3. Production/capacity planning could stop there. But a more exacting plan may be derived by calculating effects on each shop, by labor-hours and by machine-hours; shop-level capacity planning is considered next.

Step 4. A detailed production/capacity plan requires converting group capacity into smaller capacity units. Conversion factors are needed. If group capacity were in labor-hours (or machine-hours), then perhaps historical percentages could be used to translate group hours into shop hours. In the case of Quark Electronics, group capacity is in pieces per week. Therefore, labor-hours and machine-hours per piece may serve as conversion factors. These factors may be historical and not overly exact.

Figure 5–7 shows, for week 1, how such conversion factors may be used to convert planned pieces to labor-hours and machine-hours for each shop. Dividing planned pieces per week by the standard rates gives required labor-hours and machine-hours

FIGURE 5–6

Trial Production/Capacity Plan, Product Group 1

	Pieces through product group 1				
	Forecast		Trial production plan		
Week	Pieces per week (000)	Cumulative	Pieces per week (000)	Cumulative	Inventory
0					14.0
1	10.0	10.0	10.2	10.2	14.2
2	10.0	20.0	10.2	20.4	14.4
3	10.4	30.4	10.2	30.6	14.2
4	10.4	40.8	10.2	40.8	14.0

FIGURE 5–7

Production Rate Converted to Labor-Hours and Machine-Hours, Quark
Electronics

	Shop A	Shop B	Shop C	Shop D
Week 1: labor-hours				
Group 1	⑤①	68		46
Group 2	36	58	83	
Group 3	50	80		40
Total labor-hours required	137	206	83	86
Labor-hour capacity	160	200	80	80
Shortage of labor-hours	−23	+6	+3	+6
Week 1: Machine-hours				
Group 1	④①	37		51
Group 2	29	29	21	
Group 3	50	20		27
Total machine-hours required	120	86	21	78
Machine-hour capacity	120	100	36	100
Shortage of machine-hours	0	−14	−15	−22

Sample calculations (for circled figures):
  Given:
    Standard labor rate in shop A = 200 pieces per hour.
    Standard machine rate in shop A = 250 pieces per hour.
    Trial production rate for group 1 = 10,200 pieces per week.
  Therefore:
    Labor-hours required = 10,200/200 = 51.
    Machine-hours required = 10,200/250 = 41.

Sample calculations are shown at the bottom of the figure for the results in shop A, group 1. The labor rate of 200 pieces per hour is divided into the planned production rate of 10,200 pieces per week; the result is 51 labor-hours required in week 1. Similarly, the 41 machine-hours required in week 1 are derived by dividing 10,200 pieces per week by the machine rate of 250 pieces per hour.

After the calculations are completed, total labor-hours and machine-hours may be summed for each shop. Compare the totals with single-shift shop capacities, and the difference is the shortage of labor-hours or machine-hours. (Shop capacities are based on number of people or machines times 40 hours regular time per week less nonavailable time, such as break time and delay time.)

Few serious capacity problems are indicated by the results in Figure 5–7. The minus results show excess capacity, but only for shop A labor is this much of a concern. There is a greater amount of excess machine-hours, but this may be thought of as a normal margin for error, since machines constitute fixed capacity that cannot be added to on short notice.

Quark could deal with the 23 hours of excess labor in shop A by cutting the work force. Or Quark planners could make out a revised production/capacity plan with more pieces in group 1, 2, or 3—whichever would cause the least additional labor-hours in the already overloaded shops B, C, and D.

The same procedure would extend to weeks 2, 3, and 4. A computer will ease the calculating burden. But it is not necessary to achieve a highly refined match beween required and available capacity since this is only an aggregate plan.

Capacity Planning in a Just-in-Time Plant

The Japanese **just-in-time (JIT)** production system will be fully described in later chapters. There is little to be said about it here, because JIT does not directly deal with production/capacity planning. Actually, it appears that JIT production considerably reduces the need for production/capacity planning. Problems of capacity utilization tend to take care of themselves under JIT. To make a long story short, JIT cuts inventories to the bone so that workers always tend to be working on fresh orders. Furthermore, in the absence of inventories to cushion the blow of an unexpected surge in orders, the workers and other elements of capacity must be versatile and flexible. There is perhaps nothing quite so effective as flexibility for coping with the problems of capacity management and meeting customer demand.

MASTER SCHEDULE

The master schedule—or master production schedule (MPS) as it is called in industry—is formed by a merger of demand and supply plans. That is, items demanded are matched with capacity supplied to yield the MPS, which is stated by item, by period, and by capacity group. The merger is shown in the following illustration.

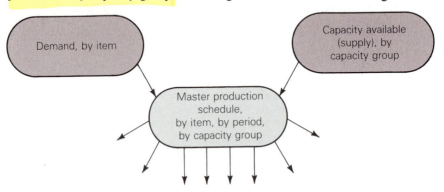

Now let us examine this merger in more detail.

Matching Capacity and Demand

Figure 5–8 is a schematic model of capacity-demand matching. There is enough detail in the model to explain the complex case of a manufacturer that fabricates and assembles in the job-lot mode. Later a reduced version of the same model is presented for a service organization.

We have already discussed blocks 1, 2, and 3, on planning in the aggregate. Blocks 4, 5, and 6 concern demand planning for specific goods or services. Block 4 refers to **actual customer orders** booked. As was pointed out in Chapter 3, a booked order may be a sale on paper, but it should not be a production commitment until it is accepted by production control, i.e., fitted into a production schedule. Production control's order promise tells sales that the booking has been accepted, partially accepted, rescheduled, postponed, or rejected.

The final master production schedule (block 8) emerges after suitable trials. The

FIGURE 5–8

Capacity-Demand Matching Process

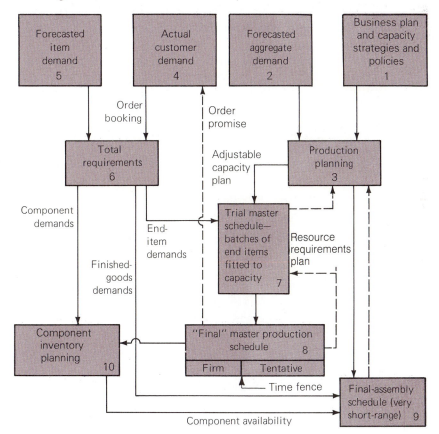

firm portion covers the total lead-time period. Since lead time covers the period in which plans are in motion, schedules need to be more stable for that zone. Still the "firm" schedule may be changed. A **time fence** separates the firm portion from the tentative portion, which covers future time buckets. Penalties for changes that far out in the future are slight; thus, changes in the tentative part of the master production schedule are to be expected.

Another dashed feedback line, block 8 to block 4, was mentioned earlier. It is the master scheduler's order promise. Traditionally in industry, communication from production to sales has been poor. The sales staff bears the burden, because they cannot give the customer reliable delivery promises. But modern, well-designed production and inventory control systems, with feedback-controlled MPSs as the hub, are finally able to provide decent order promise and order-status information. The competitive advantages should be impressive.

Final Assemblies, Component Parts, and End Items

In complex multistage production, final assembly may have its own separate schedule. The **final assembly schedule** may be developed "at the last minute" based on recent actual customer orders for end products. (See the arrow from block 6 to block 9 in Figure 5–8.)

But to assemble end products on short notice, the parts must already be made. The major modules and subassemblies that go into the end product are often called **end items.** The end items are the major capacity-consuming and time-consuming elements of production and receive by far the most planning and control attention. The schedule for end items is appropriately named: the master production schedule. (See the arrow from 6 to 7.) The MPS is not simply the demand forecast, because:

The total factory requirements are uneven from period to period, but the MPS must smooth out demands to fit planned group capacity.

Some of the end items may already be on hand or in process.

It may be economical to batch some of the demands into reasonably sized lots.

Total requirements may include one more type of item, independently demanded **component parts** such as **service parts.** Demands for components may bypass the master production schedule and go directly to component inventory planning (arrow from 6 to 10).

Master Scheduling in the Simple Case

Are capacity management and master scheduling always that complicated? Of course not. Small companies that make simple products, or make only to stock, or make to order but in standard designs may be able to omit some of the blocks in Figure 5–8. For example, a small company making picture frames to stock would be able to combine blocks 8, 9, and 10 into one master production schedule; no need for separate schedules for final assembly and for service parts. Actual customer demand, block 4 in Figure 5–8, would feed orders directly to master scheduling (block 7), and blocks 5 and 6 would be omitted. Blocks 1, 2, and 3 would still be relevant, but the production manager might be able to assess the options on the back of an envelope in a few minutes.

Master Scheduling in Make-to-Order Plants

A manufacturer of precision turntables for recording studios probably makes to order, not to stock. The bane of the make-to-order producer is lack of planning lead time. Recording studios order turntables, and want them right away. With no lead time, can a master production schedule extend long enough into the future to match demand with capacity reasonably well? The answer is yes. A flexible customer-oriented MPS procedure can achieve good results. The procedure involves what is called **consuming the master schedule.**

The method employs an MPS with three subdivisions: master schedule, actual demand, and available to promise. Figure 5–9 illustrates the three subdivisions for two models of turntable made to order. Begin with the master schedule, based on forecasting. As orders are booked, the master scheduler enters the quantities in the actual demand row. **Available-to-promise** is the computed difference between master schedule and actual demand quantities.

In Figure 5–9, one of turntable A has been sold for delivery (or completion) in week 4, and five are available to promise. In the same week both master-scheduled units of turntable B have been sold, leaving none available to promise. The master schedule is said to be "consumed" by actual orders being booked by marketing. The master schedule keeps marketing informed about quantities available to promise so that the sales force will not overconsume the schedule.

FIGURE 5–9

"Consuming" the Master Production Schedule

	Week				
	1	2	3	4	5
Turntable A:					
Master schedule	4	2	0	6	3
Actual demand	2	0	0	1	0
Available to promise	2	2	0	5	3
Turntable B:					
Master schedule	0	7	8	2	0
Actual demand	0	1	4	2	0
Available to promise	0	6	4	0	0

The master scheduler revises the MPS periodically. For example, Figure 5–9 shows six out of seven turntables Bs available to promise in week 2. With so many unsold, the master scheduler wants to reschedule the six availables to be produced in a later period, perhaps week 4.

Resource Requirements Planning

The feedback loop from block 8 to block 7 in Figure 5–8 is called resource requirements planning (RRP). Scarce resources are the focus for RRP. Typically, the scarce resource is an expensive machine, die, tool, or mold. Or it could be a worker with a hard-to-get skill, like a programmer for a numerically controlled machine, a tool and die maker, a welder, or a designer.

Resource requirements planning (RRP) is a gross check to see if the items in the master production schedule will overload a scarce resource. RRP can be reasonably accurate over a month or more but is too gross to show weekly resource requirements. To run an RRP check, data are needed to show how much of the scarce resource is required per unit of the end item to be built. For example, a plastics molder may have in its files a so-called **bill of labor** which states that an order for a certain kind of plastic fastener requires two hours of die making labor. This is the type of conversion factor that was used in step 4 of Example 5–3; in that example, the RRP concept was applied to check resource requirements for a proposed production/capacity plan. More commonly, resource requirements planning is associated with checking resource needs in the master production scheduling phase.

Rough-cut Capacity Planning. Rough-cut capacity planning is a quick and simple method of validating or "purifying" the master production schedule. It is a quick approach to resource requirements planning and helps make sure that the master production schedule does not overload bottleneck work centers.

Rough-cut planning is usually done in monthly or quarterly time periods. The first step is to convert trial MPS quantities into workload requirements in the bottleneck work centers. The workloads may be stated in pieces, pounds, machine-hours, labor-hours, or (frequently) machine cycles per time period. The method is "rough"—may overstate real needs just a bit—because there is no attempt to deduct inventories already on hand. The next step is to adjust the master production schedule if a bottleneck work center is overloaded. The adjustment is usually to reduce the offending MPS quantity or move some of the quantity to a later time period. The following is a simple example.

EXAMPLE 5–4

Rough-Cut Capacity Planning—Molded Hoses

Ajax Rubber Co. produces V-belts and molded rubber hoses for automobiles and other vehicles. The master scheduler has prepared a trial MPS, and a portion of it is shown in Figure 5–10.

In the hose-curing work center, cut lengths of extruded rubber are placed

FIGURE 5–10

Trial MPS, Molded Hoses

End item	Month 1	Month 2	Month 3
Hose 201XL	1,120	1,080	990
Hose 208S	600	300	410
.	.	.	.
.	.	.	.
.	.	.	.
Hose 618MM	870	1,050	1,100
Total hoses needed curing	91,660	95,200	94,990
Divided by conversion factor	34	34	34
Rack loads requiring curing	2,696	2,800	2,764
Capacity	2,700	2,700	2,700
Overload	696	100	64

on mandrels that protrude from racks that roll into curing ovens. Hoses are cured in an oven that is the most critical bottleneck work center in the plant. The master scheduler wants to make sure that the MPS is not overstated for that oven, which has a maximum capacity of 2,700 rack loads per month. Although the MPS is stated in weeks, rough-cut capacity planning at Ajax is by month. One reason is that the MPS will be converted to oven workload but without carefully offsetting for lead time or deducting work already in process. Another reason is that projected oven workloads cannot be very accurate on a week-to-week basis because orders get rescheduled to earlier or later weeks; but monthly totals can be reasonably good.

As Figure 5–10 shows, the total number of hoses in the trial MPS is 91,660 for month 1, 95,200 for month 2, and 94,990 for month 3. (Only a few of the hose types comprising the totals are shown.) The number of mandrels per rack depends upon the hose model number but it averages 34. For rough-cut purposes, that average is good enough to be used in converting hoses to rackloads of oven curing.

The results of the conversion show that the projected workload of 2,696 rack loads in month 1 is just below the capacity of 2,700; and in months 2 and 3 the projected workloads of 2,800 and 2,794 exceed capacity. The master scheduler sees that the trial MPS is not feasible. The hose quantities in the MPS must be reduced. Perhaps another of Ajax Rubber Co.'s plants can absorb the demand. If not, some of the projected hose demands (if they materialize) will probably be lost sales in the short term. But Ajax will be evaluating additional oven capacity as a solution in the longer term.

Load Profile. For a more precise resource requirements plan, *load profiles* instead of simple conversion factors are used. A load (meaning *work*load) profile not only shows how much of a given resource is required, but also when. However, like the rough-cut method, the profile does not deduct inventories already on hand or on order. Therefore, requirements can be overstated.

FIGURE 5–11

Load Profile for Circuit Board Manufacture

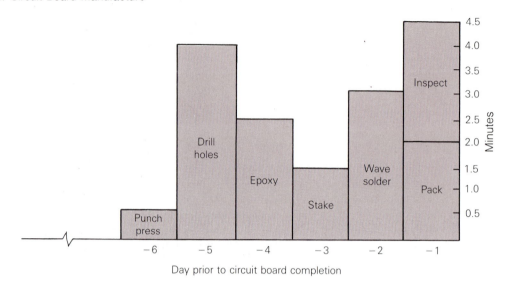

Day prior to circuit board completion

As an example, in an electronic circuit board plant, the wave soldering machine might be the scarce, or bottleneck, resource. The load profile may show that one complete circuit board of a certain type requires three minutes of wave soldering on the second day prior to board completion. A complete load profile, showing requirements for nonscarce as well as scarce resources, is portrayed in Figure 5–11. Other types of circuit boards would have their own load profiles. The profiles may exist as computer records or manual data in a file cabinet. If the master production schedule called for production of 1,000 circuit board type X, 700 of type Y, and 500 of type Z, the master scheduler may pull out the profiles and multiply the processing times by 1,000, 700, and 500 respectively. A composite workload profile is the result, and it shows whether the master production schedule will overload the resource (e.g., wave soldering) on any given day in the future. If so, the MPS quantities or timing may be changed.

Master Schedule—Services Example

A simplified example of the steps leading to a master production schedule follows. The example is simplified in that it is for services rather than goods. Thus, the master schedule and the final-assembly schedule coincide. Or putting it differently, there is a master *services* schedule but no final-assembly schedule—since services are not assemblies.

EXAMPLE 5–5

Master Scheduling in Department of Management, Funk University

Each teaching department in the College of Business Administration at Funk University must prepare a master schedule. The master schedule consists of one schedule for each course and covers the next few terms. The master schedule is prepared twice each term: One version is prepared based on preregistrations; an updated version is based on general registration data.

The master-scheduling process is illustrated in Figure 5–12. There are eight blocks in the figure. They are the same as blocks 1 through 8 in the general production/capacity-planning model of Figure 5–8. The example is for one teaching department, the Department of Management. All other

FIGURE 5–12

Master Scheduling, Department of Management

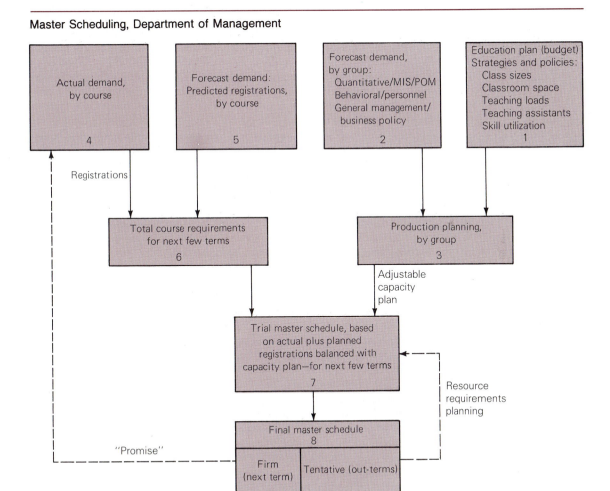

departments would follow the same steps, but the aggregate forecast groups (block 2) would be different. The Department of Management's courses—perhaps 40–50 offerings—cluster nicely into three capacity groups. These are:

1. Quantitative/management information systems (MIS)/production operations management (POM).
2. Behavioral/personnel.
3. General management/business policy.

These groups are not intended to correspond to clusters of *demand* (though student demands may cluster that way). Rather the purpose is to form natural units of *capacity*. That is, the courses in a given group should be similar enough to enable the group's faculty members to trade off on teaching assignments. The groupings shown would by no means be perfect. Someone whose speciality is personnel administration may, for example, have a secondary interest in general management instead of in behavior. Still the groupings should be all right for the purpose. That purpose is to arrive at a reasonable capacity plan for matching against total course requirements (block 6) in order to produce a trial master schedule of course offerings (block 7).

A capacity plan emerges from block 3. The unit of service in a teaching department has a rather invariable "standard time" requirement. For example, the standard three-hour course takes 45 semester hours or 30 quarter hours of class time.

A control on the capacity plan is the budget (education plan) and strategies and policies (block 1). Policies generally exist about class sizes (i.e., faculty-student ratios), classroom space, teaching loads (per faculty member), use of teaching assistants, and utilization of faculty skills. The last has to do with the extent to which faculty will be assigned to teach in their strong areas versus their weaker areas of expertise. Production planning (block 3) includes trade-off analysis, because the aggregate policies are in partial conflict with one another and also with the forecast group demands (block 2). The capacity plan, then, is a compromise.

While blocks 1 through 3 deal with aggregate demand and capacity, blocks 4 through 6 deal with unit demand, course by course. Actual demand, consisting of registrations by course, comprises block 4. Block 5 is forecast demand; this is predicted registrations, by course, based on historical patterns plus other knowledge.

Next, in block 6, assemble course requirements for the next few terms into a list. Then match this "shopping list" against what is available in the capacity plan. The result is the trial master schedule of course offerings for the next few terms. The feedback arrow from block 8 to block 7 of Figure 5–12, resource requirements planning, indicates **closed-loop control:** It makes the master schedule an honest reflection of capacity to meet demands by adjusting the master schedule until scarce resource overloads are eliminated.

Finally a master schedule emerges (block 8). It is firm for the current lead-time period, which is the upcoming term. It is tentative for all future terms. When the master schedule is set within the department, an "order promise" is sent out from Funk University's registrar to students who have registered. Their registration for a given course is either confirmed or denied; if denied, a substitute may be offered.

Master Scheduling for Repetitive and Continuous Production

To complete the discussion of master scheduling, we must look briefly at the special case of high-volume repetitive or continuous production: spark plugs, small batteries, metals, chemicals, and so forth. These industries often plan and control by cumulative units rather than by orders, jobs, and lots. Steady production of the same products month after month makes it possible to closely relate the master production schedule to production/capacity planning, including planned inventory and backlog levels. Also, the MPS may be related to elements of the firm's business plan, including the production budget and shipping forecast. The example that follows involves case data for a real company.[6]

EXAMPLE 5–6

Master Scheduling for a Continuous Processor, Pfizer, Inc.

The Easton, Pennsylvania, plant of Pfizer, Inc., produces iron oxides used in paints, plastics, cosmetics, and other products. There are about 50 types of iron oxide products. Separate master schedules for each product are prepared quarterly, and totals are cumulative over a year's time. The graph in Figure 5–13 is used to display the schedule, plus other cumulative data.

Pfizer's business plan calls for 1,800,000 pounds of this type of iron oxide to be produced this year. This is Pfizer's budgeted production.

One quarter has passed at the time represented by Figure 5–13. Actual production and actual shipments have been plotted monthly, and the difference equals actual inventory. For example, at the end of February, cumulative actual production was 400,000 pounds and cumulative actual shipments were totaled at 260,000 pounds. The difference, 140,000, is the inventory on hand, which is represented graphically by the vertical distance between 400,000 and 260,000 in Figure 5–13. (The horizontal distance in the shaded zone of the figure represents months' worth of inventory.) By the end of March, the inventory had grown to 550,000 − 360,000 = 190,000 pounds.

This quarter's actual production, at 550,000, is 100,000 pounds short of the master production schedule amount of 650,000. The reason for not meeting the schedule could be production problems. But in this quarter the reason was that customer orders, reflected by shipments, were below the forecast, and the master scheduler took action monthly to decrease the

---

[6] This example is adapted from William L. Berry, Thomas E. Vollmann, and D. Clay Whybark, *Master Production Scheduling: Principles and Practice* (Falls Church, Va.: American Production and Inventory Control Society, 1979), pp. 23–35 (TS157.5.B46x).

FIGURE 5-13

Cumulative Master Scheduling at Pfizer, Inc.

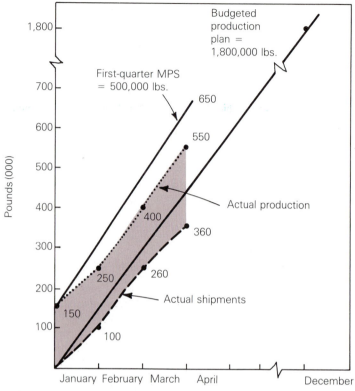

Notes: Beginning inventory = 150,000 pounds. Vertical distance in shaded zone = Inventory in pounds. Horizontal distance in shaded zone = Number of months supply of inventory.

MPS. (The decreased MPS amounts are not shown on the graph, nor is the demand forecast.) Since the first-quarter master production schedule was too high, the second-quarter MPS would probably be adjusted downward.

GLOSSARY

The terminology of capacity planning and master scheduling is not as standardized as we might like it to be. There are different terms for the same thing, and there are terms—like *capacity planning*—that have a common industrial meaning not obvious by the words themselves. The following glossary explains some of the terms that are important in this and other chapters.

Adjustable capacity – Elements of capacity that are adjustable in the medium term, including overall amounts of labor and inventory and rate of use (e.g., hours per day) of facilities, especially machine usage.

Aggregate demand forecast – Forecast of demand for a capacity group or product family, not specific as to items.

Aggregate inventory planning – Planning for the total amount of inventory to be kept on hand, not broken down into specific inventory item quantities.

Aggregate planning – See production/capacity planning.

Available to promise – The quantity of an item in the master production schedule that has not yet been promised (sold) to a customer.

Backlog – Total amount of work scheduled into a work unit but not completed.

Bill of labor – List of labor-hours needed to produce one unit of each item.

Build schedule – Term used in some companies to mean the master production schedule.

Business plan – Medium-term plan for sales, production, shipments, and cash flow; stated in dollars.

Capacity control – Short-term action to adjust labor and machine use if recent actual output is at variance from planned output.

Capacity group – Collection of related work centers, identified for purposes of aggregate demand forecasting and capacity planning. See also *product family*.

Capacity planning – Medium-term planning for overall amounts of labor and inventory and rate of use of machines, which are the adjustable elements of capacity (usually not meant to include facilities, i.e., fixed capacity).

Capacity policy – Policies that guide the management of adjustable capacity as demand changes; includes labor, inventories, backlogs, subcontractors, and facilities use.

Capacity requirements planning (CRP) – Computer-based technique for determining workloads scheduled into work centers by time period (sometimes used in a broader sense).

Capacity strategy – Strategy for planning and control in response to changing demand.

Capacity utilization – Rate of use of existing capacity, usually a percentage (existing capacity may be defined based on one, two, or three shifts).

Chase-demand strategy – Adding labor and stepping up machine use when demand is high, and vice versa.

Closed-loop control – Testing the effect of a plan and feeding back the test results to the planners (closing the loop) so that the plan can be improved. Production schedules and capacity plans may be so controlled.

Component inventory planning – Determining quantities needed and dates of need for each component part (not including the scheduling of purchase or manufacture of the components).

Consuming the MPS – Reserving quantities of items in the master schedule for specific customers as firm customer orders are received.

End item – Item that consumes large amounts of capacity and advance planning and therefore deserves status as a master production schedule item. Major subassemblies and product modules are typical; final assemblies sometimes are not included because final assembly may be possible to do at the last minute.

Facilities – Plant and equipment (capital goods, "fixed" capacity).

Final assembly schedule (FAS) – Schedule for final manufacturing stage (sometimes the finishing stage) to fill a customer order or replenish finished goods inventory. Master production schedule (MPS) generates the subassemblies and parts needed for final assembly. In some companies, the FAS and MPS are the same.

Item demand forecast – Forecast of demand for a specific end product or component part.

Level-capacity strategy – Keeping capacity (especially labor) level, and responding to demand decreases by increasing inventories or reducing backlogs.

Load profile – Statement of the timing and number of hours of workload required in a given work center in the production of one unit of an item. May be multiplied by number of units scheduled to show capacity required.

Master production schedule (MPS) – Statement of what goods the company expects to manufacture, in specific quantities and by completion dates (start dates not included); sometimes limited to capacity-consuming and time-consuming end items.

Master schedule – Same as MPS only a broader term, which could mean client appointments in the service industry as well as production schedules.

Product family – Groups of products having common production characteristics, e.g., same routing; identified for purposes of aggregate demand forecasting and capacity planning. See also *capacity group*.

Production planning – Upper management's medium-term plan for amount of manufacturing output, usually by capacity groups or product families and stated in broad terms, like tons, gallons, or pieces; regulates production, inventories or backlogs, and production expenses.

Production/capacity planning – Medium-term planning of the desired overall amount of manufacturing output and/or related capacity input, usually by capacity groups or product families; stated in broad output units (tons, gallons, pieces) or broad input units (hours, workers, machine cycles) or both.

Resource requirements planning – Converting the master production schedule (or production plan) into requirements for certain scarce resources to see if the available resources would be overloaded. May be a "rough-cut" check of resources, or a more precise check employing load profiles.

Total requirements – Actual customer demand plus forecast demand, by item and by time period; may include final assemblies, end items, and component parts.

SUMMARY

One aim of production/capacity management is to regulate inventories or backlogs and production expenses, which are elements in the business plan. Another aim is to achieve a good match between capacity and demand. The time period is medium term, typically months or quarters. Over that time range facilities—plant and equipment—are mostly fixed. Thus capacity/demand matching concerns more adjustable resources; these include the work force, inventories, and subcontractors. Other ways of adjusting to aggregate demand include use of marginal facilities, slower customer service, and off-peak price adjustments.

A chase-demand capacity strategy provides responsive service but at a cost of fluctuating capacity. A level-capacity strategy has opposite traits. Policies may be set up as guidelines for achieving the chosen strategy, and aggregate demands for logical capacity groups may be forecasted. The production/capacity plans, by families or groups, cover aggregate demand subject to policy limitations.

Companies that have little competition may safely plan capacity in detail for months into the future. The plan can maximize capacity utilization, while customer demands are simply backlogged. The quarterly ordering system includes this type of capacity planning.

Competition cuts out the luxury of backlogs. Capacity planning becomes more complex. Learning-curve planning is helpful for the case of large end products. As each added unit is made, its production time and cost tends to drop. The learning rate can be estimated and used in capacity planning and in scheduling the output, and it is a valued concept for managing productivity improvement in Japan.

In make-to-order plants, options for production/capacity planning for a given capacity group may be tested on recent demand data. Effects on order backlogs and lead time are revealed, and the plan that best fits company policy may be chosen.

In make-to-order plants, production/capacity planning is also by capacity groups. Based on a forecast of demand, the planners can calculate the effects of a trial production rate on inventory levels and on labor-hour and machine-hour requirements. The plan that most closely yields the desired inventory level and stays within available capacity may be selected.

The Japanese just-in-time (JIT) system tends to force capacity to be flexible and versatile, which makes capacity management easier.

The master production schedule (MPS) states the completion dates and quantities of end items to be produced. The capacity plan puts an upper limit on MPS quantities; sales bookings and item forecasts provide the demands to be covered by the MPS. The master scheduler's order promise commits the plant's output to certain customers. This basic approach applies to services providers as well as goods producers.

The MPS is the schedule of items that require large amounts of time and resources. Separate schedules may be developed for independently demanded component parts and for final assembly (which may take very little time). In simple cases the MPS may be the same as the schedule for final assembly.

In make-to-order plants the problem is lack of planning lead time. But an MPS based on a forecast can still work well. A good approach is to "consume the MPS" by deducting actual orders as they come in. MPS quantities not consumed are "available to promise." If too many units are available to promise, the item may be rescheduled to a later date.

Resource requirements planning (RRP) helps provide closed-loop control of the MPS. The RRP idea is to see how the trial MPS affects scarce resources. This can be done in the "rough cut" mode or using precise load profiles correctly timed. If there are no overloads or scarce resources, the final MPS may be released.

Master scheduling in continuous and repetitive production may employ cumulative graphical techniques. The graphs can show actual shipments, MPS quantities, and the yearly budgeted quantity. Shipments can be watched to see if master schedules need to be changed.

REFERENCES

Books

Berry, William L.; Thomas E. Vollman; and D. Clay Whybark. *Master Production Scheduling: Principles and Practice.* American Production and Inventory Control Society, 1979.

Orlicky, Joseph. *Material Requirements Planning.* New York: McGraw-Hill, 1975 (TS155.8.O74).

Plossl, G. W., and O. W. Wight. *Production and Inventory Control: Principles and Techniques.* Englewood Cliffs, N.J.: Prentice-Hall, 1967 (HD55.P5).

Sasser, W. Earl; R. Paul Olsen; and D. Daryl Wychoff. *Management of Service Operations.* Boston: Allyn & Bacon, 1978 (HD9981.5.S27).

Wight, Oliver W. *MRP II: Unlocking America's Productivity Potential.* Williston, Vt.: Oliver Wight Limited Publications, Inc., 1981 (TS161.W5x).

Periodicals (societies)

Production and Inventory Management (American Production and Inventory Control Society); numerous articles on capacity management.

REVIEW QUESTIONS

1. How can the master scheduler promote the goal of high use of capacity?

2. Is "chase demand" a capacity policy or a capacity strategy? Explain.

3. How do capacity plans for goods producers differ from those for services providers?

4. What determines whether a plant should have a single overall production/capacity plan, or more than one plan?

5. Why might one department in a company follow chase demand and another in the same company follow level capacity?

6. What types of production environments are best for using learning-curve planning? Why?

7. Why did the quarterly ordering system give way to demand forecasting by capacity groups?

8. Given the uncertainty of customer demand in make-to-order businesses, how can a business plan capacity intelligently?

9. In a make-to-order plant, how can a target inventory level (desired inventory after so many weeks) be translated into required machine hours?

10. What is a time fence (in master scheduling)?

11. Why might a manufacturer have three separate schedules—a master production schedule, a component-parts schedule, and a final assembly schedule?

12. Explain how a master schedule may be "consumed."

13. How does rough-cut capacity planning improve the validity of the master schedule?

14. What does the load-profile approach to RRP do that the rough-cut approach does not do?

15. How does the graphical cumulative master scheduling approach help keep master schedules valid for the continuous processor?

PROBLEMS

1. Assume that you are president of a large company and that you have a strong aversion to laying off employees. Devise a several-step policy governing what your company would do if demand in certain product lines dropped, creating excess labor. Your last step should be employee terminations.

2. How has IBM been able to avoid laying off employees, given the competition and short life cycle of many products in the fast-changing computer and business machines business? You may need to research the subject or interview IBM people to answer this question adequately.

3. City Sod is a small business that sells and lays sod (rolled strips of grass). The owner has devised a forecasting procedure based on demand history from previous years plus projection of demand in recent weeks. The forecast for the next six weeks, in labor-hours of sod laying, is:

    860   880   900   920   930   940

    Currently City Sod has a staff of sod layers consisting of four crew chiefs and 15 laborers. A crew chief lays sod along with the laborers but also directs the crew.
    The owner has decided on the following staffing policies:

    (1) A two-week backlog will be accumulated before adding staff.
    (2) Plans are based on a 40-hour work week; overtime is used only to absorb weather or other delays and employee absences or resignations.
    (3) The ideal crew size is one crew chief and four laborers.
       a. Devise a hiring plan for the six-week period covered by the forecast. In your answer, assume that there is a current backlog of 1,200 labor-hours of sod-laying orders.
       b. Does City Sod follow more of a chase-demand or a level-capacity strategy of production planning? Explain.

4. Bright Way Janitorial Service (case study, end of chapter) is considering a shift from a level-capacity to a chase-demand strategy of production/capacity planning. Bright Way managers know that chase demand would greatly simplify production/capacity planning. Explain why this is so. What new management problems would chase demand tend to create?

FOR THE LEARNING-CURVE PROBLEMS
COMPUTER PROGRAMS TO SIMPLIFY CALCULATIONS

Learning-curve calculations are easy to set up and run on a computer. Programs are given below in Basic (good for a personal computer) and in FORTRAN. Both are written for the special case of: 90 percent learning curve, first unit = 100, and total units = 60. For other problems change the R, A, and L variables.

	Basic program		FORTRAN program
10	YCUM = 0		YCUM = 0.0
20	R = .9		R = .9
30	A = 100		A = 100.
40	L = 60		L = 60
50	B = LOG(R) / LOG(2)		B = LOG(R) / LOG (.2)
60	FOR I = 1 TO L		DO 1 I = 1, L
70	Y = A * I ∧ B		Y = A * I ** B
80	YCUM = YCUM + Y		YCUM = YCUM + Y
90	Print I, Y, YCUM	1	WRITE (5,*) I, Y, YCUM
100	NEXT		STOP
110	END		END

Where

R = Learning-curve rate
A = Time to produce first unit
L = Last unit
Y = Time to produce Ith unit
YCUM = Cumulative time for first through Ith unit

---

5. Iridion, Inc., has been awarded a contract to produce 200 of a new type of rail-driven passenger car for a large city. Based on Iridion's previous experience in guided rocket manufacturing, an 80 percent learning curve is planned for the passenger-car contract. The first passenger car takes 1,400 direct-labor hours to make.

   a. If the city pays Iridion's accumulated direct-labor costs after the fourth unit, how many direct-labor hours should the city expect to owe right after the fourth unit is produced?

   b. The actual direct-labor usage for the first eight units produced is as follows:

   | 1,400 | 1,206 | 1,172 | 1,145 | 1,101 | 1,083 | 1,033 | 1,005 |

   Would you recommend that Iridion stay with its planning estimate of an 80 percent learning curve? Explain.

   c. Same as part b, except for the following changes in actual direct-labor usage:

   | 1,400 | 1,089 | 887 | 801 | 728 | 684 | 600 | 586 |

6. Bellweather Electronics (Example 5–1) already has a production plan for the generator contract. It is shown in this problem, and is based on a projected 90 percent learning curve. Bellweather planners have decided to prepare a contingency plan based on the possibility of an 80 percent learning curve.

   a. Prepare and run a computer program resulting in a listing similar to that shown here, but based on an 80 percent learning curve. *Or* perform the calculations on a hand calculator and prepare the listing manually.

   b. Devise a master schedule *on a time scale* that Bellweather could use to produce the generators following a level-capacity strategy. Show the number of generators to be completed every four weeks until all 60 are done. Use the 90 percent learning-curve data, and assume a generator-shop capacity of 100 labor-hours per week. Also, assume that generators are produced one at a time in a single work bay.

   c. Follow the instructions for *b* above, but use an 80 percent learning curve. Comment on the number of weeks to complete the contract at an 80 percent versus a 90 percent learning-curve rate.

Generator number	Labor-hours required	Cumulative labor-hours required
1	100	100.0
2	90	190.0
3	84.6	274.6
10	70.5	799.4
20	63.4	1,460.8
30	59.6	2,072.7
40	57.1	2,654.3
50	55.2	3,214.2
60	53.7	3,757.4

7. A manufacturer of ceramic products has been awarded a NASA contract to produce ceramic-based heat shields for space vehicles. The contract calls for a total of 20 heat-shield units. If the estimated learning-curve rate is 94 percent, and the first unit takes 60 hours to produce, how long will it take to produce the 5th, 10th, and final units?

8. Coast Limited Railways has a car-repair yard in Kansas City to repair the line's own cars. In the six most recent months, Kansas City's car-repair workload has been:

Month	Cars
1	83
2	72
3	71
4	90
5	49
6	56

   a. Coast Limited headquarters has directed Kansas City to plan for a capacity level not to exceed cumulative demand by more than half a month's average demand during the six-month planning period. Prepare the capacity plan, following the backlogging method of Example 5–2 in the chapter. Explain the positive and negative deviations.

b. What important factors in *a* could be analyzed in terms of dollars?

c. Is it necessary that this production-planning method be based on *cumulative* demand and planning figures? If it were Coast's policy to divert all excess orders to independent repair yards, would cumulative calculations be suitable? Explain and illustrate by an example.

9. Concrete Products, Inc., makes reinforced concrete structural members (trusses, etc.) for large buildings and bridges. Each order is a special design, so no finished-goods inventories are possible. Concrete members are made by using molds that are bolted onto huge "shake tables." A shaking or vibrating action causes the wet concrete to pack, without air pockets, around reinforcing steel in the molds. Concrete Products uses a chase-demand strategy of hiring labor to assemble the molds, fill them with concrete, and later disassemble them. If it takes a week to hire and train a laborer, how can Concrete Products make the chase-demand strategy work well? That is, what sort of labor (capacity) policies would work? The following is a representative sample of recent workloads, in labor-hours on the shake tables:

Week	Labor-hours
1	212
2	200
3	170
4	204
5	241
6	194
7	168
8	215
9	225

10. At a fiberglass products company, the dominant product line is fiberglass bathtub and shower units, which sell to the high-quality segment of the market. The company's best employees work in tubs and showers, which is treated as a separate capacity group. Forecast demands for this capacity group are in labor-hours; for the next three months demand is forecast at 300, 370, and 380 labor-hours. The present inventory is 620 labor-hours' worth of tub and shower units—in all sizes and colors. The plan is to reduce the inventory to 300 after three months, because the slow season is approaching.

a. Prepare a production plan for the next three months that minimizes labor fluctuation.

b. How would the master production schedule differ from the production plan?

11. The production control staff of Quark Electronics, Example 5–3 in the chapter, is preparing alternative trial production plans.

a. The production rate for a second trial plan is set at 15,300 pieces per week (50 percent greater than in the first trial) for product-group 1. The production rates for groups 2 and 3 are unchanged. Calculate labor-hour and machine-hour effects for week 1 only. (That is, redo Figure 5–7, using 15,300 pieces for product-group 1.) Is the second trial plan feasible? Or does it seriously overload capacity?

b. A third trial production plan is simpler to prepare. The simpler method is based on a single forecast in pieces, which is the composite of the three product-group forecasts. This requires a single average labor rate and a single average machine rate for each shop—instead of separate rates for each of the three product groups. Assume that for week 1 the composite forecast is for 50,000 pieces and that the shop production rates are:

Rate (pieces per hour)	Shop A	Shop B	Shop C	Shop D
Labor	300	222	650	830
Machine	500	750	2,000	600

Prepare the trial production plan for week 1 (similar to Figure 5–7 in the chapter). Compare the results of the third trial production plan with those of the first. Where has accuracy been lost in the third plan? In spite of this loss of accuracy, why might the production control chief prefer plan 3 (that is, where has there been a gain in precision)?

12. Gulf Tube and Pipe Co. prepares monthly production/capacity plans for three capacity areas, one of which is the pipe-forming, -cutting, and -welding (FCW) processes. The forecast FCW demand for next month is given below.

Week	Forecast lineal feet (000)
1	6,000
2	5,800
3	5,400
4	4,600

The present inventory is 16 million lineal feet.
   a. Devise a production plan, following a chase-demand strategy, that results in an ending inventory of 14 million lineal feet.
   b. Devise a production plan, following a level-capacity strategy, that results in an ending inventory of 14 million lineal feet.
   c. The following rule of thumb is used for purposes of capacity planning: Two workers are required for every million lineal feet produced. Develop two capacity plans (i.e., work force), one using data from part *a* and the other using data from part *b*.
   d. Citing data from parts *a* through *d*, explain the contrasting effects on inventories and labor of chase-demand and level-capacity strategies.

13. Devise a master scheduling diagram similar to Figure 5–12, but for draftsmen in an engineering firm. Explain your diagram.

14. Devise a master scheduling diagram similar to Figure 5–12, but for a maintenance department. Assume that maintenance includes janitorial crews and repairmen such as plumbers and electricians but does not include construction or remodeling. Explain your diagram.

15. At Gulf Tube and Pipe Co. the master scheduler has developed a trial master production schedule. Lately the growing demand for pipe products has strained capacity in the pipe-cutting work center. The work center consists of a single Dynacut cutoff machine, with a single-shift daily capacity of 120,000 lineal feet. The master scheduler has been running a rough-cut capacity plan to assure that the MPS quantities do not overload the Dynacut

machine. Engineering has provided the master scheduler with a list of all end-item numbers that require cutoff, and those items are starred in the trial MPS shown (partially) below.

End-item number	Week				
	1	2	3	4	5
0263	400	—	—	—	—
0845*	—	300	—	—	300
0997*	300	—	—	300	—
1063	—	200	800	—	—
.	.	.	.	.	.
.	.	.	.	.	.
.	.	.	.	.	.
Totals for *-items (000 of lineal feet)	600	680	470	550	590

    a.   Assuming a five-day-per-week single-shift operation, what does rough-cut capacity planning suggest should be done?

    b.   Can you tell from the data given what Gulf's production/capacity planning strategy is (i.e., level-capacity or chase-demand)? Explain.

16. In general registration at your college, registering for classes probably requires you to pass through several work centers. Which work center would you consider to be a bottleneck? Do you think the registrar's office would find the rough-cut capacity-planning idea useful in planning for that bottleneck work center? Explain. You will probably need to consider what the MPS would consist of in this case. (If you prefer, you could answer this question using drop-and-add or another administrative procedure, instead of general registration.)

17. At Piney Woods Furniture Co., the "scarce resource" that the master scheduler is most concerned about is the wood drying kiln. One product, a cabinet, uses three types of wood, which go through the kiln at different times in the manufacture of the cabinet. A load profile showing the total kiln workload resulting from one minimum cabinet order (50 cabinets) is given below. The unit of measure is cubic yard-hours, which accounts for size of the drying load and time in the kiln.

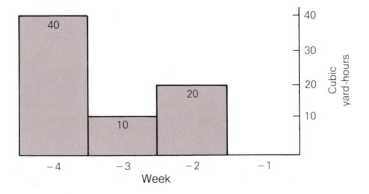

The current master production schedule (MPS) includes an order for 1,000 cabinets in week 6 (six weeks from now). Projected kiln workload for all products *other than the cabinet* is as follows for the next six weeks:

	Week					
	1	2	3	4	5	6
Cubic yard-hours	5,000	5,200	5,300	5,800	5,700	6,000

a. Calculate the week-by-week kiln loads (workloads) for the cabinet order. (Assume that week −1 on the load profile means one week prior to the week in which an order is due on the MPS.)

b. If the kiln has a maximum weekly capacity of 6,000 cubic yard-hours, will the MPS overload the kiln? Explain.

c. If the cabinet order is adjustable (customer would accept a change in delivery date), what MPS changes would you recommend, if any?

18. Pecos, Inc., produces cooking and salad oils in a continuous-process plant. Budgeted annual production is 130,000 gallons. The master production schedule calls for 40,000 gallons of production in the first quarter (January, February, and March). There are 30,000 gallons on hand as of January 1.

   Two months have passed. Actual production was 16,000 gallons in January and 13,000 gallons in February. Actual shipments were 10,000 gallons in January and 8,000 in February.

a. Draw a graph showing the budgeted production, master production schedule, actual production, and actual shipments. Use cumulative graphing and label all lines and points.

b. What is the inventory on hand after two months?

c. Production of oil normally is high in the winter months because raw materials (corn, sunflower seeds, etc.) are plentiful and at their minimum prices. That being the case, is the master scheduler doing a good job?

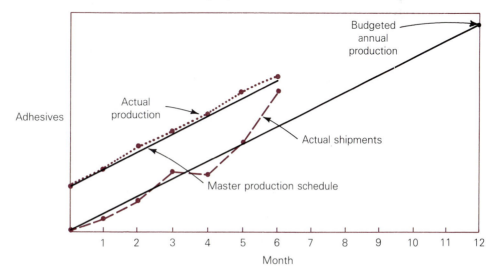

19. The above graph shows cumulative actual and planned production and shipment data for National Adhesives Corp., a continuous-process manufacturer of adhesives and related products. Explain what happened in the first four months and then in the last two months. What action would you suggest be taken by the master scheduler?

20. Great Lakes Paint Company's major product is a base white paint which is produced in batches continuously year-round. Cumulative master scheduling is used, and key information is plotted on a cumulative graph. The following data apply to the first six months of this year; beginning inventory was 38,000 gallons:

	Month					
	1	2	3	4	5	6
Master production schedule*	22	20	19	15	15	15
Actual production*	22	21	20	13	13	16
Actual shipment*	20	18	16	15	18	19

* In thousands of gallons.

a. Graph the given data in the cumulative graphical format. Label all lines and points.
b. Tell what the inventory on hand is after each month.
c. Explain the actions of the master scheduler.
d. Speculate on the causes of the actual production figures in months 3, 4, 5, and 6.

21. Technocratics, Inc., has developed a new type of corrugated aluminum shingle that is highly durable. The shingles are formed 10 at a time (per cycle) on a punch press. Maximum capacity is 2,500 shingles per 24-hour day. In the next 12 months Technocratics plans to sell 400,000 shingles. Expected demands in the next two months are 28,000 and 30,000. Current inventory is 25,000 shingles; the plan is to build inventory to 50,000 shingles in the next two months so that even a large order can be filled from stock. Punch press operation is easy to learn, and Technocratics is able to hire unskilled workers off the street at a low wage to quickly expand production when it needs to. If production were to drop off, workers would be laid off. In the case of a serious machine breakdown, the tooling (dies and fixtures) would be moved to another local company that had agreed to produce the product on its own identical punch press. Technocratics currently has 12 workers who put in a total of 96 production hours a week. Planned output is 32,000 shingles per month next month, at 96 production hours per week.
a. From the given data what can you tell about the company's business plan?
b. What is the capacity strategy, and what capacity policies are there?
c. Discuss the company's production/capacity plan and master production schedule. Will any labor changes be necessary in the next month or two? In the next year?

CASE STUDY: BRIGHT WAY JANITORIAL SERVICE

Bright Way Janitorial Service has established three categories of capacity:

1. Wet processes (mopping, buffing, etc.).
2. Dry processes (vacuuming/dusting).
3. Glass cleaning.

These categories were set because they define three separate kinds of worker/equipment processes. Each may be forecast based on historical data. Bright Way uses the forecasts, along with its labor, service, and pricing policies, to arrive at a production/capacity plan for a three-week period, by week.

The forecast and the production/capacity plan are updated (rolled over) every two weeks. The short forecast interval is suitable because hiring and training require less than two weeks. Updating the production/capacity plan need not be done every week, because there is a staff of irregular workers on call. They serve as a cushion against inaccurate forecasting.

Bright Way has a strategy of seeking "higher-quality" customers, paying a bit higher wage, and gaining a somewhat more stable workforce than its competitors. In support of that strategy the following capacity policies have developed:

Labor:
Priority 1—18–22 percent full-time labor, no overtime.
Priority 2—65–75 percent part-time labor.
Priority 3—8–12 percent irregular laborers.
Priority 4—20 percent of full-time and part-time staff cross-trained for possible temporary transfer to secondary work category.
Priority 5—subcontract (make advance agreements) for excess short-term demands, where possible.

Service (responsiveness):
Priority 1—maintain all schedules for regular customers.
Priority 2—next-week response to new customers—up to limits of staffing—for routine cleaning; that is, work categories 1 and 2.
Priority 3—work special cleaning demands into the schedule as soon as possible without disrupting regular schedules.

Pricing: No pricing incentives. This policy subject to change if competition warrants it.

With those policies as a basis, Bright Way's production/capacity plan for the next three weeks is as shown in Exhibit 1. The plan shows forecast labor-hours of demand for each work category and for each week. The forecast labor-hours are assigned to full-time, part-time, overtime, and irregular labor. In this three-week period there is no planned need for subcontracting. The totals at the bottom include percentages. These fit the percentage goals that Bright Way set in its capacity policies.

For example, in week 1, the total forecast demand for category 1 (wet processes)

EXHIBIT 1

Three-Week Group Forecast and Production/Capacity Plan—Bright Way
Janitorial Service

Work cate-gory	Labor type	Labor-hours, by week					
		1		2		3	
		Fore-cast	Assigned	Fore-cast	Assigned	Fore-cast	Assigned
1		1,240		1,160		1,100	
"Wet"	Full-time		240		240		240
	Part-time		860		860		860
	Irregular		140		60		
	Subcontract						
2		1,900		2,000		2,260	
"Dry"	Full-time		400		400		480
	Part-time		1,320		1,320		1,400
	Irregular		180		280		380
	Subcontract						
3		480		520		480	
"Glass"	Full-time		120		120		120
	Part-time		360		360		360
	Irregular						
	Subcontract						
	Totals	3,620		3,680		3,840	
	Full-time		760 (21%)		760 (20%)		880 (21%)
	Part-time		2,540 (70%)		2,620 (70%)		2,820 (69%)
	Irregular		320 (9%)		340 (9%)		380 (10%)
	Subcontract						
	Change in hours			+60		+160	
	Staffing plan			Hire 2 PT; assign to "glass." Add 20 hours irregular.		Hire 2 FT and 2 PT; assign to "dry." Add 40 hours ir-regular.	

is 1,240 labor-hours of business. Janitorial staff assignments for that demand are: 240 labor-hours of full-time labor, 860 of part-time labor, and 140 of irregular labor. Since 240 + 860 + 140 = 1,240, the plan meets forecast demand with no need for subcontracting.

Forecast demand for all three work categories in week 1 totals 3,620 labor-hours. To meet that demand without subcontracting, the plan calls for 760 labor-hours full-time, 2,540 part-time, and 320 irregular. In percentages full-time labor is 21 percent, which falls within the priority 1 goal of 18–22 percent; part-time is 70 percent, which is within the priority 2 goal of 65–75 percent; and irregular is 9 percent, which is within the priority 3 goal of 8–12 percent.

All priorities are met in week 1. The production plan is to do the full amount of business that the demand forecast indicated is available. The capacity plan that enables demand to be met is the staffing plan at bottom of Exhibit 1.

In weeks 2 and 3, hiring is called for because forecast demand is on the increase.

Since hiring is normally possible in less than two weeks, this plan provides the necessary lead time.

DISCUSSION QUESTIONS

1. As compared with its competitors, is Bright Way's strategy chase demand or level capacity? Develop a table like Figure 5–1 with Bright Way's strategy in one column and the more typical janitorial service as the other. Discuss each row in your table.

2. If Bright Way changed to the capacity strategy of its competitors, would capacity planning—and overall management—be simpler or more difficult? Explain.

3. What demand forecasting techniques would you recommend for Bright Way? Why?

Chapter 6

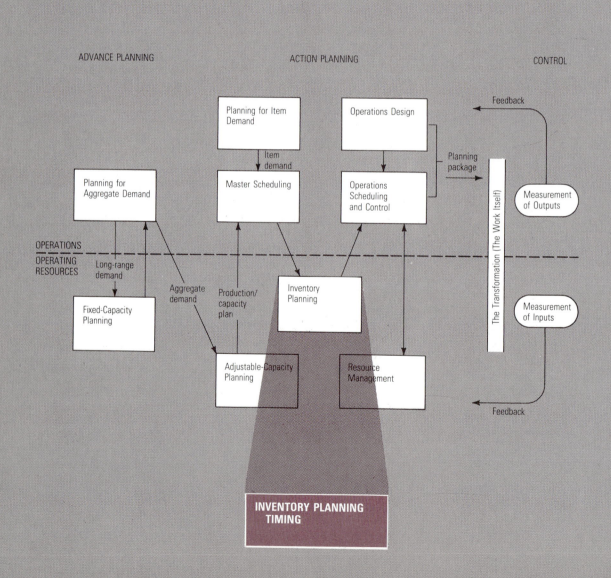

ADVANCE PLANNING

ACTION PLANNING

CONTROL

Planning for Item Demand

Operations Design

Feedback

Planning for Aggregate Demand

Item demand

Master Scheduling

Operations Scheduling and Control

Planning package

Measurement of Outputs

OPERATIONS
OPERATING RESOURCES

Long-range demand

Aggregate demand

Production/ capacity plan

Inventory Planning

The Transformation (The Work Itself)

Measurement of Inputs

Fixed-Capacity Planning

Adjustable-Capacity Planning

Resource Management

Feedback

INVENTORY PLANNING TIMING

Inventory Planning—Timing

In the most general sense an inventory is any idle resource. Strickly speaking, concepts of inventory management apply to inventories of:

Facilities—plant and equipment.

Manufacturing materials—materials that go into manufactured items.

Support materials—often referred to as MRO, for *m*aintenance, *r*epair, and *o*perating supplies.

Work-in-process (WIP) inventories—materials in a partial stage of completion.

Finished goods—materials, parts, modules, end items, or final assemblies for external customers; sometimes called *distribution inventories.*

Tools—implements used to perform work; can include reference information, the tool of the professional.

Labor—even the work force may be considered an inventory.[1]

Planning for facilities, labor, and tools is discussed in other chapters. Planning for facilities is a unique problem since they are fixed capital assets. Labor and tools, which are reused, are unlike materials, which flow in and out of the organization. It is the inventories that *flow*—that is, materials—that are discussed in this and the next two chapters. Planning for material inventories takes up three chapters because material flows are so dominant a part of operations management. It is not uncommon for material inventories to absorb over half of a firm's total expenditures. There may be thousands of items to manage and hundreds of thousands of inventory transactions per year.

The central concern in inventory planning is providing items at the right time and in the right quantities. For some 50 years, most of the attention was on quantities and lot sizes. Within the past 20 years, emphasis in American industry shifted to timing, especially a computer-based technique called materials requirements planning (MRP). At the same time Japanese industry has developed new concepts for both inventory timing (the *kanban* technique) and quantities (minimum lot sizes and just-in-time production). In the midst of these new developments, a very old technique for inventory timing—the reorder point (ROP)—remains fundamental in wholesaling, retailing, some types of manufacturing, and replenishment of supplies.

In this chapter we examine timing, which includes ROP, MRP, and kanban. In Chapter 7 the topic is quantities, and in Chapter 8 it is purchasing and materials management. Let us begin with the technique most familiar to the laymen, replenishment by reorder point methods.

REPLENISHMENT

The reorder point (ROP) is probably as old as man (maybe older, since some animals, such as squirrels, exhibit manlike behavior in replenishing low stocks). The ROP

---

[1] The airlines, for example, maintain inventories of pilots during slack periods. The pilots are under contract and must be paid (at least partially) whether or not they have flights. Their idleness pay may be considered as an inventory carrying cost.

and its variations provide for replenishing stocks when they get down to some low level. Let us look at some of the ROP variations.

Perpetual System

The classic reorder point is a **perpetual** inventory system. This means that every time an issue is made (perpetually), the stock on hand is checked to see whether it is down to the ROP. If it is, an order is placed. In the small informal case, it is the physical stock level that is perpetually examined. In the more formal case, it is the stock record balance that is examined.

Reorder points are all around us. We may reorder (go get) postage stamps when our stock is down to three. There used to be a perforated tab on the side of Kleenex boxes; the customer was to tear out the tab and then follow ROP-like instructions—something like, "When the Kleenex gets down to here, that's the time to buy two more boxes of Kleenex." (You were not only being told the reorder point; you were also being told that your lot size should be two boxes.)

Two-Bin System

A version of perpetual reorder point called the *two-bin system* is often used in small stockrooms. Two adjacent storage bins are assigned to hold a single item. Users of the stockroom are told to withdraw from bin 1 first. The rule is, when the first bin empties, place an order. The second bin contains the ROP, a quantity that covers the lead time for filling the order and allows for some additional safety stock.

There are many variations. In the forms storeroom, a colored sheet of paper may be inserted in a stack of forms on a shelf to show when the ROP (second "bin") has been reached. Indirect material or free stock, such as washers, screws, and nails, is often placed in trays on the shop floor; a painted line partway down inside the tray can designate the ROP (second "bin"). Transistors, diodes, and so on, are often stored in corrugated boxes on shelves; a small box in the larger box may be used to contain the ROP (second "bin"). Figure 6–1 shows some of these two-bin variations.

The two-bin system works best where a single person is in charge of the stockroom or is in charge of a daily check to see which items are down to the ROP. Otherwise people will get too busy to note the need for an order; each person can conveniently blame the next person when the second bin is emptied without anyone having reordered.

If the two-bin system exists in a firm that has partial computer control of inventories, order cards can be placed near bin 2. Then, when bin 2 is entered, it is an easy matter to initiate the reorder: Just pull a machine-readable card. The card would contain identifying data; nothing need be written down. People are less likely to "forget" to order when ordering is so simple.

FIGURE 6–1

Two-Bin System Variations

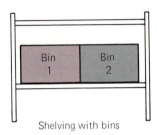

Shelving with bins

Rule: Use from bin 1 first:
when empty, reorder

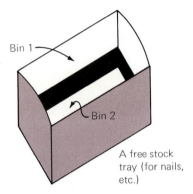

A free stock
tray (for nails,
etc.)

Rule: When down to black zone,
reorder.

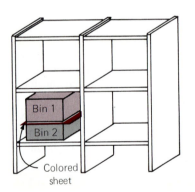

Colored
sheet

Open shelving (for forms)

Rule: When down to colored
sheet, reorder .

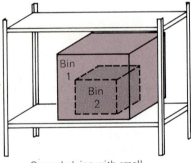

Open shelving with small
box inside larger box

Rule: When small box must be
broken open, reorder.

ROP Calculation

The reorder point (the quantity in bin 2) may be set by judgment and experience or by an ROP formula. Usually one's judgment would tend to follow the concepts on which the basic ROP formula is based. The formula is:

$$ROP = DLT + SS = (D)(LT) + SS$$

where

ROP = Reorder point
DLT = Demand during lead time
SS   = Safety stock
D   = Average demand per time period
LT   = Average lead time

Demand during lead time may be computed using a recent average demand amount and a recent average lead time. An explanatory example follows.

EXAMPLE 6–1

ROP Calculation, Fuel Oil Example

Assume that a building heated by fuel oil averages 600 gallons consumed per year and that the average lead time is two weeks. Thus,

D   = 600 gallons per year
LT   = 2 weeks/52 weeks per year = 0.04
DLT = (D)(LT) = (600)(0.04) = 24 gallons

Then, if safety stock is 40 gallons,

ROP = DLT + SS = 24 + 40
= 64 gallons

Replenishment Cycle

Use of the reorder point may be shown by a graph. Figure 6–2 is a common form of a graph for illustrating ROP replenishment cycles. Example 6–2 explains.

FIGURE 6–2

ROP Replenishment Cycles, Radiator Cap Example

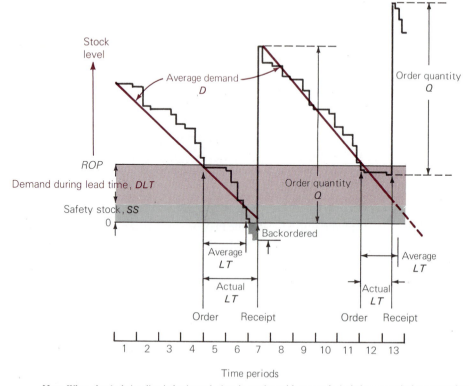

Note: When the depletion line is horizontal, time is passing with no stock depletion; a vertical segment shows a depletion.

EXAMPLE 6–2

Replenishment Cycles for Discrete Demand, Radiator Cap Example

Radiator caps are issued in discrete units; that is, there cannot be an issue of half a radiator cap. (By contrast, a continuous item like fuel oil can be issued in fractional parts of a gallon.) Figure 6–2 shows two replenishment cycles for radiator caps. The graph shows a stairstep depletion pattern; and it shows early and late order arrivals, including a case in which backordering occurs.

In the first cycle radiator caps are being issued at a slow pace, slower than past average demand, that is. Then in the fourth time period there is a spurt. At the end of the fourth time period, stock on hand drops below the ROP. An order is placed. During lead time, stock issues start out slowly, then speed up in periods 6 and 7. All radiator caps are gone by the beginning of period 7, and still orders come in.

The shaded zone below the zero line indicates orders unfilled because of the stockout condition. Orders accepted when stock is out are said to be *backorders*. They are usually filled first when stock does arrive.

In this case the stockout is caused by the late spurt in demand plus slow delivery; the actual lead time is shown to be greater than average. It is a case in which safety stock did not fully protect because of the combination of high demand and slow delivery.

The second cycle begins when the order arrives in period 7. The order quantity or lot size, *Q*, brings the stock level up from zero to *Q* units, and the backorders are immediately filled, dropping the stock level somewhat. Stock depletion is at about an average rate through period 10. In period 11 there is a surge in demand for radiator caps. The surge in demand continues into period 12, and it reduces stock to below the ROP. An order is placed.

This time, delivery is faster than average (see actual LT as compared with average LT) and there is little demand during the lead-time period. This combination of events results in little use of the DLT quantity and no use of the SS amount. Stock is high when the order quantity, *Q*, arrives. The order arrival pushes the stock level up to near the maximum possible, which is the ROP plus *Q*.

Safety-Stock Influences

Safety stock provides protection against stockout. Safety stock is influenced by a number of factors. Figure 6–3 lists some of the factors in three categories: demand protection, supply protection, and internal factors.

Under **demand protection,** demand variability (factor 1 in the figure) is usually

FIGURE 6–3

Factors Influencing Safety Stock

Demand protection	Supply protection	Internal factors
1. Demand variability	4. Lead-time variability	7. Consequences of stockout
2. Confidence in demand estimate	5. Confidence in lead-time estimate	8. Item cost
3. Exposure to stockout	6. Security of supply	9. Obsolescence
		10. Scrap rate
		11. Space requirements

thought to be the most important safety-stock factor. Demand is usually variable, and safety stock protects for variability on the high side of mean demand.[2]

Confidence in the demand estimate (factor 2) refers mainly to the amount of past data or experience. If the item has been in stock for years, its mean demand and demand variability may be estimated with confidence. If not, more safety stock is needed.

Exposure to stockout (factor 3) is the amount of time that stock is low and in danger of running out. Exposure could be measured in number of days per year that an item is down to a one-day supply or less. It is often sufficient to measure exposure in number of order cycles per year instead of in time (days). The idea is that more order cycles mean more chances to run out—when stock gets low near the end of each cycle. Thus, if stock is ordered often (in small lots), more safety stock is needed.

Factors 4 and 5, under **supply protection,** are like 1 and 2. More lead-time variability or less confidence means more safety stock.

Factor 6, security of supply, is especially important when there are raw material shortages. (Worldwide shortages in 1974 were especially severe.) Undependable suppliers also raise the issue of security of supply. Larger safety stocks provide general protection. Stockpiling, a purchasing action, is a more extreme measure.

Consequences of stockout (factor 7) is an **internal factor.** A stockout sometimes has little effect. On the other hand, lack of a particular bolt could shut down an assembly line; if that is likely, safety stock is needed.

If item cost (factor 8) is very high, you cannot afford to invest in safety stock. If it is low, safety-stock protection is obtained cheaply.

High risk of obsolescence (factor 9) is like high item cost: You do not want much of such items in safety stock. A high scrap rate (factor 10) has the opposite effect: The potential for scrap may call for more safety-stock protection.

The final factor (11) is space requirements. Bulkier items require more space, and therefore fewer of them are desirable for safety stock.

Safety stock is often expressed in terms of days, weeks, or months supply. Then safety-stock protection among items may be compared. A firm that has a safety stock of 10 cases of nails for an annual demand of 60 cases has a two-month supply in safety stock. The simple calculation is:

$$\frac{\text{Safety stock}}{\text{Demand}} = \frac{10 \text{ cases}}{\dfrac{60 \text{ cases}}{12 \text{ months}}} = \frac{10}{5} = 2\text{-month supply}$$

---

[2] Another name for safety stock is *reserve.* This alternative term may be especially familiar to the public in view of the energy crisis and publicity about oil reserves and natural gas reserves. But, as Tom Bethel points out in a magazine article, the general public thinks that the term *natural gas reserves* means total quantity in the earth. Bethel notes that in the gas industry gas reserves are proven (drilled) inventories and that these inventories are based on recent demand forecasts (and, presumably, demand variability). If that is true, then gas reserves are safety stocks; more wells may be drilled to keep the safety stocks in line with demand forecasts. Tom Bethel, "The Gas Price Fixers," *Harper's Magazine,* June 1979, pp. 37–44+.

Equivalently

$$\frac{10 \text{ cases}}{\dfrac{60 \text{ cases}}{52 \text{ weeks}}} = \frac{10}{1.15} = 8.7\text{-week supply}$$

Statistical Safety Stock

In some firms, supply protection (factors 4, 5, and 6 in Figure 6–3) is up to the purchasing department; internal factors (factors 7–11) are accounting and production department concerns, and inventory planning has the responsibility for demand protection (factors 1, 2, and 3). Inventory planning may want a streamlined, perhaps computerized, process for setting safety stocks to provide the proper level of demand protection. One such process is based on statistical service levels, considered next.

Statistical Service Levels. The cost of a stockout to the firm is often obscure. An approach that avoids wild estimates of stockout cost is the concept of statistical service levels. Under this concept, the firm sets a service-level target. The target is stated as a frequency of running out of stock. For example, if the service level is 0.98, that means customer orders would be filled 98 percent of the time, with a stockout 2 percent of the time.

The service level may then be converted to a safety factor, which is multiplied by a measure of variability of demand to give safety stock. The measure of variability of demand is either the standard deviation (SD) or the mean absolute deviation (MAD). Safety factors for a range of service levels are found in Table 6–1. Formulas for using the table are:

$$\text{Safety stock} = SF_{SD} \times SD$$

Or

$$\text{Safety stock} = SF_{MAD} \times MAD$$

For example, assume that mean demand for bread at your house is 100 slices per order cycle but that demand varies by a standard deviation of 40 slices. If the desired service level is 97.72 percent, we see from Table 6–1 that the safety factor$_{SD}$ = 2.00. Therefore,

$$\text{Safety stock} = 2.00 \times 40$$
$$= 80 \text{ slices (or about 4 loaves)}$$

Now let us find the safety stock using the MAD. Again, assume that demand is 100 slices per order cycle, but this time demand variability is a MAD of 32 slices. Table 6–1 gives a safety factor$_{MAD}$ = 2.50. Then,

$$\text{Safety stock} = 2.50 \times 32$$
$$= 80 \text{ slices}$$

TABLE 6–1

Safety Factors for Various Service Levels Based on Mean Absolute
Deviation of Normally Distributed Demand

Service level (percent of order cycles without stockout)	Safety factor using standard deviation SF_{SD}	Safety factor using MAD SF_{MAD}
50.00%	0.00	0.00
75.00	0.67	0.84
80.00	0.84	1.05
84.13	1.00	1.25
85.00	1.04	1.30
89.44	1.25	1.56
90.00	1.28	1.60
93.32	1.50	1.88
94.00	1.56	1.95
94.52	1.60	2.00
95.00	1.65	2.06
96.00	1.75	2.19
97.00	1.88	2.35
97.72	2.00	2.50
98.00	2.05	2.56
98.61	2.20	2.75
99.00	2.33	2.91
99.18	2.40	3.00
99.38	2.50	3.13
99.50	2.57	3.20
99.60	2.65	3.31
99.70	2.75	3.44
99.80	2.88	3.60
99.86	3.00	3.75
99.90	3.09	3.85
99.93	3.20	4.00
99.99	4.00	5.00

Source: G. W. Plossl and O. W. Wight, *Production and Inventory Control: Principles and Techniques.* © 1967, p. 108. Reprinted by permission of Prentice-Hall, Inc., Englewood Cliffs, New Jersey.

Notice that for the same service level the safety factors were 2.00 and 2.50. From this we can see that

$$SD = 1.25 \ MAD$$

The SD-to-MAD ratio is approximate rather than exactly 1.25. Use of the MAD instead of the standard deviation can introduce some error (for reasons that are beyond the scope of this discussion). It is true that the MAD is easier to calculate manually than is the SD. But most companies that use statistical safety stock routines do so with the aid of a computer. Since it is about as easy to program the computer for the standard deviation as for the MAD, the more accurate SD method is generally the best choice.

Lead-Time Effects. The safety-stock formulas provided above apply when the forecast period is about equal to the lead time. If lead times are abnormally long, the calculated safety stock must be adjusted. For example, if you were a homesteader in the back-woods of Alaska, replenishing your bread supply could take weeks. If you calculate mean demand and SD over a one-week period but go to buy bread only once every two months, then the SD will be over too short a period to capture the full range of variability of the two-month period. It turns out that the correct safety stock should be several times greater than the 80 slices of bread calculated above.

There is a mathematical procedure for making the correction; the procedure is reserved for advanced studies. For our purposes, we should be alert for the case when lead times greatly exceed the forecast period—and understand that in such cases the safety stock should be larger than the calculated amount.

Uses of the Statistical Safety-Stock Method. The method being discussed usually is unsatisfactory for manufacturers' direct materials. The statistical safety-stock method only considers the demand variability factor, but most factory safety stocks are there for several other reasons—see Figure 6–3.

On the other hand users of quickly replenished, locally available staples—foods, liquors, two-by-fours, nails—tend to keep safety stocks mainly for reasons of demand variability. Large grocery chains and other similar businesses are among the most likely users of the statistical safety-stock method. Also, the wholesalers and maybe the producers of grocery (or similar) products may want to use the method—in order to make sure that they can keep the grocers' shelf spaces full and not a target for a competitor's product.

Frito-Lay, for example, is said to take great pride in maintaining a service level of 99.5 percent for stores that carry Frito-Lay products.[3] To do that, Frito has to have dedicated people in its distribution system to assure that deliveries to a store in need are always fast. In other words, Frito must control lead-time variability to assure that safety stocks are not needed for lead-time reasons. In its distribution centers, Frito would need to calculate demand variability for each product, use it to compute safety stocks, and then add safety stock to demand during lead time to yield the reorder point. Of course, Frito-Lay computers would do the calculating of standard deviation of demand, safety stock, mean demand, demand during lead time, and ROP. Computer listings of ROPs for each product may be scanned by Frito product managers, who may decide to change some of the safety stocks and ROPs in light of some of the other 10 safety-stock factors given in Figure 6–3.

---

[3] Thomas J. Peters and Robert H. Waterman, *In Search of Excellence* (New York: Harper & Row, 1982), pp. 164–65 (HD70.U5P424).

Periodic System

Another type of replenishment system is the periodic system. In the perpetual system, replenishment is triggered by stock depletion to the reorder point, which is a *quantity*. In the periodic system, replenishment action occurs at fixed *points in time,* i.e., periodically.

Often the periodic system of *timing* orders is combined with **maximum-minimum quantity** criteria. For example, a grocery store might periodically reorder laundry soaps, with two days as the order interval. The maximum shelf space for one item, say Whiter-White Detergent might be four cases. Then maximum inventory is probably set at four cases. The desired minimum might be one case. The periodic system would work like this:

1. Check stock of Whiter-White on Monday, Wednesday, Friday, and so on.
2. If shelf stock is below one case, reorder enough to bring the stock as close to four cases as possible without exceeding four cases.
3. If stock is above one case, reorder zero cases.

Note that the minimum is really a reorder-point *quantity* used in conjunction with the reorder-point interval; the maximum governs what the lot size shall be to bring stock up to the maximum level.

Lead times are usually short (e.g., one day) in the grocery business. In most other businesses, lead times are longer, and the quantity ordered under the periodic system should probably include factors other than just minimum and maximum. Let us consider an elaborate example.

EXAMPLE 6–3

Periodic Reordering with Long Lead Times

Assume that an inventory planner in a manufacturing firm reorders a certain type of wire once a month and that the lead time is one month. The amount ordered, Q, might be:

$$Q = SOQ + DLT + SS + AL + BO - OH$$

where

SOQ = Standard order quantity
DLT = Demand during lead time
SS = Safety stock
AL = Allocated quantity, i.e., quantity earmarked for a particular use
BO = Backorder quantity
OH = On-hand balance

Assume further that SOQ = 400, DLT = 50, and SS = 20, and that on the date of periodic reordering AL = 15, BO = 30, and OH = 30. What this means is that 30 are on hand, including the safety stock of 20; 15 of that 30 on hand are allocated to a customer who has not yet taken delivery; and 30 are backordered for another customer who apparently does not want to take the remaining 15 as a partial delivery. Thus, today's order is for:

$$Q = 400 + 50 + 20 + 15 + 30 - 30 = 485$$

If normal events take place, 50 units will be demanded during lead time. Since only 30 are on hand, the shortage is 20. That 20 plus the AL of 15 and the BO of 30, equals a total demand of 65 when the order of 485 arrives. Immediate coverage of that current demand reduces the balance to 420, and that is exactly what is desired: 400 as the SOQ in addition to 20 as the safety stock.

MATERIAL REQUIREMENTS PLANNING

At one time reorder point systems were "state-of-the art" in manufacturing. Not any more. Let us see what changes have taken place.

MRP versus ROP

We are all aware of a major advance in *retail* inventory *control* in the 1970s: the computer-based control afforded by point-of-sale terminals. What the layman is largely unaware of is a major advance in the same decade in *manufacturing* inventory *planning*. It is called material requirements planning (MRP), and it is also computer-based.[4]

MRP is a procedure for time-phasing component-parts orders. It is an alternative to the traditional method of timing orders, the reorder point (ROP). The major difference between MRP and ROP may be stated concisely:

MRP *plans future orders.*
ROP *determines the next order.*

We see that MRP is future-oriented. ROP is present-oriented; that is, it determines if there is a need right *now* to release the next order.

The development of MRP is linked to the discovery of the concept of dependent and independent demand. These concepts are a good starting point for understanding ROP-MRP differences.

Dependent Demand

Demand for a given item is said to be dependent when the item is to go into or become part of another item. Component parts go into what are referred to as *parent* items. A tuner, for example, is a component part that goes into the parent radio

---

[4] MRP was implemented in a few firms in the 1960s, but it enjoyed explosive growth in the 1970s, as computing costs plummeted.

receiver. Treating parts demands as being dependent makes good sense only if it is easy or economical to see which parent items are to receive the parts.

A certain model of auto tire in a service station is not planned as a dependent-demand item, because there is no reasonable way to project a schedule of customers' autos needing that model of tire. By contrast, the same model of tire in an auto assembly plant depends on how many "Super XK-9" autos will be made.

Demand for most manufacturing stocks are dependent on demands for parent items. A multilevel product structure forms a dependency chain. As an example, Figure 6–4 shows a dependency chain with five levels below the end item (an automobile). For the product structure shown, demand for raw metal depends on demand for the gear that the metal is formed into; demand for the gear depends on demand for the gear shaft that that gear is mounted on; demand for the shaft depends on demand for the gear box that it goes into; demand for the gear box depends on demand for the engine; and, finally, demand for the engine depends on demand for the finished auto. With such a long dependency chain, it is worthwhile to make an

FIGURE 6–4

Partial Product Structure Showing Dependency Chain

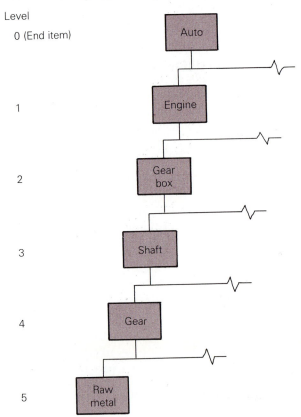

effort to carefully estimate end-item demands, since accuracy of all lower-level requirements depend on accuracy of end-item demands that they are dependent on.

Sometimes the dependency chain is short. In pottery manufacturing, demand for potters' clay and glazing chemicals depends on demand for pots. That is the extent of it. With so short a product structure there is less need for computer-based MRP as a means of planning for minimum inventories.

Independent Demand

Demand for a given item is said to be independent where there is no clearly identifiable parent or parents or where parent-item demand cannot be determined economically. This is the tendency when, for example, many small orders make up total demand for a given item. Lack of parent-item demand data rules out MRP. Time-phased order point (TPOP) or reorder point (ROP) must be considered. Demand must be forecast rather than calculated.

While many manufacturing materials are clearly dependent, a few are not. For a cabinetmaker, glue and screws would be treated as independent-demand items. They go into certain cabinets (parent items), but it is not very economical to try to order glue and screws for specific cabinets. Instead glue and screws may be ordered when stocks get low: the reorder-point method. Orders for fine woods for cabinets, on the other hand, may be planned as dependent-demand items, with the timing of wood orders coordinated with cabinet job-order schedules (the MRP idea).

Lumpiness of Demand

A related condition that makes MRP attractive is that MRP works well for "lumpy" demand streams. Lumpy demand—high one period, low or maybe zero the next, and so forth—is common in job-lot manufacturing. In contrast, distribution inventories tend to have rather smooth, steady demand from period to period, because with numerous independent sources of demand, if one customer doesn't order, the next one will. MRP handles lumpy demands very simply: It calculates the net requirement as zero when demand is zero, 500 when demand is 500, and so forth. Reorder point is based on past *average* demand and therefore will incorrectly call for orders even if there is no demand.

MRP Time Phasing

In MRP, orders for dependent demand are planned so that the items will be available at the place of need in the period when they are needed—if everything goes right. When things do not go according to plan, inventory may build or due dates may not be met. The following example illustrates.

EXAMPLE 6–4

MRP for a Caterer

Imagine that you are a caterer. Assume that you have a master schedule of parties to cater every night for the next two weeks. Your inventory policy is zero inventories (except for incidentals like seasonings). To plan for zero inventories, you consult menus for every food dish to be provided for every one of the catering orders in the next two weeks. Menu quantities times number of servings equals gross requirements. Let us say that gross requirements for salami are as shown in part A of Figure 6–5. Salami is required in the quantities shown on days 3, 6, 11, and 13.

FIGURE 6–5

Planned-Order-release Determination—Salami

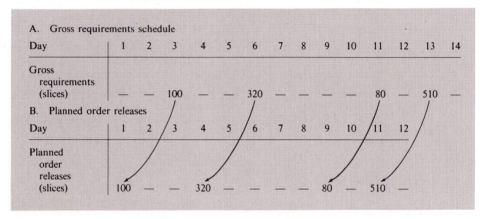

You normally order salami from a butcher shop two days ahead of time. That is, purchase lead time is two days for salami. Therefore you plan to release salami orders as is shown in part B of Figure 6–5. Each planned order release is two days in advance of the gross requirement shown in Figure 6–5A.

The schedule of planned order releases is correctly timed and in the exact quantities needed. It is a material requirements plan for one of the components that go into the foods to be catered. It is a plan for zero inventory, and zero inventory is achieved if the butcher delivers the salami orders in the planned two days. If deliveries come a day early, then inventory builds. Also, if an order of salami arrives on time, but a customer cancels the catering order calling for salami, inventory builds. Such supply and demand uncertainties cause some inventory when MRP is used, but MRP cuts inventory considerably from what it is when the producer (caterer) *plans* to keep components in stock.

MRP Computer Processing

Clearly MRP is a simple idea. The MRP calculations for salami were easy too, because there is only a single level of dependency from salami slices to a master schedule of catered food dishes. From the earlier discussion of dependent demand, recall the case of raw metal (1), cut into a gear (2), fit onto a shaft (3), placed in a gearbox (4), installed in an engine (5), assembled into a vehicle (6). That is five levels of parts below the end item (vehicle). The timing and quantities of parts to be ordered at each level are dependent on needs for parts by the parent item directly above. **Planned-order-release** calculations must cascade, that is, proceed from the first level to the second to the third, and so on. Cascading calculations are good reason for computers, especially for products having thousands of parts.

But cascading **(level-by-level)** calculations are not the only complication. The same raw metal that is cut into a gear might also go into a number of other parent items that ultimately become the given vehicle. Furthermore, the raw metal and perhaps the gear, the shaft, the gearbox, and the engine may go into other parent items that become various other vehicle types. Finally, dependent demands (i.e., demands that descend from parent items) for parts at any level must be combined with independent demands. Independent demands arise, for example, from orders for spare parts (service parts). Computers are needed to total and properly time-phase all of these requirements for the same part.

Computer power makes MRP practicable. Figure 6–6 shows the necessary inputs and outputs of an MRP computer run. The inputs are a master production schedule, an item master file, a bill-of-materials file, and an open-order file. The outputs include a planned-order-release listing, rescheduling notices, and management reports.

Master Production Schedule. The *master production schedule* (MPS) is the action input. The MPS provides the end-item schedule, which drives MRP. In most firms using MRP, the MPS has weekly time buckets (periods) extending 52 weeks (a year) into the future. The master production schedule is normally updated once a month. As days go by during the month, the MPS gets increasingly out of date. That is, toward the end of the month some of the scheduled quantities turn out to be out of line with orders that marketing is actually booking. The MPS might be updated during the month to correct for this or other problems. More often, the master production schedule is left as it is, and inaccuracies are dealt with via the weekly MRP runs, by component-parts schedule changes, and by activity control measures on the shop floor.

Item Master File. The item master file is a file that holds control data (rather than acting as driver, as the MPS does). The control data in the file includes on-hand stock balances and planning factors for every component item. The on-hand balance is simply the quantity that is supposed to be in storage. The stock balance may be verified by periodically counting what is in storage. The balance is kept up to date by posting transactions (receipts, issues, new items, etc.) to the master file.

The on-hand balance is necessary in the MRP computation of planned orders. In an MRP run, gross requirements for a given part are computed. Then projected

FIGURE 6–6

MRP Computer Run

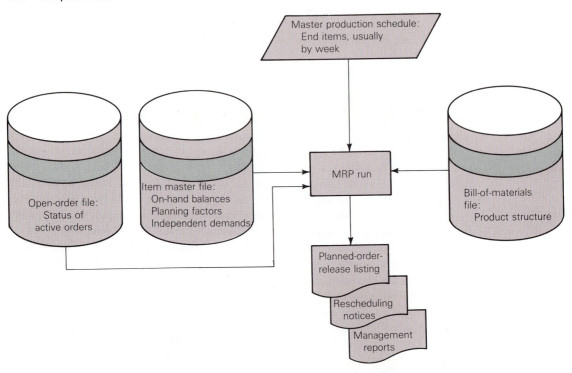

stock balance is computed to see if there is a need for a planned order. A need exists if there is a negative projected stock balance, as indicated by the following formula:

$$\text{Projected stock balance} = \text{Previous stock balance} - \text{Gross requirements} + \text{Planned and scheduled receipts}$$

In the earlier example of the caterer, stock balances were not introduced. The example is changed and extended here to allow for an on-hand stock balance. Since a caterer would hardly use computerized MRP, the salami is changed to salamite, a hypothetical chemical compound. MRP is usually run weekly rather than daily in industry, and the gross requirements for salamite are changed from a 14-day to a 14-week schedule.

EXAMPLE 6–5

MRP for a Chemical Product

Let us say that 220 units of salamite is the on-hand balance at time zero (the start of week 1). The gross requirements are as shown in Figure

FIGURE 6–7

MRP Computations—Salamite

A. MRP display

Lead time (LT) = 2

Week		1	2	3	4	5	6	7	8	9	10	11	12	13	14
Gross requirements				100			320					80		510	
Scheduled receipts															
Projected stock balance	220	220	220	120	120	120	0 −200	0	0	0	0	0 −80	0	0 −510	0
Planned order releases					200					80	510				

(Planned order releases: LT = 2 from week 4 → week 6; LT = 2 from week 9 → week 11; LT = 2 from week 11 → week 13)

B. MRP with fixed order quantity

Q = 500

LT = 2

Week		1	2	3	4	5	6	7	8	9	10	11	12	13	14
Gross requirements				100			320					80		510	
Scheduled receipts															
On hand	220	220	220	120	120	120	300 −200	300	300	300	300	220	220	210 −290	210
Planned order releases					500							500			

6–7, but with the days changed to weeks. The projected stock balance in week 3 is:

$$\text{Projected stock balance} = \text{Previous balance} - \text{Gross requirements} \\ + \text{Receipts} \\ = 220 - 100 + 0 = 120$$

The positive projected stock balance, 120, shows that there is no need to order. The projected balance stays at 120 in week 4 and 5. In week 6 the projected balance is:

$$\text{Projected balance} = 120 - 320 + 0 = -200$$

Now the projected stock balance is a negative 200. In MRP a negative stock balance is covered by a planned order. The planned order quantity is 200, and the planned order release is two weeks earlier, since the planned lead time (LT) is two weeks.

Figure 6–7, part A shows MRP results as a four-row display. This type of display might be available for viewing on a video display terminal or as printed output. (The scheduled-receipts row, empty in this example, is explained later.)

In the display we see that the projected stock balance goes negative in week 6. The projected shortage is shown as −200. The planned order release for 200 in week 4 prevents the negative stock balance, and so the −200 is crossed out and replaced by a zero balance. Recomputation of the stock balance in week 6 to account for the planned receipt of 200 is as follows:

$$\text{Projected stock balance} = \text{Previous balance} - \text{Gross requirements} \\ + \text{Receipts} \\ = 120 - 320 + 200 = 0$$

The projected balance goes negative twice more, in weeks 11 and 13. Ordering actions will correct for the negative balances, so the negative quantities are crossed out and replaced by zeros.

Planning factors stored in the item master file include lead time, lot size, safety stock, and so forth. Unlike stock balances, the planning factors in the file seldom need to be updated. In Example 6–5 the lead time (LT) of two weeks would have been extracted from the item master file. A lot size, Q (for quantity), may also be found in the file. The following modified example provides for a fixed order quantity, Q, instead of ordering just what is needed, as in Example 6–5.

EXAMPLE 6–6

MRP for a Chemical Product—Fixed Order Quantity

Assume that salamite is produced in a vat that holds 500 units. Even though 500 units is not likely to be the net requirement, it seems economical to make the salamite in full 500-unit batches. The excess is carried as a stock balance.

Figure 6–7B shows the MRP computation results for the case of a fixed order quantity, Q, equal to 500 units. A negative stock balance of 200 is computed for week 6. The computer plans an order two weeks earlier (since LT = 2). The order is for Q = 500, the fixed order quantity, which brings projected stock balance in week 6 to +300. The balance drops to 220 in week 11 and to −290 in week 13. The computer acts to prevent the negative balance in week 13 by planning an order for 500. The planned order release is in week 11, which eliminates the negative balance in week 13 and leaves 210 units to spare.

Clearly, fixed order quantities compromise the MRP goal of low or zero inventories. The debate about what order-quantity policy to use is reserved for the next chapter.

Bill-of-Materials File. A *bill of materials* (BOM) is not the kind of bill that demands payment. Bill of materials is industry's term for a list of component parts that go into a product—often a structured list. The BOM names the parts detailed on the engineer's blueprints.

Like the item master file, the computerized BOM file serves as a control file for MRP processing. In an MRP system, BOMs must be accurately structured and must be stated in terms of the same end items that are found on the master projection schedule.

The bill-of-materials file keeps track of what component parts and how much of each go into a unit of the parent item. In each MRP run the computer (1) calculates planned order timing and quantity for the parent item, (2) consults the BOM file to see what goes into the parent, and (3) translates the parent's planned order requirement into gross requirements for each component. For example, if there are three of a certain component per parent, the gross requirement for that component will be equal to triple the planned order quantity for the parent. (The grand total of gross requirements for the component would also include requirements derived from other parents and from independent demands.) A continuation of the salamite example demonstrates the role of the BOM file.

EXAMPLE 6–7

MRP for a Chemical Product with Two Levels

Planned order releases for salamite have been calculated. The computer consults the BOM file to find what goes into salamite. The first ingredient is a chemical compound known as sal. There are two grams of sal per unit of salamite. Therefore the planned order quantities for salamite are doubled to equal gross requirements for sal. This simple translation of salamite orders into sal needs is shown in Figure 6–8. (The salamite data come from Figure 6–7B.)

Projected stock balances and planned order releases may now be calculated for sal, as is shown in the figure. Then the computer does the same for the next ingredient or component of salamite.

FIGURE 6–8

BOM Reference Data and Scheduled Receipts in MRP

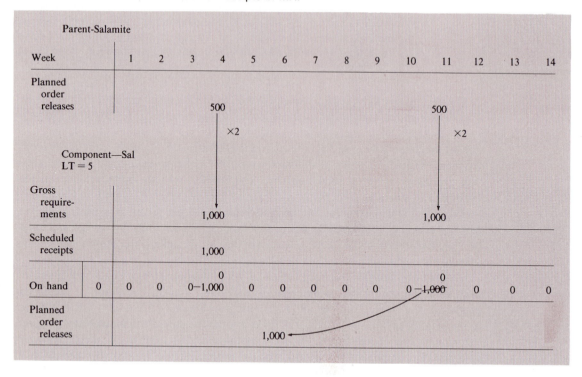

The bill-of-materials file in which salamite and sal might be found could have a structure similar to Figure 6–9. Salamite is shown as a level 2 subassembly that goes into a level 1 subassembly, which combines with other level 1 items to form an end item. The MRP processing sequence begins at the end-item level (zero) and works its way down through the BOM structure. The figure shows that sal is made from level 4 parts (or perhaps subassemblies that are made from level 5 parts).

It is cumbersome to develop the master production schedule and to forecast MPS requirements if there are a large number of products in the BOM file. For that reason, some engineering BOM numbers may be judiciously combined into modular bills, and phantom bills (or superbills). Engineering bills are often streamlined in this and other ways at the time that MRP is introduced into an organization. The process is referred to as restructuring the bills of materials.[5]

---

[5] See Joseph Orlicky, *Material Requirements Planning* (New York: McGraw-Hill, 1975), "Product Definition," ch. 10 (TS155.8.O74).

FIGURE 6–9

Sample BOM or Product Structure

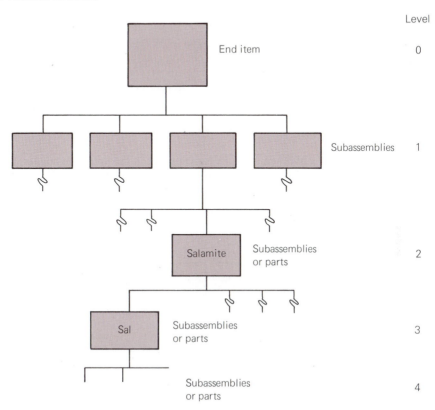

Scheduled Receipts and the Open-Order File

Another material requirements planning factor is scheduled receipts. Returning to Figure 6–8, we see that in week 4 there is a scheduled receipt of 1,000, which is the gross-requirement quantity in week 4. A scheduled receipt represents an **open order** instead of a **planned order.** In this case, an order for 1,000 has already been released, for make or buy, and it is scheduled to be delivered in week 4. Since the lead time is five weeks, it appears that the order would have been released, opened, and scheduled last week.

Let us examine the events that change a planned order into a scheduled receipt. The following sketch is a partial MRP for sal as it might have appeared on Monday morning this week.

		1	2	3	4	5	6
Gross						1,000	
Scheduled receipts							
On hand	0	0	0	0	0	0 −1,000	0
Planned order releases		1,000					

Any time a planned order release appears in the first time bucket, action to schedule the order is called for. Therefore, sometime on Monday, the scheduler writes up a shop order to make 1,000 grams of sal. The effect of scheduling the order is to remove it from the planned-order-release row and to show it as a scheduled receipt, as is shown below:

		1	2	3	4	5	6
Gross						1,000	
Scheduled receipts						1,000	
On hand	0	0	0	0	0	0	0
Planned order releases							

Next time the computer runs the MRP program the scheduled receipt for 1,000 grams will be included. The order is shown as a scheduled receipt each week until the shop delivers the 1,000 grams. (But the order could get canceled or changed in quantity or timing. Also the shop may produce more or less than the planned quantity of 1,000 grams.)

Referring back to Figure 6–6, we see that computer processing for MRP makes use of an *open-order file*. The file holds data on open orders (scheduled receipts). Each time a scheduler releases a shop order or a buyer releases a purchase order, the order is recorded in the open-order file. (Alternatively, item master file records may contain fields indicating if there is an open order for a given item.) When orders are received (or canceled), the order is closed and removed from the file.

In MRP computer runs, open orders are evaluated as follows: Timing and quantities of planned order releases are calculated in the usual fashion (based on the projected stock balance going negative). The open-order file is checked to see if quantities and timing are still correct. A given open order may still be needed, but perhaps a week later or earlier or in a different quantity. Or perhaps the order is no longer needed at all. The computer issues **rescheduling notices,** which highlight the difference between present requirements and open orders. If the open order is overstated, the shop scheduler or buyer will often ignore the rescheduling notice and allow the order to be completed early or in a quantity in excess of current need, because rescheduling every time there is a new requirement would be too disruptive for the suppliers or shops doing the work.

Regenerative and Net Change MRP

In many firms MRP computer runs are weekly; a total **regeneration** of material requirements is performed, generally over the weekend. A few companies regenerate every two or three days or even daily. An alternative to regeneration is **net change MRP.** Net change computer software is designed to update only the items that are affected by a change in quantity or timing for a related item. Since all part numbers need not be regenerated, net change saves on computer time.

Distribution Requirements Planning

Traditionally finished goods inventories in distribution centers have been planned independent of manufacturing: The distribution centers use reorder points, which randomly trigger orders from the manufacturing plants. It makes more sense to fit distribution requirements into master production schedules, a procedure known as *distribution requirements planning* (DRP).

There are various approaches to DRP, but one sound approach is to centralize the planning of distribution requirements. Some of the key steps are:

1. Central planning sends history-based demand forecasts (usually weekly, for perhaps a year into the future) to each distribution center.
2. Each distribution center manager adjusts the forecasts, based on local factors. Any known large orders or expected demand surges resulting from product promotions are added to the forecast.
3. Forecasts are returned to central planning and totaled: The master scheduler uses the totals as the basis for developing the master production schedule. Some of the requirements will probably be for lower-level components needed in the distribution centers as service parts. In that case, the totals bypass the MPS and are added directly to gross requirements for the component when the next MRP run is made. This was explained in the earlier discussion of "independent demands for component parts."

Under DRP, requirements are based on actual forecast needs, not just shelf replenishment. Thus, inventories may be cut even as service to customers improves. The manufacturing side of the business operates better as well, because the MPS may be developed based on long-term projections rather than sudden demands from distribution centers who find out that shelf stock is low.

DRP may be broadened to include planning warehouse space, shipping loads, stock picking, and other distribution activities. The broadened form of DRP is sometimes called distribution *resource* planning.

Other MRP Features

More advanced examples of MRP processing are included in the chapter supplement. The examples demonstrate other MRP features, including:

Multiple parents

Scrap allowances

Independent demands for component parts

Safety stocks

Computer program packages for MRP, which are widely available, allow for these and other features. The computer must be able to find where a component part goes into more than one parent (multiple parents) and consolidate requirements. Scrap allowances may be handled by increasing the planned-order-release quantity by the usual or expected scrap loss amount, but not increasing the scheduled-receipts amount. That is, order extras, but do not expect them to be received (in usable condition). Independent demands for component parts anywhere in the product structure are separately forecast; then they are added to parent-item demands to equal gross requirements. Safety stock is expressed as a minimum stock balance (greater than zero). Most MRP packages allow safety stocks to be entered as planning factors in the item master file. (But some authorities feel that component safety stocks are undesirable in MRP; see the chapter supplement.) The computer package not only processes new orders based on the latest planned requirements; it also has access to an open-order file so that rescheduling notices may be printed for those open orders that need adjusting.

The computational steps in MRP processing may now be summarized, with inclusion of the "other" MRP features:

1. Compute gross requirements, by time bucket. At level 1, gross requirements extend downward from the MPS. At lower levels, gross requirements in a given time bucket equal outside independent demand plus planned-order-release quantities for the parent parts. The quantity extended downward from the parents is multiplied by the **quantity per** (often one).

2. Compute needs for planned orders by detecting negative projected stock balance: old balance plus receipts minus gross requirements, minus safety stock (if any). This is done one time period at a time, beginning with the first.

3. Compute planned order quantity. A planned order is needed to cover a negative projected stock balance. A planned order release *for at least that amount* is needed. Fixed order quantities or other order-batching policies may result in planned order quantities larger than net requirements. A **scrap allowance** also makes the planned order quantity larger than the negative projected balance.

4. Compute planned-order-release timing. The planned-order-release time is computed by subtracting the lead time from the time period in which the positive net requirement occurs. Where this computation and those in numbers 2 and 3 (above) affect an open order, a rescheduling notice (changing open-order quantity or timing) is issued.

5. Convert planned orders to open orders. Time passes, and planned orders move toward the first time bucket. When a planned order is in the current period (first time bucket), inventory planners may *open* an order. That is, the planned order is converted to an open (active) order. The open order is processed by purchasing if it is a buy order, and by production scheduling if it is a make order. The next MRP run then deletes the planned order and shows its quantity in the *scheduled-receipts* row, properly offset for lead time.

ROP/Shortage List (Pseudo-MRP) System

Steps 1, 2, and 3 of the preceding list of MRP processing steps constitute what is known as **bill-of-materials explosion.** Many companies were doing BOM explosion—but for only one time period into the future—for 20, 30, or 40 years prior to the advent of MRP. The BOM explosions could be done manually (with stock balances on index cards) or using simple tabulating equipment.

Some companies still do this, perhaps on a computer, and they may refer to it as MRP. It is not. Simple BOM explosion does not produce *planned* orders, because it does not go far enough into the future to allow for the necessary planning lead time. Instead, old-style BOM explosion yields a **shortage list.** The shortage list shows shortages of items in the next time period. Expediters try to chase down the parts on the shortage list.

In nearly all of these systems, reorder point is the primary inventory system, and the shortage lists, produced by BOM explosion, are a backstop. That is, ROP puts enough of most items into the storeroom and BOM explosion reveals shortages of the few items that the ROP has failed to provide. The term, ROP/shortage list, is a suitable descriptor.

Maintaining Valid Schedules

By one estimate, as of mid-1981, there were about 8,000 MRP-using companies in the United States.[6] Most of those MRP users profited from it, even though they were missing out on a key potential benefit of MRP: maintaining valid schedules.

---

[6] Oliver W. Wight, *MRP II: Unlocking America's Productivity Potential* (Williston, Vt.: Oliver Wight Limited Publications, 1981) p. 75 (TS161.W5x).

Rescheduling.   An easy-to-obtain benefit of MRP is having component-part orders planned by computing requirements from parent-item requirements. This is a big improvement over planning orders by reorder points. But after a component-part order is planned and launched, many of the planning factors begin to stray off course.

Lead time estimates turn out wrong. This can happen when machines break down, delivery trucks are delayed, goods are damaged, the power fails, and so forth. If one such incident delays the arrival of one part number out of, say, 100 that go into an end item, then the schedules for all of the remaining 99 are thrown off.

A second planning factor that can go wrong is quantities. You plan for 1,000 of the component part, but 200 are ruined or don't pass quality inspection. The order may be on time but short. The other 99 part numbers going into the end item are affected by the shortage.

A third factor is customer requirements. The master production schedule, which drives MRP, is partly actual customer orders and partly forecast orders. The forecasts will be off by some amount, and customers will also change their minds about actual orders. Customers may ask for more or for earlier or later delivery. So the MPS changes, throwing off all component orders.

Finally, your own engineering staff is continually tinkering with product designs and issuing **engineering change notices.** These change the component parts that go into end items. How may valid schedules be maintained in the face of all these changes? First of all, up-to-date information about changing conditions must be fed into the computer regularly. If a component part order is completed late or short, the stock balance in the item master file will be short of what was planned. The next MRP run will therefore see the need to issue **rescheduling notices.** Engineering changes fed into the bill of materials file also may trigger rescheduling or other notices.

If MRP is to be effective, the using company must learn to react cautiously to the rescheduling notices coming out of the computer. As one expert puts it, "To let the computer automatically reschedule all parts to the same degree of lateness deprives the user of [the chance] to focus attention on the lagging part and correct the impediment in its schedule by alternative routing, subcontracting, multiple setups, flowing, or other corrective measures."[7] In other words, try first to meet the schedules; if it cannot be done, *then* reschedule all related parts in the bill of materials. A good deal of human analysis, decision making, and action comes before rescheduling is done. The computer does not reschedule, and it does not even recommend rescheduling; it simply issues the notice, and people take it from there.

As we have seen, material requirements planning routinely calculates valid schedules for new orders. MRP also routinely issues rescheduling notices for open orders (released in an earlier week), but the validity is less certain, because getting valid up-to-date change information into the computer files is not easy to do, and many MRP users do it poorly. Rescheduling notices are only as valid as the change data.

---

[7] R. L. Lankford, "Scheduling the Job Shop," *1973 Conference Proceedings, American Production and Inventory Control Society,* pp. 46–65.

Production Activity Control. But let us assume that the rescheduling notices are valid. The notices are acted upon by shop schedulers for made items and by buyers for purchased items. New due dates and quantities go out to the shop and to supplier companies. Then the fun begins. How do the new dates and quantities get acted upon by shops and suppliers that have the jobs already in progress based on the old schedule, perhaps already set up on a machine or in transit on a truck? Many other orders are out in the shops, each requiring work in from one to as many as 20 or 30 work centers. The jobs may spend time in queues (waiting lines) at each work center. Which jobs get run first? How can you even *find* a given job in order to change its priority?

The answer is that there must be a system whereby the work centers receive up-to-date information about job priorities and the "system" (e.g., a computer) is fed data on each move from one work center to another. It is called a **production activity control system,** and it is an adjunct to the MRP system. Production activity control is out of the realm of inventory planning, and therefore the topic is reserved for a later chapter. It is sufficient to note here that probably the majority of the 8,000 MRP users in the United States (as of mid-1981) had only a basic bare-bones MRP system in operation. That is, the system could plan new orders and reschedule old ones. Most did not have the computer-based production activity control routine in full operation, though some have reasonably good manual or partly computer-based systems.

Benefits of MRP[8]

In the narrow sense the chief benefit of MRP is its ability to keep schedules valid, as was discussed above. Valid schedules have broader benefits for the company as a whole. These include the following, roughly in order of importance.

1. Improves on-time completions. In industry this is called *improving customer service,* and on-time completion is a good way to measure it. MRP companies typically achieve 95 percent or more on-time completions. This benefit is highly likely, because with MRP, completion of a parent item is less likely to be delayed for lack of a component part.

2. Cuts Inventories. Yes, we can have our cake and eat it too. The remarkable feature of MRP is that inventories can be reduced at the same time as customer service is improved. Stocks are cut because parts are not ordered if not needed to go into parent items. Typical gains are 20 to 35 percent.

3. Provides data (future orders) for *planning work center capacity requirements* for many periods into the future. This benefit is attainable if basic MRP is enhanced by a **capacity requirements planning** (CRP) routine. Chapter 10 tells more about CRP.

4. Improves direct labor productivity. There is less lost time and overtime because of shortages and less need to waste time halting one job to set up for a shortage-

---

[8] Some of the figures on MRP gains come from Oliver W. Wight, *MRP II: Unlocking America's Productivity Potential* (Williston, Vt.: Oliver Wight Limited Publications, 1981), chap. 4 (TS 161.W5x).

list job. Reduction in lost time tends to be from 5 to 10 percent in fabrication and from 25 to 40 percent in assembly. Overtime cuts are even more dramatic, in the order of 50 to 90 percent.

5. **Improves productivity of support staff.** MRP cuts expediting (fire-fighting), which allows more time for planning. Purchasing can spend time saving money and selecting good suppliers. Materials management can maintain valid records and plan inventory needs better. Production control can keep priorities up to date. And foremen can plan capacity and assign jobs better. In some cases fewer support staff are needed.

6. **Provides a foundation for manufacturing resource planning,** sometimes called MRP II. MRP II extends requirements planning into the financial end of the business, as is explained next.

MRP II

In MRP II, cash flow is treated almost like materials. The master production schedule is exploded into component parts requirements as usual. Then the planned order releases are converted into cash outflows using unit cost data. Normal delays for paying the bills are fed into the computer, and the output is a prediction of future cash outflows. The outflows include payments to suppliers and shippers for bought items and payment of wages, power consumption, and so forth for made items. Budgeting is simple under MRP II. Cash outflows may be projected, by expense category and by organizational unit, out to a year or more. The projection may be refined into budgets.

Projected cash outflows also are valuable for predicting excessive needs for cash, for example, in periods when purchasing is heavy. Knowing this in advance, the finance department has time to shop around for favorable loans and lines of credit and to consider other options for raising short-term cash. The master production schedule (or shipping schedule) is also converted to cash inflows for projected goods sold. Past rates of payment on accounts receivable are used to project the timing of cash inflows for goods sold. Different price structures may be simulated to see the projected effects on profitability.

As to overall impact, Wight states that "MRP II results in management finally having *the numbers to run the business.*" And with "everybody using the same set of numbers," MRP II serves as "a company game plan." [9] Despite its logic, MRP II is costly and complex. Thus far, its use is limited.

KANBAN

MRP-using manufacturers in North America had thought that MRP was the ultimate. MRP is based on carefully integrated planning of all items. Furthermore, MRP reacts

---

[9] Oliver W. Wight, *MRP II: Unlocking America's Productivity Potential* (Williston, Vt.: Oliver Wight Limited Publications, 1981), p. 58. (TS161.W5x)

to changes, so that planning is dynamic. Then along came *kanban* (pronounced kahn-bahn), a Toyota invention. Kanban proved to have some attributes that MRP lacks. Chief among these are:

1. Kanban is simpler and cheaper, since it is manual not computerized.
2. Kanban ordering is triggered by actual usage rather than planned usage, so that planning (demand forecasting) errors are sidestepped. Kanban is said to be a *pull* system in which the parts user "pulls" materials from parts supply and production points as needed. MRP is a *push* system in which a schedule *pushes* materials forward; the schedule is based on average planned usage rather than actual usuage.

The Toyota kanban system has limitations that make it impractical in many cases. Before considering the limitations, let us examine the workings of the kanban system.

Toyota Dual-Card Kanban

Kanban is a Japanese word meaning *card*. There is a pair of cards, henceforth called kanban, for each part number. One is the conveyance, or C-kanban, which goes with each delivery container full of a given part number. The other is a production, or P-kanban, which signals the need to produce more of the part number. The kanban states the part number, location, and container capacity.

Figure 6–10 is a sketch of the flow pattern of containers and kanban between user and producer areas. The following is the sequence of events:

1. A user in need of parts takes an empty container and its C-kanban to the producer area.
2. The user attaches the C-kanban to a full container and detaches the P-kanban. The user takes the full container and its C-kanban back to the user area for immediate use.
3. The detached P-kanban goes into a dispatch box (behind other P-kanban) in the producing area. The P-kanban in the box are production orders. The producer makes the part numbers in order of arrival of their P-kanban in the producing area. The P-kanban is attached to the container as each container is filled.

The producer area is a shop or work center that makes different part numbers, perhaps for different users. Similarly, the user area uses different part numbers from different producer areas. "Producer area" may be broadly interpreted to include outside suppliers as well as work centers in the same factory complex. Thus, to correctly interpret Figure 6–10, you need to visualize a vast network of user-producer pairs. Two rules of the Toyota kanban system are:

1. No production takes place without a P-kanban.
2. Each container holds the exact quantity stated on its kanban, no more, no less.

The first rule enforces production discipline; it prevents producers from making parts just to keep busy. The kanban goal of immediate usage permits no buildup of parts not requested.

FIGURE 6–10

Dual-Card Kanban

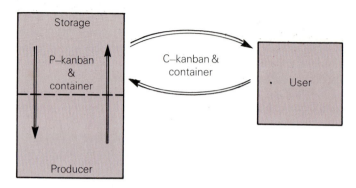

The second rule enforces rigid stock control discipline. There are as few as two containers per part number in the system, i.e., one in use and one empty needing to be refilled by the producer. Usually there are a few more containers than two. A few more full containers may be in the system as safety stock. The safety stock (or buffer stock) is there in case the producer is not able to provide a needed part right away. Still, the total quantity of a given part number is small; at Toyota the convention is that the total should be less than one-tenth of a days' usage for Toyota's own containers (not those of its suppliers). Thus, each container gets used and filled 10 times or more per day.

Special Kanban Features and Limitations

The shop foreman adds containers with kanban if the producing area is experiencing difficulties. The foreman removes containers when the producer area is running smoothly. In fact, the Toyota scheme calls for removing containers to the point where the producer area begins to have problems in keeping up. The idea is to cut buffer stocks to the point where *problems are exposed.* Exposed problems are then attacked and solved, either on the spot or over time. By this device, productivity is increased. That is, a solved problem eliminates a certain recurring type of work stoppage for all time so that output is higher per unit of input. Thus, Toyota's version of kanban is not only an inventory system but also a *productivity improvement* technique.

A limitation of kanban is that it works only for part numbers that are used regularly. If a part is not used at least every day, it is planned some other way, perhaps by reorder point or MRP. Certain other items, e.g., large or costly ones, may also be withheld from the kanban system.

Other limitations—actually prerequisites—have to do with the extensive preparation, engineering, training, and discipline that are needed to make kanban work.

Chief among these is setup time reduction. It must be possible for the producing area to set up fast to make a given part number. Setup time is further explained in the following chapter.

Single-Card Kanban

Toyota's dual-card kanban system is in use in only a small number of end-product manufacturing companies (plus a number of their supplier companies). A variation, single-card kanban, is much more widely used. (The first U.S. plant to employ kanban was Kawasaki's motorcycle plant in Lincoln, Nebraska. They began using single-card kanban.)

The technique makes use of conveyance kanban but not production kanban. Production (or purchase) is *scheduled* instead of "pulled" with P-kanban. See Figure 6–11. The schedule tries to push out the parts even when usage slows, but in practice some kind of stop signal—or denial of storage space—would halt production before too long. With no P-kanban, it is not so easy to employ the Toyota scheme of removing kanban to expose and solve problems in order to improve productivity.

Single-card kanban appears to be a version of the two-bin system: Order more when you see that there is only one container of parts left. But, by following these characteristics of Toyota kanban, single-card kanban improves upon the two-bin system:

1. Standard containers are used.
2. The quantity per container is exact, so that inventory is easy to count and control.
3. The user area keeps very few full containers on hand, usually only one or two; user areas therefore avoid the confusion of excess inventory.
4. With inventory buildups not allowed at the *user's* end, responsibility for inventory control is pushed back to the *producer's* end. This single point of responsibility eliminates "finger-pointing."
5. The quantity per container is small—several containers per day are likely to be used up—which also helps keep the user area uncluttered.
6. Producers make the parts and fill the containers in small lot sizes, which keep inventory low at the producer end.

The C-kanban serves as the signal to go get to another full container. The usual procedure is for the worker using the parts to remove the C-kanban from a just-emptied container and place it in a collection box. Another shop worker or a material control department worker regularly picks up all kanban from the collection boxes and takes them to producer areas to retrieve full containers. Sometimes a signal other than a card is used. At a Kawasaki motorcycle engine plant in Japan, a user and a producer area communicate by painted golf balls rolling down a pipe. When more of a certain number are needed, the user rolls a golf ball down the pipe, and the ball's color tells which part number is needed.

FIGURE 6–11

Single-Card Kanban

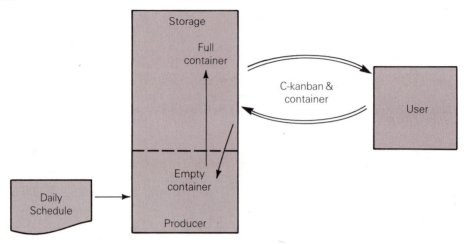

SELECTING THE RIGHT INVENTORY SYSTEM

Is material requirements planning better than reorder point? Is kanban better than MRP? The answer to both questions is, it depends. Probably it depends on several factors, but let us bundle most of those factors into two: The first is ease of associating parts requirements with end-item requirements. That factor is the basis for Figure 6–12. In the figure, the inventory-planning approaches presented in this chapter are related to the "ease of association" factor. The second factor is item cost, which is not shown in the figure but is included in the discussion.

In the fifth position in Figure 6–12 is reorder point, which is least effective in controlling inventories. ROP is widely used nevertheless, especially in companies with many different part numbers and with a long lead time between purchase or fabrication of component parts and delivery of the end product. Time unravels careful plans and calculations, so such companies do not try to plan and calculate component parts requirements. They just replenish the shelves using reorder point. However, shelf replenishment is generally too costly if the item cost is very high.

MRP is fourth in Figure 6–12. MRP controls inventory more tightly inasmuch as orders for component parts are tied to production schedules for parent items. MRP companies have learned how to meet the challenge of long lead time and complex product structures. The computer keeps abreast of the many unpredictable events that cause original plans to get out of date during lead time. The MRP system issues change notices to keep schedules valid. In other words, computer power is harnessed to keep parts requirements reasonably associated with end-product schedules.

But MRP is schedule-driven—a push system. That means that parts are bought

FIGURE 6–12

Manufacturing Inventory Systems

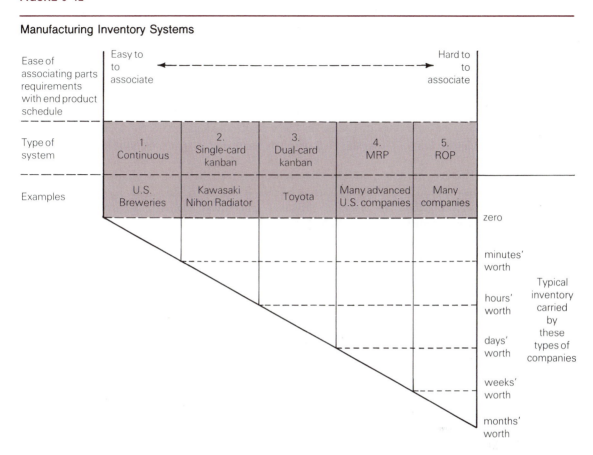

and made according to the schedule. This goes on even when the using work center is experiencing a work stoppage and cannot use those parts right away. Dual-card kanban, number 3 in the figure, solves that problem. When the using work center is "down," it ceases to send C-kanban back to the producer area, which stops the movement of P-kanban and stops the production of the part. Kanban can yield especially high payoffs if the item cost is high. (However, very high-cost items perhaps should be personally managed by a planner rather than by a set of procedures.)

Kanban's ability to keep production closely in tune with usage *could* be approximated by an MRP system: Just ask the system to issue change notices more often, perhaps once or twice an hour. But the effect is that the shops would receive a continual stream of orders countermanding previous orders. MRP professionals call it excessive "system nervousness." Such are the limitations of a push system—as compared to the simplicity of the kanban pull system.

Single-card kanban, second in Figure 6–12, is less effective than dual-card kanban. Note that the figure is arranged by ease of associating parts requirements with end-product schedules, not by inventory system effectiveness. Dual-card kanban, the system that controls inventories most tightly, is in the middle. A company (or certain shops within a company) may not *need* the dual-card version if their part-to-end-product linkage is clean and simple. That might be true if the lead time is short, the product structure is simple, the end product schedules do not change much, or the end products always take the same parts (no options). In such cases, a push system for production can work reasonably well. It requires that production schedules for component parts be changed periodically (at least daily) to match actual parts usage. But there are not many schedules to change in these environments.

Even when the producer is another company, it may be simple to adjust the schedule. For example, at Kawasaki in Lincoln, Nebraska, a buyer places a phone call every morning to TRI-CON Industries, their supplier of motorcycle seats. The buyer asks TRI-CON either to deliver a few more or less than the daily schedule calls for. TRI-CON, located only two miles away, delivers two or three times a day in quantities small enough that the seats may be delivered right to the production line from the receiving dock. Other suppliers located farther away—many in Japan—also deliver to a schedule, but usually in larger quantities (for reasons of freight economics). Quantities received are too large to be sent right to the line. Kawaski stores them. Then the station where a given part is used signals the need for more parts by putting a C-kanban into a small collection box; a material control worker comes by every two hours to pick up C-kanban and deliver more parts to the users.

Inventory control is tightest—potentially down to a few minutes' worth—in case number 1 in Figure 6–12. This is the type of company in which parts usage and end product schedules match up almost perfectly day in and day out. In petroleum refineries, the fuels and lubricants that emerge as end products associate well with known quantities of crude oil and additives that go in. In breweries, full cans of beer coming out match can-for-can with empties going in (at least as long as the production line does not jam and damage cans).

Planning component parts is so simple in these repetitive or continuous production situations that it hardly matters what inventory system is used. A simple ROP system is often good enough.

The real problem is not planning orders but planning deliveries and shipments. At Anheuser-Busch in St. Louis, a nearly continuous stream of trucks of empty cans is unloaded. Arrivals are planned well enough that the average inventory of empty cans is only about two hours' worth.

STRATEGIC EFFECTS

Inventory planning has always played a key role in operations strategy and business strategy as well. But prior to MRP and kanban the strategic effects were as much negative as positive: Safety stocks help the firm to meet the desired level of customer service, but safety stocks tie up capital that could be invested profitably elsewhere.

Material requirements planning allows the company to further improve customer service and the overall competitive position of the company. At the same time, MRP cuts inventories and capital tied up. Manufacturing resource planning (MRP II) extends the simulation power of MRP directly into financial and business planning. A new strategy of integrated business planning is a potential benefit of MRP II.

Kanban has MRP-like effects. Furthermore, Toyota's dual-card kanban technique includes a productivity improvement feature: removing kanban to expose and solve production problems. But kanban does not have MRP's simulation powers. It seems likely that certain companies in Japan and in the United States will link kanban with MRP II. In the resulting system, parts ordered could be partly kanban and partly MRP driven, and financial planning, pricing, and so forth could be simulated by the regular MPS explosion techniques of MRP II. The strategic advantages of such a system should be impressive.

SUMMARY

Planning to have the right materials at the right time is a matter of timing. The oldest inventory-timing approach is replenishment by reorder point (ROP) methods.

In the perpetual system, stock is replenished when it drops to a reorder quantity, the ROP. The ROP equals enough stock to cover average demand over an average lead time, plus some safety stock to protect against nonaverage surges in demand or lengthy lead times. In one approach, safety stock is set to equal demand variability (standard deviation of demand) times a safety factor, which is a measure of the desired customer service level. Safety stock may also depend on various other factors relating to supply and demand protection and certain internal goals. An ROP system may be run visually or using stock records.

In a periodic replenishment system, reorders are at fixed intervals rather than when stock gets low.

Replenishment is suitable for the independent demand situation found in retailing and wholesaling. In manufacturing, where component part demands are dependent on parent-item requirements, there is a better way: computer-based materials requirements planning (MRP). In MRP a master production schedule for many periods into the future is exploded into gross requirements for all component parts in the bill of materials. Present stock balance for each part is found in the item master file, and projected stock balances are calculated for each future period. Where a negative projected balance is found, the computer back-schedules (offsets for lead time) in order to plan an order in a quantity large enough to prevent the negative balance. Scrap allowances, independent demands for service parts, and safety stocks can be included in MRP processing. MRP also issues rescheduling notices for parts already in process.

The unique feature of MRP is not the explosion of bills of materials for items in the master schedule. That was done years before MRP was developed (the method produced a shortage list of items that the reorder point system failed to provide enough of). What is unique is that MRP plans far enough into the future to allow the necessary lead time to obtain the parts.

MRP is effective in that it plans for materials to arrive when needed for use, not just to refill a stockroom shelf. Furthermore, MRP can provide better information for capacity planning in the work centers and for financial and marketing planning at high levels in the company. The extension of MRP into financial planning is called manufacturing resource planning or MRP II.

A Japanese inventory system called *kanban,* meaning card, has MRP's goal of providing the right parts when needed for use. But in kanban "when needed" generally refers to the right hour or day, whereas in MRP it is usually the right week. In kanban, a card called a conveyance kanban signals the need for more parts at a using area; in some companies that card serves to release a second card called a production kanban, which triggers an order to produce more of the parts. Since the cards do their signaling only when the user truly needs more parts, kanban is said to "pull" parts from stock or production areas. In contrast, MRP is a schedule-based system that "pushes" parts forward even if usage has temporarily been halted by a problem. Thus, kanban provides even tighter control than MRP, and without the need for a computer.

ROP systems are found especially where it is hard to associate parts requirements with a master schedule. MRP becomes feasible in the dependent demand case, and it is effective in keeping schedules valid where the linkages from component parts to the end product schedules are long or changeable.

When parts and end products are more closely associated, kanban is feasible and effective. Finally, when parts requirements follow end-item schedules almost exactly, as in repetitive and continuous operations, ROP may be good enough, because the real problem is shipping and receiving, not planning orders.

Companies that use ROP must suffer the consequence of money tied up in inventories that sometimes are the wrong items. MRP improves competitive position and reduces capital requirements. Kanban does that and also can solve problems and improve productivity. A merger of kanban with MRP II could strengthen total business planning from the component part level all the way to the top.

REFERENCES

Books

Fuchs, Jerome H.   *Computerized Inventory Control Systems.* Englewood Cliffs, N.J.: Prentice-Hall, 1976 (TS160.F8).

Love, Stephen F.   *Inventory Control.* New York: McGraw-Hill, 1979 (HD55.L68).

New, Colin.   *Requirements Planning.* London: Gower Press, 1973 (TS160.N48).

Orlicky, Joseph.   *Material Requirements Planning.* New York: McGraw-Hill, 1975 (TS155.8.O74).

Plossl, G. W., and O. W. Wight.   *Production and Inventory Control.* Englewood Cliffs, N.J.: Prentice-Hall, 1967 (HD55.P5).

Schonberger, Richard J.   *Japanese Manufacturing Techniques: Nine Hidden Lessons in Simplicity.* New York: Free Press, 1982 (HD70.J3S36).

Wight, Oliver W.   *MRP II: Unlocking America's Productivity Potential.* Williston, Vt.: Oliver Wight Limited Publications, 1981 (TS161.W5x).

Periodicals (societies)

Journal of Operations Management (American Production and Inventory Control Society).

Journal of Purchasing and Materials Management (National Association of Purchasing Management).

Production and Inventory Management (American Production and Inventory Control Society).

REVIEW QUESTIONS

1. How can such operating resources as machines, space, and people be thought of as *inventory?*

2. Why is the ROP system considered to be a perpetual system?

3. Given a safety stock, what else is needed to arrive at a reorder point? Explain.

4. Contrast visual and records-based ROP.

5. To what extent can safety-stock determinations be computerized? Does it depend on type of industry? Explain.

6. Is the periodic system simpler or more complex than the perpetual system? Explain.

7. An inventory system breaks next week's demand forecast into requirements for materials. What else is needed to make this an MRP system? Explain.

8. Why is MRP associated with dependent demand?

9. What is the role of the item master file in MRP?

10. How does an open order differ from a planned order?

11. How does DRP improve on the usual way that distribution centers are managed?

12. Compare ROP/shortage list with ROP; with MRP.

13. What is the hazard in using the computer and MRP to reschedule whenever any manufacturing variables change?

14. How can MRP be helpful to marketing?

15. How can MRP be useful in cash flow planning?

16. How does kanban help keep a manufacturer from providing parts before they are needed?

17. How does Toyota use the kanban system to improve productivity?

18. Contrast the way that parts get produced in the dual-card and single-card kanban systems.

19. Why is it that the highly continuous or repetitive maker often does not need an inventory system that plans stocks tightly?

20. What is the difference between a "push" and a "pull" system?

PROBLEMS

1. The following is a list of inventory items that might be found in various locations in a hospital. For each item, pick what you feel are the two most dominant factors that should influence safety stock for the item. (Factors influencing safety stock may be found in Figure 6–3.) Also state whether you feel that the item should have a high, medium, or low safety stock, as measured in weeks' supply. Explain.

Toothpicks	Pillows
Disposable hypodermic syringes	Rare blood
X-ray film	Aspirin
Coffee cups (pottery)	Soap solution for mopping floors
Daily newspapers (for sale)	Prosthetic devices (artificial limbs)

2. A beer distributor reorders when a stock item drops to a reorder point. Reorder points include statistical safety stocks with the service level set at 95 percent. For PBR beer, the forecast usage for the next two weeks is 500 cases and the standard deviation of demand has been 137 cases (for a two-week period). Purchase lead time is one week (a five-day work week).
   a. What is the safety stock? How many working days' supply is it?
   b. What is the ROP?
   c. How many times larger would the safety stock have to be to provide 99 percent service to PBR customers? How many working days' supply does the 99 percent level provide?
   d. Statistical safety stock protects against demand variability. What two other factors do you think are especially important as influences on size of safety stock for this item, PBR beer? Explain.

3. Brown Instrument Co. replenishes replacement (service) parts based on statistical reorder point. One part is a 40-mm. thumbscrew. Relevant data for the thumbscrew are:

   Planned stockout frequency = Once per year
   Planned lead time = 1 week
   Forecast for next week = 30
   Batch size = 300
   Mean absolute deviation of demand = 25

   a. What is the reorder point? (Hint: Convert planned stockout frequency to service level.)
   b. What would the effect on ROP be if lead time were four weeks instead of one? Discuss the effect; don't try to calculate it.

4. An auto muffler shop reorders all common mufflers and the like once a week—on Tuesday mornings. (Rarely needed mufflers are not stocked.) Two of the biggest selling mufflers are muffler *A* and muffler *B*. Each is ordered if stock is below three, and enough are ordered to bring the supply up to 10. Under this reordering system the average inventory of each is about eight. It takes two days to replenish.

   A reorder-point policy with a service level of 90 percent is being considered as a replacement for the present policy. To see whether ROP would reduce costly inventories, the following data are provided:

	Muffler A	Muffler B
Item cost	$7	$39
Daily usage (average)	2	2
Standard deviation of daily usage	1.5	1.5

a. What kind of reorder policy is the present one? Are there names for it?

b. What safety stocks and ROPs would there be for mufflers A and B under a perpetual system?

c. Should the muffler shop go to a perpetual system? Stay with the present system? Devise a hybrid system? Discuss, including pros and cons.

5. One item in the storeroom has an average demand of 1,200 per year. Demand variability, as measured by mean absolute deviation, is 25 for an order cycle of one month.

a. If the desired service level is 90 percent, what is the statistical safety stock?

b. The item is bulky, costs over $1,000 per unit, and is bought from a variety of suppliers. What effects should these factors have on the safety stock? Explain.

6. Star City Tool and Die has been using a certain two-inch square metal insert at an average rate of 200 per five-day week, with a standard deviation of 125. Star City makes the inserts itself on its punch press. Only one day is needed to make more of the insert.

a. The insert is so critical that management wants the item to be available (in stock) 99.9 percent of the time. What is the statistical safety stock? What is the statistical reorder point?

b. The insert has been required for only the past six weeks, and it is inexpensive to make. Should these factors affect safety stock and reorder point? Explain.

7. Fuel oil is one source of heat in a Northern university. Average fuel demand in winter is 6,000 gallons per month. The reorder point is 6,400 gallons; the average lead time is two weeks; and the order quantity is 8,000 gallons.

a. How many orders are there in an average five-month winter season?

b. What is the demand during lead time? What is the safety stock?

c. Draw a graph showing three replenishment cycles for the fuel oil. Construct the graph so that:

(1) In the first cycle, delivery takes more than two weeks (with normal demand during lead time).

(2) In the second cycle, delivery takes less than two weeks (with normal demand during lead time).

(3) In the third cycle, lead time is average, but demand during the lead-time period is low.

Note: Since fuel-oil usage for heating is continuous (not discrete), your line showing actual usage should waver downward rather than follow a stairstep pattern downward.

8. One of the products manufactured by a maker of hand tools is a pliers. There are four parts, shown in the accompanying illustration. The parts are ordered by ROP/shortage list. At a given point in time the status of each part is as shown below; reference data are also given.

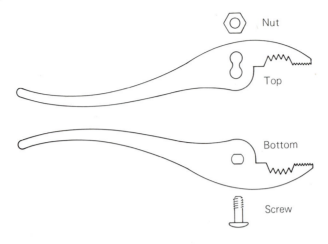

Item	Inventory status	ROP	Q	LT
Nut	8,000 on hand, none on order	4,000	10,000	10 days
Top	2,200 on hand, none on order	2,000	5,000	10 days
Bottom	3,800 on hand, none on order	2,000	5,000	10 days
Screw	1,700 on hand, 10,000 ordered two days ago	4,000	10,000	5 days
Pliers	2,700 on hand, none on order	3,000	3,000	5 days

a. For the given data, the following partial table lists required ordering actions and resulting inventory status. Complete the table (determine the correct ordering actions and inventory statuses for the blank cells in the table).

Item	Ordering actions	Inventory Status
Pliers	Shop order for 3,000 to replenish low (below ROP) stocks.	2,700 in stock 3,000 on order
Nut	Release 3,000 from warehouse for pliers shop order.	
Top		
Bottom		
Screw		

b. Inventory records (stock balances) do not have to be very accurate in the ROP/shortage list system. Explain why. Use the pliers example in your explanation.

9. Acme Wood Products Corp. makes wooden picture frames. One size is 10″ × 12″, and it is made with three finishes: oak stained, walnut stained and mahogany stained. The parts needed for final assembly and finishing are (for each frame) two 10-inch and two

12-inch wood pieces and four corner brackets. Inventory planning is by MRP. Lot sizes are 10,000 for wood parts and 5,000 for brackets.

a. Construct the BOM structure. You need not limit yourself to the given data.

b. What should go into the item master file? Be as specific as possible, given the above data. But you need not limit yourself to the given data.

c. Assume that for every oak-stained frame, two walnut-stained and three mahogany-stained frames are made. Also assume that gross requirements for 10-inch wood pieces in the next five weeks are: 0, 600, 0, 240, and 300. Compute all parent-item planned orders based on these gross requirements for the wood pieces (Work backward.)

d. Based on the gross requirements information from part c, compute the planned-order-release schedule for 10-inch wood pieces (no other item). Assume a current on-hand balance of zero and a lead time of one week.

10. The sketch below is of the two main parts of a transparent-tape dispenser: molded plastic housing and roll of tape. A master production schedule for the dispenser is shown below the sketch.

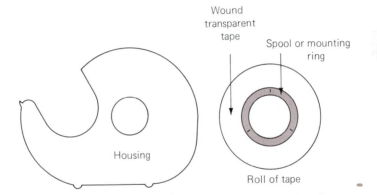

a. Draw a structured bill of materials for the tape dispenser. Include the main parts and one level of parts below that.

b. Assume that lead times are one week for the roll of tape and two weeks for the spool (mounting ring). Beginning on-hand balances are zero for the roll of tape and 3,000 for the spool. Draw the MPS, with MRPs for the roll of tape and the spool below it. (Do *not* include housing and wound transparent tape.) Compute gross requirements, scheduled receipts (if any), on-hand balance, and planned order releases for the roll of tape and the spool. Use lot-for-lot order quantities (*not* fixed order quantities). Show your results in the usual MRP display format.

c. Explain your entries or lack of entries in the scheduled-receipts row for both the roll of tape and the spool.

d. Assume that the rolls of tape are sold separately as well as being a component of the tape dispenser. Make up a forecast of independent (external) demand for rolls of tape for each of the seven time buckets. Merge your forecast of independent demand with the dependent demand from the parent item. Also assume an on-hand balance of 2,000 for the roll of tape and a scheduled receipt of 4,000 in week 2 for the spool. Recompute the MRPs as in part *b.* What could be the explanation for the *quantity 4,000* as a scheduled receipt in week 2?

11. Assume that you are employed by a company that makes a type of simple chair (you decide on the chair's design). MRP is to be the method of inventory planning for the chair.

    a. Draw a bill-of-materials structure for the chair. Briefly explain or sketch the type of chair.

    b. Develop an 8–10-week MPS for the chair.

    c. Develop MRPs for three or four of the chair's components, with the following restrictions:

        (1) Include level 1 and level 2 components (e.g., a chair arm might be level 1 and the raw material to make the arm might be level 2).

        (2) Make your own assumptions about lead times, order quantities, and beginning inventories.

        (3) (Optional—feature explained in chapter supplement): Include a safety stock for one of the parts.

        Your answer should be realistic; no two students should have the same answer.

12. Same as preceding problem, except that your product is a ball-point pen.

13. Select a product composed of fabricated parts (*not* a product referred to in the chapter explanation of MRP or in preceding MRP problems). In *one page,* develop an MPS for the product, plus a level 1 MRP for a major module and a level 2 MRP for a part that goes into the level 1 module. Include the following in your plan:

    a. An 8–10-week planning period.

    b. Draw the MPS at the top of your page, with time buckets for the two levels of parts MRPs lined up below it. The material requirements plans for the parts should include four rows: one for gross requirements, one for scheduled receipts, one for projected stock balance, and one for planned order releases. Make up the following data: realistic quantities for the MPS; beginning on-hand balances, lead times, and order quantities for each part, but make one order quantity fixed and the other lot-for-lot; and one or more scheduled receipts based on a previous order, already released (be careful about the timing and quantity of scheduled receipts).

    c. For level 1 and level 2 parts, calculate the timing and quantities of gross requirements, scheduled receipts, on-hand balance, and planned order releases. Display results on your charts.

        (*Optional for part c*—features explained in chapter supplement):

        (1) Include a safety stock for one of the parts.

        (2) Include a scrap allowance for one of the parts.

        (3) Include demands from an external source (rather than from parent planned order releases) for one of the parts.

14. Bills of materials are shown for two sizes of kitchen knife. There are two parts that are common to both knives: rivets and eight-foot wood bars. Also, a six-inch cut wood block is common to two different parents—handle, left and handle, right—for the medium knife. There are no parts of any kind on hand or on order now. Order quantities are lot-for-lot, rather than fixed. The master schedule for the next seven weeks is as follows:

					Week		
	1	2	3	4	5	6	7
Small knife	0	0	0	0	1,200	0	960
Medium knife	0	0	0	800	0	1,200	400

a. What is the first planned order release for rivets? Calculate quantity and week.

b. What is the total number of four-inch cut wood blocks that should be ordered to cover MPS demands in weeks 1 through 4?

c. How many eight-foot wood bars should be ordered in week 3?

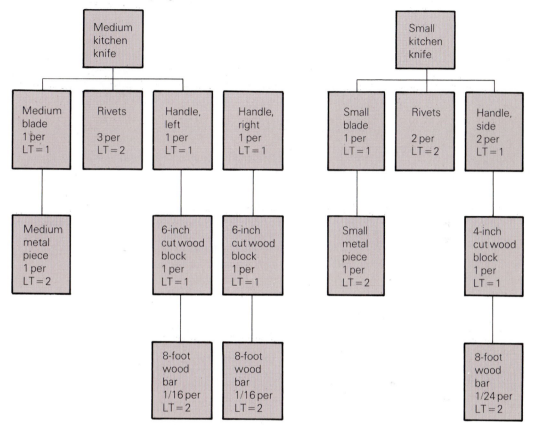

15. The matrix below shows partial MRP data for one component part. Lead time is two weeks.

	Week					
	0	1	2	3	4	5
Gross requirements		80	0	80	90	90
Scheduled receipts				70		
Projected stock balance	90					

a. If the order quantity is lot-for-lot (order just enough for requirements), when should there be a planned order release?

b. (*Optional:* see chapter supplement): If safety stock is five units, when should there be a planned order release?

c. (*Optional:* see chapter supplement): If there is a scrap allowance of 10 percent included in planned order releases, what should the planned order release quantity be? Assume zero safety stock.

16. The matrix below shows partial MRP data for one component part. Scheduled receipts are missing, as is the planned order release row. Lead time is 3 weeks. A fixed order quantity (rather than lot-for-lot) is used.

	Week					
	0	1	2	3	4	5
Gross requirements		80	80	90	90	90
Scheduled receipts						
Projected stock balance	190	270	190	100	10	80

What fixed order quantity is used? When is a scheduled receipt due in? In what period is there a planned order release?

17. A partial master production schedule and material requirements plans for a bicycle manufacturer are shown in the accompanying figure.
    a. Complete the calculations of gross requirements, projected stock balances, and planned order releases for handlebars and cut tubes.
    b. Recalculate the planned order release, given a safety stock of 20 for the handlebars and a scrap allowance of 3 percent for the cut tubing.

0-level
Master schedule—
26-inch bicycles

	Weeks							
	1	2	3	4	5	6	7	8
	40	0	50	0	0	60	0	60

1st level MRP
handlebars
1 per bicycle

			1	2	3	4	5	6	7	8
Gross requirements			40	0	50	0	0	60	0	60
Scheduled receipts					100					
Projected stock balance		80								
Planned order release										

LT = 4   Q = 100

From 1st Level MRP—24-inch Bike

From 1st Level MRP—27-inch Bike

2d Level MRP Cut tubes	Gross requirements		50					120	
¼ tube per handlebar	Scheduled receipts								
	Projected stock balance	190							
LT = 5 Q = 200	Planned order release								

18. Five companies produce and sell irrigation equipment in the same region of the country. Company A has a reorder-point system. Company B uses MRP, but only to "launch" orders. Company C has full closed-loop MRP. Company D uses MRP plus distribution requirements planning. And Company E has an MRP II system (including DRP). Discuss the likely competitive strengths and weaknesses of each company.

19. An American manufacturer of small power tools has a fully developed MRP II system. What strategic advantages might the company enjoy over its competitors?

20. The Japanese automotive industry has been the leader in implementing kanban. The electronics industry has been slower to adopt kanban. A chief reason is the high cost of automotive components compared with the low cost of many electronic components. Think about this and try to explain why. (Consider what costs of production kanban is capable of controlling.)

21. What is the right inventory system for each of the following cases? (see Figure 6–10). Explain your reasoning.

    Grocery store (groceries).

    Newspaper (newsprint).

    Furniture manufacturer (high quality wood and upholstered items).

    Washing machine manufacturer (a few models of washer).

    Dairy (milk).

    Farm machinery manufacturer (tractors, combines, balers, etc.).

22. Musicord, Inc., has a plant that manufactures reed instruments (clarinets, saxophones, etc.). The plant currently has a reorder point/shortage list system. The chief of production control wants to convert to material requirements planning. The plant manager is arguing for the Toyota (dual-card) kanban system.
    a. What are the main differences between the two proposed systems? Consider production scheduling and ordering, lot sizes, and deliveries.
    b. Discuss the difficulties involved in converting to MRP as compared with kanban.

23. A plant manufacturing telephone sets presently plans orders using material requirements planning. What sorts of storage and space-usage changes would be likely if the plant adopted single-card kanban?

24. A camera manufacturer has been using single-card kanban for a few years. The company is now considering upgrading to dual-card kanban, at least for some of its camera parts, like costly lenses. What would be the advantage in doing so?

25. How does Toyota's treatment of buffer stock (safety stock)—in the kanban system—differ from the classical safety stock approach? (Consider the way that each deals with variable output in the production process.)

26. A television manufacturer operates distribution centers in several cities in North America. The centers provide several models of TV sets and certain repair (service) parts to retailers. The factory manufactures its own circuit boards, but a certain percentage prove to be defective and not usable. The company has developed its planning beyond basic MRP. Based on the given information, which of the following would you expect the company to be using? Explain.

MRP II

ROP/shortage list

DRP

MRP, with some scrap allowances

Single-card kanban

TPOP

27. A Japanese maker of auto air conditioners uses dual-card kanban. What strategic advantages might that company enjoy over its worldwide competitors?

Supplement to Chapter 6

MRP Logic

In this supplement material requirements planning is more fully explained. The examples are more realistic than the simple cases presented in the body of the chapter, and MRP logic, including ways of treating certain special problems, is examined more closely.

Discussion centers on planning parts for bicycle manufacturing. The bicycle example is introduced in the first section and carried through three more topic sections:

1. BOM for a bicycle.
2. MRP processing—multiple parents and scrap allowances.
3. Independent demands for component parts.
4. Safety stock in MRP.

BOM for a Bicycle

Figure S6–1 is a partial bill of materials for a bicycle. There is enough room to show only a sample of the 300-odd component parts that would go into such a bicycle. The complete BOM breaks down into as many levels as are necessary to get to the *purchased* part. The breakdown of the front and rear wheels illustrates: Each wheel has a tire, an axle assembly, a rim assembly, 28 spokes, and 28 nipples (28 per wheel); and each spoke is fabricated (cut, bent, and threaded) from raw wire stock, 11 inches per spoke. The nipple is a second-level purchased part, and the wire is a third-level purchased item. Both spoke nipples and wire stock occur at two locations in the BOM; they would also occur in the BOMs for other bicycle sizes. Data-processing power is helpful in totaling the quantities needed for these kinds of parts that occur in multiple locations. (This is the BOM explosion process, which was done manually before computers and MRP were available.)

FIGURE S6–1

Partial Bill of Materials for a Bicycle

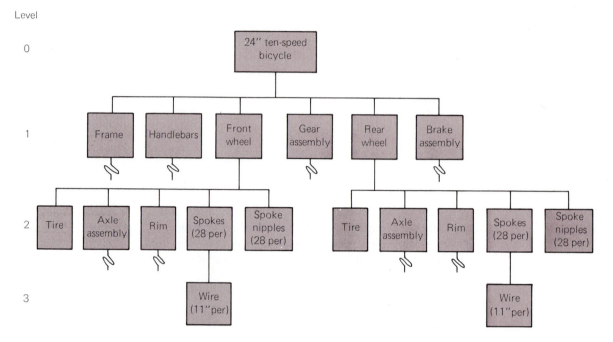

MRP Processing—Multiple Parents and Scrap Allowances

In this section, the **MRP** method of consolidating gross requirements for a component that has multiple parents is examined. Also, the method of including a scrap allowance is explained.

EXAMPLE S6–1

MRP Processing, Bicycle Spoke Nipples

Figure S6–2 shows the generation of gross requirements for spoke nipples and the translation of those requirements into planned order releases. In the figure, planned order releases for front and rear wheels are given for three sizes of bicycles, 20-inch, 24-inch, and 26-inch. Requirements for wheels would have been derived from master production schedules (level 0) for all bike models. Planned order releases for spoke nipples emerge after higher levels of **MRP** processing have been completed.

Figure S6–2 shows how orders for more than one parent are consolidated to become gross requirements for a next-lower-level part. The requirement for nipples in week 5 is based on $84 + 60 + 24 + 24 = 192$ wheels. At 28 nipples per wheel the gross requirement is $192 \times 28 = 5,376$. For week 6 the basis is $36 + 36 + 72 + 84 = 228$ wheels. The gross requirement is

FIGURE S6–2

MRP Generation of Planned Order Releases, Spoke Nipple Example

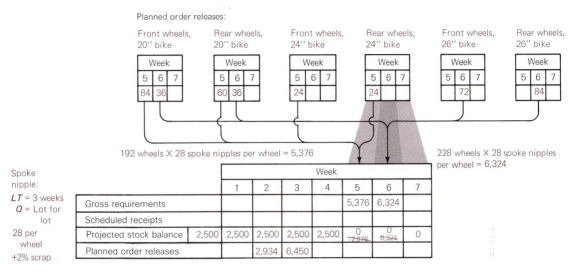

Planned order releases:

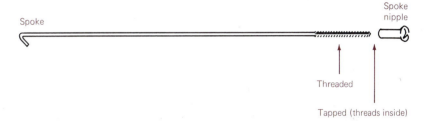

228 × 28, which equals 6,324. (Front-wheel and rear-wheel planned orders may be unequal, because there may be extra demands for one or the other as service parts, to make up for scrap losses, and so forth.)

The 2,500 nipples on hand at week 0 are projected to stay on hand (in stock) through four weeks. In week 5, 5,376 are needed, but only 2,500 are available; there is a projected shortage of 2,876. The possibility of a shortage triggers the following: The MRP program subtracts the purchase lead time (LT), three weeks, from week 5, giving week 2; an order must be released then to avert the shortage in week 5. The lot size is lot-for-lot, that is, no batching of orders. Therefore the quantity to be ordered is 2,876 plus 2 percent scrap allowance, which equals 2,934. The shortage of 6,324 in week 6 triggers a planned order in week 3. The quantity is 6,324 plus 2 percent for scrap, which equals 6,450.

Note the treatment of the 2 percent scrap factor: The planned-order-release amount includes the 2 percent so that the extra amount will be placed on order. Planned receipts do not include it, since you expect 2 percent to be scrapped.

Independent Demands for Component Parts

Independent demands for component parts may be entered into the item master file. The subset of **MRP** for handling independent demands is often called **time-phased order point** (TPOP). TPOP requires that the independent demands be forecast since they cannot be computed—no parent demands to compute from.

Independent demands may be forecast offline or determined by a computer subroutine. For example, the subroutine may project trends, perhaps with seasonal adjustments. Exponential smoothing could be used to save on past demand data storage. If exponential smoothing is used, the exponential smoothing projection for next period is also the forecast for periods 2, 3, 4, and so on, all the way out through the six-month or year planning horizon. Not very accurate, but exponential smoothing has not been touted as being accurate; rather, exponential smoothing is expedient. If most of the gross requirements for a component part are independent demands, then exponential smoothing should probably be avoided in favor of a multiperiod pattern-projection (trend, seasonal, etc.) method. Treatment of independent demands may be illustrated by a continuation of the bicycle spoke example.

EXAMPLE S6–2

Independent Demands, Bicycle Spokes

For a bicycle manufacturer, most of the gross demand for spokes would probably be dependent demands from planned orders for wheels. Some inde-

FIGURE S6–3

TPOP, Spoke Example

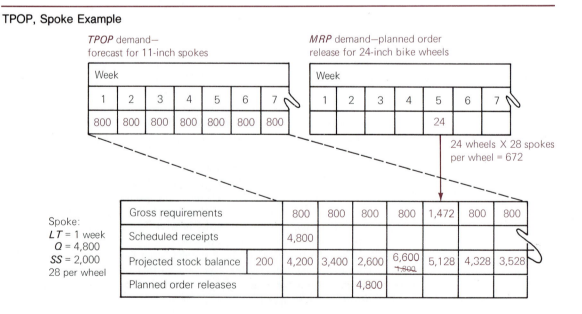

TPOP demand— forecast for 11-inch spokes

Week						
1	2	3	4	5	6	7
800	800	800	800	800	800	800

MRP demand—planned order release for 24-inch bike wheels

Week						
1	2	3	4	5	6	7
				24		

24 wheels X 28 spokes per wheel = 672

Spoke:
LT = 1 week
Q = 4,800
SS = 2,000
28 per wheel

		1	2	3	4	5	6	7
Gross requirements		800	800	800	800	1,472	800	800
Scheduled receipts		4,800						
Projected stock balance	200	4,200	3,400	2,600	6,600 ~~1,800~~	5,128	4,328	3,528
Planned order releases				4,800				

pendent demands are also likely. Examples are demands for spokes from parts wholesalers or from other bicycle manufacturers that do not make their own spokes.

It is not common for buyers to make their requirements known to producers very far in advance. This means that the producer—the bicycle maker in this case—must forecast. Let us assume that exponential smoothing is used to forecast independent demand for 11-inch spokes. The most recent forecast is for 800. That quantity, 800, is used as the forecast for the next 52 weeks. Figure S6–3 shows the 800-per-week source of independent demand at the upper left. At the upper right is the MRP source of dependent demand. The two sources of demand merge and comprise gross requirements for spokes. The independent-demand quantities, 800 per period, are extended directly; the single dependent demand of 672 is computed from the planned order of 24 wheels times 28 spokes per wheel. From this point on, MRP logic applies.

To summarize, *dependent* demands are *calculated* based on parent-item needs, while independent demands (TPOP) are *forecast.*

Figure S6–3 includes one other planning factor, a safety stock, SS. Safety stock is considered next.

Safety Stock in MRP

Safety stock is a cushion or reserve. It protects against unplanned surges in demand and other uncertainties.

Discussion in the body of the chapter indicated that safety stock is basic to reorder point (ROP) systems. It is not so basic to MRP. In fact, Orlicky recommends that safety stock generally be avoided at component levels in MRP. Instead safety stock may be provided at the MPS level; since component orders are linked to the MPS, safety stock in the master production schedule provides a balance of safety at all lower BOM levels. To add more safety stock at component levels tends to unbalance the protection. Worse, it tends to erode people's confidence in MRP, because people know there are component safety stocks to fall back on when MRP plans are not followed.

Still, MRP can be designed to allow for safety stock at component levels, and it appears that many MRP-using firms do carry some amount of safety stock for certain components. Safety stocks are most often used for purchased parts that have long lead times, that are hard to get, or that are obtainable from only one (perhaps unreliable) source.[1] Safety stock at the MRP component level may be illustrated by continuing the bicycle spoke example.

---

[1] According to Orlicky, these are legitimate exceptions, but they can be overused. Joseph Orlicky, *Material Requirements Planning* (New York: McGraw-Hill, 1975), pp. 78–80 (TS155.8.O74).

EXAMPLE S6–3

MRP Safety Stock, Bicycle Spokes

Referring back to Example S6–2, we see that Figure S6–3 shows the generation of gross requirements for spokes. The figure also shows the translation of gross requirements into planned order releases, with safety stock allowed for.

Safety stock (SS) is given as 2,000, and the stock balance is well below that at week 0. Being below the safety stock is a matter for mild concern but not alarm. After all, safety stock is not worth having around if it is never used.

The scheduled receipt of 4,800 in week 1 is to be expected in view of the low on-hand balance. That order for 4,800 spokes would have been released in an earlier period. Receipt of 4,800 and issue of 800 (to cover week 1 gross requirements) leaves a projected stock balance of 4,200. The balance drops by 800 in each of the next three weeks. That leaves 1,800 in week 4; since 1,800 is below the 2,000-unit safety stock, an order is planned for receipt in week 4. The lot size, Q, is 4,800, and lead time, LT, is one week. Thus, the planned order release is for 4,800 spokes in week 3, which keeps the projected stock balance from going below the safety stock of 2,000 in week 4.

How would safety stock ever be used when you plan always to be above it? *Unplanned* events will take care of that—unplanned events like hot orders booked too late to plan for.

Chapter 7

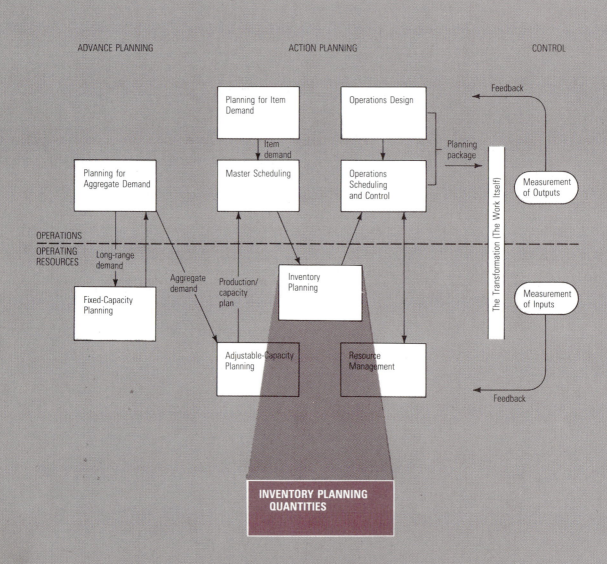

ADVANCE PLANNING   ACTION PLANNING   CONTROL

Planning for Item Demand

Operations Design

Feedback

Item demand

Planning for Aggregate Demand

Master Scheduling

Operations Scheduling and Control

Planning package

Measurement of Outputs

OPERATIONS
OPERATING RESOURCES

Long-range demand

Aggregate demand

Production/ capacity plan

Inventory Planning

The Transformation (The Work Itself)

Measurement of Inputs

Fixed-Capacity Planning

Adjustable-Capacity Planning

Resource Management

Feedback

INVENTORY PLANNING QUANTITIES

Inventory Planning—Quantities

Planning inventory quantities is called lot sizing. In the 1970s, leading Western experts were saying that lot sizing is not as important as inventory *timing*. You can order too much, or perhaps even too little, but still provide service to the customer or user. A late order, however, may be worthless. Now there is new interest in lot sizing—actually minimizing the lot size. We shall consider minimum lot-sizing concepts after first becoming familiar with basic lot-sizing economics.

LOT SIZING—BASICS

While there are many lot-sizing techniques, we shall focus on just three: lot-for-lot, part-period, and economic order quantity.

Lot-for-Lot

Lot-for-lot is the simplest lot-sizing approach. **Lot-for-lot** simply means no batching of orders into lots. In lot-for-lot, orders are frequent and order-processing costs are high, but planned inventory—and therefore planned carrying costs—are zero. From the narrow perspective of a single inventory item lot-for-lot seems uneconomical because of the high order-processing costs. But lot-for-lot has advantages for the system as a whole, especially as part of an MRP system. A collection of lot-for-lot orders tends to keep purchasing and fabricating workloads fairly even from period to period. Large lots or batches, on the other hand, tend to cause **lumpy workloads,** which call for greater peak capacity. An example will illustrate.

EXAMPLE 7–1

Lot-Sizing Effects on Workloads, Chain Manufacturing Example

The two parts of Figure 7–1 show contrasting effects of lot-for-lot versus batched orders. Figure 7–1A shows a smooth demand pattern for four styles of chain, and the smooth demand/production pattern is carried downward through the two levels to the purchased-part level (steel rod). Thus, the purchasing/receiving workload (for steel rod) is level and invariable; the workload for cutting two-inch pieces and five-inch pieces in the cutting work center is level and invariable; and the workload to make four styles of chain in fabrication work centers is level and invariable. The even workloads allow the work centers to run at nearly full capacity and without sporadic overtime.

On the other hand, order batching transforms smooth demands and even loads (workloads) into lumpy ones. Not only that, but the lumpiness is amplified downward through bill-of-materials levels. This is shown in Figure 7–1B. At the finished-chain level, batching results in lot sizes varying from 0 to 20. At the cut-piece level, lot sizes vary from 0 to 40. And at the steel-rod level, lot sizes vary from 0 to 60. With uneven workloads, sometimes the work center has too little to do, and at other times there is too much to do.

Part-Period

The **part-period algorithm** (PPA) is aimed at minimizing average cost per time period of ordering and carrying inventory.[1] While lot-for-lot has the benefit of minimiz-

---
[1] PPA is also known as the least-total-cost (LTC) method.

FIGURE 7–1

Lot-for-Lot versus Batched Ordering

A. Lot-for-lot ordering

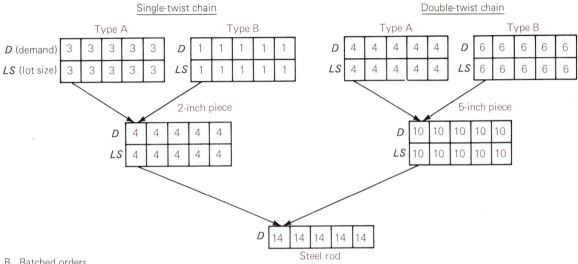

B. Batched orders

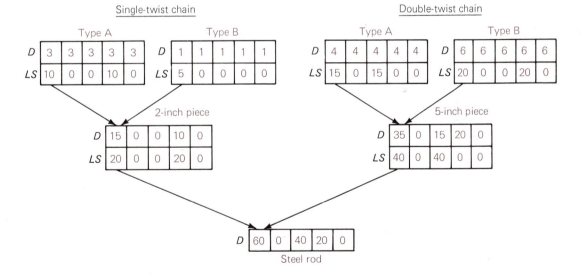

ing lumpiness in demand for a group of part numbers, PPA is concerned only with the inventory costs of a single part number. Like lot-for-lot, PPA operates well for lumpy as well as smooth planned demand.

PPA makes use of an **economic part-period** (EPP) factor. The EPP is the quantity that would make setup cost equal to carrying cost if the item is carried in stock for one period. The EPP computation is

$$EPP = \frac{S}{CC}$$

where

$$S = \text{Setup cost}$$
$$CC = \text{Carrying cost per period}$$

The part-period algorithm calls for successively computing cumulative part-periods of inventory carried for each lot-size option. The chosen lot size is that whose part-period total most nearly equals, but does not exceed, the EPP.

A part-period of inventory means one part carried for one period. (Part-period does *not* mean part *of a* period.) Twelve part-periods could be four parts carried for three periods or three parts carried for four periods or any similar multiple of 12.

PPA is demonstrated in the following example.

EXAMPLE 7–2

Part-Period Algorithm

Net requirements for the next six weeks for a certain manufactured part are: 20, 0, 20, 25, 35, 10, 10. If setup cost is $600 per lot and carrying cost is $10 per unit per week, what lot size is recommended by PPA?

Solution:

1. Calculate EPP.

$$EPP = \frac{S}{CC} = \frac{\$600}{\$10} = 60$$

2. Calculate cumulative part-periods carried, beginning with the first period, for each lot-size option. Stop and back up when EPP is reached. Calculations follow:

Trial lot size = Parts produced in period 1	Period (week)	Parts required	Part-period calculation	Cumulative part-periods
20	1	20	20 parts × 0 weeks carried = 0	0
20	2	0	0 parts × 1 week carried = 0	0
40	3	20	20 parts × 2 weeks carried = 40	40
65	4	25	25 parts × 3 weeks carried = 75	115

The first trial lot size is 20, which only covers the first period's demand. If 20 are made and used in period 1, there is zero inventory to carry. So 20 times zero equals zero part-periods. The second trial lot size covers a zero-demand period, and so there still are zero part-periods to be carried. The third trial lot size adds the demand for period 3. That demand, 20, will be covered by a lot of 40 that is produced in period 1. But the 20 units for period 3 are carried in stock for the entire first and second periods, which equals 20 times 2, or 40 part-periods to be carried. The fourth trial lot size adds another 75 part-periods, calculated by the same logic. The cumulative total becomes 115 part-periods. The EPP, 60, is exceeded by the 115 for the fourth trial lot size. Therefore, select the previous lot size, 40, which covers net requirements for weeks 1–3. The whole PPA procedure starts over again at week 4, and it yields a second lot size of 70, which covers net requirements for weeks 4 and 5. (Computation of this lot size is reserved as an end-of-chapter problem.)

The results of the PPA calculations are summarized below:

			Period				
	1	2	3	4	5	6	7
Net requirements	20	0	20	25	35	10	10
Planned order (lot size)	40			70			*

* Not computed because of lack of net requirements for periods 8 and beyond.

PPA, like lot-for-lot, provides for variable lot sizes, in which the calculated lot size is equal to projected net requirements. This is in contrast to fixed-lot-size methods, in which any excess in the produced lot must be carried in stock until the next requirement occurs.

The part-period algorithm yields a lot size that roughly minimizes the sum of setup and carrying costs.[2] Fixed lot sizes, such as the economic order quantity discussed next, *precisely* minimize that sum.

Economic Order Quantity

The **economic order quantity** (EOQ) is one of the oldest tools of management science; a basic EOQ formula was developed by F. W. Harris in 1915. The newer PPA method is actually an offspring of EOQ. And like PPA, EOQ is concerned with the inventory costs of a single part.

Unlike PPA, EOQ does not provide varying lot sizes to match varying projected demand. Instead, EOQ is based on the past *average* demand. Recall from Chapter

[2] Actually PPA does not *exactly* minimize these costs. The reason why not is explained in Joseph Orlicky, *Material Requirements Planning* (New York: McGraw-Hill, 1975), pp. 128–29 (TS155.8.O74).

6 that reorder point (ROP) is also based on past average demand, whereas MRP is based on future projected demand. EOQ and ROP have been a knife-and-fork-like pair.

Costs of Inventory.   The period inventory costs that EOQ seeks to minimize are of three types: order-processing cost, carrying cost, and item cost. Each is further explained below.

1. Order-Processing Cost.   In a given period of time, say a year, an item may be reordered once, or twice, or three times, and so on. If it is ordered once, the lot size is large enough to cover the whole year's demand; if it is ordered twice, a half year's demand is the lot size; and so on.

The costs of processing an order include clerical costs of preparing the purchase order or shop order. If it is a purchase order, costs of order expediting and processing the invoice are included; if it is a shop order, the main cost may be machine setup cost. As before, let S be the average cost of processing an order (S stands for *s*etup). Also, let Q (for *q*uantity) be the lot size and D be average annual *d*emand for a given item. Then, for the given item:

$$\frac{D\,\text{emand}}{Q\,\text{uantity}} = \text{Number of orders per year}$$

$$S\left(\frac{D}{Q}\right) = \text{Annual cost of processing orders}$$

Demand, D, could cover a period other than a year. For example, if D represents average monthly demand, then $S(D/Q)$ equals monthly cost of processing orders.

2. Carrying Cost.   Carrying cost is the cost to finance inventory and hold it in storage. Thus, carrying cost increases as number of units in storage increases. If an item is reordered infrequently in large lots, its carrying costs will be large; if it is ordered often in small lots, its carrying costs will be small.

The finance-cost component of carrying cost refers to the capital tied up in inventory. It is an interest or opportunity cost. More visible are the holding costs. These include storage facilities, insurance, inventory taxes, handling, and losses from shrinkage and obsolescence. Total carrying costs per period divided by total dollar value of inventory yields what is known as the annual inventory-carrying-cost rate, I. One rate may be set for all items carried in a given firm. To compute annual carrying cost for a single item, we need the unit cost, C, for the item. Then,

$$IC = \text{Cost to carry one unit for one year}$$

How much does I amount to? For many years, inventory experts quoted about the same figures. A typical figure is one from a 1955 handbook, which stated that the annual cost of carrying manufacturing inventory averages about 25 percent of the value of the inventory.[3] Since the interest rate in the current decade is much

---

[3] L. P. Alford and J. R. Bangs, eds., *Production Handbook* (New York: Ronald Press, 1955), pp. 396–97.

higher, today's firms are more likely to set I at 30–35 percent. In the same firm, I can be different for different classes of items.

In the 1970s some companies were persuaded that they should set I equal to the prevailing interest (or cost of capital) rate, which would be 10–15 percent at today's rates. The argument was that the carrying cost rate should include only those costs that truly vary with the quantity in the lot size; holding costs—rent, etc.—were viewed as being fixed and so should be left out. This argument now seems misguided. In recent years, the business press has been filled with stories castigating the shortsightedness of U.S. business managers. If decisions are to be made with longer-term results in mind, then surely the full costs of carrying inventory should be included in I.

Let us take a look at a few lot-sizing concepts that apply in the typical situation. (Nontypical cases are brought up later.) For any given lot size, Q, annual carrying cost equals annual cost to carry one unit times average units in stock, $Q/2$. Symbolically we have, for a given item:

$$IC\left(\frac{Q}{2}\right) = \text{Annual carrying cost}$$

Why is average inventory equal to $Q/2$? Because the average is halfway between planned maximum inventory, Q, and minimum inventory, zero (or half the sum of the maximum and the minimum). Safety stock pushes maximum inventory above Q, but by a constant amount that may be ignored in lot-size analysis.

3. *Item Cost.*   The annual cost to make an item, or the total price paid for it, is, in the most basic EOQ model, treated as a constant. You pay the same per year whether it is bought in small or large lots. Thus, the annual item cost, demand *(D)* times cost *(C)*, is omitted in basic lot-size analysis. Quantity discount effects are introduced later.

EOQ Calculations.   Since item cost is omitted, there are just two annual costs that vary with lot size: order-processing cost and carrying cost. The EOQ must minimize their sum. Algebraically the minimum occurs where

Annual order-processing cost $=$ Annual carrying cost

Substituting and collecting terms yields a basic EOQ formula, as follows:[4]

$$S\left(\frac{D}{Q}\right) = IC\left(\frac{Q}{2}\right)$$

$$Q^2 = \frac{2DS}{IC}$$

$$Q = \sqrt{\frac{2DS}{IC}}$$

---

[4] The EOQ formula may also be derived by calculus. The method is to differentiate total annual cost with respect to Q and to solve for Q at minimum total cost.

FIGURE 7–2

Graph of Annual Inventory Cost and Lot Sizes

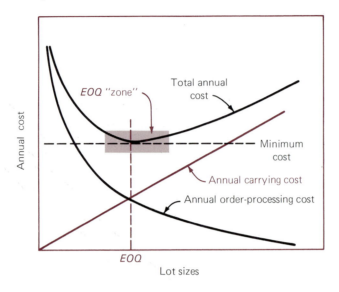

FIGURE 7–3

Effects on EOQ of Errors in Carrying-Cost Rate

Carrying-cost rate, I	Percent error in I	EOQ	Percent error in EOQ
True rate $= 0.10$		True $EOQ = 3.16\sqrt{\dfrac{2DS}{C}}$	
Erroneous rate $= 0.12$	20	Erroneous EOQ $= 2.89\sqrt{\dfrac{2DS}{C}}$	-8.5%
Erroneous rate $= 0.15$	50	Erroneous EOQ $= 2.58\sqrt{\dfrac{2DS}{C}}$	-18.4
Erroneous rate $= 0.20$	100	Erroneous EOQ $= 2.23\sqrt{\dfrac{2DS}{C}}$	-29.4

Sample calculation:

$$EOQ = \sqrt{\frac{2DS}{IC}} = \sqrt{\frac{1}{I}} \cdot \sqrt{\frac{2DS}{C}}$$

$$= \sqrt{\frac{1}{0.10}} \cdot \sqrt{\frac{2DS}{C}} = \sqrt{10} \cdot \sqrt{\frac{2DS}{C}}$$

$$= 3.16\sqrt{\frac{2DS}{C}}$$

Percent error in EOQ:

$$\frac{2.89 - 3.16}{3.16} = -8.5\%$$

Basic EOQ may be illustrated graphically. Figure 7–2 is a general form of the graph. It shows the EOQ at the minimum total annual cost, which is also where annual carrying cost equals annual order-processing cost. As has been discussed, annual order-processing cost decreases and annual carrying cost increases with larger lot sizes.

Notice that the minimum cost is shown in a shaded zone. In that zone, which is fairly large horizontally, total annual cost does not deviate much from the minimum. Thus, in a practical sense EOQ may be thought of as a zone or range of lot sizes, not just the exact EOQ quantity.

The practicality of EOQ is also enhanced by the square-root relationship between the four data inputs and the EOQ result: A large error in a data input translates into less error—the square root of the error, to be exact—in computing the EOQ. Figure 7–3 shows this effect for the carrying-cost rate, I. (The effect is similar for D, S, and C.) If the true rate is 0.10, but a rate of 0.12 is used, the error is 20 percent. For that 20 percent error in I, the EOQ error is only -8.5 percent; see the sample calculation at the bottom of Figure 7–3. For a 50 percent error in I, the EOQ error is -18.4 percent; and for a 100 percent error in I, the EOQ error is -29.4 percent. Thus, the data inputs need not be exact and one set of cost inputs may often be used for a group of like items.

Development of input data and use (and misuse) of basic EOQ are demonstrated in the following example of a small bookstore.

EXAMPLE 7–3

Economic Order Quantity, Bookstore

B. K. Worm, manager of Suburban Books, is thinking of purchasing best-selling titles in economic order quantities. Worm has assembled the following data:

Inventory on hand:	
Estimated average last year	8,000 books
Estimated average cost per book	$10
Average inventory value	$80,000
Annual holding cost:	
Rental, building and fixtures	$7,000
Estimated shrinkage losses	700
Insurance	300
Total	$8,000
Annual capital cost:	
Capital invested	$80,000
Interest rate	15%
Total	$12,000
Annual carrying cost (Annual holding cost + Annual capital cost):	
$8,000 + $12,000	$20,000

Carrying-cost rate, I (Annual
   carrying cost ÷ Average
   inventory value):
$20,000/$80,000   0.25
Purchase order processing cost, S:
   Estimate for preparation and
     invoice handling $4 per order

Now Worm has the cost data to calculate EOQs. He selects his biggest seller as the first book to be ordered by EOQ. It is *Gone with the Wind,* which is enjoying a burst of renewed popularity in Worm's store. The book in paperback recently sold at a rate of 80 copies per month and wholesales for $5 per copy. Thus, for the EOQ equation,

$$C = \$5 \text{ per unit}$$
$$D = 80 \text{ units/mo.} \times 12 \text{ mo./yr.}$$
$$= 960 \text{ units/yr.}$$

Then,

$$EOQ = \sqrt{\frac{2DS}{IC}} = \sqrt{\frac{2(960)(4)}{0.25(5)}} = \sqrt{\frac{7,680}{1.25}}$$
$$= \sqrt{6,144} = 78 \text{ copies/order}$$

The EOQ, 78 copies, is about one month's supply (78 copies/order ÷ 80 copies/month = 0.98 months/order); it is also $390 worth ($5/copy × 78 copies/order = $390 per order).[5]

Mr. Worm's assistant, M. B. Ainsworth, cannot resist pointing out to his boss a fallacy in this EOQ of 78 copies. M.B.A. puts it this way:

"Mr. Worm, I'm not so sure that *Gone with the Wind* is the right book to order by EOQ. The EOQ is based on last month's demand of 80. But demand might be 120 next month and 150 the month after. Also, the average carrying-cost rate, I, was based mostly on larger hardcover books, which cost more to store. Maybe we should use EOQ only on our stable sellers in hard cover. How about Webster's *New Collegiate Dictionary*?"

EOQ Variations

By the above example, we can see that successful use of basic EOQ depends on certain conditions. Some of the conditions are:

1. The item being reordered is about average in regard to cost of holding; for example, it has no unusual temperature, humidity, security, or bulk characteristics.

---

[5] The basic formula may be modified to directly yield an EOQ in months supply or in dollars worth:

$$EOQ \text{ (in months)} = \sqrt{\frac{288S}{ICD}}$$

$$EOQ \text{ (in dollars)} = \sqrt{\frac{2DCS}{I}}$$

2. Cost per unit is relatively fixed and known; quantity discounts are not provided for.
3. The whole quantity is delivered at one time; this is typical of purchased items, but it may not be true of made items.
4. Demand should be relatively stable, and without pronounced seasonality.

Variations on the basic EOQ model are available to offset some of these conditions. Three EOQ variations are considered next. They are: carrying-cost variations, quantity discounts, and economic manufacturing quantity.

Carrying-Cost Variations.   Two variations on the basic EOQ treatment of carrying cost warrant some discussion. In the first, annual carrying cost is based on maximum inventory rather than half of the maximum. The second is a variation in which capital cost and holding cost are treated separately rather than together.

In basic EOQ, annual carrying cost equals *IC* times *Q*/2; in a few situations it is more valid to use **IC times Q**. The former is proper when a large number of items share the same storage space. In that case, the total storage space needed is *not* based on the sum of the maximum inventory quantities (*Q*'s) for all the items, because it is unlikely that all the items will be at their maximums at one time. Instead some items will be low when others are high, and we may assume that space needs are equal to the sum of *half* the maximums (*Q*/2) for all items stored.

IC times *Q* is proper when only one item is to be stored in a given storage space. In that case, there must be space enough to hold the whole order quantity, *Q;* since the cost of the space is not shared with other items, annual carrying cost for the given item must be based on maximum inventory, *Q*. Examples of items of this kind are:

Sides of beef in a walk-in freezer.

Autos in a parking lot.

Fuel in a storage tank.

For special items like this, EOQ is derived from annual carrying cost $= ICQ;$ the result is

$$EOQ = \sqrt{\frac{DS}{IC}}$$

The second carrying-cost variation separates carrying cost into holding cost plus capital cost. Let *H* be equal to the cost of physically holding one unit in storage for one year. And let *iC* be equal to the capital cost per year,

where

$i =$ Interest rate (or discount rate or cost of capital)
$C =$ Unit cost of the item

Then,

Annual carrying cost $= \frac{1}{2}$ (Annual holding cost $+$ Annual capital cost)
$= \frac{1}{2} (H + iC)$

And

$$EOQ = \sqrt{\frac{2DS}{H + iC}}$$

This version of EOQ is a bit more precise than basic EOQ for two reasons: First, it allows an inventory planner to separately estimate H according to how costly it is to store an item or items. For example, items that are bulky or that need special storage for reasons of security or temperature and humidity control would cost more to hold in storage; a higher estimate of H could be used in EOQ calculations for such items. Second, this EOQ version properly provides for item cost, C, to affect only the interest cost of tied-up capital. (The simpler, but cruder, basic EOQ multiplies C by I, which is a factor that includes holding cost as well as interest cost.)

EOQ with Quantity Discounts.   In basic EOQ, periodic item cost is treated as constant and is omitted. The item cost for purchased items may, however, be variable—in steps—via quantity discounts. Annual item cost then becomes a relevant cost—along with annual carrying cost and order-processing cost. (optimum order quantity)

An EOQ may be calculated for each price, but the true economic order quantity is the amount that minimizes total annual cost, including item cost. A method for finding the true EOQ is:[6]

1. Calculate EOQs for each price. Reject any EOQ that is not within the allowable quantity range for the price used.
2. For feasible EOQs, calculate total annual cost.
3. Calculate total annual cost at each higher price break.
4. Pick the quantity having the lowest total annual cost. It is the true economic order quantity.

The following, a continuation of the bookstore example, employs the method.

EXAMPLE 7–4

EOQ with Quantity Discount, Bookstore

B. K. Worm, manager of Suburban Books, has applied basic EOQ to *Gone with the Wind*. But Worm didn't allow for quantity discounts. Popular Publications, Inc., offers the following price breaks for *GWTW:*

Quantity range	Price per copy
1–48	$5.00
49–96	4.70
97 up	4.40

Other data, from Example 7–3 are:

---

[6] This is not intended to be the most efficient algorithm. We can leave that matter to the computer programmers.

$$I = 0.25$$
$$S = \$4 \text{ per order}$$
$$D = 960 \text{ units/yr.}$$

Worm's first step in finding the true economic order quantity is to calculate EOQ's for each price:

$$EOQ_5 = \sqrt{\frac{2DS}{IC}} = \sqrt{\frac{2(960)(4)}{0.25(5)}} = \sqrt{6,144} = 78$$

Reject this EOQ; not within the allowable quantity range, 1–48.

$$EOQ_{4.70} = \sqrt{\frac{2(960)(4)}{0.25(4.70)}} = \sqrt{6,536} = 81$$

This EOQ is within the allowable range, 49–96. It is feasible.

$$EOQ_{4.40} = \sqrt{\frac{2(960)(4)}{0.25(4.40)}} = \sqrt{6,982} = 84$$

Reject this EOQ; not within the allowable quantity range, 97 and up.

The next step is to compute total annual costs for the feasible EOQ, 81, and also at the next higher price break, 97.

$$\text{Total annual cost} = \text{Annual order-processing cost} +$$
$$\text{Annual carrying cost} + \text{Annual purchase price}$$
$$= \frac{D}{Q}(S) + IC\left(\frac{Q}{2}\right) + DC$$

$$\text{Total annual cost}_{81} = \frac{960}{81}(4) + 0.25(4.70)\left(\frac{81}{2}\right) + 960(4.70)$$
$$= 47.41 + 47.59 + 4,512 = \$4,607.00$$

$$\text{Total annual cost}_{97} = \frac{960}{97}(4) + 0.25(4.40)\left(\frac{81}{2}\right) + 960(4.40)$$
$$= 39.59 + 44.55 + 4,224 = \$4,308.14$$

The true economic order quantity is 97, since its total annual cost, $4,308.14, is less than the total of $4,607.00 for a quantity of 81.

The cost-volume pattern for *Gone with the Wind* has been clarified. Figure 7–4 is Mr. Worm's rough sketch of the cost-volume pattern. The figure shows that annual order-processing cost drops smoothly and is not affected by the quantity discounts. The annual carrying cost line has two small bumps in it, one at each price break. The annual item cost plunges at each price break, and those effects are dominant in the makeup of total annual cost. The feasible EOQ of 81 at a unit price of $4.70 is not economical compared to the true economic order quantity of 97 at the $4.40 price break.

Economic Manufacturing Quantity. Basic EOQ is suitable for purchased items—an economic *purchase* quantity—because the whole lot is usually delivered at one time; this simplifies determining average inventory and, therefore, EOQ. When an item is made instead of bought, the quantity ordered is available in trickles as it comes off the production line. This complicates figuring average inventory, upon

FIGURE 7–4

Annual Cost Graph of Lot Sizes with Quantity Discounts

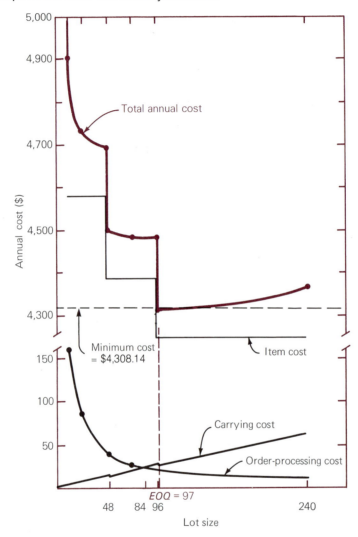

which annual carrying cost is based, and it results in a modified EOQ formula. The modification may be called an **economic *manufacturing* quantity,** EMQ, formula. (Note: Purchased items are sometimes delivered in trickles rather than all at once; if so, this EMQ modification would apply.)

The EMQ formula calls for one new term, the production rate, P. P is measured in the same units as D, the demand rate—typically in units per year. P must be greater than D in order for the demand to be covered. $P - D$ is the rate of inventory buildup. That is, you produce at rate P and at the same time use at rate D; the difference equals the rate of increase in stock.

If the lot is made in time, T, then

$$\text{Lot size} = Q = \text{Rate} \times \text{Time} = (P - D)\ (T)$$

Since Q is maximum planned inventory and $Q/2$ is average inventory,

$$\text{Average inventory} = \frac{Q}{2} = \frac{(P - D)(T)}{2}$$

The extra term, T, may be eliminated by substitution: The time needed to produce a lot, Q, is

$$T = \frac{\text{Quantity}}{\text{Rate}} = \frac{Q}{P}$$

By substitution,

$$\text{Average inventory} = \left(\frac{P - D}{2}\right)\left(\frac{Q}{P}\right) \text{ or } \left(\frac{P - D}{P}\right)\left(\frac{Q}{2}\right)$$

Now the EMQ equation may be derived in the same way that the basic EOQ equation was: by setting annual order-processing cost equal to annual carrying cost and solving for Q. The result is:

$$EMQ = \sqrt{\frac{2DS}{(IC)\,(1 - D/P)}}$$

Differences between basic EOQ and EMQ may be shown graphically. Figure 7–5A shows the general pattern of usage and replenishment for basic EOQ. It looks like a ripsaw blade: The vertical line represents the increase in stock that occurs

FIGURE 7–5

Basic EOQ and EMQ Replenishment Patterns

A. Basic *EOQ* pattern of instantaneous replenishment

B. *EMQ* pattern of noninstantaneous replenishment

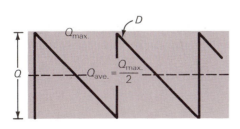

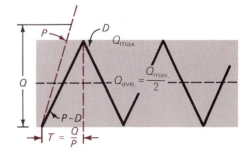

when the whole EOQ is received at one time (sometimes called *instantaneous replenishment*). The downward-sloping line is the average demand rate, *D*. Maximum quantity, $Q_{max.}$, is equal to *Q*, and average quantity, $Q_{ave.}$, is equal to $Q_{max.}/2$.

Figure 7–5B shows the general inventory pattern for EMQ. It looks like a crosscut saw blade: The upward-sloping solid line represents the rate of inventory buildup, $P - D$; *P*, the production rate, is shown as a dashed line for reference purposes. The downward-sloping line is the average demand rate, *D*. Maximum inventory, $Q_{max.}$, is not equal to *Q*; the stock level never reaches *Q*, because some of *Q* is being used up (delivered) as it is being produced. $Q_{max.}$ is, instead, equal to $(P - D)(T)$ or $(P - D)\left(\dfrac{Q}{P}\right)$, as was shown earlier, and $Q_{ave.}$ equals half of $Q_{max.}$

Note that for otherwise equal conditions, EMQ is larger than basic EOQ. Inspection of the EMQ formula shows this to be mathematically obvious, because the factor $1 - D/P$ in the denominator makes the denominator smaller and the EMQ larger. The logical reason is that with EMQ there is less stock to carry since part of *Q* is used as it is produced; with less to carry, it is economical to produce a bit more per lot.

Capturing Lot-Sizing Savings

Economic order quantity and its variations seem to offer clear-cut ways to reduce lot-size (cycle-stock) inventory costs. Here are a few obstacles in the way of capturing all of the savings:

1. Storage space may be fixed. Then if EOQs result in less inventory, expected savings on rent, storage racks, and insurance are not realized (but capital cost and inventory taxes *will* be reduced).
2. The business plan may limit the amount of money that can be invested in inventory. Then if EOQs result in more inventory, management may not allow the EOQs to be adopted.
3. The staff who process orders may be fixed. Then if EOQs result in fewer orders, expected reductions in order-processing cost do not materialize.
4. Setup staff size may be fixed. Then if EOQs result in fewer shop orders and setups, expected reductions in setup cost do not materialize.

These and other similar obstacles may be overcome over the long run. But it can be seen that capturing the savings is by no means automatic. It takes a lot of management effort.

Comparison of Lot-Sizing Methods

There are other, more elaborate lot-sizing algorithms besides those just discussed. There is neither the space nor the need to present all of them. The Wagner-Whitin algorithm,[7] for example, is theoretically important. (That is, it serves to expand the limits of our understanding of the reordering phenomenon.) Wagner-Whitin has been proven, on paper, to result in lower total inventory costs than a variety of other lot-sizing methods. But the costs are valid only if projections of demand are accurate. We have seen that forecasting accuracy drops as you go into the future; thus, a lot-sizing plan that depends on future projections will rarely achieve the economies predicted on paper.

This argument applies equally to other methods, including lot-for-lot, PPA, and EOQ. With computer power any of the methods can be run *dynamically;* that is, lot sizes can be recomputed every time demand projections change, which could be monthly, weekly, or even daily. The effect, however, is unstable planned lot sizes. That is, the lot size for a given planned order may be driven up and down by changing forecasting signals, which typically are not very reliable. The system becomes overly "nervous." For these reasons, many feel that one lot-sizing method is about as good as another. In practice, simpler methods—for example, lot-for-lot, PPA, and EOQ—are usually preferred, because they are more easily understood by operating-level people.

TOWARD PIECE-FOR-PIECE (LOTLESS) OPERATIONS

After being held in high esteem for 70 years, the economic order quantity concept is now being seriously questioned. Western industry that learned that Japanese companies tend to reject EOQs in favor of very small lots; the ideal is piece-for-piece, or lotless, production and purchase.

Severe overcrowding in Japan makes space expensive and holding costs high. Consequently, a calculated EOQ in Japan might be smaller than one in a similar case in North America. But that does not explain why the ideal should be a lot size of one, rather than the calculated economic order quantity.

Hidden Benefits

The reason is the discovery of hidden benefits of smaller lots. One is that smaller lots get used up sooner so that defective parts are caught earlier. This reduces scrap and rework and allows sources of problems to be caught and corrected quickly—*while the evidence of possible causes is still fresh.* A second benefit is that with small lots, factory floor space to hold inventory may be cut, and work stations may be positioned very close together. Then workers can see and talk to each other; learn each other's jobs, which improves staffing flexibility; and function as a team. A third benefit is that with small lots, tasks become closely linked. A problem at one work station has a ripple effect; subsequent work stations are soon starved of parts to

[7] H. M. Wagner and T. M. Whitin, "Dynamic Version of the Economic Lot Size Model," *Management Science* 5, no. 1 (October 1958), pp. 89–96.

work on. The work team considers one worker's problem the whole team's problem, and joint efforts to solve problems become common practice. A fourth benefit is that shop activity control is simplified, and costs of control of staff, forklifts, conveyors, racks, control systems, and so forth are reduced.

A new EOQ model incorporating the hidden costs could be developed. But what benefits (or negative costs) would you enter into the equation for such intangibles as better teamwork and commitment to solve problems? Perhaps because such a question has no easy answer, the Japanese have not attempted to create a new EOQ model. Instead, they simply set forth a goal of lotless operations and strive for it by making small improvements month after month, year after year.

Reducing Setup Cost

Cutting setup cost is a key to reducing production lot size. Setup cost is largely the cost of labor for such preparatory tasks as installing dies, jigs, fixtures, or cutting tools; tearing down, cleaning, sterilizing, and rebuilding food or drug equipment; and changeover to different parts and tools along a production line. Special setup crews, material handlers, crane and forklift drivers, engineers, plant maintenance workers, and quality control people can be needed to help set up to make the new part. It can take hours or days to complete one setup or production-line changeover.

When it costs a lot to set up, it is logical to make quite a few of the part before setting up again for a different part. The Western tradition is to accept that logic. The goal of lotless production does not allow acceptance of that logic. Instead, the idea is to attack the factors that add setup time so that it becomes reasonable to cut the lot size.

There is no standard formula for cutting setup time. It depends on the equipment and the products. Some kinds of machines may be outfitted with levelers, shims, stops, and locator pins that guide a die or tool into the precisely correct position.[8]

The goal is "single setup," which means a single-digit number of minutes to setup, i.e., one to nine minutes. If single setup is achieved, the next goal is "one-touch setup," which means virtually no setup time at all. How is it possible to have zero setup time? An example, this one an actual case, explains.

EXAMPLE 7–5

Setup Time Reductions, Motorcycle Frame Parts

At the Kawasaki motorcycle plant in Lincoln, Nebraska, parts for motorcycle frames are cut, bent, notched, and beveled from tube stock on punch presses. Then the cut pieces are welded into frames, painted, and assembled into motorcycles.

Typically, it took half a day or more in 1979 to set up a 60-ton punch

---

[8] See, for example, Yasuhiro Monden, "Part II: Production Smoothing at Toyota," *Industrial Engineering* 13, no. 9 (September 1981), pp. 22–30.

FIGURE 7–6

Punch Press Equipped for Quick Die Change

press to make a lot of a given frame part. Dies were heavy and had to be moved by a crane or forklift. Many adjustments and machine settings had to be made. Then a few trial pieces were punched out and inspected; more adjustments and more trial pieces. Finally everything was right for production.

In 1980 the presses were modified. Common roller conveyor sections were welded around the press to form a carousel-like surface as shown in Figure 7–6. Dies were shimmed up so that all were the same height. Various other small improvements were made. The new procedure was to line up 10 to 15 dies around the carousel conveyor first thing in the morning. During the day, dies were rolled into place one at a time, and each die produced a different part. The average die setup time: about nine minutes, which is single setup.

In 1982, setup time was cut essentially to zero, or one-touch setup. This was achieved by dissolving the punch press work center and moving small screw presses into the welding area. Each screw press was equipped with a permanent die that can make only one part number. Since the die is fixed, there is no die-insert time; only load, run, and unload time. In the new procedure, a welder makes a part on a screw press, welds it to another piece, makes another, welds it, and so forth. The punch press operator positions were eliminated since the welders could do the press work themselves.

Fast setup is not unknown in the West. A concept called "quick die change" (QDC) has been known for years in metal processing industries in North America.[9]

Reducing Order-Processing Cost

There is an order-processing cost in addition to the setup cost each time a different part number is to be produced. The kanban system (discussed in Chapter 6) is very simple and cheap compared with computer-based order scheduling and control. Kanban ordering along with quick setup makes small production lots economical.

Order-processing cost is the impediment to buying in small lots. Kanban sometimes is used for ordering purchased items as well as made items. Other ways of cutting purchase ordering costs include use of long-term purchase agreements with the same set of suppliers and dealing with nearby suppliers to cut shipping costs. With low purchase order-processing costs, it is economical to buy in small lots; piece-by-piece buying, however, is quite unlikely in view of the costs of transporting items from supplier to buyer.

---

[9] See John McElroy, "Quick Die Change Presses: QDC Is PDQ," *Automotive Industries* 162, no. 5 (May 1982), pp. 47–49.

The New Economics of Lot Sizing

Figure 7–2, earlier in the chapter, graphically shows the components of the economic order quantity. With small-lot or lotless production the graph changes a good deal. Figure 7–7 displays the effects.

Figure 7–7A is the classical EOQ graph. Part B is the modified graph showing wholesale changes. First of all, in part B the setup/order-processing cost curve has lost its steepness. The cost of ordering frequently in small lots is not much more than ordering seldom in large lots. Why? Because for made items, setup times have been engineered downward, first to single setup and finally toward one-touch setup. And for bought items, kanban has simplified ordering, and stable contracts with a few nearby suppliers have cut the costs of negotiations with suppliers.

The second major change is in carrying cost per year. The cost to carry one unit for one year is modest in part A; the modest rate is represented (arbitrarily) by a 30-degree angle. In part B the angle goes up to 60 degrees. The reason is the hidden costs of carrying inventory that have been discussed. These costs are most simply stated in the converse form, i.e., benefits of *not* carrying large lots; the benefits are: (1) catching defectives and correcting errors sooner and thereby reducing scrap and rework, (2) reducing floor space and moving workers close together so that

FIGURE 7–7

Modifying the EOQ Concept

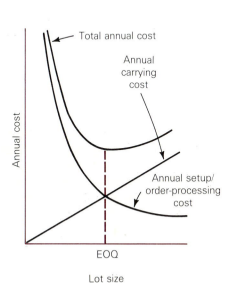

A. Classical EOQ graph

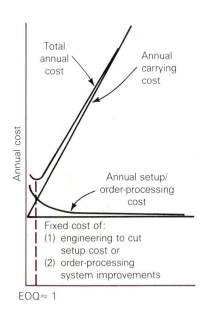

B. EOQ graph modified for small-lot or lotless production

they may interact, (3) linking processes together (because small lots cut time intervals between process stages) so that each problem is the joint concern of the whole team, and (4) simplified inventory management and costs of staff and equipment. The costs of staff, equipment, and floor space *should* be included in the carrying cost rate, *I*, in classical EOQ. But there may be a tendency for some companies to consider most resources on the factory floor—including computer terminals, conveyors, and storage areas—as production costs or factory overhead rather than inventory carrying costs. If so, the carrying cost rate would be understated. One more benefit of smaller lots that Western experts in MRP have been aware of is the avoidance of lumpy workloads in the work centers; this was discussed in the early part of the chapter.

The last modification in the EOQ graph is simply to place a layer of fixed costs underneath the variable costs. The fixed costs actually would not affect a given EOQ calculation; the fixed costs are shown only to avoid the biased impression that reducing setup/order-processing cost is free. It is not. Setup cost cuts are paid for by investing in engineering to reduce setup time. Order-processing costs are paid for by investing in system improvements like kanban and stable contractual relations for purchased items.

In sum, the modified concept of EOQ revealed by Figure 7–7 has two tenets: One is that lot sizes should be smaller than the classical EOQ, because classical EOQ neglects hidden benefits of smaller lots (and therefore understates the carrying-cost rate). The second is that the hidden benefits of smaller lots may be captured sooner if investments are made to keep reducing the costs of setup and order processing.

SUMMARY

The size of an order—the lot size—must be determined each time an order is planned. Several future orders for an item may be batched to save on setups and order-processing costs, but this increases inventory carrying costs (holding cost plus capital cost). Also larger batches of orders in the system tend to result in unbalanced workloads in the producing work centers. Therefore lot-for-lot (no batching) ordering has some advantages.

Some degree of batching is normal, especially where order-processing (setup) cost is high. The part-period algorithm (PPA) for lot sizing is suitable for minimizing the sum of annual order-processing and carrying costs, given a planned future demand schedule (as in MRP). Order-processing cost is mostly the cost of equipment setup for manufactured items; it is mostly the cost of processing purchase orders for bought items. Carrying costs include interest on capital tied up in inventory, plus physical holding (storage) costs. PPA lots vary in size from one order to the next; thus, PPA is a good method when demand is lumpy.

The more traditional lot-sizing method is the economic order quantity (EOQ). EOQ is like part-period except that EOQ is based on past demand *averages*. The EOQ is the quantity for which the sum of annual order-processing and annual carrying cost is minimized. Since the sum does not vary much on either side of the minimum cost point, the EOQ may be treated as a fairly wide zone. The basic EOQ formula requires four inputs: annual demand, order-processing cost rate, carrying cost rate, and unit cost of the item. These inputs are under a square root sign in the EOQ formula, and input estimating errors are dampened by the square root computation.

EOQ variations include: (1) special treatment of carrying cost for an item that requires unique storage, (2) separate treatment of the holding and the capital cost components of carrying costs, (3) allowing for item-cost effects in cases where quantity discounts are offered, and (4) including a production-rate input factor in cases where the lot is made and delivered at the same time as it is used up.

Classical EOQ concepts are being questioned today. Japanese manufacturers have enjoyed successes that seem attributable to a policy of producing and buying in much smaller quantities than the EOQ. The ideal is piece-for-piece or lotless making and buying.

The economics of lotless operations are obvious, but four hidden benefits of small lots have been revealed by the Japanese experience: catching and correcting errors sooner, reducing space for inventory so workers may be moved together for better teamwork, linking operations together (less inventory delay between steps) so that problems are faced jointly by work team members, and simplifying the inventory management system. Thus, it appears that lot sizes should be smaller than EOQs. By continually cutting setup/order processing costs, lot sizes can be cut economically to approach one unit.

REFERENCES

Books

Brown, Robert G. *Materials Management Systems.* New York: John Wiley & Sons, 1977 (TS161.B76).

Orlicky, Joseph. *Material Requirements Planning.* New York: McGraw-Hill, 1975 (TS155.8.O74).

Plossl, G. W., and O. W. Wight. *Production and Inventory Control.* Englewood Cliffs, N.J.: Prentice-Hall, 1967 (HD55.P5).

Prichard, James W., and Robert H. Eagle. *Modern Inventory Management.* New York: John Wiley & Sons, 1965 (HD55.P68).

Periodicals (societies)

Decision Sciences (American Institute for Decision Sciences).

Journal of Purchasing and Materials Management (National Association of Purchasing Management).

Production and Inventory Management (American Production and Inventory Control Society).

REVIEW QUESTIONS

1. Why does lot-for-lot tend to ease the problem of lumpy workloads?

2. Why are lumpy workloads a problem?

3. What is an advantage of PPA over EOQ?

4. What is a part-period?

5. How does S differ for made versus bought items?

6. Storage costs are semifixed. Should they be included as part of the variable costs of carrying stock? Explain.

7. Explain how order-processing/setup costs relate to lot size; how carrying costs relate to lot size.

8. Why omit item cost from basic PPA and EOQ? Why neglect the costs of carrying safety stocks?

9. In what sense is the EOQ a zone?

10. Why is there one more variable in the EMQ equation than in the EOQ equation?

11. Why does it take management effort to gain the economies promised by using EOQ?

12. What hidden benefits are there in following the Japanese preference for lotless piece-for-piece production?

13. Why is setup time reduction important?

14. How may order-processing costs be cut, thereby making it economical to buy in small amounts?

PROBLEMS

1. Door handles that fit onto several different models of refrigerator are scheduled by MRP. It costs $40 to set up for a production run of door handles, and carrying cost is estimated at $0.20 to carry one door handle for one week. Net requirements for the next five weeks for the door handles are:

800   500   100   100   600

    a. What is the economic part-period?
    b. Calculate the first lot size, using PPA.
    c. Carrying cost is often a rough estimate or an average that is figured for a variety of items. The estimate of $0.20 may not be accurate. Conduct a sensitivity analysis to see whether it makes much difference. That is, recalculate the PPA lot size by using a smaller and a larger carrying cost than $0.20 to see the effects on lot size.

2. In Example 7–2 a planned lot size of 70 is shown in week 4. Verify the correctness of that lot size by making the necessary PPA calculations.

3. The setup cost to produce an electronic component is $100. It costs about $1 to carry one unit for one period. Demands for the next four periods are 120, 80, 0, and 130. Calculate the first lot size using the part period algorithm. How many periods of demand does it cover?

4. Provincial government uses massive quantities of computer printer paper, which is bought centrally. The purchasing department calculates an economic order quantity based on an assumed carrying cost rate of 30 percent per year. A box of printer paper costs $40, it costs $60 to process an order, and annual demand is for 36,000 boxes of paper.
   a. What is the economic order quantity?
   b. The buyer finds that by ordering 10 percent more than the EOQ, a whole truck can be filled. Should she do it? Think about this carefully and explain your answer.

5. Shoes-R-Us, Inc., sells a high-quality line of running shoe. Demand for each of the six models carried is highly variable. For example, a typical monthly demand pattern for a year (in cases of shoes) looks like this (mean monthly demand is 23):

50	10	2	30	22	3	45	40	16	28	0	31

   With this demand pattern, would it be better to calculate purchase order quantities using PPA or EOQ? Explain.

6. Continental Plate and Boiler Co. has one storeroom that holds various sizes of pipe and steelplate. The following are costs and other data associated with pipe and plate buying and storage.

Average inventory on hand	$1.5 million
Purchasing department wages and overhead	$33,000/year
Purchases of pipe and plate	$4.5 million/year
Number of purchase orders processed	500/year
Interest rate	18 percent per year
Depreciation on storeroom and its storage racks	$38,000/year
Overhead and expenses (including taxes and insurance to operate store room)	$10,000/year

   a. What is the average cost of processing a purchase order *(S)*?
   b. What is the annual capital cost? Annual holding cost? What is the carrying-cost rate *(I)*?

7. Each Chompin' Chicken restaurant buys mixed pieces of frozen precooked chicken from a corporate distribution center for $1.00 per pound. The cost of placing and handling an order is estimated at $5, and the inventory carrying cost rate is estimated as 0.35. The frozen chicken is stored in a special freezer that holds *nothing else*. If your local Chompin' Chicken restaurant uses 10,000 pounds of frozen chicken per year, what is the economic order quantity. (Be careful to choose the right EOQ formula.)

8. Maple Tree Insurance Co. uses 2,000 boxes of staples per year. The boxes are priced at $3 in quantities of 0–99 boxes or $2.60 in quantities of 100 boxes or more. If it costs $15 to process an order, and the annual carrying cost rate is 0.30, how many boxes should be ordered at one time?

9. A chemical plant consumes sulfuric acid in a certain process at a uniform rate. Total annual consumption is 25,000 gallons. The plant produces its own sulfuric acid and can set up a production run for a cost of $4,000. The acid can be stored for $0.60 per gallon per year. This includes all carrying costs (cost of capital as well as cost to hold in storage).

The production rate is so rapid that inventory buildup during production may be ignored.

a. What is the economic order quantity?

b. How many times per year should the acid be produced?

10. A cannery buys knocked-down cardboard boxes from a box company. Demand is 40,000 boxes per year. The inventory carrying cost is 0.25 per year. The cannery's purchasing department estimates order-processing cost at $20. The box company prices the boxes as follows:

For a purchase of 100–3,999 boxes—$0.60 each (minimum order = 100).

For a purchase of 4,000 or more boxes—$0.50 each.

a. Determine the economic purchase quantity.

b. Express your EPQ in months' supply. In dollars' worth.

11. A company manufactures plastic trays in several models. One model has a forecast annual demand of 16,000. It costs $80 to set up the molding machine (insert mold, adjust, clamp, etc.) to run that model, which is then produced at a rate of 90,000 per year and for a cost of $10 each. Annual carrying cost is estimated to be 40 percent.

a. What is the economic manufacturing quantity?

b. A pallet holds 20 percent less than the calculated EMQ. Should the company adopt a lot size of one pallet load instead of the calculated EOQ? Explain your answer.

12. A printshop manufactures its own envelopes. Each production run costs $150 to set up and provides envelopes at a production rate of 2,000 per hour. Average usage of the envelopes is 10,000 per month. Envelopes cost $10 per thousand to produce. The annual inventory carrying cost is estimated at 15 percent of average inventory for this item. A working month averages 160 hours.

a. What is the economic manufacturing quantity for envelopes? How many months' supply is it?

b. The printshop is thinking of buying the envelopes instead of making them. If the order-processing cost is $150 (same as the setup cost), what would the EOQ be? Compare your answer with that in part *a.* Is the difference large or small? Explain why?

c. If the production lead time is two days, what is the reorder point?

13. A manufacturer of wooden furniture carries in its warehouse only one type of inventory: lumber. The following is a list of various costs that may or may not be associated with that inventory:

Rent on warehouse—$23,000/year
Wages and salaries, purchasing department—$80,000/year
Inventory taxes—$18,000/year
Cost of capital—14%/year
Value of average inventory on hand—$680,000
Insurance on warehouse contents—$3,500/year
Operating supplies, purchasing department—$1,400/year
Operating budget, production control department—$160,000/year
Expenditures on inventory—$3,400,000/year
Cost of a 12-foot 1″ × 4″ board—$1
Overhead, purchasing department—$25,000/year
Wages and salaries, warehouse—$48,000/year
Overhead, warehouse—$8,000/year
Miscellaneous expenditures, warehouse—$4,200/year

    a. What is the inventory-carrying-cost rate, I (for the total inventory stored)?

    b. What is the average cost of processing a purchase order, S? Assume that 3,000 purchase orders per year are processed.

    c. What is the EOQ for 1″ × 4″ boards? Assume that 30,000 of these boards are used annually.

    d. What is the annual cost of capital for the investment in 1″ × 4″ boards? (Ignore safety stock.)

14. An irrigation-system manufacturer makes its own pipes from coils of steel strip. Three sizes of pipe—three-inch, four-inch, and six-inch—are produced on a rotating schedule, on a single production line. Each size is used at a steady rate in assembly. The following are inventory data for the pipes:

> Cost to set up for a new size of pipe—$130
> Cost of capital—12 percent/year
> Cost to store one pipe (any size)—$2/year
> Manufactured cost of three-inch pipe—$20/section
> Manufactured cost of four-inch pipe—$22/section
> Production rate for pipes (all sizes)—120 sections/day
> Usage (demand) rate, same for each size of pipe—90 sections/day

    a. What is the economic manufacturing quantity for three-inch pipe? For four-inch pipe?

    b. Assume that each of the three types of pipe is stored in a rack that is made to fit the pipe diameter. That is, a storage rack for one size of pipe may not hold another size. (This changes the method of calculating EMQ.) What is the EMQ for three-inch pipe? Explain why this answer is different from the answer in part *a.*

15. A small company adopts buying by economic order quantities for all items in its stockroom. The EOQs show that many items had formerly been ordered in quantities that are far larger than their EOQs. The company has one buyer and one enclosed stockroom with one storekeeper. What savings can the company expect to derive from its EOQ ordering? What potential savings may prove to be difficult to "capture?"

16. Ordinaire, Inc., has calculated, for the first time, economic order quantities for items that are carried in stock. The calculations show that for years the supplies stockroom has been ordering quantities that are too large, and the direct material stockroom has been ordering in quantities that are too small. The comptroller is convinced that adopting the EOQs will save over $100,000 per year in reduced inventory cost. Criticize the comptroller's viewpoint. (Hint: What expected savings may fail to be captured?)

17. Among other things, Marksman Industries makes gun-cleaning rods—10 different models. Presently the 10 models are manufactured one at a time, each for about one week's worth of production (average). The schedule is supposed to provide enough of a given model, during the week-long production run, to satisfy about 10-weeks consumer demand (since it will not be made again for 10 weeks). The problem is, by the end of the 10-week cycle for a model, expected consumer demand may have changed. By the time of the next production run, Marksman may have run out of a given model—or may have a large excess. How could Marksman be more responsive to actual consumer demand?

18. Federal Time Corporation makes and sells clocks. Plastic lenses to go on clock faces are molded in Federal's own facilities. One popular table model has an annual demand of 40,000 clocks. The lens for that clock costs $0.60 to make. Setup to mold the lens, consisting of inserting and clamping the correct die in the injection molding equipment, costs $80 per production run. (Setup time is about four hours.)

a. Federal has been using EOQ to determine number of lenses per production run.
They use an inventory carrying cost rate of 0.25 and the formula, $EOQ = \sqrt{\dfrac{2DS}{IC}}$
What is the EOQ for this lens?

b. The plant manager has decided to run lenses in much smaller lots than EOQs (as competing Japanese firms like Toshiba and Sanyo do). The four-hour setup time must be reduced in order to make small lots economical. What kinds of improvements do you think would need to be made to achieve single setup? To achieve one-touch setup?

19. Kobe Electronics has a subsidiary plant in Wisconsin producing electronic games and various other products. The plant produces its own circuit boards, which are used at a steady rate on the assembly line. Demand for one type of board is 7,000 per year, and the production rate for the board is 40,000 per year. The standard cost is $6.00 per circuit board. It costs $200 to set up a production run for that kind of board.

a. If 0.30 is used as the carrying-cost rate, what is the economic manufacturing quantity for circuit boards?

b. Plant management chooses to ignore the EOQ and instead produce that model of circuit board (and other models as well) in smaller quantities. How can the decision be justified? Explain.

20. A well-known phenomenon in the semiconductor industry (making microprocessors and memory chips) is that fast processing of a production lot has a higher process yield than slow processing of the lot. (Process yield means number of *good* chips from a wafer, i.e., chips that pass electronic tests of quality.) The reason is the wafers are susceptible to handling, dust, and other kinds of damage, which are reduced if the production run is completed and the chips sealed over quickly.

One semiconductor manufacturer has several models of memory chip to run, one at a time. A production run of a given model normally takes five weeks, but a few small special runs have been completed in as little as two weeks—with high process yields. How can a manufacturer gain these advantages *all the time* instead of only in special cases?

21. A producer of precision instruments has initiated a Japanese-style just-in-time program. One of the early achievements was reducing setup time on a milling machine for making a key component part. The old setup cost was $200. Now it is $8. As a result, the new economic lot size is only 16 units, whereas the old one had been much higher.

a. If the company is serious about obtaining full just-in-time benefits, what lot size should be run? Explain.

b. What was the old EOQ? (Hint: Use the new EOQ along with the ratio of new to old setup cost. No other data are needed.)

CASE STUDY: GOODYEAR TIRE AND RUBBER COMPANY LINCOLN V-BELT AND HOSE PLANT

In late October 1982, a just-in-time (JIT) project was started in the Lincoln, Nebraska, V-belt and hose plant of the Goodyear Tire and Rubber Co. It was decided to begin in the press-cure V-belt shop, whose product is a type of long-length belt that is made in numerous models and that requires certain special process steps. The shop is a relatively self-contained operation with 60 employees, which is fewer than in most other shops in the plant. A JIT team was formed, and it included the production manager, merchandise manager, department foreman, supervisor, accountant, two schedulers, and two process engineers.

An early step was to call all shop people together and to explain how JIT works, why it is necessary, and how the production workers can help. The team decided that the next step would be to take direct action: Simply proceed with removal of work-in-process (WIP) inventory all over the shop.

The inventory was highly visible. The long V-belts hang on "trees" beside each machine. When the JIT project began, there were nearly 100 trees full of belts on a typical day, and the average WIP inventory was calculated as a 5.4-day supply of belts. Within six weeks the average WIP had been cut to a 2.4-day supply.

TECHNIQUES

A vital aid to making these cuts feasible was the work of the two process engineers. They worked full time on standardizing belt designs. They combined design features so the variety of sizes and dimensions could be greatly reduced and still meet customer demands. With fewer belt models to carry, fewer racks of different sizes in process were necessary. At the same time, the number of different gauges to measure dimensions of the belts was considerably reduced, which made quality control inspection simpler.

The choice of the press-cure belt shop for the pilot test was deliberate. Press cure was one of the few shops that had been planning jobs through use of "backward scheduling." That is, the scheduler began with customer due dates for belt orders and subtracted lead times to yield scheduled start dates at each stage of belt manufacture. Most other shops in the plant simply started orders out at initial belt processing stations and then allowed the jobs to move through remaining processes without further scheduling attention. (Since all belts follow the same basic flow process or routing, this does work.) The new rule that went into effect in the press-cure shop was: When usage stops, production stops. Thus, when the scheduler learns that, say, a fabric-wrap work station has been halted for some problem, then preceding processes that feed belts to be wrapped also need to be stopped. The scheduler tries to change the schedule for those preceding stations, or else the supervisors try to reassign the workers somewhere else where they can keep busy. (In other shops, where belts move relentlessly forward, there is no scheduling system in operation that is capable of calling for production to stop when usage stops.)

One effect of the WIP cuts was that production workers ran out of work more often than before. A worker at a slitting machine may be slowed down for a variety of reasons, which starves the next work stations (e.g., wrapping the belts with fabric, cure, etc.) of parts to work on. When this happens, the workers who are starved of parts may be able to set up their machines to make some other belt model than what was scheduled. Or they may be asked to leave their usual work stations and go help somebody else or go work on a different machine. A few years ago, these unionized workers might have resisted, because the plant had a history of locking horns with the URW (United Rubber Workers) over work rules. But labor and management had been getting along much better recently, and in this pilot JIT project, the workers turned out to be generally responsive to the need to be flexible. One result was that there actually was less idleness than before the JIT project began.

IMPACT

While the workers were busy more of the time, the time spent setting up machines for new models—always a time-consuming endeavor that produces no belts—increased significantly. This was frustrating to shop supervisors, because more unproductive setup time shows up on monthly reports as a higher labor cost per belt.

An unanticipated benefit of the WIP cuts was that faulty but repairable belts got discovered and fixed right away—e.g., by cementing poorly bonded belt areas. Before, when WIP was everywhere, it sometimes took days to discover the repairable belts, and by then many of them had to be scrapped, because the rubber had cooled or cured to the point where repairs will not "take." An increased number of good belts resulted from the JIT project, thus improving the process yield and countering some of the losses in productivity attributable to more time in setup.

To make sure that old habits of allowing WIP to build up—as a way of coping with problems—did not creep back in, over half the tree-racks were permanently removed from the shop and from the building. With the WIP and trees removed, you now can see across the large shop, and there is a good deal of empty space everywhere.

With such immediate success in cutting WIP after only six weeks, the JIT team was eager to carry on. They recognized that further problems had to be resolved in the press-cure shop and that new and different problems would be confronted in other shops.

The next target for the JIT treatment had been selected: cut-edge V-belt, a shop with 100 employees. That project would begin the first of the year.

DISCUSSION QUESTIONS

1. What problems are unresolved in the press-cure shop?
2. What are some further steps that need to be taken in press cure?
3. What, if any, changes in approach do you suggest as the JIT project moves on to other shops? Discuss.

Chapter 8

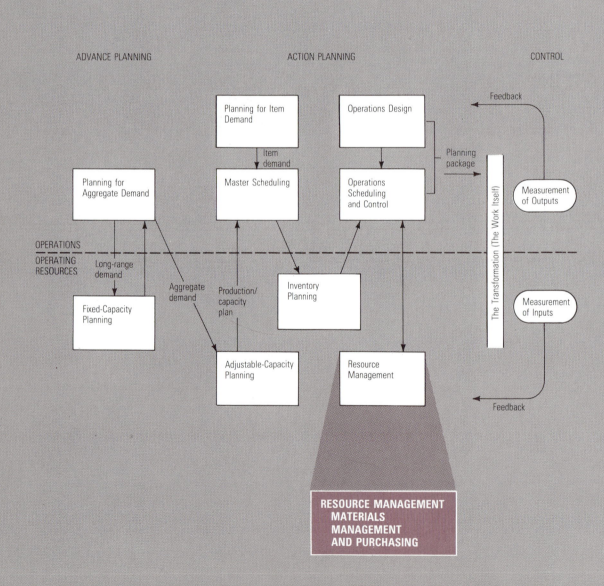

ADVANCE PLANNING ACTION PLANNING CONTROL

Planning for Item Demand

Operations Design

Feedback

Planning for Aggregate Demand

Item demand

Master Scheduling

Operations Scheduling and Control

Planning package

Measurement of Outputs

OPERATIONS
OPERATING RESOURCES

Long-range demand

Fixed-Capacity Planning

Aggregate demand

Production/ capacity plan

Inventory Planning

The Transformation (The Work Itself)

Measurement of Inputs

Adjustable-Capacity Planning

Resource Management

Feedback

RESOURCE MANAGEMENT MATERIALS MANAGEMENT AND PURCHASING

Materials Management and Purchasing

This is the last in a three-chapter sequence on inventory management. Whereas the two preceding chapters concerned planning, this chapter is concerned with strategies, policies, and controls.

MATERIALS ORGANIZATION

Material costs may account for more than 90 percent of the budget in retail and wholesale firms. Even in manufacturing, where labor and equipment costs are often the center of attention, material costs may consume half or more of the budget. High material costs might suggest high status for the materials function. Yet the organization charts of many companies show the following as the major functions: manufacturing, marketing, comptroller, personnel, engineering, production control, and quality control. Where is materials management?

That question began to be asked persistently in the 1960s. Computers had become a valued tool for inventory planning and control. Airfreight had become useful in expediting vital shipments. But coordination of material flows was missing. Materials-management functions tended to be scattered about the organization chart.

New ways of organizing materials activities were developed in the 1960s. At one extreme is the **materials-management** structure, in which materials specialties are combined. At the other extreme is the idea of wiping out some of the materials specialties by turning over their functions to line departments, especially the production department; this approach is referred to as **despecialization.** The materials-management structure and despecialization are explained in the following sections.

Materials-Management Department

Purchasing people were the strongest early advocates of the materials-management structure. *Purchasing* magazine ran a series of articles on the concept. Materials management would be a department at the vice-presidential level, and it would bring together far-flung materials activities.

Figure 8–1 is a before-and-after example of the effects of adopting the materials-management structure. Figure 8–1A shows how materials activities might be scattered on a traditional organization chart. Purchasing might be under the comptroller. Traffic (shipping) might be in marketing. Receiving might be in quality control. Material handling might be in manufacturing. Stores and inventory control might be in manufacturing, with physical inventory counting under the comptroller.

Figure 8–1B shows one possible way of putting the materials functions into one department. Production control is sometimes included. This is perhaps most likely in highly repetitive manufacturing, because there production control is heavily concerned with feeding purchased materials to manufacturing; in job-lot, job-shop, and project operations, production control is more concerned with scheduling, priorities, and capacity management, rather than being dominated by materials management.

Perhaps the major goal of a materials-management structure is to forge a link between purchasing and inventory control. Inventory control includes planning for what purchasing buys, and in firms using material requirements planning the computer helps link these two functions. A materials-management structure helps assure that the information processing linkages will function properly—with consistent managerial oversight.

FIGURE 8–1

Organization of Materials Activities

A. Traditional

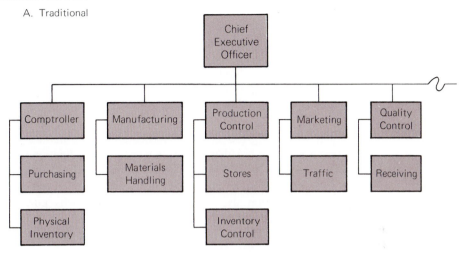

B. Materials management

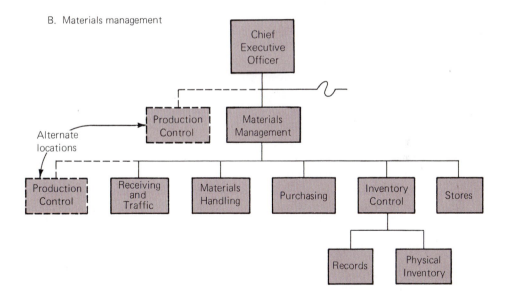

The cause of materials management was taken up by another magazine, *Materials Handling,* in the mid-1960s. *Materials Handling* was the official organ of the American Materials Handling Society. The society was so taken with the idea that it changed its name to the International Materials Management Society and the name of the magazine to *Materials Management.*

The reasons why purchasing and material-handling practitioners favor the materials-management structure may have something to do with their image as bottlenecks. Neither purchasing nor material handling contributes tangible value to the product, but both are sources of delay. When schedules are not met or quality is poor, manufacturing and engineering look for someone to blame. Purchasing is blamed for buying poor-quality or wrong items from vendors who can't deliver on time; material handling is charged with being too slow and too careless. The main advantage of grouping all materials activities together is *coordination,* and coordination reduces delay; perhaps it also improves communication in ways that can lead to better *quality* of materials. These real benefits of materials management could dampen criticism. Increased power and improved position are, of course, other reasons why purchasing and material-handling people like materials management.

Today the materials-management structure is quite common. Surveys suggest that most large industrial firms have adopted some form of materials management.

Despecialization

The traditional organization, as we have seen, places the various specialties in line and staff departments all over the organization chart. The materials-management department is an extreme in which all materials specialists are together. There is an opposite extreme in which the specialists are done away with.

Robert Townsend partially implemented that extreme, which may be called despecialization, when he took over Avis in 1963. At that time, Avis had been suffering losses for some years. As Townsend tells it,[1] he found that profit-center managers at Avis wanted to blame failures to achieve profit goals on bottleneck departments like purchasing. Townsend's reaction: He fired the purchasing department. (He also fired the personnel and public relations departments for much the same reason.) Purchasing funds were turned over to the profit centers with the challenge to "put up or shut up." In other words, the generalists in the profit centers could no longer blame the specialists in purchasing for delays, unwanted substitute items, poor materials, and so forth. Authority to control their own fate, equal to responsibility for results, was in the hands of the profit-center managers.

This extreme, which may have helped Avis get back into the black, has obvious weaknesses. It may be a useful emergency measure in some cases, but most firms would find themselves paying exorbitant prices for shoddy goods to fly-by-night vendors if purchasing experts were not in control of the buying.

The question of how to organize the materials functions loses some of its importance

---

[1] Robert Townsend, *Up the Organization* (New York: Alfred A. Knopf, 1970) (HF5549.T6).

in industrial companies that adopt American MRP or Japanese just-in-time (JIT) production. In MRP and JIT companies, inventory plans come from schedules and production plans, which are driven by business plans. Concern with the materials organization structure seems most likely in companies whose inventories are so large as to lack a close linkage to schedules.

Regardless of the organization structure, a key strategic issue of materials management is **sourcing,** i.e., finding the best source of materials. The sourcing decision, a key function of the purchasing department, is considered next.

SOURCING STRATEGIES

Traditionally, purchasing jobs or careers have not attracted many ambitious people. But a 1981 story in the *New York Times* proclaimed a "New Status for Purchasing."[2] The article pointed to the large potential for savings and influence on profitability. Procter & Gamble, General Electric, General Motors, and B. F. Goodrich were cited as companies that had put more talent into their purchasing departments to try to capture large savings. Goodrich had moved a top financial executive into the chief of purchasing position at a base salary of $99,000.

Part of the reason for the new awareness of potential savings was the oil shock of 1973 and the subsequent worldwide runaway inflation spiral. With material costs going up rapidly, finding a reliable low-cost source and properly timing the purchases became important.

Periodic material shortages have also raised the stature of buyers. In 1971 there were severe shortages of primary metals, which led to shortages of processed steel, copper, lead, titanium, chrome, and so forth. Those shortages translate into long purchase lead times for machined components and finished goods from bearings to buses to boxcars. Engineers hurry to redesign products from alternative materials, which inflates demand and causes shortages of still other materials. For example, petrochemical scarcities have led to shortages in the materials from which plastics may be made, and the primary metals scarcities have bid up demands for plastics, which further aggravates petroleum shortages. Material shortages have a way of becoming material excesses a few years later. Purchasing departments must have the flexibility to shift tactics quickly as the material availability cycle rolls over.

Backward Integration versus "Focused Factories"

When materials are scarce panic sets in. In their anxiety, some companies will opt for **backward integration.** This means setting up to make the materials formerly bought or perhaps buying your supplier company and making it a subsidiary. One result is that purchasing no longer has to scramble to get delivery commitments; the company makes the items in its own plant or subsidiary.

---

[2] Thomas C. Hayes, "New Status for Purchasing," *New York Times* July 2, 1981, pp. D1, D6.

Backward integration is a major financial commitment, and it consumes a lot of managerial energy. When the material shortage evaporates, the company that absorbed its supplier may wish that it hadn't—unless the backward integration step was taken for more reasons than just to secure a reliable supply in a period of scarcity.

The authors of an acclaimed 1980 article, "Managing Our Way to Economic Decline," comment on backward integration. They observe that companies with stable commodity-like products, such as metals and petroleum, can often gain economies and profit improvements through backward integration. The strategy may backfire, however, for companies in technologically active industries. Backward integration "may provide a quick, short-term boost to ROI figures in the next annual report, but it may also paralyze the long-term ability of a company to keep on top of technological change."[3]

Concentrating on doing a few things well in a given plant and acquiring the rest outside (perhaps from another division) is sometimes called the **focused-factory** concept.[4] This concept, which runs counter to plant expansion through backward integration, may have gained more ground with respect to buying services than buying materials. Companies hire caterers to run employee cafeterias and vending machines, janitorial services to clean the premises, contract truckers to haul goods, and consultants to provide advice.

Many Japanese manufacturers fit the focused-factory mold. Japanese end-product manufacturers sometimes have an ownership interest in certain supplier plants, but regardless of the ownership situation, each plant is likely to be small and focused on a single stage of manufacture. Sony in San Diego and Kawasaki Motors in Lincoln, Nebraska, are two Japanese subsidiaries whose managements have publicly declared their intent to focus on assembly and to avoid most parts fabrication.

The U.S. auto industry—General Motors in particular—has been reassessing its longtime belief in backward integration. At GM, 80 percent of an auto's labor cost is for items made at high United Auto Workers' wages—largely in GM's own plants. Ford buys more parts outside and thus pays UAW wages for only 60 percent of a car's labor input.[5] And while purchased materials account for less than 50 percent of GM's sales dollar, they account for nearly 80 percent at Toyota.[6]

With all the attention that the backward integration issue has received, a related, possibly more important issue sometimes is neglected: the issue of *supplier reliability*. For the buyer company the ideal is to have supplier reliability and yet not to have to totally control the supplier. In both North America and Japan methods have been devised to control only a few factors vital to maintaining a reliable supply. Beyond those factors, the supplier plant (including owned subsidiaries) is left free to innovate and to stay current in its area of manufacturing expertise.

---

[3] Robert H. Hayes and William J. Abernathy, "Managing Our Way to Economic Decline," *Harvard Business Review* 58, no. 4 (July–August 1980), pp. 72–3.

[4] Wickham Skinner, "The Focused Factory," *Harvard Business Review,* May–June 1974, pp. 113–21.

[5] "GM's 'New Alliance' with UAW Is Starting to Look Rather Shaky," *The Wall Street Journal,* Wednesday, June 8, 1982, pp. 1,18.

[6] William J. Abernathy, Kim B. Clark, and Alan M. Kantrow, "The New Industrial Strategy," *Harvard Business Review,* September–October 1981, pp. 68–81.

Gaining Supplier Reliability, American-Style

In the North American purchasing environment, the factor of greatest concern appears to be "the failure of suppliers to deliver material on the promised date." This assessment comes from Doyle Selden, director of materials management at McDonnell Douglas and a frequent speaker for the National Association of Purchasing Management. Selden feels that purchasing departments often bring the problem of late deliveries on themselves by not being aggressive. The buyer places an order, and it disappears into the supplier's system. The attitude of the nonaggressive buyer is that "it is not my business" to know what happens to the order in the supplier's system. The supplier is viewed as a vending machine or the electronic engineer's black box; see Figure 8–2. You may inquire about the order at any time, and you may ask for changes in the order (e.g., an earlier delivery). Such inquiries and requests also enter the black box, and limited replies come back to you, but you do not understand how the inquiries and requests were processed.

Selden's view is that the buyer's job is to probe the black box. The buyer should find out what specific problems the supplier is having in meeting delivery dates; the buyer then may act on the information. For example, the buyer may notify production control of likely delivery delays, modify or cancel orders, arrange for substitute materials or alternate suppliers, assist the supplier in some way, or expedite the order. Expediting actions range from impressing the supplier with the importance of the order to your firm to threatening the supplier with loss of future orders. Modifying orders includes cutting the order quantity (if it appears that the supplier could meet delivery for a smaller order), taking partial shipment, delaying the order, changing to a faster mode of transportation, and paying a premium for more supplier attention. Some buyers go so far as to assist the supplier. For example, the buyer might put pressure on one of the supplier's suppliers if there is a raw-material problem; or engineers from the buyer's own plant could be called upon to help straighten out an engineering problem that the supplier is having. But any of these actions requires knowing what is really happening in the supplier's plant.

A longer-range reason for knowing all about the supplier has to do with better supplier selection. Assume that your firm has dropped an otherwise excellent supplier because of late deliveries. Assume further that the supplier corrects problems that have caused the late deliveries. Under the black-box approach, your buyer selects

FIGURE 8–2

Black-Box View of the Supplier's System

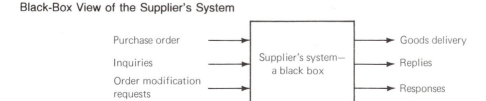

suppliers mainly on past records (perhaps in a formal supplier-selection system); nothing is known about why suppliers are late and what they are doing about it. Your buyer may pass up suppliers that are becoming good and may continue to order from some whose systems are becoming overloaded.

The aggressive, probing buyer may visit a key supplier's plant, study the supplier's production-control system, and establish personal relationships with the supplier's personnel. Or information may be obtained by asking the right series of questions over the phone. The following hypothetical exchange is an example.

Buyer: What is the status of my order?

Supplier's Representative: According to my current information, it is on time.

Buyer: What do you mean by current information?

SR: Well, I haven't received a delay notice.

Buyer: Do you receive regular delay reports?

SR: Yes.

Buyer: How often?

SR: Monthly.

Buyer *(mentally noting that month-old delay reports are badly out of date):* Could you please check to see where the order is in your shops?

SR: No, I've tried that before. Manufacturing tells me there are just too many orders on the floor to go searching for a particular one.

Buyer: OK. Then could you just check with your master scheduler to see where my order is on your MPS?

SR: MPS?

At this point it is clear that the supplier's representative is not in the habit of checking with production control or manufacturing. The aggressive buyer will press

FIGURE 8–3

Buyer-Supplier Information Network

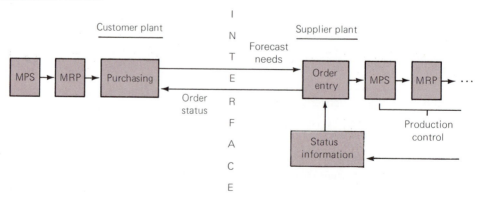

on and will have scored a coup if the supplier's rep is induced to go to production control for order-status information—and succeed in getting it.

The trend seems to be for the buyer-supplier interface to evolve into an information network with benefits both ways. The buyer gains better status information and better deliveries; the supplier, in return, may get advance notice of the customer's future materials needs. In one version of this type of information network, MRP-generated planned orders in the buyer's company are transposed into demands against the master production schedule (MPS) in the supplier's company. As Figure 8–3 indicates, purchasing at one end and order entry at the other manage the information transfer at the interface. Each company's MRP system takes it from there.

Gaining Supplier Reliability, Japanese-Style

In Japan, historical materials scarcities have driven the purchasing function in a different direction than in the United States. Japanese companies have sought reliability and long-term commitment from their suppliers, and searching for the best price has been a lesser concern. Japanese end-product makers typically buy from the same suppliers—a relatively small number—year after year. With that kind of stability the suppliers can feel safe in building their plants close to the buyer company. General Motors has more than 3,500 suppliers for just its assembly plants, and some suppliers are a long distance away. By contrast, Toyota has only 250 suppliers, and they are mostly clustered within an hour's drive of the Toyota plant. Not long after Kawasaki Motors opened its U.S. motorcycle manufacturing plant in Lincoln, Nebraska, its seat supplier, Tokyo Seat Co., opened a seat manufacturing plant just two miles away. Later Tokyo Seat Co. opened a plant in Marysville, Ohio, to make itself similarly indispensable as a supplier to the Honda plant in the same city. Numerous other Japanese suppliers have also opened plants in the United States, always very near the company they intend to sell to.

North American companies, especially those that compete with the Japanese, have been reevaluating the way they select suppliers. For example, in 1982 General Motors made it known that about half of its suppliers of parts for GM assembly plants were to be eliminated. Also, half of GM's 12 or so steel suppliers would be eliminated.[7] Distant suppliers were to be prime candidates for elimination. GM thereby could expect to gain improved service and cuts in inventories in transit. One GM executive had estimated that at any given time over half of the company's inventory was in transit.[8]

When Toyota and other Japanese companies transformed basic Japanese frugality into the just-in-time (JIT) production system, purchasing practices needed to be tight-

---

[7] "GM Spreads the Misery," *Newsweek,* April 5, 1982, p. 54.

[8] "Auto Makers Have Trouble With 'Kanban'," *The Wall Street Journal,* Wednesday, April 7, 1982, p. 1.

ened up. Under JIT, reliability is central. JIT squeezes buffer inventories out of the system; then a late delivery of parts from a supplier can cause a chain reaction of work stoppages.

Besides on-time deliveries, the JIT system requires dependable quality. A batch of bad parts from a supplier can have the same kinds of effects as a late order. The bad parts perhaps will not fit, and that can slow or stop production. Therefore, Nissan, Canon, Toshiba, and other end-product manufacturers send their buyers—plus quality control and engineering people—to their supplier plants to conduct extensive audits. The audits are aimed chiefly at finding out if the supplier is capable of delivering a quality product day in and day out. The visitors leave a long list of demerits, which may cover even indirect factors like worker absenteeism or the food in the company cafeteria. The supplier values the security of a stable relationship with the buyer company, so it acts on the demerits as if they came from company headquarters. The supplier conducts the same kinds of rigorous quality audits on *its* suppliers.

Supplier evaluation systems—in which points are awarded for on-time deliveries, low defectives, and so forth—have been used by larger Western companies for years. But the evaluations are done from afar based on records. Japanese-style supplier audits take place at the supplier's plant and are far more comprehensive. Western manufacturers that have initiated just-in-time production systems are finding it necessary to adopt the same practices. With very low just-in-time inventories, a producer is simply too vulnerable to persist in dealing with suppliers at arm's length.

Classical Make-or-Buy

We have seen that there are vital strategic issues involved in some sourcing decisions. Less critical decisions on making or buying a certain part may sometimes be aided by a type of break-even analysis. Figure 8–4 portrays the factors in this make-or-buy break-even analysis.

If the item is bought, then there is no fixed cost. Instead the total cost, *TC,* is simply the unit price, *P,* times demand, *D:*

$$TC_{\text{buy}} = P \times D$$

If the item is made, there is a fixed cost, *FC,* to set up for production. The other element of total cost is the variable cost of production, which equals unit variable cost, *V,* times demand, *D.* Then,

$$TC_{\text{make}} = (V \times D) + FC$$

In Figure 8–4 we see that the break-even demand, *B,* occurs where the total costs are equal. For demand less than *B* the total cost to buy is lower, so buy is preferred. For demand greater than *B* offsetting of the fixed cost by the lower unit cost results in a lower total cost to make, so make is preferred. The analysis should be based on annual demand and cost if the item is a stocked item that is bought year after

FIGURE 8–4

Make-or-Buy Break-Even Analysis

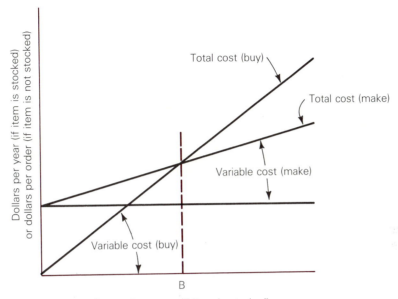

year. The demand and cost of a single order should be used for a nonstocked item that may or may not be reordered in future years.

Since the total costs are equal at the break-even point, a break-even formula is easily developed. Using B (for break-even demand) instead of D, we have:

$$TC_{buy} = TC_{make}$$
$$P \times B = (V \times B) + FC$$
$$(P \times B) - (V \times B) = FC$$
$$B(P - V) = FC$$

$$B = \frac{FC}{P - V}$$

As a brief example, assume that you can buy candles at the store for $1 each. Or you can pay $50 for candle-making apparatus, and make your own candles for a unit variable cost (wax, wicks, etc.) of $0.75. What volume is necessary to recover your fixed cost, i.e., break even?

Solution:

$$B = \frac{50}{1 - 0.75} = \frac{50}{0.25} = 200 \text{ candles}$$

MATERIALS MANAGEMENT POLICIES

While sourcing strategies have long-term impacts, materials management policies are guides for short- to medium-term activities. Perhaps the oldest—and most venerable—materials management policy is based on **ABC analysis.** ABC analysis provides a basis for more control over key materials and less control over lesser items.[9]

ABC Analysis

In ABC analysis all stocked items are classified by annual dollar-volume, that is, annual demand times cost per unit. Class *A* items, needing close control, are the high-dollar-volume group. They may include 80 percent of total inventory cost but only 1 percent of total items stocked. Class *B* is a medium-dollar-volume group—perhaps 15 percent of dollars and 30 percent of items. Class *C* is the rest—say, 5 percent of dollars and 69 percent of items. Some firms do not stop with *A, B,* and *C* but add *D* and perhaps *E* categories.

Computer processing makes ABC analysis easy to do. Item cost is available in the inventory master file. Any measure of annual usage—such as actual usage last year, actual usage last month times 12, or a forecast—may be used. The computer multiplies item cost by annual usage, giving annual dollar volume. The ABC formula is fed into the computer, and the output is a complete list of items in descending dollar-volume order. The listing is grouped into three parts: *A* items come first, *B* items second, and *C* items third.

Examples of how ABC analysis may be used follow (the details will vary from firm to firm):

1. **Purchasing.** Have each purchase order for a class *A* item signed by the president, for a class *B* item by the chief of purchasing, and for a class *C* item by any buyer.
2. **Physical inventory counting.** Count *A* items monthly, *B* items annually, and *C* items biennially.
3. **Forecasting.** Forecast *A* items by several methods on the computer with resolution by a forecasting committee, *B* items by simple trend projection, and *C* items by best guess of the buyer.
4. **Safety stock.** No safety stock for *A* items, one month's supply for *B* items, and three months' supply for *C* items.

While computers can help with ABC analysis, some authorities take a dim view of including ABC in the high form of computer-based inventory management known as material requirements planning. Orlicky,[10] for example, suggests that the MRP

---

[9] This idea of giving an item the degree of attention it deserves is sometimes called the *principle of parsimony* (parsimony means frugality). The more general principle, widely applicable in society, is the *Pareto principle;* it is named after Vilfredo Pareto (1848–1923), an economist who observed that 90 percent of wealth is in the hands of 10 percent of the population.

[10] Joseph Orlicky, *Material Requirements Planning* (New York: McGraw-Hill, 1975), p. 161 (TS155.8.O74).

system should treat all items alike (except for especially hard-to-get items). MRP plans priorities (i.e., it plans the order in which parts will be scheduled), and *C* items must contend for productive capacity and purchasing attention along with *A* and *B* items. Including *C* as well as *B* and *A* in the MRP system accounts for all loads on capacity and also helps to assure that all items will be on hand when needed.

ABC Example

While there are doubts about ABC as a component of MRP, ABC can be valuable in ROP (reorder-point) systems. A wholesaler is a good example, as is demonstrated next.

EXAMPLE 8–1

ABC Analysis, Wholesaler

Universal Motor Supply Co. has arranged its 10 inventory items in order of annual dollar-volume. Figure 8–5 shows the ordered list, with dollar-volume also expressed in percentages. The ordered list is examined in order to arrive at an ABC classification of the items.

Figure 8–6 shows the same 10 items grouped into classes *A, B,* and *C.* The groupings seem natural: The three *B* items account for about nine times as much annual dollar-volume as the five *C* items; the two *A* items account for about six times as much as the three *B* items. It is clear that *A* items should receive major attention, *B* items moderate attention, and *C* items little attention.

FIGURE 8–5

Inventory Items in Annual-Dollar-Volume Order, Universal Motor Supply Co.

Stock number	Annual demand	Unit cost	Annual dollar-volume	Percent	
407	40,000	$ 35.50	$1,420,000	59.5	} A → 88.8%
210	1,000	700.00	700,000	29.3	
021	2,000	55.00	110,000	4.6	
388	20,000	4.00	80,000	3.4	} B → 9.7%
413	4,400	10.00	44,000	1.7	
195	500	36.00	18,000	0.7	
330	40	214.00	8,560	0.4	
114	100	43.00	4,300	0.2	} C ~ 1.5%
274	280	1.00	280	0.1	
359	600	0.25	150	0.1	
Totals			$2,385,290	100.0%	

FIGURE 8–6

ABC Classification, Universal Motor Supply Co.

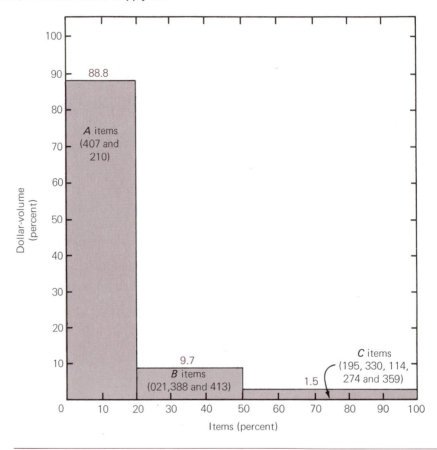

Materials management strategies are backed up by policies—like the ABC policies. Policies in turn are backed up by procedures. The next two sections are on procedures for inventory control and for purchasing.

INVENTORY CONTROL PROCEDURES

Inventory control includes control over:

1. **Inventory records and files.** Stock records and files show what has occurred and what the current inventory status is.

2. **Physical stocks on hand.** What the records show may be verified by a physical inventory count of what is in storage.

These are considered in more detail below.

Stock Record Keeping

The very small organization may get by without stock records. The small amounts of stock carried may be mentally and visually managed. Growth in stock brings the need for stock records. A file of stock records may consist of index cards or computer records. Either way, the record holds about the same information. Let us examine a typical index-card version. See Figure 8–7.

The figure shows an order quantity and a reorder point at the right edge. A running balance (stock on hand) is maintained by date in the lower portion. Each time an issue is made and posted to the card, the amount is deducted from the balance; then the balance is compared with the reorder point to see if it is time to reorder the given order quantity. If the record were computerized and used in a

FIGURE 8–7

Stock Record Card

			STOCK RECORD								
Name or description				Stock number						Location	
Primary users or uses										Order quantity	
Jan.	Feb.	Mar.	Apr.	May	June	July	Aug.	Sept.	Oct.	Nov.	Dec.	Reorder point
Monthly usage summary											
Date	Orders or allocations	Qty. on order	Receipts	Issues	Balance	Date	Orders or allocations	Qty. on order	Receipts	Issues	Balance

material requirement planning system, the current balance would serve as the starting point for period-by-period projection of the stock balance. Allocations, on-order quantities, and receipts may also be entered on the card. The stock record may also provide usage data—see the monthly usage summary in the figure—which is useful in review for standardization and disposal, for inventory valuation, and for performance assessment. Supplier lead times, stockout and backorder frequency, and other information may also be gleaned from data on the stock record.

Record Accuracy

Stock records are never perfectly accurate. The stock balance is sure to be off for at least a few items. A certain amount of inaccuracy is tolerated in reorder-point companies, because ROP orders are not intended to reflect actual need—but only the "need" to replenish a low stock. If the stock is really less than the records show, it means that the reorder will be triggered on a later date, but there may not be a stockout.

On the other hand, inaccurate records are the bane of an MRP system. In MRP, orders are recommended only when there is a real need; if the record is inaccurate, the need will not be real, and people will come to disbelieve the system. MRP experts recommend 95 percent record accuracy as a minimum for MRP companies.

The just-in-time system calls for still better record accuracy (or stock accuracy; there may not even be any records). There may not be so much as one unit of safety stock in case the planned quantity is not there.

Happily—for the MRP and the JIT user—the less overall inventory there is in the system, the less there is to go wrong. To keep even the few records from becoming inaccurate—and to correct errors when they occur—physical inventory controls are necessary.

Physical Inventory Control

Most of us are aware of retailers or other businesses that are sometimes "closed for inventory." This means closed to count the goods in stock. Counting is in natural physical units like pieces, gallons, yards, boxes, and pounds. For accounting purposes the counts are converted to dollars. For operations management purposes—record accuracy and stock protection—the natural units are sufficient. Besides counting, physical inventory control may be attained by stockroom security and by tight shop-floor procedures. Each of these methods of physical inventory control is discussed below:

The Physical Count. Taking a physical inventory count is the means of finding inaccurate records and fixing them. The count is compared with the stock record balance, and any discrepancy may call for a recount and, if necessary, a correction on the record.

Many companies still shut down once a year (or more) for a complete count. In the jargon of the trade, this is called a **complete physical inventory**. Many companies, especially MRP users, have changed over to a more accurate and less disruptive method called **cycle counting**. In cycle counting, a small fraction of items are counted each week or day, year around. Cycle counting may be tied to ABC classes. For example, *A* items might be counted monthly, *B* items semiannually, and *C* items annually.

Other counting alternatives include **event-based counting** and **stock-location counting**. One form of event-based counting is counting an item whenever it is issued; thus more active items get counted more often. Another is counting when stock is low, for example, just before a scheduled receipt; the advantage is that there is less to count. In stock-location counting, the counting moves from one storage area to another; an advantage is that "lost" items may be found in the process.

Counting is also valued in that it serves as a deterrent to theft and improper storage or use of materials. In reorder-point systems, where inventories are large, deterrence is the greater purpose of counting. In MRP systems, where there is less total inventory—zero for some items—accuracy is the greatest purpose. (There is less to steal.) Therefore, MRP companies may allow stockkeepers to count their own goods, but counting is more frequent.

Stockroom Security.   Counting and stock records actually are a secondary kind of deterrent. Primary deterrence is, first of all, assuring that materials are issued out of the stockroom only on a properly executed document. Related to this is some form of stockroom security. Lockable storage cabinets are one type. Limited-access stockrooms (which are strongly favored by most MRP experts) are another. Controlled access to buildings holding materials provides more general security. And perimeter controls—fences, gates, guards, badges, and random searches—provide boundary security.

Tight Shop-Floor Procedures.   In the just-in-time system inventories move quickly. There is not time to count and check records, and there are few stockrooms to provide security for. Yet inventory control must be at its tightest in a JIT system. The JIT plant gets tight control by buying, producing, and transporting in exact readily countable quantities. U.S. companies typically accept deliveries of purchased lots as long as they are within ± 10 percent of the amount of the purchase order, and production quantities on the shop floor are equally erratic. In the growing number of JIT companies $\pm$ *zero* performance is expected. To make sure that suppliers of materials—whether external or internal—are delivering exact quantities, special containers are used. Containers may be segmented into "pigeon holes" that will hold only the correct amount, and usually the container (or rack or hanger) is designed so that a count discrepancy would be seen at a glance.

PURCHASING PROCEDURES

Inventory control procedures apply to materials already owned. Now let us turn to procedures for buying the materials in the first place.

Purchasing Goods versus Services

Purchasing goods, or *tangibles,* differs from purchasing services, or *intangibles.* The quality of tangibles is physically measurable; the quality of intangibles is not. The distinction has an impact on purchasing practices.

Besides *quality,* the objectives of purchasing are *price, delivery,* and *favorable supplier relations* (or service). The four objectives are not independent. A buyer may sometimes deal with a loyal supplier even if that supplier's current prices are higher than, deliveries slower than, or quality not quite as good as that of another supplier.

Tangible Goods. Purchasing effort may be related to dollar-volume for standard (stocked) goods or to item cost for nonstandard (nonstocked) goods. Thus, low-dollar-volume items, for example, class *C* and low-cost items, do not warrant extensive search for the lowest price; class *A* and high-cost items do.

A class *A* item may be an expensive item that is seldom ordered or a low-cost item that is ordered often or in large quantities. Common purchasing measures are described below:

Soliciting competitive bids on specifications. An *invitation to bid* or a *request for quotation* is mailed to prospective suppliers. The item to be bought is specified in detail; the description may consist of *technical specifications* (physical or chemical properties) and *performance specifications* (mean time until failure, rated output, etc.). Specifications may be necessary because the item is nonstandard or because the buying firm wishes to exclude low-quality suppliers. And specifications can provide a sound basis for determining compliance with the requirements of the buyer. Engineering often plays a key role in developing "specs," as they are called, and engineering blueprints may be attached. Attorneys may assure that contractual obligations are legally clear.

Governments, especially the federal government, intermittently buy based on publicly available specs. Regulations require that, for many types of purchases, the invitation to bid be published in a widely circulated government document.

Negotiation. Where sources of supply are stable, there may be no need to solicit formal bids. Instead, the buying firm may just periodically negotiate with the regular source for better price or delivery terms. Typically, negotiation applies to nonstandard high-dollar-volume items produced to the buyer's specs.

Buying down and speculation. Buying down means trying to buy an item with a history of cyclic price swings when its price is down. Buying down is a form of speculative buying. In pure speculation, purchases are made for price reasons rather than to meet an actual need for the goods.

Hedging. Hedging applies especially to commodities such as wheat, corn, silver, and lumber. Organized futures markets exist for some commodities. A buyer can pay cash to buy a commodity now and at the same time sell a like amount of a future of the commodity. Price changes will mean that losses on one order are offset by gains on the other.

Class *B* or medium-cost items usually warrant less purchasing effort. Specifications may be necessary if the items are nonstandard. But the expense of soliciting bids is harder to justify for such items than for class *A* items. Many items of this kind are standard "off-the-shelf" goods, such as MRO (maintenance, repair, and operating supplies). Simpler order procedures, such as the following, may be used.

Approved supplier lists. For medium-dollar-volume purchasing, buying from proven suppliers is a reasonable substitute for seeking the lowest bid. A formal or informal supplier-rating procedure may be set up. Suppliers who get high ratings on price, quality, delivery, and service may be placed on an approved supplier list. Then, for certain types of purchases, only approved suppliers are considered.

Catalog buying. Perhaps the most common purchasing procedure for off-the-shelf (MRO) goods is buying out of current catalogs, sometimes with the help of salespeople. Most buyers have shelves full of suppliers' catalogs for this purpose.

Blanket orders. Where there is a continuous but varying need for one or several rather low-cost items, a blanket-order contract may be drawn up with a supplier. The blanket order covers a given time period, and deliveries are arranged by sending a simple "release" document to the supplier. Price and other matters are covered in the contract.

Systems contract. A systems contract is similar to a blanket order, but the systems contract is longer-term and more stringently defined. The purchasing department negotiates the systems contract; purchasing then typically becomes a monitor but not a participant in ordering. The contract may name certain foremen and other managers who may order—by mail, phone, or other means—directly from the supplier.

Stockless purchasing. Stockless purchasing is a way for the buying firm to rid itself of the costs of carrying inventories of certain commonly used goods. The supplier owns the inventories, even when they are physically located at the buyer's plant. The supplier may get a higher-than-usual price in return for dependability and relief from the financial burden of carrying the inventories. By signing up several stockless purchasers, the supplier consolidates and saves on safety-stock inventories.

Class *C* or low-cost items are worthy of little attention by purchasing specialists. Attempting to buy such items from a supplier on an approved supplier list provides a measure of control. For many items, even that is too much control and red tape, and to avoid these, using departments are provided with *petty cash funds* and may buy directly and pay cash.

Intangibility. An intangible item, as the designation suggests, is difficult to specify. Without clear, physically measurable specifications, the buyer is at the mercy of the seller.

Intangibility is relative, as Figure 8–8 attempts to show. The top end of the scale represents one extreme—high tangibility. Highly tangible items include simple parts,

FIGURE 8–8

Tangibility of Purchased Goods

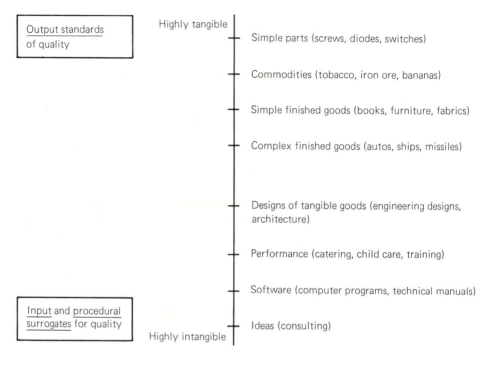

such as screws, diodes, and switches. Commodities, such as tobacco, iron ore, and bananas, are near to the tangible end, but some of their key physical properties may be costly to measure; less tangible "eye-ball" judgments on quality may be used to some extent in evaluating commodities. Simple finished goods are a bit less tangible than commodities; for example, books, furniture, and fabrics have several measurable physical properties, but for items of this kind visual inspection for scratches, flaws, and so forth, may be as important as physical measurements. Complex finished goods (e.g., autos, ships, and missiles) have thousands of measurable physical properties; yet partly subjective judgments as to their effectiveness (e.g., how well the destroyer protects the fleet) are quite important.

Procedures for buying these mostly tangible goods are rather well established. Purchase contracts may be based to a large degree on clear *standards of output*— that is, on physically measurable properties of the end product.

Intangibles, at the other end of Figure 8–8, do not have physically measurable properties. Therefore, purchase contracts may, at best, be based on input and procedural factors. In a contract with a consultant, input factors may include the consultant's level of education and years of experience; procedural factors may include number of people interviewed and number of pages on the final consultant's report. These do not comprise the quality of the consultant's services, but they are often treated as surrogates for output quality. A consultant may meet all the terms of a contract specifying input and procedural factors and yet end up with totally worthless, incorrect, and irresponsible findings and recommendations. With such poor quality, the consultant does not deserve to be paid in full, but since the specifications of output quality were too intangible to be in the contract, the consultant is legally entitled to full pay.

Slightly more tangible than ideas is software, such as computer programs and technical manuals. You can count lines of code in a computer program and number of words in a technical manual, and the contract may set limits on these factors. But no one would say that these are measures of quality. However, the software firm is legally entitled to full pay, even for a shoddy job, if it has met the input and procedural contract terms.

Contracting for performance is growing explosively; catering, child care, and employee training are examples. Enterprising college students have capitalized on the trend by starting part-time businesses to provide janitorial, yard-care, computer-dating, and a variety of other services. The end products or outputs are good food, well-adjusted children, requalified employees, clean floors, weed-free lawns, and well-matched dating couples. It is difficult to write standards for these outputs into a contract. Consequently, there has been a growing use of measures of compliance such as mean number of complaints by customers and opinion polling involving customers, experts, or impartial panels using some form of Likert scale (i.e., a rating scale from 1 to 5 or 1 to 7, etc.).

This may seem nearly as objective as measuring the diameter of a shaft with a micrometer. It isn't. The weakness lies in the difficulty of getting a representative sample. A random sample of shafts is easy to get because the shafts have no will and no bias. Selecting people to poll, on the other hand, depends on willingness to be polled, and there are many possible biases that are hard to control for.

In the center of Figure 8–8 is the purchase of designs for tangible goods, such as engineering and architectural designs. The output is like software or consulting reports, and the above remarks on the use of input and procedural contract terms apply. But there is a distinct difference: The engineer's or architect's design *becomes a tangible good*. If the bridge collapses or the roof caves in, the engineer or architect may be legally liable. This makes contracting for these services less risky.

We see that the most serious problems exist in buying performance, software, and ideas. Buying from firms with good reputations (such as the firms on an approved supplier list) would seem to be one helpful measure. But performance services tend to come and go rather than to stay and build clientele and reputation. Software firms and consulting firms are somewhat more stable. Ironically, poor software or poor consulting is not notably destructive to the reputations of firms. The reason is that dissatisfied customers tend not to admit their displeasure *(a)* because of the risk of defamation suits, since bad quality is difficult to prove and *(b)* because dissatisfaction would be an admission of having wasted a perhaps large sum of money on poor software or consulting service.

Public and corporate officials rely increasingly on consultants to help them with sticky decisions. Inability to write tough contracts leaves the officials at the mercy of the consultants. Fortunately most consultants are professionally dedicated and motivated to maintain self-respect. Still, contracting for these kinds of intangibles has become a major challenge for people in the purchasing field.

"Making Money" in Purchasing

Purchasing is spending money. The buyer can spend less money by searching for the best price, and that is how buyers spend a good part of their work day. But purchasing professionals also may become involved in projects that offer long-term substantial savings ("making money") for their company. Value analysis projects and standardization projects, considered below, are of this type.

Value Analysis.   Value analysis (VA) was developed in the purchasing department of General Electric in 1947. In VA, a team analyzes existing product design specifications with the aim of improving value. In large organizations file cabinets in purchasing and engineering may be filled with specifications developed by engineers years ago. New technology outdates some of the old specifications. Each time such items are reordered, the obsolescence becomes more apparent and purchasing takes some of the heat for not "buying modern." It is no surprise that the VA procedure was developed and promoted by purchasing people. As engineers got more involved, the concepts were extended to include new designs as well as old specifications.

In some companies and in the federal government engineers conduct the analysis, and in such cases it is called value engineering (VE). While value analysis could be applied to services, it mostly is restricted to goods, especially where material costs and usage rates are high.

The VA step-by-step procedure has been adopted worldwide. The steps (a variation of the scientific method) are:

1. **Select.** Select a product that is ripe for improvement.
2. **Gather information.** The team coordinator collects drawings, costs, scrap rates, forecasts, operations sheets, and so forth before the team first meets. Team members are asked to send in whatever information they have.
3. **Define function.** The team meets and defines each function of the product. A function is defined in two words, a verb and a noun. (A barrel *contains fluid*.) Only essential functions are included. Next the team determines the present cost of each function. This reveals which functions are costing far too much. (Note: Defining functions in this way is unique and sets VA apart from less formal cost-reduction techniques.)
4. **Generate alternatives.** Team members suggest ideas for new and different ways to accomplish the functions. This is known as brainstorming. The ideas are recorded, and later they are culled to a list of manageable size.
5. **Evaluate alternatives.** Alternatives are evaluated based on feasibility, cost, and other factors, which cuts the list to one or two (or a few) good ideas.

6. **Present proposals.** The final alternatives are refined and presented to a management committee as change proposals.

7. **Implement.** The approved change proposal is translated into an engineering change order (ECO is a common industry abbreviation) and put into effect.

Value Analysis Example.   The description of a real VA study helps show how the procedure works.[11]

EXAMPLE 8–2

VA Procedure for Improving a Bearing Housing-Support

A value analysis team was given a dust-collector valve as a study project. In the information phase, it reviewed the assembly and subassembly parts and their costs. During this information search, the team noted that two bearing housing-supports were listed on the bill of materials, that is, right- and left-hand gray iron castings.

The team found that these bearing housing-supports were used in the main assembly to locate the bearings, which, in turn, supported and located the main shaft of the dust-collector valve. Also, each of these assemblies required a bearing housing-support, a bearing, and inner and outer bearing seals. The direct material and labor costs of the two subassemblies totaled $36. See the part drawing in Figure 8–9A.

The problem attack now centered on the last two functions. The team searched a number of bearing manufacturers' catalogs. All of the catalogs included a sealed, self-mounting bearing as a standard item. When the team's

FIGURE 8–9

Bearing Housing-Support Undergoing Value Engineering

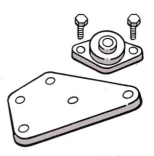

A. Before *VA*   B. *VA*-proposed design

Source: Arthur E. Mudge, *Value Engineering: A Systematic Approach* (New York: McGraw-Hill, 1971), p. 263 (TS168.M83). Used with permission.

---

[11] Arthur E. Mudge, *Value Engineering: A Systematic Approach* (New York: McGraw-Hill, 1971), pp. 263–64 (TS168.M83). Used with permission.

solution to the functions "reduce friction" and "provide seal" was combined with its solution to the functions "provide support" and "provide location," the team knew that it had a workable solution.

The team realized that the self-mounting bearing could be mounted on either side of a common piece of steel plate, as shown in Figure 8–8B. This design cut the total housing subassembly cost by 33 percent, to $25 per pair. Since only minor engineering changes were required and no tooling was needed, the annual net saving of about $3,100 began in the first year.

Impressed by the results of VA or VE in private industry, the Department of Defense issued VE regulations that were applicable to all DoD contracts costing more than $100,000. In 1964 the American Ordnance Association conducted a survey that randomly sampled 124 successful VE changes in the DoD.[12] The survey report showed not only impressive cost savings but also, in many cases, collateral gains in these areas: reliability, maintainability, producibility, human factors, parts availability, production lead time, quality, weight, logistics, performance, and packaging. The DoD then implemented a formula for sharing some of the VE savings (usually 20 percent) with contractors; this gave the contractors' VE teams added incentive to squeeze savings out of the design specifications.

Value Analysis and Just-in-Time Production.   In America, value analysis is generally done in a conference room in the office part of the plant. In the Japanese just-in-time system, value analysis is often treated as one more way to do on-the-spot problem solving. When a design problem threatens to stop production, perhaps a buyer or engineer will quickly go to the shop floor.

A foreman and perhaps a worker or two will join in the problem analysis. Blueprints may be marked up and taken right away to the inside or outside maker of the parts that are causing the problem.

One reason that the Japanese are able to conduct value analysis "on the fly" is that their blueprints and design specifications tend to be nonrestrictive. Western design engineers generally try to specify every dimension, type of material, finish, etc. Then the production people are left to sweat and curse over how to make the item. The "minimal specs" concept in Japanese industry is aimed at giving the maker latitude over nonessential design attributes so that easy, cheap ways to make the part may be used. As an example, Kawasaki Motors calls for only "an appropriate polymer coating" on some parts.

The purist might say that making design decisions on the floor should not be called value analysis, because the formal steps—defining functions, generating alternatives, and so forth—are bypassed. While that is true, the Japanese approach has the advantage of giving more attention to how product design affects producibility, a key element in overall product cost. And producibility is a vital concern in just-in-time production where a production problem can starve later production stages of parts and bring operations to a halt.

---

[12] "Reduce Costs and Improve Equipment through Value Engineering," Directorate of Value Engineering, Office of the Assistant Secretary of Defense for Installations and Logistics, January 1967. (TS168.U5).

Standardization.   Industrial standardization means settling on a few rather than many sizes, shapes, colors, and so forth for a given part. Value analysis sometimes leads to standardization. But many companies have a permanent standardization committee, often headed by an engineer or buyer.

Lee and Dobler state that "standardization is the *prerequisite* to mass production." They credit Eli Whitney's development of standardization, initially of musket parts, as having triggered the emergence of the United States as the world's dominant mass producer in the first half of the century.[13] The idea is not to make standardized end products but to make a wide variety of end products from a small number of standardized parts and materials. The cost savings can be substantial: Fewer items means less purchasing, receiving, inspection, storage, and billing. Internally, fewer different kinds of production equipment and tooling are required, and production of some parts may be relatively continuous—which is efficient—instead of stop-and-go.

The American National Standards Institute (ANSI) is a federation of over 100 organizations that develops industrial standards. After research and debate, ANSI may approve a recommended standard for adoption nationwide. Perhaps the most vexing standardization issue in America is metrics since the United States is the only nonmetric country among major industrial countries. However, most American companies with good export markets have gone metric on their own.

MATERIALS MANAGEMENT AS A PROFIT CENTER

A final materials management issue is that of overall control. Cost variance reports provide a common basis for overall control of production. Can materials management have such a control system? The answer is yes, and this brief section explains one way it may be done: establishing materials management as a profit center.

Materials management does not add tangible value to materials. But it does add intangible value, that is, time and place value. The materials management (MM) department serves, and their services cost money. MM service costs must be passed along to the using department in some way. One way is through overhead charges; another way is through transfer prices. Transfer price means the price charged by MM to the user, and the price would be the purchase cost of the item plus MM's service charge. If transfer prices are held constant from year to year, then the MM department would earn a profit if it were able to lower its service costs or to buy goods for a lower purchase cost. Similarly, MM would earn a loss if its costs or prices paid went up.

To set up MM as a profit center requires a special (artificial) bookkeeping manipulation to set transfer prices. A sound approach is to set transfer prices so that MM earns the same return on assets as the firm does as a whole. The following example will illustrate.

---

[13] Lamar Lee, Jr., and Donald W. Dobler, *Purchasing and Materials Management: Text and Cases,* 3d ed. (New York: McGraw-Hill, 1977), pp. 54–55 (HD52.5.L4).

EXAMPLE 8–3

Materials Management as a Profit Center, Energistics, Inc.

Energistics, Inc., earns 20 percent (before taxes) on assets. Therefore, in setting up its materials management (MM) department as a profit center, Energistics provides MM with a 20 percent profit to be used to set transfer prices. The 20 percent rate is applied to MM department assets, namely:

Assets:	
Facilities (floor space and equipment)	$1,000,000
Inventories of purchased goods	5,000,000
Total	$6,000,000

Profits on assets = 20% of $6,000,000 = $1,200,000

In the same year MM's service expenses are $800,000 and cost of purchased goods is $40,000,000. Determining transfer prices requires working backward from the normal way that an income statement is prepared:

MM department profit	$ 1,200,000
MM service expenses	800,000
Gross margin	2,000,000
Cost of goods sold (purchased goods)	40,000,000
"Sales" (transfer-priced)	$42,000,000

That $42 million is the revenue that MM should earn by charging using departments for materials. MM's average markup is 5 percent, that is,

$$\frac{\$2,000,000}{\$40,000,000} = 0.05$$

In the following year, the MM department mounts an internal campaign to *(a)* lower inventories, *(b)* get rid of excess facilities, *(c)* get better prices from suppliers, and *(d)* lower its operating expenses. At year's end the result is a small increase in MM profitability:

Income statement:	
"Sales" (transfer-priced)	$42,000,000*
Cost of goods sold (purchased goods)	40,100,000
Gross margin	1,900,000
MM service expenses	700,000
MM department profit	$ 1,200,000

* Transfer prices and volume of goods "sold" stayed the same as the previous year.

Assets:	
Facilities (floor space and equipment)	$ 900,000
Inventories of purchased goods	4,900,000
Total	$5,800,000

Return on assets = $\dfrac{\$1,200,000}{\$5,800,000}$ = 0.207, or 20.7%

The 0.7 percent improvement in profitability is in spite of failure to get lower prices from suppliers. In fact, because of inflation, prices paid went up from $40 million to $40.1 million. (If the general rate of inflation had been normal that year, Energistics buyers would have done very well to keep prices paid that low.) Successes were in cutting service expenses (from $800,000 to $700,000), facilities investment (from $1,000,000 to $900,000), and inventories (from $5,000,000 to $4,900,000).

The example shows that treating MM as a profit center has important motivational advantages. The profit-center concept is good for managerial development in that it exposes managers to challenges, risk-taking, investments aimed at operating savings and profits, and so forth.

If the profit-center concept is so great, why not apply it then to capacity management, maintenance, and other operations management areas? In some cases, other operations management areas might be set up as profit centers, but MM is a more natural place to apply the concept because, commonly, materials are a large part of operating costs. Accounting costs are higher for profit centers; an inordinate amount of time may be spent by profit-center managers to gain accounting advantages. Thus profit-center management is best applied where the cost impact and potential for cost improvements is great.

SUMMARY

Materials management and purchasing concern overall material strategies, policies, and controls, as well as actions, such as purchasing, to carry out inventory plans.

Inventory functions have tended to be scattered about the organization chart. The materials-management department changes this by consolidating many of the functions. The new department, often at the vice-presidential level, may gain coordination, thereby cutting red tape and delivery time and improving services. The materials-management department might include receiving and traffic, material handling, purchasing, inventory control, and stores; it sometimes includes production control.

An opposite extreme in organizing material functions is to despecialize, that is, to break up specialist units like purchasing and material handling and transfer those duties to line departments. The purposes—which are often related to the rescue of a faltering company—are to cut costs and to give line departments more authority and control.

A purchasing function that is often vital strategically is sourcing, which means securing a source for needed materials. The importance of sourcing escalated with the oil shock of 1973, which dramatically raised oil prices and also prices of many petroleum derivatives and substitute materials. In affected companies finding reliable low-cost sources of materials has a major impact on company success.

One sourcing strategy that has been historically popular in industry is backward integration. The strategy calls for making your own materials rather than buying. The strategy gains control and assures a reliable supply. More recently the focused-factory concept has gained favor. It suggests that doing a few things very well in one plant is preferable to trying to do it all. Some observers have noted that a number of Japan's most successful industrial companies follow a focused factory concept, which may help to explain their success.

For lesser items the make-or-buy decision may be aided by a type of break-even analysis. The break-even point is the point at which total cost to make equals total cost to buy. Below this point buying is cheaper, because there is not enough volume to justify the fixed cost of setting up a manufacturing capability.

For those materials that are bought, not made, supplier reliability is a key concern. Some leading American companies have adopted aggressive approaches that include visiting a supplier's plant to find out why the supplier cannot always deliver on time. The knowledge may be used to improve schedules or even to help suppliers to do better.

Reliability of supply has been a more serious concern over the years in resource-poor Japan. The Japanese company tends to carefully select a few good suppliers and then stay with them forever. The supplier reciprocates by locating near to the buying plant in order to provide better service, including deliveries more than once a day.

In the medium and short term, materials management policies are often based on the ABC concept in which inventory items are given attention based on their annual dollar volume. High-dollar-volume (class *A*) goods may be intensively managed, for example, by thoroughly searching for best prices and by carefully matching orders to current needs. Low-dollar-volume (class *C*) goods may be loosely controlled.

Day-to-day materials control requires careful physical control of stocks and, usually, good stock record keeping. The records may be contained on index cards or a computer file. The record contains item identification, keeps a running balance, and may hold other data. The balance may be used in deciding when to reorder and in acting as a deterrent to stock misuse. Records are compared with an actual stock count periodically; the cycle count method, in which a few items are counted daily, is a modern alternative to a yearly complete physical count. High record accuracy is vital in an MRP system and even more so in a just-in-time system, but in these systems the low inventories make inventory easier to count and control. While good stockroom security is important in an MRP system, careful shop-floor counting and container design is typical in a just-in-time system.

Purchasing procedures are influenced by the greater importance of purchasing in today's environment of materials scarcity, price escalation, high interest rates, and the challenges of buying intangibles that cannot be specified by physical and chemical properties.

Value analysis is a procedure that purchasers developed in order to meet material needs (functions) with lower-cost materials and designs. Engineers were commonly invited to serve on value-analysis teams, and value engineering (VE) emerged. VE has been promoted by the federal government, which offers higher profits to contractors that are able to lower costs through VE studies of government specifications.

Japanese companies tend to underspecify their products so that value analysis may iron out the details on the shop floor or in the supplier's plant; the advantage is that production and design attributes are more closely matched.

Some companies have standardization committees to try to cut down on proliferations of parts, sizes, colors, and so forth. This smooths the flow of parts and cuts inventories and inventory management. National and international bodies assist in the industrial standardization effort.

Overall control of the materials management function may be sought by establishing materials management as a profit center. The department may earn a profit by cutting costs or investment or by getting better prices. The high costs of materials may justify the trouble of running it as a profit center.

REFERENCES

Books

Aljian, George W. *Purchasing Handbook.* 3d ed. New York: McGraw-Hill, 1973.

Ammer, Dean S. *Materials Management.* Homewood, Ill.: Richard D. Irwin, 1974 (TS161.A42).

England, Wilbur B., and Michael R. Leenders. *Purchasing and Materials Management.* 6th ed. Homewood Ill.: Richard D. Irwin, 1975.

Lee, Lamar, Jr., and Donald W. Dobler. *Purchasing and Materials Management: Text and Cases.* 3d ed. New York: McGraw-Hill, 1977 (HD52.5.L4).

Love, Stephen F. *Inventory Control.* New York: McGraw-Hill, 1979 (HD55.L68).

Mudge, Arthur E. *Value Engineering: A Systematic Approach.* New York: McGraw-Hill, 1971 (TS168.M83).

Orlicky, Joseph. *Material Requirements Planning.* New York: McGraw-Hill, 1975 (TS155.8.O74).

Periodicals (societies)

Journal of Purchasing and Materials Management (National Association of Purchasing Management)

Production and Inventory Management (American Production and Inventory Control Society)

Purchasing

REVIEW QUESTIONS

1. Why did purchasing and material-handling people support the change to the materials-management structure?

2. Why is Townsend's approach not for everybody?

3. How did the "oil shock" affect the purchasing function?

4. Why has the focused-factory concept become popular?

5. Contrast the "black box" and the "probing" approaches to dealing with suppliers.

6. Why does Japanese industry tend to select suppliers differently than U.S. industry?

7. Why do Japanese JIT plants conduct extensive quality audits in supplier plants?

8. What constitute the fixed and variable costs that may be entered into break-even formulas for deciding whether to make or buy?

9. What is the purpose of ABC analysis?

10. How do stock records deter theft and misuse of materials?

11. Compare the needs for stock record accuracy in ROP, MRP, and JIT plants.

12. What is the overall objective of the purchasing department in buying class *A* items?

13. Should MRO items be bought with petty cash? Explain.

14. What special problems does the buying of intangibles present for the purchasing department?

15. How can buyers make money for their companies?

16. Explain how value analysis and standardization are used in a JIT plant.

PROBLEMS

1. From the chapter discussion four kinds of organization for materials activities may be identified: (1) traditional (see Figure 8–1A); (2) materials management, including production control (Figure 8–1B); (3) materials management, without production control (Figure 8–1B); and (4) despecialization. A number of organizational settings are listed below. For each one, state which of the four forms is most suitable. Explain your reasoning. (A reference on materials management is: Jeffrey G. Miller and Peter Gilmour, "Materials Managers: Who Needs Them?" *Harvard Business Review,* July–August 1979, pp. 143–53.)

   Aerospace company that is highly project-oriented.
   Chemical company.
   Foundry.
   U.S. Navy shipyard.
   Private shipyard faced with severe cost problems.
   Fabric manufacturer.
   Machine-tool manufacturer.

2. Buick has found that 80 percent of its bought materials (in dollar value) come from suppliers located within 75 miles of Buick's Flint, Michigan, manufacturing center. What special advantages does this present to Buick in its efforts to adopt the just-in-time system? Explain.

3. In an earlier chapter it was noted that there are generally fewer staff specialists in Japanese than in western manufacturing. Is Robert Townsend's form of "despecialization" similar to the Japanese tendency? Explain. (Note: Japanese manufacturers *do* have purchasing departments.)

4. A story (*Iron Age,* September 15, 1982) about Nissan's truck manufacturing plant in Smyrna, Tennessee, notes the following: "Nissan . . . wants to buy 455 parts from U.S. suppliers" and wants suppliers to build plants "near Smyrna and then deliver just-in-time." "The huge plant, which covers 69 acres, is divided into three plants [each with its own plant manager]: stamping and body assembly, paint, and trim and chassis assembly. In most U.S. plants, stampings are made in one plant and shipped to the assembly plants, [but] Nissan will make 45 percent of its stampings at Smyrna—as many outer stampings as possible."

   a. Is Nissan trying to follow the Japanese way of gaining supplier reliability? Explain.
   b. Does Nissan appear to be following the focused-factory concept? Explain.

5. A home remodeling contractor presently subcontracts concrete work, which is mainly for pouring concrete patios. The patios cost an average of $400 each. If the remodeling company were to do the patios itself, there would be an initial outlay of $8,000 for a concrete mixer, wheelbarrows, and so forth. But the cost per patio for labor, materials, and extras would drop to $200.

   a. What is the break-even volume?
   b. Draw and fully label the break-even graph.

6. Othello Corp. has a company uniform that employees may wear if they choose. Othello spends $60 for each new uniform. If Othello made its own uniforms the variable cost (labor, materials, etc.) would be only $50 each. But a sewing machine would have to be leased for $200 per year.

   a. What is the number of uniforms per year that is required to break even on the $200 lease cost for the machine?
   b. If 15 new uniforms per year is the projected need, is it better to make or buy uniforms? Explain.
   c. Draw and fully label the break-even graph.

7. A large corporation is considering the establishment of its own travel department, which would earn commissions on airline tickets. The current cost of airline tickets averages $122 per trip. With an internal travel department earning commissions, it is estimated that the ticket cost will drop to $105 per trip. The salaries and expenses of the travel department would come to $40,000 per year.

   What number of tickets per year would the corporation need to process in order to break even on writing its own tickets instead of buying tickets from an outside agency? If the corporation projects 2,000 trips per year, should it buy or make?

8. Below are eight items in a firm's inventory. Devise an ABC classification scheme for the items. Show which class each item fits into.

Item	Unit cost	Annual demand
A	$ 1.35	6,200
B	53.00	900
C	5.20	50
D	92.00	120
E	800.00	2
F	0.25	5,000
G	9,000.00	5
H	15.00	18,000

9. Several examples of uses of ABC inventory classification were discussed in the chapter.
   a. Suggest five more uses, and discuss their value.
   b. How could ABC analysis be used for MRP component parts?

10. Arrange the following six item numbers into logical *A, B,* and *C* classes (put at least one item into each class):

Item number	Quantity demanded last year	Unit price
24	2	$ 800
8	10	15,000
37	1,000	0.05
92	3	12
14	80	50
35	20	1.25

11. Arrange the following five item numbers into logical *A, B,* and *C* classes (put at least one item into each class):

Item number	Quantity demanded last year	Unit cost
109	6	$1,000
083	400	0.25
062	10	10
122	1	280
030	10,000	3

12. Stock record cards for three inventory items are shown below:

Item:
Stock no.: 3688 $Q=$
Location: $ROP=$

Remarks	Purchase/ manufacture order no.	Unit cost	Date	Receipts/ issues	Balance
Adjust for cycle count			2–1	−10	1,100
			2–17	−400	700
			3–1	−25	675
Order	P-110		3–1		
			3–15	−80	595
Receipt	P-110	$50	3–28	+1,000	1,595
			4–4	−65	1,530
			4–20	−100	1,430
Adjust for cycle count			5–1	−5	1,425

Item: Stock no.: 1011 Location			Q= ROP=		
Remarks	Purchase/ manufacture order no.	Unit cost	Date	Receipts/ issues	Balance
Adjust for cycle count			2–1	+2	1,820
			2–10	−500	1,320
			2–18	−700	620
Order	M-88		2–19		
			2–21	−250	370
Backorder 30			2–28	−370	0
Receipt	M-88	$2.10	3–2	+2,000	2,000
			3–3	−30	1,970
			3–11	−350	1,620
			3–16	−650	970
			3–20	−500	470
Order	M-110		3–21		
			3–27	−300	170
Receipt	M-110	$2.20	3–30	+2,000	2,170
Adjust for cycle count			4–1	0	2,170

Item: Stock no.: 7092 Location:			Q= ROP=		
Remarks	Purchase/ manufacture order no.	Unit cost	Date	Receipts/ issues	Balance
Adjust for cycle count			2–1	0	15
			2–4	−2	13
			2–9	−3	10
			2–12	−3	7
			2–13	−2	5
			2–18	−1	4
Order	P-78		2–18		
			2–22	−2	2
Receipt	P-78	$1,500	2–23	+20	22
			2–26	−2	20
			2–27	−2	18
Adjust for cycle count			3–1	0	18

a.   What are the order quantities and approximate reorder points for each item?

b.   What are the average annual demand rates and the average lead times for each item?

c.   For each item, make the computation needed for ABC classification of items. What classes would you expect for each of these items? Why?

    d. Discuss the firm's physical inventory policies. Include explanation of the cycle-count adjustments for each item.

13. Below are four descriptions of inventory *counting* situations. One is an example of good practice; the other three are examples of poor practice. Find the good one and explain why it is good—and the three poor ones and explain why they are poor. (Note: Pay no heed to the correctness of practices other than counting.)

    a. Allegheny Electric Co. is a large electric products wholesaler that carries large stocks. Allegheny uses the cycle-counting variation in which class *A, B,* and *C* items are counted every time an issue is made.

    b. Shadow Mountain Brass Co., an MRP user, does complete annual physical inventories.

    c. At the Abalone Naval Base, the evening duty officer frequently lets production supervisors into the parts warehouse when they want to return excess materials after hours. The supervisors are supposed to look up the stock locations and put stock away in correct shelves (since stockkeepers don't work the late shifts). The warehouse cycle-counts by the stock-location method.

    d. The Flat Beer Bottling Works cycle-counts materials (such as cans and labels) held in the stockroom using the method of counting after a new order for an item has been received.

14. The purchasing department at OK Industries uses different buying techniques for different items bought. What are two appropriate buying techniques for each of the following items?

    a. Bearings and seals for the factory machinery.

    b. Gear assemblies bought as direct materials in quantities of 8,000 per year.

    c. A special bottle of drafting ink for the company's one draftsman.

    d. Nails used in the maintenance department.

15. Several types of organizations are listed below. Each has different kinds of purchases to make.

Fashions (apparel)	Car-rental company
Liquor wholesaler	Glass manufacturer
City government	Plastics manufacturer
Major home-appliance manufacturer	Computer manufacturer
Electric power company	Food wholesaler
Furniture manufacturer	Shipbuilder
Construction contractor	Aerospace company

    a. Discuss some key purchasing techniques that would be useful for four of the types of organizations listed above.

    b. Which types of organizations on the list are most likely to be heavily involved in buying intangibles? Explain.

    c. Which types of organizations on the list are most likely to use an approved supplier list? bid solicitation based on specifications? blanket orders? Explain.

    d. Which types of organizations on the list are most likely to use value analysis? Explain.

16. Some years ago, the public school system in Gary, Indiana, contracted with a company to run the Gary schools. The contract featured incentive payments for raising scores on standardized math and verbal tests. What weaknesses do you suppose were present in this contract? Discuss.

17. Value analysis often begins by selecting VA projects from old specifications from the design engineering files. How is value analysis modified in companies using the just-in-time production system, and why?

18. The following is a list of products to be analyzed by value analysis.

A classroom desk	Bookends
A mousetrap	An electric fan
A backpack-style book toter	Handlebars on a bike
The grate in a fireplace	A bike lock
A coaster on which to set drinks	The lamp part shown in the accompanying sketch

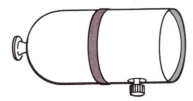

a. Select any four of the above, and define its function or functions in two words, as discussed in the chapter.

b. Why is function definition an early and precisely done step in value analysis/value engineering? Explain what this step accomplishes, using some of your examples from part a.

19. Jane A. Doe has just moved to another city and taken a job with a company that manufactures lawn sprinklers, which was exactly the kind of company she had worked for in her prior city of residence. She finds that her new company has three or four times as many different part numbers going into essentially the same models of sprinklers. Is this good or bad? Discuss.

20. Consolidated Game Corp. is establishing its materials management (MM) department as a profit center. The following data were collected and may be useful:

Cost of purchased materials last year	$ 8,000,000
MM department's operating expenses last year	120,000
Total assets, whole firm	5,000,000
Fixed assets (facilities) in MM dept	150,000
Sales last year, whole firm	16,000,000
Earnings before taxes last year, whole firm	500,000
Present inventory of purchased items	1,000,000

a. What should the MM department's average markup be if its profit rate is set to equal the rate of return on assets for the whole firm?

b. Next year the department is able, through aggressive purchasing, to do the same level of business but for a cost of $7,950,000 for purchased materials. If all other data are unchanged, what is the MM department's new rate of return on assets? Compare the new rate with last year's rate.

21. In Energistics' second year it earned a 22 percent profit. The MM department's new profit target for the third year thus became 22 percent.

    a. What revenue and what average markup should MM plan for in the third year? (See Example 8–3 for second-year results which are used in third-year planning.)

    b. Assume that MM's "sales" to other departments drop to $40 million and that aggressive buying yields a 5 percent improvement in the purchase cost of goods "sold." If service expenses and assets are unchanged, what is MM's third-year profit performance?

    c. In part *b* it seems that purchasing carries most of the load in achieving a given rate of profitability in MM. But purchasing is only one of several MM divisions. Discuss the effects on MM profitability that can be attributed to other divisions normally found in an MM department.

PART TWO CASE STUDY: HEWLETT-PACKARD— GREELEY DIVISION

The Greeley Division of Hewlett-Packard manufactures small disc drives (3½, 5¼, and 8 inch) for desk-top or other small computers. It is a product line appealing to more of a mass market than H-P, best known for its exotic electronics, is accustomed to.

The Greeley Division is presently crammed into space shared with other H-P divisions in Ft. Collins, Colorado. A new building is going up in Greeley 25 miles away. It will be ready for occupancy in four months. Wiring for phones, electrical outlets, etc., must be final in three months. A first-draft floor plan has been prepared by industrial engineering.

A just-in-time (JIT) project was kicked off one-and-a-half months ago. A JIT core group consisting of four people has been meeting every day trying to make decisions that could be built into the floor plan at the new Greeley plant site. The core group consists of Dave Taylor, materials manager; Gus Winfield, process engineering manager; Doug McCord, production manager; and Mark Oman, a production section manager. Gary Flack, manufacturing manager, is the group's boss and enthusiastic backer of the JIT project. About 40 more people have been meeting in various JIT project task forces to make recommendations to the core group.

PLANT TOUR

It is now the 29th of December 1982, and John Richards, a JIT consultant, has just spent two days at the plant. Richards spent his first morning touring the Ft. Collins operation, which is housed in three connected buildings—Buildings 1, 2, and 3—plus one warehouse for incoming materials a mile away. The tour followed the natural process flow to manufacture a disc drive: in the warehouse building, receiving, quality check, prepack, and storage; and in the main building complex, kitting, printed circuit board processing, final assembly, and shipping. Here are some of the things that Richards found out:

Quality Check

The division must spend a lot of time in receiving inspection. The defect rate on a key purchased item, the mechanical disc drive units, ranges from 5 percent from one supplier to 20 and 30 percent for two others. It takes three hours to inspect 50 drive units. The division's hope of doing away with most receiving inspection, as mature JIT operations in Japan do, does not seem near at hand.

Prepack

Goods such as transistors, diodes, and memory chips do not arrive counted out in packages in the same quantities as are being used in production. So a number of people work full time opening cartons, counting pieces (sometimes by weighing) and inserting them into packages.

Storage

Bulk storage consists of three long rows of racks served by two semiautomatic stock-picking vehicles, which allow the driver to pick by hand and also have forks for picking a whole pallet load. A card file keeps track of all storage locations.

A small-parts storage area is equipped with four long, horizontal carousel storage units, which are something like those used in dry cleaning businesses to hang cleaned clothes. Cardboard boxes holding hundreds of small electronic components and hardware are on trays hung from the carousel's frame. Across from one end of the carousel units there are several inclined roller conveyors. An order is filled as follows: One person keys in a stock number at a computer terminal, which rotates the carousel so that the right bin is facing the stock-picking area; and puts the selected parts into sacks, which go into tote boxes, which move down the roller conveyors. A person at the other side of the flow racks puts delivery labels on the tote boxes to note where they are to be delivered, and the boxes are put on pallets for later delivery to the main production complex in Buildings 1 and 3.

Computers drive the put-away and order-filling activities in the bulk and carousel storage area (and also a third storage area consisting of ordinary shelving). The computers are linked up to online terminals in all production areas. Material requirements planning (MRP) issues lists of parts needed, and storage has four days to deliver.

An "electric kanban" system conveys a message (by computer) when a using work center needs material sooner. Delivery is within 24 hours for electric kanban items. Fifty (of 4,000) parts presently are covered by the kanban system, and 50 more will soon be put on it. Connie Weichel, the supervisor in bulk storage, told the touring group that "we will never be able to handle 50 more." The kanban procedure dates back to August 1981, and it went online ("electric") in October of 1982.

The storage area is obviously sophisticated—but also, by JIT standards, elaborate and containing a large quantity of materials. Examples of items kept in particularly large quantities are:

1. Circuit boards (CBs). An eight-month supply is on hand, partly because CB suppliers require long purchase lead times.

2. Aluminum top covers. Almost a three-month supply is on hand right now—and it has been four or five times greater than that—even though the supplier is only two miles away.

3. Packing materials and manuals. Of some 600 pallet loads of material in bulk storage, about 100 hold cardboard used in packing, and 100–200 hold manuals sent out in final product cartons.

Kitting

A kit is a set of parts that goes into one unit of product. The division prepares kits of diodes, resistors, and so forth that are to be inserted into printed circuit boards. The kitting is done in Building 1. Mostly the kits consist of trays or circular racks of parts used in semiautomatic insertion machines. The concept, according to Doug McCord, is to "prearrange and predevelop locations where assemblers will not need to search." Kitting has become very efficient, going from a staff of four down to about one worker in three to four months.

PC Process

The printed circuit process is in Building 1. It consists of:

1. Silk screening. Place dots of solder resist on the circuit board places where solder is not intended.

2. Preform. Tapes of resistors, etc., are fed through a machine that cuts wire ends to length and bends them so they will fit into CB holes.

3. Insertion. Insert components into CB holes—either using a Royonic machine, which aids in hand loading, or a semiautomatic machine that inserts parts from a plastic carousel tray. One factor that slows down insertion is the large number of different CB designs, including a lot of variation in spacing of holes in the different CB models. Richards asked about product standardization. The reply was that H-P engineers are used to a lot of freedom to innovate and follow their own inclinations. However, there are some process engineers who work with design engineers.

4. Wave soldering. A wave of molten solder passes under the CB to connect the ends of the wires. The single large expensive wave-soldering machine is located in the middle of Building 1. The machine can run mixed models but only if they are all the same thickness; the different models now come in several thicknesses. Richards noted that the machine seemed very well vented so that no fumes or heat were noticeable.

5. Wash. Wash foreign matter off the CBs.

6. Add on. Add various nonwashable components to the CB.

7. Test. Place each CB on a sophisticated H-P-designed electronic testing machine, called a "bed of nails"; "nail" points make contact with various circuit locations, and a sequence of tests is run. There are several of these machines, each set for a different size board. It takes less than a minute to key in the proper instructions to test a different model of CB.

8. Board age. Plug in each CB for up to 24 hours of "burn in."

The PC process is not as automated as it is in various other large electronics companies. One reason is that H-P's volumes are small and variety of designs is large. So cheaper, more flexible machines are used. For example, H-P's semiautomatic insert machines (step 3 above) cost about $20,000, as compared with $100,000–$150,000 for highly automated machines available on the market. The core group is pleased with the low-cost equipment, since it gives them the kind of flexibility that JIT plants normally need to keep going without cushions of inventory.

Assembly

Assembly consists of a small subassembly step—making line filters—and then final assembly, in which a CB, filters, memory devices, drive units, and so forth, are assembled and installed into a metal and/or plastic case. Assembly is not paced, that is, not regulated by the pace of a powered conveyor. Instead, assembly jobs involve doing a number of operations. It is consistent with "the H-P way" for jobs to consist of a collection of tasks leading to a tangible product that workers can take some personal pride in.

In the assembly area for one of the higher-volume disc drives, assemblers sit at stations along a roller conveyor. A material handler feeds drive units, CBs, etc., down the conveyor; assemblers pick the components off the conveyor, perform the assembly, set completed units aside for transport to packing, and grab more parts. Before the JIT project began, the conveyor was always crammed with components awaiting assembly. Mark Oman, the section manager, had changed the procedures so that just enough work is on the conveyor to keep the assemblers going. The idea is to cut the in-process inventory so that it piles up at an earlier stage of production—then cut it there, etc., which results in more of a just-in-time process from start to finish.

One low-volume line of disc drives called the Sparrow has been designated as a special JIT pilot-test product. Gail Johnson, a production worker in Sparrow assembly, showed Richards the results of an initial JIT effort: a prominently displayed chart of the number of units produced per day for about the past month. The goal is to make exactly the same number every day, so that all stages of manufacture and purchase connected with the Sparrow line can depend on the number needed. The chart showed almost perfect achievement of a daily level production rate—referred to as "linearization." In order to make this possible, Mark Oman, the section manager, had instituted the concept of less-than-full-capacity scheduling for the Sparrow operation.

Packing

Cathy Cameron, packing supervisor, told the touring group that her three largest-volume products were presently being shipped in quantities of 800 per month, 700 per month, and 250 per month. An "instapack" machine is central to the packing operation. The machine operator's tasks are to place a cardboard box on a stand, put a disc drive wrapped in clear plastic into the box, and squirt a liquid into the space between the wrapped drive and the box. The liquid is stored under high pressure in a tank; when it is released, it expands and quickly hardens into a lightweight rigid foam, molded around the plastic-wrapped drive. Then the box is closed and sent to taping and stenciling. One concern about instapack is that it can yield an odor. Another is that the high-pressure vessels containing the liquid could be a safety hazard. These matters are of concern partly because of being inconsistent with "the H-P way," discussed next.

"THE H-P WAY"

During the morning tour, John Richards, the consultant, learned that some H-P employees refer to the company rather affectionately as the "H-P Land and Building Co." On seeing the main building complex for the first time, Richards had thought he was probably seeing a modern part of Colorado State University campus. The buildings and landscaping are quite lovely and unlike almost any factory. The inside is immaculately clean, light, airy, open, quiet, and full of plants. Richards learned that H-P spends far more on buildings than the average for the industry and that such expenditures are another element of "the H-P way," which is the name for a humanistic corporate culture molded over the years by Mr. Hewlett and Mr. Packard, the founders. One concern that Richards expressed was that the present buildings did not have much dock space, which can mean a good deal of congestion and extra handling to unload frequent JIT deliveries.

Labor policies also reflect the H-P way. All employees are covered by flex time, in which workers receive a liberal number of flex days off per year, based on seniority. There is no separate allowance for sick leave. The flex days are used for everything. They may be taken an hour at a time, a day at a time, or any way desired, as the employee chooses. Employees may pick their own hours of the day to work. H-P plants are not unionized, and H-P has never had a layoff.

PRESENTATIONS

During the rest of the day and at dinner that evening, Richards met with the core group, Gary Flack, and the task forces. Plans, hopes, strategies, and concerns were presented and discussed. A few of the topics covered are as follows.

ABC

Dave Taylor explained to Richards that all inventory items in the computer data base had been sorted out by traditional ABC analysis. The results were surprising. Instead of the usual smooth Pareto curve, H-P has a rather small number of high-dollar-usage (class *A*) items and a very large number of small-dollar-usage (class *C*) items—but hardly any in-between (class *B*) items. But included in the class *C* group are a number of items that are very bulky—mainly cardboard boxes and packing materials. These were upgraded to class *B*, where *B* is for "bulky."

Taylor and Jim Heckel, the purchasing manager, feel that the ABC results provide special advantages in moving toward JIT. They may focus their JIT energies on the very modest number of class *A* and *B* items; class *C* items can be largely uncontrolled without much cost.

The present ABC policy guidelines are to order and deliver class *A* items weekly, class *B* items monthly, and class *C* items semiannually. The core group wants the new policies under JIT to be daily for class *A* and *B*, and quarterly for class *C*.

Purchasing

Getting suppliers to convert to small frequent lots is a major concern of the core group and Heckel. The problem is that H-P's order quantities are a drop in the bucket for most of their suppliers. H-P does not have the clout to get suppliers to treat them in a special manner. One hope is that other users will also begin demanding JIT deliveries from the same suppliers; also, some of the suppliers will probably get involved in just-in-time programs of their own.

Heckel's plans include bringing in some of the key suppliers for a group meeting to explain what H-P is trying to do and why. Richards mentioned that Kawasaki in Nebraska did exactly that early in its own JIT program. Kawasaki called it a "vendor day."

Richards also noted that a few other companies that have started up JIT programs have elected to make a daily truck circuit to pick up small quantities of boxing and packing materials from their suppliers of those items, instead of their former practice of getting separate large infrequent deliveries from each. Dave and Jim could see no reason why the Greeley Division couldn't do the same thing.

Heckel said paper towels, cups, napkins, and so forth were class *B* items that could be reduced to one-day supplies, delivered every day.

Inventory Control

Being in the computer business, H-P has been partial toward extensive use of computers for manufacturing control. MRP is used in most H-P plants, and use of online terminals to track the flow of WIP inventory is widespread. The core group's objective is to move products through the plant so fast that there is no need to track WIP—and the same goes for labor, which could just be allocated over the total number of circuit boards at month's end. One core group member speculated that "accounting and Price-Waterhouse will tear their hair out when we start doing that." The irony of a computer company reducing its use of computer controls also was not lost on the group.

Taylor noted during the morning plant tour, and reiterated in the afternoon, the existence of many "stockroom Us" throughout the plant. "Stockroom U" is a term sometimes used by MRP people to describe stock on the production floor treated by the MRP system as if it were in a stockroom. That is, the computer logs all flows of stock into and out of that shop-floor area stockroom. These stockroom Us and their inventory are prime candidates for reduction in the JIT project.

Gary Flack participated in part of the presentations to Richards. Gary stated the plant presently had an average of 2.8 months' inventory on hand; his goal or edict is to reduce it to 1.9 months' worth by the end of the fiscal year (October 31). (Dave later noted that his own target was a more ambitious 1.5 months' supply.) Gary also noted that, in his division, material costs account for 25 percent of end product cost, whereas labor accounts for only $8/10$ of 1 percent! Gary feels strongly that far too much attention has been paid in the past to controlling labor costs and far too little in controlling material costs. Just-in-time control seems to be just what is needed.

Flack also suggested a way to reduce the huge stock of manuals in bulk storage. H-P has state-of-the-art laser printing facilities in the plant, and Flack thought that perhaps they could print their own manuals, a few every day "just in time."

Training

The core group considered training and understanding to be keys to JIT project success. They had prepared a demonstration of the effects of job-lot versus just-in-time production. The demonstration was partially captured on slides, which were shown at an afternoon meeting attended by many of the task forces and Richards. The slides showed the four core-group members around a U-shaped mock production line consisting of tables in a conference room. They were making a "product" out of styrofoam packing materials and cardboard packers. The first slides showed tables heaped with materials and production in lots of six. The next slides showed somewhat less material for a lot size of three; but a quality defect introduced toward the end caused an inventory buildup at that point. Next slides showed nearly clear tables, achieved by one-piece-lots and full JIT production. Final slides summarized results, which were based on careful counts and timing: dramatic reductions in space, lot size, cycle time, and WIP; also, quality and rework problems that had been buried in inventory were shown to be immediately visible under JIT.

Redundant Tasks

Gus Winfield, core group member and head of a containerization task force, felt that too much counting and prepacking is done—that the suppliers should do it as much as possible. Also, there was debate about the need for kitting and packing everything to improve production line efficiency. One suggestion was to have certain purchased items delivered right to the using work center with as little handling by material control as possible. Gail Johnson (Sparrow line) thought that this might create a lot of packing litter that would present disposal problems.

Plant Layout

The liveliest discussions centered around plant layout. In one of the afternoon meetings blueprints of the proposed floor plan were laid out on the table. The prints showed a more logical arrangement of processes than was possible in their present shared buildings. Everything, including storage, would be in one building. Instapack, with its potential fumes and safety problem, would be isolated somewhat in a separate room on an outer wall. Although the design of the new building does not provide for an appreciable increase in dock space for JIT deliveries, Flack observed that a wall could be knocked out if necessary.

Richards was asked for his impressions on the layout. He replied that an alternative would be to totally abandon the process-oriented layout. That is, instead of putting all kitting in one location, all assembly in another, and so forth, separate production lines could be developed for each product. The underlying concept is known as group technology (GT), which the core group was familiar with, but had not had time to fully consider. For a given product, one long production line could be planned from receiving to shipping, with work stations so close together that work can be handed from one station to another. Alternatively, one product, say the Sparrow, could be made in two or three GT cells, perhaps U-shaped for maximum staffing flexibility. A natural separation might be wave soldering: Since there is only one wave machine, GT cells for each product could end at the wave machine; then, more GT cells could complete the production process for each product. There was some discussion about the feasibility of small simple table-top alternatives to the large wave machine—so that each product could have its own wave process capability.

One option discussed was doing a pilot test of the GT-cell concept—probably for the Sparrow. The results could then be used to decide whether to extend GT cells or production lines to all products.

Another point of controversy was whether to break up assembly jobs so that each assembler has a few operations to perform in a GT cell. Presently each assembler works rather independently and is self-paced. There was some sentiment for going to divided tasks in GT cells in order to get the benefits of teamwork and mutual dependency.

The implications of going to GT cells were considerable. The core group members, especially material manager Dave Taylor, could see their jobs being eliminated or significantly altered. For example, if work stations are butted up against each other with no handling in between, the material handling staff could be reduced to almost nothing; if the production line receives, inspects, and unpacks its own materials, there go several other functions now under material control. The storage area shrinks to the point where the need for semiautomatic stock pickers, carousel storage systems, and computer-based planning may be greatly reduced. There was a lot of good-natured joking about all this and a surprisingly cavalier attitude about the prospect of eliminating one's own job.

Consultant's Presentation

After lunch on December 29, Richards gave a one-hour presentation to a group of about 40—the core group, Gary Flack, and many of the task force people. Richards gave his views on the advantages of JIT, told about other Japanese and American companies doing it, and detailed a few of the alternative ways to proceed in the Greeley Division, especially focusing on the provocative issues of plant layout by processes or by GT cells. After the meeting broke up, Richards was saying goodbye and getting ready to catch a plane. Dave and Gus were marveling at the groups of task force members out in the halls buzzing about the issues before them and the hard decisions that had to be made.

DISCUSSION QUESTIONS

1. What type of production is the Greeley Division engaged in? Continuous, repetitive, job-lot, job, project, or limited-quantity large-scale? Explain.

2. What do you think of the electric kanban approach? Discuss.

3. What should be done about prepack? About kitting?

4. Can the Greeley Division achieve its inventory reduction goals? Fully discuss, including your perception of major obstacles to be overcome.

5. Should assembly stay as it is—in mostly self-contained jobs? Or should jobs be divided up and apportioned to a mutually dependent assembly team?

6. What decision should be made on plant layout, and why?

7. Are there any major JIT techniques that have been overlooked?

8. Are there any broad external kinds of steps that should be taken (e.g., with regard to outside suppliers, accounting, design engineering, the corporate staff)?

Part Three

Translating Planned Orders into Operations

Work, jobs, tasks, activities, projects, operations. These are the outcomes of the efforts of operations managers. In Part Three we see how the operations are scheduled and controlled. First, in Chapter 9, are the continuous, repetitive, and automated operations. The next topic, in Chapter 10, is job-lot operations. Then, in Chapter 11, the topic is large-scale operations and the PERT/CPM and LOB techniques for planning and controlling those kinds of operations. Chapter 12, concluding this section, is on the control of quality.

Chapter 9

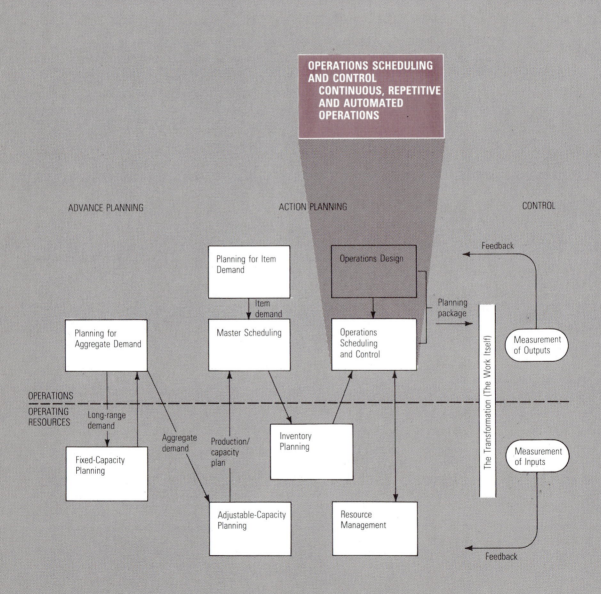

OPERATIONS SCHEDULING AND CONTROL
CONTINUOUS, REPETITIVE AND AUTOMATED OPERATIONS

ADVANCE PLANNING   ACTION PLANNING   CONTROL

Planning for Item Demand

Operations Design   Feedback

Item demand

Planning package

Planning for Aggregate Demand   Master Scheduling   Operations Scheduling and Control   Measurement of Outputs

OPERATIONS
OPERATING RESOURCES

Long-range demand

Aggregate demand   Production/capacity plan   Inventory Planning

Fixed-Capacity Planning

The Transformation (The Work Itself)

Measurement of Inputs

Adjustable-Capacity Planning   Resource Management

Feedback

Continuous, Repetitive, and Automated Operations

Continuous or repetitive operations are found in steel and aluminum mills, power generation, gas transportation, crude oil and sugar refining, canneries, breweries, processing insurance claims, and mailing out social security checks. In these and other like endeavors, planning and control are made simple by the steady quantities flowing through the process. Whole blocks of capacity—a whole production line, for example—may be dedicated to the production of a single product or model, and products of a given type all follow the same flow path one after another. You feed raw materials in one end, and finished goods come out the other end. Scheduling tends to take care of itself at all stages in between.

This does not mean that there is nothing to worry about. Regular flow paths (routings) make it easier to justify capital equipment to replace labor. But then if problems develop—machine breakdown, material shortage, and so forth—a whole production line may be shut down. To avoid these costly shutdowns, the company tries to make the process so reliable that problems rarely occur or to become adept at reacting to problems quickly.

In this chapter, we consider ways to make continuous and repetitive operations work smoothly and also how to make stop-and-go operations more streamlined. Just-in-time (JIT[1]) production serves as a useful goal or "rallying point"; there are a variety of JIT techniques that help streamline productive operations. The techniques range from use of robots and flexible manufacturing systems, to controlling the transportation system, to use of the kanban ordering technique.

TOWARD STREAMLINED OPERATIONS

In the mainstream of the history of production is a movement toward more continuous or repetitive operations. The earliest successes were in commodity-like products whose uniformity paves the way for continuous production: coal, steel, grain, newsprint, glass, sugar, oil, plastics, and many more. These industries today are highly capital-intensive and produce goods in a steady flow. They are often called the process industries (meaning relatively continuous flow process).

But discrete producers—even the services sector—also want to enjoy the advantages of smooth-flow operations; that is, they want high efficiency, low inventory, low labor cost, uniform quality, simple planning and control, and few surprises. The best discrete goods producers indeed are coming to resemble the continuous processors, in results if not in methods nor in uniformity of product. In other words, repetitive producers of discrete goods are achieving some of the benefits enjoyed by continuous producers of goods that flow or pour. Industries that bottle, can, package, or box meats, fruits, vegetables, food mixtures, drugs, cosmetics, and cleaning products have developed relatively repetitive processing methods. McDonald's and other fast-food restaurant chains have made similar achievements at the retail end of the food industry.

---

[1] JIT also stands for *job instruction training,* a procedure for training supervisors who then train the employees. The term was in wide use during World War II but not much today.

Smoothing Out Irregularities

In hundreds of other industries turning out industrial and consumer goods, final assembly may be largely repetitive, but the preassembly stages of manufacture have been mostly job-lot. Job-lot means stop and go rather than smooth and steady.

Some of the irregularity of job-lot parts fabrication is removed by using material requirements planning and shop activity control. MRP permits tighter and more accurate scheduling of orders for parts made or bought; this results in less inventory expense and less risk of failure to meet due dates for lack of the right materials. Queue control on the shop floor (covered in the next chapter) provides quick reaction to problems, which also has smoothing effects.

Just-in-time production, discussed in earlier chapters, offers further potential to smooth the irregularities of job-lot production. JIT can help to transform job-lot into a more streamlined, perhaps repetitive, mode of production. Just-in-time calls for wiping out buffer stocks and for producing and delivering parts just in time for use. A unique feature of JIT is enforced problem solving: Without extra inventory, small ripples in the rate of production or delivery at one stage of manufacture appear as large waves; all hands rally to correct the problem causing the ripples, because next stages of production are being starved of parts. The idea is to accept the consequences—temporary parts starvation—in order to get at the underlying problems. The short-term pain is worth the long-term gain.

Quick-fix solutions may warrant more thorough study. Workers and foremen learn to collect data, conduct problem-solving analyses, and recommend corrective action. Usually engineers and other experts follow through with a detailed solution to the problem. There is a wide variety of solutions—ways to smooth the ripples and curtail production slowdowns and stoppages. The solutions include better raw materials, better worker training, simpler setup or production methods, better equipment and tools, better maintenance, more thorough process control of quality, automatic quality checking and parts counting, robots and other automation equipment, kanban, group technology, overlapped production, multimodel production—the list goes on and on.

Products and Processes

Until recently, the potential for becoming more streamlined in all types of operations (including even low-volume production, but excluding artistic and philosophical endeavors) was poorly understood. We thought that streamlined production was inherent for commodity processes but not possible for custom jobs. Today we see many industries trying to become more like commodity processors—and with a good deal of success.

At one time all products—even what we now call commodities—were made in the job-shop mode. For example, put yourself in Placerville, California, in 1849 during the gold rush. Say that you have a toothache, and you are lucky enough to find a dentist in the camp. The dentist says you need a tooth filled. He melts down freshly panned gold from the South Fork River and by the light of a lamp burning the oil

FIGURE 9–1

Product-Process Matrix

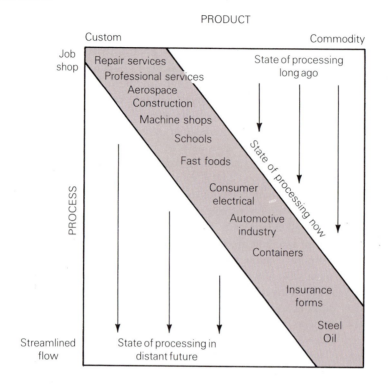

of a muskrat trapped near the same river, he fills your tooth. Fuel and gold are commodities today, produced more or less continuously. But they were custom products made in the job-shop mode when your hypothetical tooth was filled in 1849.

Figure 9–1, called a product-process matrix,[2] is useful for showing roughly how far selected industries have progressed toward streamlined flow processing. (The figure is a bit congested on the left since there are so many different industries that are more in the custom and job-shop categories.) The arrangement of selected industries along the diagonal in the figure is based on best guesses. Repair service workers and white-collar professionals in offices work in the pure job-shop mode, and an aerospace vehicle is a custom product also produced in a halting job-shop manner. Consumer electrical products are part way between custom and commodity: There is a moderate amount of product commonality in the sequence of products to be

---

[2] The original idea for the matrix comes from Robert H. Hayes and Steven C. Wheelwright, "Link Manufacturing Process and Product Life Cycles," *Harvard Business Review,* January–February, 1979, pp. 133–40; this version of the matrix is adapted from Sam G. Taylor, Samuel M. Seward, and Steven F. Bolander, "Why the Process Industries Are Different," *Production and Inventory Management,* Fourth Quarter, 1981, pp. 9–24.

made, and most of the world's electrical products companies make products in a mode that is somewhere in the middle between job shop and streamlined flow. In the lower right corner of Figure 9–1 are two examples of commodity-like products, steel and oil, which are produced in a mostly streamlined flow manner.

Industry Leaders

Within each industry there can be large differences among companies. Figure 9–2 gives two examples. First, in the middle of the figure, is the power tools industry. Black and Decker, an advanced user of material requirements planning, is an industry leader. MRP, including a well-developed shop activity control module, allows Black and Decker to keep inventories low and not have many work stoppages for lack of the right parts. Production is fairly smooth.

In the automobile industry, the Japanese have pioneered streamlined assembly, fabrication, and even purchasing. The just-in-time system is well developed by most of the Japanese automotive and related companies, especially Toyota, the JIT origina-

FIGURE 9–2

Streamlined Flow Capabilities Among Companies in the Same Industry

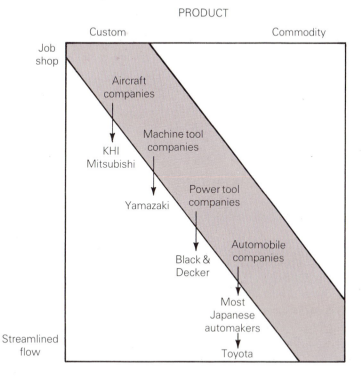

tor. Thus, Figure 9–2 shows "most Japanese automakers" somewhat below the diagonal band and shows Toyota well below it, i.e., highly streamlined.

Farther left in Figure 9–2, we see Yamazaki Machinery Works, which has built an $18 million "factory of the future" in Nagoya, Japan, to produce lathes and punch presses (machine tools). The plant is quite streamlined and efficient, even though volumes are not high and there is a fair degree of product variety. Computer-controlled production and robotized handling play a central role in streamlining this kind of production. The graveyard shift is run without any human workers.

The final example in Figure 9–2 is the aircraft industry, which is a case of complex manufacturing in small volumes. While Boeing and other U.S. producers dominate this industry, a few Japanese companies (e.g., Kawasaki Heavy Industries and Mitsubishi) are attracting attention for their methods in moving toward streamlined production. Streamlining this type of manufacturing calls for a blending of basic concepts and sophisticated equipment. Ultimately, the equipment and manufacturing stages may be closely monitored by process-control computers linked to a central mainframe computer. This degree of computer control is called **computer-integrated manufacturing** (CIM). Since the cost of CIM is very high, good examples of it may not yet exist—and the aircraft industry is merely suggested as one where CIM is likely to develop in the future. But many companies are moving toward CIM by installing pieces of computer-controlled equipment and locating them close together to form manufacturing cells; this creates pockets of streamlined production.

These few examples help to show the evolution toward streamlined production. In the next sections, we take a closer look at success factors in the different industries from commodity to custom.

THE PROCESS INDUSTRIES

In many of the process industries that are most visible to the consumer, the raw materials enter as flows, and the end products emerge as units. Sugar, chocolate, water, and other ingredients flow into a candy factory and cartons of candy bars or boxed candy come out. Potatoes, salt, vegetable oil, and so forth flow into a potato chip plant and cartons of sacked chips emerge. Sugar, water, flavoring, and active ingredients flow into a drug producing plant, and out come boxes of bottled cough medicine.

Success Factors

From an operations standpoint, some of the key success factors in this general type of production are:

1. Process design and capital investment. Most stages from mixing through packaging tend to be quite automated (capital-intensive). Some advantages can be gained by having more modern equipment than one's competitors, but it is often more important to keep the equipment in good condition so that the process yield is high and dependable.

2. **Rigorous maintenance.** An equipment breakdown idles a whole process, e.g., the whole mixing or the whole bottling process in the case of a food or drug company. When the product is perishable, there is further reason for wanting to avoid breakdowns. Perishability is also reason for not being able to use buffer stocks between process stages as protection against breakdowns; in other words, perishability forces more of a just-in-time (stockless) mode of production.

3. **Close monitoring of the process.** In the process industries, federal law or industry-wide standards often govern product quality, purity, sanitation, and so forth. Process monitoring must be rigorous to assure that the standards are met and the products safe and saleable.

4. **Reliability of supply and freight.** This can mean careful selection of a plant site close to raw materials supplies and markets. Regardless of where the plant is located, the freight haulers bringing in raw material must be reliable, because raw materials are the life blood of the process industries. Stockpiling, as protection for shaky supply or freight, is possible. But most of the process industry produces in such large volumes that even a few days' supply of ingredients can take up too much storage space.

5. **Fast changeover time.** Most, but not all, process industry plants are able to change production lines to run different blends and container sizes. Sometimes it takes several days for a line changeover, which may include completely cleaning out all equipment. The company that can make changes fast has an edge.

6. **Optimal mixtures.** One of the more important uses of linear programming, a mathematical technique, is in determining optimal (best) mixtures of ingredients in some process industries. For example, most companies that produce dog food, chicken feed, and so on use linear programming. The technique selects the lowest-cost mix of ingredients that will meet nutrition and other standards. Volumes are usually large, so saving a few cents per pound can be significant.

Process-Industry Examples

There is widespread concern in the process industries for each of the six success factors explained above. Two examples will illustrate.

Potato Chips. In North America, most cities of moderate or large size have their own local potato chip plant. The end product is bulky and susceptible to breakage; also, heat and light are hard on potato chips, which have only a 50-day shelf life. Those factors help explain why potato chip plants are everywhere. While plant site selection is not a critical issue, reliability of supply and delivery of raw materials is. One central-states producer, Weaver's Potato Chips, has potatoes grown to its specifications elsewhere in the state. They are stored at remote sites, and contract truckers bring one to three semi loads of potatoes to the plant every day. Drivers have their own key to the building so they can deliver after hours if necessary. The rate of potato deliveries is closely matched with plant production; only one day of lead time is required to get a delivery. A grain processor in the same city delivers cooking oil on an average of every six days and can deliver the same day if necessary. Thus, critical raw materials are not a problem for Weaver's. Regulations on plant cleanliness dictate that the plant be thoroughly cleaned every night, and, therefore, Weaver's produces only during the day shift. The nightly shutdown for cleaning provides ample time for equipment maintenance, which is a vital success factor.

Pasta.   Spaghetti packages are more compressed and less damage-susceptible than potato chips. Also, spaghetti has a longer shelf life. Pasta factories are few and far between (except perhaps in Italy), because spaghetti may be shipped to fairly distant markets. A local source of flour is an advantage that could help sway the decision on where to locate a pasta plant. But the best pasta is made from hard durum wheat, and most of the world's supply of good durum comes from the Dakotas and Minnesota. Thus, pasta makers (even those in Italy) can make "budget" pasta from locally milled flour and also pay the freight to ship good durum in for higher-grade products.

Making spaghetti is more complex than making potato chips, because spaghetti includes mixing and requires transformation from powder to fluid to solid states through numerous stages of production. Large American pasta factories are quite automated. (At one pasta plant, it typically takes a year to put in a new pasta line.) There are many pieces of mechanical equipment susceptible to breakdown. Since breakdowns in one process soon bring other processes to a halt for lack of materials, equipment maintenance is a major function. Maintenance people are a high proportion of the total workforce. Changes from one type of spaghetti to another require simply changing the dies through which the spaghetti strands are extruded. A die change may take only half an hour; changing packaging equipment is often more time consuming. A pasta plant can operate three shifts. But a plant shutdown for sanitation is necessary every two or three weeks. Pasta plants have a flow time that is short enough to be able to fill a private-label order (e.g., for a grocery chain) in as little as one week.

These two examples—potato chips and pasta—do not begin to capture the breadth of characteristics of the process industries. But they do project an image that is useful in further chapter discussion. The image is one of smooth, streamlined product flow with very low inventories, short leadtime, high efficiency and resource utilization, and dependably high quality. These are characteristics that nonprocess industries once believed were unattainable. But today they provide challenges and goals that nonprocess industries may reasonably aspire to.

REPETITIVE PRODUCTION

Repetitive production is doing about the same thing over and over again in the production of discrete units. There can be variety—within limits. In a Mister Steak restaurant, the cook who grills steaks has a repetitive job, but the steaks vary in size and meat quality. Final assembly of cars, trucks, tractors, and small aircraft is repetitive in much the same way. Each successive unit may have its own set of options, but the assemblers perform about the same tasks over and over.

It is useful to think of repetitive in relative terms. Highly repetitive is the most like continuous flow processing: The product rarely stops moving (little storage, little in-process inventory) and is nearly always in a process of being transformed into a product of greater value. Marginally repetitive has more of the stop-and-go character of job-lot production. That is, much of the time the product is out of production and instead in transit, in buffer storage, waiting for a problem to be fixed, or waiting for setup. It is possible to have high setup time without disrupting the repetitive product flow; for example, set up one machine while the product is in process on another.

Becoming repetitive or more repetitive may be brought about by a variety of techniques for streamlining the production process. These techniques, considered below, include implementing several old and well-known ones, plus several that have emerged from the just-in-time movement. (In the broad sense, all could be thought of as fitting beneath the just-in-time umbrella.)

Just-in-Time Production

Just-in-time techniques can pave the way for more repetitive—less irregular—production. Taiichi Ohno, the brilliant Toyota vice president who was a chief architect of JIT, likens it to a Western supermarket. Goods are received and put on the shelf just in time to be sold. The supermarket does not schedule its purchases weeks in advance; rather, when consumers stop buying an item, the store stops ordering it, and vice versa.

As the term suggests, just-in-time shrinks lead time. It also shrinks space, distance, time lag between when an error is made and when it is found out, and inventories. JIT provides broad control over production so that, in Ohno's words, "If the meaning of production control is truly understood, inventory control is unnecessary."[3]

The most obvious visible *results* of JIT are the lower inventories. But evolving toward just-in-time may employ changes in equipment, plant layout, vendor selection, freight arrangements, material handling, quality control, work procedures, scheduling, labor training, labor assignments, and the role of staff experts—in addition to changes directly affecting inventories.

As has been mentioned, just-in-time may be thought of as a system of **enforced problem solving.** In the JIT environment of minimal inventories, problems—in equipment, plant layout, vendor selection, and the rest of the above list—have to be solved; otherwise production comes to a halt for lack of parts. In traditional production control, extra parts are added to cope with problems; JIT production takes the opposite tack of removing inventory to expose and deal with the problems.

---

[3] Taiichi Ohno, "Toyota Production System; Part One," in Pakorn Abdulhan and Mario T. Tabucanon, eds., *Decision Models for Industrial Systems Engineers and Managers* (Bankok, Thailand: Asian Institute of Technology; and Elmsford, N.Y.: Pergamon Press, 1981), p. 354 (TA168.I545x)

Becoming a JIT Producer

It may seem rational to become a just-in-time producer by solving problems *first* and then removing inventory. For the most part, that will not work. The reason is that inventory hides problems. You can't solve problems until they are exposed, their severity is judged, and they are broken down into work improvement projects.

In the well-oiled JIT factory, a bit of inventory is removed, and the supervisor or workers are ready with pencils or chalk to record what problems occur and how often. The worst problems are studied further. For example, perhaps a bearing in one type of machine is prone to failure, causing machine malfunction and a stoppage in the flow of parts to the next stage of production. Is it the bearing manufacturer's fault? Is it the housing for the bearing within the machine? Is it misuse of the machine by the operator? Is it a failure to properly lubricate the bearing? Or is it some other problem? An investigation into the causes is begun. Then the problem cause is corrected, which justifies the removal of inventory that exposed the bearing problem in the first place. That is, without any more bearing problems, production can keep going longer so that there is less need for an emergency inventory.

Before just-in-time was well understood, there was a prevailing impression that Japanese production workers and foremen get involved in solving production problems (1) because they are trained in group problem solving, (2) because Japanese management encourages worker participation and involvement, and (3) because of cultural traits of the Japanese people that somehow carry over from an earlier age of collective endeavor in the rice fields. If those impressions were correct, then our challenge would be to train workers and managers to be participators and problem-solvers. But those impressions are mostly incorrect. It is good to have everyone trained to study and solve problems. But, if that is all the company does, few problems will get solved, *because workers will not know what problems to solve.* Let us examine why.

In a typical plant (or office, for that matter) the major bottleneck operations are well known. Maybe one bottleneck is a paint drying oven. Perhaps it runs day and night—except when down for cleaning, repair, or changeover—and still it can't produce painted parts fast enough for next operations. Whatever the drying oven produces is moved quickly to next processes. There is no inventory of painted parts, and so whenever the drying oven hiccups, everyone hears about it; workers, foremen, engineers, maintenance technicians, and others hover around the oven analyzing its problems and correcting the causes. There is enforced problem solving. Problems are visible and their correction is imperative, because there is no inventory of painted and dried parts to serve as a "solution." Solving drying-oven problems forestalls the day when a second costly oven needs to be added.

This is a familiar example of the kind of problem solving induced by lack of buffer stock. But in our Western tradition, this kind of problem solving goes on only at a few major bottleneck points. Everywhere else there is enough overcapacity to be able to build up a buffer inventory. And that is what we do. The inventory hides the underlying problems.

Today, many Western companies are reversing their old practices. They are deliberately removing buffer stocks throughout the plant in order to expose problems rather than adding inventory to cover up the problems. And they are resisting the impulse to keep making parts just to keep machines or workers busy.

TECHNIQUES FOR STREAMLINING PRODUCTION

There are a variety of techniques that can be employed to streamline production. A number of the techniques are discussed below. While some are separately presented in other chapters, the techniques are discussed here together in order to show the full scope of a campaign to become "lean and mean" as a producer.

Setup Time/Lot Size Reductions

An item of buffer stock looks the same as an item of lot-size inventory. Cut either one and the effect is the same. However, when lot sizes are cut, there is one more negative effect: Number of setups increases. For example, assume that you use 1,000 machined bolts per month, and once a month you set up for a bolt production run of 1,000. If you cut the lot size to 250, then you must set up to run 250 every week instead of once a month. This is four times as many setups.

One U.S. company, in the early stages of its just-in-time program, directed all of its plants to make swift inventory reductions. At one plant, managers dutifully cut lot sizes and then watched as setups consumed more time, leaving less time for production. Process yields (output per day) immediately went *down*. Many of the plant's managers knew enough about JIT to realize that engineering to reduce setup was needed. They quickly broadened the JIT program to include it, and the yield problem was soon resolved. One might conclude that the setup time reductions should have come first. Not necessarily. It is not all that bad for the control system to tell plant people that setup time needs to be cut. Then it will be viewed as a real need, not an exercise.

Re-Layout

As a deterrent to backsliding, some companies follow up on inventory removal with immediate re-layout to deprive the shop of *room* to let inventory sneak back in. Re-layout, minus storage racks, forklift trucks, conveyors, and other storage and handling gear, moves machines and work stations close together. Work stations are arranged by the way products travel so that products travel through processes fast. In the ideal, the work never touches the floor, never pauses in a queue, never is held in a state of storage. Production workers who formerly had allegiance to their own process now take an interest in the whole product flow—or at least in the preceding and following processes and work groups. Space is freed for adding another production line or product.

Material Control Discipline

When there isn't much inventory, every piece counts. Therefore, in streamlining the plant, it is necessary to be precise about stock quantity, identification, and location. Work centers must produce in exact predetermined quantities (*small* quantities) and place produced items in exact quantities in precise locations with clear identification. Standard containers holding a fixed quantity should be used at all times.

Traditionally, industry has lacked such disciplined material control. "In" and "out" areas may be painted on the floor near each shop. But containers are often poorly labeled and nonstandard. A fair amount of shop time is wasted searching for the right parts, and with excess quantities present, no one worries much about precise counts.

In one of General Electric's small appliance plants, an early JIT step was to remove inventory and collapse storage space; then the small remaining storage areas were painted to designate specific areas for specific parts. Material handlers were directed never to deliver parts to the wrong space; this virtually eliminates search time, permits fast, accurate visual counting, and as a bonus, prevents delivery of unwanted extra stock—which helps enforce the just-in-time ideal of producing and delivering only as needed.

Group Technology

The concept of group technology (GT), which dates back at least to the work of Mitrofanov in Russia in the 1950s,[4] turns out to be a key to achieving just-in-time results where item variety is high. GT is a way of grouping machines and work centers based on parts that require the same technology. A group-technology cell may be set up for several parts that follow about the same flow path. For example, perhaps 50 part numbers all require work on machines B, F, G, L, and W. Those five machines could be grouped into a GT cell. (Another aspect of group technology is selecting jobs requiring similar technology to be run through a machining sequence as a group.) The machines may be positioned close enough together that as each unit is completed on one machine, it may be loaded into the next. In effect, a small production line making an irregular mix of 50 part numbers is created, with little or no idle inventory between stages. An obstacle to this brand of just-in-time of production is setup time. Each of the 50 different parts would require its own machine settings, tool changes, and so forth. But parts following the same flow path are likely to have similar setup characteristics so that a quick-setup idea adopted for one of the parts may work for the other 49 parts as well.

An example of categorizing parts by shape for GT processing is shown in Figure 9–3. These are parts used in building a ship. The example comes from a manual describing a streamlined approach to shipbuilding.[5] (The manual pictorially shows

---

[4] S. P. Mitrofanov, "Scientific Organization of Batch Production," AFML/LTV Technical Report TR-77–218, III, Wright-Patterson AFB, Ohio, December, 1977.

[5] "The National Shipbuilding Research Program," U.S. Department of Transportation, Maritime Administration, in cooperation with Todd Pacific Shipyards Corporation (Revised December 1982).

FIGURE 9–3

Parts Used in Shipbuilding; Categorizing by Type for Group Technology

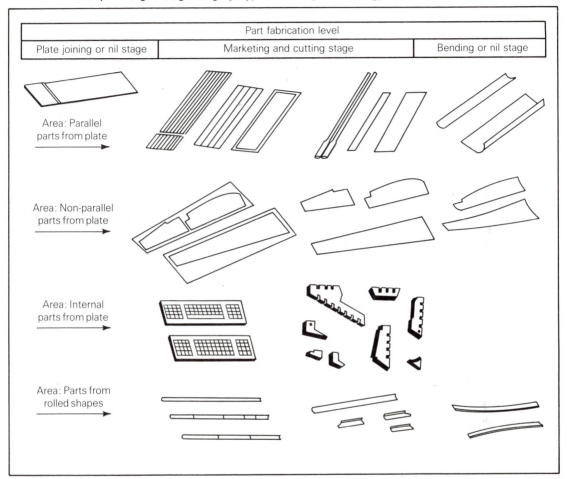

the manufacture of a 22,000 metric ton oil tanker being built in 43 working days.) The approach, developed by Ishikawajima-Harima Heavy Industries in Japan, is sweeping the shipbuilding world. The thousands of pieces of pipe and steel that go into a ship are categorized and then produced on GT flow lines. Then pieces are combined into larger pieces, still larger subassemblies, and so forth, all the way up to sections of hull, engine, superstructure, and outfitting. Work units are very small and of the same time content so that they may move in concert from one GT cell or flow line to the next, with little buildup of inventories in between. Some parts are too irregular to suit the group technology concept and so are made in the slow and high inventory job-shop manner.

In its years of experience in setting up GT cells, Toyota has developed a fondness for the number five and for the shape of a *U*. That is, such a cell would have a maximum of five manned work stations arranged into a *U*-shaped configuration. When the cell is operating at less than full capacity, fewer than five workers may be assigned, with each worker running more than one machine. At the limit a single worker handles all five machines, which are conveniently grouped into a *U*—like an efficiency kitchen.

Dedicated Production Lines

Group-technology cells are comprised of general-purpose machines, i.e., machines that can be set up to run different part numbers. But there may be one part number that is made in enough volume to warrant its own **dedicated production line.** A dedicated line justifies special-purpose machines, tooling, handling aids, and, to some extent, labor skills. If a plant with a lot of GT cells achieves low enough costs and high enough quality for its sales to grow fast, then dedicated special-purpose lines will begin to become attractive. In other words, hundreds of small improvements add up to market success so that the plant's production volume finally is sufficient to pay for fully dedicated, special-purpose streamlined production lines—with virtually no idle stock or wasted time between work stations (a just-in-time operation).

Overlapped Production

A general-purpose job shop can gain some of the benefits of dedicated production lines by employing **overlapped production.** The usual job-shop approach is to complete a whole lot (e.g., pallet load) of parts at one work center before sending it to the next work center. Overlapping means steadily moving completed parts out of the first and into the second work center so that production is going on in both places at the same time. Overlapped production is well known in Western industry. In the past, it was thought of mainly as an expediting tool. That is, a production controller may expedite a late order by having a portion moved ahead while another portion is still in process in the preceding work center. In a just-in-time plant, overlapped production is routine and not treated as an expediting action. Re-layout to move work centers and shops close together then becomes an obvious need.

Mixed Models

Companies that have a steady but moderate demand for a variety of models and options generally cannot afford to set up a dedicated production line for each model. But an attractive alternative is a single production line running a sequence of mixed models. Mixed-model production in final assembly has been common for years in our farm equipment and automotive industries and in some major home appliance plants.

An obvious benefit of mixed-model assembly is being able to produce today the mix of models that were put on order by end customers just a few days ago. That avoids cycles of finished goods buildup and depletion for first one model and then another, which is bad for customers who must wait until the next cycle of their preferred model. (People who order furniture and carpeting from samples know about this phenomenon.)

But there is a greater potential benefit of mixed-model production—a benefit that we mostly did not recognize until recently: If mixed-model production is extended backward to subassembly, component parts fabrication, and material purchasing, there can be significant streamlining effects. Producing mixed models of component items shaves peak capacity, because you no longer need to make a large batch of anything. Large-batch production requires large-batch machines and other production facilities.

For example, suppose that a toy company makes five models of toy car by pouring molten metal into molds. If each car model is made in a batch of 10, one model at a time, a large machine with apertures for 10 molds may be used; then 50 mold apertures would be needed for the five models. If, on the other hand, the toy cars are made on a mixed-model molding machine, perhaps the total number of mold apertures would be just 2 per model, or 10 apertures. Cutting down on the number of toy mold apertures from 50 to 10 is probably a modest saving. But, extend the example to real cars and the huge dies to form fenders and other body parts, and the savings can be massive.

Synchronized Scheduling

Synchronized scheduling is another benefit of extending mixed-model production backward. The final-assembly schedule is used as the schedule for subassembly, parts fabrication, and material purchasing—with offsets for lead time. There is no longer much need for production control people to handle scheduling and control, nor for elaborate computer-based scheduling systems (e.g., material requirements planning).

Regularity in End-Product Scheduling[6]

It is possible to give everybody, from suppliers to final assemblers, the same schedule but then change it all the time. That will not do. Dividing up the work into job assignments is chaotic if the schedule is irregular. Thus, the number and sequence of models should be repeatable from hour to hour. Also, the end-product schedule must be relatively frozen for a fixed number of days. Over the years, however, the time span over which the schedule is frozen should be reduced, because there are marketing advantages in doing so.

---

[6] This is sometimes called *level scheduling*. But "level" can be misunderstood. It can mean a level *amount* of work, or *the same* work over and over. Regularity means the same work over and over.

Zero Deviation from Schedule

In traditional manufacturing, we try to come fairly close to the schedule. But there is rarely much concern when production is late or early and above or below the scheduled amount. There are usually extra inventories and extra time allowances everywhere. The just-in-time plant may not treat schedules so casually, because the extra inventories and time allowances have been removed.

In most JIT plants, meeting the schedule from hour to hour is too much to ask. But some firms encourage workers to try it anyway. To make that objective visible, hourly production counts may be written on display boards for everyone to see, and problems are recorded, as well, so that there is good data for improvement.

Undercapacity Scheduling

It is important to set the daily schedule at less than maximum daily capacity. This concept, called "undercapacity scheduling," helps make zero deviation from schedule attainable. For example, schedule perhaps seven hours worth of work for an eight-hour day. On most days the work group will meet the schedule early—without being pressured into making defectives. The extra time at the end of the day should be used for training, informational meetings, machine maintenance, problem-solving projects, and so forth.

At the Greeley Division of Hewlett-Packard, a JIT program was launched as a pilot test on a production line making 3½ inch flexible disk drives. One of the first acts was to set an attainable daily schedule in final assembly and to have the assemblers plot the daily percent deviation from schedule on a large chart in the work area. The assemblers were able to plot a nearly straight line throughout the first two months of the test. This chart was used to convince supervisors and workers at earlier stages of production that they ought to strive for exactly the same regular output and that inventories and time delays between stages could be cut nearly to zero.

Standardization

Standardizing the component parts that go into the end products makes it much easier to achieve just-in-time objectives. Fewer different part numbers is as sure a way to cut inventories as lot-size reductions are. The ideal is to have a small number of standardized parts that may be plugged in or bolted on in a number of ways so that end-product variety is high. End-product variety is good for marketing reasons. With fewer part numbers, fewer kinds of equipment are necessary, and equipment maintenance is easier. Quality control is simpler to automate and make foolproof. Worker training—to make the small variety of parts—is simplified, and better-trained workers make fewer mistakes and find it easier to meet the daily schedule.

Multifunctional Workers

Rigid work rules or customs are an impediment to a just-in-time campaign. On the other hand, JIT has its own way of convincing workers—and managers—of the folly of rigid work rules. When the production system encourages people (and machines) to keep busy producing parts even when usage of those parts has been halted by a problem (or by stop-and-go scheduling), workers become accustomed to staying at one machine and one job; they come to feel they "own" that job (and perhaps are afraid to try another). But JIT requires production to stop when usage stops, and it requires people's job assignments to change when models and quantities demand change. Workers see the need to move to other jobs when theirs is halted. They may move either to other direct labor or to indirect labor (fixup and cleanup). The flexible worker is said to be **multifunctional.** Sometimes, the pay system is set up for pay increases based on number of different jobs mastered, which is rather opposite to the practice of some companies of pay increases based on longevity in a *single* job.

The multifunctional worker not only is mobile but also may be capable of running more than one process or machine at the same time. For example, one worker may handle five stations in a *U*-shaped group-technology cell. The work cycle may be: Setup and start machine one; then do the same for machine two, three, four, five and back to one.

Worker-Centered Quality Control

Under traditional quality control, inspectors work for a quality control department. The low-inventory just-in-time system cannot tolerate many interruptions caused by bad quality, and so a JIT plant must prevent, not just detect, defects. In the prevention mode, workers are given responsibility for not sending bad items forward. To meet the responsibility they may need to check every piece right after making it. Automatic checking or error-prevention devices can make this feasible and foolproof. There are a host of other quality improvement measures that may be taken both to improve quality and to make it easier to live with small inventories.

Rigorous Preventive Maintenance

Just as quality problems are not easily tolerated in a just-in-time plant, neither are equipment failures. The JIT production worker needs to follow a daily regimen of checking equipment and performing simple preventive maintenance before starting production; usually a checklist serves as a guide. This is in addition to more extensive preventive maintenance performed by the maintenance department.

Ford Motor Co. was one of the first Western firms to experiment with Toyota's plan in which preventive maintenance is done in special shifts. The plan calls for two instead of three eight-hour production shifts, and these are nested between three four-hour shifts reserved for maintenance. (Special setup work, training, pilot testing, and so forth may also fit into the maintenance shifts.) Even though production time is reduced by a third, daily output does not drop much, if at all, because there are large reductions in down time.

Kanban

JIT firms may be able to signal the need for more parts with kanban (cards) sent from user to maker. For example, one American electric lamp (light bulb) manufacturer has several plants in the same state. Some are fabrication plants feeding components to the lamp assembly plant. Before the company initiated JIT, a typical shipment between plants was a whole month's supply of a given part. One of the first JIT actions taken was to change to small quantities delivered once a day on the average. The day-to-day delivery frequency varied around that average based on production ups and downs in the using plant. Kanban were used to signal the need for each delivery.

Just-in-Time Purchasing

Just-in-time buying is the same as in-plant JIT production—with one critical difference: distance. The cost of shipping from a distant supplier argues against small purchase quantities. But the many advantages of doing business in small quantities can offset a good deal of the shipping cost disadvantages. Each time a purchase lot is cut, the shipping cost problem is magnified and begs attention. In the long run, the best solutions are to deal with nearby suppliers and stick with them year after year.

Dynamics of Streamlined Production

All of the previously mentioned techniques may work in concert to keep inventory levels falling and productivity and quality rising. Lot-size reductions plus inventory removal and re-layout are the chief triggering devices. To some degree, the rest are forced responses for getting along with less inventory. But for a maximum rate of improvement, all of the techniques should be active.

It appears the best way to drive the improvements is by a series of project assignments. All managers, engineers, buyers, material control staff, quality control people, and staff technicians should be on work improvement projects, one project after another. Many American companies have created an overall JIT coordinating group or steering committee. Task forces are often formed to plan and monitor particular aspects of the program, e.g., a preventive maintenance task force. Detailed redesign work and studies are assigned as temporary projects to small groups or individuals.

Production workers are automatically caught up in the work improvement crusade. They are in the spotlight whenever problems occur—which is repeatedly at random points throughout the plant every day. The worker is conspicuously idle when these problems occur (because of lack of inventory to keep it going). The worker's natural reaction is to try to think of a quick-fix solution so that more work stations don't grind to a halt. Leadmen (workers with some leadership duties) and veteran workers are likely to be asked to serve on projects from time to time. And most workers sometimes will be assigned to carry out improvement ideas: preventive maintenance, re-layout, machine modification for faster setup, and so forth.

In companies with mature JIT programs, a natural next step is to more formally involve the workers in the improvement efforts. A small natural group of production workers and their foremen may become a formal problem-solving group, and they are given training in problem-solving techniques. Toyota calls them small group improvement activities; many other companies call the groups quality control circles—though their mission covers any kind of improvement, not just quality.

While workers and foremen can contribute many small but valuable ideas, the backbone of the work improvement campaign is engineering. And sooner or later much of the work improvement focus shifts toward robotics and automation. These important topics are discussed next.

AUTOMATION

Webster's New World Dictionary tells us that automation is: "in manufacturing, a system or method in which many or all of the processes of production, movement, and inspection of parts and materials are automatically performed or controlled by self-operating machinery, electronic devices, etc." Webster also notes that the term *automation* was coined in about 1949, not all that long ago.

In view of the recency of the term *automation,* it is not surprising that there still are rather few examples of it. Industry has focused on mostly piecemeal mechanization, which is generally rational in view of the prohibitive cost of full automation. It is common to find factories with mixtures of conventional and automatic machine tools, gravity and powered conveyors, both human-run and operatorless tractors and stock pickers, and packaging mechanisms fed by packaging workers.

Mechanization has been strongly affected by computers. Numerically controlled (NC) machines, which are fed directly by computers or indirectly by computer-produced tape, have enjoyed sure and steady growth since the 1950s. They are common today even in many modest-sized machine shops. Computer-aided manufacturing (CAM) and computer-aided design (CAD) have increased the flexibility and scope of what could be done with computers.

NC equipment and CAD/CAM, while not well known to the general public, are at the core of advanced factory automation. The layman is more likely to associate automation with robots, which actually have developed more slowly than NC equipment and CAD/CAM. The public's fancy was captured by R2D2, the lovable robot in *Star Wars*. North American industry's interest in robotics was stimulated by reports of rapid growth of robotics in Japan. Today these technologies—NC equipment, CAD/CAM, and robotics—are all mature and affordable enough that we may expect to see accelerated growth in mechanization and in full automation as well. The business press speaks of the "factory of the future," which operates largely without production workers. A few examples already exist. Each of the components of such a factory deserve further comment.

Flexible Automated Manufacturing

NC machines are used mainly in fabricating parts out of metal. Milling, grinding, boring, drilling, lathing, and so forth are metal-cutting tasks that require exacting machine adjustments and settings. Since these adjustments and settings must be specified, why not specify them to a computer rather than to a human machinist? NC machines were developed for exactly that purpose.

Initially, NC machines were run by paper tape, developed by a technician who has both engineering and machinist skills. Microcomputers instead of paper tape control many of today's NC machines; the augmented term is computer numerically controlled (CNC) machines. When several CNC machines are linked and controlled by a central computer, the term is direct numerically controlled (DNC) machines, and the overall concept is called computer-aided manufacturing (CAM).

Most people, when they first hear about NC machines, begin with the impression that they are learning about tools for mass production. Since an NC machine may cost half a million dollars, the manager naturally presumes that there must be high-volume production to pay for it. The impression is false. NC machines are for *low-volume* machining, especially multistep complicated jobs likely to require several tool changes and setups. These are jobs for an efficient infallible machine. A human machinist may be physically just as fast, but there is so much blueprint reading to do—to say nothing of coffee breaks and so forth—that the machine is often idle and the expensive part stays too long in a state of partial completion (as work in process, or WIP).

The advantages of NC machines are high machine utilization, high quality, fast throughput (short production leadtime), low scrap and cutoff, low inventory, flexibility to change easily from one part to another, and low cost. NC machines combat stop-and-go production and allow the low-volume job-shop or custom producer to become somewhat streamlined.

Several DNC machines may be linked to a computer-controlled material handling system. The linkage is known as a **flexible manufacturing system** (FMS). Gunn explains the FMS operations as follows: "In such a system families of parts are selected through group technology for machining. Once a pallet of workpieces is set in place the workpieces proceed automatically from tool to tool, where they are machined in the proper sequence. The entire system may require loading and unloading only once a day."[7]

---

[7] Thomas C. Gunn, "The Mechanization of Design and Manufacturing," *Scientific American* 247, no. 3 (September 1982), pp. 115–30.

Computer-Aided Design

Complex machining is preceded by complex design. Harnessing the computer makes sense on both accounts, the latter being referred to as computer-aided design (CAD). In the CAD mode, the designer manipulates dimensions and product characteristics shown on a video display terminal. Blueprints may be printed out at the touch of a key, saving a large amount of work at a drafting table.

CAD and CAM may be linked to allow the design engineer and manufacturing engineer to be one and the same. That is, a design may be translated into process instructions at the same terminal. This extension is sometimes called **computer-aided process planning** (CAPP). The computer data base may contain machine alternatives and costs so that machine utilization and process efficiency may be optimized. A notable benefit is that the designer is able to look for designs that are easier and cheaper to make. Material costs, which for many manufacturers consume over 50 percent of total product cost, may be cut substantially. In conventional machining, parts designs are cylindrical or linear. The human skeleton shows, however, that a design with large ends and a narrow center is stronger and more economical. The CAD/CAM designer is able to produce such designs—or, for even greater material savings, net-like designs. Computer-controlled lasers are coming into use to improve cutting precision and quality. Lasers are becoming equally valuable in tool and die making. A laser may, for example, scan the body of a prototype automobile and cut master panels out of metal. (So far the linkage of CAD and CAM is uncommon because it is so expensive.)

Robots

While automated machine tools can make complex products, they do it on materials that are generally clamped in a fixed position. Robots, on the other hand, handle many kinds of tasks in which the material is free to move or there is a large surface to cover. Assembly, packaging, material handling, tool handling, spot welding, spray painting, and inspection are examples. Robots must possess humanlike motion capabilities to be able to handle such tasks. Still, a robot is no good at searching; locations for objects must be predictable and within the reach of the robot.

A robot has a manipulator or arm, to which a special-purpose hand may be attached. A power supply—hydraulic, electric, or pneumatic—provides strength. And a controller remembers the programmed tasks and controls motions.

Robots usually have six axes of motion—seven if you put the robot onto a traversing slide. In one type of robot, a teacher uses control buttons to teach the robot to perform a sequence of motions. In more advanced robots, an operator physically moves the manipulator through a path of motion, which the robot remembers. Sensory devices are not native to the robot but may be added to it. For example, light sensing, heat sensing, force or pressure sensing, and bar-code reading devices may be used to give the robot powers of discretion.

Computer-Integrated Manufacturing

> It's 1 P.M., the middle of the second shift. The factory floor is quiet and cool, with bright spotlights in the center creating shadows in the corners. A robotic carrier silently glides down the aisles, between rows of shining, metallic machines. It stops. A silver arm reaches out and grasps a hunk of metal from the bin the carrier holds. The carrier moves on, while the machine cuts the metal into three distinct shapes. A second arm extends and picks up a piece from a conveyor that feeds the machine automatically. Swivelling on its axis, the machine then welds one of the shapes to the new piece, and places all three pieces on a ledge. A crane bends to retrieve them, transports them across the room, and delivers them to a second machine. This machine then combines them with two parts of its own making. In a glass-enclosed control room, technicians monitor the lights and whirring discs of the computers that cover the wall. The people watch. The machines work. Science fiction? Not anymore.[8]

This vignette describes what is sometimes called "the factory of the future." Robots, direct numerically controlled machines, and CAD/CAM designers are linked to a single computer, which results in computer-integrated manufacturing (CIM). A few such powerful systems exist, some of which are able to run for a whole shift without any human intervention.

The productivity and quality benefits of computer-integrated manufacturing in the factory of the future are clear. Furthermore, CIM may link up with computer-based marketing and financial functions to help make decisions that are optimal for the entire business. But CIM is still a long way off in the plans of most companies. Pieces of it will be added year by year, a prudent approach in view of the high cost and many problems to be resolved along the way.

Office Automation

In the mid-1970s, white-collar workers exceeded blue-collar workers for the first time in the U.S. economy. In one sense, that fact is symptomatic of a national problem: too many planners, counters, controllers, and adjudicators per line worker—as compared with Japan, Germany, and a few other industrialized countries. On the other hand, the number of government officials per capita in the United States is relatively modest, and the efficiency of many of our service providers is high by world standards; services are fairly efficient, for example, in sales, distribution, travel services, material control, banking, securities, and insurance.

Since these services are information-intensive, the keys to efficiency seem to lie in data handling, information processing, and communications. The U.S. services sector has long been blessed with excellent telephones, typewriters, and copiers. In recent years, the United States has generally been the world leader in developing

---

[8] Harry Thompson and Michael Paris, "The Changing Face of Manufacturing Technology," *The Journal of Business Strategy* 3, no. 1 (Summer 1982), pp. 45–52.

and adopting computer-based data processing, which has caused service-sector productivity to soar in some industries, especially banking.

Now technology is available at the right price to transform clerical, professional, and managerial work practices. As we have seen, computer-integrated manufacturing is able to streamline stop-and-go production processes; computer-based information-communication networks are doing the same for service work. One key factor in streamlining service work is the computer-based work station, which is used especially for:

1. **Online data entry and information processing.** This technology has been available to airline travel agents for a number of years. Now it is widely available to hospital workers, insurance agents, sales people (those who travel as well as those in stores), police, stockbrokers, material controllers, schedulers, and many others. Voice output and voice entry are replacing keyboards and printers in some cases.

2. **Word processing.** Electronic word processors are rapidly making electric typewriters obsolete. A word processor, with its editing and sometimes spelling capability, can make a bad typist look good. Both quality and productivity go up.

3. **Message handling.** Our best-paid white-collar workers have traditionally spent a good deal of time handling internal memos, arranging appointments, waiting to see somebody, and so forth. The new technology, now in use in larger companies, is to send a message from your desk-top terminal to the other person's. Computer-based telecommunications networks take care of the message handling. Facsimile copiers are in use for making a hard copy ("fax") of a message, document, or photo.

4. **Information processing and retrieval for decision making.** Managers may be coaxed into using desk-top terminals for message-handling and sometimes for doing their own word processing. At that point the manager may find that the terminal also can access a multitude of home-grown and commercially available data bases. Software is available to transform the data into multicolored charts and graphs. Decision analysis models and artificial intelligence (AI) software are also coming on the scene, which offer the manager what is known as a decision support system (DSS).

The effects of office automation are not unlike those of factory automation. As Giuliano notes, with work-station information systems "information is updated as it becomes available." Furthermore, "there is no such thing as 'work in process.'" Therefore, there is a "decrease in the delay and uncertainty occasioned by the inaccessibility of information that is being typed, is in the mail, has been misfiled, or is simply in an office that is closed for the weekend."[9]

Effects on People

Automation puts people out of work. We know that to be true. But does it also put people into work—on other jobs created by the prosperity that high productivity from automation creates? Surely it does. The problem is the displacement of people

---

[9] Vincent E. Giuliano, "The Mechanization of Office Work," *Scientific American* 247, no. 3 (September 1982), pp. 149–64.

in the interim between putting people out of work and creating new jobs. Society—or industry—needs to address the issue.

An ideal solution is for industry to retrain people to perform higher-skill tasks such as robot programmer, equipment technician, and troubleshooter. Indeed this is what is going on in most companies that are automating. But that measure can employ only a portion of those displaced by automation.

In the future, our companies may become accustomed to high increases in labor productivity afforded by automation. Then they may see fit to set up permanent programs to develop new products and retrain displaced workers to staff the plants making the new products. That, at least, is what we may hope is the outcome of the issue of what to do about the human problems arising from automation.

Automation across Various Industries

To wrap up this discussion of automation, let us look at how the technologies apply to different industries. The product-process matrix in Figure 9–4 offers a rough categorization.

THE WALL STREET JOURNAL

"As director of personnel, I feel *I* should purchase the robots!"

From The Wall Street Journal, *with permission of Cartoon Features Syndicate.*

FIGURE 9–4

Applications of Automation Techniques

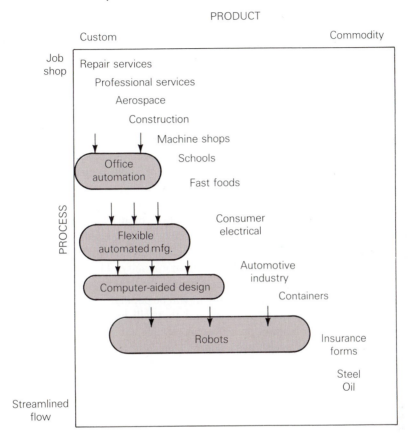

Office automation serves to streamline white-collar work, which consists mostly of custom jobs, each a bit different from another. Thus, office automation is shown under custom products, at the left in Figure 9–4.

Flexible automated manufacturing is useful mainly for goods producers in the leftmost third of the figure; examples are aerospace, machine shops, and machine tools. These industries require the precision and the flexibility of numerically controlled machines and flexible manufacturing systems.

Computer-aided design stretches across the leftmost half of Figure 9–4. CAD is widely useful in processes ranging from aerospace and construction to consumer electronics and automobiles. (It is also useful in designing steel mills, oil refineries, and the like, but that may be considered a construction application.)

Robots occupy the center of Figure 9–4. These are the industries that are the most labor intensive, and robots hold great promise as substitutes for labor in assembly work and also in repetitive jobs involving small tools or packaging.

In summary, the automation techniques have much the same purpose as material requirements planning and just-in-time techniques: streamlining the operation by squeezing out sources of delay.

Troubles in Automationland

In recent years, the public has been inundated with stories about our outdated factories on the one hand and the marvel of robots and automation of factories and offices on the other. After a time, all of this is likely to penetrate even the thick skins of hard-nosed buck-pinching executives. And so it has. In the 1980s, corporate purse strings were loosened, especially in the well-heeled companies, and vast sums were and are being spent on automation. In some industries, giant new high-speed machines that incorporate the functions of several older machines and manual processes are being installed. Often they take months to hook up; then more months of debugging before they perform as they are supposed to—if they ever do.

The justification for these supermachines is that unit costs will be low and quality will be high when they are running at capacity. The technical problems of getting them to run at capacity may be solvable. But then there is the question of whether the products made on the equipment will be popular in the marketplace. The landscape is littered with product failures, and that will never change. When products fail in companies with manual processes and simple equipment, the processes are converted to make something else, with some of the simple and cheap equipment simply being disposed of at little loss. When the failure is in products made on supermachines that have consumed enormous amounts of capital, the consequences are more serious. A factual example will illustrate.

EXAMPLE 9–1

Equipping a Plant—for Flexibility

One American company that makes video display devices experienced a costly failure of the kind just described. Glowing marketing projections led to equipping a large two-floor plant with high-capacity equipment; big expensive clean rooms and test equipment; and fast-moving conveyors and elevators that move the product quickly in, through, and out of the plant. The forecasts were that the plant would be running three shifts a day by summer of 1983. As it turned out, the product was not a hit. Demand was only high enough to run the plant at half a shift per day. With so little volume, unit costs were high not low, which means that the product could not be priced low to stimulate demand. The plant was an enormous drain on corporate assets. Furthermore, the huge investment was in yesterday's technology, and much of the equipment was tightly bolted to the structure or in immobile clean rooms.

FIGURE 9–5

Flexible Equipment and Layout

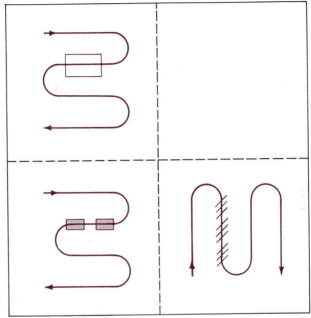

First line (with
clean room) for first
six months demand

Second line (with
modular clean tunnels)
for second six months
demand

Third line (with
laminar-flow benches)
for third six months
demand

A new group of managers and engineers in the same company has the job of equipping a plant for another new product, again one that looks great based on market testing. They are determined not to make the same mistakes. The engineers are buying *small* machines and mobile equipment. Initially, they will equip only one corner of the plant, with enough capacity to meet projected demand growth for just six months into the future. Then, if that demand actually occurs, a second production line will go in next to the first. Six months later, a third line will go in beside the second, and so forth. Figure 9–5 illustrates the plan for expansion.

There seems to be no way to avoid a clean room in the first line, and clean rooms are costly and immobile. The engineers think that the quality of component parts will improve enough that the second line will be able to get by with "modular clean tunnels," which are more flexible than a clean room. And they plan to go to "laminar flow benches" (a curtain of air to keep the work bench area free of dust) instead of clean tunnels for the third or fourth line. If the product is a failure, the latter lines will not get built.

What this example illustrates is a greater concern for flexibility and caution, a concern that has arisen in some companies after getting burned. Some rules of thumb in these companies are:

Avoid putting equipment into pits or on special platforms, attaching equipment to the structure, and building it into special rooms. If the equipment requires these immobilizers, see if alternate, simpler equipment will do the job. Put equipment on wheels, if possible. (Sometimes, of course, there is no avoiding the immobility.)

Add machine capacity like we add people, a unit at a time as demand builds.

Avoid a single multiprocess machine or line, which is vulnerable to total shutdown. Several smaller units or lines can assure that production can continue when one machine is down. Furthermore, each unit or line *could* be dedicated to one model, size, or color, which can improve efficiency and quality. Alternatively, each line could produce a mixture of models.

The operations managers need to understand not only the power of automation and robotics but also the pitfalls. Management must learn to manage technology (and the technocrats) rather than be managed by it.

SUMMARY

Throughout industrial history, manufacturing in every industry has improved by becoming more streamlined, i.e., more continuous with fewer stops and starts. While it is easiest to streamline the production of commodities such as primary metals and foodstuffs, the manufacturing of products having design variety may also become relatively continuous. The Japanese developed just-in-time (JIT) techniques to transform job-lot production of automotive and other products into repetitive processing. The Americans developed material requirements planning, which enables companies with even more product variety—like hand-tool manufacturers—to speed up the flow of products through the manufacturing process and thereby become more like continuous processors. And in all industrialized countries, flexible computer-controlled machines are enabling even custom products to be made rather smoothly instead of in the old, slow job-shop way. The flexible machines, sometimes aided by robots, do so by reacting quickly to design changes.

The process industries, whose products flow more or less continuously, have the easiest time becoming streamlined. Since the product is stable for years, they can afford to invest in automated processes. Rigorous equipment maintenance, close monitoring of quality, and reliability of supply and freight are vital, because disruptions are so costly in automated plants. Some plants run different grades of a commodity through the same process and so must be able to change over fast. Linear programming is sometimes used to develop low-cost mixtures of ingredients.

In companies that employ just-in-time techniques and become more repetitive, compressed lead times and inventory cuts are the most obvious results. But the more profound effect may be that lower inventories enforce problem solving. Attention is on all problems that would bring a work station's production to a halt for lack of parts. By contrast, the usual approach is for inventory to be added to keep problems out of sight and therefore unsolved—except for the few major bottleneck operations that are obvious in every plant.

The techniques for streamlining operations include the following:

1. Cut lead time and cycle stock by reducing setup time and lot sizes.
2. Each time inventory is removed, relocate machines to eliminate storage space so that inventory cannot creep back in.
3. Require exact counting and placement of the materials to prevent search delays when materials are needed.
4. Arrange work stations close together in cells according to dominant flows of similar parts—the group technology (GT) idea; a *U*-shaped arrangement provides added staffing flexibility.
5. Where a single model is made in high volume, set up a production line dedicated to that model.
6. In the job-shop environment use overlapped production instead of making and moving whole lots at a time between work stations.
7. Run similar models down a single mixed-model production line, thereby shaving peak capacity requirements for any given model; prepare for this by reducing time to change from model to model.
8. Use the final assembly schedule as the schedule for subassemblies and components.
9. Make the schedule regular from day to day and exercise discipline to meet it every day—which gives all parts suppliers the certainty they need to deliver just the number of parts exactly when needed.
10. Standardize parts design so that inventory does not exist solely because of proliferation of component parts.
11. Gain flexibility and achieve high utilization of workers by training them and sometimes assigning them to do more than one job at a time.
12. Give workers, not inspectors, the responsibility to check their own quality; this is the surest way to hold down parts shortages and delays caused by bad quality.
13. Rigorously maintain equipment to avoid parts shortages and delays caused by machine malfunction.
14. Use the kanban order-card system to assure that parts are not made and delivered before they are needed.
15. Buy in small amounts delivered every day or more often.
16. Get all employees, including white-collar workers, involved in JIT through a succession of team projects to solve problems revealed by lack of inventory.

Streamlining the production of highly variable product designs had not been thought to be attainable. But now flexible automation is being introduced to do just that. Computer numerically controlled (CNC) machines are the foundation. CNC machines combined with computer-controlled material handling is called a flexible manufacturing system (FMS). Putting FMSs under the control of a main computer results in the so-called "factory of the future," which is largely unmanned. Then computer-aided design and computer-aided manufacturing (CAD/CAM) modules may be added to make engineering a part of the whole grand computer-integrated manufacturing (CIM) system.

Robots may be a part of it all—doing programmable tasks that do not require search, like handling tools and common parts. Robots also have a role in more labor-intensive operations, replacing workers on some of the hard-to-do tasks. Just-in-time implementation steps, such as moving machines close together and exactly positioning tools and parts, are also excellent ways to prepare for robots.

Office work is also being automated. Desk-top computer terminals can make anyone an accurate typist. They also permit data entry and storage, message handling (instead of hand-written memos), and information processing for decision support.

All of the techniques and technology discussed in this chapter lead in the same direction: less inventory; smoother, steadier, faster production and delivery; higher quality; and higher productivity. Automation and robotics do, however, carry the risk of costly failure, especially if the equipment is not adaptable to other purposes.

REFERENCES

Books

Hall, Robert W. *Zero Inventories.* Homewood, Ill.: Dow Jones-Irwin, 1983.

Monden, Yasuhiro. *Toyota Production System.* Atlanta, Ga.: Institute of Industrial Engineers, 1983.

Quain, Mitchell, and James Townsend. *Factory Automation.* New York: Wertheim and Co., 1981.

Schonberger, Richard J. *Japanese Manufacturing Techniques: Nine Hidden Lessons in Simplicity.* New York: Free Press, 1982 (HD70.J3S36).

Shingo, Shigeo. *Study of "Toyota" Production System from Industrial Engineering Viewpoint.* Tokyo: Japan Management Association, 1981.

Periodicals (societies)

"The Mechanization of Work," a special issue of *Scientific American* 247, no. 3 (September 1982).

REVIEW QUESTIONS

1. In what sense are discrete goods producers coming to resemble the continuous-flow processors?

2. How can it be said that both MRP and JIT have streamlining effects on the production process?

3. How can custom producers ever achieve flow-like production?

4. Since job-lot and custom producers are trying to emulate the continuous-flow processors, does that mean that the latter should not tamper with their successful production techniques? Discuss.

5. Some companies have a program to train workers to be problem solvers. Compare the effectiveness of that approach to problem solving with the JIT approach.

6. Why should machine setup times be reduced when lot sizes are cut?

7. Why should plants be re-layed out and material control be more disciplined when JIT is adopted?

8. How is re-layout (to move shops or processes close together) related to overlapped production?

9. Contrast universal scheduling with regularity in end-product scheduling.

10. Why are undercapacity scheduling and zero deviation from schedule desirable in a JIT plant?

11. How does parts standardization improve the effectiveness of worker-centered quality control?

12. Why are multifunctional workers particularly important in connection with streamlined production?

13. Why are rigorous preventive maintenance and worker-centered quality control helpful in achieving streamlined production?

14. Can kanban be used in JIT purchasing? Explain.

15. In what sense can automation be thought of as a JIT technique?

16. What technologies are necessary in designing the "factory of the future"?

17. What similarities are there between CAD and office automation?

18. Compare robots with automated machine tools.

19. How can office automation lead to just-in-time information processing?

20. How can a company that automates avoid layoffs?

21. Why is the use of robots less likely for making custom and commodity-like products than for all types in between?

22. Why is it risky to automate, and what may be done to lessen the risk?

PROBLEMS

1. Modesto Farms operates a high-volume cannery for tomato products: canned whole tomatoes, tomato sauce, tomato paste, etc. Discuss three vital success factors, in the area of manufacturing, for this company; be as specific as you can even though you have to speculate on the nature of this type of company.

2. Detergent is manufactured in a continuous process through a network of pipes, vessels, and pressure chambers. First, petroleum is distilled into paraffin, which is oxidized and then catalytically hydrogenated under pressure to form fat alcohols. Sulphuric acid is added, and water cools the mixture to yield fat alcohol esters. Bleaching agents and alkalies are injected, and an emerging paste of fat alcohol sulphate is processed through a "spray tower" into finished detergent. Discuss two vital manufacturing success factors for a detergent manufacturer; be as specific as you can.

3. In the following industries, what stages of manufacture are best considered as continuous-flow and what stages repetitive production? Discuss.

   A cigarette manufacturer.

   An aspirin tablet producer.

   A breakfast cereal producer.

4. What would a high-class restaurant have to do to transform itself from a job shop into more of a repetitive producer? Be imaginative in your answer. Think futuristically.

5. What would a medical clinic have to do to transform itself from a job shop into more of a repetitive operation? Be imaginative in your answer. Think futuristically.

6. When production volume is high and product variety is low, dedicated production facilities may be used to run a streamlined just-in-time operation. How may JIT be achieved in the opposite condition of low volume, high variety?

7. A flexible manufacturing system (FMS) moves materials and changes tools automatically and quickly, often while the previous operation is in process, and therefore can run mixed models in a streamlined fashion. A labor-intensive final-assembly line running mixed models is also streamlined.

   What kinds of preparations and prerequisites are necessary to make both of these feasible (automated FMS and labor-intensive mixed-model assembly)?

8. Zeus, Inc., makes three models of personal computers: large, medium, and small. One purchased part is an internal cooling fan: large fan for the large computer, medium fan for the medium, and small fan for the small. Zeus produces and buys components purely just-in-time. The end-product schedule calls for producing one large, two medium, and four small computers every 10 minutes during the day, and the schedule is frozen for four weeks into the future. Suppliers deliver component parts (like fans) once a day.
   a. What are the advantages of the daily mixed-model delivery schedule for the fan supplier? (One supplier provides all three sizes.)
   b. During one period of five days, Zeus has trouble meeting its daily schedule, falling short by 30 units one day, five units on the second, two on the third, 25 on the fourth, and eight on the fifth day. What difficulties does this create for the "just-in-time" supplier?
   c. Zeus' schedule works out to 48 large, 96 medium, and 192 small computers per

eight-hour day. What is wrong with the schedule (a possible contributor to the problem described in part *b*)?

9. During their first year under a full-scale JIT program, Pacific Co., an airplane seat manufacturer, has drastically reduced machine failures, rework, setup times, and number of component part types.
   a. How does each of these permit inventory cuts?
   b. After inventory is cut, what should be done next to make sure it does not creep back in?
   c. Workers inspecting their own quality keep records on incidence of several kinds of problems. What should be done about the most common and severe problems recorded?

10. Ohio Webpress has set up a few GT cells for some of its main repeat-business printing jobs. In each cell workers have been trained to operate several different kinds of machines (e.g., machines for printing, collating, binding, etc.).
    a. How could overlapped production fit in—if at all?
    b. How could kanban be employed—if at all?

11. Barney Hogan confided to his wife that he was a little afraid of the desk-top terminals—all linked together by a host computer—that were on order for all of his staff, and for other departments as well. He and a few of his people—staff economists, statisticians, planners, etc.—had been testing the terminals for a few months and had become aware of the impact. Barney said, "I don't know if we can make good decisions as fast as the system will beg for them. Also, I wonder if next they won't be asking me to cut my staff."
    Are Barney's concerns well-founded? Explain.

12. a. Arrange the following industries on a product-process matrix: fast-food restaurants, motels, shoe manufacturing, electric power generation (nonnuclear), meat packing, furniture manufacturing. Discuss.
    b. For any three of the above, discuss the potential impact of robots in the next 10 years.
    c. For any three of the above (excluding motels and electric power), discuss the potential impact of just-in-time techniques in the next 10 years.

13. Hasty Mills is a fabric manufacturer. On each weaving line, it is typical for a lot of a given fabric to run for 16 weeks. Then it takes about four hours to convert the line to run the next fabric. There are several earlier stages of manufacture that feed the weaving lines; they must be set up—in advance of weaving—to make the materials that are consumed in the 16-week weaving runs. The process is substantially automated and very high speed. What just-in-time measures could be taken to streamline the process?

14. Local 354 of the union is generally supportive of Triple-A Manufacturing Company's just-in-time program. For example, when lot sizes were slashed, Local 354 saw the need to relax rigid work rules (the old "one worker, one job" concept). And the local readily accepted the idea of worker-centered quality control. The need to meet daily schedules was also supported by the union. But shop stewards regularly complain that the schedules are too hard to meet. (Industrial engineers have carefully determined what a fair day's work is, and that amount of work is the daily schedule.)
    a. Why do you suppose cutting lot sizes helped make the local receptive to relaxing work rules?
    b. Regarding the scheduled amount of work per day, who is right and who is wrong? What's the problem?

15. ABC Electric Co., which manufactures fans, receives fan blades from an outside supplier. A number of sizes of fan and blade are involved. ABC has adopted the following policies: (1) fan blade supplier delivers once a month; (2) fan blade supplier must deliver an *exact* quantity, no shortages or overages; (3) ABC inspects a sample of each lot of fan blades upon receipt and returns the whole lot to the blade supplier if the sample is too high in defectives; (4) ABC runs a mixed-model fan assembly line.

    ABC is striving to be a just-in-time producer. Which of the four policies help and which hinder ABCs JIT progress? Discuss fully.

16. Sunny Corp. operates a TV assembly plant in San Antonio. In one area of the plant specially designed video display terminals are assembled in small volumes for scientific applications. In a second area a few different medium-volume consumer TV models are assembled. And in a third area Sunny's two high-volume models are assembled.

    Three techniques for streamlined just-in-time production are: Dedicated production lines, group technology, and mixed-model production. Match up these three techniques with the three assembly areas at the Sunny Corp. plant. Explain your match-ups—and what their advantages are.

17. Argonics, Inc., operates two plants making about the same mix of products. Plant A has recently been heavily involved in a conversion to the just-in-time mode of production. Plant B, a conventional job-lot facility, has invested a good deal of time on an employee-involvement program, which includes training the production workers in problem-solving skills.

    Which plant is likely to produce the most significant quality and productivity improvements from its production workers? Explain.

18. The County Welfare Office has two main "products": welfare clients and paperwork (forms, reports, letters, etc.). The office administrator wants to apply some of the concepts he has read about for streamlining manufacturing to his service function. His goals: Improve service and cut costs. Which of the concepts from the following list offer the greatest potential to streamline the Welfare Office function? Discuss.

Multifunctional workers	Material control discipline
Robots	Office automation
Mixed models	Kanban
Standardization	

19. Jeans by Jean, Inc., runs a high-volume plant making jeans. CNC machines, automated fabric transporters, and robot fabric feeding devices have been installed in a new automated production line. President Jean herself has assured the workforce that there will be no layoffs. How can she make such assurances? Be specific.

20. Robotamatic Corp. is a small but fast-growing company that manufactures robots. Sharon H. has just been hired as sales manager and is developing a sales strategy, including which market to focus on. Three local industries on Sharon's list are: (1) automotive parts manufacturers (hub caps, bumpers, windshield wipers, and a few others), (2) paper manufacturers, and (3) automotive, electronic, and appliance repair services. Which may Sharon rule out as likely users of robots? Which have fair or good potential as robot users? Explain your reasoning.

21. Alpha Corp., a maker of office wall panels, has purchased a 75-foot long machine to manufacture steel panel sections. The machine integrates these eight functions, which had been performed in separate steps: (1) uncoil and straighten steel coil, (2) trim both sides, (3) cut to length, (4) apply a cement and feed a "honeycomb" insert between an over-under pair of the cut panels, (5) heat-bond the steel panels to the honeycomb insert, (6) weld a steel rail on each side, (7) turn the unit 90 degrees and weld steel top and bottom rails in place, and (8) stack the completed section on a pallet. All steps are done automatically, except for setting up the machine and resupplying it with raw material. It has taken a year to install and debug the machine. Now the first five steps work well, but the automatic welders work properly less than half the time. One engineer wonders "if we will ever get the welders to work right."

What risks of automation does this example demonstrate? Are there any good alternatives? Discuss.

22. An automatic home dishwasher is a simple example of a single machine that incorporates several functions. Imagine that you must wash huge quantities of dishes all day long day after day, but the automatic dishwasher—one just like the home type but much larger—breaks down a lot.

   a. How could the advantages of automated dishwashing be gained but without such serious breakdown problems? Consider the rules of thumb in the chapter, and think of some other type of equipment design besides the single multifunctional machine.

   b. Now imagine that your dishwashing tasks change: Some days are very heavy on plates with few glasses or utensils; on other days it's many glasses, few plates; etc. What kind of automated equipment might respond well to this need?

CASE STUDY: LINCOLN ELECTRIC COMPANY*

The Lincoln Electric Company is the world's largest manufacturer of welding machines and electrodes. Lincoln employs 2400 workers in two U.S. factories near Cleveland and about 600 in three factories in other countries. This does not include the field sales force of more than 200 persons. Lincoln's market share has been more than 40 percent of the United States market for arc-welding equipment and supplies, according to one estimate.

The main plant is in Euclid, Ohio, a suburb on Cleveland's east side. The layout of this plant is shown in Exhibit 1. There are no warehouses. Materials flow from the half-mile long dock on the north side of the plant through the production lines to a very limited storage and loading area on the south. Materials used at each work station are stored as close as possible to the work station.

A new plant, just opened in Mentor, Ohio, houses some of the electrode production operations, which were moved from the main plant. The main plant is currently being enlarged by 100,000 square feet and several innovative changes are being made in the manufacturing layout.

* Source: Adapted from George A. Steiner, John B. Miner, and Edmund R. Gray, *Management Policy and Strategy: Text, Readings, and Cases* © 1982, pp. 958–80. Used with permission of A. D. Sharplin, author of the case.

EXHIBIT 1

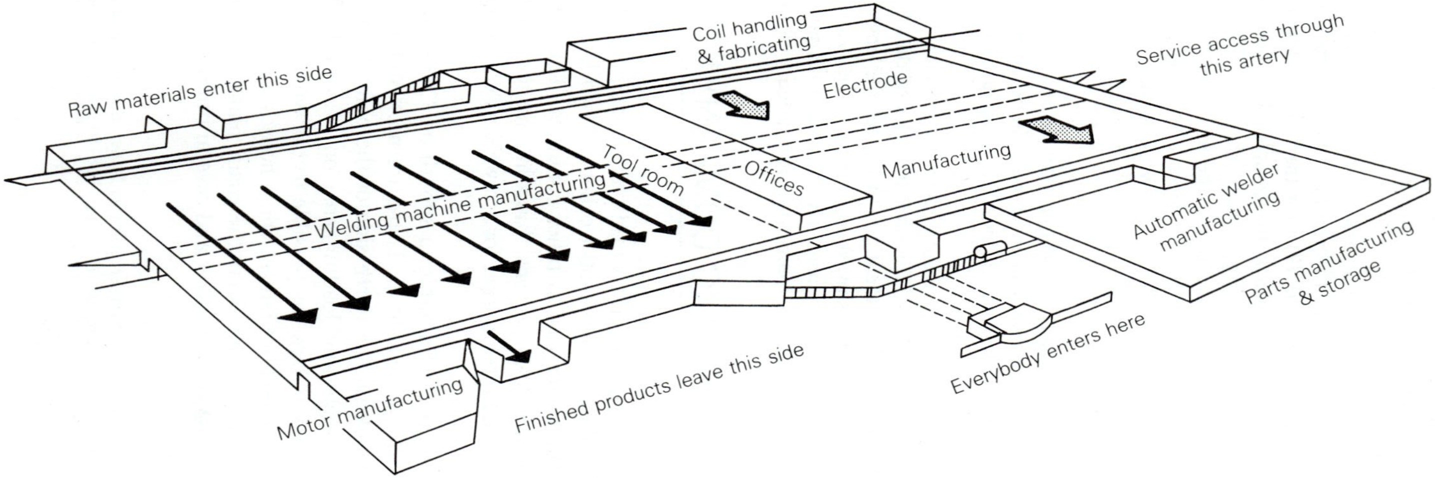

Service access through this artery

Automatic welder manufacturing

Parts manufacturing & storage

Manufacturing

Electrode

Coil handling & fabricating

Everybody enters here

Offices

Tool room

Finished products leave this side

Welding machine manufacturing

Raw materials enter this side

Motor manufacturing

PRODUCTION AND MARKET INFORMATION

Products

The company's main products are electric welding machines and metal electrodes used in arc-welding. Lincoln also produces electric motors ranging from 1 horsepower to 200 horsepower. Motors constitute about 8–10 percent of total sales.

The electric welding machines, some consisting of a transformer or motor and generator arrangement powered by commercial electricity and others consisting of an internal combustion engine and generator, are designed to produce from 130 to over 1000 amperes of electrical power. This electrical current melts a consumable metal electrode, and the molten material is transferred in a superhot spray to the metal joint being welded. Very high temperatures and hot sparks are produced. Operators usually must wear special eye and face protection and leather gloves, often along with leather aprons and sleeves.

Welding electrodes are of two basic types: (1) Coated "stick" electrodes, usually 14 inches long and smaller than a pencil in diameter. The operator holds these electrodes in a special insulated holder and must manipulate the electrode to maintain a proper arc width and pattern of deposition of the metal being transferred. Stick electrodes are packaged in 6- to 50-pound boxes. (2) Coiled wire, ranging in diameter from 0.035 to 0.219 inch. The wire is designed to be fed continuously to the welding arc through a "gun" held by the operator or positioned by automatic positioning equipment. The wire is packaged in coils, reels and drums weighing from 14 to 1,000 pounds.

Manufacturing Processes

Electrode manufacturing is highly capital intensive. Metal rods purchased from steel producers are drawn or extruded down to smaller diameters. Then they are cut to length and coated with pressed-powder "flux" for stick electrodes or plated with copper (for conductivity) and spun into coils or spools for wire. Some of Lincoln's wire, called Innershield, is hollow and filled with a material similar to that used to coat stick electrodes. Lincoln is highly secretive about its electrode production processes, and the casewriter was not given access to the details of those processes.

Welding machines and electric motors are made on a series of assembly lines. Gasoline and diesel engines are purchased partially assembled, but practically all other components are made from basic industrial products, for example, steel bars and sheets and bare copper conductor wire, in the Lincoln factory. Individual components, such as gasoline tanks for engine-driven welders and steel shafts for motors and generators, are made by numerous small "factories within a factory." The shaft for a certain generator, for example, is made from a raw steel bar by one operator who uses five large machines, all running continuously. A saw cuts the bar to length, a digital lathe machines different sections to varying diameters, a special milling machine cuts a slot for a keyway, and so forth, until a finished shaft is produced.

The operator moves the shafts from machine to machine and makes necessary adjustments. Another operator punches, shapes, and paints sheetmetal cowling parts. One assembles steel laminations on a rotor shaft, then winds, insulates, and tests the rotors. Crane operators move finished components to the nearby assembly lines.

Market Information

Although advances in welding technology have been frequent, arc-welding products, in the main, have hardly changed over the last 30 years. The most popular Lincoln electrode, the Fleetweld 5P, has been virtually the same since the 1930s. The most popular engine-driven welder in the world, the Lincoln SA-200, has been a gray-colored assembly, including a four-cylinder Continental "Red Seal" engine and a 200-ampere direct-current generator with two current-control knobs for at least three decades. A 1980 model SA-200 even weighs almost the same as the 1950 model, and it certainly is little changed in appearance. It also seems likely that changes in the machines and techniques used in arc welding will be evolutionary rather than revolutionary.

Lincoln and its competitors now market a wide range of general purpose and specialty electrodes for welding mild steel, aluminum, cast iron, and stainless and special steels. Most of these electrodes are designed to meet the standards of the American Welding Society, a trade association. They are thus essentially the same as to size and composition from one manufacturer to any other. Every electrode manufacturer has a few unique products, but these typically constitute only a small percentage of total sales.

Lincoln's research and development expenditures have recently been less than 0.2 percent of sales. There is evidence that others spend several times as much as a percentage of sales.

Lincoln's share of the market has been between 30 and 40 percent for many years, and the welding products market has grown somewhat faster than industry in general. The market is highly price-competitive. Variations in prices of standard products normally amount to only 1 or 2 percent. Lincoln's products are sold directly by its engineering-oriented sales force and indirectly through its distributor organization. Advertising expenditures amount to less than 0.25 percent of sales, one third as much as a major Lincoln competitor with whom the casewriter checked.

A HISTORICAL SKETCH

In 1895, after being "frozen out" of the depression-ravaged Elliott-Lincoln Company, a maker of Lincoln-designed electric motors, John C. Lincoln took out his second patent and began to manufacture his improved motor. He opened his new business, then unincorporated, with $200 he had earned redesigning a motor for young Herbert Henry Dow, who later founded The Dow Chemical Company.

Started during an economic depression and cursed by a major fire after only one year in business, Lincoln's company grew, but hardly prospered, through its first quarter century. In 1906, John C. Lincoln incorporated his company and moved from his one-room, fourth-floor factory to a new three-story building he erected in east Cleveland. In his new factory, he expanded his work force to 30 and sales grew to over $50,000 a year. John Lincoln was more an engineer and inventor than he was a manager, though, and it was to be left to another Lincoln to manage the company through its years of success.

In 1907, after a bout with typhoid forced him from Ohio State University in his senior year, James F. Lincoln, John's younger brother, joined the fledgling company. In 1914, with the company still small and in poor financial condition, he became the active head of the firm, with the titles of general manager and vice president. John C. Lincoln, while he remained president of the company for some years, became more involved in other business ventures and in his work as an inventor.

One of James Lincoln's early actions as head of the firm was to ask the employees to elect representatives to a committee that would advise him on company operations. The first year the Advisory Board was in existence, working hours were reduced from 55 per week, then standard, to 50 hours a week. In 1915, the company gave each employee a paid-up life insurance policy. A welding school, which continues today, was begun in 1917. In 1918, an employee bonus plan was attempted. It was not continued, but the idea was to resurface and become the backbone of the Lincoln Management System.

The Lincoln Electric Employees' Association was formed in 1919 to provide health benefits and social activities. This organization continues today and has assumed several additional functions over the years. By 1923, a piecework pay system was in effect, employees got two-week paid vacations each year, and wages were adjusted for changes in the consumer price index. Approximately 30 percent of Lincoln's stock was set aside for key employees in 1914 when James F. Lincoln became general manager, and a stock purchase plan for all employees was begun in 1925.

The Board of Directors voted to start a suggestion system in 1929. The program is still in effect but cash awards, a part of the early program, were discontinued several years ago. Now, suggestions are rewarded by additional "points," which affect year-end bonuses.

The legendary Lincoln bonus plan was proposed by the Advisory Board and accepted on a trial basis by James Lincoln in 1934. The first annual bonus amounted to about 25 percent of wages. There has been a bonus every year since then.

By 1944, Lincoln employees enjoyed a pension plan, a policy of promotion from within, and continuous employment. Base pay rates were determined by formal job evaluation and a merit rating system was in effect.

By the start of World War II, Lincoln Electric was the world's largest manufacturer of arc-welding products. Sales of about $4,000,000 in 1934 had grown to $24,000,000 by 1941. Output per employee more than doubled during the same period.

During the war, Lincoln Electric prospered as never before. Despite challenges to Lincoln's profitability by the Navy's Price Review Board and to the tax deductibility of employee bonuses by the Internal Revenue Service, the company increased its profits and paid huge bonuses.

Certainly since 1935 and probably for several years before that, Lincoln productivity has been well above the average for similar companies. Lincoln claims levels of productivity more than twice those for other manufacturers from 1945 onward. Information from other sources tends to support these claims.

James F. Lincoln died in 1965, and there was some concern that the Lincoln system would fall into disarray, profits would decline, and year-end bonuses might be discontinued. Quite the contrary, 15 years after Lincoln's death, the company appears stronger than ever. Each year since 1965 has seen higher profits and bonuses. Employee morale and productivity remain high; employee turnover is almost nonexistent except for retirements; and Lincoln's market share is stable.

COMPANY PHILOSOPHY

James F. Lincoln was the son of a Congregational minister, and Christian principles were at the center of his business philosophy. There is no indication that Lincoln attempted to evangelize his employees or customers—or the general public for that matter. The current board chairman, Mr. Irrgang, and the president, Mr. Willis, do not even mention the Christian gospel in their recent speeches and interviews.

Attitude toward the Customer

James Lincoln saw the customer's needs above all else. "When any company has achieved success so that it is attractive as an investment," he wrote, "all money usually needed for expansion is supplied by the customer in retained earnings. It is obvious that the customer's interests, not the stockholder's, should come first" [Lincoln, 1961, p. 119]. In 1947 he said, "Care should be taken . . . not to rivet attention on profit. Between 'How much do I get?' and 'How do I make this better, cheaper, more useful?' the difference is fundamental and decisive" ["You Can't Tell . . . ," p. 94]. Mr. Willis still ranks the customer as Lincoln's most important constituency. This is reflected in Lincoln's policy to "at all times price on the basis of cost and at all times keep pressure on our cost . . ."

Attitude toward Stockholders

Stockholders are given last priority at Lincoln. This is a continuation of James Lincoln's philosophy: "The last group to be considered is the stockholders who own stock because they think it will be more profitable than investing money in any other way" [1961, p. 38]. Concerning division of the largess produced by incentive management, Lincoln writes, "The absentee stockholder also will get his share, even if undeserved, out of the greatly increased profit that the efficiency produces" [1961, p. 122].

Attitude toward Unionism

There has never been a serious effort to organize Lincoln employees. Although James Lincoln criticized the labor movement for "selfishly attempting to better its position at the expense of the people it must serve" [1961, p. 18], he still had kind words for union members. He excused abuses of union power as "the natural reactions of human beings to the abuses to which management has subjected them" [1961, p. 76]. Lincoln's idea of the correct relationship between workers and managers is shown by this comment: "Labor and management are properly not warring camps; they are parts of one organization in which they must and should cooperate fully and happily" [1961, p. 72].

Beliefs and Assumptions about Employees

If fulfilling customer needs is the desired goal of business, then employee performance and productivity are the means by which this goal can best be achieved. The Lincoln attitude toward employees, reflected in the following quotations, is credited by many with creating the company's success [all taken from Lincoln, 1961]:

> The greatest fear of the worker, which is the same as the greatest fear of the industrialist in operating a company, is lack of income. . . . The industrial manager is very conscious of his company's need of uninterrupted income. He is completely oblivious, evidently, of the fact that the worker has the same need [p. 36].

> If money is to be used as an incentive, the program must provide that what is paid to the worker is what he has earned. The earnings of each must be in accordance with accomplishment [p. 98].

> Status is of great importance in all human relationships. The greatest incentive that money has, usually, is that it is a symbol of success. . . . The resulting status is the real incentive. . . . Money alone can be an incentive to the miser only [p. 92].

ORGANIZATION STRUCTURE

Lincoln has never had a formal organization chart. An open door policy is practiced throughout the company, and personnel are encouraged to take problems to the person most capable of resolving them. Perhaps because of the quality and enthusiasm of the Lincoln work force, routine supervision is almost nonexistent. A typical production foreman, for example, supervises as many as 100 workers, a span-of-control that allows only infrequent worker-supervisor interaction.

Position titles and flows of authority do imply something of an organizational structure. For example, the vice president—sales, and the vice president—electrode division, report to the president, as do various staff assistants such as the personnel director and the director of purchasing. Using such implied relationships it appears that production workers have two or, at most, three levels of supervision between themselves and the president.

PERSONNEL POLICIES

Recruitment and Selection

Every job opening at Lincoln is advertised internally on company bulletin boards, and any employee can apply for any job so advertised. External hiring is done only for entry level positions. People are selected for these jobs by personal interviews—there is no aptitude or psychological testing. Not even a high school diploma is required except for engineering and sales positions, which are filled by graduate engineers. A committee of vice presidents and superintendents interviews candidates initially cleared by the personnel department. The supervisor who has a job opening makes the final selection. In 1979, out of about 3500 applicants interviewed by the personnel department fewer than 300 were hired.

Job Security

After one year, each employee is guaranteed not to be discharged except for misconduct. Each is guaranteed at least 30 hours of work each week. There has been no layoff at Lincoln since 1949.

Performance Evaluations

Each supervisor formally evaluates all subordinates twice a year on "quality," "dependability," "ideas and cooperation," and "output." Employees who offer suggestions for improvements tend to receive high evaluations. Supervisors discuss individual performance marks with the employees concerned.

Compensation

Basic wage levels for jobs at Lincoln are determined by a wage survey of similar jobs in the Cleveland area. These rates are adjusted quarterly with changes in the Cleveland Area Consumer Price Index. Insofar as possible, base wage rates are translated into piece rates. Practically all production workers and many others—for example, some forktruck drivers—are paid by piece rate. Once established, piece rates are never changed unless a substantive change in the way a job is done results from a source other than the worker doing the job. In December of each year, a portion of annual profits goes to employees as bonuses. Incentive bonuses since 1934 have averaged about the same as annual wages and somewhat more than after-tax profits. The average bonus for 1979 was about $17,000. Individual bonuses are exactly proportional to merit-rating scores. For example, a person with a score of 110 would receive 110 percent of the standard bonus as applied to his regular earnings.

Work Assignment

Management has authority to transfer workers and to switch between overtime and short time as required. Supervisors have undisputed authority to assign specific parts to individual workmen, who may have their own preferences due to variations in piece rates.

Employee Participation in Decision Making

When a manager speaks of participative management, he usually thinks of a relaxed, nonauthoritarian atmosphere. This is not the case at Lincoln. "We're very authoritarian around here," says Mr. Willis. James F. Lincoln placed a good deal of stress on protecting management's authority. "Management in all successful departments of industry must have complete power," he said. ". . . Management is the coach who must be obeyed. The men, however, are the players who alone can win the games" [1951, p. 228]. Despite this attitude, there are several ways in which employees participate in management at Lincoln.

Richard Sabo, manager of public relations, relates job-enlargement to participation. "The most important participative technique that we use is giving more responsibility to employees." Mr. Sabo says, "We give a high school graduate more responsibility than other companies give their foremen."

The Advisory Board, elected by the workers, meets with the chairman and the president every two weeks to discuss ways of improving operations. This board has been in existence since 1914 and has contributed to many innovations. The incentive bonuses, for example, were first recommended by this committee. Every Lincoln employee has access to advisory board members, and answers to all suggestions are promised by the following meeting. Both Mr. Irrgang and Mr. Willis are quick to point out, though, that the advisory board only recommends actions. "They do not have direct authority," Mr. Irrgang says, "and when they bring up something that management thinks is not to the benefit of the company, it will be rejected" [Incentive Management in Action . . .].

A suggestion program was instituted in 1929. At first, employees were awarded one half of the first year's savings attributable to their suggestions. Now suggestions affect the performance evaluation scores that determine individual incentive bonus amounts.

Training and Education

Production workers are given brief on-the-job training and then placed on piecework pay. Lincoln does not pay for off-site education. The idea is that everyone cannot take advantage of such a program, and it is unfair to expend company funds for an advantage to which there is unequal access. Sales personnel receive on-the-job training in the plant followed by a period of work and training at one of the regional sales offices.

Fringe Benefits and Executive Perquisites

A medical plan and a company-paid retirement program have been in effect for many years. A plant cafeteria, operated on a break-even basis, serves meals at about 60 percent of usual costs. An employee association, to which the company does not contribute, provides disability insurance and social and athletic activities. An employee stock ownership program, instituted in about 1925, and regular stock purchases have resulted in employee ownership of about 50 percent of Lincoln's stock.

As to executive perquisites, there are none—crowded, uncarpeted austere offices; no executive washrooms or lunchrooms; and no reserved parking spaces. Even the company president pays for his own meals and eats in the cafeteria.

FINANCIAL MANAGEMENT

James F. Lincoln felt strongly that financing for company growth should come from within the company—through initial cash investment by the founders, retention of earnings, and stock purchases by those who work in the business.

Lincoln Electric Company uses a minimum of debt in its capital structure. There is no borrowing at all, and debt is limited to current payables. Even the new $20,000,000 plant in Mentor, Ohio, was financed totally from earnings.

The pricing policy at Lincoln is succinctly stated by President Willis: "at all times price on the basis of cost and at all times keep pressure on our cost." Recently, the SA-200 Welder, Lincoln's largest selling portable machine, decreased in price from 1958 through 1965. According to Dr. C. Jackson Grayson of the American Productivity Center in Houston, Lincoln's prices in general have increased only one fifth as fast as the Consumer Price Index since 1934. This has resulted in a welding products market in which Lincoln is the undisputed price leader for the products it manufactures. Not even the major Japanese manufacturers, such as Nippon Steel for welding electrodes and Osaka Transformer for welding machines, have been able to penetrate the U.S. market.

Huge cash balances are accumulated each year preparatory to paying the year-end bonuses. The bonuses totaled $46,500,000 for 1979. This money is invested in short-term U.S. government securities until needed.

WORKER PERFORMANCE AND ATTITUDES

Exceptional worker performance at Lincoln is a matter of record. The typical Lincoln employee earns about twice as much as other factory workers in the Cleveland area.

Yet the labor cost per sales dollar at Lincoln, currently 23.5 cents, is well below industry averages.

Sales per Lincoln factory employee currently exceed $157,000. An observer at the factory quickly sees why this figure is so high. Each worker is proceeding busily and thoughtfully about his task. There is no idle chatter. Most workers take no coffee breaks. Many operate several machines and make a substantial component unaided. The supervisors, some with as many as 100 subordinates, are busy with planning and recordkeeping duties with hardly a glance at the people they supervise. The manufacturing procedures appear efficient—no unnecessary steps, no wasted motions, no wasted materials. Finished components move smoothly to subsequent work stations and crane operators keep materials conveniently on hand.

Worker turnover at Lincoln is practically nonexistent except for retirements and departures by new employees.

The appendix summarizes interviews with several Lincoln employees.

HOW WELL DOES LINCOLN SERVE ITS "PUBLIC?"

Lincoln Electric believes it differs from most other companies in the importance it assigns to each of the principal groups it serves. Mr. Willis identifies these groups, in the order of priority Lincoln ascribes to them, as (1) customers, (2) employees, and (3) stockholders.

Certainly Lincoln customers have fared well over the years. Lincoln prices for welding machines and welding electrodes are acknowledged to be the lowest in the marketplace. Lincoln quality has consistently been so high that Lincoln "Fleetweld" electrodes and Lincoln SA-200 welders have been the standard in the pipeline and refinery construction industry, where price is hardly a criterion, for decades. The cost of field failures for Lincoln products was an amazing 0.04 percent in 1979. A Lincoln distributor in Monroe, Louisiana, says that he has sold several hundred of the popular AC-225 welders and, though the machine is only warranted for one year, he has never handled a warranty claim.

Perhaps best served of all Lincoln constituencies have been the employees. Not the least of their benefits, of course, is the year-end bonus, which effectively doubles an already-average compensation.

A CONCLUDING COMMENT

It is easy to believe that the reason for Lincoln's success is the excellent attitude of Lincoln employees and their willingness to work harder, faster, and more intelligently than other industrial workers. However, Richard Sabo, manager of publicity and educational services at Lincoln, suggests that appropriate credit be given to Lincoln executives whom he credits with carrying out the following policies.

1. Management has limited research, development and manufacturing to a standard product line designed to meet the major needs of the welding industry.

2. New products must be reviewed by manufacturing and all production costs verified before being approved by management.

3. Purchasing is challenged not only to procure materials at the lowest cost, but also to work closely with engineering and manufacturing to assure that the latest innovations are implemented.

4. Manufacturing supervision and all personnel are held accountable for reduction of scrap, energy conservation, and maintenance of product quality.

5. Production control, material handling, and methods engineering are closely supervised by top management.

6. Material and finished goods inventory control, accurate cost accounting and attention to sales costs, credit and other financial areas have constantly reduced overhead and led to excellent profitability.

7. Management has made cost reduction a way of life at Lincoln and definite programs are established in many areas, including traffic and shipping, where tremendous savings can result.

8. Management has established a sales department that is technically trained to reduce customer welding costs. This sales technique and other real customer services have eliminated nonessential frills and resulted in long-term benefits to all concerned.

9. Management has encouraged education, technical publishing, and long-range programs that have resulted in industry growth, thereby assuring market potential for The Lincoln Electric Company.

REFERENCES

"Incentive Management in Action: An Interview with William Irrgang, Chief Executive Officer, The Lincoln Electric Company." *Assembly Engineering,* March 1967. Reprinted by the Lincoln Electric Company, Cleveland, Ohio.

Lincoln, James F. *Incentive Management.* Cleveland, Ohio: The Lincoln Electric Company, 1951.

Lincoln, James F. *A New Approach to Industrial Economics.* New York: The Devin-Adair Company, 1961.

"You Can't Tell What a Man Can Do—Until He Has the Chance." *Reader's Digest,* January 1947, pp. 93–95.

APPENDIX: EMPLOYEE INTERVIEWS

During the late summer of 1980, the author conducted numerous interviews with Lincoln employees. Typical questions and answers from those interviews are presented below. In order to maintain each employee's personal privacy, the names used for the interviewees are disguised.

I

Interview with Ed Sanderson, 23-year-old high school graduate who had been with Lincoln four years and who was a machine operator in the electrode division at the time of the interview.

Q: How did you happen to get this job?

A: My wife was pregnant and I was making three bucks an hour and one day I came here and applied. That was it. I kept calling to let them know I was still interested.

Q: Roughly what were your earnings last year including your bonus?

A: $37,000.00.

Q: What have you done with your money since you have been here?

A: Well, we've lived pretty well and we bought a condominium.

Q: Have you paid for the condominium?

A: No, but I could.

Q: Have you bought your Lincoln stock this year?

A: No, I haven't bought any Lincoln stock yet.

Q: Do you get the feeling that the executives here are pretty well thought of?

A: I think they are. To get where they are today they had to really work.

Q: Wouldn't that be true anywhere?

A: I think more so here because seniority really doesn't mean anything. If you work with a guy who has 20 years here and you have two months and you're doing a better job, you will get advanced before he will.

Q: Are you paid on a piece rate basis?

A: My gang does. There are nine of us who make the bare electrode and the whole group gets paid based on how much electrode we make.

Q: Do you think you work harder than workers in other factories in the Cleveland area?

A: Yes, I would say I probably work harder.

Q: Do you think it hurts anybody?

A: No, a little hard work never hurts anybody.

Q: If you could choose, do you think you would be as happy earning a little less money and being able to slow down a little?

A: No, it doesn't bother me. If it bothered me I wouldn't do it.

Q: What would you say is the biggest disadvantage of working at Lincoln, as opposed to working somewhere else?

A: Probably having to work shift work.

Q: Why do you think Lincoln employees produce more than workers in other plants?

A: That's the way the company is set up. The more you put out, the more you're going to make.

Q: Do you think it's the piece rate and bonus together?

A: I don't think people would work here if they didn't know that they would be rewarded at the end of the year.

Q: Do you think Lincoln employees will ever join a union?

A: No.

Q: What are the major advantages of working for Lincoln?

A: Money.

Q: Are there any other advantages?

A: Yes, we don't have a union shop. I don't think I could work in a union shop.

Q: Do you think you are a career man with Lincoln at this time?

A: Yes.

II

Interview with Roger Lewis, 23-year-old Purdue graduate in mechanical engineering who had been in the Lincoln sales program for 15 months and who was working in the Cleveland sales office at the time of the interview.

Q: How did you get your job at Lincoln?

A: I saw that Lincoln was interviewing on campus at Purdue and I went by. I later came to Cleveland for a plant tour and was offered a job.

Q: Do you know any of the senior executives? Would they know you by name?

A: Yes, I know all of them—Mr. Irrgang, Mr. Willis, Mr. Manross.

Q: Do you think Lincoln salesmen work harder than those in other companies?

A: Yes. I don't think there are many salesmen for other companies who are putting in 50- to 60-hour weeks. Everybody here works harder. You can go out in the plant or you can go upstairs and there's nobody sitting around.

Q: Do you see any real disadvantage of working at Lincoln?

A: I don't know if it's a disadvantage, but Lincoln is a Spartan company, a very thrifty company. I like that. The sales offices are functional, not fancy.

Q: Why do you think Lincoln employees have such high productivity?

A: Piecework has a lot to do with it. Lincoln is smaller than many plants, too; you can stand in one place and see the materials come in one side and the product go out the other. You feel a part of the company. The chance to get ahead is important, too. They have a strict policy of promoting from within, so you know you have a chance. I think in a lot of other places you may not get as fair a shake as you do here. The sales offices are on a smaller scale, too. I like that. I tell someone that we have two people in the Baltimore office and they say "You've got to be kidding." It's smaller and more personal. Pay is the most important thing. I have heard that this is the highest paying factory in the world.

III

Interview with Jimmy Roberts, a 47-year-old high school graduate who had been with Lincoln 17 years and who was working as a multiple drill press operator at the time of the interview.

Q: What jobs have you had at Lincoln?

A: I started out cleaning the men's locker room in 1963. After about a year I got a job in the flux department, where we make the coating for welding rods. I worked there for seven or eight years and then got my present job.

Q: Do you make one particular part?

A: No, there are a variety of parts I make—at least 25.

Q: Each one has a different piece rate attached to it?

A: Yes.

Q: Are some piece rates better than others?

A: Yes.

Q: How do you determine which ones you are going to do?

A: You don't. Your supervisor assigns them.

Q: How much money did you make last year?

A: $47,000.

Q: Have you ever received any kind of award or citation?

A: No.

Q: What was your merit rating last year?

A: I don't know.

Q: Did your supervisor have to send a letter—was your rating over 110?

A: Yes. For the past five years, probably, I made over 110 points.

Q: Is there any attempt to let others know. . . ?

A: The kind of points I get? No.

Q: Do you know what they are making?

A: No. There are some who might not be too happy with their points and they might make it known. The majority, though, do not make it a point of telling other employees.

Q: Would you be just as happy earning a little less money and working a little slower?

A: I don't think I would—not at this point. I have done piecework all these years and the fast pace doesn't really bother me.

Q: Why do you think Lincoln productivity is so high?

A: The incentive thing—the bonus distribution. I think that would be the main reason. The pay check you get every two weeks is important too.

Q: Do you think Lincoln employees would ever join a union?

A: I don't think so. I have never heard anyone mention it.

Q: What is the most important advantage of working here?

A: Amount of money you make. I don't think I could make this type of money anywhere else, especially with only a high school education.

Q: As a black person, do you feel that Lincoln discriminates, in any way, against blacks?

A: No. I don't think any more so than any other job. Naturally, there is a certain amount of discrimination, regardless of where you are.

DISCUSSION QUESTIONS

1. To what degree is Lincoln Electric a "streamlined" producer? a just-in-time plant? Explain.

2. The case describes the plant layout and inventory conditions but does not comment on their contributions to Lincoln's success. What may we conclude about those contributions?

3. How important is labor flexibility in the way that Lincoln operates?

4. While Lincoln Electric has much in common with some of the best Japanese manufacturing companies, it is rare for a Japanese company to use piece rates (extra pay for extra output). Are piece rates a vital part of Lincoln's success? Discuss.

5. What techniques for streamlining production is Lincoln probably using (you may be able to make a few inferences where the case does not provide enough direct information)?

6. Comment on weaknesses, if any, that you can think of in the way that Lincoln manages its operations.

Chapter 10

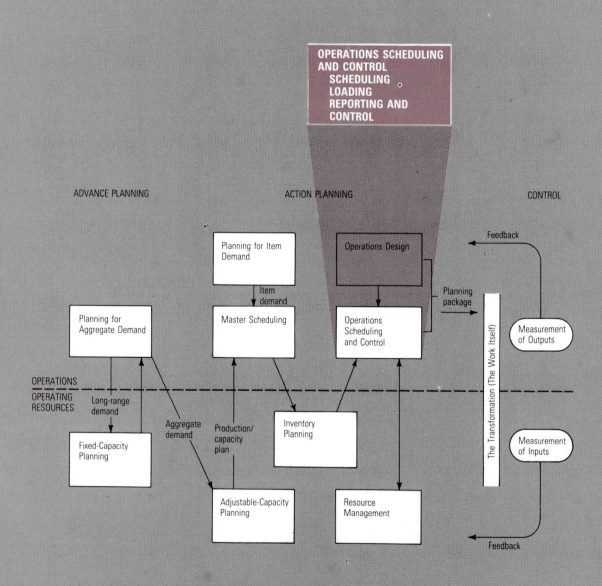

OPERATIONS SCHEDULING AND CONTROL
SCHEDULING
LOADING
REPORTING AND CONTROL

ADVANCE PLANNING   ACTION PLANNING   CONTROL

Planning for Item Demand

Operations Design

Feedback

Planning for Aggregate Demand

Master Scheduling

Operations Scheduling and Control

Planning package

Measurement of Outputs

OPERATIONS
OPERATING RESOURCES

Long-range demand

Item demand

The Transformation (The Work Itself)

Fixed-Capacity Planning

Aggregate demand

Production/ capacity plan

Inventory Planning

Measurement of Inputs

Adjustable-Capacity Planning

Resource Management

Feedback

Job-Lot Operations

We have seen the advantages of streamlined operations. But much of the world of work resists being streamlined. Job and job-lot operations are common in manufacturing and almost universal in services. We must manage them as best we can (and keep trying to streamline). Good scheduling and control are proven techniques.

The chart on the chapter title page shows three inputs into operations scheduling and control. The downward arrow signifies the flow of methods and time standards data that are useful in scheduling operations. The two-headed arrow going down to resource dynamics suggests that the schedule for operations should dovetail with the schedule for operating resources.

The arrow from inventory planning drives the scheduling function. That is, planned orders for component parts are passed to the scheduler, and the scheduler writes shop orders to make the parts. In services, where there are no parts, inventory planning is bypassed: The master schedule of *services* drives the services scheduling or dispatching function.

The difference between scheduling and control for goods and for services is shown more clearly in Figure 10–1. There is a master production schedule (MPS) for goods. For services by appointment there is an appointment book, which is a master services schedule. End items on the MPS explode into component parts, which are planned (timing and quantities) and scheduled (shop orders). Dispatching applies to both

FIGURE 10–1

Differences in Order Scheduling and Control for Goods and Services

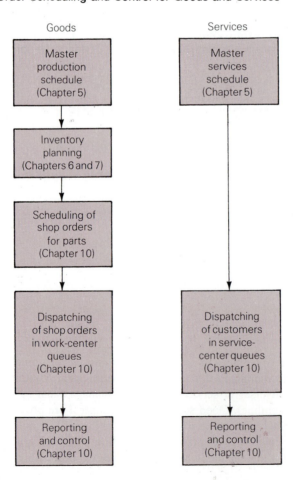

goods and services. For goods, shop orders in work-center queues (waiting lines) are dispatched; that is, the jobs in queue are arranged in some order of importance and passed along to the workers one at a time. For services, customers in queue are dispatched (arranged for processing) at each service center.

Reporting and control are similar for goods and services. Both require measurement of outputs and resource inputs. Measurement data on outputs and inputs are fed back to the planners and schedulers for corrective action, if necessary. (See measurement and feedback in the chart on the chapter title page.)

Our discussion begins with job-lot production control; then considers scheduling, loading, dispatching, and shop-activity control; and concludes with reporting, feedback control, measurement, and reports.

JOB-LOT PRODUCTION CONTROL

In job-lot or job-shop production, which is probably more common than repetitive production, there is a changing mix of jobs produced in moderate or small quantities. In goods-producing job-lot firms, many people are employed in production-control (PC) departments. A large PC staff is needed because orders for goods spawn job orders for a variety of parts, which must be planned and controlled.

In Chapter 6, we saw how material requirements planning can lead to correct planning for the parts. In the following sections we see how inventory plans are translated into scheduled manufacturing orders, how order priorities are kept current, and how progress data are collected and formatted for control purposes. Scheduling, progress reporting, and control of services are also considered.

Scheduling, priority control, and reporting in job-lot manufacturing are hard to understand. The difficult issues are not omitted in our discussion. Without examining the difficult issues, the reader would be hard put to see why production-control staffs are large, what the role of the computer is, why production-control people are still needed even with computerization, and why production control is a challenging area to work in.

A difficulty in understanding job-lot production control seems to be keeping straight the difference between a *job* and an *operation,* which are planned and controlled by the scheduler and the dispatcher. Definitions and an example may make the upcoming discussion easier to understand. First the definitions:

Job: A job is the whole work activity that is required to produce a **component part.** In some firms a job is called a lot. The job or lot (or job lot) is also known as an order, job order, or lot order. A document about the job may be called a shop order, manufacturing order, work order, or job order.

Operation: An operation is one step or task in a job. But more importantly each operation requires a new **setup.** Usually the new setup is at a different work center. There are good reasons to separately plan, schedule, and control each operation. One reason is that a special setup crew may need to be on hand. A second reason is that material handlers and handling devices may be needed.

A third reason is that an inventory can build before each operation. Finally and most importantly, there is usually a choice of operations for different jobs queued up at a given work center. A document showing priority-ordered operations for a work center is known as a dispatch list or priority report.

We shall see that the scheduler schedules both jobs and operations. The dispatcher tries to meet the operation due dates. Dispatchers' actions may include arranging for setups and handling, arranging for jobs to be run in priority order, counting units, and reporting when operations are completed.

An example of jobs and operations follows:

EXAMPLE 10–1

Distinction between Jobs and Operations, Bookcase Shelf

In bookcase manufacturing the bookcase appears on the master schedule and is exploded into component parts. One part is a shelf. Making a quantity of the shelf involves planning and controlling one job and several operations. Figure 10–2 shows a job consisting of 10 bookcase shelves. The shelf part number is 777, and the shop order is shown as a five-operation job. Next, the figure shows each of the five operations and the inventory conditions between them. First, boards are withdrawn from the stockroom. Second, boards are sawed. Third, sawed boards are planed. Fourth, planed boards are sanded. Fifth, sanded boards are finished. The result is 10 finished shelves. These are component parts that go into the next-higher-level item on the bill of materials for the bookshelf order.

Each operation, even stockroom activities, requires setup or get-ready time. And after each operation, work-in-process (WIP) inventories form and sit idle for a time. The setups and the heaps of WIP require attention. A dispatcher is the management specialist who assists the wood-shop foreman in scheduling and controlling the operations: saw, plane, sand, and finish. But the due date for the whole bookshelf job was set earlier by a scheduler in the production control department.

JOB-LOT SCHEDULING

In production-control jargon, master scheduling applies to end items (or services), but *scheduling* pertains to component parts (or service tasks) that come before the end item (or service) due date. Three questions have to be answered in scheduling the job order for a component part (or service task):

1. When can the job be completed?—based on standard times.
2. When should the job be completed?—based on date of customer or parent-item need.
3. When will the job be completed?—based on realities in production work centers.

It makes things simple if all three questions have the same answer. For example, let us say that a patient is undergoing a complete physical examination. An early

FIGURE 10–2

Job and Operations for 10 Bookcase Shelves

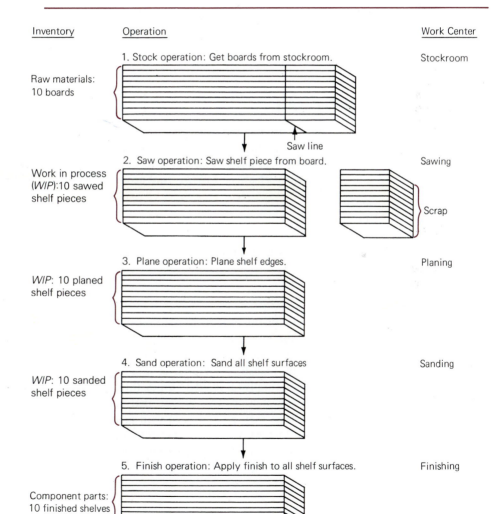

Job: Make 10 shelves,
part number 777

Shop order

1. Stock
2. Saw
3. Plane
4. Sand
5. Finish

Inventory	Operation	Work Center
	1. Stock operation: Get boards from stockroom.	Stockroom
Raw materials: 10 boards		
	Saw line	
	2. Saw operation: Saw shelf piece from board.	Sawing
Work in process (*WIP*):10 sawed shelf pieces		Scrap
	3. Plane operation: Plane shelf edges.	Planing
WIP: 10 planed shelf pieces		
	4. Sand operation: Sand all shelf surfaces	Sanding
WIP: 10 sanded shelf pieces		
	5. Finish operation: Apply finish to all shelf surfaces.	Finishing
Component parts: 10 finished shelves		

step is withdrawing specimens of various body fluids. The physician may want the results of laboratory analysis of a certain specimen to be ready at the end of the exam, say 30 minutes later; that is the answer to question 2. Perhaps the standard time, adjusted for efficiency and utilization, is also 30 minutes; that answers question 1. Suppose the lab has no higher-priority jobs that would interfere with this lab test; then the job can be expected to be completed in 30 minutes, which answers question 3. Since all three questions have the same answer, it is clear that the lab test should be scheduled to start upon withdrawal of the body fluids and to be completed 30 minutes later.

Actually, it is not very likely that a lab can complete its testing as soon as the physician would desire the results. A lab is a job shop, and in job shops queues of job orders form and jostle for priority. In repetitive production, by contrast, jobs generally do not compete for the same resources because problems and other sources of variability have been removed so that jobs may flow from station to station smoothly without queues of WIP inventory.

Production Lead-Time Elements

In job and job-lot production, realities in production work centers result in inflated production lead times—inflated, that is, beyond standard times and often beyond customer and parent-item needs. According to Orlicky,[1] the elements of production lead time for a given part are as follows, in descending order of significance.

1. Queue time.
2. Run time.
3. Setup time.
4. Wait (for transportation) time.
5. Inspection time.
6. Move time.
7. Other.

Orlicky and others maintain that in machine shops, queue time, the first element, normally accounts for about 90 percent of total lead time. Standard time—to run and perhaps to set up, inspect, and move—therefore accounts for less than 10 percent of lead time. Clearly, realistic schedules for manufactured parts must be based on total lead time and not simply on standard times. (Standard times, discussed in Chapter 13, can be set by stopwatch or other precise analysis.)

While standard times may be developed with precision, lead-time precision is elusive. Accurate lead-time estimates, and therefore accurate schedules, are likely only when work centers are uncongested, because only then may the typical job sail through without long and variable queue times at each work center. One job of the scheduler

---

[1] Joseph Orlicky, *Material Requirements Planning* (New York: McGraw-Hill, 1975), p. 83 (TS155.8.O74).

is to keep things uncongested, that is, without an unnecessary amount of work in process (WIP).

Work in Process

The WIP problem has received much attention in Western industry as well as in Japan. Good manufacturing managers recognize the benefits of keeping WIP low:

1. **Service.** Low WIP means less queue time and faster response to customer orders; also, with less queue time, there is less uncertainty in the schedule and customers may be given better status information.
2. **Forecasts.** We know that forecasts are more accurate for shorter periods into the future, that is, for the shorter lead times that result from smaller amounts of WIP.
3. **Production-control work force.** Less WIP means less congestion and less need for shop-floor control by expediters and dispatchers.
4. **Floor-space and inventory costs.** These are lower when fewer jobs are in process.

There are practical limits to work-in-process reductions. There should be enough work to keep work centers busy. The operations to produce certain parts do not spread evenly over all the work centers. They tend to cluster, overloading some work centers and perhaps underloading others. As the job mix changes, and it often changes quickly, the pattern of over- and underloading changes. There is pressure on the scheduler to overload on the average in order to hold down the number of underloaded work centers. Production supervisors get nervous about cost variances (explained later) when workloads get low.

Lead-Time Accuracy

The scheduler seems caught in a bind: Scheduling enough work to keep work centers busy means that queue times will grow and make schedules less realistic. It is difficult to predict average queue time, because the average changes with the changing job mix. It is even harder to predict queue time for a given job, because the job may queue up at several work centers as it completes its routing. Therefore, it is not uncommon for the scheduler to follow a "rule" of adding a fixed number of days for queue time and other delays. Here are two examples of possible scheduler's rules:

$$LT = 2N + 4 \tag{1}$$

$$LT = RT + I + 4 \tag{2}$$

where

LT = Lead time in days
N = Number of operations in the job
RT = Run time in days
I = Inspection time in days

Formula (1) allows two days for each operation plus four days for queue time and other delays. Formula (2) is a bit more precise. It specifies a run time and inspection time and then adds four days for queue and other delays.

A **dynamic queue-time** approach is another possibility. In the dynamic approach, queue time includes an extra-time allowance for current or projected shop congestion. A simple measure of shop congestion is the number of open job orders, which the computer could find in the open-order files. (The open-order file is discussed in Chapter 6 in connection with material requirements planning.) Another measure of shop congestion is the number of operations in all open orders. To find number of operations, the computer searches the open-order file and then the routing file, which tells the route taken by an order.

In a material requirements planning system, accurate lead times are not vital for job and priority control. If a simple, but inaccurate static approach is used, lead-time errors may be adjusted for. Changing the due date for a part that is on order is one type of adjustment. Advice about the need to change due dates is in the form of *rescheduling notices* from the weekly MRP run. While planned order releases from an MRP run trigger inventory planning (ordering) actions, rescheduling notices trigger scheduling actions. Together, these two MRP outputs provide full support for component parts planning and control. A second type of adjustment may be made each day (between weekly MRP runs): A daily dispatch list from the computer tells the dispatcher of the need to change the priorities of work in process in order to meet due dates. (Dispatch lists are discussed later.)

Inaccurate lead times have a more severe effect on capacity control. **Capacity requirements planning (CRP) is a computer-based extension of MRP in which future work-center loads are computed.** Accuracy of computed loads may be improved by including some kind of queue-time allowance in lead-time estimates; allowances based on shop congestion—the dynamic scheduling idea mentioned above—may be helpful. With more accurate load projections, work-center capacity may be planned so that there is less need for last-minute capacity control measures.

Backward and Forward Scheduling

For services offered on demand, the usual customer need date is "as soon as possible." (ASAP is a well-known abbreviation.) The customer order is scheduled forward from the current date or from the date on which resources are expected to be available.

For services provided by appointment, backward scheduling may be used. An example is deliveries of checks and deposit slips from a small bank to a larger bank's computer service center. The service center may require that the delivery be made by 9:00 P.M. each day. If so, schedules for each delivery stop are backward-scheduled. That is, operation lead times (time between stops) are successively subtracted from 9:00 P.M. The resulting schedule might appear as shown in the accompanying diagram.

Backward and forward scheduling may be used in tandem. A scheduler might be asked to estimate the earliest date on which a job can be completed, which calls

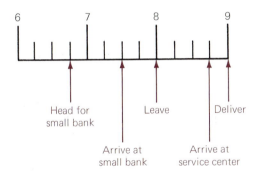

for forward scheduling. The date of need might be beyond the calculated earliest completion date; backward scheduling might then be used to determine the scheduled start date.

Goods producers also use both forward and backward scheduling. Generally, manufacturing inventories that are replenished by reorder point (ROP) are forward-scheduled. But MRP yields planned order releases that are backward-scheduled from the date of the net requirement. Actually, in most MRP systems the planned-order-release date is not the scheduled start *day*. The scheduler is advised by the computer of the (backward-scheduled) start *week*, and the scheduler then determines the start *day*. The following is an example of the scheduler's procedure.

EXAMPLE 10–2

Scheduling a Shop Order, QUIDCO, Inc.

The weekly MRP run at QUIDCO, Inc., shows a planned order in the current time bucket for Part no. 1005CX. The part is due on Monday of time bucket (week) 3, which is shop calendar date 105. (See Figure 10–3A.)

The inventory planner validates the need for the order and the order quantity and timing. The planner decides that it should be a make rather than a buy order and therefore requests a shop order.

The scheduler finds the part number in the routing file, and the routing and time standards for each operation are displayed on a video display terminal. The scheduler prepares a shop order using data from the routing file. (See Figure 10–3B.) Backward scheduling is used, along with these "rules" that QUIDCO uses for computing operation lead times.[2]

1. Allow eight standard hours per day; round upward to even days.
2. Allow one day between operations—for move and queue time and other delays.
3. Allow two days to inspect.

---

[2] Adapted from Oliver W. Wight, *Production and Inventory Management in the Computer Age* (Boston: CBI Publishing, 1974), pp. 81–82 (TS155.W533). Note that operation lead times are detailed, whereas job-order lead times, discussed earlier (for computing planned order releases), are gross.

FIGURE 10–3

Generating Shop Order from Current Planned Order Listing

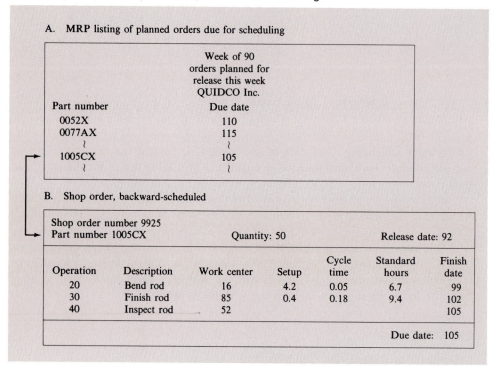

A. MRP listing of planned orders due for scheduling

Week of 90
orders planned for
release this week
QUIDCO Inc.

Part number	Due date
0052X	110
0077AX	115
⟨	⟨
1005CX	105
⟨	⟨

B. Shop order, backward-scheduled

Shop order number 9925
Part number 1005CX   Quantity: 50   Release date: 92

Operation	Description	Work center	Setup	Cycle time	Standard hours	Finish date
20	Bend rod	16	4.2	0.05	6.7	99
30	Finish rod	85	0.4	0.18	9.4	102
40	Inspect rod	52				105

Due date: 105

4. Release shop order to the stockroom five days before the job is to be started into production.
5. All dates are treated as end of the eight-hour day.

Backward scheduling begins with the due date, 105, in the lower right corner. (A **shop calendar** of consecutively numbered work days, omitting weekends and holidays, is common among manufacturing firms, because it makes computation easy.) That is the finish date for the last operation, inspect. Two days for inspect and one day between operations are subtracted, which makes 102 the due date for the finish operation. Finish takes 9.4 standard hours (0.4 + 0.18 × 50 pieces), which rounds upward to two days. Subtracting that two, plus one day between operations, equals 99 as the due date for the bend operation. Finally, one day (6.7 hours rounded upward) for bend, five days for stockroom actions, and one day between operations are subtracted, which makes day 92 the release date. Shop order 9925 is therefore held in the scheduler's **hold-for-release** file on Monday and Tuesday (days 90 and 91) and released on Wednesday (day 92).

A week goes by. The inventory planner notifies the scheduler that part no. 1005CX has a new need date: the week of 110 instead of 105. (The latest MRP run informed the inventory planner of the later date.) The sched-uler recomputes operation due dates as follows:

```
Job due date = Inspect due date = Day   110
Less inspect time              =          2  days
                          Day   108
Less move/queue time           =          1  day
Finish due date          = Day   107
Less finish time               =          2  days
                          Day   105
Less move/queue time           =          1  day
Bend due date            = Day   104
```

The scheduler enters the three new operation due dates into the computer. The computer uses the new dates in printing out a daily dispatch list. Copies of the list go to the three work centers to tell them about the changes in operation due dates.

In this system there is no need for the scheduler to issue paperwork giving initial due dates and revised due dates, because the computer issues a dispatch list telling what the operation due dates are. The scheduler does need to assemble a planning package that may include job tickets, inspection tickets, and forms on which to record such things as material usage, scrap, and labor changes.

In a manual system there may not be a daily dispatch list. In that case the scheduler will need to put due dates on job tickets or other planning-package paperwork. A problem with the manual system is keeping everybody informed of new due dates when schedules change. It can be a paperwork nightmare.

In the QUIDCO example, the backward scheduling is done by a human scheduler. The scheduler could do this at a video display terminal, with the computer handling the calculation chores following the lead-time rules.

It is gradually becoming more common for MRP systems to plan in days rather than weeks. Schedulers then may plan in hours instead of days. This is highly desirable because it cuts work-in-process inventory further and shortens lead times, which makes the firm stronger financially and competitively. Later in the chapter, we discuss shop-floor recorders, which provide the scheduler with faster feedback on how jobs are doing so that schedule changes can be more responsive.

Scheduling Operating Resources

We have been talking about the scheduling of jobs and job operations—the ends. Schedulers must, at the same time, make sure that the right operating resources (means) are there at the right time for the scheduled jobs. The schedules for ends and means must match; hence the two-headed arrow between scheduling and resource dynamics in the chart on the chapter title page.

In an earlier era, the tendency was to schedule jobs and operations with little regard for whether resources would be on hand. This was the case in manufacturing for two main reasons:

1. Labor resources were largely unskilled, and labor laws were weak. Labor could therefore be adjusted up or down, on short notice, as job schedules required.
2. Material resources, that is, purchased and made parts, were planned by reorder point, because there was too little data-processing power to *schedule* these resources based on future net requirements—today's MRP process. The same was true of reusable resources such as tools, gauges, fixtures, dies, machines, and space.

Today labor-hours, machine-hours, and aggregate inventories may be scheduled roughly to meet aggregate demand. The scheduling is done using the production planning and rough-cut capacity-planning techniques presented in Chapter 3. Component parts may be precisely scheduled using MRP. And MRP II extends the concept to allow for better scheduling of cash flow (see Chapter 6); also the MRP II idea may allow for scheduling of labor, gauges, dies, tools, and machines, all based on a master production schedule.

A picture is worth a thousand words, as the saying goes. Is it possible to present a schedule in the form of a picture? Yes, it is. A pictorial schedule, known as a Gantt chart, is covered next.

Gantt Scheduling Charts

Henry Gantt's name is attached to a type of chart that is widely used for displaying a schedule. The basic form of the Gantt chart has vertical time divisions and has the jobs or resources to be scheduled as rows. Lines, bars, brackets, shading, and other such devices mark the start, duration, and end of a scheduled entity. Schedules for a variety of operating resources may be displayed. The purpose of the charts, like that of any visual aid, is to clarify and so to improve understanding and to serve as a focus for discussion. Some common examples are shown in Figure 10–4.

The examples shown are for scheduling three different resource types: equipment, space, and workers. Each also identifies the jobs to be performed by the resources. Notice also that each is a services example. While Gantt's original chart was for the control of repetitive manufacturing, Gantt charts today, in simpler forms, are more widely used in services, where routings are short and queues have few chances to form.[3]

In goods production, Gantt charts may be usable if:

1. There are not many work centers. With many work centers a carefully developed Gantt display of schedules tends to be a piece of gross fiction, because queuing effects (discussed earlier) make lead time unpredictable. Keeping the chart up to date under such conditions would be time-consuming and pointless.

---

[3] The original purpose was to display variances from planned production rates in repetitive production. Today the Gantt chart is used almost exclusively for displaying schedules in nonrepetitive work.

FIGURE 10–4

Common Forms of the Gantt Chart

A. Schedule for machine

Scheduled computer jobs	M	T	W	T	F	S	S	M	T	W	T	F	S	S	M	T	W	T
Payroll			▓							▓							▓	
Accounts receivable				▓								▓						▓
MRP					▓								▓					

B. Schedule for classrooms

Classroom schedule	(Monday) 6	7	8	9	10	11	12	1
CBA 100				MGM 331	ACCT 101			MGM
CBA 101		ECON 205			ECON 400		FIN 394	

C. Schedule for worker

	Dentist's appointments
Mon. 8:00	Mrs. Harrison
8:30	↓
9:00	J. Peters
9:30	Steve Smith
10:00	
10:30	
11:00	↓

2. Cycle times are long—days or weeks rather than hours. An example is a construction project. Drywallers, painters, cement crews, roofers, and so on, may each spend several days or even weeks at a worksite.

3. Job routings are short. In parts manufacturing, routings can be long. A single job may pass through 5, 10, or even 15 work centers, with unpredictable queue time at each stop. In maintenance work, routings tend to be short and Gantt charts can be helpful. Maintenance is often thought of more as a service than a goods-oriented activity, even though it is goods that are being maintained. As a service, maintenance may be expected to benefit from Gantt-charted schedules, just as other services do. Later in the chapter we look at the use of Gantt charts in controlling maintenance jobs.

WORK-CENTER LOADING AND CAPACITY CONTROL

In Chapter 5, we discussed capacity planning, which is done early—before and during master scheduling. Now we may discuss **capacity control,** which goes on after work centers are loaded with jobs to make the parts that go into master-scheduled products.

Keeping the work centers loaded with work—but assuring that loads do not exceed work-center capacity—is a day-to-day management problem. The problem exists for work centers of all kinds: The typing pool in an office is a work center; so is the X-ray area in a clinic or hospital; and in a factory a machine or a group of similar machines is a work center. Staff analysts' reports constitute workload for a typing pool; hospital patients generate workload for an X-ray work center; and component-parts orders in support of a master production schedule generate workloads for machine centers.

Load is short for workload, and **loading** refers to the assigning of workload to a work center. Orders for inventory components create workloads in work centers. Thus, capacity control in work centers comes after inventory planning.

In job-lot production, loads are likely to be distributed very unevenly. For a given work center, loads will vary from week to week. And some work centers will be overloaded, some underloaded. This loading unevenness may call for short-term capacity adjustments.

The traditional approach is to make short-term capacity adjustments "at the last minute," because of lack of good information about loadings in future periods. In this older approach work-center loads are calculated for upcoming weeks based only on open orders. (An open order is a component-parts order that has been released by production control to the work centers.) No planned (future) orders are included; the traditional planning system is simply not future oriented. Therefore work-center load reports are incomplete for future time buckets, which means capacity adjustments cannot be planned very far in advance. Attention is on the current week. Production control's tendency is to overload each work center for the current week and to have expediters "pull" the high-priority jobs through. One expediting option is lot splitting; another is overlapped production, which means delivering parts as you make them to the next work center so that a single lot is in production in more than one work center at the same time. In a job shop, these options require extraordinary coordination, but they may be preferable to another costly option: overtime.

Backlog Tracking

Load reports, even incomplete ones, may be useful in projecting past loading trends into the future. The method is as follows: Each week the current load and all future

FIGURE 10–5

Work-Center Load (backlog) Trends

A. Work center 024—extrusion

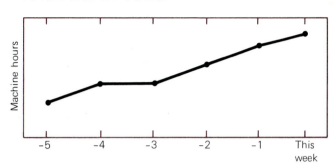

B. Work center 016—welding

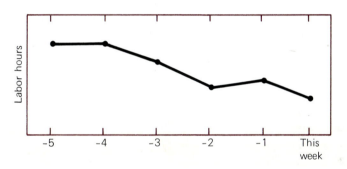

==loads (from open orders) are totaled. The total is the work center's **backlog.** The backlog may be plotted, or tracked, week by week on a graph. Trends in plotted points may suggest a need for short-term capacity (or other) adjustments.== An example is given in Figure 10–5.

Part A of the figure is a machine-oriented work center (extrusion). The load or backlog is expressed in machine-hours, and it is rising. The rising trend tells production control that more machine capacity will be needed soon. Otherwise, lead times will lengthen and service to customers will deteriorate.

Part B is a labor-oriented work center (welding). The backlog is in labor-hours, and it is falling. Production control may recommend layoffs or a similar capacity adjustment, unless marketing can generate more orders that include welding work.

Capacity Requirements Planning

==Capacity requirements planning (CRP) is a computer-based method of revealing work-center loads.== A CRP run on the computer requires three inputs. One input is planned order releases for component parts. Planned order releases are calculated by the computer in an MRP run (see Chapter 6). A second input is open orders for component parts. Open orders are orders released by scheduling (or purchasing) in an earlier period and still in process. The third input is routing data that tells what work centers each component-parts order goes through and how long it takes in each. Both the open order file and the routing file must be computerized in order to run CRP. (Many firms that adopt material requirements planning do not add CRP for several years—because of the trouble and cost of creating a computer file of valid routing and operation-timing data.)

Capacity requirements planning reports project loads in work centers that have been having difficulty in keeping up with planned output. Deficient capacity in each critical work center is projected far enough in advance to do something about it; two or three months of future projections are often enough. (There is no sense in asking the computer to run CRP projections for all work centers and for 52 weeks into the future, because the real problems are in the near future and likely only in certain work centers.) Common actions to be taken are training new workers, shifting labor to new jobs, layoffs, subcontracts, and so on. With CRP's potential to alert managers so as to keep work-center capacities reasonably close to planned loads, the usual chaotic atmosphere on the shop floor may give way to reasonable order and tranquillity. The differences between traditional and CRP load projections are examined further below.

Loading to Infinite versus Finite Capacity

In repetitive production, balanced assembly lines may be designed. The capacities of work centers are then in balance (as near as is practical) with one another and with the rate of product flow. The work centers are said to be loaded to finite capacity.

In job-lot production it is not so simple. A variable mix of orders loads unevenly on work centers. *Planning* a balanced load, that is, loading to finite capacity, is quite possible. However, *completing* work-center operations in the planned amount of time is rare. And when the plans do not work out, as they won't, a carefully developed finite-capacity loading plan falls apart. Therefore most firms do not attempt finite-capacity loading. Loading to infinite capacity can be made to work fairly well.

Loading to infinite capacity means scheduling job orders without regard for resulting work-center loads. That is, the scheduler tries to set job-order due dates based on planned dates when parts are needed; there is no attempt to smooth out lumpy groups of operations so as to ease overloads in particular work centers. In effect, the scheduler seems to be assuming infinite capacity in the work centers. Scheduling without regard for loading is not insane. The system employs production control people to see that more important jobs get run first in overloaded work centers. It works.

Infinite-capacity loading is normal in manufacturing firms that make do with incomplete load reports based only on open orders. It also is normal in firms that rely on complete computer-produced load reports via MRP-CRP. Figure 10–6 shows how a visual loading report might look for each type of firm. Figure 10–6A shows the

FIGURE 10–6

Infinite-Capacity Loading

A. Manually calculated loads

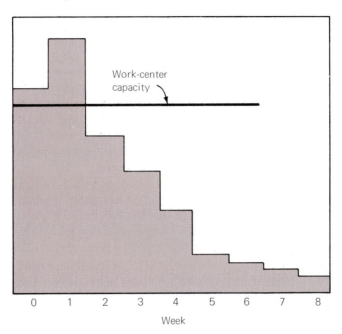

B. Computer-calculated *(CRP)* loads

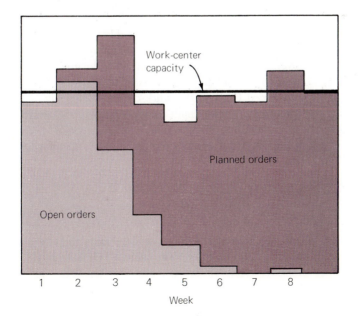

usual falling-off load projected for a work center in a firm relying on incomplete data. The load falls off because it is based only on open orders for parts that are low in the warehouse. The week 0 load is a backlog of parts orders already in the work center; the remaining loads are for parts orders due into this work center after passing through upstream work centers. The backlog and the week 1 load are shown to be more than double the work center's capacity. This is not a great problem. Only a few of the orders are needed for current production, and they will appear on a shortage list. Expediters will see that they are run first. Other orders are for stock replenishment (fill warehouse supplies) and may safely be delayed.

Figure 10–6B shows the up-and-down loading pattern common for work centers in firms that use the computer for inventory planning and loading (CRP). A heavy line divides open orders—those already released by the scheduler to the shops— from planned orders calculated by the computer to meet future needs. Overloads are shown in weeks 2, 3, and 8. Daily dispatching of more urgent jobs in those weeks can deal with most of the overload problem. When overloads are severe, a few end-item batches may be moved on the MPS. Moving batches of end items to an earlier or later time bucket also moves the dates of need for component parts that go into the end items. It may not be easy to trace a component part back to the end items in which it goes. (This kind of tracing is called "pegging," and it may be performed on a computer.) Once the linkage has been established, the master scheduler may move an end-item batch and thereby move all the other links in the chain down to the level of the overloaded work center, and the overloading may be relieved.

SHOP-ACTIVITY CONTROL

The workplace or shop floor is out of control if it is choked with partly completed jobs. This is true for a restaurant, clinic, or bank as well as for a goods producer. In Chapter 5 we studied production/capacity planning and master scheduling, which help to keep an overall balance between workload and capacity, and in the last section we considered work-center loading concepts. There are two final steps to be taken in the quest for balanced loads in the work centers. They involve the scheduler and the dispatcher. Their jobs include **input control** of work releases to gateway or bottleneck work centers (scheduling), **input/output control** over work-center loads, **priority control** of operations in work centers (dispatching), and **expediting** of urgent jobs when all else fails.

Input Control

The first half of the scheduler's job is to determine due dates for each operation and a release date for the whole job. The second half is to release orders in trickles so as not to overload the work centers; this is often referred to as input control. Two techniques of input control are discussed below.

The scheduler's hold-for-release file will typically contain a mix of priorities. There will be some shop orders due for release in the next few days, some orders due for release today, and often some new rush orders. There may also be orders that were due for release on a previous day but were withheld so as not to overload certain work centers.

The purpose of input load leveling is as the words suggest: to release or input a level load. A level load is a mix of shop orders that neither overloads nor underloads a work center. Input load leveling works well only for work centers at the input end of the operation sequence, which are "gateway" work centers. The foundry or certain work centers in the machine shop are common gateways. (The scheduler could, with computer help, work up a schedule to level not only gateway but also downstream work centers. But it won't work. Because of variable queue times at later work centers, the later operations are not likely to follow the schedule closely enough for the loads to remain level.)

The **firm planned order** is an MRP tool that may be used to overrule the automatic rescheduling feature of MRP. This can be helpful in load leveling. A firm planned order may be scheduled earlier than the actual need in order to get the order into a gateway work center in a slack (underloaded) week. Figure 10–7 illustrates this use of the firm planned order. To invoke the firm planned order, the scheduler instructs the computer to flag a particular planned order and move it to a given time bucket. In the example, planned order 688 is moved from week 3, its calculated date of need, to week 2, which helps level the load imbalance in weeks 2 and 3. The next MRP run will not reschedule the flagged job back to its need date (but will issue a reschedule message, which may be ignored).

FIGURE 10–7

Firm Planned Order for Load Leveling in Gateway Work Center

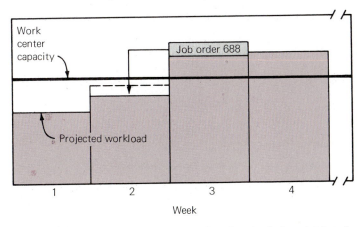

Action taken: Job order 688 is scheduled as a firm planned order in week 2 instead of week 3, its MRP-generated date of need.

The firm planned order may also be used to move a job to a later week. But there is no point in going very far into the future, since conditions will change the future before it arrives.

Input/Output Control

While the firm-planned-order technique is best for gateway work centers, the input/output control technique concerns loads on any work center. Input/output control helps control capacity by revealing where work-center outputs are too low and where inputs are too low or too high. An input/output control report provides the information. Figure 10–8 is an example.

The report is for work center 111, and it shows work-center performance against plan for the last three weeks. The note below the report explains that the planned input is the average of CRP loads. Raw, unaveraged loads are not usable, because work is not likely to arrive at the same erratic rate that is projected in the CRP computer run; too many things can happen in prior work centers for CRP loads to be valid except as averages.

The bottom half of the report in Figure 10–8 shows actual output; it drops from 725 to 704 to 698. Planned output is not getting done. The result will be a buildup of work-in-process inventory and a negative cost variance (explained later) in work center 111, and later work centers will be delayed because of the low output in work center 111.

The top half of the report shows that the output problems are not all the fault of work center 111. Not enough work is arriving, and the deficiency is growing

FIGURE 10–8

Input/Output Control Report

Work center 111		Date: Week ending 94		
Week ending	80	87	94	101
Planned input*	720	720	720	720
Actual input	700	690	710	
Cumulative deviation	−20	−50	−60	
Planned output	720	720	720	720
Actual output	725	704	698	
Cumulative deviation	+5	−11	−33	

* Calculated by averaging the loads that result from capacity requirements planning for many weeks into the future:

CRP loads | 685 | 730 | 690 | 730 ?

Average = 720

from -20 to -50 to -60. Previous work centers seem to be bottlenecks for work center 111.

Examination of input/output control reports for all work centers can show where the causal bottlenecks are. Foremen may be able to raise output, e.g., by overtime, in those work centers. If actual output is not brought up to planned output, or if actual inputs are chronically low, the master production schedule may need to be changed.

Data to produce the bottom half of the report may be available in non-MRP as well as MRP firms. Actual output is simply a count of work produced, in standard hours. Planned output is the same as planned input in the example of Figure 10–8. But sometimes planned output is set at a higher level than planned input; a reason might be to work off a backlog.

The output part of the report is beneficial with or without the input part. But the input information helps to show causes of output deviation and thus may be worthwhile. Getting actual input data requires the firm to keep track of work moved to next work centers, which are data many firms do not normally collect. Thus, new procedures for collecting data on moves between work centers might be necessary. (Some companies track the flow of work with online computer terminals.)

Priority Control (Dispatching)

Controlling **capacity** (by input/output control) is only one aspect of work-center management. **Priorities** of the jobs and lots flowing through the work centers also must be controlled. Why? Because jobs are not likely to arrive at a work center in an orderly manner. Some jobs arrive earlier than planned, some later, and often there are jobs in queue awaiting their turn. The jobs that are already behind schedule should be given a higher priority in order to go through first. **Priority rules** or policies need to be established, and a **dispatcher** may be on hand to release the jobs according to the rules. Priority control concepts, the daily priority report, shop recorders, and centralized versus decentralized dispatching are discussed below.

Priority. At retail, the priority system is simply first come, first served. Customers are considered homogeneous; one is not more important than another. First come, first served suits the retailer because it runs itself. The retailer need not pay a dispatcher to pick and choose among customers.

The wholesaler and the factory are not blessed with such simplicity. Their orders are *not* homogeneous. Some orders are more urgent than others—or more profitable, or for more important customers, or fit better with the present-plant-capacity situation. Therefore, scheduling shipments or end-item manufacturing should involve priority trade-offs among:

1. Customer importance.
2. Order urgency.
3. Order profitability.
4. Impact on capacity utilization.

For example, customer orders for items held within the Department of Defense supply system are scheduled to be filled based on a priority composed of two factors. One is urgency. The other, called the force activity designator, is importance of the customer. A combat unit deployed in a combat zone is treated as a most important customer. If the unit orders bullets, the order will probably receive a high-urgency factor. The combination of customer importance and urgency yields a priority number calculated by the computer, probably priority 1 in this case. The supply system has procedures for very fast delivery, say 24 hours, for priority 1 requisitions; orders with very low priority call for delivery to take a certain number of weeks or months. Note that priority decisions are simplified here because profitability is not a factor. Capacity utilization is also not a factor (though it affects the supply system's delivery performance).

Scheduling component parts for end items involves simpler priority decisions than does scheduling the end items themselves. At the component-parts level, orders for the same part are often batched. Customer identification is lost in batching orders, and so it would be hard to schedule parts orders based on end-item profits or customer importance. Therefore, dispatching priorities (for dependent-demand parts) are usually based on order urgency and impact on capacity utilization, not on profitability or customer importance.

Various priority rules have been proposed to aid in dispatching. Some are given in Figure 10–9 and discussed here.[4]

FIGURE 10–9

Some Work-Center Dispatching Rules

Timing-based rules
First come, first served
Shortest operation processing time
Longest operation processing time
Earliest operation due date
Earliest operation start date
Least operation slack
Critical ratio
Hot list

Other rules
Profitability rules
Cost rules
Preferred customer rules
Work-center capacity rules

---

[4] These are local priority rules, applied to operations performed at work centers. Global rules, applied to the job as a whole rather than to an operation, may be used for scheduling the job to begin with. Also, there is a less precise work-center priority system that uses the timing of the whole job rather than the operation as its basis.

First come, first served. This rule was discussed earlier. It may be applied simply by selecting jobs for the current operation in their order of arrival at the work center. We know that first come, first served is the simplest of priority rules. We also know that leading Japanese manufacturers have perfected simple just-in-time shop-floor ordering systems. If you guessed that first come, first served is the priority rule used with the JIT approaches, you are right. In formal kanban, for example, first come, first served operates by dispatching jobs in order of kanban arrival in the producing work center.

Shortest Operation Processing Time. Processing time for the current operation means setup time plus run time. Earlier in the chapter in the QUIDCO, Inc., example (Figure 10–3) the *operation* processing time for the bend operation (operation 190) at work center 16 was shown as 6.7 standard hours, of which 4.2 hours was setup time.

Shortest operation processing time is noteworthy, because in computer simulations the rule has been shown to be superior to several other rules. The simulations show more on-time completions when the rule is used. Even so, few firms have adopted the rule. Instead, more advanced manufacturers especially MRP users, usually base priority decisions on some measure of relative lateness. The next four rules are based on due date and thus measure relative lateness. Each has its adherents among MRP authorities, and all yield about the same good results.

Earliest Operation Due Date or Start Date. These rules simply consider the operation dates for jobs in queue at a work center. First priority goes to the job with the earliest operation start (or due) date.

In MRP firms, job due dates may be updated with each MRP run, typically weekly. The computer may then back-schedule from the job due date to recompute operation start (or due) dates. Thus, the operation dates that were assigned before the job was released may change while the job is out in the factory.

Least Slack and Critical Ratio. Earliest start (or due) date has a minor flaw: If an eight-hour operation and an eight-day operation each have the same operation start (or due) date, their priorities are equal, but actually the eight-day operation should begin seven days sooner (or end seven days later). Such differences in processing times are accounted for by least slack and by critical ratio, but extra computations are required.

Slack may be loosely defined as demand time minus supply time. Operation slack is computed as follows:

$$\text{Slack} = \text{Demand (need) time} - \text{Supply (make) time}$$

Or, equivalently,

$$\text{Slack} = \text{Time until operation due date} - \text{Operation lead time}$$

where

$$\text{Time until operation due date} = \text{Operation due date} - \text{Today's date}$$
$$\text{Operation lead time} = \text{Queue time} + \text{Processing time}$$
$$\text{Processing time} = \text{Setup time} + \text{Run time}$$

Critical ratio (CR) uses the same data as operation slack but expressed as a ratio, as follows:

$$CR = \frac{\text{Demand (need) time}}{\text{Supply (make) time}}$$

Or, equivalently,

$$CR = \frac{\text{Time until operation due date}}{\text{Operation lead time}}$$

The smaller the slack or the critical ratio, the more urgent the job. Negative slack or a critical ratio less than 1.0 signifies a late condition: The operation is due for completion in less than planned operation lead time.

To demonstrate slack and critical ratio, let us assume that on day 101 four jobs are in queue at work center 16, which is the punch press center, where metal bending is performed. Assume the following data (the first shop order, 9925, is from the QUIDCO example of Figure 10–3; recall that operation due dates are derived by back-scheduling from the job due date):

Shop order	Move/queue time	Punch press processing time (set up + run)	Operation due date
9925	1 day	6.7 hours, or 1 day rounded	Day 99
9938	1 day	15.8 hours, or 2 days rounded	Day 102
9918	1 day	1.8 hours, or 1 day rounded	Day 101
9916	1 day	0.8 hours, or 1 day rounded	Day 105

The slack and critical ratios for the four jobs are given in Figure 10–10, which is roughly in the form of a daily priority report for work center 16. In the figure, slack values show that shop order 9925 is 4 days behind, 9938 and 9918 are each 2 days behind, and 9916 is 2 days ahead; the jobs should be run in work center 16

FIGURE 10–10

Daily Priority Report, by Operation Slack and Critical Ratio, for Work Center 16

Shop order	Demand time (due date − today)	Supply time (move/queue + processing)	Operation slack	Critical ratio
9925	99 − 101	1 + 1	−4	−1.0
9938	102 − 101	1 + 2	−2	0.33
9918	101 − 101	1 + 1	−2	0.0
9916	105 − 101	1 + 1	+2	2.0

in that order. Using critical ratios, shop orders 9938 and 9918 are not of equal priority.

Note that if the due date and today's date are the same—as with shop order 9918—the numerator (demand time) is zero, and this always yields a critical ratio of zero, whether the denominator (supply time) is large or small. The biased result from a zero numerator is not serious; critical ratio is still a worthy priority rule, because you are looking for only a rule of thumb, not mathematical precision.

Hot List and Other Rules.   The hot list, also known as a shortage list, was partly explained in Chapter 6 in connection with the ROP/shortage-list way of planning parts inventories. Hot-listed jobs get dispatched first at each work center. The other rules listed in Figure 10–9 are based on profitability, cost, preferred customer, and work-center capacity. These are generally more complex than the timing-based rules (and they should normally be used in conjunction with timing-based rules); elaboration on these kinds of rules is reserved for advanced studies.

Daily Priority Report.   The means of setting priorities is less important than the dispatching procedure. The recommended procedure, especially for MRP-using firms, is the daily priority report, often called a dispatch list, issued by work center. Non-MRP firms could produce the report as easily as MRP firms. But without a weekly material requirements planning run to show changes in part need dates, operation priorities on the dispatch list become out of date. Still, some non-MRP firms may find benefits in the dispatch list. The key feature of the priority report is its recomputation every day.

Centralized versus Decentralized Dispatching.   Activities on the shop floor are usually controlled from the shop floor. Typically, production control department people called dispatchers or shop schedulers are assigned to work in foremen's offices. Dispatchers make sure that higher priority jobs are run ahead of lower-priority jobs. Dispatchers also handle blueprints, route sheets, shop orders, job tickets, move tickets, inspection forms, tool orders, material issue forms, and completion forms. These documents get jobs started and account for their completion at each stage of their routing. Dispatchers are on the scene and can therefore react quickly to delays. One reaction is to assign higher priority to the delayed job at the next work center. Others are to reroute upstream jobs around serious sources of delay, such as a machine breakdown, and to split a lot. A few companies have a central dispatching group, physically located away from shop-floor action. Why centralize? Consider this analogy. In an airport, decentralized air traffic control would amount to putting one air traffic controller on each runway. They would try to communicate with one another via walkie-talkies. But the results would surely be suboptimal: The peak number of planes handled per hour would be small, or else there would be frequent disasters. Thus, air traffic controllers—aircraft dispatchers—are centralized. That way they can coordinate tight scheduling and high peak volumes.

So it is with centralized dispatching in manufacturing companies. The major reason appears to be a need for high-volume production and tight scheduling with little margin for error. Automobile assembly, shoe manufacturing, and large appliance manufacturing may be among the better candidates for centralized dispatching.

Centralized dispatching does not mean that production control no longer has people in the plant. There may be a need to have PC people on the floor to report activities by phone or other electronic media so that central dispatching can make realistic, up-to-date priority-contol decisions.

Expediting

Launch orders by ROP, and have expediters pull through those that become hot: This describes the standard shop-floor control system of an earlier age. The production control department was large, and expediters were a sizable proportion of its staff. Under MRP, expediting is less common and can sometimes be managed by foremen instead of full-time expediters.

A production control chief who was guest-lecturing to one operations management class expressed his philosophy of production control: "The whole world is out there trying to stop my job, but I ain't gonna let 'em." His firm relied heavily on expediting, which is a defensive, fire-fighting approach.

Expediting often involves hurried searches for parts needed for a hot subassembly, and for this reason the expediter is sometimes called a parts chaser. Finding the parts can involve preparing shop orders and purchase orders, hand-carrying paperwork, special trips to freight terminals to meet incoming orders, Teletype messages and phone calls to search for parts orders in transit, and so forth. Expediting is disruptive, expensive, and not always successful. It is a mode of operation that many modern firms would be happy to leave behind, if only they could.

REPORTING AND FEEDBACK CONTROL OF MANAGERIAL PERFORMANCE

> The best-laid plans of mice and men
> Oft go awry.[5]

If plans did not go awry, there would be no need for reporting and feedback controls and managerial intervention. But plans do go awry, and there are two reasons why. First, best-laid plans are based on conditions at a given time and always suffer from the lack of complete information at that time. Changed conditions and unforeseen events put the original plan out of step with reality. Second, those who carry out the plans are not perfect robots but are imperfect and sometimes irrational. We cannot count on them to follow the plans exactly.

---

[5] A popular adaptation of lines from the poem *To a Mouse*, 1789, by the Scottish poet Robert Burns. The original lines are:

> The best-laid schemes o' mice an' men
> Gang aft a-gley.

In spite of all this, the best control is still a well-laid plan properly fed forward. The plan or piece of the plan that goes awry should be the exception, calling for management action based on feedback information.

The previous section was about control, but a very short-range variety. Shop-floor control decisions are highly task-related; they are made by workers and foremen in small organizations and by production-control specialists only in larger organizations. In this section, we turn to feedback control based on periodic historical reports which are able to show the larger control picture. By this means, operations management policies can be tested and supervisory and managerial performance can be assessed. The basic control cycle provides a framework for discussion.

The Control Cycle

Control is a cyclic process. Plans (or standards) are fed forward and measured results fed back. Feedback information is analyzed, and new plans (or standards or policies) may be developed and fed forward. An option is for supervisors to motivate compliance with plans—that is, get back on track—instead of developing new plans. The basic control loop, with the motivational option, is shown in Figure 10–11.

The chart on the chapter title page shows the control loop (minus the motivational option) as applied to operations planning and control. The chart also refers to the work itself, that is, the transformation of resource inputs into goods and services. There is no reason to discuss the work per se, but there is reason to discuss control over the work. In the first part of this section problems in controlling the work are discussed. Control tools, including secondary controls such as labor, material, and cost variances, are examined, in addition to primary controls over schedules. (Another type of primary control—over quality—is the topic of Chapter 12, Quality Assurance. Standards for planning and controlling labor are discussed in Chapter 13.)

FIGURE 10–11

Basic Control Loop

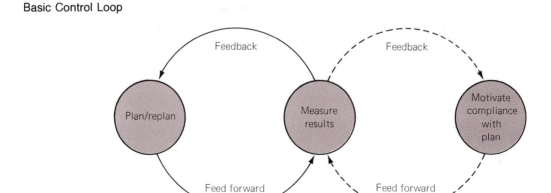

Control Responsibilities

The first-line supervisor has first-line responsibility for the transformation of resources into outputs. The scope of control can be broad. In advanced operations control systems, results are formally measured and reported. Production control departments take measurements and provide the reports, on which supervisory performance is judged. Also, the periodic reports help show how well production control did in its role as staff adviser and planner.

The chart on the chapter title page shows two types of measurements that production control is concerned with. First and foremost is *output* measurement, on the upper right side. Secondarily, below that, is *input* (resource-utilization) measurement. Direct control over operations is based on measurement of output *quality* and output *performance against schedules.* Actual costs of resources (inputs used in producing the outputs) may be compared with standard costs; this type of report relates outputs to inputs and results in a comprehensive **cost-variance report.** Finally, more detailed reports on *utilization* and *efficient use* of various resources (inputs) may help show causes of cost variance and poor output performance. The nature of these three types of measurements and reports—on outputs, costs, and utilization/efficiency—is considered next.

MEASUREMENTS AND REPORTS

Our discussion begins with cost-variance reporting. A cost-variance report compares actual costs with standard costs for a reporting period such as two weeks or a month. Actual costs are collected job by job and summed up for the period. Standard costs— what products are supposed to cost—are prepared by the cost accounting people in advance; then the standard costs are summed up job by job for the reporting period. In job-lot control systems, cost-variance reports are "the bottom line," so to speak. (Note: In repetitive and continuous production actual costs are not collected by job, because production is not divided into jobs. Cost per unit is simply all costs divided by units made for the reporting period. Such accounting and control system simplicity is one more reason for trying to transform job-lot production into repetitive production—by adopting such techniques as just-in-time.)

Besides cost-variance reports, our discussion considers resource-usage reports, which give detail on resource utilization and efficiency. Finally, we examine ways to measure and report on outputs.

Cost-Variance Reporting

Why have cost-variance reports? Aren't more detailed reports on specific operating resources sufficient? That is, can't we just hold operating managers responsible for labor and machine efficiency and for controlled usage of materials, tools, and space?

The answer is no. Detailed resource-usage (utilization) reports may be good. But cost-variance reports are even better. The reason has to do with economy of control.

Economy of Control. Economy of control has become a popular idea in regard to national policy. The deregulation movement is partly based on it. The idea is to regulate enough so that the organization is held accountable for overall results but is free to apply its own managerial talents and innovativeness to figuring out means of achieving those results. At the national level, economy of control sometimes conflicts with traditions, long-standing policies, and so on. Within the firm there is little that conflicts with the economy-of-control idea. In fact, it may be viewed as a principle of good management. Cost-variance reporting is to the operating manager what profitability reporting is to the chief executive officer.

Trade-offs. The beauty of cost variance as a primary control tool is that it allows operating managers room to make the trade-offs that are necessary to hold costs down. The manager may elect to spend more on equipment maintenance to avoid costly labor idleness from equipment failure; more on training to avoid costly rework; more on employee selection to avoid costly turnover; and so on. Without cost-variance reports, there could still be reports on labor idleness, equipment failure, training time, rework, turnover, and so forth. But those factors are often in conflict, and management of individual resources based on individual resource reports is likely to be frustrating and to produce suboptimal results.

Therefore, as the job-lot producer grows large enough to be able to afford systematic reports, cost-variance reports should be among the first. Supporting detailed reports on labor idleness, equipment failure, and so forth, may come later.

Resource-Usage Reporting

Resource-usage data are also collected. They are used to produce resource-utilization and efficiency reports. Resource utilization means, simply, "busyness." Utilization rates are often measured in percentages, but there are other measures as well. A gross measure is intensity of use of total plant or company capacity, generally expressed as a percentage. This measure was discussed in Chapter 5. More specific measures are considered here.

Utilization Rate. Sometimes measurement of resource utilization is automated, especially in the case of costly *equipment.* For example, computers often have executive software that enables them to measure and report on their own utilization. Industrial and commercial vehicles often have time- and mileage-recording meters; time-of-use readings may then be translated into utilization reports. Automated assembly lines and expensive industrial machines also may have time-recording meters. For example, Kawasaki Motors has line-stop clocks at the ends of its motorcycle assembly lines. Assemblers have "line-stop" authority, which means they may push a button to stop the line. This turns on the line-stop clock to record minutes of down time.

Space-utilization reports are common in larger organizations. The reports express space in use as a percentage of total space, which may be broken down by type of space or type of use. (Colleges and universities generally report based on several room-use categories, as specified in guidelines published by the Department of Education.)

Labor-utilization rates may be measured by work sampling. Random observations of whether or not workers are busy are taken by an outside observer using the procedure described in Chapter 13. Sampling is cheap (as compared with continuous observation). Self-reporting is another possibility, but not necessarily a good one since people may not be truthful about their own busyness. Work sampling may also be used to measure equipment utilization. Time-recording meters are preferable (over a human observer), but some equipment is not metered.

Equipment-, space-, and labor-utilization rates are usually computed by the formula

$$\text{Utilization rate} = \frac{\text{Time in use}}{\text{Time available}}$$

expressed as a percentage. Idleness rate is 100 percent minus utilization rate.

Even information resources may be controlled based on utilization rates. The measure is usually frequency of use, as compared to some standard, rather than percentage of time in use. For example, records and files may be archived based on a certain standard of use or nonuse, and records and files may be disposed of completely in the next phase of records/file control. (**Migration** is a common term for moving information from active storage to archives to disposal.) These are common techniques of records management.

There are many other measures of resource utilization. For example, for the labor resource, it is common to keep track of absences resulting from illness, jury duty, military duty, labor-union activities, tardiness, and so forth—all of which eat into productive time. Measures of materials utilization might include scrap, theft, deterioration, obsolescence, and misplacement—all of which eat into productive use of materials. Some of the same kinds of measures may be applied to tools, equipment, space, and information.

Resource Utilization in Perspective. Reports about resources tend to proliferate as organizations grow, because increasing revenue helps pay for the reporting costs. Close control is easiest to justify for resources that are expensive. But such controls can be, and often are, overdone.

It is staff organizations, such as purchasing, personnel, maintenance, and inventory control, that generate resource-utilization reports. These are operating-resources organizations—below the dashed line in the chart on the title page of the chapter—and they exist only for purpose of above-the-line operations. But preservation, growth, and power instincts conflict with the mandate to serve operations. Those instincts tend to result in too much resource management and too many reports. When large organizations fall on hard times, regaining economic health may include cutting staff employees and many of their reports.

Indiscriminate use of resource-utilization data is another possible problem to guard against. One government agency, for example, followed a rigid policy for allocating forklifts among its departments and shops. The policy required a projected forklift utilization rate exceeding (let us say) 60 percent. A shop could have its forklift removed if the time meter showed utilization falling below that figure. One result was that none of the agency's hundreds of industrial shops could justify the purchase of low-cost nonpowered "pallet movers." These are simple hand trucks, some with elevatable forks, selling for a few hundred dollars up to a few thousand. Instead, whenever a shop needed to have a pallet moved a few feet, a large vehicular forklift costing $10,000–$30,000 had to be dispatched from a central location. Meters on the central forklifts showed a high utilization rate, but mostly from driving, not lifting. Assigning a hand truck to each of the various shops might have been cheaper, quicker, and more convenient.

One hundred percent utilization of a resource is not necessarily ideal. For example, no computer center wants its computer to be 100 percent utilized. With such high use there are sure to be long backlogs, interminable delays in getting a job run, and many customers who balk at the long backlogs and do without the service. Chapter 17, on service-center management, includes a more complete discussion of trade-offs between facility (server) utilization and waiting lines.

Finally, utilization rate is a surrogate rather than a true measure of efficiency. Busyness fails to take output into consideration. Therefore, a good control system for operations management should also include efficiency reporting.

Efficiency Reporting. Labor is the only resource that is measurable in efficiency terms. Machines, tools, space, and materials have no will and cannot work at any pace other than normal. Labor efficiency is measured by the following formulas (further explained in Chapter 13):

$$\text{Efficiency} = \frac{\text{Actual output}}{\text{Standard output}} \text{ or } \frac{\text{standard time}}{\text{actual time}}$$

Labor *utilization* requires a special work-sampling study, which makes it too expensive for regular weekly, biweekly, or monthly reporting. Labor efficiency, however, comes from data that many organizations have anyway: output data, payroll data (hours worked), and time standards data.

The first version of the efficiency formula given above is in terms of output, actual divided by standard. It is nevertheless an input measure, because it is a measure of actual speed or pace or effort against standard or normal speed or pace or effort. How standard speed or pace is determined is a major topic of Chapter 13.

Output Reporting

The first priority of the first-line supervisor is online completions. That is an output statistic. The way you measure it depends on type of operations, as is shown in Figure 10–12.

FIGURE 10–12

Output Measures by Type of Operations

Type of operations	Output measures
Continuous, repetitive, or limited-quantity large-scale	Unit count
Job or job-lot	Unit count (work center) Due dates met (job orders) Percent of completion
Project	Percent of completion Milestones completed on time Events completed on time

Measures. In continuous, repetitive, or limited-quantity large-scale production, measuring output is simple. As Figure 10–12 shows, it just requires counting units produced (that meet minimum quality standards). In factories it is parts that are counted. In other organizations miles of highway, square yards of concrete, clients visited, patients seen, and so forth, are counted. The count is in units per day, per week, or per some other time unit. Bar-code, optical, or mechanical counters, and scales are sometimes used for counting. Periodic reports may show variances from scheduled output. A variance might be expressed as less (or more) actual output than scheduled output per day; or it might be expressed in hours or days late, or in overtime hours used to meet the schedule.

In job-lot production, output measurement can be costly and difficult. A parts order may be routed through multiple work centers, with output measurement taking place at each of them. As is shown in Figure 10–12, the measurement may include a **unit count** of parts successfully produced (not scrapped); time of completion is also reported, so that priorities may be recomputed for upcoming work centers. Periodically, perhaps every two weeks, a report may summarize parts moved out (after successful completion) as compared with raw materials moved into each work center; and another report may show job-order **due dates met,** which is a measure of success for all the work centers put together. Due dates met is also a suitable output measure in simpler job-shop work involving perhaps only one unit and one work center. Examples are repairing a pair of shoes, papering the walls of a room, performing a lab test, and cooking a meal. **Percent of completion** is a suitable measure in job shops in which processing time at a given work center is long—days or weeks— and the output is not readily countable. Examples are major overhauls and renovations.

Three kinds of output measures listed in Figure 10–12 for project operations are percent of completion, milestones completed on time, and events completed on time. These measures are discussed in connection with project management and the PERT/ CPM technique in Chapter 11.

Gantt Control Chart. The Gantt chart as a visual aid for scheduling services was discussed earlier, and examples of Gantt charts were given in Figure 10–4. Gantt charts are no longer used as a control tool in repetitive manufacturing. But Gantt control charts are useful in certain job-shop work. Renovation, major maintenance, and extensive overhaul work are examples.

Figure 10–13 shows a Gantt control chart for renovation work. The Gantt chart in Figure 10–13A is an initial schedule for three crews. An arrow at the top of each chart points to the current day.

Figure 10–13B shows the progress that has been made after one day. The shading indicates amount of work done, which probably is estimated by the crew chief, in percent of completion. Two thirds of the first paint job was scheduled for Monday, but the paint crew got the whole job done that day. While the paint crew is one-half day ahead of schedule, drywall is one-quarter day behind. Carpentry did Monday's scheduled work on Monday and is therefore on schedule.

Figure 10–13C, for Tuesday, shows painting falling behind, drywall on schedule, and carpentry ahead.

Various commercially available schedule boards use felt or magnetic strips, pegs,

FIGURE 10–13

Gantt Control Chart, Renovation Work

A. Schedule at first of week

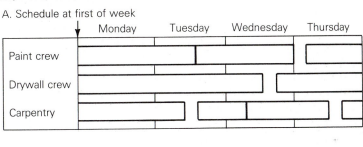

B. Progress after one day

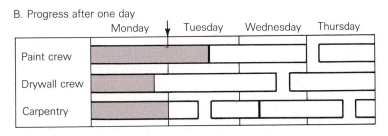

C. Progress after two days

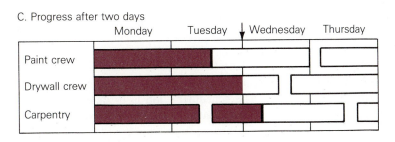

plastic inserts, and the like to block out schedules and to show progress. Such boards are common in construction offices, project managers' headquarters, and maintenance departments. But Gantt control charts are poor for parts fabrication, because parts schedules and work-center priorities change too fast to make plotting on a schedule board worthwhile.

Shop Recorders. Some years ago, large numbers of shop recorders were sold to manufacturing companies. The recorders were placed in shops for recording both output and input data, which usually included charging labor and material to a given job and recording quantities of parts successfully produced as well as parts scrapped. Foremen or workers could enter the data, which reduced the need for production-control data-collection people. The data could be entered into the computer each day or more often, and the computer could then develop new schedules and priorities.

In most companies the recorders were a failure. Why? Because it was too easy to enter false data. If the operation calls for machining 90 widgets and the operator scraps 15, the operator should enter 75 as the number produced. But the operator may "fudge" a bit and enter 80 or even 90. In a few days, after the parts have passed through several remaining operations, the job order is closed and a shortage is discovered. The operator who fudged may claim that the shortage happened before he received the order—or after. Or the operator may simply say that he miskeyed the "damn recording machine." Many of the recorders ended up on a shelf someplace gathering dust.

In recent years shop recorders have been enjoying healthy sales once again. This time they are working. A difference is that the recorders are so-called smart terminals, or they link up to smart terminals, and the terminals in turn link up to a mainframe computer. A smart terminal has some memory and computing power and can perform simple data checks. One effective check is to compare the produced quantity that is entered by one operator with the quantity entered by the operator in the preceding work center. If an operator claims to have produced 90, but the preceding operator forwarded only 75, the discrepancy is caught right away. The smart terminal may tell the second operator to try again. Increasingly, the recording is done automatically by reading a bar code on the part or its container. The operator is not involved.

With smart on-line shop recorders and bar-code readers, some firms cut priority-update time from a day or two to virtually instant updating. The daily priority report gives way to continuous recomputation of priorities. The effect is less **WIP** inventory, shorter lead times, and more responsive service to customers—but, of course, a whale of a lot of computing.

SUMMARY

Carrying out inventory plans or service plans in job-lot operations involves scheduling, reporting, and control. The scheduler's job is to determine when to release a job order for component parts, so that the order will arrive when the inventory planner says the parts are needed. Production lead time is a question mark, because parts orders spend time in queues at each work center in the process flow. Queue time should be held in check, which also reduces work-in-process inventory investment. The scheduler can help by regulating the flow of work to the shops. Lead-time estimates used in scheduling can be made more accurate, and thus better for capacity planning, if some measure of shop congestion is included. Scheduled jobs and operations should dovetail with schedules for operating resources—labor, equipment, tools, and so on. In services, it is often helpful to display schedules on a visual aid known as a Gantt chart, but scheduling with Gantt charts has limited usefulness in connection with goods production.

Having enough capacity at individual work centers to handle the parts orders routed through them is an old problem. Work-center loads that are computed manually are somewhat valid for the near future and can also be used to track the size of the backlog of open orders. But for the load report to be valid, planned orders must be added to open orders. This can be done by computer, using capacity requirements planning (CRP), an extension of MRP. CRP load reports give plenty of advance notice of capacity problems so that adjustments do not have to wait until the last minute.

The scheduler has some impact on shop-activity control, that is, the control of jobs in the work centers. For example, the scheduler can make use of the firm-planned-order feature of MRP in order to level workloads in gateway work centers. Another device, the input/output control report shows which work centers are failing to meet planned outputs and whether the preceding work centers are at fault for forwarding less-than-planned inputs to the next work centers.

When jobs queue up at each work center, there is a choice of which job to do next. Choosing the next job is known as the dispatching function, and it is a way to get delayed jobs back on schedule. Some method of computing the latest priorities provides the basis for the selection. First come, first served is almost universal for dispatching in retailing, but timing—due dates at each operation—is more important as a priority factor within the firm. Earliest operation start (or due) date is a simple way to set priorities. Least slack and critical ratio are also popular. The shop-floor dispatcher (or foreman) follows a daily priority report in assigning work and handling shop documents. Dispatchers sometimes work in a centralized office instead of on the shop floor, especially where operations must be tightly coordinated. When all else fails, expediting may be used to pull a late job through.

A variety of historical reports are useful in assessing production and production-control performance. A periodic cost-variance report is a foundation report showing weaknesses; resource-utilization and efficiency reports provide details on the causes of problems. Even more basic are reports on output, that is, on-time completions. Outputs are measured variously, depending on type of operations. The Gantt control chart is one way of displaying progress against due dates, but it is useful only for work, such as renovation and overhaul, where tasks extend over more than a day.

A modern approach is to place recording devices in shops. They may be connected on-line to computers, which can quickly verify the production data and can reschedule jobs as necessary.

REFERENCES

Books

Fogarty, Donald F., and Thomas R. Hoffman. *Production and Inventory Management.* Cincinnati, Ohio: South-Western Publishing, 1983.

Fuchs, Jerome H. *Computerized Cost Control Systems.* Englewood Cliffs, N.J.: Prentice-Hall, 1976 (HD47.5.F8).

Plossl, G. W., and O. W. Wight. *Production and Inventory Control: Principles and Techniques.* Englewood Cliffs, N.J.: Prentice-Hall, 1967 (HD55.P5).

Wight, Oliver W. *Production and Inventory Management in the Computer Age.* Boston: CBI Publishing, 1974 (TS155.W533).

Periodicals (societies)

Decision Sciences (American Institute for Decision Sciences), an academic journal.

Production and Inventory Management (American Production and Inventory Control Society).

Operations Management Journal (American Production and Inventory Control Society and American Institute for Decision Sciences), an academic journal.

REVIEW QUESTIONS

1. Planning for production of goods includes inventory planning and scheduling of shop orders. Why aren't these two functions included in planning for services?

2. What is the difference between a job and an operation?

3. Why is it hard to estimate production lead time accurately?

4. Why is it important to minimize work-in-process inventory?

5. Contrast backward and forward scheduling.

6. Explain how a due date for a shop order may be translated into finish dates for each operation in the job.

7. Why is the Gantt chart so limited in its applicability?

8. What is the purpose of backlog tracking?

9. How do CRP reports get produced and what are they used for?

10. When work-center workloads are calculated manually in a non-MRP system, why do the workloads end up looking like the bar chart of Figure 10–6A; that is, why the load in week 0 and the tapering-off pattern?

11. In MRP systems infinite-capacity loading is usual; does this make the MRP data invalid? Discuss.

12. How do the firm planned order and input/output control help to assure that the right amount of work is released by the scheduler?

13. There are eight timing-based dispatching rules listed in Figure 10–9. What do the last five do that the first three don't?

14. Distinguish between scheduling, loading, and dispatching.

15. Why are least slack and critical ratio about equal in effectiveness?

16. Who receives the daily priority report (or dispatch list) and what is it used for?

17. When is it wise to do centralized dispatching?

18. How can expediting be decreased?

19. The control cycle calls for what action when things go wrong?

20. Why are cost-variance reports useful in job-lot production, even when there are other reports on resource utilization, efficiency, etc.?

21. Why are accounting data important in job-lot production control?

22. Why are outputs measured differently in project, job or job-lot, and continuous, repetitive, or limited-quantity large-scale production?

23. What does the Gantt control chart do that the Gantt scheduling chart does not do?

24. What can be done to overcome the temptation to falsify shop-floor data?

PROBLEMS

1. A manufacturer of stereo speakers produces five main types of high-quality speakers. The company considers itself a job-lot producer: The single production line produces job lots of each type of speaker on a rotating schedule. Price competition has been severe, and the company's profits have eroded. A conglomerate is buying the stereo manufacturer, and it intends to invest a considerable amount of cash to improve production control and cut production costs.
   a. What should the money be invested in if the decision is made to continue as a job-lot producer?
   b. What should the money be invested in if the decision is made to convert to small lots?

2. A scheduler at QUIDCO, Inc., is working up a schedule for making 20 of Part no. 0077AX. The inventory planner advises that the order should be released this week, week of day 90, and that the order is due on the week of day 115, when it will be needed to go into a parent item.
   a. How would the inventory planner have determined the week due and the week of release? If the inventory planner has determined these dates, doesn't that constitute rescheduling and eliminate the need for the scheduler to do anything? Discuss.
   b. The *A* in the part number signifies a costly item. For *A* items the following rules are followed for computing operation lead times:

(1) Allow eight standard hours per day; round upward to even (eight-hour) days.

(2) Allow *no time* between operations. *A* items receive priority material handling.

(3) Allow one day to inspect.

(4) Release the job to the stockroom four days before it is to be started into production.

(5) All dates are treated as of the end of the eight-hour day.

Schedule a shop order for the item, assuming that the part goes through three operations, plus inspection. You make up the setup times and operation times such that the schedule will fit between days 90 and 115. Explain.

c. Compare the operation lead-time rules for Part no. 0077AX with the rules in Example 10–2 for Part no. 1005CX. Why should a more expensive item have different lead-time rules? (Hint: WIP has something to do with it.)

d. A week passes. Inventory planning notifies scheduling that Part no. 0077AX is now due (to go into a parent item) in week 120 instead of 115. The shop order, along with a planning package (blueprints, job tickets, etc.), has already been released. There is no need to issue new paperwork, because QUIDCO has a computer-produced daily dispatch list for each work center. Least operation slack is the dispatching rule. The scheduler merely gets on a terminal and inputs updated scheduling information. Explain how that information would be used in generating dispatch lists. Also explain how the dispatch lists serve the purpose of adjusting for the new due date.

3. The maintenance department has two renovation orders that are being scheduled. Order No. 1 requires these three jobs or tasks: 14 days of wiring, then 7 days of drywall work, then 9 days of painting. Order No. 2 takes five days of drywall followed by six days of painting.

a. Draw a Gantt chart showing the workloads (backlogs) for each of the three trades (wiring, drywall, and paint).

b. Draw a Gantt chart showing the two orders back-scheduled, the first with completion due at the end of day 35 and the second due at the end of day 14.

c. Draw a Gantt chart with the two orders forward-scheduled. In what situation would forward scheduling for these three trades be useful?

4. Open Air Furniture Co. makes patio furniture. There are just three work centers: rough saw, finish saw, and assemble.

Production control uses loading charts for short-term scheduling and capacity management. Each week's component-parts orders are translated into machine-hours in rough saw and finish saw and into labor-hours in assemble. Current machine-hour and labor-hour loads are given below:

	Rough saw	Finish saw	Assemble
Current week	270	470	410
Week 2	40	110	100
Week 3	—	40	50
Week 4	—	30	15
Weekly capacity	150	225	190

a. Discuss probable reasons for the load pattern given for each work center.

b. Is this the type of firm that is likely to rely heavily on expediting? Explain.

5. Part of a daily open-order file and part of a routing file are shown below.

Daily open-order file   Date: 93

Part no.	Shop-order no.	Quantity	Work centers and dates in routing sequence (current location signified by X)					
00112	836	10	11–91	X18–94	40–96	22–100	42–103	. . .
00810	796	48	11–84	X21–88	18–93	38–95	. . .	
00901	816	6	X16–88	26–91	12–98	18–100	40–103	. . .
00904	821	20	21–90	12–92	X18–95	28–98	. . .	
00977	801	30	21–83	51–86	28–90	X40–94	18–96	16–99
00989	806	18	09–84	40–88	X18–98	13–102	. . .	
01016	844	4	X12–94	41–98	29–102	18–104	23–107	. . .

Routing file (only selected part numbers are included)

Part no.	Work center	Setup time	Cycle time
00112	11	—	0.8
	18	2.2	0.2
	09	0.6	1.2
	31	1.1	0.1
	14	5.0	0.7
00810	18	0.5	0.1
00901	18	1.0	2.0
00904	18	3.0	0.6
00977	18	1.5	0.3
00989	18	5.0	1.0
01016	18	1.2	3.1

Note: The complete routing is given only for the first part number.

a. Using the information in the files, compute the load on work center 18 (WC18) for the weeks beginning on days 94, 99, 104 and 109. Plot the computed totals for each week on a load chart similar to Figure 10–6A and the open-orders part of Figure 10–6B.

b. Backlogs in the recent past for WC18 were:

As of week	Backlog
79	96 hours
84	97 hours
89	91 hours

In week 94, the WC18 backlog is 70 hours, plus the load that you calculated in part *a*. (Your part *a* results are incomplete since they are based on only *part* of a daily open-order file—only seven part numbers.) What concerns should the foreman over WC18 have in view of the backlog pattern?

c. Why is it necessary to state "rules" for computing operation lead times for scheduling purposes but not for loading purposes?

  d. Explain how your load chart (from part *a*) could be augmented to include planned orders.

6. The chart below shows projected loads for one work center.
  a. What may the scheduler do to help correct the imbalance between load and capacity in some weeks? Discuss, including any limitations or difficulties in correcting the imbalance.
  b. How would the load report be produced?
  c. Assume that the foreman has set work-center output (via planned staffing) at 590 per week for these five weeks. A report after five weeks shows actual output in the five weeks as:

     585 590 575 590 585

  What may be concluded about the five-week results?
  d. A second part of the five-week report shows actual inputs of:

     565 650 650 570 600

  What should be listed as planned inputs for the period? Now what may be concluded about the five-week results? Discuss fully.

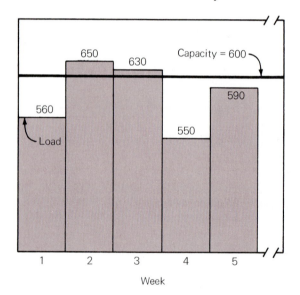

7. On day 280 the daily priority report for the nickel plating work center includes job number 2228. That job is due out of plating on day 279, and its planned run time is one day. If an additional day is allowed for move and queue time, what is the critical ratio? What is the operation slack? Show your calculations. How should these calculated results be interpreted?

8. Jerrybuilt Machines, Inc., uses the least-operation-slack priority rule. On shop calendar day 62 the following shop orders will be in work center 30:

Shop order	Move/queue allowance	Operation time	Operation due date
889	2 days	3 days	68
916	2 days	1 day	64
901	2 days	1 day	69

Calculate the slack for each shop order and arrange your calculated results in list form as they would appear on a daily dispatch list.

9. Two shop orders are in the slitting work center on day 28. Order 888 is due out of slitting on day 32; it requires 1.8 hours of run time. Order 999 is due out of slitting on day 33; it requires 18.0 hours of run time. Determine which job should be run first by calculating critical ratio. Assume that run time is rounded up to even eight-hour days.

10. The following data apply to three shop orders that happen to end up in the same work center on day 120:

Shop order	Preceding work center	Completion date (day moved to next work center)	Next (current) work center	Queue time plus run time in work center 17	Date due out of work center 17
300	28	119	17	3 days	122
310	14	117	17	2 days	123
290	13	118	17	1 day	121

Moves from one work center to another take virtually no time.

a. Arrange the shop orders in priority order, first to last, using the first-come, first-served priority rule.

b. Calculate critical ratios for the three jobs and arrange them in priority order, first to last.

11. Today is day 12 on the shop calendar, and three jobs are in work center 67, as shown in the accompanying table.

Jobs in work center 67	Scheduled operation start date	Scheduled operation finish date
A	12	18
B	8	16
C	13	17

Calculate critical ratios and operation slack for the three jobs. Arrange the jobs in priority order, and indicate which should be done first.

12. On day 12 shop order number 222 is in the blanking work center; the order requires two days in blanking (including all waits, setups, moves, etc.) and is due out of blanking on day 15. Also on day 12 shop order 333 is in the same work center; it requires three

days in blanking and is due out on day 17. Furthermore on day 12, shop order 444 is in the work center; it requires one day and is due out on day 12.

Determine which order should be run first, which second, and which third. Calculate slack for each order to prove your answer. What is the meaning of the slack value you get for order 444?

13. An antenna manufacturer produces in job lots. Part of the daily dispatch list on day 314 is shown below for the chrome-plating work center.

Shop order	Part	Setup time (standard hours)	Operation time (standard hours)	Operation slack
910	AS65	0.5	3.5	−3
914	AS41	2.0	12.0	0
.				
.				
885	AL88	4.5	10.0	+6

a. If shop order 885 is as shown below, what is the critical ratio of the plating operation on day 314 (a Friday)?

Shop order 885   Part no. AL88   Quantity: 5 loads

Operation	Setup hours	Run hours	Finish
Cut	1.0	6.0	320
Move			321
Chrome plate	4.5	10.0	323
Trim		8.0	324

b. What rules for computing operation lead times can be detected from shop order 885?

c. On day 315 (Monday morning) inventory planning notifies scheduling that the due date for Part no. AL88 is now day 319 instead of 324. The chrome-plating operation has not yet been done for the part. What is the new operation slack in the chrome-plating work center? What is the new critical ratio? Is shop order 885 now urgent?

d. On day 315, where are shop orders 910 and 914 likely to be? Base your answer only on the above information.

e. Assume that on day 316 the (partial) daily dispatch list is as follows:

Shop order	Part number	Setup time (standard hours)	Operation time (standard time)	Operation slack
898	AL26	1.5	4.0	−4
914	AS41	2.0	12.0	−1
885	AL88	4.5	10.0	−1
.				
.				
.				

Explain what has happened to yield this dispatch list.

f. Will shop order 885 also appear on the daily dispatch list for the trim work center? Explain.

g. Is this company likely to use centralized or decentralized dispatching? Explain.

h. Would on-line shop recorders make sense for this firm? Explain.

14. An aggressive new chief of production control has developed full computer-based MRP and CRP plus a wide assortment of feedback reports. The feedback reports include the following, in order of importance according to the PC chief:

Input/output control report.

Efficiency report.

Report of percent of job orders completed on time.

Quality-control report of defectives.

Scrap report.

Report of stockroom parts-shortage rate.

Various other minor reports and special audits.

One effect of these reports is that foremen complain about all the paperwork and about the continual need to defend their performance as indicated in the reports. What is missing in the reporting system? Explain.

15. In chapter discussion the cost-variance report was stated to be a cornerstone of an effective feedback control system. Is the grade that a student gets in a course similar as a performance indicator to the cost-variance report in manufacturing? Fully discuss this analogy.

16. The following is a list of the ways in which the results in a given organization or program are measured.

Agency, firm, or program	Measurement of results
Library	Books circulated per full-time employee
Highway safety program	Expenditures on safety advertising
Tax service	Cost per tax return prepared
Computer center	Minutes of downtime
Personnel department	Expenditures versus budget
Sales department	Number of clients visited
Hospital	Average length of stay
School lunch program	Average pounds of uneaten food from plates
Antismoking program	Number of antismoking clinics established
School	Student credit hours per full-time equivalent instructor
Maintenance department	Percent of repair orders completed on time
Welding shop	Tons of scrap produced

a. The above list includes (1) output measures, (2) input efficiency measures, (3) input utilization measures, (4) input cost measures, and (5) other less precise input measures. Which of the five types of measures applies to each item on the list? Explain each answer briefly.

b. Suggest an improved (but similar) type of output measure for each item on the list. Explain.

17. Vacation Hotels, Inc., has each of its hotels report monthly on hours of use of all hotel conference rooms. For example, each hotel has an identical "grand ballroom." The corporation uses 420 hours per month as the maximum possible usage of a grand ballroom.

    One hotel reports 180 hours of use of its grand ballroom. Calculate the utilization rate for that hotel's ballroom. Is this a good and useful control measure for the corporation, or is it deficient? Discuss.

18. Acme Trucking Co. generates monthly reports on the following: driver hours consumed, truck utilization rate, maintenance hours, customer complaints, and fuel consumption. Which of these are output reports, and which are input reports? Explain each briefly. Think of two output reports that would be valuable for a trucking company and explain why.

19. Four jobs are on the desk of the scheduler for the minor construction department in a firm. Each of the four jobs begins with masonry and is followed by carpentry and wiring. Work-order data are given below:

Work order	Estimated task time, masonry	Estimated task time, carpentry	Estimated task time, wiring
58	2 weeks	3 weeks	1½ weeks
59	1 week	1½ weeks	1 week
60	3 weeks	2 weeks	3 weeks
61	5 weeks	½ week	1½ weeks

a. Prepare a Gantt chart scheduling the four jobs through the three crafts (crafts are rows on the chart). Use first come, first served as the priority rule for scheduling (first *job* first—the *whole* job). Assume that a craft cannot divide its time between two work orders. How many weeks do the four jobs take?

b. Repeat part *a*, but use the shortest-job-processing-time rule instead of first come, first served. Now how many weeks are required?.

c. Three weeks pass. The following progress is reported to the scheduler:

    Masonry completed on WO 58.

    Masonry not started on WO 59, 60, or 61.

    Carpentry half completed on WO 58.

    Show the progress on a Gantt control chart.

d. In this problem situation each shop is fully loaded as the jobs are sequenced and scheduled. It is finite-capacity loading. What is there about minor construction work of this kind that makes scheduling and loading so uncomplicated (as compared with job-lot parts fabrication)?

20. The accompanying Gantt chart shows a scheduled project task and progress as of a given date.

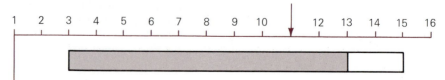

a. What is the present date, and what is the percent of completion for the task? How many days ahead or behind schedule are shown?

b. Redraw the chart as it will look tomorrow if the entire task is completed. How many days ahead or behind schedule does your chart represent?

c. Saturdays and Sundays are not worked—and are not identified on the chart. Explain how the dating system treats weekends (and holidays).

Chapter 11

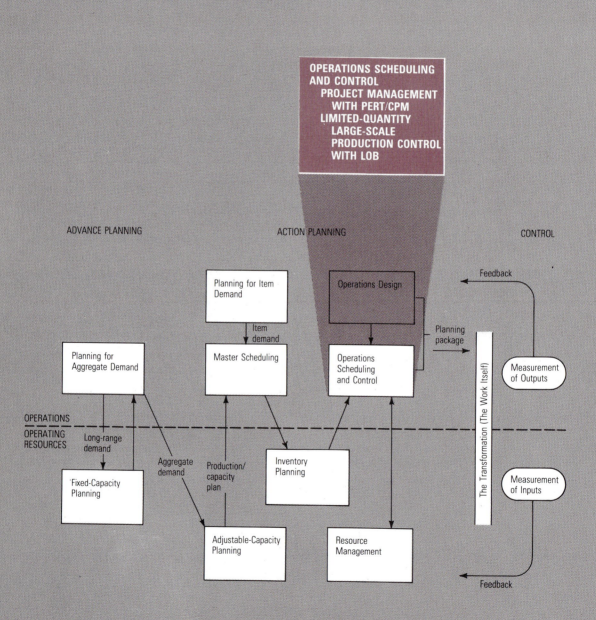

OPERATIONS SCHEDULING AND CONTROL
PROJECT MANAGEMENT WITH PERT/CPM
LIMITED-QUANTITY LARGE-SCALE PRODUCTION CONTROL WITH LOB

ADVANCE PLANNING

ACTION PLANNING

CONTROL

Planning for Item Demand

Operations Design

Feedback

Item demand

Planning package

Planning for Aggregate Demand

Master Scheduling

Operations Scheduling and Control

Measurement of Outputs

OPERATIONS

OPERATING RESOURCES

Long-range demand

Aggregate demand

Production/ capacity plan

Inventory Planning

The Transformation (The Work Itself)

Measurement of Inputs

Fixed-Capacity Planning

Adjustable-Capacity Planning

Resource Management

Feedback

Large-Scale Operations with PERT/CPM and LOB

This is the third of three chapters on operations planning and control. The previous two covered continuous, repetitive, job, and job-lot operations. Now we shall see what is done for projects and for limited-quantity large-scale production.

PERT/CPM

The critical path method (CPM), a project management tool, was developed by Catalytic Construction Company in 1957. Catalytic developed CPM as a method for improving planning and control over a project to construct a plant for Du Pont Corporation. CPM was credited with having saved time and money on that project, and today CPM is well known and widely used in the construction industry.

The program evaluation and review technique was developed in 1958 by Booz, Allen, and Hamilton, a large consulting firm, along with the U.S. Navy Special Projects Office. PERT was developed to provide more intensive management of the Polaris missile project. Polaris was one of the largest research and development projects ever undertaken. Nevertheless, Polaris was completed in record time—about four years. PERT got much of the credit, and soon it was adopted throughout the R&D industry as a tool for intensive project management.

Networks

Both CPM and PERT are based on a task sequence chart known as a network (also called a PERT chart or arrow diagram); see Figure 11–1 for an abbreviated sample of a network. A few early differences between CPM and PERT have mostly disappeared, and it is convenient to think of PERT and CPM as being one and the same, referred to by the combined term PERT/CPM. The construction industry still calls it CPM, and the R&D people still usually call it PERT; a few other terminological differences are mentioned later.

FIGURE 11–1

A PERT/CPM Network

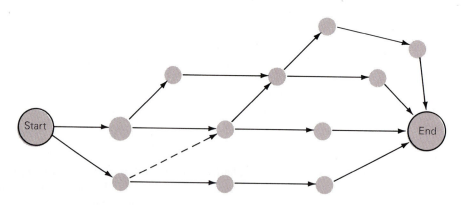

Project Phases and PERT/CPM Subsystems

PERT/CPM is among the more interesting and written-about management techniques. Actually PERT/CPM may be more than a technique. Perhaps it is, or can be, a management system.

A system has subsystems, and our discussion of PERT/CPM will identify four subsystems. We shall see that most projects are not complex enough to justify the expense of all four. But managing grand projects may call for a full computer-based PERT/CPM system, which, throughout the project, can help cope with sequence and time-management problems and also aid in resource allocation and cost control. The four subsystems that would be found in a full computer-based system are:

Project planning and sequencing. This is about the same as the product design and process planning/routing activities in repetitive and job-lot operations.

Time estimating and path analysis. Time estimating for projects is like time estimating in a job shop, but path analysis is unique to project operations.

A project scheduling subsystem. Scheduling projects has some elements of both repetitive and job-lot scheduling. But since a project is a self-contained unit of work, scheduling options are looked at differently.

Reporting and updating. Treating the network as a self-contained unit permits intensive project control using the management-by-exception principle.

PROJECT PLANNING AND SEQUENCING SUBSYSTEM

The initial PERT/CPM subsystem is to develop the network. In planning job-lot operations, we begin with a bill of materials (BOM); in planning project operations, the same is true, but it is labeled a work breakdown structure (WBS) rather than a BOM. The WBS defines major project modules, secondary components, and so on.

In job-lot production, the sequence of tasks to produce a part is merely listed on a route sheet, but in projects, sequences of tasks for parts are linked to form a network. Why the fancy sequence display? Because projects, by common definition, are complex, with multiple tasks in progress at any given time; and projects tend to be large, sometimes having tens or hundreds of thousands of tasks. The PERT/CPM network responds to the need to know how these tasks fit together.

Work Breakdown Structure

An example of a work breakdown structure (WBS) for building a house is presented next. Actually building houses is so routine that it is more like repetitive than project production. But since house building is familiar, it will serve to illustrate the WBS concept.

EXAMPLE 11–1

Work Breakdown Structure, House Construction

A WBS for building a house is shown in Figure 11–2. Figure 11–2A is a preferred way to construct a WBS; the project is broken down into tangible products at levels 2 and 3. Figure 11–2B is a process-oriented way to draw it—not recommended. The process-oriented chart does not have tangible products whose completion may be assigned to a single manager. Carpentry, for example, is a process that results in several tangible products or parts: forms for footings, the frame of the house, finished cabinets, and so forth. Painting, landscaping, and masonry also are found throughout the project and result in several outputs. When the project is delayed or resources

FIGURE 11–2

Work Breakdown Structures for House-Building Project

A. Product-oriented *WBS*

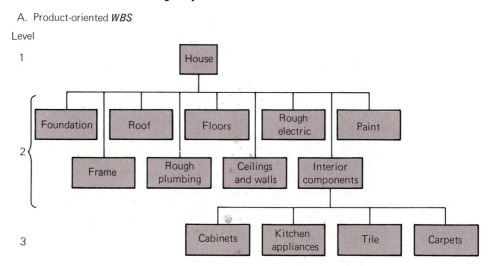

B. Process-oriented *WBS*

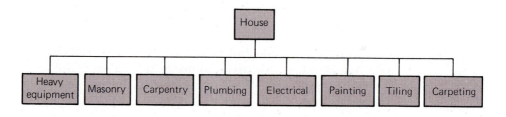

are idled, it may be convenient for painters to blame carpenters, and so forth. If managers are appointed to "honcho" given parts of the project—instead of having foremen only for each craft or process—the managers may work to secure cooperation from the various crafts; this may save time and cut the costs of idle resources.

Task Lists, Network Segments, and Whole Networks

Once the project has been broken down into products as in Figure 11–2A, tasks for each product are listed. Finally the tasks are arranged into a PERT/CPM network. The following example demonstrates.

EXAMPLE 11–2

Networking, House Construction

Figure 11–3 shows how a work breakdown structure (WBS) evolves into network segments, which combine into networks. The figure is a continuation of the house building example. The lowest level in the WBS is for three parts: cabinets, kitchen appliances, and tile. Task lists for each part are identified in Figure 11–3A.

Without the task lists for all of the other parts of the house, it is not possible to properly sequence all of the tasks into networks. But Figure 11–3B demonstrates the kind of sequencing logic that must occur. Kitchen wall cabinets go first since they are easier to install if the lower cabinets are not in the way. Floor cabinets are installed with gaps for the range and dishwasher, which are installed next. Kitchen tile is laid after the kitchen cabinets and appliances have been installed; if it were laid sooner, it might not butt closely against the cabinets and appliances and it might also get marred. Bathroom tile follows the bathroom vanity for the same sort of reason. Since there appears to be no reason why the hood/fan and the hall tile should come either before or after the other tasks shown, they are drawn unlinked to the other tasks (but they would link to tasks not shown when the full network is constructed).

The rectangles, numbered (1), (2), and (3) in Figure 11–3B, are not essential. They merely show craft groupings. Later, during scheduling, each craft may use Gantt charts to show when its project tasks occur. Note that it would serve no purpose to group all kitchen activities together, all bathroom activities together, and so forth; the kitchen is a room, but it is neither a product to be separately managed nor the responsibility of a separate craft.

Task lists and network segments go together to form a whole-project network. Figure 11–4 is an example of a whole-project network. It is a continuation of the house-building example, but further simplified; for example, this house has no tile, carpets, or bathroom vanity.

FIGURE 11–3

Translating Task Lists into Network Segments

A. Task lists for project parts

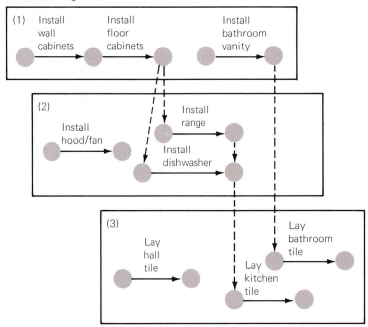

Cabinets (1)	Kitchen appliances (2)	Tile (3)
Install kitchen wall cabinets	Install range	Lay kitchen tile
Install kitchen floor cabinets	Install dishwasher	Lay bathroom tile
Install bathroom vanity	Install hood/fan	Lay hall tile

B. Network segments

Source: Adapted from Fred Luthans, *Introduction to Management: A Contingency Approach* (Richard J. Schonberger, contributing author) (New York: McGraw-Hill, 1976) (HD31.L86), p. 375. Used with permission.

Networking Conventions

A few rules and conventions of networking may be mentioned:

1. One destination. A PERT/CPM network (except segments) has only one start event and one end event. (In Figure 11–4 these are numbered 1 and 18.) To bring this about, all arrows must progress toward the end, and there can be no doubling

FIGURE 11–4

Network for House Construction

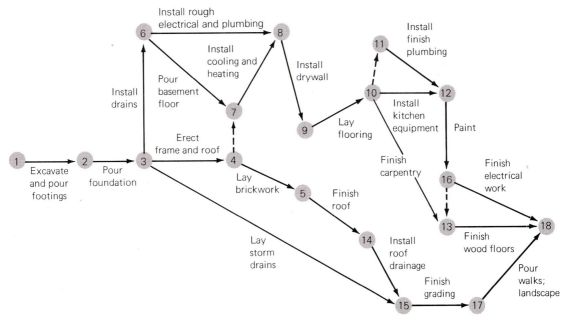

Source: Adapted from Jerome D. Wiest and Ferdinand K. Levy, *A Management Guide to PERT/CPM,* © 1969, p. 16. Reprinted by permission of Prentice-Hall, Inc., Englewood Cliffs, New Jersey.

back and no loops.[1] Figure 11–5 shows these two no-no's. In large networks it is not uncommon to make a few such errors inadvertently; for example, an arrowhead may be carelessly placed at the wrong end of a line. This results in event numbers going into wrong data fields on computer records—if the network plan is computerized. Most PERT/CPM computer packages will detect such errors and print error messages.[2]

2. Event completion. A network event (or node) stands for the completion of all activities (or arrows) leading into it. Furthermore, in PERT/CPM logic no activity may begin at an event until *all* activities leading into that event have been completed. For example, consider event 8 in Figure 11–4. If rough plumbing is installed and *inside* cooling and heating work is completed, it should be all right to install drywall, which is strictly inside work. But the network logic says no. An outside cooling compressor would be a part of activity 7–8, so event 8 includes it. The network

---

[1] But these two and other options *are* allowed in a PERT/CPM variation called GERT (graphical evaluation and review technique).

[2] For a listing of commercially available PERT/CPM computer programs, see Larry A. Smith and Joan Mills, "Project Management Network Programs," *Project Management Quarterly,* June 1982, pp. 18–29.

FIGURE 11–5

Networking Errors

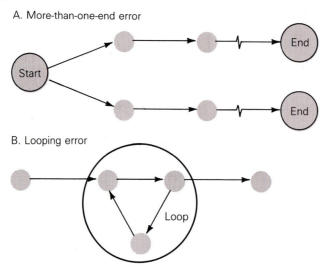

A. More-than-one-end error

B. Looping error

must be drawn differently and the activities labeled differently if we prefer that drywall not depend on the completion of all cooling work.

3. Dummy activity. A dummy activity is a dashed arrow; it takes no time, and it consumes no resources. Four of the five dummies in Figure 11–3 merely connect subnetworks. They are not essential and may be left out when the full network is drawn.

In Figure 11–4 two of the dummies are necessary for project logic. These are activities 4–7 and 16–13. Activity 4–7 is there in order to assure that both 3–4 and 6–7 precede 7–8 but that only 3–4 precedes 4–5. The logic is thus: You want cooling and heating to be installed on top of a basement floor (6–7) and through holes drilled in the frame (3–4). You want brickwork to go up against the frame (3–4), but it need not wait for a basement floor (6–7) to be poured. The dummy, 4–7, decouples the two merging and the two bursting activities to correctly show the logic. There is no other way to show it. Dummy activity 16–13 has the same sort of purpose.

Dummy activity 10–11 is there only to avoid confusing the computer—if the network is computerized. The problem is that two different activities occur between events 10 and 12. Most PERT/CPM computer packages identify activities and their direction by predecessor and successor event numbers. For example, the dummy activity 10–11 goes *from* 10 *to* 11. The computer knows this because the 10 is input into a predecessor field and the 11 into a successor field in a computer record for that activity. (Each activity gets its own record.) In Figure 11–4 an extra event, 11, creates a dummy activity, 10–11. This assures that finish plumbing and kitchen equipment have unique numbers. Three equivalent ways to do this are shown in the accompanying illustration.

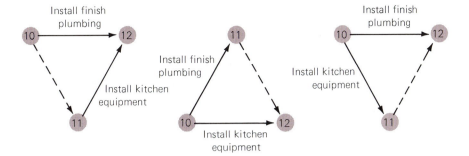

4. Event numbering. Most computer software for PERT/CPM does not require that event numbers go from smaller to larger. Larger to smaller (e.g., 16 to 13 in Figure 11–4) is all right, because the *from* event (16) is entered into the predecessor field in the computer record and the *to* event (13) is entered into the successor field. Thus, the computer has no difficulty keeping the sequence straight.

5. Level of detail. Every activity in Figure 11–4 could be divided into subactivities. In fact, the activities could be subdivided all the way down to therbligs (basic hand and body motions), which would result in tens of thousands of activities instead of the 24 shown. Besides the burden that more activities impose, there is no need to plan for a level of detail beyond what a manager would want to control. On the other hand, there should be enough detail to show when one activity should precede another.

6. Plan versus actual. The network is only a plan. It is unlikely to be followed exactly. Maybe, for example, walks and landscapes will get poured (17–18 in Figure 11–4) *before* finished grading (15–17). Or maybe money will run out and finished grading will be cut from the project. Thus, the network is not an imperative, and it is not "violated" when it is not followed. The network is just your best estimate of how you expect to do the project. Your best estimate is far better than no plan at all.

Alternative Forms of Networks

The original and most common form of the PERT/CPM network shows activities as arrows. Figure 11–3B and Figure 11–4 are of this type. The rationale is that an activity takes time, and a line or arrow tends to imply the passage of time. The circle before and after each arrow signifies an instant in time: the start or end of an activity. Other ways to draw and label networks follow:

1. Activity-oriented networks. There are two forms of the activity-oriented network. One is called activity-on-arrow (AOA); that is, the activity is signified by the arrow itself. The other form is called activity-on-node (AON), in which the node or circle represents the activity. Figure 11–6 shows both forms. It is a good idea to pick one form and stick with it, and in this book AOA is the choice. AON is shown only because some students seem naturally inclined to want to draw networks that way

FIGURE 11–6

Activities and Computer Inputs

A. Activity-on-arrow network segment and computer inputs

B. Activity-on-node network segment

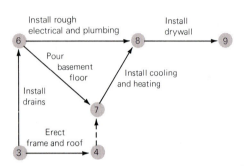

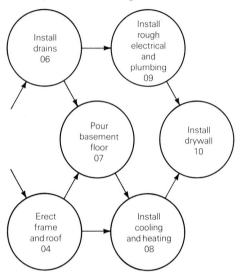

and then wonder why their networks do not look like those of other students. (There is one special advantage of the AOA form and a different advantage of the AON form. These are beyond the scope of this discussion.)

2. **Event-oriented networks.** Operating people think in terms of actions, which in PERT are called **activities.** Upper managers are more interested in completions, or **events.** The event-oriented network is created from an activity-oriented network, and its purpose is to give upper managers a basis for reviewing project completions. Figure 11–7 shows two forms of event-oriented networks. Figure 11–7A is a portion of the construction project example stated as an event-oriented network. Nodes are drawn large to hold event descriptions. Descriptions use present-tense verb forms in activity-oriented networks, but they use past-tense forms in event-oriented networks. For example, "Pour basement floor" in Figure 11–6 becomes "Basement floor poured" in Figure 11–7A. At merge points (nodes where two or more activities converge), the event description can get long and cumbersome. For example, event 8 is "Rough plumbing, cooling, and heating installed."

Networks for big projects may include tens or even hundreds of thousands of events. Upper managers surely do not care to review the project event by event. It is common instead to create a summary network for upper managers. The summary network may be limited to certain key events, called **milestones.** The large arrows from Figure 11–7A to Figure 11–7B show how five events (4, 7, 8, 9, and 10) are condensed into two milestone events. Milestones are usually events that signify the end of major project stages. In house construction, most people would think of comple-

FIGURE 11–7

Events and Milestones

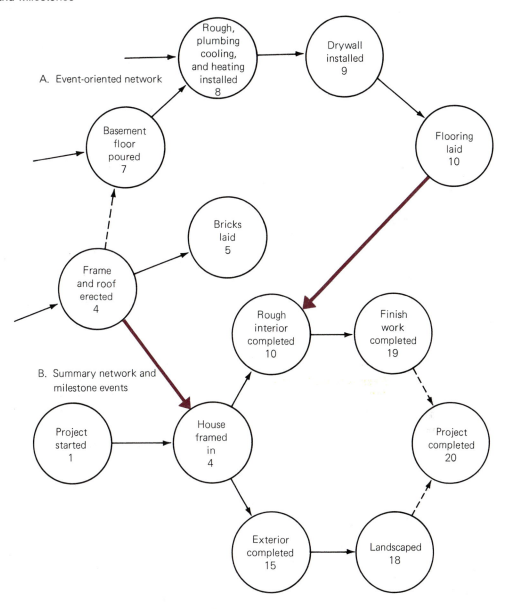

A. Event-oriented network

B. Summary network and milestone events

tion of framing and completion of rough interior work as major stages; these are milestones 4 and 10 in Figure 11–7B.

Some sequential accuracy is lost in condensing a network. For example, milestone event 4 subsumes events 2 and 3 (from Figure 11–4). But in cutting out event 3, two "branches" of the "tree" at that point—branches 3–6 and 3–15—are unceremoniously chopped off, as is shown in the accompanying illustration. From an upper-management perspective, however, the inaccuracy is of little concern.

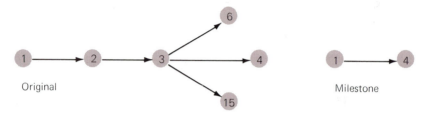

Original   Milestone

TIME-ESTIMATING AND PATH-ANALYSIS SUBSYSTEM

The time-estimating and path-analysis subsystem is next. It begins with estimates of the time to complete each activity in the network. The sum of time estimates from the beginning to the end of the network yields the estimated project duration. There are multiple paths through a given network, and each path may have a different total time.

Activity Times

It is harder to accurately estimate times for projects than for repetitive and job-shop operations because of project uncertainty and task variability. Engineered time standards are unlikely for project activities, except for activities that tend to recur from project to project. Instead the project manager obtains technical estimates from those in charge of each project activity. (A technical estimate is a type of historical, nonengineered time standard; see Chapter 13.)

The person doing the estimating tends to "pad" the estimate, because an overestimate is easier to achieve. In construction projects, usually enough experience and historical data are available to keep estimators from getting away with gross padding of estimates.

Not so with research and development projects. R&D projects often include advanced state-of-the-art activities; historical benchmark data are scarce. Because of this, PERT, the R&D-oriented half of PERT/CPM, was originally outfitted with a special statistically based routine. PERT project managers asked not for one activity time estimate but for three: a most likely estimate, an optimistic estimate, and a pessimistic estimate. Next the three time estimates are converted into most likely times and variances, and probabilities of completing any given event by a given date are calculated.

The apparent rationality of the statistical procedure has been confounded in practice by human behavioral problems. First of all, for an activity never done before, it is hard to pry one time estimate out of people, much less three. A request for three estimates may result in drawn-out discussion of the definitions of most likely, optimistic, and pessimistic. Second, the estimators for R&D activities often are scientists, engineers, and other professionals. They tend to be strong-willed, and unafraid to withhold their cooperation. If pressed to provide three estimates, they may give meaningless estimates like 5–10–15 or 8–10–12.

For these reasons, the PERT three-time-estimating procedure has mostly fallen into disuse. Today in both PERT and CPM a single best estimate is the norm, and best estimate is simply defined as how long the activity is expected to take under normal conditions and with normal resources.

Path Analysis

The most time-consuming path is the **critical path.** That path is *time*-critical because a delay in completing any of its activities delays the whole project. A continuation of the house-construction example, as follows, demonstrates path analysis.

EXAMPLE 11–3

Path Analysis, House Construction

The house-construction network of Figure 11–4 is reproduced in Figure 11–8. Time estimates, shown on each activity, have been added. Path durations are given below the network. Although this network is very small— for illustrative purposes—there are still 17 paths to add up. Computers are efficient at adding path times, and path-analysis subroutines are usually included in PERT/CPM software.

In the figure, path 12 is critical, at 34 days. It is shown by colored lines in the network. Several other paths—6, 7, 8, 9, 10, 11, 13, 14, and 15—are nearly critical, at 31 to 33 days. The critical-path and nearly critical-path activities deserve close managerial attention. Other activities have *slack* or *float* time and need not be managed so closely. The more slack, the more flexibility there is for managers to schedule the activities.

Activity Slack

Slack time may be explained by an extension of the example, as follows. Calculating slack by comparing slack-path segments with critical-path segments seems fairly simple. It becomes tedious, however, for larger networks. An algorithm has been developed to avoid much of the tedium. The algorithm is demonstrated in Figure 11–9 for a portion of the house-construction example. The three-step calculation procedure is explained below for the positive-slack example of Figure 11–9A.

EXAMPLE 11–4

Slack Time, House Construction

In Figure 11–8, paths 7, 11, and 14 take 33 days, or 1 day less than the critical path. This means that relative to the critical path, paths 7, 11, and 14 contain a day of **slack** (in PERT lingo) or **float** (in CPM lingo). The day of slack does not apply to the whole path, but rather to one or more path activities. Which ones? Consider path 7 first.

Path 7 is identical to critical path 12 except in the segment from event 3 to event 7. The critical-path segment from 3 to 4 to 7 takes four days; the slack-path segment from 3 to 6 to 7 takes three days. Activities 3–6 and 6–7 are said to have one day of slack. This means that 3–6 *or* 6–7 (but not both) could be delayed by one day without affecting the planned project duration. By like reasoning, activity 16–18 on path 11 has a day of slack and activity 10–12 on path 14 has a day of slack.

Slack analysis is complicated when an activity is on more than one slack-path segment. Activity 3–6, for example, is on slack-path segments 3–6–7 and 3–6–8. Slack segment 3–6–8 takes four days, as compared with eight days for the critical-path segment 3–4–7–8. It may seem that activities 3–6 and 6–8 have four days of slack and that either could be delayed four days without affecting the planned project duration. But we learned above that activity 3–6, on slack segment 3–6–7, may be delayed no more than one day. Slack on 3–6 is therefore one day, not four days; the larger value is rejected. Activity 6–8, however, does have four days of slack.

1. **Earliest start.** Starting with the first event, earliest activity start times are determined in a *forward pass* through the network. In the figure, the project start time (event 1) is set equal to zero, and the earliest start (ES) for activity 1–2 is also zero. *ES* for each successive activity equals the previous *ES* plus the previous activity time, *t.* For activity 2–3, then, $ES = 0 + 4 = 4$; for activity 3–4, $ES = 4 + 2 = 6$; and so forth.

2. **Latest start.** Beginning with the final event, the latest activity start times are found in a *backward pass* through the network. In the figure, the project due date at event 8 is set equal to 14, the critical-path time. The latest start (LS) for each preceding activity equals the *LS* minus the preceding activity time, *t.* For activity 4–7, then, $LS = 10 - 0 = 10$; for activity 3–4, $LS = 10 - 4 = 6$; and so forth.

3. **Slack.** Slack for each activity simply equals $LS - ES$. In Figure 11–9A slack is 4 for activity 6–8, 1 for activities 6–7 and 3–6, and 0 for each of the critical-path activities.[3]

---

[3] *Event* slack may be computed by a similar procedure. Instead of using *ES* and *LS* for each activity, event slack is based on T_E and T_L for each event. T_E stands for time earliest (to complete the event) and T_L stands for time latest. Event slack $= T_L - T_E$.

FIGURE 11–8

Path Analysis

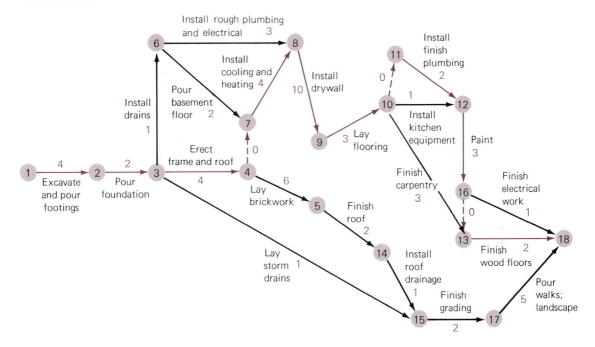

* Activity times are in days.

Path number	Paths	Path time	
1	1–2–3–6–8–9–10–11–12–16–18	29 days	
2	1–2–3–6–8–9–10–11–12–16–13–18	30	
3	1–2–3–6–8–9–10–12–16–18	28	
4	1–2–3–6–8–9–10–12–16–13–18	29	
5	1–2–3–6–8–9–10–13–18	28	
6	1–2–3–6–7–8–9–10–11–12–16–18	32	
7	1–2–3–6–7–8–9–10–11–12–16–13–18	33	Nearly critical paths
8	1–2–3–6–7–8–9–10–12–16–18	31	
9	1–2–3–6–7–8–9–10–12–16–13–18	31	
10	1–2–3–6–7–8–9–10–13–18	31	
11	1–2–3–4–7–8–9–10–11–12–16–18	33	
12	1–2–3–4–7–8–9–10–11–12–16–13–18	34 ←	Critical path
13	1–2–3–4–7–8–9–10–12–16–18	32	Nearly critical paths
14	1–2–3–4–7–8–9–10–12–16–13–18	33	
15	1–2–3–4–7–8–9–10–13–18	32	
16	1–2–3–4–5–14–15–17–18	26	
17	1–2–3–15–17–18	14	

FIGURE 11–9

Calculating Activity Slack

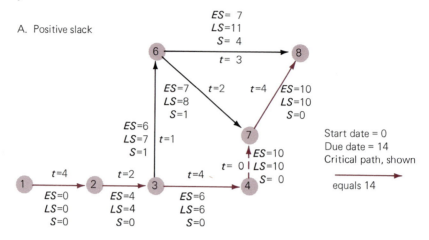

A. Positive slack

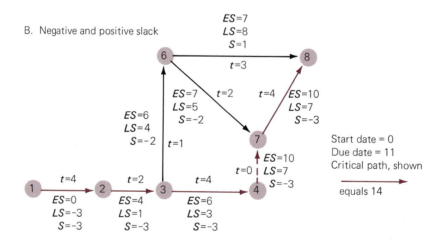

B. Negative and positive slack

Negative Slack

If *LS* is less than *ES*, negative slack results. Negative slack means that the activity is late. Not only is this possible, but it is almost the norm—at least for critical-path activities. It is rare enough for projects to be on time that *The Wall Street Journal* published a front-page story some years ago with headlines proclaiming that a certain large construction project was completed on time. (The project was the domed stadium in Pontiac, Michigan, which also met targeted costs!)

Figure 11–9B illustrates negative slack. What produces the negative slack is an earlier due date, day 11 instead of day 14. For activity 7–8, *LS* = 11 − 4 = 7;

slack = $LS - ES = 7 - 10 = -3$. Each of the other critical-path activities also has a slack of -3, which means that the project is three days late while still in the planning stage. The network plan could be changed to make the planned completion time equal the due date. Or the project could start out three days late in the hope of catching up.

Slack-Sort Computer Listing

Computers are needed in the path-analysis stage of PERT/CPM. The most common computer output is a slack-sorted list of all project activities. An example follows.

EXAMPLE 11–5

Slack-Sort Computer Listing, House Construction

Figure 11–10 is an example of a slack-sort computer listing. Slack sort means sorting or listing activities in order of how much slack they have. Critical-path activities have the least slack and therefore appear first; next most critical activities, usually from more than one path, appear next; and so on. In the figure a space separates each group of activities having common

FIGURE 11–10

Computer Listing for Path Analysis

Slack-Sorted Activity Report

Activity number	Description	Time	Earliest start	Latest start	Activity slack	
1–2	Excavate, pour footings	4	0	−3	−3	⎤
2–3	Pour foundation	2	4	1	−3	⎟
3–4	Erect frame and roof	4	6	3	−3	⎟
4–7	Dummy	0	10	7	−3	⎬ Critical path
.	.	.	.	.	.	⎟
.	.	.	.	.	.	⎟
13–18	Lay flooring	2	32	29	−3	⎦
3–6	Install drains	1	6	4	−2	
6–7	Pour basement floor	2	7	5	−2	
10–12	Install kitchen equipment	1	27	25	−2	
16–18	Finish electrical work	1	32	30	−2	
10–13	Finish carpentry	3	27	26	−1	
.	.	.	.	.	.	
.	.	.	.	.	.	
15–17	Finish grading	2	19	24	+5	
17–18	Pour walks and landscape	5	21	26	+5	
3–15	Lay storm drains	1	6	23	+17	

slack times. Bottom-most activities are least critical; the last one, activity 3–15, has +17 days of slack, which means that it may be delayed by 17 days without affecting the project due date.

The slack-sorted computer listing helps a manager more than a network. Indeed, most managers rely on this type of listing and never need to see a network.[4]

Network Simulation

As we have seen, the critical path is easily computed by successive path-time addition. Unfortunately the method treats each path independently of all other paths. It fails to allow for time variation, which affects all event completion times and the total project duration. It is easy to prove by Monte Carlo simulation that the deterministic critical-path time understates the likely project duration.[5] Figure 11–11 illustrates.

The figure presents the simplest possible project network: two activities occurring at the same time. (A single activity is a job; multiple activities going on simultaneously are a key distinguishing feature of a project.) In Figure 11–11A both paths are critical at five days, so it is a five-day project. In Figure 11–11B the mean or expected task time on each path is still five days. Yet, as the table shows, the simulated mean project duration is 5.4 days. In the Figure 11–11 table the variability—four, five, and six days—is simulated by considering all time combinations and allowing equal chances for each time value on each path. For each combination the higher path time is the project duration, which pushes the expected (mean) project duration up to 5.4 days.

If more variability is added, the expected project duration increases further. For example, if path time is 3, 4, 5, 6, or 7, each equally probable, expected duration by simulation is 5.8 days. If more paths are added, expected project duration also goes up. As a general rule, then, the fatter the network and the more variable the activity times, the greater the project duration is in excess of the simple critical-path time. This provides a mathematical explanation of why projects tend to be late.

Since the critical path understates reality, why is it widely used? The key reason is path addition is simple and cheap, whereas Monte Carlo simulation is costly. A second reason is Monte Carlo simulation is harder to understand. A third reason is activity time estimates are rough anyway, and there are diminishing returns from applying increased analytical rigor to rough data. A fourth reason is it is difficult to know what to do with simulated network data. Do you add a percentage to each estimated activity time? If so, then perhaps those new times should be inputs to another round of simulation. Where would these rounds of simulation end?

---

[4] Often the listing is event- rather than activity-oriented; for example, instead of earliest- and latest-start activity times (*ES* and *LS*) there will be time-earliest and time-latest event times (T_E and T_L).

[5] An explanation is given in A. R. Klingel, Jr., "Bias in PERT Project Completion Time Calculations for a Real Network," *Management Science* 13, no. 4 (December 1966), pp. B-194–201.

FIGURE 11–11

Effects of Variable Activity Times on Project Duration

A. 5-day project

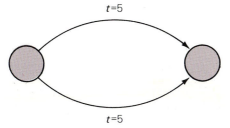

B. 5.4-day project

t=4, 5, or 6; equal (1/3) probabilities

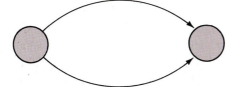

t=4, 5, or 6; equal (1/3) probabilities

	Possible time combinations		
	Top path	Bottom path	Project duration
1	4	4	4
2	4	5	5
3	5	4	5
4	5	5	5
5	4	6	6 } Mean = 49/9 = 5.4 days
6	5	6	6
7	6	6	6
8	6	5	6
9	6	4	6

The question will be left unanswered. The point is project managers should be aware that the critical path understates reality.

PROJECT SCHEDULING SUBSYSTEM

Path analysis reveals how long the project is expected to take using normal resources. But forward scheduling may yield a project completion date that is too late. Upper management may elect to spend more on resources to cut the expected project duration.

Numerous combinations of cost and time are possible. A time-cost trade-off procedure shows these combinations. Then one time-cost pair is selected for implementation, and activities are scheduled. This section explains the procedure; project and work-center scheduling are also considered.

"Crashing" the Network

Expected project duration may be cut by spending more on resources. The extra expenditures must be applied to critical-path activities if the total project duration is to be reduced or "crashed." As time is cut on the critical path, new critical paths may emerge. The cost to cut more time from the project may then involve extra resource costs to reduce activity times on multiple paths. The analysis can get complicated.

If resource costs are inconvenient to collect, the choice of which critical-path activity to crash is not clear cut. Crashing an early activity on the critical path may seem wise, because the reduction will apply to other paths that could become critical later; but money spent early is gone. The opposite wait-and-see approach seems wise for another reason: Perhaps some critical-path activities will be completed earlier than expected, thus averting the need to crash at all; but if that does not happen, late options for crashing may be few and costly.

Time-Cost Trade-Off Analysis

When it is convenient to collect resource costs, a technique known as time-cost trade-off analysis may be used. The technique is explained in the following example.

EXAMPLE 11–6

Time-Cost Trade-Off Analysis

A small network and related time and cost data are shown in Figure 11–12. The critical path is B–D–E, eight days long. The cost for that eight-day project is shown to be $390. This plan need not be accepted. More money would be spent—for extra shifts, airfreight, and so on—to reduce the time required to complete various tasks. For example, activity A costs $50 to do in three days (normal), $75 to do in two days (paying for overtime perhaps), and $100 to do in one day (paying still more, perhaps for extra shifts).[6] The linear assumption—$25 for each day reduced—may be somewhat erroneous, but it is generally accurate enough for planning purposes.

---

[6] The normal and crash costs are often engineering estimates or managers' estimates based on current known direct labor and overhead rates; a careful cost accounting estimate may not be necessary. Also, the cost estimates may be incremental costs rather than full costs.

FIGURE 11–12

Network and Time-Cost Data

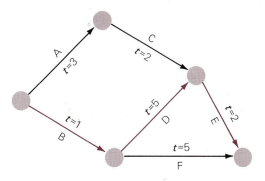

(critical path ⟶ is B-D-E at 8 days)

	Normal		Crash		Cost
Activity	Time	Cost	Time	Cost	per day
A	3	$ 50	1	$100	$25
B	1	40	1	40	—
C	2	40	1	80	40
D	5	100	3	160	30
E	2	70	1	160	90
F	5	90	2	300	70
		$390			

Source: Adapted from Fred Luthans, *Introduction to Management: A Contingency Approach* (Richard J. Schonberger, contributing author) (New York: McGraw-Hill, 1976) (HD31.L86), p. 378. Used with permisison.

The method of calculating average cost per day may be expressed as a formula:

$$\text{Cost per day} = \frac{\text{Crash cost} - \text{Normal cost}}{\text{Normal time} - \text{Crash time}}$$

For activity A, the calculation is:

$$\frac{\$100 - \$50}{3 \text{ days} - 1 \text{ day}} = \frac{\$50}{2 \text{ days}} = \$25 \text{ per day}$$

Cost per day for each of the other activities is calculated the same way. Activity B cannot be crashed and thus does not have a cost-per-day entry.

The question is, If it costs $390 to do the project in eight days, what would it cost to do it in seven? If you pick the lowest total in the cost-per-day column, $25 for A, you are wrong. Spending $25 more on A would reduce A from three days to two days. But it would not affect the eight-day projection duration. A critical-path activity—B, D, or E—must be selected. B is out because its crash time is no better than its normal time. The choice between D and E favors D—at an extra cost of $30, as opposed to $90 for E. Thus, doing the project in seven days requires $30 more, for a total cost of $420.

The next step is to try a two-day reduction. But the above reduction of D to four days results in two critical paths, B–D–E and A–C–E, both seven days long. Reducing the project duration to six days is possible by crashing A and D together at a cost of $55, D and C together at $70, or E alone at $90. The first option is cheapest, and it is selected, bringing the total project cost up to $475.

Next try a three-day reduction. After the above step, all paths are critical at six days. The only choice (since B and D are already crashed to their minimum times) is to crash E and F by one day. The added cost is $160, with a total project cost of $635. No further reductions in times are possible since the B–D–E path is fully crashed.

If this were a construction project with a penalty of $100 for every day beyond a six-day project duration, then alternative 3 below looks best since it has the lowest total cost, $475.

Alternative	Time	Construction cost	Penalty cost	Total cost	
1	8 days	$390	$200	$590	
2	7	420	100	520	
3	6	475	0	475	← Minimum
4	5	635	0	635	

Time-cost trade-off analysis came from the CPM people in the construction industry. It remains more suitable for construction projects than for R&D projects. One reason is that construction costs and perhaps times tend to be easier to estimate than R&D costs and times. The cost per day to crash is thus more meaningful in construction projects. Use of late penalties in construction contracts is further reason why time-cost trade-off analysis tends to be associated with construction and CPM.

Event Scheduling

After a time-cost alternative has been selected, dates are put on each event in the final network. Dating is based on the final activity times, allowing appropriate time off for holidays and weekends. Dating, as well as the trade-off analysis itself, may be done by a computer. Event-dating subroutines are usually available in PERT/CPM programs. The planned date of the first event is input, and the program computes the rest. The resulting computer listing will usually show time-earliest (T_E) and time-latest (T_L) to complete each event, and event slack $(T_L - T_E)$ will be listed in another column.

Each subcontractor, department, or work center that is involved in a given project is also likely to be in on other projects, jobs, and perhaps repetitive operations. Fitting their activities into multiple projects is the next management concern.

Figure 11–13 illustrates this concern. The work center, a grading crew, has developed a Gantt chart showing three upcoming activities that are on the PERT/CPM networks for three different projects. The figure helps make the point that the goals of project managers and work-center managers sometimes conflict. The work-center manager strives for high utilization of capacity, but this may conflict with the timing of work-center activities on project managers' networks. Each project manager strives to get work crews to the job according to PERT/CPM schedules, but work crews are often wanted by more than one project manager at the same time. These conflicts require compromise (although some multiproject-scheduling computer software exists). In most cases, tasks can be scheduled earlier or later within available slack-time limits. This meets the needs of the project manager and also helps spread the work more evenly on the work-center manager's Gantt chart. The tasks that appear on a critical path do not have flexibility for rescheduling, so they are most apt to cause conflict.

FIGURE 11–13

Decomposition of **Network** Activities into Work-Center Schedules

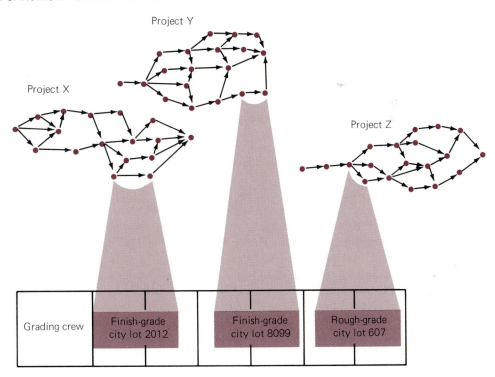

REPORTING AND UPDATING SUBSYSTEM

PERT/CPM management may be applied in the project control phase as well as in project planning. PERT/CPM control centers on periodic reports. The reporting periods are generally every two weeks or once a month.

Reporting

Figure 11–14 shows a typical reporting scheme. The partial network at the top of the figure divides into monthly reporting periods. At the end of each reporting period event-completion data go to the project management office, where they are prepared for entry into the computer. In Figure 11–14, the current month is February and February-planned events 1, 2, 3, 5, and 6 have been completed. A card (or direct data-entry record) is prepared for each; on the first card, for example, an 01 is punched in the event field and the completion date—020482, for February 4, 1982— is punched in another field.

Event 4 was scheduled for February, but no notice of completion has been received. Instead, an activity reestimate notice is received; the first reestimate card has the activity 03–04 punched (without the hyphen) in the key field, and 21 (days) is the new time estimate punched in another field. The reestimate pertains to why event 4 has not been completed: Event 3, completed on February 12, plus 21 days for activity 3–4, pushes the planned completion date for event 4 into March. Future activities may also be reestimated, as 08–10 has been in Figure 11–14.

Updating

With event completions and activity reestimates as inputs, the PERT/CPM network is updated by the computer. A new slack-sort report is produced. It shows the new slack status of each activity. The report is like the report shown in Figure 11–10, except it gives start and due dates for events. The report tells all parties what the new project schedule is for all events. Other reports may be printed—for example, a report listing activities by work center (or department or subcontractor); various resource, budget, and cost reports; and summary (milestone) reports for upper managers. Some of the reports get wide distribution, and in some firms those responsible for activities completed late must explain why.

Replanning is inherent to control. It is possible to rerun a time-cost trade-off analysis each month after the network has been updated, using event-completion data and activity reestimates. Without this analysis, the computer will replan (re-schedule) all events anyway, but without considering using more or less resources on given activities.

Another major type of replanning is altering the network. Activities may be added or subtracted, and sequence may be changed. All that is required is adding, removing, or repunching a few cards. The ease of making such changes is a key asset of PERT/CPM, because project uncertainty demands planning flexibility.

FIGURE 11–14

PERT/CPM Periodic Reporting

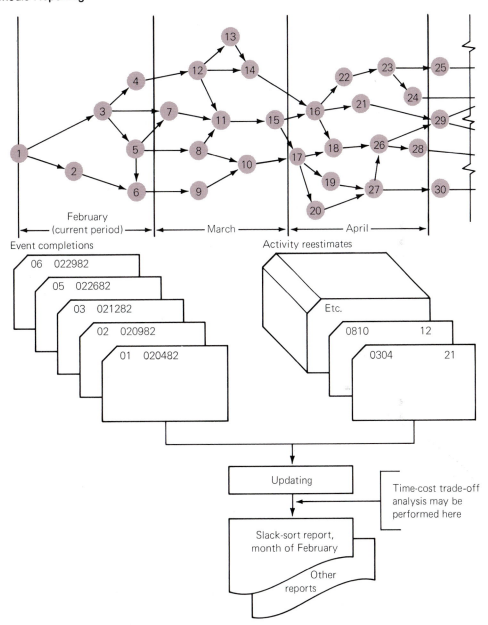

USES AND MISUSES OF PERT/CPM

PERT/CPM is, like many management techniques, expensive. Fully computerized PERT/CPM may eat up an additional 1 or 2 or 3 percent of the total project cost, because it is not a replacement for conventional management. Conventional forecasting, scheduling, inventory control, quality control, budgeting, and so forth, are still done in each functional area (e.g., department or work center). A project management group and PERT/CPM systems hardware and software costs are additional. PERT/Cost, considered next, is even more expensive than ordinary PERT/CPM. The discussion of PERT/Cost is followed by a section on the PERT/CPM environment and reaction to it.

PERT/Cost

In the early 1960s, a PERT extension known as PERT/Cost was tried in the Department of Defense (DoD) and the National Aeronautics and Space Administration (NASA). In PERT/Cost, cost as well as time estimates are made for each activity; actual cost and time data are collected as project activities are done, and cost as well as time variances are reported. But the cost side of PERT/Cost generally proved to be unacceptably expensive to administer, because it required a new and additional bookkeeping system. PERT/Cost may yet be resurrected—if the bookkeeping burden can be eased somehow. But the DoD and NASA abandoned PERT/Cost long ago, and probably few other organizations use it today, except in diluted forms.[7]

PERT/CPM Environment

Some organizations have tried out and abandoned ordinary PERT/CPM as well, because it seemed not to pay for itself. In some such cases the problem is trying to apply full computerized PERT/CPM to small-scale projects. Figure 11–15 reemphasizes a point partially made early in the chapter: that PERT/CPM consists of distinct and separable subsystems. The figure further suggests that only projects that are grand in scope warrant the full PERT/CPM treatment. At the other extreme, projects of modest scope may justify the expense of only the first subsystem.

Project scope is expressed in Figure 11–15 in terms of four characteristics: size, uncertainty, urgency, and complexity. Size and urgency are self-explanatory. Project uncertainty is of two types:

1. Task uncertainty—doubts about what is to be done.
2. Time uncertainty—doubts about activity time estimates.

---

[7] PERT/Cost should not be confused with time-cost trade-off analysis. In the latter, costs are estimated for scheduling purposes only. But PERT/Cost includes a full range of accounting: budgeting, cost accounting, and cost-variance reporting.

FIGURE 11–15

Matching PERT/CPM Subsystems to Project Scope

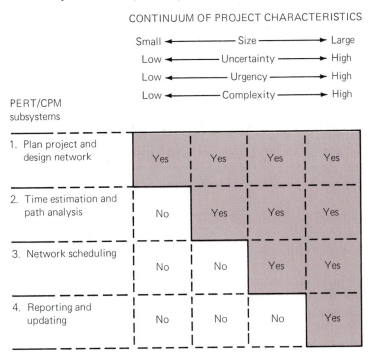

Similarly, complexity may be thought of in two ways:

1. Organizational complexity—many organizations involved in the project.
2. Activity complexity—many activities in progress at the same time.

To illustrate, consider the kinds of construction projects managed by a typical Army Corps of Engineers district: dams, manmade lakes, dredging, channel straightening, levees, bridges, and riverbank stabilization, to name a few. Perhaps 100 projects are in progress at a given time.

A project like a major dam may be only moderately urgent and uncertain, but it is likely to be very large and complex. In sum, the project characteristics seem to be far enough to the right in Figure 11–15 to warrant full computer-based PERT/CPM, including all four subsystems (four yeses in the figure). Without computer-based scheduling, reporting, and control, coordinating the many simultaneous activities of the numerous participating organizations might be chaotic.

Most bridge-construction jobs are much smaller and less complex. For such intermediate-scope projects the project engineer should probably design networks, conduct path analysis, and perhaps use the computer to schedule project events, which may include time-cost trade-off analysis (two or three yeses). But subsystem 4, reporting and updating, may not be warranted. It is the costliest subsystem to administer—it probably costs a lot more than subsystems 1, 2, and 3 combined; a typical bridge is not so urgent as to require the tight time controls of subsystem 4.

Channeling and riverbank stabilization projects are still less urgent, and they are not often large, complex, or uncertain. The project engineer may expend a small amount of time, effort, and cost to accomplish subsystem 1, designing PERT/CPM networks (one yes, left column of the figure). The benefits—seeing who has to do what and in what order—are large for the modest cost. There seems to be little reason to perform path analysis and the other subsystems.

In R&D projects the model seems equally valid. Designing a major aircraft, such as a B-1 bomber, is a project of massive scope—and urgency as well, in view of the capital that it ties up. Full PERT/CPM is easily justified. Redesign of a wing for an existing aircraft is a modest project; subsystem 1 may be sufficient.

The good sense of this situational approach to using PERT/CPM subsystems may be clear. Nevertheless, some organizations have viewed PERT/CPM in only one way: as a single, indivisible system to be used for every project. Disappointment is likely.

LINE-OF-BALANCE ANALYSIS

Line-of-balance (LOB) analysis is useful in controlling *limited-quantity* production of a *large-scale* item. A project does not qualify, for a project involves only one unit of a large-scale item. Neither does repetitive production qualify, because LOB analysis applies when the quantity is not repetitive but limited. Limited quantity is in the range of, say, 25 to 400 units. If the quantity were smaller, the production run might be over before the LOB reporting system were fully operational. If the quantity were in excess of 400, production control would normally settle into a standardized routine, as in mass production.

It is the intermediate-quantity realm that may benefit from the special management control that LOB can exert over large-scale items. Good examples are aircraft, missiles, ships, large boats, tanks, earth-moving equipment, large dynamos, and large generators. Delivery schedules for such items generally spread out over a period of months.

There are four steps in LOB analysis: The first two are planning steps, done in advance; the last two are control steps, done each reporting period in the control phase:

1. **Objective.** A cumulative delivery schedule is the objective.
2. **Process plan.** The second step, the process plan, shows the total sequence (for a single unit) in the form of control points on a lead-time chart.
3. **Progress.** The third step, is plotting progress on a bar chart for each control point and against the objective. This is done each reporting period (usually once a month).
4. **Line of balance.** The line of balance, which is calculated each reporting period, shows what *should* be done. That is, it shows the cumulative quantities required

to date to meet the objective (schedule) in the future. The "line" indicates the "balance" quantity. The line of balance is plotted on top of the bars on the progress chart, and discrepancies are studied to see how to catch up.

LOB Example

The following example explains the LOB method.

EXAMPLE 11–7

Line-of-Balance Analysis, Solar Power Generators

Solesource, Inc., has been awarded a federal energy agency contract for 50 of a new type of solar power generator. The contract calls for deliveries over five months, as shown in Figure 11–16A. The cumulative delivery schedule is curved: The increasing rate allows for increased production efficiency as the contract moves forward (the learning-curve idea).

The process plan for producing one solar generator is shown in Figure 11–16B. There are nine **control points,** that is, completion points, to be monitored. The process plan is based on the industrial engineers' best estimates. The total process time for one unit is 24 working days. The first activity, "Fabricate gyro," takes 10 days—from 24 days (at control point 1) to 14 days (at control point 5) prior to shipment. (Lead time for acquiring gyro parts is not included in the lead-time chart; material deliveries are assumed to be no problem.) Each of the other activity times is also defined as the time between control points.

Figure 11–16C shows the status of the nine control points as of June 30. Such a status report is developed each month, beginning with April 30. The only conclusion that may be safely drawn from the bar chart alone is whether the final control point, 9, is on schedule. The bar for point 9 is at 16 units; a check on the cumulative delivery schedule, Figure 11–16A, reveals that 15 are due, so shipments are slightly ahead of schedule.

This is not a complete picture. Shipments may be slightly ahead, yet other control points may be far ahead or far behind. The final step, laying down the line of balance, is necessary to show the status of the other control points.

Figure 11–17 shows the LOB laid on top of the bars. The LOB height is determined graphically. The graphic method is demonstrated in the figure for control points 6 and 7. Both have nine days' lead time (see Figure 11–16B). Therefore, June 30 performance for those control points has its impact on the delivery schedule nine workdays into July. The vertical arrow in Figure 11–17 intersects the cumulative delivery schedule as of the ninth July workday. The point of intersection, 20 units, is the quantity that should be done today, June 30, at control points 6 and 7 in order to have 20 ready for shipment on the ninth workday of July. That amount, 20, is the proper height of the line of balance at points 6 and 7.

Each of the other LOB heights is calculated in the same way. (If the

FIGURE 11–16

Delivery Schedule and Lead-time Chart, Solar Power Generator

A. Cumulative delivery schedule

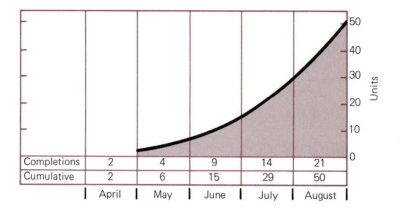

	April	May	June	July	August
Completions	2	4	9	14	21
Cumulative	2	6	15	29	50

B. Process plan

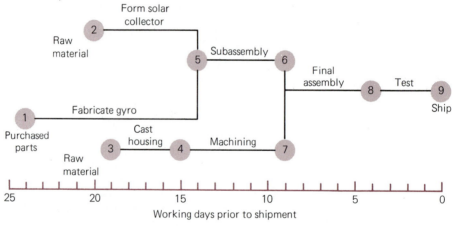

C. Progress as of June 30

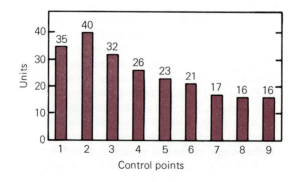

FIGURE 11–17

Constructing the Line of Balance

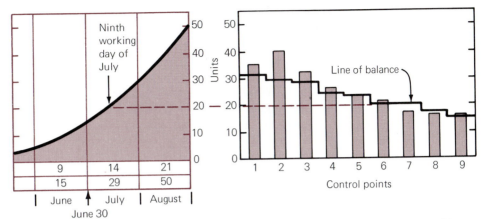

Cumulative delivery schedule

Progress and line of balance as of June 30

delivery schedule were a straight line, the LOB could be calculated by an easy algebraic procedure instead of graphically.)

Each month the officers at Solesource review progress on the solar-generator contract. The LOB chart is displayed at the monthly review meeting, and it serves as the focal point for discussion.

At the July 1 meeting the LOB of Figure 11–17 is displayed. The contract administrator points out the following to the officers:

1. Shipments, control point 9, are slightly ahead of schedule.
2. The solar subassembly, control points 1, 2, 5, and 6, is on or ahead of schedule.
3. Casting of the housing, control points 3 and 4, is ahead of schedule, but machining of the castings, control point 7, is behind.
4. Final assembly, control point 8, is a bit behind schedule. In fact, there are the same number of final assemblies completed (16) as there are shipments, even though four days of testing are required between final assembly and shipment.

It is clear to the officers that a potentially serious problem has arisen in machining. Castings are ahead of schedule, but the castings are not being machined on time. Furthermore, it appears that lack of machined castings is the reason why final assemblies have fallen behind schedule.

Two actions are needed. One is investigation to find out the cause of the machining delay. The second action, which depends on what is learned in the investigation, is to get machining and final assembly back on schedule. Overtime, hiring, expediting, or other actions may be taken. A more extreme measure is to change the process plan to provide more lead time for machining.

LOB Advantages

In the LOB technique there are usually more control points than in the above simplified example. With more control points the periodic review pinpoints problem areas more precisely. Two special advantages of LOB analysis are suggested by the example:

1. **LOB is simple and inexpensive.** The graphic simplicity makes LOB effective for management review meetings. Little effort and cost are needed to update the bar charts and construct the line of balance each month.

2. **LOB is future-oriented** (unlike most periodic reporting methods). A discrepancy between the LOB and the bar for a given control point is not a problem today; instead, it points to upcoming contract delivery problems if action is not taken now to get the earlier activity back on schedule. LOB analysis is aimed at forestalling future contract delivery failures.

SUMMARY

The program evaluation and review technique (PERT) and the critical-path method (CPM) are useful in planning and controlling projects. Both are based on a type of sequence chart called a network.

PERT/CPM consists of four subsystems: designing the network, path analysis, scheduling, and reporting and updating. Designing the network begins with planning project goals; the project plan may be displayed as a work breakdown structure (WBS). Task lists are then drawn up and arranged into networks. Networks may be activity-oriented for lower managers or event-oriented for high-level managers.

Time estimates may be collected for each network activity. Activity times for each of the paths through the network may be added up, and the sum for the most time-consuming path—called the *critical path*—is the estimated project duration. Path analysis also includes determining slack for each activity. Slack is the amount that an activity may be delayed without making the whole project late. Negative slack is possible, and in fact is common, especially on the critical path.

The project scheduling subsystem is aimed at determining due dates for each network event. If forward scheduling yields a late project completion time, certain activities may be "crashed." Crashing (cutting activity time) is done by spending more for resources, for example, overtime. Combinations of project times and costs may be produced via time-cost trade-off analysis. One time-cost alternative is selected, and the selected times are the basis for scheduling network events. Finally, organizations having a role in more than one project must fit in the scheduled project tasks so that their capacities are not overloaded.

The reporting and updating subsystem may come into play after the work begins. Reports are usually monthly or every two weeks. A basic report displays slack time for each activity, and the report lists most critical activities first, then next most critical activities, and so forth. The reports are valuable for replanning and rescheduling.

Each of the PERT/CPM subsystems is more costly than its predecessor. All four should be used only if project size, uncertainty, urgency, and complexity are sufficient to justify the cost.

Line-of-balance (LOB) analysis applies only to limited-quantity large-scale production, for example, a contract for 80 ballistic missiles. LOB analysis begins with a cumulative delivery schedule and a process plan in the form of a lead-time chart. Then, as the project progresses, line-of-balance charts are produced at periodic intervals, often monthly. A bar chart showing units completed for each control point on the process plan is developed, and the line of balance is laid on top of the bars. The line of balance, for a given control point, equals the cumulative deliveries that the contract calls for, LT (lead time for that control point) days into the future. Thus, the LOB shows future contract impacts of present progress. Discrepancies between the height of the LOB and the bars suggest the need for investigation and corrective action.

REFERENCES

Books

Harris, Robert B.   *Precedence and Arrow Networking Techniques for Construction.* New York: John Wiley & Sons, 1978 (TH438.H37).

Wiest, Jerome D., and Ferdinand K. Levy.   *A Management Guide to PERT/CPM.* 2d ed. Englewood Cliffs, N.J.: Prentice-Hall, 1977 (TS158.2.W53).

Periodicals (societies)

Project Management Quarterly (Project Management Institute); sometimes cataloged as a monograph series (HD69.P75p76) instead of a periodical.

REVIEW QUESTIONS

1. Why is a process-oriented WBS not recommended?
2. How is a WBS translated into a PERT/CPM network?
3. Why must we have dummy activities in networks?
4. Why is the network not a correct way to display activities (or tasks) occurring in repetitive production?

5. Why might a project manager prepare both an activity-oriented and an event-oriented network for the same project?

6. What is done with time estimates in PERT/CPM?

7. What is the purpose of path analysis in PERT/CPM?

8. What is the critical path?

9. Where and under what conditions is negative slack likely to be found?

10. What is a slack-sort report used for?

11. Why is the deterministic critical path likely to understate the project duration?

12. Why is it often sufficient for the project manager to develop the network but not carry the PERT/CPM technique any farther?

13. What data are needed to perform time-cost trade-off analysis, and where are the data obtained?

14. In the time-cost trade-off analysis procedure, why is it necessary to check to see what paths are critical after every change?

15. How are PERT/CPM data translated into scheduled jobs or tasks? Why might those scheduled task dates cause conflict for those who are to do the work?

16. Given the uncertainties inherent in R&D and construction projects, how can PERT/CPM adapt?

17. Why is PERT/CPM a costly system to administer?

18. What management role does the LOB technique play?

19. What does the line of balance show, and how is it used?

20. What are the uses of the cumulative delivery schedule and the process plan in the LOB technique?

PROBLEMS

1. Develop a product-oriented work breakdown structure for a nonconstruction project of your own choice. (Examples are a market research project, a political campaign, a disaster-relief project, a research and development project, and a large-scale computer-based information system development.) You may need to speculate about the nature of your chosen project—since most of us have little actual experience in large projects. In addition to drawing the WBS, explain the nature of your project. Show part of at least three levels on your WBS.

2. The R&D group of Home Products Company (HOPROCO) is developing a prototype for a new gasoline-powered lawn mower. The project is to be managed using PERT/CPM. Project activities include all design, manufacturing, and testing for the single prototype mower. The mower engine is to be designed and made by another firm, an engine manufacturer. All other major modules are to be designed and made by HOPROCO's own employees.

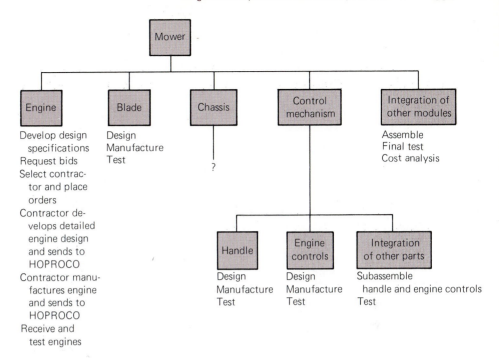

Engine

Develop design
  specifications
Request bids
Select contrac-
  tor and place
  orders
Contractor de-
  velops detailed
  engine design
  and sends to
  HOPROCO
Contractor manu-
  factures engine
  and sends to
  HOPROCO
Receive and
  test engines

Blade

Design
Manufacture
Test

Chassis

?

Control
mechanism

Integration of
other modules

Assemble
Final test
Cost analysis

Handle

Design
Manufacture
Test

Engine
controls

Design
Manufacture
Test

Integration
of other parts

Subassemble
  handle and engine controls
Test

a. A partial WBS and task lists are shown for the mower. One module, the chassis, has not been broken down into major parts and task lists. Your first assignment is to do this. You must decide, as best you can, what major parts the chassis would need to include. Then decide on tasks for each major part. Notice that the WBS is product oriented, except for an integration activity whenever there is a need to combine other modules or parts.

b. Some of the beginning and ending activities for the mower project are shown as a partial PERT/CPM network in the accompanying illustration. Network activities are taken from the task lists in the WBS. Your second assignment is to complete the network. (Note: Engine-design data are needed before certain HOPROCO tasks can begin. You must reason where this is the case and draw the network that way.)

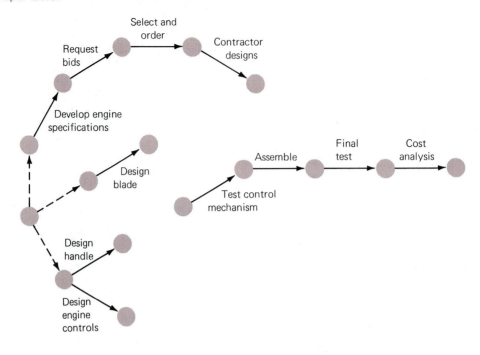

c. Some of the dummy activities in your network are not needed. Redraw portions of the network to show the elimination of all unnecessary dummy activities.

3. Explain the purpose of activity 16–13 in Figure 11–4.

4. You and several others have been appointed as a planning committee by the president of your social organization. It has been decided that in order to obtain additional funds for operating expenses you will produce a play (or a variety show). You have been asked to submit a plan for the next meeting. This plan is to include all of the activities or tasks that will have to be accomplished up to the opening of the play. Publicity, tickets, the printed program, and so on, as well as the staging for the production, should be part of the plan. It has already been decided that the scenery will be constructed in a member's garage and that the costumes will be rented.

   To facilitate presentation of the plan, a network diagram of about 30 activities is to be drawn. Brief descriptions of the activities should appear on the network diagram.

5. A manufacturer of tape and record players buys turntables from outside contractors. A new contract is to be awarded for a new style of turntable. The company has developed an activity-on-node network for the turntable project. The accompanying network includes an initial contract for turntable development and a second contract (assuming that the turntable tests are OK) for production. Redraw the network in the activity-on-arrow form.

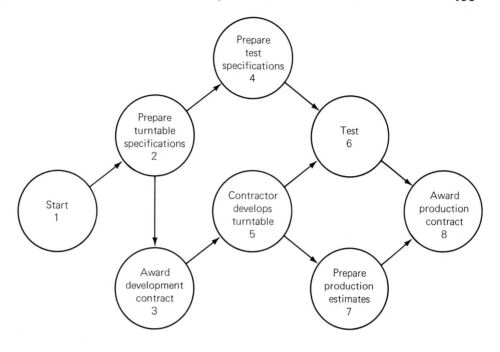

6. The manager for a project to develop a special antenna system is preparing a **PERT**-based project plan. Data for the plan are given below:

Activity number	Description	Expected time (days)
1–2	Design frame	4
1–3	Procure mechanism	5
2–4	Procure parts	1
3–4	Dummy	0
3–7	Determine repair requirements	4
4–6	Assemble	2
4–7	Hire maintenance crew	3
6–7	Test	1

a. Draw the network.
b. Compute and indicate the critical path.
c. Compute slack times for all activities, assuming that the project is scheduled for completion in the number of days on the critical path.
d. Five working days have passed, and status data have been received, as follows:
   (1) Activity 1–2 was completed in five days.
   (2) Activity 1–3 was completed in four days.
   (3) Activity 4–6 has been reestimated at four days.
   Based on the data, recompute the critical path and slack on all of the remaining project activities. (Assume no change in scheduled project completion dates.)

7. Aeropa, Inc., has a contract to develop a guided missile. A PERT/CPM network and activity times are given in the accompanying illustration. Times are in weeks.

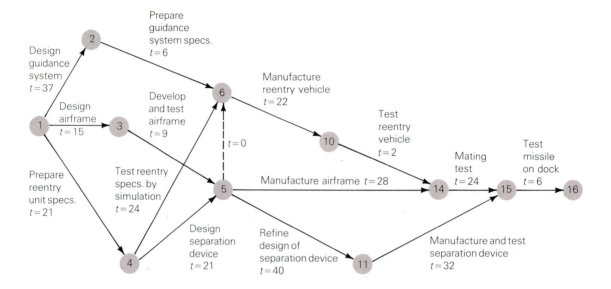

a. Compute ES, LS, and S for each activity. Assume that slack = 0 on the critical path. Identify the critical-path activities and the critical-path duration.

b. Draw a condensed event-oriented network with only five milestone events in it. The five events should be designated: 1. Start. 5. Shell specs completed. 6. Guidance specs completed. 14. Modules completed. 16. Missile tested.

Put activity times on the arrows between your events. Compute ES, LS, and S for each activity. Verify that the critical-path duration is the same as in part *a* above. What activity time goes on the arrow 1–6? Explain the difficulty in deciding on a time for this activity.

c. Assume the following project status at the end of week 50:

Activity	Actual duration
1–2	39
1–3	17
1–4	20
2–6	7
3–5	9
4–5	28
4–6	20

No other activities have been completed.

Develop a slack-sorted activity report similar to Figure 11–10 for the project as of the end of week 50. What is the new projected project duration?

8. Figure 11–11 shows a simulation of a simple network with equally possible activity times of 4, 5, or 6. In discussion of the figure it was stated that expected project duration increases to 5.8 for the five equally probable activity times—3, 4, 5, 6, and 7. Verify the figure 5.8.

9. A network consists of two activities that occur at the same time. Each is expected to take one, two, or three weeks to complete, and the probabilities of each of those possible times are 1/3, 1/3, and 1/3. What is the expected project duration based on the critical path? What is it based on PERT simulation?

10. A network consists of two activities that occur at the same time. Each is expected to take one or two months to complete, and the probabilities of each of those possible times are 1/2 and 1/2.
    a. What is the expected project duration based on the critical path? What is it based on PERT simulation?
    b. What would the expected project duration be using PERT simulation if the network had three instead of two activities, each with equally probable activity times of one or two months?

11. The following data have been collected for a certain project:

Activity		Normal		Crash	
Predecessor event	Successor event	Time (days)	Cost ($)	Time (days)	Cost ($)
1	2	6	250	5	360
2	3	2	300	1	480
2	4	1	100	1	100
2	5	7	270	6	470
3	4	2	120	1	200
4	5	5	200	1	440

    a. Draw the network.
    b. Compute and indicate the critical path and the normal project cost.
    c. Compute the slack time for each activity in the network, using 12 days as the project due date.
    d. Perform time-cost trade-off analysis, crashing down to the minimum possible project duration. Display each of the time-cost alternatives.

12. Normal and crash data are given below for the accompanying network. Compute all time-cost options. Which is best if there is a $40 per day penalty for every day beyond a seven-day project duration?[8]

---

[8] Adapted from J. S. Sayer, J. E. Kelly, Jr., and M. R. Walker, "Critical Path Scheduling," *Factory*, July 1960.

	Normal		Crash	
Activity	Days	Cost	Days	Cost
A	3	$ 50	2	$ 100
B	6	140	4	260
C	2	25	1	50
D	5	100	3	180
E	2	80	2	80
F	7	115	5	175
G	4	100	2	240
		$610		$1,085

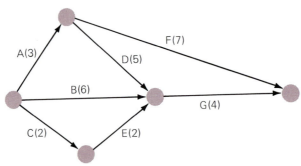

13. *a.* For the accompanying network, what is the critical path and expected project duration? What is the second most critical path and its duration?

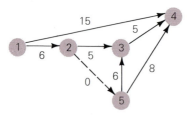

b. What is the largest that the time value may be for activity 3–4 to be sure that it is not a critical-path activity? (Ignore the present time of 6 days for that activity in answering the question.)

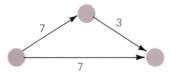

14. *a.* For the accompanying network, if there is positive slack of +6 on the upper path, what is the slack on the lower path?

    b. If the slack is −4 on the upper path, what is the slack on the lower path?

15. *a.* For the accompanying network, if there is slack of +5 on the lower path, what is the slack on the upper path?

    b. If there is slack of +1 on the upper path, what is the slack on the lower path?

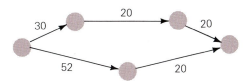

16.

	Normal		"Crash"	
Activity	Time	Cost	Time	Cost
1–2	2	$10	1	$15
2–3	6	8	5	18
2–4	2	15	1	21
2–5	8	30	6	52
4–3	2	7	2	7
3–5	3	21	1	33
1–5	8	20	5	41

    a. For the accompanying time-and-cost table, what is the least costly way to reduce the project time by one day? (You may wish to draw the network for better visualization of the problem.)

    b. What is the least costly way to reduce the expected project duration by three days (i.e., "crash" the project by three days)?

17.

	Normal		"Crash"	
Activity	Time	Cost	Time	Cost
1–2	6	$100	5	$205
1–4	17	200	12	600
2–3	5	100	4	190
3–4	5	150	3	360
5–3	6	80	5	185
5–4	8	300	7	360

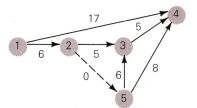

    a. For the accompanying network and time-and-cost table, what is the least costly way to reduce ("crash") the project by one day?

    b. What is the fastest that the project could be done if you used crash times?

18. A number of kinds of projects are listed below. The projects range from small and simple to grand. As is indicated in Figure 11–15, modest projects warrant only the first PERT/CPM subsystem, whereas grand projects warrant all four subsystems; in-between projects warrant subsystems 1 and 2 or subsystems 1, 2, and 3. Decide which subsystems should apply for each of the listed projects. Explain each.

    Computer selection and installation for company of 200 employees.

    Moving the computer facility for a large bank to a new building in a major city.

    Moving the computer facility (same size as bank's) to a new building at a major university.

    Community project to attract new industry in three large abandoned factory buildings (town of 10,000 people).

    Five-year overhaul of a nuclear submarine.

    Implementing MRP in a manufacturing company of 1,000 employees.

    New product development and testing (including market research) for a major food company.

    Moving an army division from one closed-down post to a new one in another state.

    Planning an NCAA-sponsored national sports championship event.

    Building a 500-room hotel in Lincoln, Nebraska.

    Building a 500-room hotel in Manhattan.

19. The accompanying network segments are all part of the same home-construction project. Where is a dummy activity needed, and why?

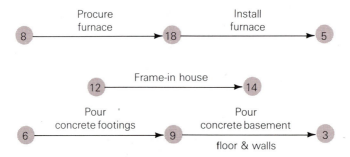

20. A firm contracts to manufacture a fixed number of theater televisions. The lead time for starting the picture tube testing is four weeks. The first six are supposed to be delivered four weeks from today, and today three picture tubes are ready for testing. Where is the line of balance for "begin picture tube testing"? How far behind or ahead of schedule is that task?

21. A firm making modular homes uses the LOB system. In two weeks the firm should have delivered 25 completed homes, and now 20 are framed in (and ready for interior finishing). If the lead time for frame completion is two weeks, where will the line of balance be on today's LOB chart for that control point (i.e., "home framed in")? How

many units ahead or behind schedule are they for the same control point? (Hint: The first step is to consider the cumulative delivery schedule requirements.)

22. On February 1, 1984, Global Associates, Inc., was awarded a contract to produce 130 Doppler search units. The contract calls for completion by the end of December 1985. Lead-time information was developed by company engineers. It is shown in the accompanying lead-time chart.

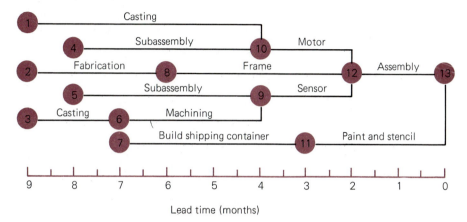

Lead time (months)

The following delivery schedule has been agreed upon:

Month (1985)	Deliveries	Month (1985)	Deliveries
January	2	July	12
February	4	August	14
March	5	September	16
April	7	October	18
May	9	November	17
June	11	December	15

a. It is now one year later (February 1985). The following status information has just been received:

Control point	Completions	Control point	Completions
1	90	8	64
2	80	9	18
3	72	10	20
4	100	11	15
5	80	12	8
6	72	13	0
7	64		

Use graph paper to plot the delivery schedule, plot the status information in the form of a bar chart, and lay down the line of balance.

b. What areas need corrective action, and why?

23. A contract calls for delivery of five swamp buggies per week for 30 weeks. The process plan is shown below. (Note: Deliveries begin in week 9 since there is a nine-week lead time. Therefore the total contract covers 39 weeks.)

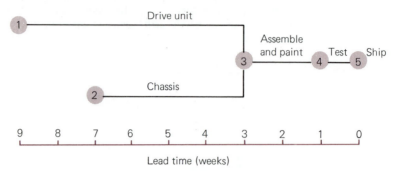

Lead time (weeks)

a. Calculate the line-of-balance quantity for each of the five control points as of the end of the 19th week (in the 39-week contract period). If a completion report shows that 50 swamp buggies have been assembled and painted after 19 weeks, what is your assessment of the assembly and paint operation?

b. The delivery schedule makes it easy to calculate line-of-balance quantities. Is this form of delivery schedule realistic? Discuss briefly.

Chapter 12

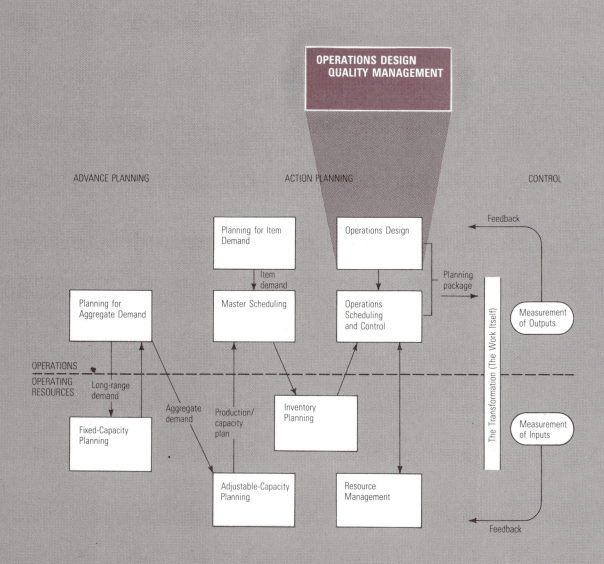

Quality Management

Quality. What is it? A good answer (in the words of Joseph Juran) is, "Quality is fitness for use." That definition pulls in all aspects of quality management, from the "gleam in the customer's eye," to design and production, to delivery, use and customer service.

QUALITY: ART AND SCIENCE

Quality management is part art and part science. The artful or subjective side is interpreting what the customer wants and will pay for. Of course, there are often different kinds of customers for a type of product. Some will pay top dollar for the very best, and others look for lesser cost-quality combinations. Deciding on which segments to appeal to depends broadly on the company's competitive strategy; and it depends narrowly on the nature of the product, the demand, and the capability to produce the desired quality at the right price. Based on these factors, the product and its performance characteristics are decided.

Different designs will meet the performance characteristics: perhaps build out of plastic, glass, or metal; forge or weld; punch or drill. Here science—rational decision making—begins. Value analysis (discussed in an earlier chapter) is a systematic way to judge the merits of different designs while cutting costs. Finally, design specifications are set, or at least critical specifications are.

Making a product that conforms to the specifications is also, largely, science: controlling the process through the science of quality control. Process control failures may be found by inspecting and testing items already made.

Quality management also includes careful packing and shipping, servicing of goods already sold, and handling warranty claims. These are, again, more art than science.

These aspects of quality management may be coordinated by a **quality assurance** (QA) department, sometimes called **quality control** (QC) instead. But having a QA department is no guarantee of assuring quality, as is explained below.

THE QUALITY-ASSURANCE FUNCTION

Quality assurance was once in the hands of the craftsperson. The industrial revolution brought about the factory system and labor specialization, which serve to increase output and decrease cost. But sometimes the factory worker, office and human services "factories" included, loses touch with the quality of the end product or service.

An early solution was to inspect after the product was made or the service provided. Inspection became a specialty. Inspectors identified defectives, which could be removed before passing the work on to the next process or to the end user. But relying on inspectors lets the maker off the hook, and concern for quality by those making the parts begins to erode. In many companies, quality fell apart. Consumers began to scream.

Consumerism

Increased public interest in product quality and safety began in the mid-1960s. Contributing to that interest were Ralph Nader, the Consumer Federation of America and its affiliates, action-line columns in the newspapers, and investigative TV and newspaper journalists. In 1965, the American Law Institute issued its "Restatement of the Law of Torts," which defined *strict liability:* making manufacturers liable for product defects even without proof of negligence. In 1972 the U.S. Congress passed the Consumer Product Safety Act, which aims at preventing hazardous or defective products from reaching the consumer. Some companies extended their product warranties in the 1970s, but newspaper stories about massive product recalls seemed to say that quality on the warranty paper was not quality in fact. At the same time, in affluent nations large numbers of a new and demanding type of consumer were emerging: the consumer of average means who prefers to do without rather than pay for second best. Neglected crafts like handweaving, the stone-grinding of flour, and the creation of stained-glass windows resurged. Consumers once again sought the quality of the earlier age of the craftsperson.

FIRST, YOU HAVE TO HAVE QUALITY TO CONTROL!

Competition

With higher demands for quality, North American industry went on the defensive. Industry tended to react to consumer complaints and legal and regulatory challenges as they occurred. But in the 1980s, the quality emphasis has shifted to the offensive. The impetus is competition. A heavy amount of it has come from Japan, where quality improvement has been spectacular. The competition also comes from Germany and certain other European countries where quality has been steadily good for many years. We may consider German quality management first, then Japanese, and finally North American.

Quality in Germany.   Causes and effects are not easy to pin down in regard to Germany's consistently high quality. Limprecht and Hayes cite fuzzy factors such as German determination to "get everything 'just right' " and insistence "that what goes out the door of their factories be as close to perfect as possible."[1] The two authors argue, however, that these are not cultural traits but rather are based on imitable industrial practices. One of these practices is managerial pursuit of **technical strength.** Technical strength serves as a marketing asset that is more enduring than the quick sale based on special options, colors, or styles. A second practice is an extensive apprenticeship system. In this system most young people go from school into a full-time three-year apprentice program by age 16. Industry provides most of the training, with the support of labor and government.

Quality in Japan.   A massive effort to upgrade product quality has been going on in Japan since the late 1940s. Japan had lost the war and needed capital to rebuild its bombed-out industries and put people back to work. Lacking natural resources to sell, Japan could obtain capital only through exports. But at that time Japanese export goods were held in low regard by the rest of the world. To make a long story short, allied occupation forces, plus two U.S. experts, W. Edwards Deming and Joseph P. Juran, began teaching quality control to the Japanese, and today nearly everyone, from production worker to chief executive officer, is knowledgeable in quality control techniques. The result is that Japan has become dominant in numerous quality-sensitive international markets. Good quality also avoids the high costs of rework, scrap, extra inventories, warranty work; bad feelings and finger-pointing within the firm; and loss of customers. These factors translate into lower prices for Japanese goods and a healthy environment for further improvements.

Quality in North America.   It took a long time for North America to catch on. An awakening seems to have started in the current decade. Training of our managers and foremen in quality concepts began on a large scale. Deming and Juran—both in their 80s—became esteemed at home as they had long been in Japan. They and other quality experts have been conducting intensive QA courses for industry all over North America. Just how far and fast we have come is evidenced by a statement

---

[1] Joseph A. Limprecht and Robert H. Hayes, "Germany's World-Class Manufacturers," *Harvard Business Review,* November–December 1982, pp. 137–45.

made at a Chicago seminar on Japanese management techniques in early 1983. The quality manager at F. D. Farnam, a supplier of gaskets and seals to the auto industry, stated that in his company there were cases of production workers running formal training in statistical process control for other production workers.

Thus it appears that Western industry has launched its own assault on bad quality. Responsibilities and practices are changing in order to make the assault successful, as is explained next.

Quality at the Source

In 1961, A. V. Feigenbaum, an American, stated in his book, *Total Quality Control,* that "the burden of proof for quality rests with the makers of the part."[2] Japanese industry uses Feigenbaum's title, **total quality control,** or TQC, as the name of its quality movement. But the meaning of the quotation was changed slightly to make it work: The *responsibility for* quality rests with the makers of the part. That is, in TQC primary responsibility for quality goes to the production department, and all others, including the quality control department itself, have secondary responsibility. The popular slogan, "Quality at the source," describes this vesting of primary responsibility with the line production people.

Principles. What should production do with that responsibility? The answers, in TQC, are found in these principles:

1. Design error-proof machines or machines with automatic checking devices, and keep equipment in perfect condition.
2. Make every work station a quality control point, cutting the chance of bad products passing onward.
3. Where inspection is necessary, inspect every piece right after it is made.
4. Where defects are not found out until a later process—or until the end consumer uses the product—provide for fast feedback right to the makers of the product or component.
5. Give each worker the authority to stop production—even a whole production line—to avoid making a bad product.
6. Make every work group responsible for correcting its own defects; if at all feasible, send defective but repairable batches back to where they were made (rather than to separate rework crews).
7. Provide enough time to do the job right. (This is the "under-capacity-scheduling" concept, which is also a just-in-time production practice.)
8. Train supervisors and workers in how to measure quality, to collect quality data, and to analyze quality statistics in order to isolate causes of defects.
9. Formally organize workers and supervisors into quality-improvement projects or quality control circles—to apply data analysis and problem-solving techniques.

---

[2] A. V. Feigenbaum, *Total Quality Control: Engineering and Management* (New York: McGraw-Hill, 1961).

FIGURE 12–1

Process Control and Quality Information Feedback

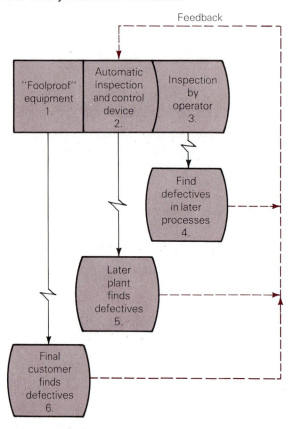

Principles 1 through 4 describe levels of process control. Figure 12–1 explodes the four into six. First and most effective—the ideal—is building quality into the equipment. The Japanese word, *pokayoke,* meaning foolproof, is a good descriptor. Second are automatic inspection and control devices attached to the process. Third is inspection by the operator, which, of course, introduces chances of human error. Fourth is finding defectives in a later process in the same plant. Fifth is finding defectives in a later plant. And sixth is the final customer finding defectives.

The last three involve feedback delay; the trail begins to grow cold. Fast feedback about the defect, once it is found, can keep the trail from getting too cold—so the error can be corrected before too many bad products are made.

Role of Quality Department. With "quality at the source" is there a need for a quality department? Yes. All of the major Japanese manufacturers have them (as do Western manufacturers). Their roles include helping to get ideas for quality improvement implemented, performing final product testing, providing quality control training, conducting onsite audits of quality at supplier plants, and auditing quality in their own plants.

By contrast, North American quality departments traditionally have focused on the inspections themselves. The department chose where inspections were to be done, and inspectors were sent out to draw samples and conduct the tests. There never were enough inspectors to inspect at every process, so the department also selected which processes would be inspection points.

Now that TQC is thriving in North America, the quality assurance department's role is changing. A major job for many years surely will be training, because there are so many to train, and the QA people have the know-how to do it. There may be some resistance to a sudden shift of primary responsibility for quality to the production department. But roles such as quality auditing and training are in some ways more prestigious for the QA people than actual inspecting. Some QA people may welcome their new role, which includes training everybody in the techniques of quality control and improvement, considered next.

QUALITY CONTROL AND PROCESS IMPROVEMENT

Improving a product or service means going through cycles of measuring, controlling for consistency, and improving the process; measuring, controlling, improving; and so forth. These cycles should never end, but the amount of measurement may decrease over time, and the measurement procedure should become simpler. The whole process should improve. This can mean less scrap, less labor content, fewer equipment failures, better tooling, and, of course, better quality of the part itself. In the past, we tended to divorce control of product quality from control and improvement of other process variables. Today there is better understanding of the close linkages among the process variables and the tools for improving them.

Improvement Cycle

As an example, consider the excess plastic, called "flash," that must be trimmed off plastic parts coming out of an injection molding machine. Collect and weigh the flash for every piece. If the weight of flash per piece is trending up or down, or there are occasional pieces with a great amount of flash (or none at all), then there is no consistency. The injection molding process is out of control.

Bringing it under control means searching for a **special cause.** Perhaps the machine is experiencing heat buildup, which might explain an increasing amount of flash. Perhaps the hopper gets low on raw material now and then, which might explain an extreme value. Or perhaps the person running the machine has a bad habit, like adjusting the timer once in awhile instead of leaving it alone; that also could explain an extreme value. Whatever the special cause, it must be found and eliminated. Verify its removal by weighing more pieces. When consistency has been attained, there will still be some variability in the weights of flash from piece to piece, but normal variability arises from **common causes** instead of special causes.

When the process is in control, we may want to cut back on the number of pieces checked. Perhaps weighing flash for a sample of five pieces every hour will be enough to see if the process is staying in control.

During the time the process is in control, thought should be given to improving the process. Note that *control* is not a measure of quality level, but of consistency. Improving the quality level of the process requires a good idea, and a management decision to implement it. The solution may be to improve the mold, install a more precise raw material feeding device, or buy a better grade of raw plastic pellets. Or maybe the worker is consistent, but not a good injection molding machine operator— even after becoming fully trained to run it; the answer may be to assign another person to the job.

After implementing an idea for improving the process, the flash again should be weighed for every piece for a time to assure consistency. This time, perhaps an automatic weighing device can do the weighing, which saves money on human inspection and avoids human inspector error, and makes 100 percent inspection (every piece) possible for the long run. Automated 100 percent inspection can be a powerful quality-control tool—one that has been instrumental in some companies in producing strings of defect-free parts numbering into the hundreds of thousands.

Repeat the cycle, and keep repeating it. We always want the process to be better than it is, and we can never achieve perfection. But we keep trying.

What Was Improved?

In improving the injection molding process, was product quality improved? No. We didn't mention the plastic part being made, or its specifications. It was the flash or waste that was the center of attention. Cutting the flash lowered the product cost by reducing the amount of material consumed per unit of product made. And labor per unit to check for and trim off flash may have been reduced, too. It may be that product quality improved as a by-product of reducing the amount of flash. For example, if heat buildup were avoided as a way to reduce flash, the plastic piece may also end up with a smoother finish or more uniform dimensions. The point is that the technique is for controlling and improving the *process*.

Now the example is changed a bit to make product quality the foremost concern.

Conformance to Specifications

Assume that the specifications for the part being made in the injection molding machine call for an outer diameter of 5.0, plus or minus 0.05, centimeters. The 5.0 cm. is the desired dimension, and the plus or minus 0.05 cm. is the tolerance. What kind of quality control technique should be used? The answer is to do just about what was described for controlling and reducing flash. This time the example will show how two types of charts are used. The two are a **run diagram** and **statistical process control (SPC)** charts. The example is long, but that is because there are several phases of quality measurement and improvement to explain.

EXAMPLE 12–1

Quality Control, Injection-Molded Parts

Specifications: Outer diameter = 5.00 cm., ±0.05 cm.

Quality control objective: Continually improve quality and productivity and continually reduce fraction of injection-molded parts that do not meet the specifications, i.e., that do not stay within the tolerances (plus or minus 0.05 cm.). Pursuit of the objective takes us through a six-phase cycle of improvement—and then repeats.

Phase 1. Operator measures every piece; plots results on a *run diagram*. Figure 12–2 shows the outer diameters of 30 pieces plotted on the run diagram. Pieces 7 and 23 look way out of line, and there is also a trend downward. The process is out of control—not consistent.

FIGURE 12–2

Run Diagram, Outer Diameters of 30 Pieces

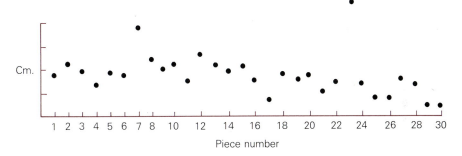

Cm.

Piece number

Phase 2. Operator and supervisor look for special causes; correct them (may need to call maintenance, engineering, etc., for help). The operator *knows* why the diameters are decreasing: heat buildup (same thing mentioned earlier as a possible cause of excess flash). Maintenance is called in to work on the thermostat. The supervisor thinks he knows the cause of bad pieces 7 and 23: impurities in the raw material. The solution is to put a sheet of clear plastic over the containers of plastic pellets so that people walking by will not think the open box is a trash receptacle.

Phase 3. New run diagram. Figure 12–3 shows 30 more measures. They look consistent, so no need to measure every piece any more. Most of the diameters are greater than 5.0 cm., the specification, but that is not the concern yet.

FIGURE 12–3

Run Diagram, Outer Diameters of 30 More Pieces

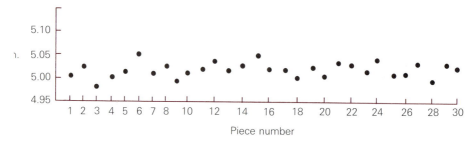

Phase 4. Use sampling and SPC charts. Figure 12–4 gives mean diameters and ranges for 20 samples. The sample size is four pieces, and a sample is drawn and plotted hourly. The means tell whether the diameters are abnormally high or low. The ranges tell whether the consistency is still OK. Note: The range is simply the highest minus the lowest of the four measures in a sample. (Standard deviation is a better measure of consistency, but it

FIGURE 12–4

Measurements for Designing $\bar{x}$ and R Charts

Sample number	Date	Measurements (cm.)				Mean ($\bar{x}$)	Range (R)
		x_1	x_2	x_3	x_4		
1	10/10	5.01	5.00	5.03	5.06	5.025	0.06
2		4.99	5.03	5.03	5.05	5.025	0.06
3		5.03	5.04	4.99	4.94	5.000	0.10
4		5.05	5.03	5.00	5.01	5.022	0.05
5		4.97	5.04	4.96	5.00	4.992	0.08
6		4.97	5.00	4.99	5.02	4.995	0.05
7		5.06	5.00	5.02	4.96	5.010	0.10
8		5.03	4.98	5.01	4.95	4.992	0.08
9	10/11	5.05	5.03	5.05	4.98	5.028	0.07
10		4.99	5.03	5.01	4.96	4.998	0.07
11		4.98	5.05	5.05	4.94	5.005	0.11
12		4.95	5.04	4.99	4.99	4.992	0.09
13		5.00	5.05	5.01	4.97	5.008	0.08
14		4.96	5.03	5.05	5.00	5.010	0.09
15		5.08	5.01	5.02	4.96	5.018	0.12
16		5.02	4.98	5.04	4.95	4.998	0.09
17	10/12	5.02	4.99	4.99	5.04	5.010	0.05
18		4.99	5.00	5.05	5.05	5.022	0.06
19		5.03	5.02	5.01	4.96	5.005	0.07
20		5.02	5.04	5.04	5.04	5.040	0.02
Totals						100.195	1.50

takes more calculations. The range has always been used instead in SPC work, because it is simple and quick.)

Now some calculations are necessary in order to create SPC charts. Results of some of the calculations are given in Figure 12–4. The mean, $\bar{x}$, is the simple average of the four units in the sample. Thus, for sample 1,

$$\bar{x}_1 = \frac{\Sigma x}{n} = \frac{5.06 + 5.00 + 5.03 + 5.01}{4} = 5.025$$

The range, R, is the largest minus the smallest of the four units in each sample. For sample 1, the largest is 5.06; the smallest is 5.00. So,

$$R_1 = 5.06 - 5.00 = 0.06$$

Next step is calculating control limits. In SPC the limits are set at three standard deviations (3σ) above and below the mean. (The Greek letter sigma, σ, is the symbol for standard deviation.) The confidence interval between control limits at $\pm3\sigma$ is 99.7 percent. What this means is that 99.7 percent of the sample means are expected to fall within the control limits and that only 0.3 percent, or 3 out of 1,000, are expected to fall outside the limits—if the process quality has not changed. With such wide control limits, if a sample plots outside them, the process appears to be out of control—not consistent. If so, go back to searching for a special cause, and remove it; then begin sampling again to build new SPC charts.

The 3σ control limits are calculated with the aid of a value from a table. The means, $\bar{x}$, of sample measurements of a wide variety of phenomena are known to be normally distributed (they describe a bell-shaped frequency distribution). We mention this because the reader may wonder where the tables come from that are used in calculating the 3σ limits. The tables were derived from the basic mathematics of the normal distribution and of the special distribution of ranges. For the $\bar{x}$ chart the "A" table is used. A factor from the A table times the average range, $\bar{R}$, serves as an estimate of 3σ. Symbolically,

$$A\bar{R} = 3\sigma,$$

where

A = A factor from the A table that is related to sample size, n
$\bar{R}$ = Average (mean) range for the samples
σ = Sigma, the Greek letter commonly used to represent standard deviation

From the data in Figure 12–4, the sum of the ranges for the 20 samples is 1.50. Therefore, where m = number of samples, the mean range is

$$\bar{R} = \frac{\Sigma R}{m} = \frac{1.50}{20} = 0.075 \text{ cm.}$$

The A-factors are given in Table 12–1. The A-factor for a sample size, n, of 4 is 0.729. Then, our estimate of 3σ is:

$$A\bar{R} = (0.729)(0.075) = 0.055$$

TABLE 12–1

Factors for Computing 3σ Control Limits

Number of observations in sample, n	A-factors for control limits about the mean	B-factors for UCL for range	C-factors for LCL for range
4	0.729	2.282	0
5	0.577	2.115	0
6	0.483	2.004	0
7	0.419	1.924	0.076
8	0.373	1.864	0.136
9	0.337	1.816	0.184
10	0.308	1.777	0.223

One more piece of data, the center line of the $\bar{x}$ charts, is needed. The mean of the sample measures is the sum of the sample means, 100.195 (from Figure 12–4), divided by the number of sample means, m:[3]

$$\bar{\bar{x}} = \frac{\Sigma \bar{x}}{m} = \frac{100.195}{20} = 5.010$$

Control limits above and below $\bar{\bar{x}}$ are:

Upper control limit $(UCL_{\bar{x}}) = \bar{\bar{x}} + A\bar{R}$
Lower control limit $(LCL_{\bar{x}}) = \bar{\bar{x}} - A\bar{R}$

Since $\bar{\bar{x}} = 5.010$ and $A\bar{R} = 0.055$,

$$UCL_{\bar{x}} = 5.010 + 0.055 = 5.065$$
$$LCL_{\bar{x}} = 5.010 - 0.055 = 4.955$$

Next is the R chart. The center line is $\bar{R}$, which we have found to be 0.075. The control limits, at $\pm 3\sigma$, are easily computed using the B- and C-factors from Table 12–1:

$$UCL_R = B\bar{R}$$
$$LCL_R = C\bar{R}$$

For $n = 4$ Table 12–1 gives $B = 2.282$ and $C = 0$. Then,

$$UCL_R = (2.282)(0.075) = 0.171$$
$$LCL_R = (0)(0.075) = 0.0$$

---

[3] The double bar over the x indicates that this is the grand mean, or the mean of the 20 sample means. A simpler way to calculate the mean of the entire group of 80 measurements is to total them and divide the total by 80; a slightly different answer results from this method. Why do it the hard way? The reason is the central limit theorem, which the reader may have encountered in statistics studies. The theorem says that, regardless of how data in the population are distributed, the grand mean of sample means from that population will be normally distributed. The SPC tables (e.g., the A table) used to compute estimates of 3σ are based on an assumed normal distribution, and $\bar{x}$ is used in order to assure a normal distribution.

FIGURE 12–5

$\bar{x}$ and R Charts, including Plotted Data

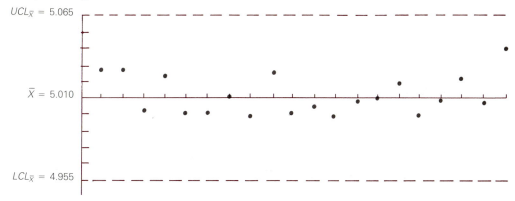
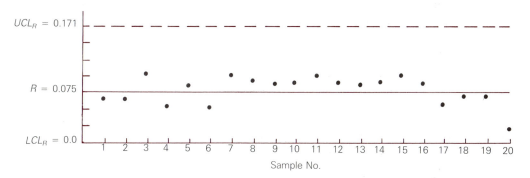

The $\bar{x}$ and R charts are drawn as shown in Figure 12–5, and the 20 samples are plotted on the charts. Since all points are within the control limits on both charts, the process looks to be in control. That is, the charts tell us what the quality of the process is. "The control chart is the process talking to us."[4]

Phase 5. Cease sampling. If SPC charts continue to show that the process is in control, there may be no need to keep it up. However, measurement and plotting on SPC charts should still be done on an audit basis occasionally in order to make sure that the process does not stray out of control. There are exceptions, of course. If defectives absolutely cannot be tolerated—such as checking radiation levels in containers of materials coming out of a nuclear power plant—then inspection must continue. But probably in that case quality control would never be relaxed to the SPC phase; instead measuring 100 percent of items—perhaps automatically—and plotting on run diagrams would remain in force.

---

[4] I. W. Burr, *Engineering Statistics and Quality Control* (New York: McGraw-Hill, 1953).

Phase 6. Improve the process. This is *not* the same as removing a special cause of inconsistent quality (e.g., defective thermostat or raw material contamination). It is a wholesale improvement, usually requiring improved grade of raw material, mold, fixtures, tools, or equipment—or, possibly, a design change. These changes may be recommended by production employees, but usually some management action is needed to make the change occur. Management decides on how much to spend to improve the process and how quickly to make the change.

Now, finally, the issue of meeting design specifications arises. In Figure 12–4 the first *x* value, 5.01 cm., exceeds the 5.00 cm. specification, but it is within the ±0.05 cm. tolerance. However, if we look at more of the data in Figure 12–4, we see that five samples out of 80 are outside of the tolerance limits: In sample 1, x_4 is 0.01 cm. too large; in sample 3, x_4 is 0.01 cm. too small; in sample 7, x_1 is too large; in sample 11, x_4 is too large; and in sample 15, x_1 is too large. Five out of 80 "off-spec" parts is a defective rate of 6.25 percent, which seems poor. Perhaps management will choose to place a high priority on improving the process.

What if the process is improved to the point that *no* parts are off-spec? That is not possible. There will always be some fraction, however small, defective or off-spec. Therefore, process improvement never ends. But of course the urgency and pressure to improve lessens as defectives drop, especially if your quality is better than your competitor's.

Each time the process is improved a new round of run diagrams and SPC is called for, because the improvement may introduce some new inconsistency. A special cause of the inconsistency must be rooted out before the next round of process improvement is begun.

Overview of Process Control

The process-control phases that we have just seen may now be summarized, with comments about reasons why. The phases are:

1. Operator measures every piece and plots results on a run diagram. The purpose is to see if the process is in control, i.e., is consistent.

2. Operator and supervisor look for special causes of inconsistency and correct them. The purpose is not to control the *level* of quality but to make sure the quality is steady with only random ups and downs resulting from common causes.

3. Repeat phase 1 to see that the change has truly erased the inconsistency.

4. Relax the frequency of measurement. Take small samples (like 4, 5, or 6 pieces) and average the results. Plot on $\bar{x}$ and R charts. The $\bar{x}$ chart plots the mean level of quality. The R chart plots the range of variability within a sample, which is the consistency check. As long as no points are plotted above upper control limit or below lower control limit on both charts, the process is presumed to be in control.

5. Cease sampling, but reintroduce it periodically to see that the process has not strayed out of control.

6. Improve the process, which usually takes a management decision to spend money for better resources or designs. Management is eager to spend the money if the defect rate is high, i.e., a high percent of pieces that are not within specified tolerances. Once the process has been improved, repeat the above phases.

The philosophy behind this six-phase procedure is what Juran calls "the precious habit of improvement." Get the process consistent, then improve it; get it consistent, then improve it; and so forth. Keep it up for the life of the part. Why? Because every defective is bad; it costs money, causes the customer (if any) problems, and results in losses in customer (if any) goodwill. The "if any's" in the preceding sentence are there because sometimes it is the quality of the product going to a customer that is being improved, and other times the goal is cost or waste reduction (for example, the earlier example of reducing flash).

The reader might wonder why it is necessary to bring the process under control before improving it. One reason is that special causes are severe, and it is urgent to correct them. A second reason is that trying out new ideas for improving the process—new chemical formulations, new fixtures, new source of raw materials—may yield phony results if special causes are still present. For example, using a higher grade of plastic beads to reduce flash may not work if the thermostat on the injection molding machine is defective. The flash may actually worsen and make it seem that the new raw materials are the cause!

Thus process control is the first order of business. Deming quotes William E. Conway (president of Nashua Corp.) as noting that "engineers and chemists then become innovative, creative toward improvement, once they see that the process is in statistical control. They sense that further improvement is up to them."[5]

What about Low-Volume Production?

Does the process improvement philosophy just described apply to low-volume production—the pure job shop? The answer is, yes and no. Assuring quality in such a case is more prevention than cure:

1. Run diagrams and SPC charts are important for the *suppliers* of raw materials, parts, tools, and equipment. The purchasing department for the job shop should try to select suppliers who are willing to certify "quality at the source" and demonstrate that they use TQC techniques.

2. A high level of equipment, tool, and die maintenance is important to prevent errors caused by mechanical defects.

3. The tradespeople in the job shop should be treated as craftspeople, who would naturally take personal pride in good work. The craftsperson gets good results by following accepted procedures (there's a right and a wrong way even to pound a nail). Use of gauges and other measurement devices is often a part of the craftsperson's training.

4. In controlling the process for a small lot, a typical procedure is for the operator to do a *first-piece inspection* using a proper gauge. If the piece is not within tolerances,

---

[5] W. Edwards Deming, *Quality, Productivity, and Competitive Position* (Cambridge: Massachusetts Institute of Technology, Center for Advanced Engineering Study, 1982), p. 121.

adjust the machine. Then another first-piece inspection. When the process succeeds in making a good piece, inspection may cease until the *last piece*. Gauge the last one, and if it is good, the presumption is that the process did not stray off course, e.g., the tool did not lose its sharp edge. A widespread and not quite so effective practice is to do the first-piece but skip the last-piece inspection.

In the future, with the trend toward flexible automation, the craftsperson may become more a machine programmer than an operator. In flexible manufacturing cells complex metal, plastic, or ceramic parts may be made in one-piece lots without stopping. With no pauses for possible inspection the TQC concept of controlling the processes becomes even more vital. Product designers, machine-tool designers and makers, machine maintainers, and raw material buyers will then have nearly all of the responsibility for making sure the process is capable of making good products.

Process Control for Attributes

Is it necessary actually to *measure* the output of a process? Can't we just judge a piece good or bad without recording how many grams or centimeters or ohms? Certainly we can. The battery tester with a red zone and a green zone is just such a tester. We do not care to measure the voltage. Similarly we test a night light by putting it into a socket and flipping the switch. It either lights, or it doesn't. We are not taking a reading of lumens or footcandles. A table setting in a fancy restaurant may be checked by the headwaiter. If one fork or glass is out of place, the headwaiter may judge the table setting to be defective. Diameters of ball bearings could be checked by rolling them across a hole-filled surface. Those that fall through are too small; no one has measured their diameters.

This type of yes-no, go-no go, or good-bad testing is known as **attribute inspection,** whereas taking an actual measurement is called **variables inspection.** Attribute inspection is not powerful since a yes-no judgment yields little information about the process. By contrast, measurement of a variable tells us *how* good the process is. Although variables inspection is usually best, attribute inspection has the advantage of being easy to do and does have its place as a process control technique.

Attribute inspection operates a bit differently from variables measurement. For one thing, there is no piece-by-piece run diagram in attribute inspection. Instead, the fraction or percent defective out of a sample is the logical unit of analysis. That is, collect a few, check them, and plot the fraction defective; collect a few more, check, plot; and so forth. The points plotted may be averaged and nested between an upper control limit (UCL) and a lower control limit (LCL). The chart is called a *p* **chart,** for percent defective, or a *c* **chart,** for number of defects per unit. The SPC phases of checking for consistency; eliminating special causes; checking; and improving the process may follow.

Now another reason why variables measurement is more powerful may be mentioned: A variable may be measured right after the piece is made, which permits very close monitoring of the process for consistency. But inspection for an attribute awaits the accumulation of a group large enough to reasonably judge the percent (or fraction) defective, and that builds in some delay between making an error and discovering it. Thus, true process control is less of a reality with attribute inspection. Nevertheless, it has its uses. Let us consider an example.

EXAMPLE 12–2

Attribute Inspection, Light Bulbs

There are many operations in the manufacture of a light bulb. There are hundreds of process variables that could be inspected for. It might be economical to formally inspect for some of them: Perhaps the width of filament-wire samples could be measured, and perhaps the strength of glass-bulb samples could be tested by applying measured degrees of force to the glass surfaces. But a likely final test of samples of completed bulbs is a simple attribute inspection: Apply current, and reject those that do not light—or are cracked, improperly mounted, and so on.

Phase 1. In conducting SPC analysis based on attribute inspection, the first step is to develop p charts. First, choose the sample size, number, and frequency. Frequent sampling—every half hour or hour in some cases—provides better process control than infrequent sampling. Attribute sample size is usually somewhere between 50 and a few hundred.

In this case the sample size, n, is 200 light bulbs; samples are taken once a day for 20 days ($m = 20$). Figure 12–6 is a summary of the data collected.

FIGURE 12–6

Attribute Inspection Data for Designing p Chart

Sample number	Number of defective lights	Fraction defective
1	4	0.020
2	1	0.005
3	6	0.030
4	3	0.015
5	8	0.040
6	10	0.050
7	7	0.035
8	3	0.015
9	2	0.010
10	2	0.010
11	6	0.030
12	12	0.060
13	7	0.035
14	9	0.045
15	9	0.045
16	6	0.030
17	2	0.010
18	4	0.020
19	5	0.025
20	1	0.005
Total	107	

Phase 2. Now the p chart calculations are made. Like the $\bar{x}$ and R charts, the p chart has control limits $\pm 3\sigma$ from the centerline. The p chart is based on the binomial statistical distribution (instead of the normal distribution). *Bi-nominal* means two numbers, which is fitting since an attribute can have only two degrees of quality: good or defective. The formula for σ in the binomial distribution is:

$$\sigma = \sqrt{\frac{\bar{p}(1-\bar{p})}{n}}$$

where

$\bar{p} = $ Average (mean) fraction defective (or percent defective)
$n = $ Number in each sample

Therefore the control limits, at 3σ from the centerline, $\bar{p}$, are:

$$UCL = \bar{p} + 3\sqrt{\frac{\bar{p}(1-\bar{p})}{n}}$$

$$LCL = \bar{p} - 3\sqrt{\frac{\bar{p}(1-\bar{p})}{n}}$$

The average fraction defective, $\bar{p}$, is total defectives divided by total items inspected, where total items inspected equals number of samples, m, times sample size, n:

$$\bar{p} = \frac{\text{Total defectives found}}{mn}$$

Since 107 defectives were found (from Figure 12–5),

$$\bar{p} = \frac{107}{(20)(200)} = \frac{107}{4,000} = 0.027$$

The control limits are:

$$UCL = \bar{p} + 3\sqrt{\frac{\bar{p}(1-\bar{p})}{n}}$$
$$= 0.027 + 3\sqrt{\frac{(0.027)(1-0.027)}{200}}$$
$$= 0.027 + 3\sqrt{\frac{0.0263}{200}}$$
$$= 0.027 + 3\sqrt{0.00013}$$
$$= 0.027 + 0.034 = 0.061$$
$$LCL = 0.027 - 0.034 = -0.007 \text{ or } 0.0$$

(The control limit may not be negative.)

Figure 12–7 shows the resulting p chart. As is proper, the data used in its construction are plotted back on the chart. All points are within the control limits. If there were a point out of control, then a search for a special cause would be undertaken. For example, the machine that bonds the base to the globe may be set to apply too little of the bonding agent. Changing the machine settings may clear up the problem.

FIGURE 12–7

Trial and Final *p* Chart for Attribute Inspection

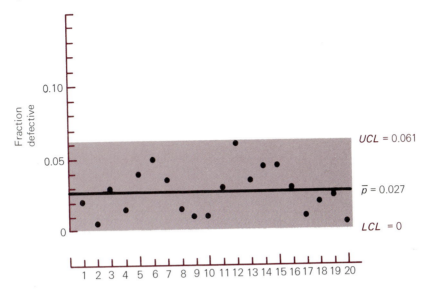

Sometimes the special cause is found in an earlier process. For example, the metal base may sometimes be bent out of round in handling. More care in handling could make the process consistent.

Phase 3. Cease sampling. Probably no need to continue to sample since the process is in control. But inspection should resume on an audit basis from time to time to make sure that the process does not stray away from control.

Phase 4. Improve the process. This usually requires a management decision to spend money for a better raw material, an equipment improvement, or some other upgrade in the process.

Phase 5. Repeat.

SPC for Attributes—The *c* Chart

A single control chart, the *c* chart, is used in statistical process control when inspection consists of counting the number of defects found on a surface area or unit. There are far fewer uses for *c* charts than for $\bar{x}$ and *R* or *p* charts. The best applications of *c* charts seem to be in industries that produce sheets of a basic product: glass, steel, plastics, paper, and fabric. Some products in a more finished state may also be suitable for *c* charts: a keg of nails, the wing of an aircraft, or the hull of a ship. Scratches, bubbles, and breaks per sheet, per surface, or per 10 lineal yards are examples of ways in which defects might be counted for such products.

The basis for the c chart is the Poisson statistical distribution rather than the normal or binomial distribution. In the Poisson distribution the formula for standard deviation, σ, is very simple:

$$\sigma = \sqrt{\bar{c}}$$

where $\bar{c}$ = Average (mean) number of defects per surface area. Thus, the control limits, at 3σ, are:

$$UCL = \bar{c} + 3\sqrt{\bar{c}}$$
$$LCL = \bar{c} - 3\sqrt{\bar{c}}$$

The centerline, $\bar{c}$, is the sum of the defects found on the sampled surface areas (or units) divided by the number of samples, m (m should be at least 25):

$$\bar{c} = \frac{\Sigma c}{m}$$

Design, inspection, correction for consistency, and process improvement with use of c charts follow the same general steps as for p charts.

OTHER PROCESS-IMPROVEMENT TECHNIQUES

Run diagrams and SPC charts are the stars of process improvement. Supporting actors are the process flowchart, Pareto analysis, the fishbone chart, and the scatter diagram.

The process flowchart comes first in a process-improvement project; the chart identifies the operations in a production process and how they are sequenced. Pareto analysis, used to identify which of the operations are major and which are minor, is second. The third step is the fishbone chart, which keys in on a major factor needing improvement; the fishbone chart identifies subfactors and sub-subfactors. Fourth is the run diagram and SPC charts, which provide data on out-of-control factors. Fifth and last is the scatter diagram, which is used to check potential causes of error in processes where error causes are not obvious. While other steps or techniques could be used in a process improvement, these five are a solid core group. In many process-improvement projects only two or three of the five will need to be done formally. In tougher cases all five, summarized below, may be necessary.

1. Process flowchart.
2. Pareto analysis.
3. Fishbone chart.
4. Run diagrams and SPC charts.
5. Scatter diagram.

Steps 2, 3, and 5 are discussed below. Step 4 has already been presented, and we will save step 1, the process flowchart, for discussion in the next chapter—as a methods study technique.

Pareto Analysis

Pareto analysis is a way of separating the important few from the trivial many. (ABC analysis, discussed earlier as an inventory-management technique, is one type of Pareto analysis.) Pareto analysis, as used in process improvement, goes like this:

1. Identify the factors affecting product quality.
2. Keep track of how often a measurable defect is related to each factor.
3. Plot the results on a bar chart, where length of a bar stands for (or is proportional to) how often the causal factor occurs. More-serious causes (longest bars) are positioned left of less-serious causes.

Figure 12–8 is a sample Pareto chart for a certain product being supplied to an important customer. The process flow is from raw materials, to fabrication of component parts, to subassemblies, to final assembly, to delivery. The Pareto chart shows that by far the most critical errors—about 85 percent—are made in delivering the finished product to the customer and in raw materials. The process improvers will probably want to focus their efforts on those two factors and save the other three for a later round of improvement.

FIGURE 12–8

Pareto Chart, Occurrences of Errors in Providing a Product to a Customer

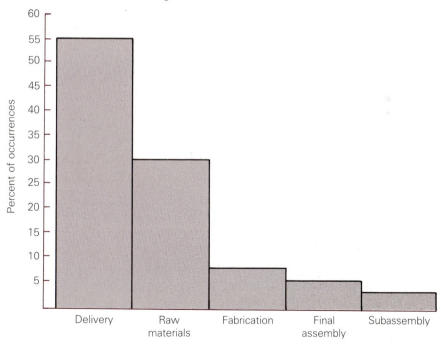

Fishbone Chart

The **fishbone chart** was developed by Dr. Kaoru Ishikawa, Japan's revered quality authority. (The chart is also known as an Ishikawa diagram and a cause-and-effect chart.) The chart looks like the skeleton of a fish. The central spine represents an important process or quality characteristic. Primary bones connecting to the spine are main contributors, and secondary bones are secondary contributors.

Figure 12–9 shows a fishbone chart for a quality-of-service characteristic: on-time truck deliveries of goods in the right amount, which is the spine. That characteristic was identified in the earlier Pareto analysis as being a trouble spot. Four main contributors are shown: trucking, packing, shipping documents, and container labeling. Trucking quality is influenced by four secondary factors, each shown as small bones: latest traffic and road conditions, truck maintenance, leave at right time, and driver knows route. Packing is also influenced by four factors (bones): quantity in the container, protective packing, container labeling, and right container. Shipping has two factors, invoice and packing list. And container labeling is influenced by three: right information, label stuck on well, and label location.

Generally the chart is produced by people who know the process: trucker, packer, material handler, material controller, supervisor. The group may then post the chart in the shipping area and begin thinking about or working on controlling and improving each process factor. Some of the factors, like "driver knows route," are not well suited to run diagrams and SPC charts. (While you could chart "number of times

FIGURE 12–9

Fishbone Chart, Delivery of Goods by Truck

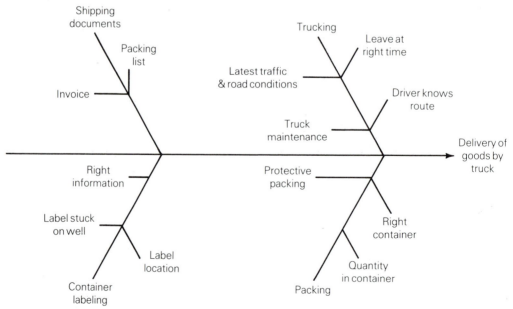

driver got lost," good driver training might be more effective overall than measuring errors.) Others are. For example, "label location" may be measured and plotted in centimeters from the edge of the container. Percent of defective labels—wrong stock number, shipping location, etc.—could be judged by a second person following up on the person who prepares and attaches the labels. (These two examples happen to be actual cases that the author observed in practice in two different companies.)

Scatter (correlation) Diagram

A scatter, or correlation, diagram is used to plot effects against experimental changes in process inputs. The correlation coefficient (discussed earlier as a demand-forecasting tool) may be calculated, although the strength of the correlation is often obvious just by looking at the diagram.

Scatter diagrams are most useful when the process is complex and causes of error are not well understood or obvious. That tends to rule out our previous simple example of deliveries by truck. As a more realistic example, suppose samples of rubber inner tubes are tested by blowing them up. This is known as **destructive testing.** In a previous process the formed tubes are cured in ovens, with the cure time varied experimentally. A scatter diagram—see Figure 12–10—is used to show the correlation between cure time and strength. Each point on the diagram represents one tube; cure time is a point's horizontal location, and strength is its vertical location. The points seem to follow an upward but bending pattern. Natural conclusions are: (1) Tube strength does correlate well with cure time, since there is a definite clustering of points about the curving dashed line. (2) Tube strength increases with cure time

FIGURE 12–10

Scatter Diagram, Cure Time for Inner Tubes

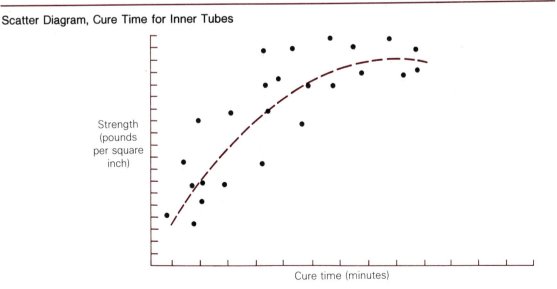

Strength
(pounds
per square
inch)

Cure time (minutes)

up to a point, and then further cure time does no more good and may be harmful. Next, look for other factors that might correlate with tube strength.

The scatter-diagram approach is particularly useful for chemical, biological, metal-lurgical, paint, and similar complex processes. The approach is less useful for simple standard processes, where most cause-effect relationships are already well known. For example, the carpenter already knows that two nails in a board provide more strength than one, so there is no point in plotting number of nails on a scatter diagram.

LOT INSPECTION

Lot inspection takes place well after production and therefore is not used for control. As the term implies, it is lots, literally, that are to be inspected. A lot is generally large, perhaps hundreds or thousands of units. The lot to be inspected may be an incoming shipment of raw materials, a completed production order for parts or end items, or an impending shipment of finished goods. One purpose is to remove the bad parts from the lot. When sampling inspection is used, another purpose is to find out if the lot is good enough to let it go forward or bad enough to stop it.

Lot inspection has been derogatorily called the "death certificate" approach: Separate good ones from bad ones, and then sign death certificates for the bad ones—too late to be saved. Obviously process control—controlling while the pieces are being made—is a better way. But all too often process control does not take place. That is when lot inspection comes into use.

Types of Lot Inspection

Sometimes in lot inspection 100 percent of the lot is checked. This may be necessary for a new part or a new supplier, when suspicion is high that something is wrong with the process that made the parts, or when it is vital for all parts to meet the specification.

More often lots are sample-inspected, which cuts inspection time and cost. Also, sampling can be nearly as effective as 100 percent inspection, because the inspector may become fatigued or bored and make judgmental errors if 100 percent of a large lot must be checked.

In lot sampling inspection, the sample size is often set by use of statistical tables. Then the inspector will try to select a random or stratified sample. A stratified sample would be one in which pieces are drawn from the back, middle, front, top, and bottom strata in a pile (and not just selected from an area of the lot that the maker might prefer the sample to be drawn from).

If a bad sample is found, the whole lot is presumed unacceptable. Then, in some cases, every piece in the lot is inspected so that all bad ones may be taken out and replaced with good ones. This is called a **100 percent rectifying inspection.** In other cases, if the item is cheap, the rejected lot may be discarded, melted down and reprocessed, or sold as scrap or seconds.

Like SPC, lot inspection may be for variables or attributes, but acceptance inspection for attributes is more common. Attribute inspection of lots and use of sampling tables deserves further explanation.

Lot Inspection with Sampling Tables

In sample-inspecting large lots for attributes, two sampling plan characteristics must be determined. First, what is the **sample size?** Second, what is the maximum number of defectives allowed—called the **acceptance number**—in the sample before the lot is rejected? The sample size and acceptance number may be found in sampling tables. The most popular set of tables is the Military Standard Sampling Procedures and Tables for Inspection by Attribute, which is better known as MIL-STD-105D. Though MIL-STD-105D was devised for military purchasing, it has become the standard for attribute inspection for all industry. (It is known internationally as ABC-STD-105D or International Standard ISO/DIS2859.)

MIL-STD-105D includes tables for various types of lot sampling. Figures 12–11 and 12–12, which go together, constitute the most popular type. Figure 12–11 is used to arrive at a sample-size code letter. The code letter is found by selecting the proper lot-size range from the 15 listed and the level of inspection from the seven options.

FIGURE 12–11

Sample-Size Code Letters, MIL-STD-105D

Lot or batch size	Special inspection levels				General inspection levels		
	S–1	S–2	S–3	S–4	I	II	III
2– 8	A	A	A	A	A	A	B
9– 15	A	A	A	A	A	B	C
16– 25	A	A	B	B	B	C	D
26– 50	A	B	B	C	C	D	E
51– 90	B	B	C	C	C	E	F
91– 150	B	B	C	D	D	F	G
151– 280	B	C	D	E	E	G	H
281– 500	B	C	D	E	F	H	J
501– 1,200	C	C	E	F	G	J	K
1,201– 3,200	C	D	E	G	H	K	L
3,201– 10,000	C	D	F	G	J	L	M
10,001– 35,000	C	D	F	H	K	M	N
35,001–150,000	D	E	G	J	L	N	P
150,001–500,000	D	E	G	J	M	P	Q
500,001 and over	D	E	H	K	N	Q	R

Source: Acheson J. Duncan, *Quality Control and Individual Statistics,* 4th ed. (Homewood, Ill.: Richard D. Irwin, 1974), p. 223.

FIGURE 12–12

Master Table for Single-Sampling Plans (Normal Inspection), MIL-STD-105D

Acceptable Quality Levels (normal inspection). Each cell shows **Ac Re** (Ac = Acceptance number, Re = Rejection number). ↓ = Use first sampling plan below arrow. ↑ = Use first sampling plan above arrow.

Sample size code letter	Sample size	0.010	0.015	0.025	0.040	0.065	0.10	0.15	0.25	0.40	0.65	1.0	1.5	2.5	4.0	6.5	10	15	25	40	65	100	150	250	400	650	1000
A	2	↓	↓	↓	↓	↓	↓	↓	↓	↓	↓	↓	↓	↓	↓	↓	↓	0 1	1 2	2 3	3 4	5 6	7 8	10 11	14 15	21 22	30 31
B	3	↓	↓	↓	↓	↓	↓	↓	↓	↓	↓	↓	↓	↓	↓	↓	0 1	1 2	2 3	3 4	5 6	7 8	10 11	14 15	21 22	30 31	44 45
C	5	↓	↓	↓	↓	↓	↓	↓	↓	↓	↓	↓	↓	↓	↓	0 1	1 2	2 3	3 4	5 6	7 8	10 11	14 15	21 22	30 31	44 45	↑
D	8	↓	↓	↓	↓	↓	↓	↓	↓	↓	↓	↓	↓	↓	0 1	1 2	2 3	3 4	5 6	7 8	10 11	14 15	21 22	30 31	44 45	↑	↑
E	13	↓	↓	↓	↓	↓	↓	↓	↓	↓	↓	↓	↓	0 1	1 2	2 3	3 4	5 6	7 8	10 11	14 15	21 22	30 31	44 45	↑	↑	↑
F	20	↓	↓	↓	↓	↓	↓	↓	↓	↓	↓	↓	0 1	1 2	2 3	3 4	5 6	7 8	10 11	14 15	21 22	30 31	44 45	↑	↑	↑	↑
G	32	↓	↓	↓	↓	↓	↓	↓	↓	↓	↓	0 1	1 2	2 3	3 4	5 6	7 8	10 11	14 15	21 22	30 31	44 45	↑	↑	↑	↑	↑
H	50	↓	↓	↓	↓	↓	↓	↓	↓	↓	0 1	1 2	2 3	3 4	5 6	7 8	10 11	14 15	21 22	30 31	44 45	↑	↑	↑	↑	↑	↑
J	80	↓	↓	↓	↓	↓	↓	↓	↓	0 1	1 2	2 3	3 4	5 6	7 8	10 11	14 15	21 22	30 31	44 45	↑	↑	↑	↑	↑	↑	↑
K	125	↓	↓	↓	↓	↓	↓	↓	0 1	1 2	2 3	3 4	5 6	7 8	10 11	14 15	21 22	30 31	44 45	↑	↑	↑	↑	↑	↑	↑	↑
L	200	↓	↓	↓	↓	↓	↓	0 1	1 2	2 3	3 4	5 6	7 8	10 11	14 15	21 22	30 31	44 45	↑	↑	↑	↑	↑	↑	↑	↑	↑
M	315	↓	↓	↓	↓	↓	0 1	1 2	2 3	3 4	5 6	7 8	10 11	14 15	21 22	30 31	44 45	↑	↑	↑	↑	↑	↑	↑	↑	↑	↑
N	500	↓	↓	↓	↓	0 1	1 2	2 3	3 4	5 6	7 8	10 11	14 15	21 22	30 31	44 45	↑	↑	↑	↑	↑	↑	↑	↑	↑	↑	↑
P	800	↓	↓	↓	0 1	1 2	2 3	3 4	5 6	7 8	10 11	14 15	21 22	30 31	44 45	↑	↑	↑	↑	↑	↑	↑	↑	↑	↑	↑	↑
Q	1250	↓	↓	0 1	1 2	2 3	3 4	5 6	7 8	10 11	14 15	21 22	30 31	44 45	↑	↑	↑	↑	↑	↑	↑	↑	↑	↑	↑	↑	↑
R	2000	↓	0 1	1 2	2 3	3 4	5 6	7 8	10 11	14 15	21 22	30 31	44 45	↑	↑	↑	↑	↑	↑	↑	↑	↑	↑	↑	↑	↑	↑

↓ = Use first sampling plan below arrow. If sample size equals, or exceeds, lot or batch size, do 100 percent inspection.

↑ = Use first sampling plan above arrow.

Ac = Acceptance number.

Re = Rejection number.

After finding the code letter, go to the "master table," Figure 12–12, to find the sample size, *n,* and the acceptance number, *Ac.* To use the master table, an **acceptable quality level** (AQL) must be specified. Acceptable quality actually is expressed as acceptable defects. Today the very idea that there can be an *acceptable* number of defects is frowned upon by people in the total quality control movement; current thinking is that whatever the defect level is, it should be made better. Still, an AQL must be specified to use the table. (Actually, specifying a set number has some advantages in *contracting* for a certain level of quality.)

The AQL may be specified as either a percent defective or a number of defects per 100 units (where more than one defect per unit may be counted). An example demonstrates use of the sets of tables.

EXAMPLE 12–3

Attribute Sampling, Reeds for Musical Instruments

Problem:

Reeds are produced in lots of 2,000 for the replacement market of owners of clarinets and other reed instruments. Samples of reeds are visually inspected for cracks, chips, and so on. MIL-STD-105D is used to find the sampling plan. The acceptable quality level (AQL) for the reeds is set at 1.5 percent, and general inspection level II is chosen. What is the sampling plan?

Solution:

Go to Figure 12–11 to find the sample-size code letter. The lot size of 2,000 is in the row 1,201 to 3,200. For that row and general inspection level II the code letter is K.

Find code letter K in Figure 12–12. The sample size for code letter K is 125. For an AQL of 1.5 and code letter K, an arrow points downward to an acceptance number (Ac) of 5. (The rejection number, Re, of 6 is also given.)

The sampling plan is $n = 125$ and $Ac = 5$. This means that if more than five defective reeds are found in a sample of 125, the whole lot of 2,000 is rejected.

In future sampling of reeds, if defects should rise sharply, it would be prudent to shift to general level III, which results in a larger sample size and tighter control. When defects drop, go back to level II or even to I. (The four special levels in Figure 12–11 are for certain special conditions that need not be explained here.)

Clearly the MIL-STD-105D set of tables that we have just seen are designed to hold down inspection costs. If lot size is large, then the tables point toward the large sample size, because when the lot is large it makes good economic sense to be more careful with evidence about lot quality. And after all, the sample is only giving us evidence, not proof, of the quality of the lot. There are other tables, and mathematical procedures, too, for calculating how much error there is in relying on sampling to judge the quality of the lot. The other approaches are left for advanced studies in quality control.

QUALITY COMMITMENT

The techniques for gaining conformance to quality specifications date back to the works of Walter Shewhart of Bell Labs, circa 1930.[6] The techniques are sure, almost cut and dried. Yet rather few industrial companies in North America have made a strong effort to put them to use. But it appears, as this book is being written, that a commitment to quality improvement is gathering momentum in many, perhaps most, large industrial corporations—and the better small ones, too. Here are some examples:

At Xerox, management became alarmed about loss of market share to high-quality competitors, especially foreign ones. Twenty-five of Xerox's most senior managers spent a good portion of December 1982, and January–February 1983, on the quality problem. They listened to W. Edwards Deming and Joseph Juran and attended Philip Crosby's Quality College in Florida, and then they developed a quality policy with a full set of implementation actions. The quality policy: "Quality is *the* basic business principle for Xerox. Quality means providing our external and internal customers with innovative products and services that fully satisfy their requirements. Quality improvement is the job of every Xerox employee."[7]

IBM has made a similar quality commitment. For example, IBM divisions in California's "Silicon Valley" rented the San Jose city auditorium and invited W. Edwards Deming to speak to some 5,000 IBM employees. In some IBM divisions, SPC charts are posted on doors or walls of even the offices (charting number of data entry errors, invoicing errors, and so forth).

Tennant Company in Minneapolis sent scores of its people to Crosby's Quality College. Today quality control displays are everywhere in Tennant's plants. In 1982 Tennant had its second "Quality Day." A theatrical group had been hired some months earlier to write and choreograph an original one-and-a-half-hour series of skits, music, and dance on the theme, *quality* in a factory. On the evening of Quality Day, all employees and their spouses were invited to the Guthrie Theater, which Tennant had rented for the occasion. They were treated to the show, plus dinner and other events.

What these stories show is a commitment to quality improvement that comes from top management. It is not an easy commitment to make, because these companies, like most in North America, are run mostly by people who have a financial or legal background. Operations experience, with exposure to quality matters, has been scarce

---

[6] For example, W. A. Shewhart, *The Economic Control of Quality of Manufactured Product* (New York: Van Nostrand Reinhold, 1931; American Society for Quality Control, 1980).

[7] Frank J. Pill, "Management Commitment to Quality: Xerox Corp.," *Quality Progress,* August 1983, pp. 12–17.

at high levels of the organization. Top management in most companies are now aware of the problem, and as a result they are sponsoring massive quality-control training efforts—and sometimes including themselves in the training.

Quality Circles

An easier but less sure path toward quality is for top officials to delegate the quality responsibility; that is, set up programs in which middle managers and lower-level people have the responsibility for quality improvement. For example, thousands of Western companies have set up *quality circle* programs. A quality circle is a small work group that meets periodically to discuss ways to improve quality, productivity, or the work environment. In Japan, quality control circles (as the Japanese call them) are everywhere, and they accomplish a good deal. But the circles are just one piece of a many-faceted total quality control (TQC) program. Furthermore, in many cases TQC is spurred on by a just-in-time production system, in which small-lot production exposes defectives early and lack of buffer stock requires that the cause be corrected right away.

Quality circle members are trained in the use of run diagrams, statistical process control (SPC) charts, fishbone charts, Pareto analysis, scatter diagrams, and a few other tools of analysis. They also learn how to conduct a presentation on a proposed improvement. These skills are unlikely to flourish, however, in the absence of a high commitment to quality and work improvement throughout the organization.

Quality of Service

Commitment to quality "throughout the organization" means that services are included as well as tangible goods. The quality of services often can be measured with some objectivity. What is the cook-down weight of the hamburger patty? How many trees survived after planting? How many pages had to be reprinted or retyped? How many tax forms had errors?

For such services the usual tools may be useful: Run diagrams and SPC charts sometimes may be used in tracking process consistency in preparation for improving the process that provides the service. Fishbone charts, Pareto analysis, and scatter diagrams are also usable.

Some of these tools do not work as well for *human* services. The reason is that measuring the quality of human service usually means asking the client or patron for an opinion. The answer depends somewhat on what kind of mood the patron is in at the time. The mood bias tends to wash out if the population is large. But then there is the problem of getting a representative sample.

Consider, for example, a rest area alongside a major highway. The highway department may place questionnaires in the rest area to solicit opinions about the quality of rest rooms, tourist brochures, state roads, state police, and so on. Travelers' opinions may be measured in numbers, perhaps on a scale of one to seven, just as a micrometer might measure diameters from one to seven centimeters. Should the data then be plotted on statistical process control charts? No, because it is impossible to judge how representative the sample is. The process could appear out of control when it really is simply that a motorcycle gang filled out a disproportionate number of questionnaires in one time period, truckers in a storm filled out a large number in another period, and so forth. The questionnaire data are helpful but in this case not usable in the SPC mode.

Sampling people's opinions is not like sampling goods. Goods do not have the will to resist being sampled; humans, on the other hand, have the option of participating or not.

SUMMARY

Quality management is partly an art, in regard to determining the level of product quality that is right for intended customers. After the product specifications are set, the science of quality control may be used in assuring compliance with specifications.

Western industry's recent efforts to manage quality better have been spurred by demanding consumers and consumer legislation plus competition from high-quality imports, especially from Japan. Japan has spent over 35 years on a "total quality control" (TQC) campaign, and now other countries are following suit.

Keys to TQC include vesting quality responsibility with the production people rather than a staff group; imposing quality control at every process rather than relying on inspection of lots; and giving people the time and training to do the job right and the authority to slow or stop production if necessary to avoid bad output. Process controls should be built in to the process itself, and as a backstop, there must be a good way of getting feedback from users on their satisfaction with quality.

There is a well-established cycle of process improvement that may yield direct quality improvement, reduction of waste, higher labor productivity, or other benefits. First, measure every piece to see if the variability is normal. If there is an abnormal trend or extreme values, look for a special cause, and eliminate it. Then measure every piece for a time to assure that the process really has been brought under control. If so, it may make sense to reduce to sampling instead of 100 percent inspection; then perhaps cease inspecting altogether, except for an occasional check. Or, perhaps automate inspection so that 100 percent inspection makes sense. The last step is to improve the process, which usually takes a management decision to spend funds on better equipment, materials, tools, designs, and so forth.

At the point where sampling replaces 100 percent inspection, statistical process control (SPC) practices may be used. Measure small samples (such as four, five, or six pieces). Then translate those measures into SPC charts: an x-bar chart reflecting sample means and an R chart for variability within samples. Each SPC chart has an upper control limit (UCL) and a lower control limit (LCL) set three standard deviations away from the mean. From then on, plot all sample means and ranges on the charts. Assume that the process is in control if all points stay between the UCL and LCL; look for a special cause and fix it if a point strays outside the limits.

SPC charts do not work well for low-volume production where there are not enough pieces for statistical sampling to be valid. Craftsmanship, plus first- and last-piece inspection, are substitutes for SPC.

A variation on the process control improvement technique is checking for the existence or absence of a desirable attribute. This is a yes-or-no judgment, not a measurement of a variable. Take a number of sizable samples and see what percent in each sample does not possess the attribute, i.e., is defective. The mean of those percents defective becomes the center line on an SPC chart, and a UCL and LCL are added. The chart is used similar to the way that x-bar and R charts are used. One other type of attribute inspection requires counting *number* of defects per surface area (instead of percents of pieces defective); the mean number, c-bar, goes on a c-chart with LCL and UCL in place.

Other process improvement techniques (besides SPC) include the process flowchart, Pareto analysis, the fishbone chart, and the scatter diagram. The process flowchart identifies how the product is produced so that each step in the process may be analyzed as a cause of error.

Pareto analysis works on those causes. The causes are arranged on a bar chart from most to least frequent. The most frequent are the factors to be given the most attention.

On the fishbone chart, a main quality characteristic is displayed as the spine bone on a drawing that looks like the skeleton of a fish. Secondary and tertiary bones represent factors that contribute to that quality characteristic. The chart helps focus attention on causes of defects, which then may be plotted on run diagrams and SPC charts to isolate out-of-control factors.

The scatter diagram correlates experimental changes in process inputs (amount of water added, time of cure, etc.) with results of a test. It shows what set of inputs is best.

Less adequate than process control—but sometimes necessary anyway—is lot inspection. Every piece in a lot may be inspected, or the lot may be sample-inspected. Where sampling is used, the sampling plan may be made "statistically correct" by using sampling tables or formulas. MIL-STD-105D is the abbreviation for a set of tables that is used worldwide. Using it requires three inputs: the lot size, an "acceptable quality level," and a choice of how tight the desired inspection is to be. The tables yield the sample size and the acceptable number of defects in the sample. Accepted lots are passed along (minus the bad ones found in the sample). Rejected lots are often subjected to a "100 percent rectifying inspection," which means inspect every piece in the lot and replace bad ones with good ones.

Dramatic gains in quality come to the firms that have a quality commitment in upper management. That commitment has been missing, but lately many companies have taken steps to correct the deficiency. But some companies have taken the less sure path of delegating quality improvement roles to lower-level work groups, sometimes formally designated as quality circles. Such groups need strong leadership from the top.

Quality of service can be improved by run diagrams, SPC charts, and other process improvement tools—if the service is measurable physically. If the measure is a human perception, tools like SPC sometimes are unsound, because of the problems of getting stable, representative perceptions from humans.

REFERENCES

Books

Besterfield, Dale H. *Quality Control.* Englewood Cliffs, N.J.: Prentice-Hall, 1979 (TS156.B47).

Deming, W. Edwards. *Quality, Productivity, and Competitive Position.* Cambridge: Massachusetts Institute of Technology, Center for Advanced Engineering Study, 1982.

Drury, C. G., and J. G. Fox, eds. *Human Reliability in Quality Control.* New York: Halsted Press, 1975 (TS156.2.I57).

Feigenbaum, Armand V. *Total Quality Control.* 3d ed. New York: McGraw-Hill, 1983.

Juran, J. M., Frank M. Gryna, Jr., and R. S. Bingham, Jr., eds. *Quality Control Handbook.* 3d ed. New York: McGraw-Hill, 1974 (TS156.Q3J8).

Periodicals (societies)

Journal of Quality Technology (American Society for Quality Control).

Quality Assurance.

Quality Progress (American Society for Quality Control).

REVIEW QUESTIONS

1. What is quality?

2. Is quality getting better or worse in the world? Explain, and consider regional differences in your answer.

3. How has consumerism affected quality?

4. How has competition affected quality?

5. Under total quality control (TQC) what is the role of the worker? Of the QA department staff?

6. What is the most advanced form of process control, and why? What is the role of feedback from users of a producer's product?

7. In process improvement, what are the roles of run diagrams and SPC charts? What are the similarities and differences?

8. Do specifications and tolerances play a role in process improvement? Explain fully.

9. Does process improvement mean the same thing as quality improvement? And are process improvement techniques restricted to improving product quality? Discuss.

10. Why, in SPC for variables, are there *two* kinds of charts, namely x-bar and R charts?

11. Compare and contrast x-bar, R; p; and c charts and their uses.

12. Why is SPC not very suitable for low-volume production? What *is* suitable?

13. Compare the effectiveness of process control with that of lot inspection.

14. How is a fishbone chart constructed, and what is it for?

15. How is Pareto analysis used in process control or process improvement?

16. How is a scatter diagram used in process control or process improvement?

17. In using MIL-STD-105D how does a larger lot size affect the sampling plan? Why are the tables designed so that lot size is one of the inputs?

18. What is the role of quality circles, and what does it take to make them produce maximal benefits?

19. In what ways are improving processes in services different from improving processes in goods production?

PROBLEMS

1. Some years ago the Bon Vivant Company went bankrupt. There were quality problems in its line of canned soups (e.g., Bon Vivant Vichyssoise). Find recorded accounts of the bankruptcy in your library. What went wrong? Suggest quality-assurance steps that Bon Vivant might have taken to avert the bankruptcy.

2. What sorts of quality-assurance programs are used by the more successful fast-food franchisors?

3. Guarantee Seed Co. has a statistical process control program for checking the weight of packages of seeds. Inspectors weigh samples of packages after they have been filled and fastened shut. In one set of five samples, each sample size equal to seven bags, the mean sample weights in grams are 5.0, 5.1, 5.1, 4.9, and 4.4.
   a. To the extent possible with the data given, perform all calculations needed to construct SPC charts. (Note: Normally five samples is not enough, but assume that it is—to make the calculations simpler.)
   b. What data are needed to do the remaining calculations necessary for constructing SPC charts? Explain.

4. Sixteen-ounce chunks of longhorn cheese are packaged by a cheese processor. Quality control has designed $\bar{x}$ and R charts: $\bar{\bar{x}}$ is at 16.09 ounces, with $UCL_{\bar{x}} = 16.25$ and $LCL_{\bar{x}} = 15.93$; $\bar{R}$ is at 0.376, with $UCL_R = 0.723$ and $LCL_R = 0$.
   a. What sample size, n, would have been used? (It may be calculated.)
   b. Although the cheese packages are labeled as 16-ounce chunks, $\bar{\bar{x}} = 16.09$. What is a reasonable explanation of the difference?

5. Hypodermic needles are subjected to a bend test, and the results, in grams, are to be

plotted on $\bar{x}$ and R charts. A suitable number of samples have been inspected. The resulting $\bar{\bar{x}}$ is 26.1, and the resulting $\bar{R}$ is 5.0.

a. For $n = 8$, calculate the control limits for the SPC charts.

b. What should be done with the data calculated in part a?

c. Assume that SPC charts have been developed for the data given above and that the operator has been using the charts regularly. For one sample of hypodermics, $\bar{x} = 26.08$ and $R = 0.03$. Should there be an investigation for a special cause? Explain.

6. Random samples, each with a sample size of six, are periodically taken from a production line that manufactures one-half-volt batteries. The batteries sampled are tested on a voltmeter. The production line has just been modified, and a new quality-control plan must be designed. For that purpose, 10 random samples (of six each) have been taken over a suitable period of time; the test results are given below:

Sample number	Tested voltages					
	V_1	V_2	V_3	V_4	V_5	V_6
1	0.498	0.492	0.510	0.505	0.504	0.487
2	0.482	0.491	0.502	0.481	0.496	0.492
3	0.501	0.512	0.503	0.499	0.498	0.511
4	0.498	0.486	0.502	0.503	0.510	0.501
5	0.500	0.507	0.509	0.498	0.512	0.518
6	0.476	0.492	0.496	0.521	0.505	0.490
7	0.511	0.522	0.513	0.518	0.520	0.516
8	0.488	0.512	0.501	0.498	0.492	0.498
9	0.482	0.490	0.510	0.500	0.495	0.482
10	0.505	0.496	0.498	0.490	0.485	0.499

a. Compute and draw the appropriate SPC chart(s) for the data.

b. What should be done next? Discuss.

7. Current loss in a circuit is being measured, and the means of sample measurements are plotted on a statistical process control chart. Most of the means fall below the lower control limit—less current loss than before. What is the implication of this—on such factors as pricing, marketing, purchasing, production, training, design, and SPC charts?

8. A manufacturer of coat hangers has decided what constitutes a defective hanger. Samples of 200 hangers have been inspected on each of the last 20 days. The numbers of defectives found are given below. Construct a p chart for the data. What should be done next? Explain.

Day	Number defective	Day	Number defective
1	22	11	21
2	17	12	21
3	14	13	20
4	18	14	13
5	25	15	19
6	16	16	24
7	12	17	14
8	11	18	8
9	6	19	15
10	16	20	12

9. Determine the control limits for a *p* chart using the data from the table below. If there are any out-of-control points, suggest what should be done. Graph the control chart or charts.

Sample number	Number inspected	Number defective
1	400	6
2	400	2
3	400	8
4	400	9
5	400	4
6	400	10
7	400	3
8	400	3
9	400	11
10	400	8
11	400	7
12	400	3
13	400	6
14	400	2
15	400	9

10. OK-Mart, a chain retailer, contracts with Electro Corp. to manufacture an "OK" brand of photo flash bulb. OK-Mart states that it wants an average quality of 99 percent good flash bulbs, i.e., 99 percent that actually flash. Electro's marketing manager states that their goal should be for 99.9 percent to flash (better than OK-Mart's stated goal). After production begins at Electro, sampling on the production line over a representative time period shows 0.2 percent defective.
    a. Where should the center line (or lines) be drawn on a statistical process control chart, and why?
    b. What, if anything, needs to be done about the differences between goals and actual quality?

11. Guarantee Seed Co. has a statistical process control program applied to germination rates on its line of seeds. For one new type of seed, the inspection plan is to pull out samples of 100 seeds from bags before they are fastened shut and test them to see what the germination rate is. After production starts up, five samples of 100 are drawn, and they contain 1, 3, 3, 3, and 5 seeds that will not germinate. Calculate the center line and upper and lower control limits for an SPC chart that plots germination rates. (Note: Usually 20 or more samples are taken to produce the charts, but in this problem use only five—so that calculations are simpler.)

12. Statistical process control charts are being constructed in a pottery manufacturing firm. Thirty pottery samples are taken, and the mean percentage of pottery samples that fail a strength test is 0.02, which becomes the center line on a *p* chart. Control limits are put in place, and the 30 defect rates are plotted on the chart. Two of the 30 fall above the upper control limit but all 30 are less than the major customer, a department store, requires. Explain the situation. What should be done?

13. Draw a chart like the one shown. Fill in your chart to show the type of inspection for process control that is suitable for each of the products on the left; briefly explain each of your answers.

	Run diagram	$\bar{x}$ & R chart	p chart	c chart
Alcoholic content in beer batches				
Billiard balls—ability to withstand force in a destructive test				
Vibration of electric motors; right after a process improvement				
New electronic component				
Number of fans that do not turn when plugged in				
Percent of lenses that have a scratch				
Number of scratches per table surface				

14. Orville's Ready-Pop Popcorn is packaged in jars. The jars are supposed to contain a certain quantity of popcorn, and the fill-machine operator inspects for quality using statistical process control. Which of the three SPC methods—$\bar{x}$, R; p; and c charts—could or could not be used for SPC inspection of this product? Explain.

15. Explain why each of the three SPC inspection techniques—$\bar{x}$, R; p; and c—could be used in inspecting tabletops.

16. American Pen and Pencil has had most of the market for ballpoint pens, but it now is under great pressure from a competitor whose product is clearly superior. AmPen workers have identified several quality problems. They include: Viscosity of ink, which is affected by temperature of the mixing solution, purity of powdered ink, and amount of water; the ballpoint assembly, which is affected by diameter of ball, roundness of ball, and trueness of the opening of the tube in which the ball goes; strength of the clip, which is affected by the thickness of the metal and the correctness of the shape after stamping.
    a. Draw a fishbone chart for these ballpoint pen factors. How should the chart be used?
    b. An inspection procedure at the ink mixing stage reveals that 80 percent of bad samples are caused by impurities, 15 percent by wrong temperature, and 5 percent by wrong amount of water. Draw a Pareto chart. How should it be used?

17. A waiter is trying to determine the factors that increase tips. Some of his ideas are: how long it takes to serve, how many words he speaks to a table of patrons, how long it takes the kitchen to fill the order, time between taking away dishes and bringing the check, and how far the table is from the kitchen.
    a. Arrange these few factors into a *logical* fishbone chart. Explain your chart.
    b. Which one of the factors is likely to plot on a scatter diagram as an upside down U. Explain.

18. This problem includes a scatter diagram showing inches of deviation from the correct length of wooden blinds and humidity in the shop.
    a. What does the shape of the scattered points indicate?
    b. Sharpness of the saw blade is known to also have an effect on the correctness of length of blind. Make a drawing of how the scatter for those two factors (sharpness and deviation of length) would probably look.

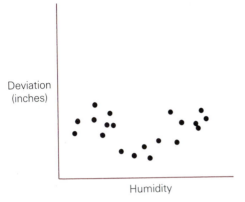

19. Two columns of products/services are shown below. Select two from each column, and do the following:
    a. For each of your four selections decide on two attributes and/or variables that you think are most suitable for inspection. Explain your reasoning.
    b. Discuss whether a formal statistical sampling method or an informal inspection method is sensible for each of your four selections.

Column 1	Column 2
Telephone	Auto tire mounting
Ball-point pen	Bookbinding
Pocket calculator	Keypunching
Dice	Proofreading
Space heater	Wallpaper hanging
Electric switch	Library reference
Glue	services
Bottle of Coke	Nursing care
Watch	Food catering
Handgun	Cleanliness of dishes
Light bulb	Bank teller service
	Roadside rest stop

20. Components International makes connectors for the electronics industry. A major connector is made in lots of 200,000. Rejected lots are subjected to 100 percent rectifying inspection.
    a. If the company uses MIL-STD-105D, general inspection level II, and an AQL of 0.25, what is the sampling plan?
    b. If a sample has eight defective connectors in it, what happens?

21. A machine shop has a contract to supply pistons to an engine manufacturer. The pistons are made in lots of 1,200, and the contract stipulates that MIL-STD-105D, general inspection level II, will be used in single-sampling inspection of the lots. AQL is set at 2.5.
    a. Use the sampling tables for MIL-STD-105D to arrive at a sampling plan for the pistons.
    b. Now consult the tables to see what the sampling plans would be if general inspection level I were used. Is the level I plan tighter (more discriminating) or looser than the level II plan.
    c. If the lot size were 1,201, the sampling plan would change. Explain how it would change and why lot size should make a difference.

22. A manufacturer of office furniture (employment = 1,000 people) is planning to adopt a total quality control program. The following are some characteristics of its present production system: There is a quality assurance department of 50 people, including 30 inspectors. Rejected products discovered at the end of final assembly are sent by a conveyor to a rework area staffed by 120 people. All purchased raw materials and parts are inspected on the receiving docks using MIL-STD-105D. All direct laborers are paid by how much they produce, which is measured daily. What changes would you suggest?

23. Hali-fish, Inc., in the Province of Nova Scotia has a contract to supply one-pound packages of cod to a grocery chain. If a package is 0.4 oz. less than one pound, the package fails to meet the contract specifications. Hali-fish sample-inspects each lot of 400 dozen (4,800) packages to try to assure that the grocery chain will be satisfied. If the AQL is 0.04, and general inspection level I is used, what is the sample size and acceptance number? Explain their use. (Use the MIL-STD-105D tables.)

MINICASE STUDY: GE LAMPS FOR IBM COPIERS

IBM copiers, made in Boulder, Colorado, take high-wattage lamps, which are made by General Electric's lamp division in the Cleveland area. The lamps had been produced and delivered in lots of 5,000. Over the early years of the contract, IBM found a small proportion of the lamps to be defective. Bad lamps were sent back to GE. Then, as part of a vigorous quality program, IBM altered this arrangement. The IBM copier division told the GE lamp division that henceforth if even one bad lamp were found in a lot, the whole lot would be sent back to G.E.

Of course it happened. IBM found a bad lamp. The whole lot went back to GE. The GE folks in Cleveland thought IBM's action a bit extreme. After all, perhaps the other 4,999 out of 5,000 were good. But the action triggered a massive effort to find the cause of the occasional bad lamps that were turning up at IBM.

One change was to impose a lot-control system: Numbers were assigned to every lot so that any bad lamps could be traced back to their raw materials and conditions of manufacture. No help.

The plant was virtually turned upside down in the search for a *special cause*. Finally, a breakthrough. An ancient water de-ionizer was found to be yielding water contaminated by ions. One process in the production of lamps required de-ionized water but was not getting it. The problem was that the filters were clogged, because there was no procedure for checking and cleaning them. A filter-maintenance procedure was established, and the incidence of defective lamps dropped dramatically— not only for the copier lamps going to IBM but for *all* of GE's lamps. The lamp division, in the end, was very pleased that IBM had sent back the whole lot.

DISCUSSION QUESTIONS

1. What principles of total quality control was IBM following?

2. Since the lamp division was searching for a special cause, what was the probable state of quality? Explain.

3. What else needs to be done in regard to quality improvement, and why?

CASE STUDY: AMERICAN CERAMIC AND GLASS PRODUCTS CORPORATION*

The American Ceramic and Glass Products Corporation employed approximately 13,000 people, each of its three plants employing between 4,000 and 5,000 of this total. About three quarters of its sales volume came from standard glass containers produced on highly automatic equipment; the balance of the company's sales were of specialized ceramic and glass items made in batches on much less automated equipment. John Parr, production manager for American Ceramic and Glass Products, had just completed a trip that covered eight states, seven universities, and three major industrial centers. The purpose of his trip was to recruit personnel for American's three plants. He felt that his trip had been extremely successful. He had made contacts that would, he hoped, result in his firm's acquiring some useful and needed personnel.

Parr was anxious to hire a capable person to head up the inspection and quality control department of the largest of American's plants located in Denver, Colorado. The position of chief of inspection and quality control had just been vacated by George Downs, who had taken an indefinite leave of absence due to a serious illness. There was little chance that Downs would be able to resume any work duties within a year and a substantial chance that he would never be capable of working on a full-time basis. During the ten years that Downs was chief of inspection and quality control, he had completely modernized the firm's inspection facilities and had developed a training program in the use of the most modern inspection equipment and techniques. The physical facilities of Downs's inspection department were a major attraction for visitors to the plant.

---

* Adapted from Robert C. Meier, Richard A. Johnson, William T. Newell, and Albert N. Schrieber, *Cases in Production and Operations Management,* © 1982, pp. 8–18. Reprinted by permission of Prentice-Hall, Inc., Englewood Cliffs, N.J.

THOMAS CALLIGAN

During his trip, Parr interviewed two men whom he felt were qualified to fill Downs's position. Although each appeared more than qualified, Parr felt that a wrong choice could easily be made. Thomas Calligan, the first of the two men, was a graduate of a reputable trade school and had eight years of experience in the inspection department of a moderately large manufacturing firm (approximately 800 employees). He began working as a production inspector and was promoted to group leader within two years and chief inspector two years later. His work record as a production inspector, as a group leader, and as chief inspector was extremely good. His reason for wishing to leave the firm was "to seek better opportunities." He felt that in his present firm he could not expect further promotions in the near future. His firm was known for its stability, low employee turnover, and slow but assured advancement opportunities. His superior, the head of quality control, was recently promoted to this position and was doing a more than satisfactory job. Further, he was a young man, only 32 years old.

JAMES KING

James King, the second of the two men being considered by Parr was a graduate of a major southwestern university and had about five years of experience. King was currently employed as head of inspection and quality control in a small manufacturing firm employing some 300 people. His abilities exceeded the requirements of his job, and he had made arrangements with his employer to do a limited amount of consulting work for noncompeting firms. His major reason for wanting a different position was a continuing conflict of interests between himself and his employer. King did not wish to make consulting his sole source of income, but he felt that his current position was equally unsatisfactory. He believed that by working for a large firm he would be able to fully use his talents within that firm and thus resolve conflict between his professional interests and the interests of his employer.

King's work record appeared to be good. He had recently been granted a sizable pay increase. King, like Calligan, began his career as a bench inspector and was rapidly promoted to his current supervisory position. Unlike Calligan, King viewed his initial position of bench inspector primarily as a means of financing his education and not as the beginning of his lifetime career. King was 31 years old.

ROLE OF INSPECTION AND QUALITY CONTROL

Major differences between the two men centered on their philosophies on the role of inspection and quality control in a manufacturing organization. Calligan's philosophy was:

> Quality is an essential part of every product. . . . It is the product development engineer's function to specify what constitutes quality and the function of quality

control to see that the manufacturing departments maintain these specifications. . . . Accurate and vigilant inspection is the key to controlled quality.

When asked how important process control was in the manufacture of quality products, he stated,

> Process control is achieved primarily through the worker's attitude. If a firm pays high wages and provides good working conditions, they should be able to acquire highly capable workers. . . . A well-executed and efficient inspection program will, as it has done in my firm, impress the importance of quality on the employees and motivate high-quality production. In the few cases when quality lapses do occur, an efficient inspection program prevents defective products from leaving the plant. . . . Any valid quality control program must hold quality equal in importance to quantity. . . . Quality records must be maintained for each employee and be made known to both the employee and his immediate superiors. Superior quality should be a major consideration in recommending individuals for promotion or merit pay increases.

King's philosophy paralleled that of Calligan only to the extent that "quality was an essential part of every product." King made the following comments on his philosophy toward inspection and quality control:

> If quality is properly controlled, inspection becomes a minor function. The more effective a quality control system becomes, the less inspection is required. . . . The key to quality control is process control, and inspection serves only as a check to assure that the process controls are being properly administered. . . . An effective inspection scheme should locate and pinpoint the cause of defects rather than place the blame on an often innocent individual. A good rejection report will include the seeds from which a solution to future rejections can be developed. . . . One sign of an unsatisfactory quality control system is a large, impressive inspection program.

King was asked what steps he would take to develop such a program if he were to be offered and accept the job of chief of inspection and quality control in the Denver plant. He answered.

> I would design and install a completely automatic inspection and process control system throughout the plant. By automatic I do not mean a mechanical or computer-directed system, but rather a completely standardized procedure for making all decisions concerning inspection and process control. The procedures would be based on a theoretically sound statistical foundation translated into laymen's terminology. The core of the program would be a detailed inspection and quality control manual.

When asked how long this might take, King continued,

> I constructed a similar manual for my present employer in a period of less than 12 months and had the whole process operating smoothly within 18 months after beginning work on the task. Since your firm is somewhat larger, and accounting for my added experience, I would estimate it to take no longer than two years and hopefully significantly less time. . . . As previously stated, I would place major emphasis on process control and would minimize inspection by apply-

ing appropriate sampling procedures wherever possible. . . . Employee quality performance should be rated on the basis of process control charts rather than on the basis of final inspection reports. The employee should be trained and encouraged to use these charts as his chief tool toward achieving quality output.

King further stated that one of the reasons for his desire to find a new employer was that he had developed the quality control program in his present firm to the point where it was no longer offering him any challenge. He further stated that he felt this situation would recur at American Ceramic and Glass Products but that, because of the size of the firm, he could direct his attention to bigger and more interesting problems rather than be required to seek outside consulting work to satisfy his need for professional growth.

When asked what his real interests were, King stated, "Application of statistical concepts to the nonroutine activities of a manufacturing organization." He cited worker training, supplier performance, and trouble shooting as areas of interest. King submitted several reports that summarized projects that he had successfully completed in these or related areas.

This was the extent of information that Parr had on each of the two individuals he felt might best fill the position vacated by Downs, the retiring chief of the inspection and quality control department.

DISCUSSION QUESTIONS

1. What should be the role of the chief of inspection and quality control?

2. What was Calligan's philosophy toward quality control?

3. What was King's philosophy toward quality control?

4. Under what conditions would you expect Calligan and King, respectively, to be most effective?

5. Which of the two candidates, if either, should be selected for the position of chief of the inspection and quality control department? Explain your choice.

Part Four

Operations Support

Behind the scenes are the people performing the many operations support functions. In Chapter 13, support in the areas of work improvement, standards, and productivity is the topic. In Chapter 14, the support provided by the facilities (plant and equipment) planners is discussed. In Chapter 15, we look at ways to determine locations for facilities and handling movable resources within those facilities. In Chapter 16, the topic is maintenance support. Chapter 17 more broadly examines the whole issue of running a service center, with all of the waiting-line problems that entails.

But do the support functions *have to* be performed by people once removed from the operations themselves? Certainly not! A theme of the whole book is that support functions are often performed best by those who have to live with the results: the people in charge of performing the operations on the floor. Chapter 18, the finale, summarizes that point of view.

Chapter 13

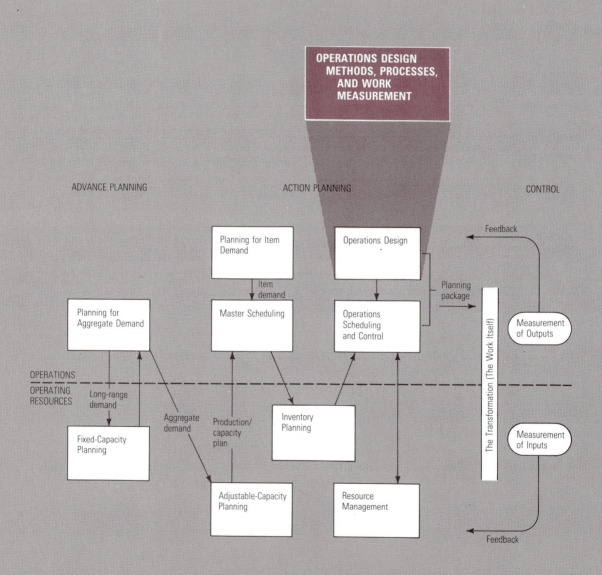

OPERATIONS DESIGN METHODS, PROCESSES, AND WORK MEASUREMENT

ADVANCE PLANNING

ACTION PLANNING

CONTROL

Planning for Item Demand

Operations Design

Feedback

Item demand

Planning for Aggregate Demand

Master Scheduling

Operations Scheduling and Control

Planning package

OPERATIONS
OPERATING RESOURCES

Long-range demand

Aggregate demand

Production/capacity plan

Inventory Planning

The Transformation (The Work Itself)

Measurement of Outputs

Measurement of Inputs

Fixed-Capacity Planning

Adjustable-Capacity Planning

Resource Management

Feedback

Work Improvement, Standards, and Productivity

Productivity improvement comes from cutting costs of labor, materials, and other resources inputs—and raising outputs. The first organized approach to improving the productivity of *labor* arose at the turn of the century from the work of the pioneers of scientific management—Americans, Frederick W. Taylor, Frank and Lillian Gilbreth, and others. Their approach was to standardize the labor element of production. Nonstandard labor practices were simply too expensive and wasteful. By standardization, we mean standard *methods* and standard *times.*

Scientific management could be thought of as the last phase of the industrial revolution. Earlier phases concerned invention, mechanization, standardization of parts, division of labor, and the factory system. Machines and parts were standardized, and labor was divided into narrow specialties, but worker productivity was controlled more by supervisors' skill than by design. Taylor's and Gilbreth's techniques for methods study (or motion study) and time study extended science into the realm of the worker, and U.S. Supreme Court Justice Louis Brandeis called the approach **scientific management.**

Since scientific management is native to the United States, its benefits came to the United States sooner than to other industrial countries. Methods and standards programs spread rapidly in U.S. manufacturing firms between 1900 and 1950, and this may help explain the phenomenal growth of industrial output in the United States in the first half of the century. Methods and time standards programs are no longer limited to manufacturing. Today they are also found in hospitals, food service, hotels, transportation, and other services. So carefully industrially engineered is the McDonald's hamburger that Levitt calls it "the technocratic hamburger."[1] It is becoming hard to compete in these industries without good methods design and labor standards.

Scientific management is not without critics. Labor unions have often resisted time standards, and some believe that under work measurement people are treated

---

IS TAYLORISM OUTDATED?

Some American writers have said that rejection of Taylorism is one reason for Japan's industrial success. That is nonsense. Frederick W. Taylor's contribution was methods study and time standards—and the industrial engineering profession. The Japanese are the most fervent believers in industrial engineering in the world. At Toyota even the foreman is often an IE, or studying to become one. In the just-in-time approach, problems surface, and then people apply methods-study (and quality-control) concepts to solve the problems. Time standards are widely used in Japanese industry, not to measure and report on performance but to plan how long to expect a job to take, to assign the right amount of labor, and to compare methods. Taylor declared that his "whole object was to remove the cause for antagonism between the boss and the men who were under him."*

* Source: Frederick W. Taylor, *The Principles of Scientific Management* (New York: Harper & Row, 1911), pp. 20–28.

---

[1] Theodore Levitt, "Production-Line Approach to Service," *Harvard Business Review,* September–October 1972, pp. 41–52. Also see Richard J. Schonberger, "Taylorism Up-to-Date: The Inevitability of Worker Boredom," *Business and Society,* Spring 1974, pp. 12–17.

like cogs in the machine. Job enrichment and nonlinear assembly concepts respond to some of the criticisms. In the final section of this chapter we consider how to design work for high efficiency without serious losses in humanity. But first we look at organization for productivity, and then at the techniques of methods study and time standards.

ORGANIZATION FOR PRODUCTIVITY IMPROVEMENT

Productivity improvement is something that can be attacked on all fronts—like an land-air-sea battle plan in a war. Some companies do just that. Figure 13–1 shows how employees and supervisors get involved as part of their jobs and how other staff specialists also fit in. The boxes on the chart are discussed below, one by one.

FIGURE 13–1

Productivity Improvement Activities throughout the Organization

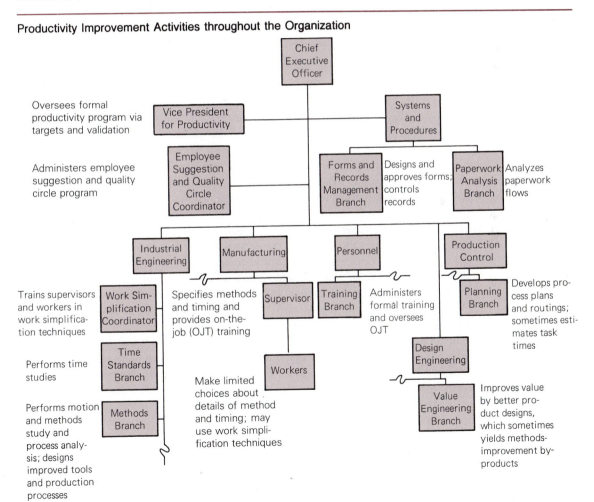

Organizational Elements

Employees and Supervisors. Employees make choices about details of methods and timing and sometimes perform work simplification studies. Supervisors—for example, foremen—give directions on methods and timing and assist in on-the-job training (OJT). A just-in-time program and worker-centered quality control spur shop people to suggest good ideas for improving methods.

Personnel. The training branch in personnel departments relieves supervisors of some of the training burden. They develop training procedures, materials, and facilities; and they may oversee the OJT process.

Production Control. Production control (PC) departments help plan and control work. PC help is especially valuable for work that moves through several work centers. Production control prepares the routing plan (route sheets) for such work. In the absence of formal time standards, PC planners also estimate labor-hours and machine-hours.

Industrial Engineering. Industrial engineering (IE) is responsible for engineered methods and time standards. Often, graduate IEs are in charge of the work-measurement program, but nongraduate IE technicians carry out the analyses. This allows the graduate IE to focus more on operations research analyses.

Industrial engineering may also run a work-simplification program, in which IEs train workers and supervisors to perform their own work studies. Work simplification was developed partly because IEs were having problems trying to impose their ideas upon production people. Work-simplification programs were abundant in the 1940s and 1950s, but they are far less common today.

Forms, Records, and Paperwork. Scientific management in the office has grown steadily in government over the years and has grown in spurts in business offices. Methods and standards programs spread to insurance companies in the 1950s and to banks in the 1950s and 1960s.[2] Part of the reason was a paperwork explosion, in which there were cases of 10- and even 15-copy forms. Paperwork flowcharts were useful for tracking the flows of copies, and these flowcharts sometimes papered the four walls of a good-sized room.

The Systems and Procedures Society of America (SPSA) was founded in 1947 for specialists in paperwork management, and a "management analyst" specialty was established by the U.S. Civil Service for the same purposes: forms design, reports control, records management, standard (office) operating procedures, and paperwork flow analysis. Commercial computers were able to absorb many paper-processing steps, thus simplifying paper flows. (In 1957 SPSA became the Association for Systems

---

[2] Donald L. Caruth cites 60 articles written about commercial—mostly banking—uses of work measurement; nearly all were published in the late 1950s and into the 1960s. *Work Measurement in Commercial Banks* (Boston: Bankers Publishing, 1971), pp. 219–22 (GH1720.W63C36).

Management, which focuses on computer systems analysis as well as traditional paper-work systems and procedures.)

Value Engineering. Value engineering (VE) is mainly directed toward improving product designs. But ideas for better method and process designs often emerge as a byproduct.

Employee Suggestions and Quality Circles. Getting employees to submit ideas for methods improvement can be a formal program. Employee suggestions programs have been around for years. Quality control circles—or quality circles, for short—are a Japanese innovation that many Western companies have adopted to get *groups* to make suggestions. Most suggestions concern methods and processes, including tools, equipment, and other resources. Suggestions may go to a coordinator and then to an expert to review the idea. Accepted suggestions sometimes mean a cash award for the suggestion—or at least praise and recognition.

Vice President for Productivity. The idea of a vice president (or coordinator) for productivity caught on in North America in the late 1970s. The person coordinates the whole productivity program. This means running training courses, setting productivity goals, and measuring results.

Assembling the Planning Package

The chart on the title page of the chapter shows the components of a **planning package,** which gives directions to the workers. The planning package is a formal set of documents in larger organizations, especially goods producers.

A common flow pattern and set of planning-package documents are shown in Figure 13–2. Design engineering is the first step. The engineer's product design goes forward as a set of blueprints, bills of materials, and product specifications.

Methods and times come next. In the less formal version, the flow is directly to the process planner in the production control (PC) department. This flow is likely for nonrepetitive tasks, especially in job-shop operations. Often the process planner began in the shop and has the background to plan the operations and estimate operation times. These go onto what is often called a **route sheet.**

Repetitive tasks may be planned in a more specialized way. A methods analyst in industrial engineering (IE) may formally study ways to produce the product in the engineer's blueprints. A proposed new method may be displayed as a flowchart of operations; new workplace layouts, tool designs, and so on, may accompany the flowchart. Documents on the new method are filed, and the training branch in personnel may use them to create training materials; the documents are also used in time-standards development.

The time-standards analyst in the IE department develops a standard time for each operation. Standard times may be developed on some sort of time-study form, and the results are kept on file.

FIGURE 13–2

Characteristic Flow in Assembling Planning Package

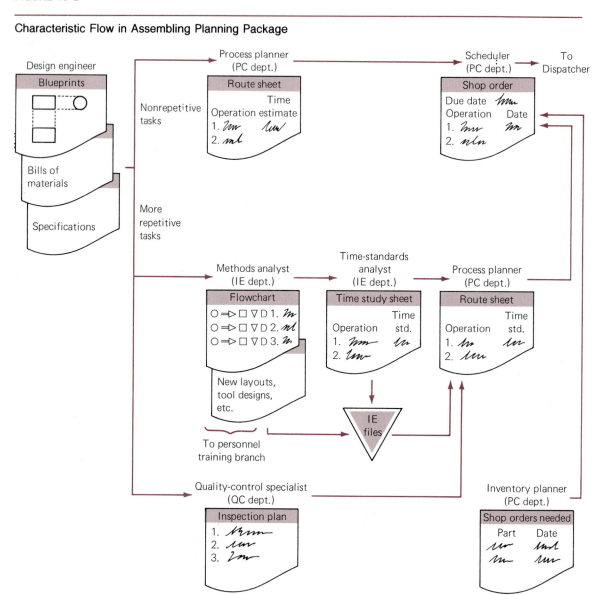

In this formal flow, the process planner develops the route sheet from routings (sequences of operations) and standard times on file. Quality-control inspection procedures may be inserted in the proper places on the route sheet.

The planning package is completed by an inventory planner, who notes the need for a parts order, and by a production control scheduler, who prepares a shop order for the parts. The scheduler computes operation due dates based on work-center lead times and enters them on the shop order. The shop order goes into the job stream, and dispatchers steer it through to completion.

The flow patterns described are general—not precise as to details, because details vary from firm to firm.

The methods and time-standards inputs to the planning package are explained further in the next two sections. Quality-control and inventory inputs are discussed in other chapters.

METHODS STUDY

Formal methods-study techniques are based on the scientific method, a general method of inquiry. The steps in one version of the scientific method are:

1. Define problem.
2. Collect data.
3. Generate alternatives.
4. Evaluate alternatives and choose.
5. Implement.

Now let us see how Taylor, Gilbreth, and other pioneers of scientific management translated the scientific method into a procedure for methods study. Figure 13–3 illustrates, and explanation follows.

FIGURE 13–3

Methods Study and Scientific Method

Scientific method	Methods study
1. Define problem.	Select a present task for methods improvement (or a new task for methods development).
2. Collect data.	Flowchart present method (the *before* chart), or synthesize a flowchart for a new task.
3. Generate alternatives.	Apply questioning attitude, principles of motion economy, etc., to arrive at alternative method and flowchart the method (the *after* chart).
4. Evaluate alternatives and choose.	Evaluate new method via savings in: Cost. Delays. Time. Transportations. Effort. Transportation distances. Storages. Choose best method.
5. Implement.	Implement—in training workers and in job planning.

Methods-Study Procedures

Methods study begins with task selection (step 1 in Figure 13–3). It may be a present task that seems inefficient or that has never been studied before, or it may be a new task.

Steps 2 and 3 often feature *before* and *after* comparison. Collected data goes onto a flowchart showing the present method—the "before" condition. Then an "after" flowchart is developed to show a better method.

In arriving at a better method, the questioning attitude may be applied. Methods analysis, like newspaper reporting, embraces Kipling's six honest serving men:

> I keep six honest serving men
> (They taught me all I knew);
> Their names are what and why and when
> and how and where and who.
>
> Rudyard Kipling
The Elephant's Child

Principles of methods improvement are also useful. Frank and Lillian Gilbreth were early developers of such principles.[3] Ralph Barnes elaborated on the Gilbreths' work in developing "principles of motion economy." Others have offered further refinements. For example, Mundel provides a list of "general principles," which attempt to incorporate the human factor. Study of the human factor is a subfield of industrial engineering known as ergonomics. Mundel's list is given in Figure 13–4.[4]

These general principles are grouped under four headings: elimination, combination, rearrangement, and simplification. Notice that some of the items emphasize the human factor. For example, A4 concerns more normal body motions; A5 concerns better posture; A8 concerns danger; B1 suggests natural, sweeping motions as opposed to choppy, irregular ones; C2 suggests use of the eyes as a substitute for use of the hands; and most of D concerns the physiology of effort. The idea is that much of the potential for productivity gain is found at the labor-machine interface, and this calls for attention to human comfort and emotions as well as physical efficiency.

Step 4 in Figure 13–3 is evaluating new the method based on cost or other criteria. Cost analysis is often itself costly, and cost estimates for methods not yet tried can be inaccurate. Therefore, other criteria are often used as surrogates for cost: time, effort, storages, delays, transportations, and transportation distances. Quality is usually *not* one of the criteria, because in a methods study a minimum level of quality is usually treated as a given.

The chosen method is implemented (Step 5) for worker-training and job-planning purposes. Sometimes the industrial engineer's chosen method must be "signed off" by the foreman and perhaps also by quality control, safety, production control, personnel, and a labor-union steward.

---

[3] F. B. Gilbreth and L. M. Gilbreth, *Fatigue Study* (New York: Sturgis and Walton, 1916). The book was written by Lillian Gilbreth.

[4] Marvin E. Mundel, *Motion and Time Study: Improving Productivity,* 5th ed. (Englewood Cliffs, N.J.: Prentice-Hall, 1978), pp. 172–73 (T60.7.M86).

FIGURE 13–4

General Principles of Methods Improvement

A. *Elimination*
  1. Eliminate all possible jobs, steps, or motions. (This applies to body, leg, arm, hand, or eye.)
  2. Eliminate irregularities in a job so as to facilitate automaticity. Provide fixed places for things.
  3. Eliminate the use of the hand as a holding device.
  4. Eliminate awkward or abnormal motions.
  5. Eliminate the use of muscles to maintain a fixed posture.
  6. Eliminate muscular force by using power tools, power feeds, etc.
  7. Eliminate the overcoming of momentum.
  8. Eliminate danger.
  9. Eliminate idle time unless needed for rest.

B. *Combination*
  1. Replace with one continuous curved motion short motions which are connected with sudden changes in direction.
  2. With fixed machine cycles, make a maximum of work internal to the machine cycle.
  3. Combine tools.
  4. Combine controls.
  5. Combine motions.

C. *Rearrangement*
  1. Distribute the work evenly between the two hands. A simultaneous symmetrical motion pattern is most effective. (This frequently involves working on two parts at the same time.) With crew work, distribute the work evenly among members of the crew.
  2. Shift work from the hands to the eyes.
  3. Arrange for a straightforward order of work.

D. *Simplification*
  1. Use the smallest muscle group capable of doing the work, providing for intermittent use of muscle groups as needed.
  2. Reduce eye travel and the number of fixations.
  3. Keep work in the normal work area, the area reached without moving the body.
  4. Shorten motions.
  5. Adapt handles, levers, pedals, buttons, and so on, to human dimensions and musculatures.
  6. Use momentum to build up energy in place of the intense application of muscular force.
  7. Use the simplest possible combination of motions.
  8. Reduce the complexity of each motion, particularly the motions performed at one location (as contrasted with motions that change the location of things).

Source: Marvin E. Mundel, *Motion and Time Study: Improving Productivity* (Englewood Cliffs, N.J.: Prentice-Hall, 1978), p. 173 (T60.7.M86). Used with permission.

The five steps in methods study may be applied to small, medium, or large units of work. In fact, the history of methods study began with motion study of workers confined to the workbench and gradually grew. Whole work stations and then work that crossed work-center and departmental boundaries were studied. There are variations on the five-step process that apply to various levels of work-unit analysis.

Figure 13–5 presents four such levels—from workbench to machine to work area to whole plant; the focus shifts from hand motions to worker and machine to mobile worker to product flow. The first of the four is described next.

FIGURE 13–5

Four Levels of Methods Study

Type	Application	Flowchart
Motion study	Manual task at workbench or desk	Right-and-left-hand chart
Worker-machine analysis	Machine tending at workplace	Worker-machine chart
Worker analysis	Task involving mobile worker	Process flowchart (worker-oriented)
Product analysis	Product flow	Process flowchart (product-oriented)

Motion Study

Frank Gilbreth is the father of motion study, which began as a laboratory approach to analyzing basic hand and body motions. In fact, basic motions such as reach and grasp are known as "therbligs," and therblig is Gilbreth spelled backward (except for the *th*). It was sensible for Gilbreth to focus on highly repetitive short-cycle manual motions. Rather small gains can yield large benefits, and the analysis is not complicated by costly machines, worker travel, and irregular activities.

The left-and-right-hand chart is suitable for before-and-after analysis. A goal is to keep both hands busy, because an idle hand is like half an idle worker. An example follows.

EXAMPLE 13–1

Left-and-Right-Hand Chart, Bolt-Washer-Nut Assembly

One repetitive task in a certain firm is to make a washer-nut-bolt assembly. The present method seems inefficient, and it is undergoing study using the left-and-right-hand charting method.

Figure 13–6 charts the present method. In this version of the left-and-right-hand chart the operation is described in symbols as well as words. The meanings of the symbols are:

FIGURE 13–6

Left-and-Right-Hand Chart for Bolt-Washer-Nut Assembly,
Present Method

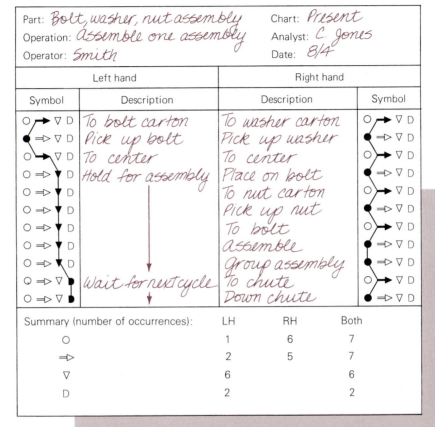

Part: Bolt, washer, nut assembly			Chart: Present	
Operation: assemble one assembly			Analyst: C. Jones	
Operator: Smith			Date: 8/4	

Left hand		Right hand	
Symbol	Description	Description	Symbol
O→▽D	To bolt carton	To washer carton	O→▽D
●⇒▽D	Pick up bolt	Pick up washer	●⇒▽D
O→▽D	To center	To center	O→▽D
O⇒▼D	Hold for assembly	Place on bolt	●→▽D
O⇒▼D		To nut carton	O→▽D
O⇒▼D		Pick up nut	●⇒▽D
O⇒▼D		To bolt	O→▽D
O⇒▼D		assemble	●⇒▽D
O⇒▼D		group assembly	●⇒▽D
O⇒▽●	Wait for next cycle	To chute	O→▽D
O⇒▽■		Down chute	●⇒▽D

Summary (number of occurrences):	LH	RH	Both
O	1	6	7
⇒	2	5	7
▽	6		6
D	2		2

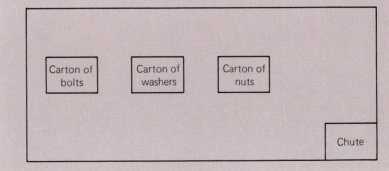

FIGURE 13–7

Left-and-Right-Hand Chart for Bolt-Washer-Nut Assembly, Proposed Method

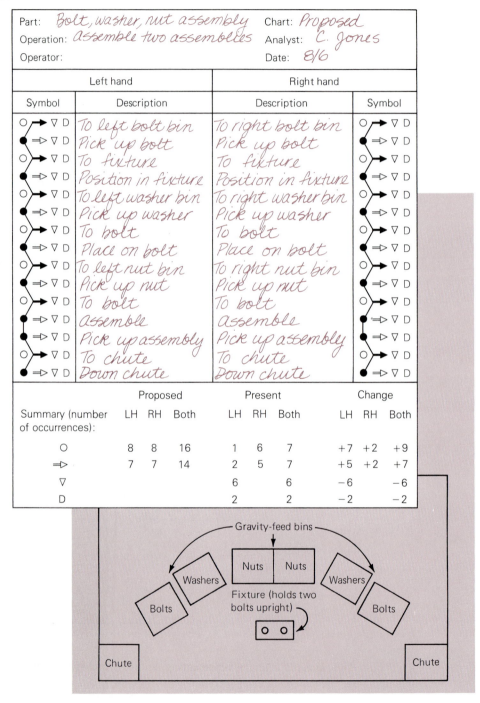

Part: Bolt, washer, nut assembly   Chart: Proposed
Operation: Assemble two assemblies   Analyst: C. Jones
Operator: Date: 8/6

Left hand		Right hand	
Symbol	Description	Description	Symbol
○→▽D	To left bolt bin	To right bolt bin	○→▽D
●⇒▽D	Pick up bolt	Pick up bolt	●⇒▽D
○→▽D	To fixture	To fixture	○→▽D
●⇒▽D	Position in fixture	Position in fixture	●⇒▽D
○→▽D	To left washer bin	To right washer bin	○→▽D
●⇒▽D	Pick up washer	Pick up washer	●⇒▽D
○→▽D	To bolt	To bolt	○→▽D
●⇒▽D	Place on bolt	Place on bolt	●⇒▽D
○→▽D	To left nut bin	To right nut bin	○→▽D
●⇒▽D	Pick up nut	Pick up nut	●⇒▽D
○→▽D	To bolt	To bolt	○→▽D
●⇒▽D	Assemble	Assemble	●⇒▽D
●⇒▽D	Pick up assembly	Pick up assembly	●⇒▽D
○→▽D	To chute	To chute	○→▽D
●⇒▽D	Down chute	Down chute	●⇒▽D

Summary (number of occurrences):	Proposed			Present			Change		
	LH	RH	Both	LH	RH	Both	LH	RH	Both
○	8	8	16	1	6	7	+7	+2	+9
⇒	7	7	14	2	5	7	+5	+2	+7
▽					6	6		−6	−6
D					2	2		−2	−2

Gravity-feed bins

Nuts Nuts

Washers   Washers

Bolts   Bolts

Fixture (holds two bolts upright)

Chute   Chute

Operations are productive, moves and holds less so, and delays not at all. The summary at the bottom of the flowchart shows mostly low-productive and nonproductive elements, i.e., seven moves, six holds, and two delays. A workbench sketch commonly goes with the left-and-right-hand chart, because a poor workbench design impedes productivity.

Figure 13–7 charts a proposed method, which is based on improved design of the workbench. The new workbench design and method follow some of the principles of methods improvement given in Figure 13–4. For example, the proposed method "eliminates the use of the hand as a holding device" (principle A3) and it "distributes the work evenly between the two hands" (C1).

The summary in Figure 13–7 shows elimination of all holds and delays. There are seven more moves, but the proposed method produces two assemblies every cycle versus one per cycle under the present method. The proposed method clearly increases productivity. Also, it provides smoother, more natural motions and shorter hand-travel distances; the proposed method may be less tiring.

If the results of the motion study appear likely to be disputed, it may be worth the extra effort to measure elements in time units. Also, having the results in minutes permits conversion into dollars, so that operating savings may be compared with the costs of new-methods development and implementation.

Worker-Machine Analysis

When the worker is a machine tender instead of a tool user, we worry about the productivity of the machine as well as the worker, since a machine is a costly resource. A worker-machine-time chart may be used to record present (before) and proposed (after) methods for work involving one or more workers and machines. For example, a two-person crew might sort, wash, dry, and iron sheets in a hospital laundry. A five-column worker-machine-time chart could be set up to record activities and durations, one column for the first crew member, one for the second crew member, one for the washer, one for the dryer, and one for the ironing machine. A workplace layout normally accompanies the chart. Time saving is the basis for comparing the new method with the old.

Worker Analysis

The activities of a mobile worker may be studied by the process flowchart, another contribution of Gilbreth. Four process flow symbols are used. The circle, the arrow, and the large *D* were discussed earlier; the fourth symbol, a square, stands for inspection. The inverted triangle, representing hold or store, is not used in worker analysis because you do not store a person.

Product Analysis

The process flowchart is also used to chart the flow of products. Five charting symbols are used: the four used in worker analysis, plus the inverted triangle, for storage. These five symbols were standardized by the American Society of Mechanical Engineers (ASME), which provided aid and encouragement in the formative years of scientific management. The ASME symbols are accepted throughout the world. The symbols and the product analysis flowchart are used in the following example.

EXAMPLE 13–2

Process Flowchart—"The Expense-Account Express"[5]

Intel Corporation has "rediscovered" the process flow chart and is using it extensively in both its paperwork and its goods production operations. For example, Intel's expense-account processing steps have been reduced from 25 to 14, as is shown in the before-and-after charts of Figure 13–8. The accounts-payable clerk took over the cash-receipts clerk's job of checking past expense accounts of the employee, steps 8, 10, and 11. This eliminates steps 5 and 7. There was no need for an accounts-receivable clerk to check the employee's past expense accounts, since another department already did that; steps 8, 10, and 11 were eliminated. Checking items against company guidelines, step 14, was done away with; it seemed more trouble than it was worth. Logging batches, step 19, was found to be unnecessary. Four delays, steps 2, 6, 9, and 18, were eliminated. Now expense accounts are processed in days rather than weeks.

For expenses under $100, the employee now just fills out a petty-cash voucher and collects right away from the cashier. After these and other simplifications, the accounts-payable department cut its staff from 71 in 1980 to 51 in April 1981.

Other Methods Analysis Tools

A number of other tools besides flowcharting are used in methods analysis. Systems flowcharting and program flowcharting are similar tools in the computer industry. Material handling and plant/office layout, discussed in a later chapter, are special-purpose process analysis techniques. Capital budgeting/engineering economy techniques are used mainly to evaluate facilities proposals, but they are also used to compare manual methods with automated facilities. Linear programming, queuing, simulation, and other models of management science are also useful in process analysis. We examine some of those tools in other chapters.

One bedrock analysis tool quite different from the flow-charting tools is work sampling. Work sampling is a tool for both process analysis and time-standards analysis and will thus be discussed twice in this chapter.

---

[5] Adapted from Jeremy Main, "Battling Your Own Bureaucracy," in *Working Smarter,* by the Editors of *Fortune* (New York: Viking Press, 1982) pp. 88–89 (HC110.I52W67).

FIGURE 13–8

Process Flowchart

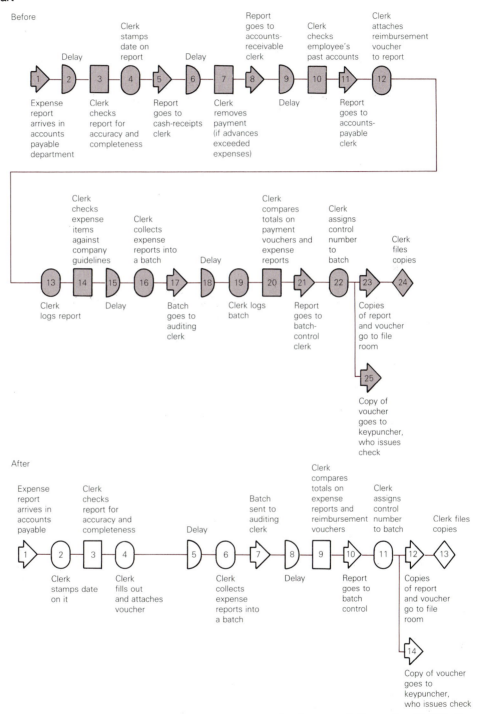

Work-Sampling Analysis.   Work sampling is like the *before* flowchart. It shows what is happening at present. The work-sampling study yields data on percentage of idle or delay time.[6] More than that, the study can be designed with idleness broken down into categories, thereby showing process bottlenecks. An example follows.

EXAMPLE 13–3

Work Sampling, Pathology Lab

The director of Midtown Pathological Labs is concerned. Costs are going up rapidly; the staff has plenty to do, yet it often is idled by assorted problems. The director decides to probe the sources of delay by conducting a one-week work-sampling study. Of special interest are lab equipment failures, shortages of supplies, delays waiting for instructions, excessive coffee breaks, and lab technicians out of the work area. The director prepares a work-sampling data sheet that includes those five categories of delay (plus an "other" category); she also works up a schedule for taking 100 sample observations (20 per day).

The schedule and the completed form are shown in Figure 13–9. The results—the staff not working 35 percent of the time—confirm the director's impression of serious delay problems. The breakdown into categories of delay yields insight into causes.

The management system can be blamed for the first 18 percent of non-working time. Equipment failure (3 percent), supplies shortage (6 percent), and wait for instructions (9 percent) are failures to provide technicians with resources to keep busy.

The 13 percent of delay for coffee breaks is an employee problem. Authorized coffee breaks are a 15-minute morning break and a 15-minute afternoon break. This amounts to 30 minutes or, in percent of an eight-hour day,

$$\frac{30 \text{ min.}}{8 \text{ hr.} \times 60 \text{ min./hr.}} = 0.0625 \approx 6\%$$

The coffee-break abuses may be dealt with immediately. The data on resource shortages do not offer a solution, but they do tip off the director as to where to look.

Avoiding Bias.   Work sampling yields delay statistics. It also yields the complement, utilization statistics. Utilization rate (65 percent in the example) means "busyness," that is, hours busy divided by hours available. But most of us are very busy at times and not so busy at other times. This means that, to avoid bias, the analyst doing work sampling must take care to do the study in a representative period of

---

[6] In fact, work sampling used to be known as *ratio delay,* a term proposed by R. L. Morrow, an early U.S. user of the technique. (L. H. C. Tippett developed the method in England in the 1920s.) Later the editor of *Factory* magazine, recognizing its usefulness in time-standards analysis as well as delay analysis, proposed the more general term *work sampling*. Ralph M. Barnes, *Work Sampling* (New York: John Wiley & Sons, 1957), pp. 8–10 (T60.T5B3).

FIGURE 13–9

Work-Sampling Data Sheets, Midtown Pathological Labs

SCHEDULE OF OBSERVATION TIMES

Mon.	Tues.	Wed.	Thurs.	Fri.

8:01
8:13
9:47
9:59
10:12
10:59
11:16
11:32

1:00
1:15
1:19
2:52
2:55
2:56
2:57
3:02
3:29
3:37
4:07
4:32

WORK-SAMPLING FORM

Category of Activity	Observations (tallies)	Percentages
Working	₩₩ ₩₩ ₩₩ ₩₩ ₩₩ ₩₩ ₩₩ ₩₩ ₩₩ ₩₩ ₩₩ ₩₩ ₩₩ (65)	65%
Not working:		
• Equipment failure	||| (3)	3%
• Supplies shortage	₩₩ | (6)	6%
• Wait for instructions	₩₩ |||| (9)	9%
• Coffee break	₩₩ ₩₩ ||| (13)	13%
• Out of area	|| (2)	2%
• Other	|| (2)	2%
Total	100	100%

time (representative of average conditions if that is the goal of the study; representative of very busy conditions if peak conditions are being examined; etc.).

There are other types of bias to guard against. Some guidelines are:

Conduct the study over a number of days or weeks—so that results are not biased by a single unusual day.

Make "instantaneous" observations so that the worker doesn't "glide" into another activity, leaving the analyst a choice of which one to record.

Vary the route of travel if the study goes to several work areas—to guard against having workers in one area alert workers in the next area that the observer is coming.

Observe at random intervals—so that workers may not come to expect and "prepare for" the observer's arrival at set intervals.

Tell the workers what you are doing, and emphasize the goal of improving resource support—to prevent hostility and deliberate attempts to foul up the study.

When in doubt, ask the worker what the observed activity is—to avoid judgmental bias.

Take a large enough sample to yield convincing results. (Probably 100, the sample size of Figure 13–9, is not enough. Statistical guidelines are available in many industrial engineering books.)

Keep in mind that utilization is not the same as efficiency. That is, one who works (is utilized) 100 percent of the time may or may not also be efficient. Efficiency measures how much work got done in comparison with a standard. Standards are considered next.

TIME STANDARDS AND THEIR USES

Methods study comes first; time study comes next. Why? Because you'd rather not set a time standard on a poor method.

Actually the ideal sequence of method first, time standard second, is not always practiced. Time standards tend to be more important—at least in the short run—than improved methods. In launching a methods and standards program, some firms therefore may reverse the process: first cover all tasks with time standards—perhaps "quick and dirty" ones; later turn to methods studies; and finally refine time standards based on the improved methods. Let us see why time standards are important.

Importance of Time Standards

Work is simply a form of exertion. But a work unit (e.g., a job, task, project, or other unit) implies the *time to do work.* Our thoughts about work time need not go beyond that notion of an implied time. But sometimes, perhaps to motivate ourselves or others, we are more specific about work time: We estimate it in advance. Time estimating—in advance—is more essential when more than one person is involved. If person B must wait for person A to finish a job, then person B will want an advance estimate of how long A's job will take. Time estimates are also useful in planning labor needs and labor costs.

These uses of time standards (estimates) suggest three sorts of purposes: One is coordination, another is analysis, and the third is motivation. The three types are listed in more detail in Figure 13–10.

Coordination—Scheduling

By coordination we mean scheduling. This may be the primary use of a time standard. Actually, by definition, a schedule is a time standard, with adjustments

FIGURE 13–10

Uses of Time Estimates or Standards

Coordinational uses

Scheduling. The time to perform a scheduled task is as shown below:

$\longleftarrow$ Time standard—with efficiency and utilization adjustments $\longrightarrow$

Start   Finish
of   of
task   task

Analytical uses

Staffing, budgeting, and estimating/bidding.

Example: Forecast of $\times$ Standard time $=$ Staff needed
work units   per unit   (e.g., in labor-hours)

Evaluating alternative methods/equipment. The labor-cost element of a method/equipment alternative might include:

Operating cost—based on standard time per unit of output.
Maintenance cost—based on standard time to repair equipment.

Motivational uses

Efficiency and productivity. Labor efficiency may be evaluated by:

$$\text{Efficiency} = \frac{\text{Standard time/unit}}{\text{Actual time/unit}} \text{ or } \frac{\text{Actual units/time period}}{\text{Standard units/time period}}$$

$$\text{Labor productivity} = \frac{\text{Standard time for all work done}}{\text{Time available for work}}$$

Targets for personal motivation. Knowing what is expected of you provides self-motivation.

for efficiency and utilization. That is, the time between the scheduled start and the scheduled finish of a task equals:

Standard time—the time that it should take under normal assumptions
. . . adjusted downward for a fast worker or upward for a slow worker.
. . . adjusted downward for less than 100 percent labor utilization (i.e., for expected idleness).

Mathematically, scheduled output for a given time period is:

$$\text{Scheduled output} = \frac{\text{Efficiency} \times \text{Utilization}}{\text{Standard time per unit}} \qquad (1)$$

or

$$\text{Scheduled output} = \text{Standard units per time period} \times \text{Efficiency} \times \text{Utilization} \qquad (2)$$

and

$$\text{Utilization} = \frac{\text{Time working}}{\text{Time available for work}} \qquad (3)$$

A useful inversion of formula (1) is:

$$\text{Scheduled time} = \frac{\text{Standard time per unit}}{\text{Efficiency} \times \text{Utilization}} \qquad (4)$$

Many firms use a single combined efficiency-utilization rate instead of two separate rates. The combined rate is a **productivity** rate. Then,

$$\text{Scheduled time} = \frac{\text{Standard time per unit}}{\text{Productivity rate}} \qquad (5)$$

Utilization goes up when workers are kept busy and provided with proper tools, materials, well-maintained equipment, and so forth. The scheduled time, for a job that is done more than once, may be cut as utilization is improved. It is up to management to provide the right resources to keep workers busy. An example follows:

EXAMPLE 13–4

Translation of Time Standard into Schedule, Tire Installation

Gate City Tire Company sells and installs tires, some by appointment, the rest to drop-in customers. Appointments are carefully scheduled so that (1) the customer may be told when the car will be ready and (2) installers are kept busy. The manager knows that under normal conditions a four-tire installation takes about 20 minutes. The time varies, depending on the speed (efficiency) of the installer and the delay (utilization) encountered.

A recent study shows efficiency to be 90 percent (where normal efficiency or speed is 100 percent); it is low because the present crew lacks experience. Utilization is predicted to be 80 percent (it would be 100 percent for a crew that is busy every minute of the eight-hour day). Delays arise mainly from tool breakdowns, parts shortages, special customer requests, and two authorized 15-minute coffee breaks; these, plus miscellaneous delays, account for the 20 percent nonutilization time.

The current scheduled daily output is found using formula (1):

$$\text{Daily output} = \frac{8 \text{ hrs.} \times 60 \text{ min./hr.}}{20 \text{ min./installation}} \times 90\% \text{ efficiency} \times 80\% \text{ utilization}$$
$$= 17.28 \text{ installations/day}$$

Seventeen installations per day is the expected output, but each of the 17 or so jobs in a day may be separately scheduled. For example, let us assume that the third job of the day, a phoned appointment, is assigned to Jeff, who has been only 80 percent efficient; but the manager expects no delays for lack of materials, tool breakdowns, or other problems, and it is not near coffee-break time. So utilization is expected to be 100 percent. The scheduled installation time, from formula (4), is:

$$\text{Scheduled time} = \frac{20 \text{ min./installation}}{80\% \times 100\%} = 25 \text{ minutes}$$

Where coordinational demands are light, work units may not be formally scheduled. But we nearly always have at least a vague time plan for starting and finishing an upcoming task. That vague time plan is an *implied* time standard.

Analysis

One of the analytical uses listed in Figure 13–10 is staffing, budgeting, and estimating/bidding. Staff needed is the product of units forecast times standard time per unit. Budgeting for staff goes one step further: staff needed times wage rate equals staff budget.

The staff component of an estimate or bid is computed the same way as the staff component of a budget. Accurate bidding is a key to success in contract-oriented businesses, for example, construction. Accurate cost estimating is important in job-shop work, because pricing is based on estimated cost plus profit margin. Physicians, attorneys, and consultants also often operate this way.

The following example shows how a time standard is translated into the staff component of a budget/estimate/bid.

EXAMPLE 13–5

Bidding Based on Time Standards, Teen Labor Services

An enterprising group of teenagers have organized themselves into Teen Labor Services. Teen Labor bids on common-labor jobs. Teen Labor is currently preparing a bid for a nearby farmer who has two acres of nearly ripe cucumbers. One member of the group is experienced, and he says that three bushels per hour is standard for one worker. The farmer estimates that the field will yield 80 bushels per acre.

The bid is based on an estimate that the inexperienced crew will work at 85 percent efficiency. With breaks, plus delays in waiting for more baskets, waiting for the pickup truck, and so forth, estimated utilization is 80 percent. The group bids at a labor rate of $4 per hour. The bid is calculated as follows—beginning with formula (2):

$$\text{Scheduled output per hour} = 3 \text{ bushels/hr.} \times 85\% \text{ efficiency}$$
$$\times 80\% \text{ utilization}$$
$$= 2.04 \text{ bushels/hr.}$$

$$\text{Total bushels} = 2 \text{ acres} \times 80 \text{ bushels/acre}$$
$$= 160 \text{ bushels}$$

$$\text{Scheduled hours} = \frac{160 \text{ bushels}}{2.04 \text{ bushels/hr.}}$$
$$= 78.43 \text{ hrs.}$$

$$\text{Labor component of bid} = 78.43 \text{ hrs.} \times \$4/\text{hr.}$$
$$= \$313.72$$

For this job, Teen Labor foresees no expenses for supplies, tools, materials, utilities, and so on, and Teen Labor never adds an overhead charge or a profit margin. Therefore, the bid consists entirely of the labor cost, $313.72.

The other analytical use of time standards is evaluating alternative methods/equipment. Most such alternatives involve some labor costs. The labor component of operating cost is based on standard time per unit of output, with adjustments for efficiency and utilization. The labor component of maintenance cost is based on standard time to repair, with adjustments.

Motivation, Efficiency, Productivity

You can ask almost anyone what they think a time standard is for, and they will say "to motivate people" or "to speed up workers" or "to control labor." We know better. We have just studied other uses. The time standard *may* also be used for motivation or speedup or control. These possible uses are considered next.

Efficiency Reports.   The control may be external—efficiency evaluation and incentive wages in Figure 13–10. Typically there is a periodic report of efficiency by worker, work center, and/or department. Efficiency is determined in two ways:

$$\text{Efficiency} = \frac{\text{Standard time per unit}}{\text{Actual time per unit}} \qquad (5)$$

or simply,

$$\frac{\text{Standard time}}{\text{Actual time}}$$

$$\text{Efficiency} = \frac{\text{Actual units per time period}}{\text{Standard units per time period}} \qquad (6)$$

or simply,

$$\frac{\text{Actual units}}{\text{Standard units}}$$

Notice that the two versions are mathematically equivalent; each is an inversion of the other. To illustrate the formulas, assume that 440 actual units are produced in a 40-hour week, and 400 is the standard output per week. Using formula (6),

$$\begin{aligned}
\text{Efficiency} &= \frac{\text{Actual units/week}}{\text{Standard units/week}} \\
&= \frac{440 \text{ units/week}}{400 \text{ units/week}} \\
&= 1.10, \text{ or } 110\%
\end{aligned}$$

To use formula (5), the data must be converted to time per unit. Since there are 2,400 minutes in a 40-hour week,

$$\begin{aligned}
\text{Standard time} &= \frac{2,400 \text{ minutes/week}}{400 \text{ units/week}} \\
&= 6 \text{ minutes/unit}
\end{aligned}$$

and

$$\text{Actual time} = \frac{2,400 \text{ minutes/week}}{440 \text{ units/week}}$$
$$= 5.45 \text{ minutes/unit}$$

Then, by formula (5),

$$\text{Efficiency} = \frac{6 \text{ min./unit}}{5.45 \text{ min./unit}}$$
$$= 1.10, \text{ or } 110\%$$

In job-lot operations, formula (5) is often adapted to cover a number of jobs over a fixed reporting period. The numerator is the total standard time for all jobs worked on in the period. The denominator is time spent on those jobs. A data-entry terminal on the shop floor may be used to record when the worker starts and stops work on a job. Then the total time clocked on all jobs for a period is the denominator. The formula is:

$$\text{Efficiency} = \frac{\text{Total standard time for all jobs done}}{\text{Actual direct labor time on those jobs}} \qquad (7)$$

Assume, for example, that in a 40-hour week a shop with six workers completes 36 jobs that have a total of 190 standard hours of work content. (That averages 5.0 hours per job and 0.83 hours per worker on each job.) The six workers report 200 actual hours of direct labor on those 36 jobs. Then, by formula (7),

$$\text{Efficiency} = \frac{190}{200}$$
$$= 0.95 \text{ or } 95\%$$

Utilization Reports.   In this example, the six employees would be paid for working a total of 240 hours for the 40-hour week. Only 200 of those hours were assigned to the 40 jobs. If we assume that the other 40 hours represent idle time (perhaps it actually includes worthy indirect activities like training), then the utilization rate, formula (3), is:

$$\text{Utilization} = \frac{\text{Time working}}{\text{Time available for work}}$$
$$= \frac{200}{240} = 0.83 \text{ or } 83\%$$

Utilization is mostly a measure of *management* performance: If utilization is low, management is at fault for not providing the resources, jobs, and attention to keep the workers busy.

Productivity.   A productivity rate (a grosser measure of results than efficiency) may also be calculated. Productivity—whether in economics, engineering, or business—

means output divided by input. Standard time can serve as an objective measure of output. The productivity formula, then, is

$$\text{Productivity} = \frac{\text{Standard time for all work done}}{\text{Time available for work}} \qquad (8)$$

In our example,

$$\text{Productivity} = \frac{190}{240} = 0.79 \text{ or } 79\%$$

Also, it happens that

$$\text{Productivity} = \text{Efficiency} \times \text{Utilization} \qquad (9)$$

So,

$$\text{Productivity} = 0.95 \times 0.83 = 0.79$$

Incentive Pay. Sometimes incentive wages are paid. There are many ways to set up an incentive-wage system.[7] A pure incentive is simply a piece rate; for example, a berry picker's piece rate might be $1 per bucket. But U.S. wage-and-hour laws require that piece-rate earnings may not fall below the minimum wage, based on hours worked.

Incentive wages may also be based on standard times. In some plans incentive wages are paid for increments of output above an acceptable productivity level (APL). The APL equals standard output or some agreed-upon percentage of it. Incentive pay can dramatically raise productivity. But the APL must be carefully engineered. Otherwise there will be disputes whenever the methods, equipment, and products change. If workers lose their incentive pay, the system unravels.

The measured daywork (MDW) system is more popular than APL-based systems. MDW is only nominally an incentive-wage system. In MDW, standard output serves as a target that methods engineers, trainers, and supervisors help the worker attain. The worker who cannot attain it is moved to another position or advised to seek work elsewhere.

The final item in Figure 13–10 is the time standard as a target for personal motivation. An open-ended job assignment invites delay. An explicit statement of how long the task should take serves as self-motivation to the worker. Some research suggests that self-motivation is greater if workers plot their own output on graphs.

TIME STANDARDS TECHNIQUES

There are common abuses (to be discussed later) as well as common uses of time standards. Some uses and abuses relate to the techniques for *developing* time standards. The techniques are of two types: engineered and nonengineered; see Figure 13–11.

---

[7] See, for example, John A. Patton, C. L. Littlefield, and Stanley Allen Self, *Job Evaluation* (Homewood, Ill.: Richard D. Irwin, 1964).

FIGURE 13–11

Techniques for Setting Time Standards

Technique	Source of times	Timing role of analyst
Engineered		
1. Time study	Stopwatch (or film)	Direct observation: record times for several cycles of the task; judge and record pace.
2. Work sampling	Percent of study period busy at given task divided by number of units produced	Direct observation: randomly check worker status; keep tallies of worker activities and pace; obtain production count.
3. Predetermined	Table look-up	Define task in basic body motions; look up time values in basic motion tables.
4. Standard data	Table look-up	Define task in small common elements (e.g., pound nail); look up time value in standard-data tables.
Nonengineered		
5. Historical (statistical)	Past records on actual task times	Determine arithmetic mean and/or other useful statistics.
6. Technical estimate ("guesstimate")	Experienced judgment	Experienced person estimates times, preferably after breaking task into operations.

Engineered and Nonengineered Standards

Four techniques may result in engineered time standards. The engineered standard is prepared at some expense following the scientific methods of the industrial engineer. Two of the engineered techniques require direct observation. These are stopwatch time study, a well-known approach, and work sampling, which was presented earlier as a process analysis technique. The other two engineered techniques, predetermined and standard data, do not require direct observation; instead, the analyst building a standard uses tables of time values. Since a real worker is not involved, these standards are sometimes called synthetic time standards.

Two techniques are listed in Figure 13–11 as nonengineered. The first is historical or statistical. It is based on past records rather than on controlled study. The second is the technical estimate or "guesstimate."[8] It comes from subjective judgment instead of recorded statistics.

---

[8] It is also known as a WAG or a SWAG, common abbreviations for slightly salty terms that some readers may be familiar with.

Requisites of an Engineered Standard

The expense of an engineered time standard is worthwhile if precision is needed: for example, in highly repetitive processes where small gains add up fast. The following steps lead to an engineered standard:

1. Clearly specify the method.
2. Obtain time values via a proper sampling procedure or from validated tables.
3. Adjust for worker pace.
4. Include allowances for personal, rest, and delay.

Each step adds precision. A precise time standard is associated with a known standard method (ideally an improved or engineered method). One way to get precise time values is to use a proper sampling procedure and direct observation; direct observation is avoided by use of a "synthetic" time value from validated tables. Where direct observation is used, the time value should be adjusted for worker pace; but validated tables of time values have built-in pace adjustments. Finally, the pace-adjusted time is adjusted further by adding reasonable allowances for workers' personal and rest time and for unavoidable delay.

The nonengineered techniques control for none of the four above factors of precision. (Even the first four in Figure 13–11 are worthy of the term *engineered* only if they are precisely developed, following the four steps.) In the following discussions, we see how the steps apply for each technique. Time study is discussed first and in some detail; the other techniques include many of the same steps.

Time Study

The most direct approach to time standards is timing a worker who is performing the task. A stopwatch is the usual timing device, but motion-picture film or videotape also works.[9] Time study is best for shorter-cycle tasks. The cost of having an analyst at the worksite and timing a proper number of cycles of the task tends to rule out time study for longer-cycle tasks. The four time-study steps and an example are explained below.

Select Task and Define Method.   Time study begins with selection of a task to study. There are choices to be made here. For example, packing and crating a large refrigeration unit might consist of packing the unit into a carton, placing the carton on a pallet, building a wooden crate around the carton and pallet, stenciling, and steel-strapping. A single time study of the whole series of tasks is one possibility. Or separate time studies could be done for each major task—packing, placing, and so forth. But each of these tasks involves lesser tasks, which could be separately time-studied. Pounding a single nail into a crate could be the task chosen for study.

Once the task has been chosen, the analyst defines the method. This involves

---

[9] Film analysis was common in the World War II era. Any idea that might help with the war effort had a good chance of being funded at that time, and industrial film labs seemed to have the potential to help increase productivity. Today few firms use film techniques.

dividing the task into elements that are easy to recognize and to time. The definition must specify clearly the actions that constitute the start and the end of each element; this is how the analyst knows when to take each stopwatch reading.

Cycle Time.   Tools of the time-study analyst include a clipboard, a preprinted time-study data sheet, and a stopwatch. The watch is mounted on the clipboard. Before timing, the analyst observes for awhile to be sure that the worker is following the prescribed method.

In the timing phase, the analyst records a stopwatch reading for each element. Several cycles of the task should be timed so that effects of early or late readings can be averaged out. Multiple cycles also provide a better basis for judging pace and for observing unavoidable delays and irregular activities. Comments on irregularities are entered in a "remarks" section on the data sheet.

The number of cycles to time could be calculated based on the statistical dispersion of individual element readings. However, most firms pay more attention to the cost of multiple cycles than to the statistical dispersion of readings. For example, General Electric has established a table as a guide to the number of cycles.[10] The table calls for timing only three cycles if the cycle time is 40 minutes or more. But it calls for timing 200 cycles if the cycle time is as short as 0.1 minute. Since 200 cycles at 0.1 minute adds up to only 20 minutes of observer time, the 200-cycle study may cost less to do than the three-cycle study of a 40-minute task.

The result of timing is an average **cycle time** *(CT)*—a raw time value.

Pace Rating.   If the analyst times a slow worker, the average cycle time will be excessive—*loose* is the term usually used; if a faster worker is timed, the CT will be tight. To avoid loose or tight standards, the analyst judges the worker's pace during the study. The pace rating is then used mathematically to adjust CT so that the result is a normal time. This is called **normalizing** or **leveling.** The normal pace is 100 percent; a 125 percent pace is 25 percent faster; and so on.

Pace rating is the most judgmental part of setting time standards. But it need not be pure guesswork. Films are available from the American Management Association and other sources for training in pace rating. The films show a variety of factory and office tasks. The same task is shown at different speeds, and the viewer writes down what the pace appears to be for each speed. The projector is shut off, and the viewer's ratings are compared with an "answer key." The correct answers were decided upon by experts or measured by film speed.

Expert opinion has been channeled to some extent. There are two widely accepted benchmarks of normal (100 percent) pace. One benchmark, for hand motions, is dealing 52 cards into four equal piles (bridge hands) in 30 seconds. The other benchmark is walking on a smooth, level surface, without load, at three miles per hour. These concepts of normal extrapolate to many other manual activities.

Most people can become good enough at pace rating to be able to come within ±5 percent of the correct ratings on training films. It is easier to rate a worker

---

[10] Benjamin W. Niebel, *Motion and Time Study,* 6th ed. (Homewood, Ill.: Richard D. Irwin, 1976), p. 325; also see a more elaborate table from Westinghouse on p. 278 (T56.N48).

who is close to normal than one who is very slow or fast. Because of this, it is a good idea for the analyst to try to find a rather normal worker to observe in doing a time study (or a work-sampling study). Sometimes pace rating is "omitted" by preselecting a worker who is performing at normal; the omission is illusory, since the rating is done in the worker-selection step.

Personal, Rest, and Delay (PR&D).   The normalized time per unit is not the standard time. We can't expect a worker to produce at that normal rate hour after hour without stopping. Personal time (drinking fountain, rest room, etc.) must be allowed. Rest time, such as coffee breaks, must also be allowed. And there may be unavoidable delays to include in the time standard.

Personal and rest time may be set by company policy or union contract. The rest (fatigue) allowance may be strictly a coffee-break allowance. This is common with clerical employees. In industrial shops the rest or fatigue allowance may be job dependent. For example, for tasks performed in a freezer or near a furnace the fatigue allowance may be as high as 50 percent.

Unavoidable delay could be set by contract or policy. More often, it is task dependent. Unavoidable delays may result from difficulty in meeting tight tolerances, from material irregularities, and from machine imbalances when a worker operates more than one machine. Interruptions by foreman, dispatcher, material handler, and so on, may also qualify. Strictly speaking, an unavoidable delay is one inherent in the method. Under that strict interpretation, delays caused by foremen or staff would be considered as avoidable delays and not included in the unavoidable delay allowance. These delays (like material or tool shortages and machine breakdowns) may be avoided by better management of resources. Unavoidable delays are sometimes determined by a work-sampling study in which occurrences of various types of delay are tallied.

The allowances are usually combined as a percentage, referred to as the **PR&D** or **PF&D allowance.** The combined allowance is then added to the normalized time. The result is the **standard time.**

Time-Study Example.   The steps in a time study are best understood by seeing them on the time-study data sheet. An example follows.

EXAMPLE 13–6

Time Study of Bolt-Washer-Nut Assembly

The proposed bolt-washer-nut assembly method (see Figure 13–7) was approved, and a time-study analyst was assigned to develop a time standard for the task. The analyst has, after observation, reduced the task to four timeable elements (as opposed to 15 elements that were defined for detailed methods study). Six cycles are timed[11] by the continuous stopwatch method, and each element is pace-rated.

The time-study data sheet is shown in Figure 13–12. The stopwatch is

---

[11] For a short-cycle task like bolt-washer-nut assembly, it would take less than an hour to time, say 30 cycles, and this would improve reliability. The six-cycle example is thus less than ideal.

FIGURE 13–12

Time-Study Data Sheet, Bolt-Washer-Nut Assembly

Element	Cycles						CT	RF	NT	Remarks
	1	2	3	4	5	6				
1. Get bolts and place in fix-ture	12 / 12	10 / 116	13 / 240	11 / 349	16 / 468	10 / 656	72 / 12	110	13.2	
2. Get washers and place on bolts	14 / 26	16 / 132	15 / 255	14 / 363	93 / 561	14 / 670	73 / 14.6	100	14.6	5th cycle: Blew nose
3. Get nuts and assemble onto bolts	75 / 101	86 / 218	77 / 332	82 / 445	79 / 640	78 / 748	477 / 79.5	95	75.5	
4. Drop assem-blies down chutes	05 / 106	09 / 227	06 / 338	07 / 452	06 / 646	07 / 755	40 / 6.7	100	6.7	

Total normalized time	110.0	
× PR&D allowance + 100%	111.25%	
Standard time	122.375, or 1.22 min./unit	

Note: CT is sometimes called the select time (ST); NT is sometimes called the leveled time (LT) or rated time (RT).

read in hundredths of a minute; the analyst does not insert decimal points until after the last computation. The stopwatch begins at zero and runs continuously for 7.55 minutes. Continuous readings are entered below the diagonal line, and elemental times are then computed by successive subtraction.

Average cycle time (CT) is the sum of elemental times divided by six; for element 2, CT is divided by five because one irregular elemental time was thrown out. The average goes below the diagonal line in the CT column. Pace ratings are in the rating factor (RF) column, with decimal points not included. Normalized time (NT) equals CT times RF. The NT column adds up to 110, or 1.10 minutes per cycle.

The firm has a PR&D allowance negotiated with the labor union. The allowance provides 3 percent personal time (e.g., blow nose), two 15-minute rest (coffee) breaks, and 2 percent unavoidable delay allowance. (These are minimum allowances; the contract allows rest time to be set higher for highly fatiguing work, and the delay allowance may be set higher for tasks involving abnormal delays.)

The two 15-minute breaks convert to percentages of an eight-hour or 480-minute day by:

$$\frac{30 \text{ min.}}{480 \text{ min.}} = 0.0625, \text{ or } 6.25\%$$

$$\text{Total PR\&D allowance} = 3\% + 6.25\% + 2\%$$
$$= 11.25\%.$$

The final computation is multiplying the total normalized time by the PR&D allowance of 11.25 percent plus 100 percent (which is mathematically the same as adding 11.25 percent to the total normalized time). The result is the standad time of 1.22 minutes per unit.

Work-Sampling Standards

Earlier we looked at work sampling as a technique for determining labor-utilization and -delay rates. To use work sampling for setting a time standard requires one extra piece of data: a production count, that is, a count of units produced or customers served during the study period. Cycle time (CT), then, is:

$$\text{Cycle time} = \frac{\text{Percent of time on task} \times \text{Total minutes in study period}}{\text{Production count}} \quad (10)$$

Cycle time is transformed into standard time by normalizing for worker pace and adding PR&D allowance—the same as for time study. An example follows.

EXAMPLE 13–7

Work Sampling for Setting Time Standards, Pathology Lab

The director of Midtown Pathological Labs has conducted a one-week work-sampling study of the lab staff. The results were that the staff was working 65 percent of the time. The director also tallied the type of work task observed. The lab performs two major types of analysis and a host of miscellaneous analyses, and the director found that the 65 percent work time was divided as follows:

Serum-blood tests (standard tests) in chemistry lab	30%
Whole-blood tests (complete blood count) in hematology lab	25
Miscellaneous tests in either lab	10
Total work time	65%

There are two lab technicians in the chemistry lab and one in hematology.

At the end of the study the director found that 48 serum tests and 32 whole-blood tests had been performed. The director's estimates of worker pace are 90 percent for serum tests and 105 percent for whole-blood tests. Midtown allows a PR&D allowance of 13 percent.

With these data, a time standard may be set for both the serum test and the whole-blood test.

Serum test:

$$\text{Cycle time} = \frac{0.30 \times 5 \text{ days} \times 480 \text{ min./technician-day} \times 2 \text{ technicians}}{48 \text{ tests}}$$

$$= \frac{1{,}440 \text{ min.}}{48 \text{ tests}}$$

$$= 30 \text{ min. per test}$$

$$\text{Standard time} = CT \times RF \times (100\% + \text{PR\&D})$$
$$= 30 \times 90\% \times 113\%$$
$$= 30.51 \text{ min. per test (per technician)}$$

Whole-blood test:

$$\text{Cycle time} = \frac{0.25 \times 5 \text{ days} \times 480 \text{ min./technician-day}}{32 \text{ tests}}$$

$$= \frac{600 \text{ min.}}{32 \text{ tests}}$$

$$= 18.75 \text{ min.}$$

$$\text{Standard time} = CT \times RF \times (100\% + \text{PR\&D})$$
$$= 18.75 \times 105\% \times 113\%$$
$$= 22.25 \text{ min. per test}$$

Are these precise (engineered) time standards? The technicians in the chemistry lab don't think theirs is. They point out to the director that their method is to run the serum tests in batches and as a two-person team. There could be one or many samples in a batch, but the time to run a batch does not directly depend on the number of samples in a batch. The time standard for serum testing is imprecise, indeed invalid, because the work-sampling study was not precise as to method.

The hematology technician has a milder objection: A mere 25 observations of the whole-blood testing were extrapolated into an assumed 600 minutes of testing time during the week. While the sample size seems rather small, the technician and the director decide that the standard time of 22.25 minutes per test is usable for short-term capacity adjustments. These include scheduling overtime, using part-time help, and subcontracting to other labs.

For example, on a given day perhaps 30 blood samples will arrive and require testing in hematology. At 22.25 minutes per test, the workload is $22.25 \times 30 = 667.5$ minutes of testing. Since an eight-hour day is only 480 minutes, the director had better tell the technician to plan on some overtime that evening. Part-time help or subcontracting are other options.

Predetermined Standards

Predetermined time standards really are part way predetermined. The predetermined part is the tables of time values for basic motions. The other part is properly selecting basic-motion time values in order to build a time standard for a larger task.

Basic-motion tables were Gilbreth's idea. But it took some 35 years of effort by many researchers to develop the tables. The best-known tables are those of the MTM (Methods-Time Measurement) Association.[12] Others include the Work-Factor, Brief Work-Factor, and Basic Motion Timestudy (BMT) systems. Our limited discussion focuses on **MTM.**

---

[12] The tables were originally developed by H. B. Maynard and associates. See Harold B. Maynard, G. J. Stegemerten, and John L. Schwab, *Methods-Time Measurement* (New York: McGraw-Hill, 1948) (T60.T5M3).

MTM and other synthetic techniques have several advantages:

1. No need to time; the data are in tables.
2. No need to observe; the standard may be set before the job is ever performed and without disrupting the worker.
3. No need to rate pace; the time data in the table were normalized when the tables were created.

A disadvantage of MTM is the great amount of detail involved in building a standard from the tables. Basic MTM motions are tiny; motions are measured in **time measurement units (TMUs),** and one TMU is only 0.0006 minute. The bolt-nut-washer assembly with a time standard of 1.22 minutes per cycle by time study (see Figure 13–12) is equal to 2,033 TMUs. One MTM motion usually takes 10 to 20 TMUs. Therefore the bolt-nut-washer assembly would be described in something like 100 or 200 basic MTM motions. The MTM analyst needs training to be able to specify tasks in that amount of detail. Still, MTM is perceived as being a fair approach to time standards, and it is widely used.

The MTM Association has developed tables for the following types of basic motions: reach; move; turn and apply pressure; grasp; position; release; disengage; eye travel and eye focus; body, leg, and foot motions; and simultaneous motions. Most of the tables were developed by film analysis.

One of the tables, the reach table, is shown in Figure 13–13. From the table we see, for example, that reaching 16 inches to an "object jumbled with other objects in a group so that search and select occur" takes 17 TMUs. That motion, abbreviated as an *RC16* motion, takes about 0.01 minute, or less than a second.

In an MTM study, the analyst enters each motion on a **simultaneous motion (SIMO) chart,** which is a left-and-right-hand chart. The total TMUs on the chart are converted to minutes. The total is the rated (leveled) time, not the cycle time, because 100 percent pace is built into the tables. Add a PR&D allowance, and you have the standard time.

Standard Data

Standard-data standards, like predetermined (e.g., MTM) standards, are synthetically produced from tables. But standard-data tables are for larger units of work. An example is the flat-rate manuals used in the auto-repair industry.[13] Flat-rate tables list times for repair tasks such as "Replace points" and "Change oil."

If precise time study, work sampling, or MTM is the basis for the tables, then the standard data may be considered to be engineered. It is normal for a firm to keep time standards on file, and it is just one more step to assemble standards from

---

[13] Auto manufacturers produce such tables for repairs on new cars. Flat-rate manuals for older cars, which take more time to repair, are available from independent companies. Best known are the Chilton manuals.

FIGURE 13–13

Reach Table for MTM Analysis

Length of reach in inches	Time in TMUs*				Hand in motion (TMU)		Case and description
	Case A	Case B	Case C or D	Case E	A	B	
¾ or less	2.0	2.0	2.0	2.0	1.6	1.6	A—Reach to object in a fixed
1	2.5	2.5	3.6	2.4	2.3	2.3	location or to object in
2	4.0	4.0	5.9	3.8	3.5	2.7	other hand or on which the
3	5.3	5.3	7.3	5.3	4.5	3.6	other hand rests
4	6.1	6.4	8.4	6.8	4.9	4.3	
5	6.5	7.8	9.4	7.4	5.3	5.0	B—Reach to single object in
							location which may vary
6	7.0	8.6	10.1	8.0	5.7	5.7	slightly from cycle to cycle
7	7.4	9.3	10.8	8.7	6.1	6.5	
8	7.9	10.1	11.5	9.3	6.5	7.2	C—Reach to ojbect jumbled
9	8.3	10.8	12.2	9.9	6.9	7.9	with other objects in a
10	8.7	11.5	12.9	10.5	7.3	8.6	group so that search and select occur
12	9.6	12.9	14.2	11.8	8.1	10.1	
14	10.5	14.4	15.6	13.0	8.9	11.5	D—Reach to a very small
16	11.4	15.8	17.0	14.2	9.7	12.9	object or where accurate
18	12.3	17.2	18.4	15.5	10.5	14.4	grasp is required
20	13.1	18.6	19.8	16.7	11.3	15.8	
							E—Reach to indefinite
22	14.0	20.1	21.2	18.0	12.1	17.3	position to get hand in
24	14.9	21.5	22.5	19.2	12.9	18.8	position for body balance,
26	15.8	22.9	23.9	20.4	13.7	20.2	next motion, or out
28	16.7	24.4	25.3	21.7	14.5	21.7	of way
30	17.5	25.8	26.7	22.9	15.3	23.2	

* One time measurement unit (TMU) represents 0.00001 hour.

Source: MTM Association for Standards and Research. Copyrighted by the MTM Association for Standards and Research. No reprint permission without written consent from the MTM Association, 16-01 Broadway, Fair Lawn, New Jersey 07410.

the files into standard-data tables. The next step is to assemble standard data for a whole trade or industry. This has been done in auto repair and other common trades, notably machining and maintenance trades.[14]

Variable working conditions and lack of common methods from firm to firm may compromise the precision built into standard data. Still, standard data are a powerful tool in that they bring time standards down to the level of the planner, the supervisor, and the operator. Experts create the tables, but you and I can use them.

---

[14] The standard data tables come in several levels. Basic motions (e.g., MTM) are at the most detailed level. Next come combinations of basic data (e.g., the MTM Association's general-purpose data), such as a joint time for reach–grasp–release. Then come elemental standard data for common elements like gauging and marking. Standard data for still larger units of work are at the level of whole tasks, such as the tasks of auto-repair mechanics or electricians.

Historical Standards and Technical Estimates

Nonengineered techniques—historical and technical estimates—are far more widely used than engineered techniques. And rightly so. Most of the work (or play) that most of us do is variable, and the cost to measure it with precision is prohibitive. Still, explicit time estimates help to improve management, and nonengineered techniques serve the purpose.

Historical standards and technical estimates are simple to develop and need not be explained further. As all six standards-setting techniques have been treated, we may turn to questions of humanity and fairness.

HUMANITY AND FAIRNESS IN SCIENTIFIC MANAGEMENT

Scientific management is a two-edged sword. It cuts waste (improves productivity), but it alienates people. Jobs with task variety and chances to exercise judgment may be chopped up into narrow and invariable jobs. Unskilled workers may be hired at less pay to perform these narrow and highly engineered jobs. The payoff is cheaper goods and services of more uniform quality.

But the unskilled worker lacks the pride and commitment of the craftsman. Quick, visible gains in productivity may be eroded by longer-term losses in motivation and growth of alienation.

One solution is to automate the boring jobs out of existence. This has been the promise of automation. But automation requires massive capital expenditure. The need for humans persists.[15]

Another solution is not to break jobs down into narrow tasks but instead to apply methods improvement and time standards to more variable jobs. Let us examine this possibility further.

Task Variety and Job Design

Methods improvement can turn interesting jobs into boring ones. That is, it can lead to decreased task variety for the jobholder. **Job design** is an approach that helps avoid that bad result. (Note: A worker holds a job and performs tasks. Job design has more to do with labor-resource planning; method or task design has more to do with operations planning.)

---

[15] The point is elaborated upon in the following quotation: .

In the automotive industry . . . many of the component-producing departments are highly automated, while there is no essential difference in assembly methods today from those used in making the Model T. As the machining departments are automated, workers are laid off or transferred to the assembly lines where the work is still manual. . . . [Assembly] is the last frontier of manufacturing automation.

Theodore O. Prenting and Nicholas T. Thomopoulas, *Humanism and Technology in Assembly Line Systems* (Rochelle Park, N.J.: Spartan Books, 1974), p. 5 (TS178.4.P73).

Job design is still more a concept or idea than a formal step-by-step technique. It is easier to point to examples of results of job design than to talk about how to do it. Prime examples of the job-design approach are **job enlargement** and **enrichment.** IBM's early efforts to enlarge jobs in its manufacturing areas have been documented. Insurance, appliance, and textile industry examples have also been publicized. As an example, one job in an insurance company home office might be to approve new policies, process all claim forms, and maybe even write the claim checks for a certain block of customers.

In the late 1960s and early 1970s, a few manufacturers began experimenting with **nonlinear assembly.** Volvo and Saab in Sweden did some of the pioneering. In this approach, assembly lines are replaced by assembly areas, and assemblers become team members who are no longer isolated at spots along an assembly line. Team members are cross-trained, and the team has a daily or weekly production quota or standard to meet. Sometimes teams are leaderless and do their own interviewing to fill vacancies. The team may have responsibility for the quality or operability of the end product (and even packaging, shipping, and office work in the case of one General Foods pet food plant in Topeka).

Nonlinear assembly is aimed at restoring task variety, social interaction, commitment, and motivation. But nonlinear assembly has not caught the fancy of many manufacturers. Part of the reason may be high training costs and greater variability (less dependability) of output. Training costs are high because methods are less well defined and jobs less specialized. Variability of output can lead to factory coordination problems, because group quotas are loose (perhaps nonengineered) as compared with the tight task time standards in assembly-line jobs. In short, some of the traditional benefits of methods and standards are lost in nonlinear assembly.

But now the nonlinear assembly idea is resurfacing in new clothes. The Japanese just-in-time system, worker-centered quality control, and group technology have some of the same good effects on workers. And they have a host of other benefits—besides direct effects on workers—as well. Those techniques are discussed in other chapters.

Responses to Variability

Work measurement seems best suited for repetitive tasks. It may seem poorly suited to variable tasks, for example, job-shop tasks. A better way of putting it is that work measurement should be applied differently to variable tasks. Four key differences between work measurement for variable tasks and repetitive tasks are:

1. For variable tasks, nonengineered time standards are often more suitable. Engineered standards are costly. And for a job just received and about to begin there is not enough time to develop more than a technical estimate. But variable jobs may be made up of tasks that have been done before; engineered standards may already exist, e.g., as standard data.

2. For variable tasks, variance from standards should be reported less often. Nonengineered standards will sometimes be unfairly high or low. High and low estimates may cancel out over a suitable reporting period; that allows efficiency reporting to be used fairly—but only if times for many jobs are aggregated over the reporting period.

Example. The U.S. Air Force Logistics Command, which operates very large job shops for aircraft repair, compares accumulated standard times against accumulated clock hours for most of its repair-shop crews. The reporting period of two weeks is long enough to include perhaps hundreds of task time standards, most of which are technical estimates.

3.   When a task covered by a time standard includes variable operations, don't use it to compare employees, unless all employees encounter the same mix of operations.

Example: Many college libraries use computers to produce catalog cards. A cataloging aide with book in hand enters data about a new book at a remote terminal, and the data are transmitted across the country to a central library cataloging service center. The center's computer data base is searched to find a Library of Congress catalog number for the book. For the search to be successful, the cataloging aide must enter the right data. This can be difficult, for example, for foreign-language books, musical compositions, and government documents.

One college library set a monthly standard rate (historical) of 300 books per cataloging aide. The standard rate was deeply resented, because some aides arrived early in the morning in order to fill their carts with easy books, which allowed them to easily exceed 300 books per month. Some of the aides who were challenged by the tough books actually looked worse when the monthly report came out. The solution: Distribute books to cataloging aides at random each morning. That way, each receives about the same variety of types of books over a period of months.

4.   For variable tasks, time standards uses may be limited. For example, in one effort to set time standards on lawyers' tasks the sole purpose was to straighten out a staffing mess. The lawyers worked in 36 program offices of the U.S. Department of the Interior, and it was hard to assign the proper number of lawyers to each office.

The department hired a consultant to help define work units and set standards.[16] The basic work unit was a **matter** (not a case, because matters often did not result in cases). Fifty-nine varieties of matters were defined, and secretaries kept records on the time spent by lawyers on each matter. The results were fairly consistent throughout the United States, and the average times served as historical (nonengineered) standards for use in staffing decisions. That is, in a given office each matter could be forecast (by trend projection, etc.) and multiplied by standard time to yield labor-hours, which converted into staff needs.

Professional work like that of a lawyer is not only variable but is often seen as something of an art and resistant to standardization. The lawyers in this example cooperated because the limited purpose—better staffing—was made clear. Probably there would have been no cooperation had the purpose been to judge efficiency or even to schedule lawyers' tasks.

---

[16] Part of the consultant's story is told in Mundel, *Motion and Time Study*, pp. 485–94.

The Element of Judgment

The engineered time standard purports to be scientific. And it is to a degree, but elements of judgment are always present. Bertram Gottlieb, an industrial engineer for the AFL–CIO, makes that point in his monograph *The Art of Time Study: An Exercise of Personal Judgement.*[17] Gottlieb cites court opinions supporting the view that company standards are not always so scientific that they are exempt from collective bargaining.

Besides collective bargaining, there is in some firms a good deal of informal negotiation ("horse trading") over time standards. The analyst produces a standard that follows engineered procedures to the letter and then is talked into loosening up the standard. The analyst's principles are compromised, but it makes life easier in future visits to the work center.

Fair Pay

Tying pay directly to output or efficiency seems fair to some people. Nevertheless, direct wage incentives are rather uncommon. Differing concepts of fair pay may be part of the reason why. Figure 13–14 helps put the concept of fair pay into perspective.

One concept of fair pay is that everyone should be paid the same, and minimum-wage laws are a means of bringing that about. Pay by time worked is a second concept of fair pay, and a popular one. Pay by job content also seems fair, especially in large organizations where unequal pay for the same work would be a visible problem; evaluating job content is a major function in larger personnel departments. A fourth concept of fair pay is pay based on output against standards, which has appealing productivity advantages. The last concept in Figure 13–14 (not necessarily a complete list) is pay by supply and demand; this seems fair to society in that it provides greater rewards for people willing to do society's messiest jobs.

What Figure 13–14 suggests is that time standards—also minimum wages, time clocks, job evaluation, and free-market labor pricing—are not the whole answer to fair pay and should therefore be used with discretion.

SUMMARY

Scientific management emerged at the turn of the century as a final phase of the industrial revolution. Its main ingredients are methods and process design and time standards.

Methods and process design may involve many parties: employees, supervisors, personnel training branch, production control planners, industrial engineers and IE technicians, paperwork specialists, computer systems analysts, and programmers.

---

[17] Center for Labor and Management, College of Business Administration, University of Iowa, October 1966 (T60.T5G65).

FIGURE 13–14

Concepts of Fair Pay

	What is fair pay?	Who subscribes to this?
1.	**Everyone paid the same** Rationale: We are all created equal; we are all products of our environments and partners in society. Means: High minimum wages applied equally to all.	Organized labor Socialists
2.	**Pay by the hour (or week, month, year)** Rationale: Though we are products of our environment, society's work must be done, and work is most easily measured in time units. Means: Have workers punch time clocks, and reprimand them for tardiness.	Supervisors (easy to figure out pay) Organized labor (workers like to "put in their time"—or their time and a half)
3.	**Pay according to job content** Rationale: It is not the person who should be paid but the position; "heavy" positions should be paid heavily, "light" positions lightly. Means: Job evaluation, using job ranking/classification, point plan, factor comparison.	Personnel managers (requires a large pay-and-classification staff) Bureaucrats (seems rational and impersonal; fits concept of rank or hierarchy)
4.	**Pay according to output** Rationale: Though we are products of our environment, society's work must be done, and work should be measured in output (not merely time on the job). Output efficiency is based on a count of actual units produced as compared to a standard. Means: Piecework, incentive pay, profit sharing.	Industrial engineers Economists
5.	**Pay according to supply and demand** Rationale: Society's messiest jobs must be done too, and greater pay for less desirable jobs is necessary to attract workers. Means: Let the labor market function (or list jobs needing to be done, and set pay according to willingness to do each job—The *Walden II* method)	Some economists (e.g., those advocating below-minimum wages for teenagers) B. F. Skinner (see his book *Walden II*)

Work-simplification, employee-suggestion and cost-reduction programs are aimed at the coordination of methods-improvement efforts.

Methods and time standards are central in the assembly of a planning package, which goes to workers and involved staff. Engineers develop the product design; methods analysts develop methods and processes, often in the form of a route sheet; standard times or estimates are entered on the route sheet; and finally the scheduler determines due dates.

Formal methods study follows the scientific method. A task is selected; data about it are collected; the data are analyzed, leading to alternative methods; the alternatives are evaluated; and the chosen alternative is implemented. It is common to use flowcharts to gather data (on a "before" flowchart), analyze data, and generate and evaluate alternatives (on an "after" flowchart). Another tool, work sampling, can yield data on employee or facilities utilization, or "busyness," and it can show percentages of work time in various delay categories of the resource-delivery system.

Time standards improve coordination by providing a sound basis for scheduling; are useful for analyzing the labor component in staff needs, for budgeting and estimating/bidding, and for evaluating operating and maintenance costs; and are also valuable for self-motivation and for external motivation derived from efficiency reporting, including incentive wages.

There are six basic techniques for setting time standards: stopwatch time study, work sampling, predetermined standards, standard-data time standards, historical standards, and technical estimates. Engineered (high-precision) standards require controls on methods, time measurement, worker pace, and allowances for personal, rest, and delay (PR&D) time.

Scientific management has contributed considerably to increasing industrial output and is rapidly being extended into the services sector, but it has some negative effects on workers. Job enrichment and nonlinear assembly help combat tendencies to mold workers into mindless cogs in the machine. While time standards may be applied in variable-task environments, their application requires careful thought to avoid variability biases.

REFERENCES

Books

Caruth, Donald L.   *Work Measurement in Commercial Banks.* Boston: Bankers Publishing, 1971 (HG1720.W63C36).

Kazarian, Edward A.   *Work Analysis and Design for Hotels, Restaurants, and Institutions.* 2d ed. Westport, Conn.: AVI Publications, 1979 (TX911.K36).

Krick, Edward V.   *Methods Engineering: Design and Measurement of Work Methods.* New York: John Wiley & Sons, 1962 (T56.K7).

Maynard, Harold B., G. T. Stegemerten, and John L. Schwab.   *Methods-Time Measurement.* New York: McGraw-Hill, 1948 (T60.T5M3).

Mundel, Marvin E.   *Motion and Time Study: Improving Productivity.* 5th ed. Englewood Cliffs, N.J.: Prentice-Hall, 1978 (T60.7.M86).

Salvendy, Gavriel.   *Handbook of Industrial Engineering.* New York: John Wiley & Sons, 1982 (T56.23.H36).

Periodicals (societies)

Industrial Engineering (American Institute of Industrial Engineering).

Journal of Systems Management (Association for Systems Management), paperwork management and systems analysis.

REVIEW QUESTIONS

1. Have methods and standards programs faded in usefulness over the years? Discuss.

2. Is the methods and standards program the responsibility of only a few specialists? Or is it more than that? Explain.

3. When a job needs to be scheduled, why can't the shop order simply consist of methods and standards records pulled out of industrial engineers' files?

4. In methods study what information is included in the "before-and-after" comparison?

5. How are principles of motions economy (or methods improvement) used?

6. Which flowcharting symbols are used in which of the four types of methods study? Explain.

7. Which of the four types of methods study measures results in *time* units? Why don't they all need to do so?

8. How do work sampling studies reveal deficiencies in the management system?

9. How can labor efficiency and utilization be allowed for in scheduling? How is productivity allowed for?

10. How can wages be based on time standards, given U.S. minimum wage laws?

11. Why is a statistical time standard *not* an engineered standard?

12. When is a nonengineered time standard not good enough?

13. In stopwatch time study how many cycles should be timed before calculating the average (CT) values? Why?

14. How can work sampling data yield CT values?

15. Why isn't the CT the time standard?

16. Which of the PR&D factors are task dependent? Explain.

17. In what sense is pace rating unfair? fair?

18. What is the difference between predetermined standards and standard data?

19. Why do workers tend to prefer standards set synthetically?

20. Why has methods study tended to make jobs boring, and what can be done to counter the tendency?

21. How can labor standards be fair if tasks are variable?

22. Is it fair to pay based on amount of work produced? Why or why not?

PROBLEMS

1. You are the president of a company that is in serious financial trouble. Your production costs are higher than the production costs of all your competitors. You realize that these

costs must be cut drastically, and that the measures used must include layoffs of nonessential people. Part of your company's organization chart is shown in Figure 13–1. Do you see any nonessentials that could be cut on this chart? Think about this carefully, since production cost is your problem, and many of these functions purport to reduce costs. On the other hand, you should reflect on the meaning of the word *essential*.

2. Refer to Figure 13–2, which shows the characteristic flow in assembling a planning package. One route generally applies to nonrepetitive tasks, and the other generally applies to more repetitive tasks.

   a. A small printing plant would probably not have staff specialists to do such things as prepare route sheets, determine time estimates or standards, and prepare shop orders. Who would perform these and other functions associated with the planning package? Or would some of the functions be unnecessary in a small printing plant? Explain.

   b. The parts-fabrication department for a machine-tool manufacturer follows the flow pattern for more repetitive tasks. The process planner sometimes finds operation and time data in IE files and must sometimes wait for IE analysts to do a special study to provide operation and time data. Explain why there should be two sources of process and time data. Also, at some times the planner must assemble the route sheet; at other times the planner finds a *standard route sheet* (or *standard routing*) in the IE files. Explain this distinction.

   c. What are the differences between the route sheet, the shop-orders-needed listing, and the shop order.

3. Figure 13–3 lists a number of ways to evaluate new methods: cost, time, effort, storages, delays, transportations, transportation distances. Explain how each of these types of evaluation data may be determined from flowcharts. Refer to one or more of the types of flowcharts in the chapter in your explanations.

4. Mundel's *general principles of methods improvement* (Figure 13–4) are newer but less well known than the *principles of motion economy* developed by Barnes. Find Barnes's principles in your library. Compare Barnes's principles with Mundel's principles. Discuss. (Barnes's principles may be found in many industrial engineering and production/operations management books, including Barnes's own work: R. M. Barnes, *Motion and Time Study,* New York: John Wiley & Sons, 1937.)

5. Find a screw-together type of ball-point pen. Take it apart and set the pieces before you. Imagine that you are an assembler in a factory making this type of pen. Develop a left-and-right-hand chart for your method of assembly. Now develop an "after" flowchart for an improved method—which may use a special workbench, feed trays, chutes, fixtures, and so on. You may wish to include a workbench sketch. Evaluate the extent of improvement.

6. The present method of reading gas meters (on a successful call) is shown below (a worker analysis chart).

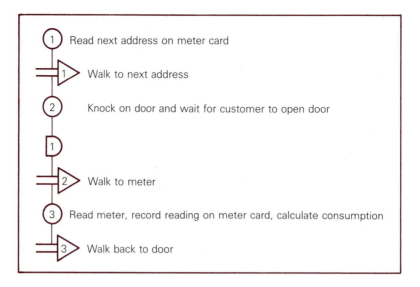

a. The gas company is considering a requirement that all gas meters be located outside or be visible through a window. Draw a new process flowchart for meter reading for the proposed new meter locations. Develop a summary of the improvements.

b. What other improvements are there that are not shown on the summary? What are the disadvantages of the new method?

7. The present method of billing, weighing, and stenciling sacks is shown in the accompanying illustration.

Develop a process flowchart for a proposed new, improved method. Include a summary of the improvements.

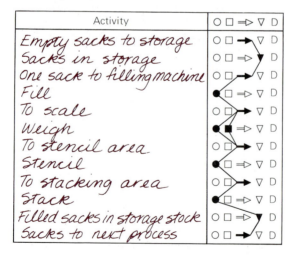

8. The accompanying chart shows five days of actual on-the-job activities of a seamstress who sews decorator pillows together. (Ten minutes is used as the smallest time increment so that time values can be read off the chart easily.) You are to conduct a 50-observation work-sampling study, taking your observations from the chart instead of from on-site observation.

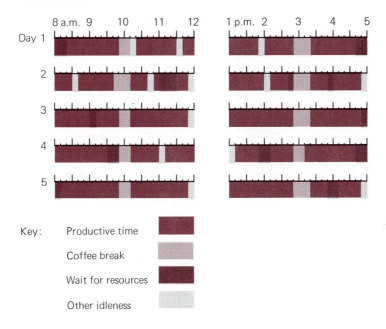

Key: Productive time

Coffee break

Wait for resources

Other idleness

a. As a first step in conducting the study, you will need a schedule of 50 random observation times. You will find a list of two-digit random numbers in Table 17–1. Select 50 of those numbers, and devise a method of translating them into 50 clock times between 8:00 A.M. and 12:00 P.M. and between 1:00 and 5 P.M. for a five-day study period. Show your 50 random numbers and 50 times.

b. Develop a tally sheet and conduct the work-sampling study. The desired end result is percentages of time in four activity areas: productive time and coffee break, wait for resources, and other idleness.

c. The unavoidable-delay component of the PR&D allowance is to be based on the wait-for-resources element of the work-sampling study in part *b.* The rest component is set at two 15-minute coffee breaks per day. And personal time is set by company policy at 5 percent. What is the total PR&D allowance?

d. Explain the difference between the time allowed for coffee breaks and the time taken, as revealed by the work-sampling data.

e. During the five-day study period the seamstress completed 760 pillows. You, the analyst, judged her pace during the study period. Your pace rating is 90 percent. Calculate the standard time. Also, express the standard in pieces per day (standard production rate).

f. Discuss possible weaknesses or sources of bias in the work-sampling study. Is the time standard engineered?

g. What should be the primary uses of this time standard? Explain.

9. A salesman has an order for 1,000 candles in the shape of an athletic team's mascot. Production control assembles the following data from the candlemaking shop, to be used in setting a price (direct cost and overhead + markup):

Cycle time	20,000 TMUs
Allowance for personal time and unavoidable delay	9%
Authorized break time	20 minutes per day

Recent candlemaking statistics:

Total clock hours for candlemakers	350 hours
Standard hours' worth of candles produced	380 hours

a. What standard time should be used in computing direct cost?
b. If there are two employees in candlemaking, how many hours should be scheduled for them to complete the order for the 1,000 special candles?
c. Assume that the candle order has been finished. It took 190 hours to complete. What rate of efficiency did the crew attain?

10. The director of a social agency is preparing next year's budget. The agency's case load averaged 42 clients per day last year, but it has been increasing at an annual rate of 15 percent. The caseworkers and directors agree that it takes 3.5 hours to handle each client properly.
a. How many caseworkers should be requested as the staff component of next year's budget, assuming the 15 percent increase in case load. Assume that caseworkers work an average 250 days per year (which allows for vacation days, sick days, etc.), at eight hours per work day.
b. What kind of time standard is used by the agency? Is there any way to improve this time standard?
c. What other reasonable uses are there for the time standard?

11. Assume that your boss is foreman of the packing and crating department and has just sent you the following memo:
"The president wants all shops, including ours, covered by time standards. I'd like you to do a preliminary study to see if reasonable time standards can be set for our type of work. Everything we pack is of a different size. So how can we have standard times?"
a. Respond to the boss's memo.
b. What technique for setting time standards is best for this type of work? Explain.

12. In an automobile plant a time standards analyst finds that the average cycle time for mounting tires onto rims is 3.6 minutes. If the personal, rest, and delay allowance is 14 percent, and the pace rating is 105 percent, what is the standard time?

13. An MTM study yields 8,500 TMUs as the total time to make one unit. If the company allows 18 minutes of personal time, 30 minutes of rest time, and no delay time per day, what is the standard time in minutes?

14. An MTM analyst predicts that installing a cord on a proposed new telephone set takes 4,250 TMUs.

a. What is the standard time in minutes if the shop allows a 20 percent PR&D allowance?

b. How can the analyst set a standard on a *proposed* telephone set? Doesn't the item have to actually exist? Discuss.

15. A worker in an electronics plant is using a lugging machine to attach a connector onto the end of a wire. (The machine automatically kicks the wire into a chute once the connector has been attached.) The data below are provided by a time study analyst. Stopwatch readings are in hundredths of a minute and cumulative from element to element and cycle to cycle.

Job elements	Cycle				Pace rating
	1	2	3	4	
Cut length of wire	21	48	74	103	100
Insert into "lugger" and press start button	30	58	86	112	90

a. What is the standard time? Assume a personal time allowance of 5 percent, a delay allowance of 3 percent, and two 20-minute coffee breaks per eight-hour day.

b. What would the advantage be in using methods-time measurement (MTM) instead of stop-watch time study?

16. A work sampling study has been conducted for the job of spray-painting a set of parts. The job consists of mounting the parts on hangers, then spraying them. The PR&D allowance is 20 percent. The analyst's tally sheet is shown below:

Job: Spray-painting
Time period: Five 8-hour days

Activities sampled	Tallies	Total	Work count	Pace rating
1. Mount	ꟷꟷꟷꟷꟷꟷ	30	20	110
2. Spray	ꟷꟷꟷꟷꟷꟷꟷꟷꟷꟷ	50	20	120
3. Nonwork	ꟷꟷꟷꟷ	20		
Total		100		

a. What is the cycle time for each task?

b. What is the rated time for each task?

c. What is the standard time for each task?

d. What is the value of the data on nonwork time? How could the data be improved to make it more useful?

17. A supervisor has done a work-sampling study of a subordinate, a clerk-typist. The purpose of the study was to set time standards for typing letters and retrieving letters on file. Therefore, those two tasks were tallied on the work-sampling tally sheet, along with a miscellaneous category for all other activities of the clerk-typist. The complete tally sheet is given below.

Subject: Typist					
Tasks: Typing letters and retrieving letters on file					
Dates: November 29–December 10 (10 working days)					
Analyst: Clerical supervisor					

Activities sampled	Tallies	Total	Per-centage	Work count	Pace rating
1. Type letters	ℕℕ ℕℕ ℕℕ ℕℕ ℕℕ ℕℕ ℕℕ ℕℕ ℕℕ ℕℕ ℕℕ ℕℕ ℕℕ ℕℕ ℕℕ ℕℕ	80	40%	60	90
2. Retrieve letters	ℕℕ ℕℕ ℕℕ ℕℕ ℕℕ ℕℕ	30	15	150	80
3. Miscellaneous	ℕℕ ℕℕ ℕℕ ℕℕ ℕℕ ℕℕ ℕℕ ℕℕ ℕℕ ℕℕ ℕℕ ℕℕ ℕℕ ℕℕ ℕℕ ℕℕ ℕℕ ℕℕ	90	45	—	—
Totals		200	100%		

a. PR&D allowance is 12 percent. Compute cycle time, rated time, and standard time for each of the tasks.

b. Discuss the possible uses of these time standards.

c. Comment on the fairness and/or validity of these time standards. Are they engineered?

18. An insurance company mail room prepares all of the company's premiums and letters for mailing. A time study has been done on the job of enclosing premium statements in envelopes. Continuous stopwatch data are given below. The readings are in hundredths of minutes.

Job elements	Cycle							Performance rating
	1	2	3	4	5	6	7	
Get two envelopes	11		55		105		151	105
Get and fold premium	22	41	65	83	116	135	162	115
Enclose in envelope and seal	29	48	73	97	123	143	169	95

a. Develop a time standard, providing 15 percent for allowances.

b. Assume that the premiums and letters are of various sizes and shapes. The get-and-fold element takes much longer if the item is large and requires several more folds than are needed if the item is small. Therefore, the time standard could be unfair to some of the employees it covers. Suggest some situations in which the standard would be unfair. Suggest some options for making it fair.

c. Assume that there is an irregular element: At every 25th envelope, 25 envelopes are wrapped with a rubber band and placed in a box. This element was timed once, and the elemental time was 15 with a performance rating of 90. With this added factor recompute the time standard from part a.

19. Wabash Airways calculates that a flight attendant needs two minutes to fully serve a meal to a passenger on one of its aircraft. That is, the standard time is two attendant-minutes per meal.
    a. If two flight attendants are assigned to an aircraft with 80 passengers on board, and they serve all of them in a flight having one hour of serving time, what is their efficiency?
    b. If the flight attendants are utilized (busy) 90 percent of the time (not counting when they are strapped in for takeoff and landing), what is their productivity?
    c. If a new jumbo aircraft seats 600 passengers, how many flight attendants are needed for a flight with 100 minutes of serving time?

20. The new office manager for Senator I. M. Fogbound has imposed a standards and productivity system for clerical workers. Last month, the crew of envelope-stuffers handled 20,000 envelopes. The time standard is 0.6 minutes per envelope, and the crew was paid for 250 hours of office time. The crew was busy (utilized) 80 percent of the time last month.
    a. How many hours of time were spent on things other than stuffing envelopes?
    b. What was the crew's efficiency rate?
    c. What was the crew's productivity rate?

21. At the Transcona Plating Co. all metal plating jobs are covered by time standards. Last week the company did 850 standard hours worth of plating jobs. Total clock time for production workers was 1,000 hours that week, and their actual hours of direct labor (hours allocated to actual plating jobs) was 800.
    a. What is the efficiency rate?
    b. What is the utilization rate?
    c. What is the productivity rate?

22. The following is a list of tasks on which time standards/estimates may be set. Suggest a suitable technique or techniques for setting a time standard for each of the tasks, and explain your choice.

    Mowing grass.

    Soldering connections in small electronic components.

    Drafting (design drawing).

    Typing and filing.

    Overhauling or adjusting carburetors.

    Cooking in fast-food restaurant.

    Computer programming.

    Installing auto bumpers on car assembly line.

23. "Equal pay for equal work" was the hot pay issue in an earlier era. Now it's "equal pay for comparable work." Which concept(s) of fair pay (from Figure 13–14) does the comparable work idea seem most consistent with? Explain.

24. In some companies the final time standard is negotiated: The analyst develops the standard, but the foreman complains that it is too "tight," so the analyst agrees to add a bit more time to it. What are the good and/or bad features of a negotiated standard? Discuss.

25. The county commissioners of Sir Galahad County hired a consulting firm to do a "staffing study" of all wage-earning employees. The consultants used standard efficiency and labor-

utilization techniques. Food-service people were affected most severely by the study: Deep cuts in the number of food handlers were recommended. One cafeteria director was quite upset. Her feeling was that the employee cuts were made without regard for customer service. That is, she felt that cafeteria lines would grow longer and customers would be lost because there were fewer employees to staff the lines. She stated, "One of the consultants came right out and told me that the consulting firm pays so much a head for each employee that can be cut."

Have the consultants been fair and professional?

CASE STUDY: LAND AND SKY WATERBED CO.

HISTORY

As of October, 1982, Land and Sky Waterbed Co., of Lincoln, Nebraska, was the fourth largest waterbed company in the United States and the largest in the Midwest. Land and Sky was founded in 1972 by two brothers, Ron and Lynn Larson. The brothers remain as co-owner/managers. The total workforce, including office staff, is 67. The oldest employee is the vice president, Jim Wood, a psychology graduate in his mid-30s. Jim has played a major role in developing the scheduling, inventory, quality, and employee payment systems at L&S.

THE PRODUCT LINE

L&S produces two lines of waterbed mattresses and liners in standard sizes (king, queen, double, super single, and twin). L&S also manufactures special made-to-order mattresses for other frame manufacturers. The Land and Sky label goes on the higher-quality gold and bronze bed sold exclusively to franchised dealers. L&S produces another brand, called the Daymaker. It is sold without advertising as a "commodity" product. The Daymaker is available to any dealer.

There is a trade group for the waterbed industry. Unfortunately the trade group has not yet been successful in agreeing on standard dimensions for king size, queen size, and so forth for the soft-sided foam frame. Therefore, over 60 sizes must be built to order. Also, some customers make beds to their own dimensions before checking to see what mattress dimensions can be readily obtained. L&S will accept special orders for such unusual sizes, but the price will be high and the order will take 30 days to be filled.

L&S also makes two kinds of soft-sided frames, which are designed to make a waterbed look like a conventional bed with box spring and ordinary mattress ("a waterbed that appeals to older people," according to Jim Wood). One kind is made of rigid foam and is cheap and easy to make. The other kind, their own unique design, has a plastic rim built in and is called Naturalizer 2000; the rim keeps the foam from breaking down.

COMPETITIVE CLIMATE

Since waterbed manufacturing is not highly technical and quite labor intensive, competitors spring up all over. Low-wage countries, like Taiwan, are becoming tough competitors.

L&S markets its product line throughout the United States and Canada. An Australian producer makes to L&S's specifications under a licensing agreement. (Jim Wood now wishes that L&S had established its own Australian subsidiary, rather than the licensing agreement.) There is not yet enough of a European market for waterbeds to be concerned about.

There are two main market outlets for waterbeds. The older market outlet is the small waterbed retailer, many of whom tend to be less sophisticated in the ways of the business world and therefore unstable. Recently waterbeds have become popular enough that a second major market outlet has emerged: old-line furniture stores. The two market types present very different demands on the waterbed manufacturer. The small waterbed retailer wants "instant" delivery responsiveness. The old-line furniture store plans orders carefully in advance and does not expect delivery right away, but does drive a hard bargain with respect to price. L&S has developed a fast-response production system aimed at filling orders faster than the competition. Most orders can be shipped within 48 hours, and same-day production and shipment is possible (not cost effectively). Since the recent emergence of price-conscious furniture stores as a second major market, L&S has instituted procedures that tightly control material storage costs, labor costs, and costs of scrap and defects.

One complicating factor is a few retailers are unsophisticated in their ordering. For example, one retailer phoned in a large order specifying the quantity but not which models he wanted. When asked which models, he said, "Just send about what I have ordered before." This was rather meaningless since prior orders had come in at different times for different models.

Some inventory of finished waterbeds is kept in bonded public warehouses in different regions of the country so orders in those regions may be filled quickly.

MARKETING

Wholesale advertising in trade journals, as well as displays at furniture conventions, are the main forms of product promotion. Then salesmen call on established and prospective accounts.

THE PLANT

L&S is located in an industrial park, and housed in three noncustom metal buildings arranged in a *U*-shaped configuration. The first building—at one leg of the *U*—houses the sales and administrative offices with a shipping and receiving warehouse in the back. The second building, forming the bottom of the *U*, is the main production area where waterbeds are manufactured and quality-checked. The third building—the other leg of the *U*—is for fiber baffle production and assembly, liner production, and injection-molding and assembly of soft-sided frames. A parking lot in the center of the *U* is also used for vinyl storage.

THE PROCESS

Producing the Waterbed

Vinyl Processes. The waterbed begins as a roll of vinyl. It is cut to size by hand. (A $20,000 cutting machine had been used, but it broke down a lot and also yielded too much scrap.) The next steps are to install valves and corner seam panels; special machines are used in these installations. Then the vinyl sheets go to machines that fuse the corners together by high-frequency radio waves. Next, the ends and sides are sealed.

Baffle Installation. High-quality waterbeds contain a fiber baffle that keeps the water from "making waves" when in use. Research and development has come up with a baffle made of polyurethane fiber that reduces the "wave time" from 25 to 3 seconds. Fusing of the side and end seams on the mattress is considered especially important, and the best workers are assigned to it. One outside observer watched the job being done and estimated that the two workers were going at a pace of around 140 percent of normal pace.

Total cycle time for these steps in making the waterbed is 35 minutes. The daily output is about 450 waterbed units.

One way that L&S holds down production lead time is by performing early stages of manufacture—such as cutting the vinyl and installing valves and fusing corners—before knowing exactly what the model mix is. Later the same day late-arriving orders are totaled by product type, and final model-mix instructions go out to the shop floor. Some of the options that are determined "at the last minute" are: (1) the number that are to be top-of-the-line beds with fiber baffles and (2) the number that are to have the L&S label vs. the Daymaker "commodity" line.

Waterbed Subassemblies and Accessories

Fiber Baffles. These are cut on a cutting machine (the one originally bought for $20,000 to cut vinyl). Then holes are drilled around the edges of a stack of fiber sheets and vinyl ties are threaded through the holes to hold the stack together for storage and transport (the vinyl-ties idea was developed after glue and plastic hooks failed).

Soft-Sided Frames. These are injection-molded and assembled. L&S has patented a plastic rim insert, for which it spent $250,000 on research and development; the insert lends support and adds life to the foam in the frame.

Cardboard-Reinforced Bottom Liner.   These liners were developed by L&S to make waterbed setup faster (it cuts setup time by about 20 percent) and easier. They have been on the market for about seven months. Retailers love this feature, because the liner is reusable—a good sales point; the bottom liners sell for $16 to $20 at retail.

RESEARCH AND DEVELOPMENT

R&D is the responsibility of one of the owners. Outside R&D consultants are called upon for assistance sometimes.

PAY SYSTEM

In July, 1982, L&S converted from a straight hourly pay plan to a piece rate system having the following features:

Base Piece Rate.   The base piece rate depends on the assigned job, e.g., $0.20 per bed.

Achievement Raise.   A worker gets a 5 percent bonus on top of base rate for each additional machine that the worker learns to operate. A few workers have learned to run 10 or 12 machines and therefore get 50–60 percent more than the base piece rate. The bonus buys flexibility for the company. Typically a worker who can run just two or three machines averages $5–7 per hour, while one who can run 12 machines might earn $9–11 per hour. Jim Wood stated that other companies send people home when a machine is down; here "we put them on another machine."

Quality Bonus.   Workers get a bonus of 25 percent of total pay per period for zero errors. The bonus decreases for each error found: 1–2 errors, 20 percent; 3 errors, 15 percent; 4 errors, 10 percent; 5 errors, 5 percent; and 6 or more errors, 0 percent. The owners were initially dubious about the 25 percent bonus (Jim Wood's idea); previously the bonus was 15 percent. Their feeling was "Why pay a large bonus for what the employees are supposed to do anyway." But they agreed to give the plan a try and were very pleased with the results. The error rate had been about 5 percent (5 out of 100 beds). It was down to about 0.5 percent by October. Some of the better workers were achieving zero error rates.

Error Penalty.   The worker has to pay a penalty of $0.65 for every error discovered by quality control inspectors. Errors are easily traced back to the worker responsible, because each worker attaches his employee number to the bed. If the worker notifies quality control of an error by marking it, then the penalty is only $0.25. Plans are in motion to make the penalty zero for an admitted error; that way there will be no temptation to try to sneak one by the inspector. Inspection is much more efficient and valid when workers mark their own errors.

Quality control does the bookkeeping for the entire piece rate and quality incentive system. QC people record daily production and quality performance data for each employee. All information is maintained on the computer.

LABOR POLICIES

Waterbeds are a somewhat seasonal product, which makes staffing difficult. The peak seasons are March–April–May and August–September–October. L&S will not build inventory just to keep workers busy. Competition from other waterbed manufacturers is fierce, especially the Taiwanese manufacturers of liners. A low inventory policy is a competitive necessity. Therefore, in the slack season workers are laid off. Layoffs are strictly by productivity, not seniority.

Workers usually work in pairs, since bed materials are too large for one person to handle easily. If one worker is tardy or absent, the partner must keep busy on lower-pay work and forego the chance for piece-rate bonuses—a sacrifice that the worker is sure to complain about. Therefore, policies are very rigid on absenteeism and tardiness. Absenteeism usually means automatic termination. Also, workers of comparable skill are generally assigned to work together.

QUALITY CONTROL AND WARRANTIES

Quality control visually inspects each bed. The surfaces are checked for blemishes, seams are checked, valves are checked, and so forth. Once in awhile a bed will be blown up with air like a balloon in a more thorough leak check. Water is not used to test beds, because it leaves a residual odor.

If no blemishes or defects are found, the bed is sent to the retailer with a five-year warranty. Beds with a flaw are sold as blems at a lower cost and with a three-year warranty.

INVENTORY CONTROL

Material costs are significantly higher than payroll costs. Thus materials are tightly controlled.

Vinyl, a key raw material, has relatively few manufacturers, and vinyl suppliers require a 30-day lead time. Vinyl suppliers ship to L&S by a regular purchase-order schedule, and any schedule changes require about 30–60 days' advance notice. Therefore demand forecasting is important for L&S. One of the owners does the forecasting, which is based on seasonal factors and past sales.

Other materials are reordered by a visual reorder point method: When stock looks low based on the projected manufacturing schedule an order is placed. The safety stock is typically about two-and-a-half days' supply.

Average raw materials inventory on hand is typically about two to three weeks' worth. In other words, inventory turns over 20 times a year or more. This is partly a matter of necessity. Fiber, which must be stored indoors because the material is bulky and there simply is not space to store more, is maintained at a two-and-a-half-day inventory level.

The main purchased material is vinyl in large rolls. Since vinyl is waterproof and may be stored cheaply outdoors, larger lots of it are ordered than is the case for other materials. Shipments are received about three times a month, 40,000 pounds at a time.

Fiber is the second most important purchased item. Since fiber must be stored inside, it is ordered in smaller lots more often: twice a week in semi loads of 8,000 pounds.

A complete physical inventory of finished goods and raw materials is taken every four weeks.

Purchasing buys from at least two sources, which provides protection in case one supplier should shut down—a serious matter since L&S's inventories are kept so low. On some occasions purchased parts have been delayed to the point where vinyl rolls are gone; then the workers do what they can with scrap materials, after which they perform other duties or shut down and go home.

Purchasing and traffic (shipping) are under the management of a single individual, Mr. Bergman.

Finished goods are stored in the warehouse for a short time prior to loading onto an outbound truck.

DISCUSSION QUESTIONS

1. In what respects is Land and Sky a just-in-time producer? (No one at L&S had ever heard of JIT at the time of the case.)

2. What serious problems are likely at L&S as it grows into a large company? Consider, especially, its production and quality incentive pay system and its present ways of filling customer orders fast.

3. How can L&S protect itself from the miseries that plague most Western companies as they grow large?

Chapter 14

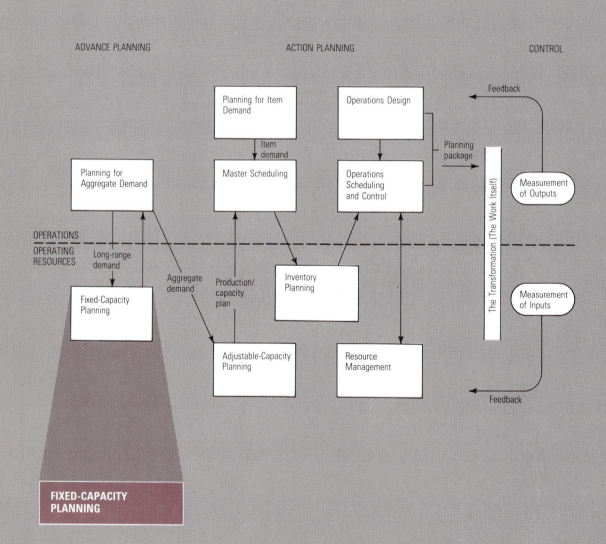

ADVANCE PLANNING   ACTION PLANNING   CONTROL

Planning for Item Demand

Operations Design

Feedback

Planning for Aggregate Demand

Item demand

Master Scheduling

Operations Scheduling and Control

Planning package

Measurement of Outputs

OPERATIONS

OPERATING RESOURCES

Long-range demand

The Transformation (The Work Itself)

Aggregate demand

Fixed-Capacity Planning

Production/ capacity plan

Inventory Planning

Measurement of Inputs

Adjustable-Capacity Planning

Resource Management

Feedback

FIXED-CAPACITY PLANNING

Facilities Planning

Facilities means plant and equipment; the fixed capacity of the organization. Planning for facilities acquisition and replacement, the subject of this chapter, is strategic because the costs of such decisions are so high and their effects are so lasting. Facilities in place set the character of the organization for years to come.

In fact, as is suggested by the upward-pointing arrow in the chart on the chapter title page, plans for fixed capacity can influence plans for aggregate demand. (The *means* influence the *ends*.) Existing facilities can turn out only a limited variety of goods and services. Planning for changes in the product line is partly limited by those existing capabilities. Existing facilities have a maximum output that puts upper limits on expansion, and the desire to fully use capacity limits the freedom to withdraw from products or markets.

FACILITIES STRATEGIES

Clearly facilities have a large impact on what a firm is able to do. The business strategy and the facilities strategy must be a matched set. Quite often they are not and something needs to be changed.

Here, for example, are three common business strategies:

1. Improve the climate between labor and management.
2. Bring out new products quickly.
3. Be the lowest-cost producer.

The first strategy, better climate, is a popular one. And North American industry seems to be adopting a facilities strategy that is a key to improving the interpersonal climate. That facilities strategy follows the **focused-factory** concept.[1] The focused factory mainly means focusing on doing one thing well. Also, it usually means keeping the plant small, a place where everyone knows everyone else.

Many of our larger manufacturers have convinced themselves that the huge vertically integrated plants of the past are unmanageable: too many people, too many technologies to master, poor climate for understanding. Some of the same thinking is found in retailing. In the department store business, appliance, TV, and furniture departments are shucked off, and specialty stores are taking over. Even universities are not immune. Budget crunches have resulted in some programs being dropped; the university becomes less universal.

The second strategy, bring out new products quickly, is especially important in high-technology industries. Inflexible facilities make the strategy hard to achieve. To make sure inflexibility of facilities is not an obstacle, high-tech companies need to build plants without many walls and with dispersed electric, water, and other utility outlets. Also, they need to avoid hard automation (generally a group of machines linked together for one purpose, without versatility), rigid material handling systems, and very high-cost super machines.

In the office "industry" the open-office concept has become popular. It features large open spaces with movable modular partitions, often with electrical and communications wiring in the partition walls.

The third strategy, be the lowest-cost producer, is often thought of as calling for a facilities strategy opposite the flexibility just mentioned. That is, sacrifice flexibility and invest in hard automation and super machines to reduce the variable costs. The risk is that today's efficient plant bristling with hard automation to drive down labor costs will be tomorrow's liability. For example, the U.S. auto industry found itself

---

[1] Wickam Skinner, "The Focused Factory," *Harvard Business Review,* May–June 1974, pp. 113–21.

with modern transfer lines for making eight-cylinder engines and big cars, when suddenly consumer demand shifted to small fuel-efficient cars. For a hot product that has sales in thousands per day—a running shoe, tennis racket, or portable battery-operated vacuum cleaner, for example—there is a great temptation for the company to "throw flexibility to the winds." Rigid (hard) automation is the way of the past, but old ways die hard. Small self-developed machines, group technology, quick setup, multifunctional workers, simple handling methods, and avoidance of storage help make industry more responsive to change and at the same time more efficient. This is the case whether volume is low or high. Assembly robots, which are reprogrammable, will replace some of the hard automation in higher volume production. Office automation has some of the same effects, because the equipment is driven by modifiable programs.

While the chapter focuses on *facilities* proposals, the concepts also apply to other high-cost pursuits. For example, consulting, market research, product design, or computer software can call for large expenditures. Also, management techniques themselves are a large investment—in the talents and time it takes to implement them. Hundreds of management techniques are presented in this and other books. All of them may be good techniques, but only in the proper place, and a given organizational unit cannot afford to use many of them. A proposed management program should compete for funding right along with proposals for buying a drill press or remodeling a wing of the plant or office.

PROPOSAL REVIEW

Review of proposals to acquire or upgrade facilities should be done with care in capital-intensive organizations. In purely service-oriented organizations, there may be little plant and equipment to worry about. Most services, however, require at least an owned or leased building. In some cases (e.g., fast foods), plans for the building can be critical to success. In manufacturing, both building and equipment planning are critical. It is in manufacturing that planning for facilities tends to be done most carefully.

Larger manufacturers often have a separate department for facilities planning. (In other firms facilities planning may be assigned to industrial engineering, to accounting, or simply to each using department.) The facilities planning department becomes the focal point for collecting and analyzing data on facilities proposals. Figure 14–1 displays facilities planning and other units having a role in the total proposal-review process.

Facilities proposals may arise anywhere in the organization: A mechanic suggests that a tool crib be installed nearer to the workplace; a foreman asks that an old drill press be replaced with a new one; an inventory manager recommends that additional warehouse space be obtained; or an engineer develops a proposal for a backup power generator. As Figure 14–1 shows, such proposals may go to the facilities planning department.

To evaluate proposals properly, costs must be determined. Industrial engineering

FIGURE 14–1

Proposal-Review Process

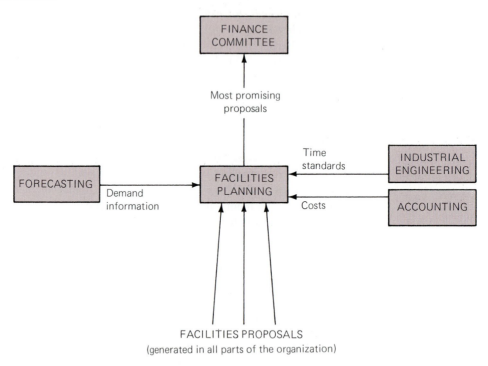

FACILITIES PROPOSALS
(generated in all parts of the organization)

may be asked to supply labor and productivity estimates. Accounting may furnish labor rates, overhead rates, tax rates, and cost-of-capital rates.

The need for a proposed facility is not based simply on the fact that someone asked for it. There should be evidence, e.g., a forecast, of sufficient demand for the product or service to be produced by the facility. In some cases the demand forecast may be translated into revenues or savings. Then the revenues or savings may be compared with costs. The analysis is wrong if the forecast is poor. A multimillion-dollar plant with no demand for its production is the kind of mistake that can be made.

Proposals approved by facilities planning may have one more hurdle: a finance committee of high-level executives. The finance committee normally puts proposals into rank order and creates a cutoff line, which is often called a hurdle, or **hurdle rate:** Those above the cutoff get funded; those below may be rejected or deferred for a year or more. While facilities planning does its work piecemeal, the finance committee considers how well the mix of projects fits into overall plans and policies and money-market conditions. Unfortunately, our finance committees have tended to focus narrowly on financial factors, in part because operating managers fail to provide good nonfinancial information. Such factors as flexibility and impact on people often have been neglected. There are signs that industry is coming to understand its past myopia. More broadly based facilities decisions may be forthcoming.

At different stages in proposal review, different analysis methods may be used. In business colleges such methods are generally referred to as **capital-budgeting** techniques. Industrial engineers prefer the term **engineering economy.** Our discussion includes nine proposal-review techniques grouped into three types:

Preliminary analysis.
> Break-even (indifference) analysis.
> Payback period.
> Average annual cost.

Detailed analysis.
> Equivalent annual cost.
> Present value of cost.
> Cost-effectiveness.

Final analysis.
> Internal rate-of-return.
> Net present value.
> Benefit-cost.

The preliminary-analysis methods are most easily understood and used by line operations managers and therefore are explained thoroughly. The detailed-analysis methods are used more often by staff specialists who serve the line managers. The staff specialist might be in a facilities planning or plant engineering department. Problem examples of detailed-analysis methods are included in the body of the chapter. The final-analysis *methods* are closely associated with money management, and problem examples of those methods are omitted. The final-analysis *stage* of proposal review is explained rather fully in the chapter, since higher-level operating resource people are among the final decision makers.

Caution: All of these techniques tend to put emphasis on financial factors. Simple, easy-to-use techniques that give weight to nonfinancial impacts are, unfortunately, not available. Goal programming, cost-effectiveness analysis, and some other multiattribute decision analysis techniques do account for other impacts. But the techniques are not yet simple to understand and easy to use, and so their uses in industry are still quite limited.

PRELIMINARY ANALYSIS

As will be shown, the preliminary-analysis methods omit **time-value-of-money** considerations and so are not entirely valid. Yet they are simple, and for this reason they are widely used. This is especially true in smaller firms that lack people capable of doing deeper analysis. In larger firms it may be customary for preliminary analysis to be done by the proposing departments; these departments may forward the good proposals to facilities planning for detailed analysis.

Break-Even

Break-even is a common term used without explanation in the nation's newspapers. **Break-even point** usually means break-even *volume.* It is the volume of sales or production that just allows you to break even: that is, to earn enough revenue to cover costs. In this chapter two kinds of break-even analysis are considered as an aid in facilities planning:

1. A single facilities proposal. Is the proposal worthy? To find out, determine how much sales or savings would be needed to pay for it, that is, what the break-even point is.

2. Two or more competing proposals for doing the same thing. A fancy but accurate term for this is **mutually exclusive alternatives:** Selection of the best alternative excludes the others. The alternatives may be analyzed by searching for the *indifference point,* the production volumes at which the costs of one alternative are exactly the same as the costs for another. Here the problem is simplified because revenue is ignored. It is proper to ignore revenue because the decision to do one or the other has already been made; it remains to find out which alternative is least costly—for various production volumes.

Single Proposals—Complete-Recovery Method. Should the company invest in a building addition, a new utility system (power, water, disposal, communications), or a new machine? To help decide, find the sales volume needed to completely recover the costs of the equipment. This is the *complete-recovery* approach to break-even.

The break-even point *(B)* for total recovery, is the point at which total revenue *(TR)* equals total cost *(TC).* Total revenue is price times volume, so total revenue at the break-even point is *(P)(B).* Total cost is fixed cost plus variable cost, so total cost at the break-even point is $FC + (V)(B).$ Therefore,

$$TR = TC$$
$$(P)(B) = FC + (V)(B)$$
$$(P)(B) - (V)(B) = FC$$
$$B(P - V) = FC \tag{1}$$
$$B = \frac{FC}{P - V}$$

EXAMPLE 14–1

Break-Even by Complete-Recovery Approach,
Treespade Proposal

Capitol Landscape Co. is thinking about buying an industrial treespade, vehicular equipment that can dig up and move whole trees. The question is, Could anticipated revenue pay for the cost? Business volume is hard to estimate. It therefore makes sense to construct a break-even chart to see how much volume is needed to completely recover the costs.

Given data:

Delivered price of treespade, 44-inch: $9,000.

Estimated cost to operate and maintain: $10 per hour of use.
  (Sales representative says $8 per hour; Capitol uses $10 to be on the safe side.)

"Going rate" for treespade service: $20 per hour of use.

Solution:

B = Break-even point, the unknown
FC = Fixed-cost = $9,000
V = Variable cost rate = $10 per hour
P = Price = $20 per hour

These data are inserted into formula (1):

$$B = \frac{FC}{P - V}$$
$$= \frac{9,000}{20 - 10} = \frac{9,000}{10} = 900 \text{ hours}$$

This means that Capital would have to operate the proposed treespade 900 hours before it could recover its fixed and continuing costs.

A graph gives more information than the formula does. Figure 14–2 is a graph of this break-even problem. Referring to the graph, we may see the amount of profit or loss for any volume. For example, it appears that for 500 hours of treespade operation, the loss would be $4,000: $10,000 revenue minus $14,000 cost. For 1,000 hours of operation the profit is $1,000: $20,000 revenue minus $19,000 cost.

How does this help Capitol decide whether or not to buy the treespade? The reasoning might be something like this: If the treespade were only operated two hours a day, it would take about 450 days (900/2) to break even. That is less than two years, which seems to be a fairly fast recovery of costs.

Sensitivity analysis may offer further insights. You want to find out if different assumptions about data inputs lead to large changes in the results; that is, you want to see whether the results are *sensitive* to the inputs.

For example, see what would happen to the break-even point if there were an increase in operating costs. This might happen if the price of fuel rose or if the operators' union won a large wage increase. Also, see how sensitive the break-even point is to a price decrease: The going rate for treespade services could be driven down by the entry of more competitors.

If preliminary analysis by break-even is favorable, the next step might be a more precise analysis using time-value-of-money methods.

Single Proposals—Annual-Volume Method. Another break-even method is the **annual-volume** approach: the result is break-even volume *per year.* It is as simple as the complete-recovery approach, except that input data correspond more closely to

FIGURE 14–2

Break-Even Graph for Proposed Treespade—Complete-Recovery
Approach

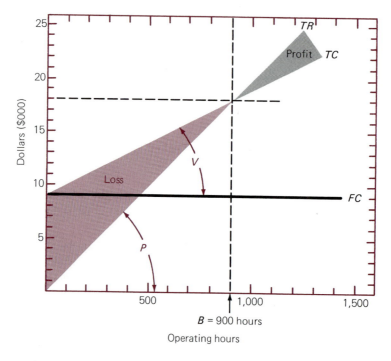

profit-and-loss accounting conventions. This means the proposing department may
need to go through the added step of requesting cost data from the accounting department. But it results in break-even and profit information based on the legal meaning
of profit. This is more valid than the general idea of a profit zone beyond a complete-
recovery point. On the other hand, the approach does not show how many years
the break-even volume per year applies to. In sum, the simpler complete-recovery
approach lends itself better to decisions about *proposed* facilities. Nevertheless, the
annual-volume approach is widely used. (Bear in mind that, either way, break-even
is a rough, preliminary-analysis method.) The formula for break-even by the annual-
volume method is the same as by the complete-recovery method. An example follows.

EXAMPLE 14–2

Break-Even by Annual-Volume Approach, Treespade Proposal

The example is the same treespade proposal for Capitol Landscape Co.
covered in Example 14–1. But the fixed cost is different.

Given data:

Fixed cost per year for 44-inch treespade *(FC):* $1,000/yr. (Provided by accounting department; includes annual depreciation charges.)

Variable cost to operate and maintain *(V):* $10/hr.

Price for treespade service *(P):* $20/hr.

Again the break-even point *(B)* is the point at which total revenue *(TR)* equals total cost *(TC).* And $B = FC/(P - V)$. So,

$$B = \frac{1,000}{20 - 10} = \frac{1,000}{10} = 100 \text{ hours/year}$$

This is shown graphically in Figure 14–3. It does not look much different from Figure 14–2. But as has been explained, the two figures are interpreted quite differently, since Figure 14–3 gives results on a per-year basis.

FIGURE 14–3

Break-Even Graph for Proposed Treespade—Annual-Volume Approach

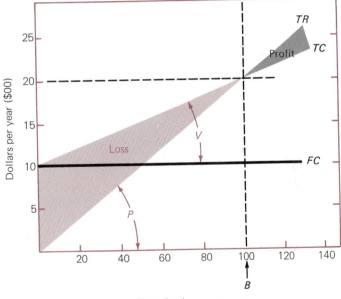

Operating hours per year

It would be prudent to see whether the break-even point is sensitive to changed assumptions about input data. Sensitivity to a fuel or wage hike could be tested by increasing *V.* A lower market price, *P,* could also be tested. And Accounting's estimate of $1,000 per year fixed cost is a prime target for sensitivity analysis, since accounting costs are often based on averages and simple cost allocation methods rather than actual cash flow.

Competing (mutually exclusive) Proposals. Now let us consider break-even for competing proposals that have the same purpose. The break-even point *(B)* may be computed based on costs alone. It is the production volume (sales volume is not at issue) for which the total costs of proposal 1 equal the total costs of proposal 2 (and proposals 3, 4, etc.). So, for just two proposals,

$$TC_1 = TC_2$$
$$FC_1 + (V_1)(B) = FC_2 + (V_2)(B)$$
$$(V_1)(B) - (V_2)(B) = FC_2 - FC_1$$
$$B(V_1 - V_2) = FC_2 - FC_1 \qquad\qquad (2)$$
$$B = \frac{FC_2 - FC_1}{V_1 - V_2}$$

At the risk of overdoing it, we shall stick with the treespade case for another example. Let us say that Capitol Landscape Co. has decided to buy a treespade. But it isn't sure whether to buy a cheap Acme or an expensive Ajax treespade.

EXAMPLE 14–3

Break-Even Analysis for Competing Treespade Proposals

Given data:

	(1) Acme	(2) Ajax
Fixed cost *(FC):* Delivered price	$7,000	$11,000
Variable cost rate per hour of operation *(V):*		
Fuel consumption	$2.50/hr.	$1.75/hr.
Repair and maintenance	0.50/hr.	0.25/hr.
Total variable cost	3.00/hr.	2.00/hr.

Two pieces of data are conspicuously absent, but for good reason: (1) Operators' wages and overhead costs are omitted because they are equal for the two brands and thus cannot affect the outcome. (2) Revenue is also omitted—for the same reason: It is the same for either brand.

For the given data,

$$B = \frac{\$11,000 - \$7,000}{\$3 - \$2}$$
$$= \frac{\$4,000}{\$1} = 4,000 \text{ hr.}$$

Interpretation: For 4,000 hours of operation Capitol is indifferent between Acme and Ajax. But 4,000 is a lot of hours. It seems doubtful that the operating economies of Ajax ($1 per hour cheaper) would justify its $4,000 higher price; it would take too many years (even if there is a large inflation in fuel costs) to recover the higher price through operating economies.

Again a graph is helpful; see Figure 14–4. It shows the $4,000 advantage

FIGURE 14–4

Break-Even Analysis for Competing Proposals—Treespades

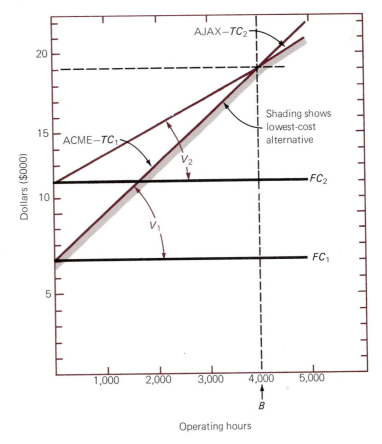

for Acme at zero operating hours; Acme maintains its total cost advantage up to the point of indifference, 4,000 hours. Beyond that, Ajax becomes cheaper.

Payback Period

The object of payback analysis is to find out how long it will take to pay off the initial cost of a facility: the payback period. A firm that relies on payback may set a maximum payback period of, say, three years. Then any proposal with a payback period shorter than three years is worthy; longer ones are unworthy.

This is a rather rough way to judge proposals. It is often best to limit payback to preliminary screening. The proposing department could, for example, drop any of its proposals that fail to pay back the investment in, say, six years.

Proposals with shorter payback periods could go to facilities planning for more precise analysis. Two ways of doing payback are discussed, along with weaknesses in the method, in the following sections.

Payback with Uniform Cash Inflow. Payback is simple if cash inflows—profit or savings—are the same every year. The payback period is simply:

$$P = \frac{I}{A} \tag{3}$$

where

P = Payback period
I = Investment
A = Annual savings or profit

The following example will illustrate.

EXAMPLE 14–4

Payback Period for Uniform Cash Inflow Case—Office Collator

MidAm Gas and Electric Company is considering buying an office collator. The collator costs $6,000. The savings in clerical costs are estimated at $1,250 per year. What is the payback period?

Solution:

$$P = \frac{I}{A} = \frac{\$6,000}{\$1,250/\text{year}} = 4.8 \text{ years}$$

Since 4.8 years is fairly slow payback, MidAm may elect not to fund the proposal or to advance it for detailed analysis.

Payback with Nonuniform Cash Inflow. Savings or profits are often not uniform from year to year. In that case the payback formula does not apply. Instead, find the payback period by adding each year's cash inflow until it equals the investment, as in the following example.

EXAMPLE 14–5

Payback Period for Nonuniform Cash Inflow Case—Kiln

As a source of income, Marblecone Abbey may buy a kiln to manufacture salable pottery. The kiln costs $2,000. Profits are expected to rise slowly as sales grow and the potter gains proficiency. Profit estimates are shown below, with the rightmost column showing progress toward payback:

Year	Profit	Investment less profit
0	—	$2,000
1	$ 200	1,800
2	500	1,300
3	1,000	300
4	1,000	—

As is shown, it takes a bit more than three years to pay back the $2,000 cost of the kiln.

Strengths and Weaknesses of Payback. Payback is enormously popular. One reason is its simplicity. Another is its adaptability: Payback works the same way for any type of organization, public or private, and for any size or type of investment. Still another reason is its independence of other data: There's no need to look at cost of capital, minimum attractive rate-of-return, capital supply, and other attractive capital expenditure proposals.

There is also a notable weakness: Payback is concerned only with the years until the investment is paid back. But what of profits or savings after that? Figure 14–5

FIGURE 14–5

Contrasting Cash Inflows and Paybacks for Equivalent Investments

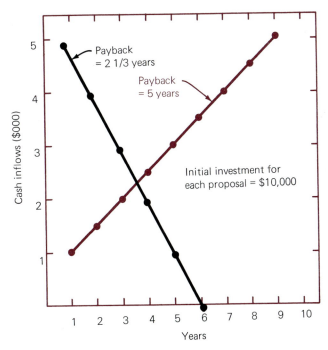

shows two contrasting cash inflow patterns, each for a proposed facility costing $10,000.

The falling cash inflow pattern (dark line) is $5,000 the first year, then $4,000, $3,000, and so forth; payback of the $10,000, then, is one third of the way—equal to $1,000—into year 3: $5,000 + $4,000 + $1,000. Cash inflow continues to decline, reaching zero in year 6. The rising pattern (light line) starts small, so that it takes five years to pay back the $10,000 investment: $1,000 + $1,500 + $2,000 + $2,500 + $3,000. But after that the rise continues, year after year. Clearly the proposal with the rising pattern is preferred. Yet its payback period is nearly four times as long as the payback period for the other proposal.

In view of the above, we may infer the following: Companies that rely on payback analysis will tend to be *shortsighted*. That is, they may reject expenditures for computers, robotics, numerically controlled equipment, and R&D, because the high cash inflows tend to come several years out.

Another weakness of the payback method is that it does not consider compound interest on the investment and on cash inflows. In the above case, interest charges (opportunity costs) on the two investments of $10,000 would be the same and would therefore be of no concern. But interest earnings on the cash inflows are quite different for the two investments. Actually, since the falling pattern has higher early cash inflows, its inflows would earn considerably more interest in the early years than the rising pattern would. This offsets some of the long-run advantage of the rising-pattern proposal. Just how much this amounts to must be determined by time-value-of-money methods, covered later in this chapter.

Average Annual Cost

The average annual cost (AAC) method is limited to mutually exclusive proposals. The reason is that *cost* alone is analyzed, not revenue. It is reasonable to do this where the need for *a* facility has been agreed upon but the particular make or model must still be chosen: You choose the one that costs least.

While the AAC method does not allow for interest, it at least considers all life-cycle costs. Therefore, in validity (if not in scope) AAC is superior to breakeven and payback.

The following example illustrates AAC and, for good measure, combines it with break-even analysis.

EXAMPLE 14–6

Average Annual Cost Method, Alternative Elevator Motors

Two 10-horsepower motors are being considered for an elevator that is to be installed in a new state office building. Motor 1 costs $450 and has operating costs of $0.16 per hour. Motor 2 costs $350 and has operating costs of $0.18 per hour. After five years, motor 1 is expected to have a salvage value of $270, motor 2 a salvage value of $175.

It is difficult to estimate annual hours of operation. Therefore, it has been decided to find the number of hours per year for which average annual costs of the motors are equal: a break-even point.

Solution:

At the break-even point, *B*, the average annual costs (AAC), are equal. And AAC, for each motor equals fixed cost (FC) per year, plus variable cost rate *(V)* per hour times number of hours per year. Therefore,

$$AAC_1 = AAC_2$$

and

$$FC_1 + V_1(B) = FC_2 + V_2(B)$$

Fixed cost of motor 1, FC_1 would be the net cash outlay, averaged over the five-year life; that is, the cash paid out, $450, minus the $270 received for salvage is divided by the five years. Variable cost is the annual operating cost; for motor 1 and at the break-even hours per year it is: $0.16(B)$. Motor 2 is interpreted similarly. Substituting in the equation, we have:

$$\frac{\$450 - \$270}{5} + \$0.16B = \frac{\$350 - \$175}{5} + \$0.18B$$

$$\frac{\$180}{5} + \$0.16B = \frac{\$175}{5} + \$0.18B$$

$$\$36 + \$0.16B = \$35 + \$0.18B$$

$$\$0.02B = \$1$$

$$B = 50 \text{ hours per year}$$

Interpretation: The cheaper motor 2 is preferred if it is operated less than 50 hours per year. Above 50 hours per year, the operating economies of motor 1 justify its higher price.

PROPOSAL-REVIEW STAGES

Having considered preliminary analysis in some detail, we may now see how it relates to detailed and final analysis in a total proposal-review procedure. There are several paths that a proposal might take through the proposal-review stages. The choice of a path hinges on what decision is needed.

Three types of decisions are shown in Figure 14–6. Type 1 is the preliminary decision (usually by the using department) on the question, Is the facility needed? This really means: Is there a function that must be performed and a facility that can perform it to economic advantage? As we have seen, the question may be partly answered by break-even and payback analysis. It may be answered more carefully, in final analysis, by time-adjusted rate-of-return, net present value, and benefit-cost analysis.

Decision type 2 is directed to the question, Which facility can perform the function less expensively? The need for the function has already been determined. Therefore, benefit analysis is not relevant; the decision is based simply on minimizing costs.

FIGURE 14–6

Facilities Proposal-Review Stages

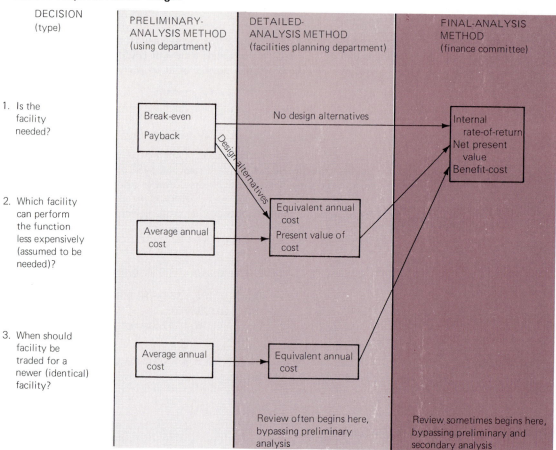

Preliminary analysis may be done by the average annual cost (AAC) method; detailed analysis is done by the equivalent annual cost (EAC) and present-value (PV) of cost methods.

Decision type 3 concerns the question, When should the facility be traded for a newer (identical) facility? This is the kind of decision that most of us face with our personal automobiles. AAC and EAC are the preferred methods. The computation is more complicated than that required in the other types of decisions. But whether to trade (replace) is a question that operating managers must raise over and over again for the same piece of equipment. The importance of the decision to operating managers makes it worthwhile to consider type 3 quite thoroughly. The topic is given emphasis in a separate section later in the chapter.

Type 2 and type 3 proposals may be passed on to the finance committee for a final analysis. Final analysis normally includes rank-ordering all proposals—type 1, type 2, and type 3—according to internal rate-of-return, net present value, or benefit-cost ratio. These techniques require additional data on revenue or savings generated by a given proposal.

Type 2 questions (*which* facility) are considered in the next section.

DETAILED ANALYSIS

The equivalent annual cost (EAC) and the present value (PV) of cost methods involve interest calculations, with which some readers are familiar. Review of the concept of interest—the time-value of money—with EAC and PV examples, may be found in Chapter Supplement A. EAC and PV examples presented in the following section are solved using six interest tables. Some readers will be familiar with methods that use only two interest tables. The two-table methods, which are commonly presented in finance and managerial accounting courses, produce the same answers as the six-table methods. The two tables (present-value tables) are provided in Supplement B for those who prefer that approach.

Equivalent Annual Cost

As is noted in Supplement A, EAC is the annualized (or annuitized) sum of all relevant costs. It is like the amount of an installment-loan payment. The following example demonstrates EAC.

EXAMPLE 14–7

Equivalent Annual Cost Method, Generating Plant

A hospital is considering two options for backup power generation:

1. Lease a portable generator at an annual cost of $5,000. The lease cost includes repair and maintenance.

2. Purchase a generator. The vendor's installed cost is quoted as $25,000. The generator's useful life is estimated at 25 years with no salvage value. Major maintenance is expected as follows: $500 cost after 5 years, $1,200 after 10 years, $2,500 after 15 years, and $4,000 after 20 years. Labor costs for operation plus routine maintenance costs (O&M costs) are estimated at $1,000 per year. Which alternative has the most favorable EAC if interest is 12 percent?

The accompanying diagrams show the cash inflows for the two generator alternatives.

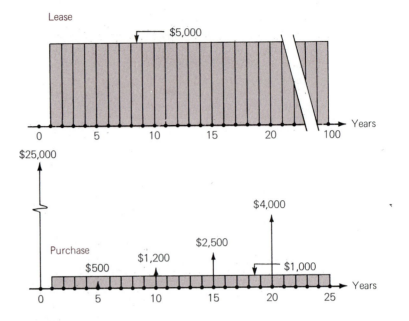

Solution:

Option 1 has an EAC of $5,000, which is the lease cost.

Option 2 must be evaluated in steps based on the following givens and relevant interest table factors (Table S14–1 in Supplement A):

$$P = \$25,000$$
$$F_5 = \$500 \qquad (P/F)^5_{12\%} = 0.5674$$
$$F_{10} = \$1,200 \qquad (P/F)^{10}_{12\%} = 0.3220$$
$$F_{15} = \$2,500 \qquad (P/F)^{15}_{12\%} = 0.1827 \qquad (A/P)^{25}_{12\%} = 0.1275$$
$$F_{20} = \$4,000 \qquad (P/F)^{20}_{12\%} = 0.1037$$
$$A = \$1,000$$

The purchase cost, $25,000, can be translated to EAC in one step, while the O&M cost, $1,000, is already EAC. The four major maintenances require two steps: First, each is converted to present value; then each present value (or the sum of the present values) is converted to EAC. It would be incorrect to try to convert directly from F to A, because each F occurs at a different point in the future. Therefore,

$$
\begin{aligned}
EAC =\ & [\$25,000 + \$500\,(0.5674) \\
& + \$1,200(0.3220) + \$2,500(0.1827) \\
& + \$4,000(0.1037)][0.1275] + \$1,000 \\
=\ & (\$25,000 + \$284 + \$386 + \$457 + \$415)(0.1275) + \$1,000 \\
=\ & (\$26,542)(0.1275) + \$1,000 \\
=\ & \$3,384 + \$1,000 = \$4,384
\end{aligned}
$$

Purchase at $4,384 per year is favored over leasing at $5,000 per year.

Present Value of Cost

PV of cost is the present (discounted) equivalent sum of all relevant costs. An example of its use follows.

EXAMPLE 14–8

Present-Value Method, NC Equipment

A firm purchased a numerically controlled (NC) jig-boring machine one year ago for $100,000. The machine was expected to last 10 years and to have no salvage value at the end of that time. The machine is operated by a highly skilled machinist at an annual labor cost of $14,000. It has now been discovered that a reputable specialty shop will contract to do the work for $15,000 per year. Investigation reveals that, because of design quirks, the jig-boring equipment would bring only $20,000 today on the used equipment market. If the firm figures its money is worth 10 percent, what is the best alternative based on present-value analysis?

The accompanying diagrams show the cash flows for the two alternatives.

Solution:

The first alternative is to continue jig-boring "in house." The given data and the relevant interest factor (from Table S14–1) are:

$$A = \$14,000 \text{ per year for labor}$$
$$n = 9 \text{ years (since one year of the ten-year life of the NC}$$
$$\text{equipment has passed)}$$
$$i = 10\%$$
$$P/A^9_{10\%} = 5.759$$

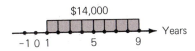

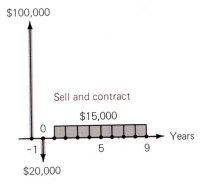

The total present value of cost is:

$$P = \$14,000 \, (5.759)$$
$$= \$80,626$$

The second alternative is to contract to have the work done and to sell the NC equipment. Given data and relevant interest factor are:

$$A = \$15,000 \text{ per year contract cost}$$
$$P = -\$20,000 \text{ proceeds on sale of equipment}$$
$$n = 9 \text{ years}$$
$$i = 10\%$$
$$P/A^9_{10\%} = 5.759$$

The total present value of cost is:

$$P = \$15,000 \, (5.759) - \$20,000$$
$$= \$86,385 - \$20,000$$
$$= \$66,385$$

Comparison: Contracting is cheaper by $14,241 ($80,626 − $66,385).

What of the equipment cost, $100,000, paid out a year ago? It must be ignored. It is a **sunk cost**—incurred in a prior period and thus not a relevant cost for the decision at hand. (But its influence on taxes *is* still relevant.)

The Users

The examples show two methods, EAC and PV, for analyzing costs of proposals. The facilities planners, who must confer with the operating people who develop many of the proposals, often favor the EAC method. The reason is that the equivalent annual cost is easy for lay people to understand. It is the same idea as installment loan payments. On the other hand, some users—up-from-the-ranks foremen, for example—may have difficulty with the concept of a present value. Financial people, by contrast, are likely to prefer the PV method, because they and their peers can appreciate the present-value idea of a single lump sum sufficient to pay off all future obligations.

Tax factors are sometimes left out at the level of detailed analysis. Ignoring taxes simplifies computations and makes it easier to explain results to users. Taxes may not be omitted in final analysis, because final analysis involves money management in which all inflows and outflows, including taxes, must be allowed for. In detailed analysis the goal is narrower: Just to decide which facility is least costly. While tax is a cost, the tax cost *tends* to affect each alternative similarly. This is less true if there are special tax write-offs. It is safer to always include tax considerations.

Replacement of Existing Facilities

In the third type of decision, replacement analysis, EAC, rather than PV of cost, is used. The method presumes replacing a facility with another of the same type.

Sometimes it is a direct trade-in. If you are upgrading to a radically different type, then replacement would not be the right term, and the replacement method would not work. In the replacement method, we assume that the new facility has all of the same life-cycle costs as the one it replaces. Assuming the same costs simplifies the calculation process.[2]

Replacement calculations are based purely on costs. A facility is already owned and assumed to be worthwhile; therefore the amount of benefit or revenue it generates is not the question. As was shown in Figure 14–6, replacement/trade-in analysis follows the average annual cost (AAC) and equivalent annual cost (EAC) methods. Both methods are treated in the following example.

EXAMPLE 14–9

Replacement Analysis by AAC and EAC Methods, Forklift Truck

A 3,000-pound forklift truck on a loading dock cost $5,000 new. It gets high use, and it is therefore generally traded in for a new one every one, two, or three years. Given the following operation and maintenance (O&M) cost and trade-in (salvage) value data, what is the most economical number of years until trade-in? Assume a 10 percent discount rate.

Year	O&M cost*	End-of-year trade-in-value
1	$ 500	$3,600
2	800	2,800
3	1,000	1,800

* As always in capital budgeting problems, O&M costs are assumed to be incurred at the end of the given year.

Diagrams of the cash flows for the three trade-in alternatives are shown in Figure 14–7.

AAC solution:

The average annual cost (AAC) is computed by adding all costs, subtracting trade-in value, and dividing the result by number of years in the trade-in period. So,

AAC for trading
after one year = $5,000 + $500 − $3,600 = $1,900 per year

AAC for trading
after two years = $\dfrac{\$5,000 + \$500 + \$800 - \$2,800}{2} = \dfrac{\$3,500}{2}$

= $1,750 per year

---

[2] In operations research replacement models concern *component* replacement. Chapter 16, Maintenance Management, includes discussion of component replacement. Replacement of *facilities*, the present subject, is different—it is a capital expenditure problem since large amounts of capital are involved.

$$\text{AAC for trading} \atop \text{after three years} = \frac{\$5,000 + \$500 + \$800 + \$1,000 - \$1,800}{3}$$

$$= \frac{\$5,500}{3} = \$1,833 \text{ per year}$$

The results suggest that it is best to trade after two years, at an average annual cost of $1,750 per year. But, of course, interest has been ignored, and the conclusion may not be valid. Detailed analysis by the EAC method, below, will confirm or deny the conclusion. Discussion follows.

FIGURE 14–7

Cash Flow Diagrams, Forklift Truck Replacement Proposals

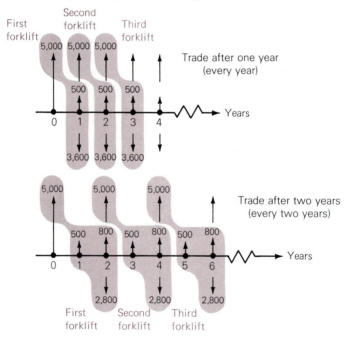

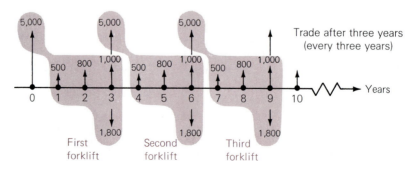

EAC solution:

Option 1. Trade after one year.

$$
\begin{aligned}
EAC &= [\text{Price} + (\text{First-year O\&M}) \ (P/F^1_{10\%}) \\
&\quad - (\text{First-year trade-in}) \ (P/F^1_{10\%})] \ [A/P^1_{10\%}] \\
&= [\$5,000 + \$500 \ (0.9091) - \$3,600 \ (0.9091)] \ [1.100] \\
&= (\$5,000 + \$455 - \$3,273) \ (1.100) \\
&= (\$2,182)(1.100) = \$2,400 \text{ per year}
\end{aligned}
$$

Option 2. Trade after two years.

$$
\begin{aligned}
EAC &= [\text{Price} + (\text{First-year O\&M}) \ (P/F^1_{10\%}) \\
&\quad + (\text{Second-year O\&M})(P/F^2_{10\%}) \\
&\quad - (\text{Second-year trade-in}) \ (P/F^2_{10\%})] \ [A/P^2_{10\%}] \\
&= [\$5,000 + \$500 \ (0.9091) + \$800 \ (0.8264) \\
&\quad - \$2,800 \ (0.8264)] \ [0.57619] \\
&= (\$5,000 + \$455 + \$661 - \$2,314)(0.57619) \\
&= (\$3,802)(0.57619) = \$2,191 \text{ per year}
\end{aligned}
$$

Option 3. Trade after three years.

$$
\begin{aligned}
EAC &= [\text{Price} + (\text{First-year O\&M}) \ (P/F^1_{10\%}) \\
&\quad + (\text{Second-year O\&M})(P/F^2_{10\%}) \\
&\quad + (\text{Third-year O\&M}) \ (P/F^3_{10\%}) \\
&\quad - (\text{Third-year trade-in}) \ (P/F^3_{10\%})][A/P^3_{10\%}] \\
&= [\$5,000 + \$500 \ (0.9091) + \$800 \ (0.8264) \\
&\quad + \$1,000 \ (0.7513) - \$1,800 \ (0.7513)][0.40211] \\
&= (\$5,000 + \$455 + \$661 + \$751 - \$1,350)(0.40211) \\
&= (\$5,517)(0.40211) = \$2,220 \text{ per year}
\end{aligned}
$$

Solution aid: The computations may be simplified by use of tables. The tables have a uniform format, easily printed as computer output. Figure 14–8 is such a table for the forklift truck problem. Each line is a replacement alternative, and all relevant costs, factors, and subtotals, as well as the final computed EAC, are given on that line. Columns 5, 8, and 9 are subtotals, and column 11 is the final EAC.

FIGURE 14–8

Tabular Format for Replacement Calculations

(1)	(2)	(3)	(4)	(5) $(3) \times (4)$	(6)	(7)	(8) $(4) \times (7)$	(9) $(2)+(5)-(8)$	(10)	(11) $(9) \times (10)$
Replacement age	Price (PV)	O&M cost	10 percent p/f	PV of O&M	Cumulative PV of O&M	Trade-in value	PV of trade-in	Total PV	10 percent a/p	Total EAC
1	$5,000	$ 500	0.9091	$455	$ 455	$3,600	$3,273	$2,182	1.100	$2,400
2	5,000	800	0.8264	661	1,116	2,800	2,314	3,802	0.57619	2,191 ←
3	5,000	1,000	0.7513	751	1,867	1,800	1,350	5,517	0.40211	2,220

* Arrow (←) shows optimal result.

Discussion:

O&M and trade-in values are figured as of the ends of each year they occur in; price is treated as of time zero. These figures may be combined only after they have been converted to common-time dollars—present value in this case. Thus, the table shows that O&M and trade-in value are first converted to present values and then combined with price, giving total present value. The total PV is then converted to EAC (annuity).

As was explained earlier in the chapter, EAC is time-independent. Thus, the result for trading in after one year is validly comparable with the result for trading in after two years, three years, and so forth.

Trading in after two years, at $2,191 per year, is preferable to the other two options: the one-year EAC of $2,400 per year and the three-year EAC of $2,220 per year.

The results make a good graph; see Figure 14–9. As the figure shows, the minimum on the EAC curve is in the middle, trading after two years. In replacement problems, the computations go on until the bottom of the curve, which is normally U-shaped, is found. Luckily, in the forklift problem the minimum was found among the first three options; there were no cost data for computing beyond that. (The trade-in point would be pushed out to a later year if the forklift truck were not used much; then O&M costs would be low each year and trade-in values would be higher.)

FIGURE 14–9

U-Shaped Replacement Curve for Forklift Truck

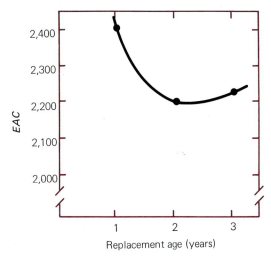

As it happens, the EAC results confirm the AAC conclusion that it is best to trade after two years. The two methods, EAC and AAC, are more likely to produce the same conclusions in short-life cases like this one than in cases where the trade-in point is several years out.

Replacement tends to be an operating-level decision: It concerns existing facilities that are assigned to operating-level managers, such as foremen and other first-line supervisors. By contrast, new facilities tend to be proposed by engineers, middle managers, and planners; their concern is more with modernization strategies than with day-to-day operating problems such as breakdowns and repairs of existing facilities.

Replacement decisions occur often, whereas new-facilities decisions are less frequent. With computers available to most organizations, it makes good sense to set forth systematic procedures to review and project O&M costs and salvage values and to use EAC methods to compute when to replace.

FINAL ANALYSIS

Middle managers may have the authority to decide on facilities proposals if the cost is modest. High-cost proposals will surely go to a high-level finance committee (or its equivalent) for a decision. The high-level group will want to decide based not only on cost but also on benefits (e.g., revenue and/or intangible gain). Cost data from the detailed-analysis stage is combined with benefits data. Methods of doing this include internal rate-of-return (IRR), net present value (NPV), and, in the nonprofit sector, benefit-cost analysis.

IRR and NPV are important analysis tools for money managers (e.g., financial analysts and accountants). Benefit-cost (BC) is an important tool of the planner in nonprofit organizations. Operating managers do not often commission proposal-review analysis using IRR, NPV, and benefit-cost, because revenues and intangible benefits come to the whole organization, not to the manager using the facility. But operating managers are among the decision makers who sit on finance committees to evaluate the results of IRR, NPV, or benefit-cost analysis. IRR, NPV, and benefit-cost are briefly examined below.

IRR, NPV, and BC Analysis

Internal rate-of-return (IRR) considers timing of cash flows. In the IRR method the interest rate, i, is the unknown. It is the compound interest rate at which cash inflows exactly equal cash outflows. Computing the IRR is a trial-and-error procedure (except in simple cases) that may be found in basic finance and managerial accounting textbooks.

Net present value (NPV) is the *net* of present value of cash inflows minus present value of outflows. PV of cost, or outflows, was presented earlier; PV of inflows works the same way.

Benefit-cost analysis is a preferred method in more complex cases. For example, governments and public utilities tend to have more complex benefits to consider because they serve diverse clientele.

Data computations in benefit-cost analysis are the same as in time-adjusted rate-of-return and net present value analysis. That is, all benefits or inflows and all costs or outflows are expressed as either equivalent annual cost (annuity) or present value. It might seem that the only difference among the techniques is in what is done with those subtotals—that is, they are translated into a rate (IRR), an amount (NPV), or a ratio (BC ratio). Not so. There is a major difference, and it is in the way that qualitative factors are treated.

In IRR and NPV analyses, qualitative factors are called *intangibles*. The private firm has profit, in dollars, as the dominant measure of worth. As mentioned earlier, some factors, such as interpersonal climate and flexibility, do not readily translate into dollars. So they are left out of the IRR or NPV computations; they may be interjected later as intangible factors at the time of final discussion and decision.

In public projects, where profit in dollars is not the measure of worth, nearly all benefits seem to be intangible. Treating benefits as intangibles, presented in prose rather than numbers, bothered some people. It seemed nonscientific. Hence, benefit-cost (BC) analysis was developed. In BC analysis *all* benefits, intangible or not, are stated in dollars (EAC or PV dollars). This is an uncertain and speculative process that is almost sure to generate arguments about dollar amounts assigned. But dollars seem to be a logical measure of benefits, because costs are expressed that way. A BC *ratio* results when the dollar sign in the numerator is canceled out by the dollar sign in the denominator. Proposals with BC ratios greater than 1.0 are worthy; those with ratios below 1.0 are not.

Ranking Proposals

Final analysis ends with comparison of proposals and selection of the best ones for funding. Selection is easier when proposals are ranked. A useful approach is ranking by IRR and by amount of investment. Consider, for example, these proposals:

Proposal	Description	IRR	Investment
A	Treespade	14%	$ 7,000
B	Building	20	70,000
C	Research project	35	50,000
D	Computer project	10	30,000
E	Collator	16	6,000
F	Replace truck	9	14,000
G	Kiln	31	2,000

Putting these seven proposals into rank order by IRR yields the following table, with cumulative investment added:

Proposal	IRR	Investment	Cumulative investment
C	35%	$50,000	$ 50,000
G	31	2,000	52,000
B	20	70,000	122,000
E	16	6,000	128,000
A	14	7,000	135,000
D	10	30,000	165,000
F	9	14,000	179,000

IRR may be the basis for selection. For example, if the firm's hurdle rate is 12 percent, then proposals C, G, B, E, and A could be funded; D and F, the computer project and the truck, are below the hurdle rate and thus would be dropped.

A bar graph is helpful in showing rankings. In Figure 14–10 the height of the bars stands for IRR; the width stands for amount of investment. Superimposed is a dashed line drawn at the 12 percent level, which is the hurdle rate. Proposals that go above the line—C, G, B, E, and A—are worth funding. Those below the line—D and F—do not return enough to pay for their investments.

In addition to the horizontal cutoff line, there may be a vertical cutoff. A vertical line signifies a limit in the amount of capital available. The firm would like to generate $135,000 to fund the five proposals that have attractive rates-of-return. But if, say, only $100,000 could be readily generated (at the 12 percent rate), then that $100,000 would have to be budgeted among the five attractive projects. The term for this

FIGURE 14–10

Proposals Ranked by Internal Rate-of-Return (IRR)

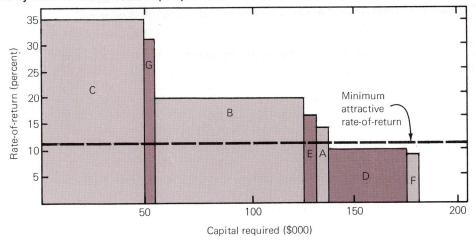

process is **capital budgeting,** and, as was mentioned earlier, a high-level finance committee is often given final responsibility in capital-budgeting.

For firms using NPV analysis instead of IRR, ranking is by NPV from most to least. Public agencies using BC analysis rank projects by BC ratio from most to least. But the rank-ordering should not be final. BC ratios are quite speculative. So sensitivity and risk analysis are needed to see whether some of the projects with high BC ratios are overly dependent on a given set of assumptions or on uncertain data.

SUMMARY

A key strategic decision is planning for facilities: buildings and equipment. Such decisions are not frequent, but they involve large amounts of capital. They also limit the company's freedom to change for years to come.

One strategy that has become popular recently is the focused factory, which means keeping the plant small and narrowly directed; the focused factory helps create a climate for good understanding among people. Flexibility is another strategic factor. Flexible plants—those that avoid hard automation and giant machines, make it easier to introduce new products. Today, with robotics and flexible automation, it is possible to pursue a strategy of both efficiency and flexibility at the same time.

The break-even (BE) point is where total revenues cover total costs, either over the life of the product or year by year. Another type of BE analysis is where the costs of one proposal equal the costs of another proposal—where either will do the job. Payback refers to the number of years it takes for annual savings (or profits) to pay off the initial investment. Average annual cost (AAC) is simply the fixed cost averaged out over the life of the facility plus the variable cost per year.

Payback and simple rate-of-return are useful for decisions on whether to make an investment at all. The form of break-even involving revenue is useful for the same thing. If there is already agreement that an investment in a facility will be made, then revenues and benefits need not be part of the analysis. Just use AAC or break-even to compare alternate facilities capable of performing the function.

Detailed analysis injects compound interest and is limited to cost comparisons. The analysis techniques are equivalent annual cost (EAC) and present value (PV) of cost. The EAC is about the same as a mortgage or installment payment: It is the annual amount that will pay for all expenditures and receipts, allowing for interest (time-value of money). PV is the present lump sum amount that would pay for all expenditures and receipts for the life of the asset—with interest properly allowed for.

A special class of facility proposal is replacement with a newer one (trade-in). The AAC method is all right for preliminary screening; the EAC method is preferable for detailed analysis.

Final analysis is also based on compound interest, but for revenue (or savings) as well as cost. The techniques are internal rate-of-return (IRR), net present value (NPV), and benefit-cost (BC) analyses. The IRR correctly allows for interest effects of all cash inflows and outflows and their *timing*. NPV treats inflows and outflows the same way as IRR; but while IRR divides inflows by outflows, NPV subtracts. BC analysis treats inflows and outflows like IRR and NPV do, but there is a big difference in the source of the cash amounts: In BC analysis, mainly used in nonprofit cases, all intangible benefits (as well as costs) are stated in dollars. These include all sorts of public benefits, which do not convert to dollars easily.

A weakness of IRR and NPV has been in their use: overreliance on that which is easily stated in dollars, not enough consideration of intangibles like effects on people and on flexibility. BC analysis deliberately allows for all the intangibles, but not in a way that avoids controversy.

Part of proposal review is to restate secondary analysis data in terms of IRR, NPV, or BC ratio. Then all proposals may be ranked so that the best get the most consideration from the finance committee, which must make the final decisions.

REFERENCES

Books

English, J. Morley, ed. *Cost-Effectiveness: The Economic Evaluation of Engineered Systems.* New York: John Wiley & Sons, 1968 (TA183.C63).

Horngren, Charles T. *Cost Accounting: A Managerial Emphasis.* 5th ed. Englewood Cliffs, N.J.: Prentice-Hall, 1982 (HF5686.C8H59).

Riggs, James L. *Engineering Economics.* 2d ed. New York: McGraw-Hill, 1982 (TA177.4R532).

Weston, J. F., and E. F. Brigham. *Essentials of Managerial Finance.* 6th ed. Hinsdale, Ill.: Dryden Press, 1982 (HG4026.W448).

Periodicals

The Engineering Economist.
Financial Management.
Management Accounting.

REVIEW QUESTIONS

1. What are *facilities* and why should they be flexible?
2. Explain the *focused factory* concept.
3. In what sense are the open-office concept and office automation *flexible* approaches?

4. Trace the flow of facilities proposals through the organization towards approval.

5. Explain the difference between the complete-recovery and the annual-volume methods of break-even.

6. If there are two mutually exclusive proposals and the anticipated demand is above the break-even point, which proposal is favored, the one with high fixed cost or low fixed cost? Why?

7. What are the weaknesses of payback? Why is it widely used then?

8. How are preliminary-analysis data recomputed in the detailed-analysis stage?

9. Will the results sometimes change for a proposal evaluated first by AAC, then by EAC? Explain.

10. If labor and operating costs are a flat $200 per week, how are they converted to equivalent annual cost? Explain.

11. If you have an overhaul in the fifth year of life for a machine that lasts 10 years, how is the cost of the overhaul converted to an EAC? to a present value?

12. Why doesn't the EAC replacement method work when trading in for a machine with different technology?

13. The EAC method can compare trade-in every two years with trade-in every seven years. Doesn't this introduce bias—since seven years of cost certainly will be greater than two years of cost? Explain.

14. A proposal has been studied using EAC or PV of cost; now it goes to the finance committee. What new data and new computations are necessary so that the committee can compare the proposal with others?

15. What are the major differences between IRR and NPV on the one hand and BC on the other?

16. Why is IRR more valid than simple rate-of-return?

17. In the finance committee how are projects ranked, and how is the decision made on which ones to fund?

PROBLEMS

1. National Aeronautics Corp. is evaluating a proposal to build an entire new factory for full production of a new supersonic aircraft. The factory is expected to cost $50 million; aircraft production costs (not including the factory and related fixed assets) are estimated at $200,000 per aircraft, and each aircraft is to be priced at $300,000. What is the break-even volume? Graph your results. How are the results interpreted, and why should this calculation be considered *preliminary* analysis?

2. Capital Landscape Co. has evaluated a proposal to purchase an industrial treespade. Analysis is based on a delivered price of $9,000, operation and maintenance (O&M) cost of $10 per hour of use, and $20 revenue per hour of use. The complete recovery

breakeven (BE) point, then, is 900 hours of use (see Example 14–1). You are to carry the analysis further, using sensitivity analysis.

a. Perform calculations to see how sensitive the BE point is to the O&M cost estimate. Hint: Increase the O&M cost (or the price for the service) by some percentage; calculate the revised BE point; and determine the percentage change in the B-E value. Decrease by a percentage, and follow the same steps. Compare percentage changes in input data with percentage changes in BE result; draw your conclusions about sensitivity.

b. What are some possible causes of inaccurate estimates—or sudden changes—in O&M cost or price for the service? How likely are those variations in input data? Discuss.

3. Suburban Hospital is considering the purchase of a CAT (computerized axial tomography) scanner for its radiology department. The amortized fixed costs for the scanner and related facilities are projected at $40,000 per year. The cost to operate and maintain the CAT system are estimated to average $300 per scan, and the hospital plans to charge an average of $400 per scan. What is the break-even volume? Plot the results on a BE graph. How are the results interpreted? Why should the BE data be considered *preliminary* analysis?

4. Two college students are starting up a lawn-care service. Two types of rider-mower are being considered for purchase. Data on each type are given below:

	Mower X	Mower Y
Fixed cost (delivered price)	$1,000	$1,600
Variable costs per 1,000 square feet mowed:		
Repair and maintenance	$0.10	$0.07
Labor	1.00	0.78

a. How much grass would the students need to cut to justify the more expensive Mower Y? Graph your results, and discuss them briefly. Recommend a decision based on the data if you can; or explain why you cannot decide.

b. If the students had a single lawn-care contract to care for a 10,000-square-foot plot—and sought no other work—break-even analysis would no longer be the logical method of analysis. Explain why, and work the problem by a more logical method.

5. A proposed new product will require buying a machine for $1,000. The product will sell for $10 and will cost $5 in labor plus $3 in material to produce.

a. What is the break-even volume?

b. Which of the following types of break-even analysis is this? Or is it all of them? Explain your answer.

                Complete-recovery.   Annual-volume.   Mutually exclusive.

6. Central Plumbing Supply Co. is considering the purchase of an $8,100 microcomputer system. The system would cut the costs of inventory posting, invoicing, billing, and financial reporting. The firm selling the microcomputer system estimates these clerical savings at $3,600 per year, based on a brief benefit-cost analysis.

a. Based on payback analysis, does the investment appear to be worthwhile?

b. What are some weaknesses of the payback analysis?

c. The son of Central Plumbing's owner, a major in business administration, disputes the vendor's savings estimate. The son's analysis is based on the assumption of an increasing cash flow from benefits and decreasing costs to program and debug. The resulting savings projection is:

Year	Net savings
1	−$4,000
2	− 1,000
3	+ 3,000
4	+ 5,000
5	+ 5,000
6	+ 5,000
⋮	⋮

What is the payback? Is further (secondary) analysis desirable, or should the project be killed?

7. Able-Baker Distributors uses mainly its own fleet of single-axle trucks for regional pickups and deliveries. For larger long-haul loads, a double-axle semitrailer tractor is rented. The rental charges are $350 per week, plus 10 cents per mile, with renters providing their own fuel. The truck was rented 20 weeks last year, and the weekly trips averaged 2,000 miles. Able-Baker management is now considering having the company purchase its own semi, which may be cheaper than renting in the long run. The following data on having the company own its own rig have been assembled for analysis of the rent-versus-buy alternatives:

Price of a double-axle tractor	$50,000
Useful life	8 years
Resale value after eight years	$4,000
Maintenance cost	$0.08 per mile

Fuel and driver wages are presumed to be the same for either alternative.
a. Which alternative is preferred, based on an average annual cost analysis?
b. Which alternative is preferred, based on an equivalent annual cost analysis using a 15 percent interest rate? What are some important nonquantifiable factors that might bear on the decision?

8. The interest rate (discount rate) is 10 percent, and a vehicle costing $3,000 is replaced with a new $3,000 vehicle every year. Trade-in value is $2,300 and it costs $400 per year for operation and maintenance expenses.
a. What is the equivalent annual cost?
b. Probably you calculated the EAC by using interest tables. Actually, for this simple problem (trading every year) it is possible to calculate the EAC with just the data given and without interest tables. Look over your solution to part a and then explain how to solve for the EAC without interest tables.

9. Snow removal from the walkways of City College Campus can be hand-loaded or machine-loaded. For an average snowfall, hand loading requires 50 men at $32 per day each. The annual cost of shovels, including storage, is $1,500. Machine loading requires snow removal equipment costing $60,000. The equipment would last ten years and have a salvage value of $2,000. Twelve operators are needed to operate the equipment; their wage rate is $44 per day. Fuel, oil, and repairs would amount to $250 per snow day.

Storage cost would be $400 per year. City College uses 10 percent as its cost of capital.

   a. Assuming that there are five days of snow removal per year, how do the two alternatives compare—based on calculations of average annual cost and equivalent annual cost? Which alternative should be selected? Explain.

   b. If an analysis of your snow removal records produced this information, would your decision change?

Days of snow removal per year	4	5	6	7	8
Probability	0.05	0.40	0.35	0.15	0.05

10. An industrial sewing machine leases for $400 per year. Sewers work 2,000 hours per year, and they get paid $3 per hour. If the cost of capital is 5 percent and the sewing machine is expected to have a useful life of six years, what is the EAC of the machine-and-sewer combination? What two pieces of data from the problem are not used in its solution, and why?

11. What is the EAC for a $1,000 machine that will last 10 years with a $345 overhaul at the end of year five? Assume 10 percent interest and no salvage value.

12. Chompin' Chicken is a national franchiser in the fast-food business. A decision is to be made on the type of chair that will be installed in new franchised outlets as the highly successful business expands. Chair A costs $25 and has a projected useful life of five years with a salvage value of $5. Chair B costs $40 and has a projected useful life of eight years with a salvage value of $10. Chompin' Chicken uses an interest rate of 12 percent in its investment calculations.

   a. Which chair is preferred? Base your answer on EAC analysis.

   b. Explain the calculation procedure that would be required using PV-of-cost analysis. Draw cash flow diagrams as part of your explanation.

13. A new performing arts center will have either tile or stone floors in the lobby and main floor hallways. The choice will be made based on a cost analysis using an 8 percent interest rate and the following data:

   Tile: Installed cost per square foot is $15. The tile will last 20 years, and it will require annual upkeep cost (for waxing, etc.) of $1 per square foot.

   Stone: Installed cost per square foot is $50. The stone will last 60 years. Upkeep costs are negligible. (Both tile and stone require dusting and mopping, but only tile requires waxing.)

   a. Which floor is preferred, based on equivalent annual costs?

   b. Repeat the analysis, but this time use PV of cost.

14. Two types of coal-car wheel are under consideration by a railroad. One type is a conventional wheel, which lasts eight years and is refurbished (cleaned, reground, and pressed onto a new axle) at year 3 and year 6. Initial cost is $250, and salvage value is $40. The first refurbishment costs $80, and the second costs $125. The other wheel type is made of specially treated metal alloys. These special wheels will last four years, but they cannot be refurbished economically. Initial cost is $350, and salvage value is $60.

   a. If the interest rate is 8 percent, which wheel is preferable? Use either EAC or PV analysis. Draw cash flow diagrams in support of your analysis.

   b. Which method, EAC or PV, is the most efficient for this analysis (i.e., the method requiring the fewest interest calculations)?

c.   Railroad executives want to be sure that lower-level supervisors understand the economics in selecting one wheel over the other. How may the calculations be best
explained so that those supervisors will understand?

15.   A machine costs $30,000, and it takes $800 per year to operate and maintain it. It will
be overhauled at the end of year 5 at a cost of $3,000, and again at the end of year 10
for $4,000. At the end of year 15 it is to be scrapped, which should yield $2,000 scrap
proceeds. What is the total present value if the interest rate is 15 percent?

16.   Paint-bake oven A costs $5,000 and consumes $2 worth of power per hour of operation.
Oven B costs $7,000 and consumes $1.50 per hour of operation. The company uses 12
percent as its discount rate and projects 400 hours as its oven usage per year. Both
ovens have a projected useful life of 15 years.
a.   Which oven is preferable by the PV of cost method?
b.   Which oven is preferable by the AAC method? Convert the PV from part *a* to an
EAC. Explain the difference between the AAC and the EAC.

17.   Paramount Linen Service has a large industrial washer. The washer has been experiencing
considerable breakdown time, and the general manager wonders whether it should be
replaced. The washer is four years old, and it has the following history and projected
future pattern of maintenance costs and resale (or trade-in) values:

Year	Maintenance cost	Resale
1	$ 300	$45,000
2	570	32,000
3	990	23,000
Current → 4	2,025	15,000
year 5	4,500	9,000
6	7,830	4,000
7	11,050	3,000
8	16,040	2,000

If that type of washer costs $60,000 new, is it time to replace? If not, when? Assume a
12 percent interest rate. Suggestion: Set the problem up in a tabular format similar to
that of Figure 14–8.

18.   Corning County has hired an MBA, who recommends that the internal rate-of-return
method be used to justify capital expenditures. One department head questions the advice,
saying, "We aren't a profit-making organization. How can we talk about a 'return'?" Is
it true that the IRR method cannot be used in a nonprofit organization? Explain.

19.   A firm wants to replace its mimeograph machine with an identical new one costing
$1,000 when its maintenance costs get too high relative to the cost of new equipment.
The costs for three alternatives are: (1) Replace every year—Maintenance = $100; trade-
in proceeds = $400. (2) Replace every two years—Maintenance = $200/year; trade-in
proceeds = $200. (3) Replace every three years—Maintenance = $400/year; trade-in
proceeds = $100.
a.   Which alternative is most economical if interest is zero percent?
b.   Which is most economical if interest is 12 percent?

20.   A high-volume office equipment manufacturer is thinking of investing $1 million in equip-
ment that will straighten steel coil, cut it, and bend it into file cabinet panels. The equipment
promises to reduce labor costs by $250,000 a year.

a. On the basis of purely financial considerations, is it a good investment? Support your answer with appropriate calculations using only the data given. What other data would make your financial analysis more complete, and why?

b. Some other factors are quality, impact on people, reliability, and flexibility. How much weight should be given to these factors? With these factors included, what do you think of the investment?

21. The airlines are being called upon to address the issue of fire- or smoke-retardant seats. The cost would surely be high. What benefits are there that could be translated into dollars? Would an analysis of cost versus dollar benefits be reasonably complete as a basis for decision making? Or would the airlines want to put weight on other factors? Discuss.

22. Here are seven proposals and their capital requirements and internal rates of return: (A) Scrap-burning power plant, $300,000, 18 percent. (B) Hire Arthur D. Little to conduct study of automation potential, $100,000, 20 percent. (C) Microwave relay facilities for interplant communications, $900,000, 30 percent. (D) Train all salaried and hourly employees in total quality control, $200,000, 50 percent. (E) Warehouse with automated storage/retrieval system (AS/RS), $1,400,000, 15 percent. (F) Worker retraining project, $250,000, 10 percent. (G) Engineering effort to cut setup times, $50,000, 70 percent.

   Arrange these data into a capital-budgeting chart similar to Figure 14–7. Insert a hurdle rate of 22 percent. What proposals do not qualify? Do any of those seem as though they might have major intangible benefits and deserve a second look? Discuss.

23. The U.S. Naval Base at Guantánamo Bay, Cuba, has several major tenants, two of which are a supply depot (SD) and a public works department (PWD). Each has its own carpentry shop. The carpentry shop at PWD serves the whole base, including housing. The carpentry shop at SD exists to build crates and shelves, and to perform minor construction and remodeling.

   In a cost-cutting drive the SD commander has assigned an analyst to study the carpentry shop. A segment of the analyst's study report follows:

   The carpentry shop has 11 large pieces of power equipment, which is about as much as the PWD carpentry shop has. For crating operations in SD only three large power saws (at the most) are needed; the remainder of the equipment is currently used for miscellaneous carpentry jobs in the slack winter months.

   Since providing carpentry and woodworking services to all base tenants is part of the mission of PWD, SD has no reason for being in the carpentry business except to construct required shipping crates. All skills and equipment in excess of those needed for crate construction are an unnecessary duplication of the PWD effort. Disposal action should be taken on this equipment, which is listed below.

Name of equipment	Original price
Planer	$2,260
Jointer-planer	2,725
Radial-arm saw	552
Radial-arm saw	n.a.
Band saw	n.a.
Jointer-planer	n.a.
Sander	n.a.
Drill press	n.a.

The analyst's report went to the commander, who presented it at a staff meeting. One SD department head who had played a role in acquiring the equipment 20–30 years earlier, objected, as did a few other old-timers. The analyst's recommendation for disposal ended up being "shelved." When the analyst heard about the result, his wry comment was,

> The noble art of losing face
> May someday save the human race.

What did the analyst mean? Assess the analyst's study and its outcome.

Supplement A to Chapter 14
Time-Value of Money

In Supplement A we examine time-value-of-money concepts, including:

1. Interest and interest tables.
2. Solution procedure.
3. Payment patterns.

Interest and Interest Tables

"A bird in the hand is worth two in the bush." Similarly $1 in hand is worth $2 five years from now. That is a true statement—if the interest rate for a savings account is 15 percent. Here is the proof (the final figure is a penny too high because of rounding error):

1st year: $1.00 at 15 percent interest equals $1.15 at year-end.

2d year: $1.15 at 15 percent interest equals $1.32 at year-end.

3d year: $1.32 at 15 percent interest equals $1.52 at year-end.

4th year: $1.52 at 15 percent interest equals $1.75 at year-end.

5th year: $1.75 at 15 percent interest equals $2.01 at year-end.

There is a much faster way to find what money today is worth in the future: Multiply (or divide) today's amount by the appropriate compound interest factor for the given interest rate and number of years. The interest factor may be found in interest tables, which are widely available in banks and finance companies; in the facilities planning and accounting departments of firms; and in appendices of textbooks in business administration and industrial engineering.

Finance and management accounting textbooks generally include two interest tables. Industrial engineering (engineering economy) textbooks[1] include the same two, plus four (or sometimes five) more, which are mathematical transpositions of the first two. Operations management textbooks tend to spend time in both camps, and

---

[1] The first major work on time-value-of-money analysis was probably J. C. L. Fish, *Engineering Economics* (New York: McGraw-Hill, 1923).

thus may include either the two tables or the six tables. In this textbook the six-table approach is demonstrated.

The six-table approach uses interest factors (Table S14–1, end of Supplement A) for

1. Finding the *future* value of a *present* sum, abbreviated as F/P_i^n, where

   F/P means "F, given P," or "Find the *future* sum, given the *present* sum."
   Note that the slash (/) stands for the word *given*.
   n stands for *number* of years.
   i stands for *interest* rate.

2. Finding the *present* value of a *future* sum, abbreviated P/F_i^n.
3. Finding the equivalent *annual* cost (or annuity) of a *future* sum, abbreviated A/F_i^n.
4. Finding the equivalent *annual* cost of a *present* sum, abbreviated A/P_i^n.
5. Finding the *future* value of a uniform *annual* amount (or an equivalent annual cost, or an annuity), abbreviated F/A_i^n.
6. Finding the *present* value of a uniform *annual* amount, abbreviated P/A_i^n.

Numbers 1 and 4 are simply the reciprocals of all the interest factors in 2 and 6, respectively. That is, P/F is the reciprocal of F/P, and A/P is the reciprocal of P/A.

Number 5 is useful only in special situations, but number 3, the A/F interest factor, is often useful. A typical situation is this: You want to find the equivalent annual cost of a proposed machine costing X dollars, having Y dollars per year operation and maintenance (O&M) cost, and returning Z dollars salvage value at the end of its useful life. To work the problem you must combine the three costs, but only after translating them into common-time-dollars—in this case equivalent annual cost (EAC).

Initial cost X is translated into EAC:

$$EAC = X(A/P)_i^n$$

O&M cost Y is already annual and uniform from year to year, so:

$$EAC = Y$$

Salvage value Z may be translated into EAC:

$$EAC = -Z(A/F)_i^n$$

Then add the three EAC components.

The salvage value step may be interpreted thus: (1) Salvage value is a receipt or negative cost and therefore bears a minus sign. (2) The equivalent annual cost of salvage value is like a prepayment plan—or a sinking fund. (3) The A/F factor allows you to "annualize" salvage value in one step (whereas this would take two steps using the two-table method).

Solution Procedure

It may seem that time-value-of-money methods make detailed analysis difficult. A few tips can help the learner cope with these difficulties:

1. Begin by labeling the given data. In the six-table method this means labeling each item of numeric data as being *P, A, F, i,* or *n;* these, of course, are the five labels found in the interest tables, Table S14–1. Recall that:

> *P* stands for *p*resent amount, or *p*rincipal, or *p*resent value, or *p*resent worth— any sum that occurs at time *zero,* the time that the decision on the proposal is to be made.

> *A* stands for uniform *a*nnual amount, or equivalent *a*nnual cost, or *a*nnualized equivalent of a present or future sum with interest included (like installment loan payments)—it must occur every year of the life of the proposal, and it is always assumed to occur at year-end.

> *F* stands for *f*uture amount that occurs at the end of some given year—typically a trade-in or salvage value at the end of a proposal's life or an overhaul in one or more intermediate years.

> *i* stands for *i*nterest rate, or discount rate, or cost of capital, or hurdle rate, or time-adjusted rate-of-return, or internal rate-of-return, or opportunity cost rate.

> *n* stands for *n*umber of years—for which a uniform annual amount is paid or received, or until a future sum occurs, or the life of the proposal.

2. Decide what the unknown is—the numeric value that is to be solved for; it will be *P, A, F, i,* or *n.* This numeric solution is used in some way to help decide on the merits of the proposed facility. Often there is a choice of unknowns to solve for. For example, results may sometimes be expressed in terms of present value *(P),* equivalent annual cost *(A),* or internal rate-of-return *(i).* Each usually results in the same decision about the proposal. The choice of unknown, then, may be based on which form is most familiar to the analyst or decision maker or which form is easiest to compute.

3. Use appropriate interest tables to compute the unknown. This may be easy and quite mechanical, because you simply choose the proper interest table and column and row by referring to the desired unknown and the given data. For example, suppose that you are given a future amount *(F)* and that the desired unknown is present value *(P).* For short, you want "*P,* given *A.*" Therefore, you go to the *P/A* column— on the page for the given interest rate *(i)* and down the page to the given number of years *(n).*

Payment Patterns

In facilities proposals there will often be a cost of operating that is about the same in each year of use. For example, it may cost $500 per year—for wages and power—to operate a proposed copying machine. If the machine is expected to last ten years, the present value equivalent, at 10 percent, is (using the appropriate *P/A* factor):

$$\text{Present value} = (\$500)(6.145) = \$3,072.50$$

Wages would probably be paid out in weekly increments, and power in monthly increments. It is convenient, however, to treat all such costs as if they were paid for in a lump sum at the end of the year; this is standard practice among accounting, financial, and engineering analysts. The resulting inaccuracy is slight.

TABLE S14–1

Six Interest Tables
1%

	To find F. given P:	To find P. given F:	To find A. given F:	To find A. given P:	To find F. given A:	To find P. given A:	
	$(1 + i)^n$	$\dfrac{1}{(1 + i)^n}$	$\dfrac{i}{(1 + i)^n - 1}$	$\dfrac{i(1 + i)^n}{(1 + i)^n - 1}$	$\dfrac{(1 + i)^n - 1}{i}$	$\dfrac{(1 + i)^n - 1}{i(1 + i)^n}$	
n	$(f/p)^1_n$	$(p/f)^1_n$	$(a/f)^1_n$	$(a/p)^1_n$	$(f/a)^1_n$	$(p/a)^1_n$	n
1	1.010	0.9901	1.00000	1.01000	1.000	0.990	1
2	1.020	0.9803	0.49751	0.50751	2.010	1.970	2
3	1.030	0.9706	0.33002	0.34002	3.030	2.941	3
4	1.041	0.9610	0.24628	0.25628	4.060	3.902	4
5	1.051	0.9515	0.19604	0.20604	5.101	4.853	5
6	1.062	0.9420	0.16255	0.17255	6.152	5.795	6
7	1.072	0.9327	0.13863	0.14863	7.214	6.728	7
8	1.083	0.9235	0.12069	0.13069	8.286	7.652	8
9	1.094	0.9143	0.10674	0.11674	9.369	8.566	9
10	1.105	0.9053	0.09558	0.10558	10.462	9.471	10
11	1.116	0.8963	0.08645	0.09645	11.567	10.368	11
12	1.127	0.8874	0.07885	0.08885	12.683	11.255	12
13	1.138	0.8787	0.07241	0.08241	13.809	12.134	13
14	1.149	0.8700	0.06690	0.07690	14.947	13.004	14
15	1.161	0.8613	0.06212	0.07212	16.097	13.865	15
16	1.173	0.8528	0.05794	0.06794	17.258	14.718	16
17	1.184	0.8444	0.05426	0.06426	18.430	15.562	17
18	1.196	0.8360	0.05098	0.06098	19.615	16.398	18
19	1.208	0.8277	0.04805	0.05805	20.811	17.226	19
20	1.220	0.8195	0.04542	0.05542	22.019	18.046	20
21	1.232	0.8114	0.04303	0.05303	23.239	18.857	21
22	1.245	0.8034	0.04086	0.05086	24.472	19.660	22
23	1.257	0.7954	0.03889	0.04889	25.716	20.456	23
24	1.270	0.7876	0.03707	0.04707	26.973	21.243	24
25	1.282	0.7798	0.03541	0.04541	28.243	22.023	25
26	1.295	0.7720	0.03387	0.04387	29.526	22.795	26
27	1.308	0.7644	0.03245	0.04245	30.821	23.560	27
28	1.321	0.7568	0.03112	0.04112	32.129	24.316	28
29	1.335	0.7493	0.02990	0.03990	33.450	25.066	29
30	1.348	0.7419	0.02875	0.03875	34.785	25.808	30
31	1.361	0.7346	0.02768	0.03768	36.133	26.542	31
32	1.375	0.7273	0.02667	0.03667	37.494	27.270	32
33	1.391	0.7201	0.02573	0.03573	38.869	27.990	33
34	1.403	0.7130	0.02484	0.03484	40.258	28.703	34
35	1.417	0.7059	0.02400	0.03400	41.660	29.409	35
40	1.489	0.6717	0.02046	0.03046	48.886	32.835	40
45	1.565	0.6391	0.01771	0.02771	56.481	36.095	45
50	1.645	0.6080	0.01551	0.02551	64.463	39.196	50
55	1.729	0.5785	0.01373	0.02373	72.852	42.147	55
60	1.817	0.5504	0.01224	0.02224	81.670	44.955	60
65	1.909	0.5237	0.01100	0.02100	90.937	47.627	65
70	2.007	0.4983	0.00993	0.01993	100.676	50.169	70
75	2.109	0.4741	0.00902	0.01902	110.913	52.587	75
80	2.217	0.4511	0.00822	0.01822	121.672	54.888	80
85	2.330	0.4292	0.00752	0.01752	132.979	57.078	85
90	2.449	0.4084	0.00690	0.01690	144.863	59.161	90
95	2.574	0.3886	0.00636	0.01636	157.354	61.143	95
100	2.705	0.3697	0.00587	0.01587	170.481	63.029	100

Source: Paul G. Hoel, *Elementary Statistics,* 4th ed. Copyright © 1976 by John Wiley & Sons, Inc. Reprinted by permission.

2%

	To find F, given P:	To find P, given F:	To find A, given F:[*]	To find A, given P:	To find F, given A:	To find P, given A:	
	$(1 + i)^n$	$\dfrac{1}{(1 + i)^n}$	$\dfrac{i}{(1 + i)^n - 1}$	$\dfrac{i(1 + i)^n}{(1 + i)^n - 1}$	$\dfrac{(1 + i)^n - 1}{i}$	$\dfrac{(1 + i)^n - 1}{i(1 + i)^n}$	
n	$(f/p)_n^2$	$(p/f)_n^2$	$(a/f)_n^2$	$(a/p)_n^2$	$(f/a)_n^2$	$(p/a)_n^2$	n
1	1.020	0.9804	1.00000	1.02000	1.000	0.980	1
2	1.040	0.9612	0.49505	0.51505	2.020	1.942	2
3	1.061	0.9423	0.32675	0.34675	3.060	2.884	3
4	1.082	0.9238	0.24262	0.26262	4.122	3.808	4
5	1.104	0.9057	0.19216	0.21216	5.204	4.713	5
6	1.126	0.8880	0.15853	0.17853	6.308	5.601	6
7	1.149	0.8706	0.13451	0.15451	7.434	6.472	7
8	1.172	0.8535	0.11651	0.13651	8.583	7.325	8
9	1.195	0.8368	0.10252	0.12252	9.755	8.162	9
10	1.219	0.8203	0.09133	0.11133	10.950	8.983	10
11	1.243	0.8043	0.08216	0.10218	12.169	9.787	11
12	1.268	0.7885	0.07456	0.09456	13.412	10.575	12
13	1.294	0.7730	0.06812	0.08812	14.680	11.348	13
14	1.319	0.7579	0.06260	0.08260	15.974	12.106	14
15	1.346	0.7430	0.05783	0.07783	17.293	12.849	15
16	1.373	0.7284	0.05365	0.07365	18.639	13.578	16
17	1.400	0.7142	0.04997	0.06997	20.012	14.292	17
18	1.428	0.7002	0.04670	0.06670	21.412	14.992	18
19	1.457	0.6864	0.04378	0.06378	22.841	15.678	19
20	1.486	0.6730	0.04116	0.06116	24.297	16.351	20
21	1.516	0.6598	0.03878	0.05878	25.783	17.011	21
22	1.546	0.6468	0.03663	0.05663	27.299	17.658	22
23	1.577	0.6342	0.03467	0.05467	28.845	18.292	23
24	1.608	0.6217	0.03287	0.05287	30.422	18.914	24
25	1.641	0.6095	0.03122	0.05122	32.030	19.523	25
26	1.673	0.5976	0.02970	0.04970	33.671	20.121	26
27	1.707	0.5859	0.02829	0.04829	35.344	20.707	27
28	1.741	0.5744	0.02699	0.04699	37.051	21.281	28
29	1.776	0.5631	0.02578	0.04578	38.792	21.844	29
30	1.811	0.5521	0.02465	0.04465	40.568	22.396	30
31	1.848	0.5412	0.02360	0.04360	42.379	22.938	31
32	1.885	0.5306	0.02261	0.04261	44.227	23.468	32
33	1.922	0.5202	0.02169	0.04169	46.112	23.989	33
34	1.961	0.5100	0.02082	0.04082	48.034	24.499	34
35	2.000	0.5000	0.02000	0.04000	49.994	24.999	35
40	2.208	0.4529	0.01656	0.03656	60.402	27.355	40
45	2.438	0.4102	0.01391	0.03391	71.893	29.490	45
50	2.692	0.3715	0.01182	0.03182	84.579	31.424	50
55	2.972	0.3365	0.01014	0.03014	98.587	33.175	55
60	3.281	0.3048	0.00877	0.02877	114.052	34.761	60
65	3.623	0.2761	0.00763	0.02763	131.126	36.197	65
70	4.000	0.2500	0.00667	0.02667	149.978	37.499	70
75	4.416	0.2265	0.00586	0.02586	170.792	38.677	75
80	4.875	0.2051	0.00516	0.02516	193.772	39.745	80
85	5.383	0.1858	0.00456	0.02456	219.144	40.711	85
90	5.943	0.1683	0.00405	0.02405	247.157	41.587	90
95	6.562	0.1524	0.00360	0.02360	278.085	42.380	95
100	7.245	0.1380	0.00320	0.02320	312.232	43.098	100

3%

	To find F, given P:	To find P, given F:	To find A, given F:	To find A, given P:	To find F, given A:	To find P, given A:	
	$(1 + i)^n$	$\dfrac{1}{(1 + i)^n}$	$\dfrac{i}{(1 + i)^n - 1}$	$\dfrac{i(1 + i)^n}{(1 + i)^n - 1}$	$\dfrac{(1 + i)^n - 1}{i}$	$\dfrac{(1 + i)^n - 1}{i(1 + i)^n}$	
n	$(f/p)_n^3$	$(p/f)_n^3$	$(a/f)_n^3$	$(a/p)_n^3$	$(f/a)_n^3$	$(p/a)_n^3$	n
1	1.030	0.9709	1.00000	1.03000	1.000	0.971	1
2	1.061	0.9426	0.49261	0.52261	2.030	1.913	2
3	1.093	0.9151	0.32353	0.35353	3.091	2.829	3
4	1.126	0.8885	0.23903	0.26903	4.184	3.717	4
5	1.159	0.8626	0.18835	0.21835	5.309	4.580	5
6	1.194	0.8375	0.15460	0.18460	6.468	5.417	6
7	1.230	0.8131	0.13051	0.16051	7.662	6.230	7
8	1.267	0.7894	0.11246	0.14246	8.892	7.020	8
9	1.305	0.7664	0.09843	0.12843	10.159	7.786	9
10	1.344	0.7441	0.08723	0.11723	11.464	8.530	10
11	1.384	0.7224	0.07808	0.10808	12.808	9.253	11
12	1.426	0.7014	0.07046	0.10046	14.192	9.954	12
13	1.469	0.6810	0.06403	0.09403	15.618	10.635	13
14	1.513	0.6611	0.05853	0.08853	17.086	11.296	14
15	1.558	0.6419	0.05377	0.08377	18.599	11.938	15
16	1.605	0.6232	0.04961	0.07961	20.157	12.561	16
17	1.653	0.6050	0.04595	0.07595	21.762	13.166	17
18	1.702	0.5874	0.04271	0.07271	23.414	13.754	18
19	1.754	0.5703	0.03981	0.06981	25.117	14.324	19
20	1.806	0.5537	0.03722	0.06722	26.870	14.877	20
21	1.860	0.5375	0.03487	0.06487	28.676	15.415	21
22	1.916	0.5219	0.03275	0.06275	30.537	15.937	22
23	1.974	0.5067	0.03081	0.06081	32.453	16.444	23
24	2.033	0.4919	0.02905	0.05905	34.426	16.936	24
25	2.094	0.4776	0.02743	0.05743	36.459	17.413	25
26	2.157	0.4637	0.02594	0.05594	38.553	17.877	26
27	2.221	0.4502	0.02456	0.05456	40.710	18.327	27
28	2.288	0.4371	0.02329	0.05329	42.931	18.764	28
29	2.357	0.4243	0.02211	0.05211	45.219	19.188	29
30	2.427	0.4120	0.02102	0.05102	47.575	19.600	30
31	2.500	0.4000	0.02000	0.05000	50.003	20.000	31
32	2.575	0.3883	0.01905	0.04905	52.503	20.389	32
33	2.652	0.3770	0.01816	0.04816	55.078	20.766	33
34	2.732	0.3660	0.01732	0.04732	57.730	21.132	34
35	2.814	0.3554	0.01654	0.04654	60.462	21.487	35
40	3.262	0.3066	0.01326	0.04326	75.401	23.115	40
45	3.782	0.2644	0.01079	0.04079	92.720	24.519	45
50	4.384	0.2281	0.00887	0.03887	112.797	25.730	50
55	5.082	0.1968	0.00735	0.03735	136.072	26.774	55
60	5.892	0.1697	0.00613	0.03613	163.053	27.676	60
65	6.830	0.1464	0.00515	0.03515	194.333	28.453	65
70	7.918	0.1263	0.00434	0.03434	230.594	29.123	70
75	9.179	0.1089	0.00367	0.03367	272.631	29.702	75
80	10.641	0.0940	0.00311	0.03311	321.363	30.201	80
85	12.336	0.0811	0.00265	0.03265	377.857	30.631	85
90	14.300	0.0699	0.00226	0.03226	443.349	31.002	90
95	16.578	0.0603	0.00193	0.03193	519.272	31.323	95
100	19.219	0.0520	0.00165	0.03165	607.288	31.599	100

605

5%

n	To find F, given P: $(1 + i)^n$ $(f/p)^5_n$	To find P, given F: $\dfrac{1}{(1 + i)^n}$ $(p/f)^5_n$	To find A, given F: $\dfrac{i}{(1 + i)^n - 1}$ $(a/f)^5_n$	To find A, given P: $\dfrac{i(1 + i)^n}{(1 + i)^n - 1}$ $(a/p)^5_n$	To find F, given A: $\dfrac{(1 + i)^n - 1}{i}$ $(f/a)^5_n$	To find P, given A: $\dfrac{(1 + i)^n - 1}{i(1 + i)^n}$ $(p/a)^5_n$	n
1	1.050	0.9524	1.00000	1.05000	1.000	0.952	1
2	1.103	0.9070	0.48780	0.53780	2.050	1.859	2
3	1.158	0.8638	0.31721	0.36721	3.153	2.723	3
4	1.216	0.8227	0.23201	0.28201	4.310	3.546	4
5	1.276	0.7835	0.18097	0.23097	5.526	4.329	5
6	1.340	0.7462	0.14702	0.19702	6.802	5.076	6
7	1.407	0.7107	0.12282	0.17282	8.142	5.786	7
8	1.477	0.6768	0.10472	0.15472	9.549	6.463	8
9	1.551	0.6446	0.09069	0.14069	11.027	7.108	9
10	1.629	0.6139	0.07950	0.12950	12.578	7.722	10
11	1.710	0.5847	0.07039	0.12039	14.207	8.306	11
12	1.796	0.5568	0.06283	0.11283	15.917	8.863	12
13	1.886	0.5303	0.05646	0.10646	17.713	9.394	13
14	1.980	0.5051	0.05102	0.10102	19.599	9.899	14
15	2.079	0.4810	0.04634	0.09634	21.579	10.380	15
16	2.183	0.4581	0.04227	0.09227	23.657	10.838	16
17	2.292	0.4363	0.03870	0.08870	25.840	11.274	17
18	2.407	0.4155	0.03555	0.08555	28.132	11.690	18
19	2.527	0.3957	0.03275	0.08275	30.539	12.085	19
20	2.653	0.3769	0.03024	0.08024	33.066	12.462	20
21	2.786	0.3589	0.02800	0.07800	35.719	12.821	21
22	2.925	0.3418	0.02597	0.07597	38.505	13.163	22
23	3.072	0.3256	0.02414	0.07414	41.430	13.489	23
24	3.225	0.3101	0.02247	0.07247	44.502	13.799	24
25	3.386	0.2953	0.02095	0.07095	47.727	14.094	25
26	3.556	0.2812	0.01956	0.06956	51.113	14.375	26
27	3.733	0.2678	0.01829	0.06829	54.669	14.643	27
28	3.920	0.2551	0.01712	0.06712	58.403	14.898	28
29	4.116	0.2429	0.01605	0.06605	62.323	15.141	29
30	4.322	0.2314	0.01505	0.06505	66.439	15.372	30
31	4.538	0.2204	0.01413	0.06413	70.761	15.593	31
32	4.765	0.2099	0.01328	0.06328	75.299	15.803	32
33	5.003	0.1999	0.01249	0.06249	80.064	16.003	33
34	5.253	0.1904	0.01176	0.06176	85.067	16.193	34
35	5.516	0.1813	0.01107	0.06107	90.320	16.374	35
40	7.040	0.1420	0.00828	0.05828	120.800	17.159	40
45	8.985	0.1113	0.00626	0.05626	159.700	17.774	45
50	11.467	0.0872	0.00478	0.05478	209.348	18.256	50
55	14.636	0.0683	0.00367	0.05367	272.713	18.633	55
60	18.679	0.0535	0.00283	0.05283	353.584	18.929	60
65	23.840	0.0419	0.00219	0.05219	456.798	19.161	65
70	30.426	0.0329	0.00170	0.05170	588.529	19.343	70
75	38.833	0.0258	0.00132	0.05132	756.654	19.485	75
80	49.561	0.0202	0.00103	0.05103	971.229	19.596	80
85	63.254	0.0158	0.00080	0.05080	1245.087	19.684	85
90	80.730	0.0124	0.00063	0.05063	1594.607	19.752	90
95	103.035	0.0097	0.00049	0.05049	2040.694	19.806	95
100	131.501	0.0076	0.00038	0.05038	2610.025	19.848	100

7%

	To find F, given P: $(1 + i)^n$	To find P, given F: $\dfrac{1}{(1 + i)^n}$	To find A, given F: $\dfrac{i}{(1 + i)^n - 1}$	To find A, given P: $\dfrac{i(1 + i)^n}{(1 + i)^n - 1}$	To find F, given A: $\dfrac{(1 + i)^n - 1}{i}$	To find P, given A: $\dfrac{(1 + i)^n - 1}{i(1 + i)^n}$	
n	$(f/p)^7_n$	$(p/f)^7_n$	$(a/f)^7_n$	$(a/p)^7_n$	$(f/a)^7_n$	$(p/a)^7_n$	n
1	1.070	0.9346	1.00000	1.07000	1.000	0.935	1
2	1.145	0.8734	0.48309	0.55309	2.070	1.808	2
3	1.225	0.8163	0.31105	0.38105	3.215	2.624	3
4	1.311	0.7629	0.22523	0.29523	4.440	3.387	4
5	1.403	0.7130	0.17389	0.24389	5.751	4.100	5
6	1.501	0.6663	0.13980	0.20980	7.153	4.767	6
7	1.606	0.6227	0.11555	0.18555	8.654	5.389	7
8	1.718	0.5820	0.09747	0.16747	10.260	5.971	8
9	1.838	0.5439	0.08349	0.15349	11.978	6.515	9
10	1.967	0.5083	0.07238	0.14238	13.816	7.024	10
11	2.105	0.4751	0.06336	0.13336	15.784	7.499	11
12	2.252	0.4440	0.05590	0.12590	17.888	7.943	12
13	2.410	0.4150	0.04965	0.11965	20.141	8.358	13
14	2.579	0.3878	0.04434	0.11434	22.550	8.745	14
15	2.759	0.3624	0.03979	0.10979	25.129	9.108	15
16	2.952	0.3387	0.03586	0.10586	27.888	9.447	16
17	3.159	0.3166	0.03243	0.10243	30.840	9.763	17
18	3.380	0.2959	0.02941	0.09941	33.999	10.059	18
19	3.617	0.2765	0.02675	0.09675	37.379	10.363	19
20	3.870	0.2584	0.02439	0.09439	40.995	10.594	20
21	4.141	0.2415	0.02229	0.09229	44.865	10.836	21
22	4.430	0.2257	0.02041	0.09041	49.006	11.061	22
23	4.741	0.2109	0.01871	0.08871	53.436	11.272	23
24	5.072	0.1971	0.01719	0.08719	58.177	11.469	24
25	5.427	0.1842	0.01581	0.08581	63.249	11.654	25
26	5.807	0.1722	0.01456	0.08456	68.676	11.826	26
27	6.214	0.1609	0.01343	0.08343	74.484	11.987	27
28	6.649	0.1504	0.01239	0.08239	80.698	12.137	28
29	7.114	0.1406	0.01145	0.08145	87.347	12.278	29
30	7.612	0.1314	0.01059	0.08059	94.461	12.409	30
31	8.145	0.1228	0.00980	0.07980	102.073	12.532	31
32	8.715	0.1147	0.00907	0.07907	110.218	12.647	32
33	9.325	0.1072	0.00841	0.07841	118.923	12.754	33
34	9.978	0.1002	0.00780	0.07780	128.259	12.854	34
35	10.677	0.0937	0.00723	0.07723	138.237	12.948	35
40	14.974	0.0668	0.00501	0.07501	199.635	13.332	40
45	21.002	0.0476	0.00350	0.07350	285.749	13.606	45
50	29.457	0.0339	0.00246	0.07246	406.529	13.801	50
55	41.315	0.0242	0.00174	0.07174	575.929	13.940	55
60	57.946	0.0173	0.00123	0.07123	813.520	14.039	60
65	81.273	0.0123	0.00087	0.07087	1146.755	14.110	65
70	113.989	0.0088	0.00062	0.07062	1614.134	14.160	70
75	159.876	0.0063	0.00044	0.07044	2269.657	14.196	75
80	224.234	0.0045	0.00031	0.07031	3189.063	14.222	80
85	314.500	0.0032	0.00022	0.07022	4478.576	14.240	85
90	441.103	0.0023	0.00016	0.07016	6287.185	14.253	90
95	618.670	0.0016	0.00011	0.07011	8823.854	14.263	95
100	867.716	0.0012	0.00008	0.07008	12381.662	14.269	100

10%

	To find F, given P: $(1 + i)^n$	To find P, given F: $\dfrac{1}{(1 + i)^n}$	To find A, given F: $\dfrac{i}{(1 + i)^n - 1}$	To find A, given P: $\dfrac{i(1 + i)^n}{(1 + i)^n - 1}$	To find F, given A: $\dfrac{(1 + i)^n - 1}{i}$	To find P, given A: $\dfrac{(1 + i)^n - 1}{i(1 + i)^n}$	
n	$(f/p)_n^{10}$	$(p/f)_n^{10}$	$(a/f)_n^{10}$	$(a/p)_n^{10}$	$(f/a)_n^{10}$	$(p/a)_n^{10}$	n
1	1.100	0.9091	1.00000	1.10000	1.000	0.909	1
2	1.210	0.8264	0.47619	0.57619	2.100	1.736	2
3	1.331	0.7513	0.30211	0.40211	3.310	2.487	3
4	1.464	0.6830	0.21547	0.31547	4.641	3.170	4
5	1.611	0.6209	0.16380	0.26380	6.105	3.791	5
6	1.772	0.5645	0.12961	0.22961	7.716	4.355	6
7	1.949	0.5132	0.10541	0.20541	9.487	4.868	7
8	2.144	0.4665	0.08744	0.18744	11.436	5.335	8
9	2.358	0.4241	0.07364	0.17364	13.579	5.759	9
10	2.594	0.3855	0.06275	0.16275	15.937	6.144	10
11	2.853	0.3505	0.05396	0.15396	18.531	6.495	11
12	3.138	0.3186	0.04676	0.14676	21.384	6.814	12
13	3.452	0.2897	0.04078	0.14078	24.523	7.103	13
14	3.797	0.2633	0.03575	0.13575	27.975	7.367	14
15	4.177	0.2394	0.03147	0.13147	31.772	7.606	15
16	4.595	0.2176	0.02782	0.12782	35.950	7.824	16
17	5.054	0.1978	0.02466	0.12466	40.545	8.022	17
18	5.560	0.1799	0.02193	0.12193	45.599	8.201	18
19	6.116	0.1635	0.01955	0.11955	51.159	8.363	19
20	6.727	0.1486	0.01746	0.11746	57.275	8.514	20
21	7.400	0.1351	0.01562	0.11562	64.002	8.649	21
22	8.140	0.1228	0.01401	0.11401	71.403	8.772	22
23	8.954	0.1117	0.01257	0.11257	79.543	8.883	23
24	9.850	0.1015	0.01130	0.11130	88.497	8.985	24
25	10.835	0.0923	0.01017	0.11017	98.347	9.077	25
26	11.918	0.0839	0.00916	0.10916	109.182	9.161	26
27	13.110	0.0763	0.00826	0.10826	121.100	9.237	27
28	14.421	0.0693	0.00745	0.10745	134.210	9.307	28
29	15.863	0.0630	0.00673	0.10673	148.631	9.370	29
30	17.449	0.0573	0.00608	0.10608	164.494	9.427	30
31	19.194	0.0521	0.00550	0.10550	181.943	9.479	31
32	21.114	0.0474	0.00497	0.10497	201.138	9.526	32
33	23.225	0.0431	0.00450	0.10450	222.252	9.569	33
34	25.548	0.0391	0.00407	0.10407	245.477	9.609	34
35	28.102	0.0356	0.00369	0.10369	271.024	9.644	35
40	45.259	0.0221	0.00226	0.10226	442.593	9.779	40
45	72.890	0.0137	0.00139	0.10139	718.905	9.863	45
50	117.391	0.0085	0.00086	0.10086	1163.909	9.915	50
55	189.059	0.0053	0.00053	0.10053	1880.591	9.947	55
60	304.482	0.0033	0.00033	0.10033	3034.816	9.967	60
65	490.371	0.0020	0.00020	0.10020	4893.707	9.980	65
70	789.747	0.0013	0.00013	0.10013	7887.470	9.987	70
75	1271.895	0.0008	0.00008	0.10008	12708.954	9.992	75
80	2048.400	0.0005	0.00005	0.10005	20474.002	9.995	80
85	3298.969	0.0003	0.00003	0.10003	32979.690	9.997	85
90	5313.023	0.0002	0.00002	0.10002	53120.226	9.998	90
95	8556.676	0.0001	0.00001	0.10001	85556.760	9.999	95
100	13780.612	0.0001	0.00001	0.10001	137796.123	9.999	100

12%

n	To find F, given P: $(1 + i)^n$ $(f/p)^{12}_n$	To find P, given F: $\dfrac{1}{(1 + i)^n}$ $(p/f)^{12}_n$	To find A, given F: $\dfrac{i}{(1 + i)^n - 1}$ $(a/f)^{12}_n$	To find A, given P: $\dfrac{i(1 + i)^n}{(1 + i)^n - 1}$ $(a/p)^{12}_n$	To find F, given A: $\dfrac{(1 + i)^n - 1}{i}$ $(f/a)^{12}_n$	To find P, given A: $\dfrac{(1 + i)^n - 1}{i(1 + i)^n}$ $(p/a)^{12}_n$	n
1	1.120	0.8929	1.00000	1.12000	1.000	0.893	1
2	1.254	0.7972	0.47170	0.59170	2.120	1.690	2
3	1.405	0.7118	0.29635	0.41635	3.374	2.402	3
4	1.574	0.6355	0.20923	0.32923	4.779	3.037	4
5	1.762	0.5674	0.15741	0.27741	6.353	3.605	5
6	1.974	0.5066	0.12323	0.24323	8.115	4.111	6
7	2.211	0.4523	0.09912	0.21912	10.089	4.564	7
8	2.476	0.4039	0.08130	0.20130	12.300	4.968	8
9	2.773	0.3606	0.06768	0.18768	14.776	5.328	9
10	3.106	0.3220	0.05698	0.17698	17.549	5.650	10
11	3.479	0.2875	0.04842	0.16842	20.655	5.938	11
12	3.896	0.2567	0.04144	0.16144	24.133	6.194	12
13	4.363	0.2292	0.03568	0.15568	28.029	6.424	13
14	4.887	0.2046	0.03087	0.15087	32.393	6.628	14
15	5.474	0.1827	0.02682	0.14682	37.280	6.811	15
16	6.130	0.1631	0.02339	0.14339	42.753	6.974	16
17	6.866	0.1456	0.02046	0.14046	48.884	7.120	17
18	7.690	0.1300	0.01794	0.13794	55.750	7.250	18
19	8.613	0.1161	0.01576	0.13576	63.440	7.366	19
20	9.646	0.1037	0.01388	0.13388	72.052	7.469	20
21	10.804	0.0926	0.01224	0.13224	81.699	7.562	21
22	12.100	0.0826	0.01081	0.13081	92.503	7.645	22
23	13.552	0.0738	0.00956	0.12956	104.603	7.718	23
24	15.179	0.0659	0.00846	0.12846	118.155	7.784	24
25	17.000	0.0588	0.00750	0.12750	133.334	7.843	25
26	19.040	0.0525	0.00665	0.12665	150.334	7.896	26
27	21.325	0.0469	0.00590	0.12590	169.374	7.943	27
28	23.884	0.0419	0.00524	0.12524	190.699	7.984	28
29	26.750	0.0374	0.00466	0.12466	214.582	8.022	29
30	29.960	0.0334	0.00414	0.12414	241.333	8.055	30
31	33.555	0.0298	0.00369	0.12369	271.292	8.085	31
32	37.582	0.0266	0.00328	0.12328	304.847	8.112	32
33	42.091	0.0238	0.00292	0.12292	342.429	8.135	33
34	47.142	0.0212	0.00260	0.12260	384.520	8.157	34
35	52.800	0.0189	0.00232	0.12232	431.663	8.176	35
40	93.051	0.0107	0.00130	0.12130	767.091	8.244	40
45	163.988	0.0061	0.00074	0.12074	1358.230	8.283	45
50	289.002	0.0035	0.00042	0.12042	2400.018	8.305	50

15%

	To find F, given P: $(1 + i)^n$	To find P, given F: $\dfrac{1}{(1 + i)^n}$	To find A, given F: $\dfrac{i}{(1 + i)^n - 1}$	To find A, given P: $\dfrac{i(1 + i)^n}{(1 + i)^n - 1}$	To find F, given A: $\dfrac{(1 + i)^n - 1}{i}$	To find P, given A: $\dfrac{(1 + i)^n - 1}{i(1 + i)^n}$	
n	$(f/p)_n^{15}$	$(p/f)_n^{15}$	$(a/f)_n^{15}$	$(a/p)_n^{15}$	$(f/a)_n^{15}$	$(p/a)_n^{15}$	n
1	1.150	0.8696	1.00000	1.15000	1.000	0.870	1
2	1.322	0.7561	0.46512	0.61512	2.150	1.626	2
3	1.521	0.6575	0.28798	0.43798	3.472	2.283	3
4	1.749	0.5718	0.20027	0.35027	4.993	2.855	4
5	2.011	0.4972	0.14832	0.29832	6.742	3.352	5
6	2.313	0.4323	0.11424	0.26424	8.754	3.784	6
7	2.660	0.3759	0.09036	0.24036	11.067	4.160	7
8	3.059	0.3269	0.07285	0.22285	13.727	4.487	8
9	3.518	0.2843	0.05957	0.20957	16.786	4.772	9
10	4.046	0.2472	0.04925	0.19925	20.304	5.019	10
11	4.652	0.2149	0.04107	0.19107	24.349	5.234	11
12	5.350	0.1869	0.03448	0.18448	29.002	5.421	12
13	6.153	0.1625	0.02911	0.17911	34.352	5.583	13
14	7.076	0.1413	0.02469	0.17469	40.505	5.724	14
15	8.137	0.1229	0.02102	0.17102	47.580	5.847	15
16	9.358	0.1069	0.01795	0.16795	55.717	5.954	16
17	10.761	0.0929	0.01537	0.16537	65.075	6.047	17
18	12.375	0.0808	0.01319	0.16319	75.836	6.128	18
19	14.232	0.0703	0.01134	0.16134	88.212	6.198	19
20	16.367	0.0611	0.00976	0.15976	102.444	6.259	20
21	18.821	0.0531	0.00842	0.15842	118.810	6.312	21
22	21.645	0.0462	0.00727	0.15727	137.631	6.359	22
23	24.891	0.0402	0.00628	0.15628	159.276	6.399	23
24	28.625	0.0349	0.00543	0.15543	184.168	6.434	24
25	32.919	0.0304	0.00470	0.15470	212.793	6.464	25
26	37.857	0.0264	0.00407	0.15407	245.711	6.491	26
27	43.535	0.0230	0.00353	0.15353	283.569	6.514	27
28	50.066	0.0200	0.00306	0.15306	327.104	6.534	28
29	57.575	0.0174	0.00265	0.15265	377.170	6.551	29
30	66.212	0.0151	0.00230	0.15230	434.745	6.566	30
31	76.143	0.0131	0.00200	0.15200	500.956	6.579	31
32	87.565	0.0114	0.00173	0.15173	577.099	6.591	32
33	100.700	0.0099	0.00150	0.15150	664.664	6.600	33
34	115.805	0.0086	0.00131	0.15131	765.364	6.609	34
35	133.176	0.0075	0.00113	0.15113	881.170	6.617	35
40	267.863	0.0037	0.00056	0.15056	1779.090	6.642	40
45	538.769	0.0019	0.00028	0.15028	3585.128	6.654	45
50	1083.657	0.0009	0.00014	0.15014	7217.716	6.661	50

TABLE S14–1 *(concluded)*

20%

	To find F, given P: $(1 + i)^n$	To find P, given F: $\dfrac{1}{(1 + i)^n}$	To find A, given F: $\dfrac{i}{(1 + i)^n - 1}$	To find A, given P: $\dfrac{i(1 + i)^n}{(1 + i)^n - 1}$	To find F, given A: $\dfrac{(1 + i)^n - 1}{i}$	To find P, given A: $\dfrac{(1 + i)^n - 1}{i(1 + i)^n}$	
n	$(f/p)_n^{20}$	$(p/f)_n^{20}$	$(a/f)_n^{20}$	$(a/p)_n^{20}$	$(f/a)_n^{20}$	$(p/a)_n^{20}$	n
1	1.200	0.8333	1.00000	1.20000	1.000	0.833	1
2	1.440	0.6944	0.45455	0.65455	2.200	1.528	2
3	1.728	0.5787	0.27473	0.47473	3.640	2.106	3
4	2.074	0.4823	0.18629	0.38629	5.368	2.598	4
5	2.488	0.4019	0.13438	0.33438	7.442	2.991	5
6	2.986	0.3349	0.10071	0.30071	9.930	3.326	6
7	3.583	0.2791	0.07742	0.27742	12.916	3.605	7
8	4.300	0.2326	0.06061	0.26061	16.499	3.837	8
9	5.160	0.1938	0.04808	0.24808	20.799	4.031	9
10	6.192	0.1615	0.03852	0.23852	25.959	4.192	10
11	7.430	0.1346	0.03110	0.23110	32.150	4.327	11
12	8.916	0.1122	0.02526	0.22526	39.581	4.439	12
13	10.699	0.0935	0.02062	0.22062	48.497	4.533	13
14	12.839	0.0779	0.01689	0.21689	59.196	4.611	14
15	15.407	0.0649	0.01388	0.21388	72.035	4.675	15
16	18.488	0.0541	0.01144	0.21144	87.442	4.730	16
17	22.186	0.0451	0.00944	0.20944	105.931	4.775	17
18	26.623	0.0376	0.00781	0.20781	128.117	4.812	18
19	31.948	0.0313	0.00646	0.20646	154.740	4.843	19
20	38.338	0.0261	0.00536	0.20536	186.688	4.870	20
21	46.005	0.0217	0.00444	0.20444	225.025	4.891	21
22	55.206	0.0181	0.00369	0.20369	271.031	4.909	22
23	66.247	0.0151	0.00307	0.20307	326.237	4.925	23
24	79.497	0.0126	0.00255	0.20255	392.484	4.937	24
25	95.396	0.0105	0.00212	0.20212	471.981	4.948	25
26	114.475	0.0087	0.00176	0.20176	567.377	4.956	26
27	137.371	0.0073	0.00147	0.20147	681.853	4.964	27
28	164.845	0.0061	0.00122	0.20122	819.223	4.970	28
29	197.813	0.0051	0.00102	0.20102	984.068	4.975	29
30	237.376	0.0042	0.00085	0.20085	1181.881	4.979	30
31	284.851	0.0035	0.00070	0.20070	1419.257	4.982	31
32	341.822	0.0029	0.00059	0.20059	1704.108	4.985	32
33	410.186	0.0024	0.00049	0.20049	2045.930	4.988	33
34	492.223	0.0020	0.00041	0.20041	2456.116	4.990	34
35	590.668	0.0017	0.00034	0.20034	2948.339	4.992	35
40	1469.772	0.0007	0.00014	0.20014	7343.858	4.997	40
45	3657.258	0.0003	0.00005	0.20005	18281.331	4.999	45
50	9100.427	0.0001	0.00002	0.20002	45497.191	4.999	50

611

Supplement B to Chapter 14
Present-Value Tables

The two interest tables in this supplement are the types commonly found in finance and managerial accounting books. They are:

Table S14–2: Present value of a sum (which is the same as the P/F column in Table S14–1).

Table S14–3: Present value of an annuity (which is the same as the P/A column in Table S14–1).

TABLE S14–2

Present Value of a Sum

Year	1%	2%	3%	4%	5%	6%	7%	8%	9%	10%
1	0.990	0.980	0.971	0.962	0.952	0.943	0.935	0.926	0.917	0.909
2	1.970	1.942	1.913	1.886	1.859	1.833	1.808	1.783	1.759	1.736
3	2.941	2.884	2.829	2.775	2.723	2.673	2.624	2.577	2.531	2.487
4	3.902	3.808	3.717	3.630	3.546	3.465	3.387	3.312	3.240	3.170
5	4.853	4.713	4.580	4.452	4.329	4.212	4.100	3.993	3.890	3.791
6	5.795	5.601	5.417	5.242	5.076	4.917	4.766	4.623	4.486	4.355
7	6.728	6.472	6.230	6.002	5.786	5.582	5.389	5.206	5.033	4.868
8	7.652	7.325	7.020	6.733	6.463	6.210	6.971	5.747	5.535	5.335
9	8.566	8.162	7.786	7.435	7.108	6.802	6.515	6.247	5.985	5.759
10	9.471	8.983	8.530	8.111	7.722	7.360	7.024	6.710	6.418	6.145
11	10.368	9.787	9.253	8.760	8.306	7.887	7.499	7.139	6.805	6.495
12	11.255	10.575	9.954	9.385	8.863	8.384	7.943	7.536	7.161	6.814
13	12.134	11.348	10.635	9.986	9.394	8.853	8.358	7.904	7.487	7.103
14	13.004	12.106	11.296	10.563	9.899	9.295	8.745	8.244	7.786	7.367
15	13.865	12.849	11.938	11.118	10.380	9.712	9.108	8.559	8.060	7.606
16	14.718	13.578	12.561	11.652	10.838	10.106	9.447	8.851	8.312	7.824
17	15.562	14.292	13.166	12.166	11.274	10.477	9.763	9.122	8.544	8.022
18	16.398	14.992	13.754	12.659	11.690	10.828	10.059	9.372	8.756	8.201
19	17.226	15.678	14.324	13.134	12.085	11.158	10.336	9.604	8.950	8.365
20	18.046	16.351	14.877	13.590	12.462	11.470	10.594	9.818	9.128	8.514
25	22.023	19.523	17.413	15.622	14.094	12.783	11.654	10.675	9.823	9.077
30	25.808	22.397	19.600	17.292	15.373	13.765	12.409	11.258	10.274	9.427

Year	12%	14%	16%	18%	20%	24%	28%	32%	36%
1	0.893	0.877	0.862	0.847	0.833	0.806	0.781	0.758	0.735
2	1.690	1.647	1.605	1.566	1.528	1.457	1.392	1.332	1.276
3	2.402	2.322	2.246	2.174	2.106	1.981	1.868	1.766	1.674
4	3.037	2.914	2.798	2.690	2.589	2.404	2.241	2.096	1.966
5	3.605	3.433	3.274	3.127	2.991	2.745	2.532	2.345	2.181
6	4.111	3.889	3.685	3.498	3.326	3.020	2.759	2.534	2.339
7	4.564	4.288	4.039	3.812	3.605	3.242	2.937	2.678	2.455
8	4.968	4.639	4.344	4.078	3.837	3.421	3.076	2.786	2.540
9	5.328	4.946	4.607	4.303	4.031	3.566	3.184	2.868	2.603
10	5.650	5.216	4.833	4.494	4.193	3.682	3.269	2.930	2.650
11	5.988	5.453	5.029	4.656	4.327	3.776	3.335	2.978	2.683
12	6.194	5.660	5.197	4.793	4.439	3.851	3.387	3.013	2.708
13	6.424	5.842	5.342	4.910	4.533	3.912	3.427	3.040	2.727
14	6.628	6.002	5.468	5.008	4.611	3.962	3.459	3.061	2.740
15	6.811	6.142	5.575	5.092	4.675	4.001	3.483	3.076	2.750
16	6.974	6.265	5.669	5.162	4.730	4.033	3.503	3.088	2.758
17	7.120	5.373	5.749	4.222	4.775	4.059	3.518	3.097	2.763
18	7.250	6.467	5.818	5.273	4.812	4.080	3.529	3.104	2.767
19	7.366	6.550	5.877	5.316	4.844	4.097	3.539	3.109	2.770
20	7.469	6.623	5.929	5.353	4.870	4.110	3.546	3.113	2.772
25	7.843	6.873	6.097	5.467	4.948	4.147	3.564	3.122	2.776
30	8.055	7.003	6.177	5.517	4.979	4.160	3.569	3.124	2.778

Source: Richard B. Chase and Nicholas J. Aquilano, *Production and Operations Management*, 3d ed. (Homewood, Ill.: Richard D. Irwin, 1981), p. 143.

TABLE S14–3

Present Value of an Annuity

Year	1%	2%	3%	4%	5%	6%	7%	8%	9%	10%	12%	14%	15%
1	.990	.980	.971	.962	.952	.943	.935	.926	.917	.909	.893	.877	.870
2	.980	.961	.943	.925	.907	.890	.873	.857	.842	.826	.797	.769	.756
3	.971	.942	.915	.889	.864	.840	.816	.794	.772	.751	.712	.675	.658
4	.961	.924	.889	.855	.823	.792	.763	.735	.708	.683	.636	.592	.572
5	.951	.906	.863	.822	.784	.747	.713	.681	.650	.621	.567	.519	.497
6	.942	.888	.838	.790	.746	.705	.666	.630	.596	.564	.507	.456	.432
7	.933	.871	.813	.760	.711	.665	.623	.583	.547	.513	.452	.400	.376
8	.923	.853	.789	.731	.677	.627	.582	.540	.502	.467	.404	.351	.327
9	.914	.837	.766	.703	.645	.592	.544	.500	.460	.424	.361	.308	.284
10	.905	.820	.744	.676	.614	.558	.508	.463	.422	.386	.322	.270	.247
11	.896	.804	.722	.650	.585	.527	.475	.429	.388	.350	.287	.237	.215
12	.887	.788	.701	.625	.557	.497	.444	.397	.356	.319	.257	.208	.187
13	.879	.773	.681	.601	.530	.469	.415	.368	.326	.290	.229	.182	.163
14	.870	.758	.661	.577	.505	.442	.388	.340	.299	.263	.205	.160	.141
15	.861	.743	.642	.555	.481	.417	.362	.315	.275	.239	.183	.140	.123
16	.853	.728	.623	.534	.458	.394	.339	.292	.252	.218	.163	.123	.107
17	.844	.714	.605	.513	.436	.371	.317	.270	.231	.198	.146	.108	.093
18	.836	.700	.587	.494	.416	.350	.296	.250	.212	.180	.130	.095	.081
19	.828	.686	.570	.475	.396	.331	.276	.232	.194	.164	.116	.083	.070
20	.820	.673	.554	.456	.377	.312	.258	.215	.178	.149	.104	.073	.061
25	.780	.610	.478	.375	.295	.233	.184	.146	.116	.092	.059	.038	.030
30	.742	.552	.412	.308	.231	.174	.131	.099	.075	.057	.033	.020	.015

Year	16%	18%	20%	24%	28%	32%	36%	40%	50%	60%	70%	80%	90%
1	.862	.847	.833	.806	.781	.758	.735	.714	.667	.625	.588	.556	.526
2	.743	.718	.694	.650	.610	.574	.541	.510	.444	.391	.346	.309	.277
3	.641	.609	.579	.524	.477	.435	.398	.364	.296	.244	.204	.171	.146
4	.552	.516	.482	.423	.373	.329	.292	.260	.198	.153	.120	.095	.077
5	.476	.437	.402	.341	.291	.250	.215	.186	.132	.095	.070	.053	.040
6	.410	.370	.335	.275	.227	.189	.158	.133	.088	.060	.041	.029	.021
7	.354	.314	.279	.222	.178	.143	.116	.095	.059	.037	.024	.016	.011
8	.305	.266	.233	.179	.139	.108	.085	.068	.039	.023	.014	.009	.006
9	.263	.226	.194	.144	.108	.082	.063	.048	.026	.015	.008	.005	.003
10	.227	.191	.162	.116	.085	.062	.046	.035	.017	.009	.005	.003	.002
11	.195	.162	.135	.094	.066	.047	.034	.025	.012	.006	.003	.002	.001
12	.168	.137	.112	.076	.052	.036	.025	.018	.008	.004	.002	.001	.001
13	.145	.116	.093	.061	.040	.027	.018	.013	.005	.002	.001	.001	.000
14	.125	.099	.078	.049	.032	.021	.014	.009	.003	.001	.001	.000	.000
15	.108	.084	.065	.040	.025	.016	.010	.006	.002	.001	.000	.000	.000
16	.093	.071	.054	.032	.019	.012	.007	.005	.002	.001	.000	.000	
17	.080	.030	.045	.026	.015	.009	.005	.003	.001	.000	.000		
18	.089	.051	.038	.021	.012	.007	.004	.002	.001	.000	.000		
19	.030	.043	.031	.017	.009	.005	.003	.002	.000	.000			
20	.051	.037	.026	.014	.007	.004	.002	.001	.000	.000			
25	.024	.016	.010	.005	.002	.001	.000	.000					
30	.012	.007	.004	.002	.001	.000	.000						

Source: Richard B. Chase and Nicholas J. Aquilano, *Production and Operations Management,* 3d ed. (Homewood, Ill.: Richard D. Irwin, 1981), p. 144.

Chapter 15

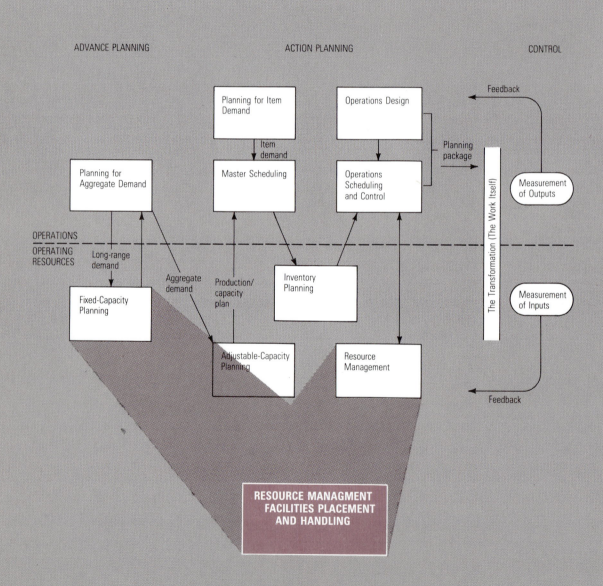

ADVANCE PLANNING

ACTION PLANNING

CONTROL

Planning for Item Demand

Operations Design

Feedback

Planning package

Planning for Aggregate Demand

Master Scheduling

Operations Scheduling and Control

Item demand

Measurement of Outputs

OPERATIONS

OPERATING RESOURCES

Long-range demand

Aggregate demand

Production/ capacity plan

Inventory Planning

The Transformation (The Work Itself)

Measurement of Inputs

Fixed-Capacity Planning

Adjustable-Capacity Planning

Resource Management

Feedback

RESOURCE MANAGMENT FACILITIES PLACEMENT AND HANDLING

Facilities Placement and Handling

Once planned, facilities need to be deployed. Deployment is the second of the four stages in the life cycle of operating resources. This is shown here.

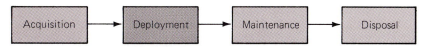

Deploy, in the broad sense, means *locate* geographically. The plant, office, warehouse, or store may be located in Memphis or Flin Flon, Albuquerque or Salem. After the building's location is set, the next question is how to deploy the equipment inside. The usual term for this is **layout** (of equipment and processes).

The handmaiden of layout is **handling.** The customers, the documents, the materials, and the tools have to move from one process or machine to the next, and the handling system provides the means.

Like facilities planning, facilities deployment is a strategic issue. Let us see why.

DEPLOYMENT STRATEGY

Deployment strategies, both geographical and intraplant, never seem to stay stable. Holiday Inn had a rural location strategy at one time, but then added urban locations, too. McDonald's had an urban strategy, but then expanded into low-population centers. The meat packers once were in the cities where the labor and the markets were, but they decentralized and now are built close to the cattle and hogs. This holds down costs to ship fed livestock and also taps lower-cost labor to run packing plants. In the cities, hospitals and clinics that once were dispersed now tend to cluster. High-tech electronics companies also cluster—in California's Silicon Valley and near Boston, Phoenix, Austin, Portland, the eastern slope of the Rockies in Colorado, and Florida's Atlantic "Gold Coast." The clustering provides a "critical mass" of talent. And "smokestack America" moves to the Sun Belt, not so much for sun as for cheap nonunion labor.

Location Strategies

Keeping up with changes in the location strategies of North American business has been fascinating. It may become more so in the latter half of the 1980s. There are signs, for example, that there will be a dispersion of supplier plants. The day of mammoth plants making components like tires, motors, hydraulics, wire and cable, seats, fabric, containers, and fasteners may be numbered. The companies that once built large centralized plants to make these component products are finding that their customers want them to build *small* plants close by. The end result may be a lot of small tire plants, hydraulics plants, etc., scattered around the country. The customers—end-product producers of machine tools, airplanes, trucks, printed matter, furniture, and so forth—are demanding better and quicker service: For example, they want daily deliveries, close engineering support, and fast response to quality requirements. The buyers intend to stick with the supplier willing to locate nearby and establish a long-term close relationship—no more rebidding every year to shave a few dollars or cents off the price.

As an example, Delco Electronics (a division of General Motors) operates a plant in Kokomo, Indiana, employing more than 10,000 people (certainly not a very focused plant at this point). Delco wants to be ringed by small supplier plants, much like "Toyota City" in Nagoya, Japan. The Indiana Commerce Department has a campaign to help. The department is trying to get suppliers now located elsewhere around the country to move a satellite operation into one of the empty buildings in Kokomo. (Kokomo had been devastated earlier by plant closings, which left many unemployed workers.) The supplier plants would be small and dedicated to Delco.[1] Many other companies around the country are doing much the same thing as Delco, and other states may adopt the kind of industrial development strategy that Indiana has.

When components plants locate close by, methods of handling between plants change: less use of rails, more use of trucks; and fewer six-axle semis, more two-and-a-half ton trucks or pickups.

The state and local help for industry is also a major factor in where plants decide to locate. For example, Nissan opened a truck manufacturing plant in Smyrna, Tennessee, in 1983. Nissan was influenced by the state's willingness to help screen and train Nissan's workforce. Some 40,000 people applied, and Tennessee's State Employment Department did the preliminary screening. Nissan hired 500 out of the initial 40,000.[2] Like several other states, Tennessee also takes an active role in providing technical training for the state's industry.

Layout Strategies

Conventional beliefs about plant layout are also changing. It has always been common to put similar facilities or functions into groups: personnel people together in the personnel department, sheet-metal equipment and people grouped into a sheet-metal shop, and so forth. The problem is that the work, the customer, or the client have long distances to go between one shop or department and the next. Just-in-time production demands that many of the common groupings—we call them **process layouts**—be broken up. Move one sheet-metal machine to the area producing housings, another to the area making fans, and so forth. This can also apply to human services: Move personnel specialists and their file cabinets and desks next to foremen's offices, into the marketing department, and wherever else there are numbers of employees and managers in need of personnel services. Alternatively, the whole personnel office could be located near the employee cafeteria in order to make it convenient for employees to stop in.

In manufacturing companies that move toward streamlined layouts there are effects on material handling: less need for forklift trucks and long distance-spanning conveyors; greater use of simple transfer devices.

We shall spend more time on these issues later in the chapter. First, we look at plant location in greater detail.

---

[1] "An Idea from Japan May Offer a Way of Recruiting Industries," *The Wall Street Journal*, August 23, 1983.

[2] "Japanese Managers Find Best Way to Direct U.S. Workers," *Iron Age*, May 21, 1982, pp. 69–74.

LOCATION

Decisions on locating a business are partly based on intangible and even emotional factors: good entertainment and educational facilities, good housing, even good fishing or scenery. Before the intangible factors take over, some hard study of costs in different locations ought to take place. Here are some cost factors that should be part of the study:

1. **Transportation costs:** incoming raw materials and parts, outgoing finished goods.
2. **Plant and equipment costs:** site, building, materials, equipment, other.
3. **Prevailing labor costs:** unskilled labor, skilled labor, professional salaries, fringe benefits.
4. **Utilities:** electric, gas, water, waste disposal.
5. **Taxes:** real estate, property, inventory, income, workmen's compensation.
6. **Ancillary service costs:** warehousing, worker training, janitorial, food, data processing, etc.
7. **Special monetary inducements:** community-offered tax incentives, road building, plant space, utility hookups, etc.

The first of these factors, transportation cost, is often very large. Sometimes transportation costs for different sites are simple to compare. But where resources move from multiple sources to multiple destinations, comparing the costs gets complicated. Linear programming (LP), considered next, helps sort out the complexity.

Transportation-Cost Analysis

The **simplex method** of linear programming, which is widely taught and perhaps familiar to the reader, *may* be used in the study of transportation costs. But there is a simpler method called the **transportation method.** Here are some differences between the simplex and transportation methods:

Transportation method—limited to a single homogeneous resource (that must be moved in quantity from multiple sources to multiple destinations).

Simplex method—suitable for a single homogeneous resource *or* a variety of unlike resources (e.g., different resource inputs transformed into various resource outputs or products).

The transportation method is in two steps. First, we need an initial feasible transportation routing—a routing pattern that fulfills demand and uses up supply. Second, improve the initial solution until the optimum is reached. There are alternative techniques for developing initial and optimal solutions:

Initial-solution techniques:
1. **Northwest-corner rule.**
2. **Vogel's approximation method** (VAM).

Optimal-solution techniques:
1. **Stepping-stone method.**
2. **Modified distribution method (MODI).**

Our discussion is limited to northwest-corner and stepping-stone. MODI, not discussed, has the same result as stepping-stone, but the procedure is different. NW-corner is a quick way to get started. If VAM (not discussed) is used for the initial solution, fewer steps are likely to be required in finding the optimum.

Transportation-Method Example

The following example shows the usefulness of the transportation method in location decisions. The example demonstrates another use as well: finding optimum transportation routings once geographic locations of sources and destinations have been set. The example is divided into parts.

EXAMPLE 15–1

Transportation Method for Locating a Printing Plant in the
Hawaiian Islands

Basic problem. The *Island Explorer,* a newspaper serving the Hawaiian Islands, is printed presently in two plants. One plant is in Honolulu on the island of Oahu, and the other is in Hana on the island of Maui. The two printing plants serve readers in the six major islands: Oahu, Maui, Hawaii, Kauai, Molokai, and Lanai.

Printing capacity has become insufficient at Honolulu and Hana. Honolulu's capacity is 300 pallets of newspapers per week, and Hana's capacity is 100 pallets per week. Demands are: Oahu, 275 per week; Maui, 60 per week; Hawaii, 60 per week; Kauai, 50 per week; Molokai, 30 per week; and Lanai, 20 per week. Total demand, 495, exceeds capacity, 400, by 95 pallets per week, which are lost sales.

The publisher has decided to locate a third printing plant either at Hilo on Hawaii or at Lihue on Kauai.[3] A transportation-cost analysis is needed to support the location decision.

Additional problem data—Hilo location. Figure 15–1 is a map of the island region. The arrows between islands in Figure 15–1A show all possible routes—and air-transportation costs—from printing plants to destinations if the new plant is located at Hilo. No arrows lead into Oahu, Maui, and Hawaii, because the Honolulu, Hana, and Hilo plants can provide newspapers to readers on their own islands at zero air-transportation cost.

For analyzing a plant location at Lihue instead of Hilo, Figure 15–1B applies. It shows three arrows leading into Hawaii instead of into Kauai.

Transportation matrix—Hilo location. In the transportation method routes and costs go into a transportation matrix. Quantities to be transported

---

[3] A note on pronounciation to those unfamiliar with the lingual heritage of the 50th state: Pronounce every letter of a Hawaiian word. Thus, Kauai is pronounced Kah-$\overline{oo}$-ah-$\overline{ee}$.

FIGURE 15–1

Map Showing Transportation Routes and Costs

A. New plant at Hilo

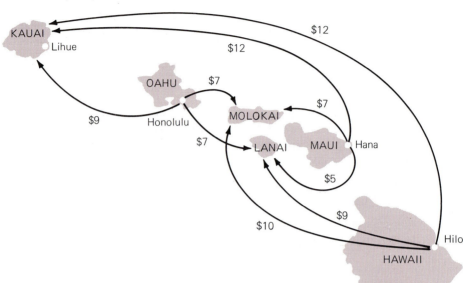

B. New plant at Lihue

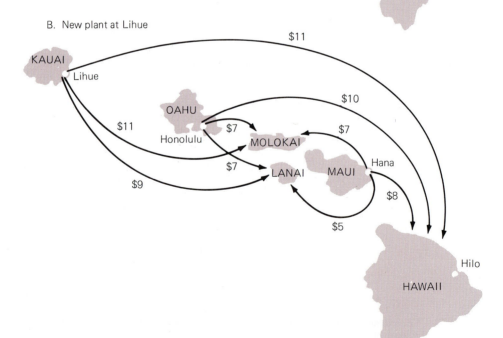

Note: Transportation costs are per pallet of newspapers.

from each source to each destination are also shown on the matrix. Figure 15–2 is the matrix for the Hilo plant-location option. Transportation costs are shown above the slash (/) in each cell of the matrix. The upper left or "northwest"-corner cell, for example, represents the route from Honolulu to the island of Lanai, with a transportation cost of $7 per pallet. Demands for the three destinations are shown at the bottom of the three destination columns: 20, 30, and 50. Supply of the three sources, at the right in the three source rows, is the net transportable capacity of each. Net capacities, computed below, are based on the logic that each printing plant services its own island:

Honolulu net transportable capacity = Honolulu gross capacity minus Oahu demand
= 300 − 275 = 25

Hana net transportable capacity = Hana gross capacity minus Maui demand
= 100 − 60 = 40

Hilo net transportable capacity = Capacity shortage minus Hawaii demand
= 95 − 60 = 35

The calculation for Hilo is based on having a gross capacity just sufficient to meet the gross capacity shortage, 95, that was mentioned at the outset.

FIGURE 15–2

Transportation Matrix, Hilo Location

Sources	Destinations: Lanai	Molokai	Kauai	Supply
Honolulu	7/	7/	9/	25
Hana	5/	7/	12/	40
Hilo	9/	10/	12/	35
Demand	20	30	50	100 \ 100

Supply and demand are totaled in the lower right corner of Figure 15–2. Both equal 100 pallets per week.

Initial solution—Hilo location. A feasible solution following the NW-corner rule is developed in Figure 15–3. We begin by making an allocation to the NW-corner cell, Honolulu-Lanai. The most that can be allocated is 20, which is Lanai's entire requirement; this leaves five more units available from Honolulu, which goes into the adjacent cell to the right, Honolulu-Molokai. Molokai needs 25 more units, which it gets from the cell below, Hana-Molokai. This leaves 15 more available from Hana, which goes into the cell to the right, Hana-Kauai. Kauai needs 35 units more, which it gets from the cell below, Hilo-Kauai. All rim requirements are now met; the solution is feasible. (An equally simple initial solution could be developed from the SW, NE, or SE corners; the NW corner has no particular significance.)

The total weekly transportation cost for the NW-corner solution is $950 per week, as calculated below:

Honolulu-Lanai:	$ 7 × 20 = $140 per week
Honolulu-Molokai:	7 × 5 = 35 per week
Hana-Molokai:	7 × 25 = 175 per week
Hana-Kauai:	12 × 15 = 180 per week
Hilo-Kauai:	12 × 35 = 420 per week
	Total $950 per week

FIGURE 15–3

NW-Corner Initial Solution, Hilo Location

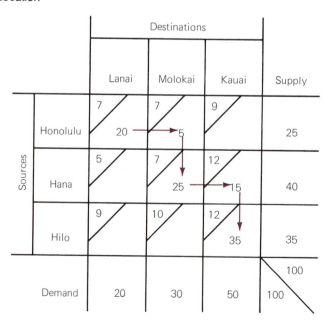

The NW-corner solution may usually be improved. Improvements would aim, for example, at avoiding the $12 cells (to Kauai from Hana and from Hilo) in favor of low-cost cells, like the $5 Hana-to-Lanai cell, which was not used in the NW-corner solution. Improvements *could* be found by trial and error. Better yet, use the stepping-stone or MODI methods, which may be computerized.

Optimal solution—Hilo location. After all improvements have been taken, we have an optimal solution. The optimum for the Hilo location is given in Figure 15–4. The total weekly transportation cost for the optimal solution is calculated below:

Honolulu-Kauai:	$ 9 × 25 =	$225 per week
Hana-Lanai:	5 × 20 =	100 per week
Hana-Molokai:	7 × 20 =	140 per week
Hilo-Molokai:	10 × 10 =	100 per week
Hilo-Kauai:	12 × 25 =	300 per week
	Total	$865 per week

The improved solution, at $865 per week, is $85 per week less than the NW-corner solution, at $950 per week. If the plant is to be built at Hilo, the optimal solution should constitute the transportation routing plan. But first we must see whether it is more economical to build at Lihue.

Additional problem data—Lihue location. The publisher of the *Island Explorer* has decided that if the plant goes up in Lihue, it will be built

FIGURE 15–4

Optimal Transportation Solution, Hilo Location

Sources	Destinations: Lanai	Molokai	Kauai	Supply
Honolulu	7	7	9 / 25	25
Hana	5 / 20	7 / 20	12	40
Hilo	9	10 / 10	12 / 25	35
Demand	20	30	50	100 / 100

FIGURE 15–5

Transportation Matrix with Dummy Destination, Lihue Location

Sources	Destination				Supply
	Lanai	Molokai	Hawaii	Dummy	
Honolulu	7	7	10	0	25
Hana	5	7	8	0	40
Lihue	9	11	11	0	50
Demand	20	30	60	5	115 / 115

with five pallets per week of excess capacity. The extra capacity will allow for projected expansion to the small island of Niihau near to Kauai. But Niihau is not included in the current transportation-cost analysis.

Transportation matrix—Lihue location. The excess capacity at Lihue results in an unbalanced transportation problem: Supply exceeds current demand by five pallets per week. The transportation method still works, but only after demand is artificially adjusted upward to equal supply. That is, add a dummy column with a dummy demand of five in the transportation matrix. (In the reverse situation, demand greater than supply, add a dummy row with the required extra supply to the matrix.)

Figure 15–5 shows the adjusted matrix. The demands, including the dummy demand of five, total 115 pallets per week. The supply (capacity) for Lihue is set at 50 in order that supply be equal to demand. The dummy's transportation costs are set at zero, because it costs nothing to ship to a dummy destination.

Optimal solution—Hawaii location. The optimal solution is shown in Figure 15–6. The chapter supplement demonstrates how to arrive at this solution using the stepping-stone method. If the *Island Explorer* builds at Lihue, $925 per week is the expected transportation cost.

Assessment. The Hilo location has an optimal transportation cost of $865 per week. For the Lihue location the optimal transportation cost is $925 per week; that is $80 or 9.2 percent more. We would expect the Lihue solution to cost more, because Hawaii's demand is 60 when the plant is

FIGURE 15–6

Optimal Solution, Hawaii Location

		Destination				
		Lanai	Molokai	Hawaii	Dummy	Supply
Sources	Honolulu	7	7 / 25	10	0	25
	Hana	5 / 20	7 / 5	8 / 15	0	40
	Lihue	9	11	11 / 45	0 / 5	50
	Demand	20	30	60	5	115 / 115

built at Lihue. That is 10 units more than Kauai's demand of 50 in the Hilo solution. That is, the total to be shipped from the three sources to the three destinations is 110 (not counting the dummy demand) if the plant is at Lihue, but it is 100 if the plant is at Hilo.

The Hilo location has the advantage in transportation costs. The costs of such other items as labor, taxes, utilities, plant construction, and raw materials would also bear on the decision. Indeed they may be more significant than transportation cost. Less tangible factors, like labor availability and future expansion, may also be important in the final location decision.

LAYOUT

Deployment is more than *plant* location; it also is location and arrangement of facilities within plants, which requires *layout planning*. Layout planning is performed under two conditions: New facilities require *new layouts*. Existing facilities occasionally get out of date and require *re-layout*.

In our discussion of layout, we consider several layout environments and also different layout types. There are four rather different layout environments: mechanized production lines, labor-intensive production lines, job-lot production, and labor-intensive services. Each raises different layout issues.

Layout-Planning Environments

In mechanized production lines, layout planning needs to be good, because it is costly to reposition large machinery and related facilities. In a petrochemical plant, for example, the layout of tanks, chambers, valves, pipes, and other equipment is so much a part of the plant itself that major re-layout may never be feasible. In steel manufacturing the cost of major re-layout is also enormous, and steel plants may close rather than retool and re-layout to improve efficiency, meet pollution control regulations, and so on. Retooling of automated transfer lines in the auto industry is undertaken every few years. But the *layout* of retooled machines changes infrequently. In each of these examples—petrochemicals, steel, autos—the initial layout choices restrict the firm's ability to respond to major changes in product line or technology for years to come.

Labor-intensive assembly lines and job-lot production facilities are less fixed, and therefore initial layout planning is less critical for these. The focus is on re-layout. For an assembly line, re-layout itself is not prohibitively costly because people and their tools are mobile. There may, however, be high costs for planning; line balancing; retraining; and rearranging benches, storage facilities, material handling aids, and any larger pieces of equipment.

Job-lot plants often have large machines and storage and handling aids. Re-layout may be attractive, however, because the equipment used tends to be general-purpose, loosely coupled, and moveable if not too large. Also, with shorter production runs, there is a need for flexibility and movability. The need for re-layout grows over time. Symptoms of the need include production bottlenecks, backtracking, overcrowding, poor utilization of capacity (including space), poor housekeeping, too much temporary storage, a high or growing ratio of handling time to productive time, and missed due dates.

Labor-intensive services tend to undergo frequent re-layouts. It is not uncommon for office workers to "wonder where my desk will be" on Monday morning. The desk may be across town in newly rented office space. There are few physical obstacles to moving; most offices could move overnight if telephone hookups could be arranged. With few physical problems, office re-layout tends to focus on people and work climate.

Layout Types

There are three or four types of layout, depending on how the lines between the categories are drawn. The first type is the process-oriented layout—**process layout,** for short: The facilities are arranged into process groups. Putting like facilities together may make it easier to provide tool and maintenance support, utility hookups, control of fumes and heat, and removal of chips. Putting people with like functions together provides a climate for mutual support and learning from one another, cross-training, and talent development. Job shops, producing either goods or services, generally have process layouts.

Product-oriented layout (**product layout,** for short), the second type, means laying out the facilities along product-flow lines. The result is a **production line.**

The product layout and the production-line method of manufacture are not new. Here, for example, is a description of a production line for equipping ship galleys at the Arsenal of Venice in about 1438.[4]

> And as one enters the gate there is a great street on either hand with the sea in the middle, and on one side are windows opening out of the houses of the arsenal, and the same on the other side, and out came a galley towed by a boat, and from the windows they handed out to them, from one the cordage, from another the bread, from another the arms, and from another the balistas and mortars, and so from all sides everything which was required, and when the galley had reached the end of the street all the men required were on board, together with the complement of oars, and she was equipped from end to end. In this manner there came out ten galleys full armed, between the hours of three and nine. I know not how to describe what I saw there, whether in the manner of its construction or in the management of the workpeople, and I do not think there is anything finer in the world.

A third type is the **cellular layout.** The idea is to arrange work stations and machines into cells that process families of parts that follow similar flow paths. The cellular layout follows the group technology (GT) concept, which includes a number of subconcepts: parts deliberately designed to have as many common features as possible; a numbering (coding) system that allows the computer to find which family a part belongs in; and the cellular layout itself. A cellular layout actually is about the same as a product layout, although most people think of product layouts (production lines) as handling only one product (or just a few) instead of a family. Cellular layout is still a somewhat new concept and one that is growing in importance.

In the fourth type, the fixed-position layout (**fixed layout,** for short), the product itself is fixed and the facilities must come to it. Construction is a good example. Another good example is the manufacture of oversized vehicles and heavy equipment— items too large to be moved easily.

Mixed layouts—two or more layout types in a single facility—are common, if not the norm. An apt example is a restaurant that sets up a buffet brunch line on Sunday mornings. The patron has the choice of going through the buffet line or sitting down and ordering from a menu. A patron entering the restaurant may be thought of as raw materials; a patron leaving is finished goods. The production process transforms an empty patron into a full one. The two types of patrons are processed through two types of facilities layouts. The buffet customer goes through a product or cellular layout (hard to narrow it down to one or the other). It is very much like an assembly line. The menu customer is processed in a fixed-position layout: Menu, waiter, food, drinks, and check come to the fixed position.

Figure 15–7 is a sketch of such a restaurant. The sketch identifies the product

---

[4] This description is from Pero Tafur's book, *Travels and Adventures* (London: G. Routledge & Sons Ltd., 1926) pp. 1435–39; R. Burlingame, *Backgrounds of Power* (New York: Charles Scribner's Sons, 1949).

FIGURE 15–7

Mixed Layout in a Restaurant

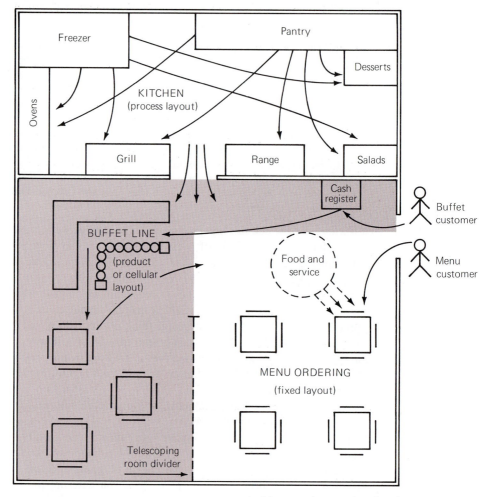

(solid arrows show product flows)

layout and the fixed layout, and it shows that the restaurant also includes a process layout. The process layout is found in the kitchen. There foods, not patrons, are the products that are being transformed. The process areas in the kitchen layout include grill, salad area, range, dessert area, ovens, freezer, and pantry.

As compared with a single-layout facility, a mixed-layout facility is more difficult to plan, more costly to equip, and more troublesome to maintain. But it is easier to keep that kind of facility busy, because it affects a wider variety of customers or products.

Layout Features.   A few of the common distinguishing features among the three primary layout types are given in Figure 15–8. The figure lists eight operating resource factors and the ways in which each factor is commonly treated for each layout type.

The first factor, facilities arrangement, deals with the main differences among the types of layout. These have already been discussed.

Type of production is the second factor. Process layout is dominant in the job shop and common in job-lot production. Product layout is typical in repetitive production and sometimes in production of larger lots in the job-lot mode. Cellular layout is becoming common for small lots of first one part in a family and then another. Fixed layout is common in construction and industrial projects and in limited-quantity large-scale production (e.g., missiles and dynamos). Fixed layout is also found where special human services are provided. For example, the resources come to the client or customer for surgery, grooming, feeding, and home TV repair.

Cost of layout/re-layout is third. In the process layout, groupings of work centers need not be closely coupled by elaborate handling devices; thus process layout is generally not costly. For a product or cellular layout the cost is high if the production line is linked by automated handling devices; the cost may be moderate if it is labor-

FIGURE 15–8

Common Characteristics of Operating Resources for Each Layout Type

Operating resource factors	Types of layout		
	Process-oriented	Product or cellular	Fixed-position
1. Facilities arrangement	Facilities grouped by specialty	Facilities placed along product-flow lines	Facilities arranged for ease of movement to fixed product
2. Type of production	Job-lot and job-shop	Continuous, repetitive and job-lot	Construction and industrial projects; medium-quantity large-scale production; special human services
3. Cost of layout/re-layout	Moderate to low	Moderate to high	Moderate to low
4. Facility utilization	Usually low	High	Moderate
5. Type of production facilities	General-purpose	Special-purpose	Mostly general-purpose
6. Handling equipment	Variable-path	Fixed-path	Variable-path
7. Handling distance	Long	Short	Moderate
8. Worker skill level	Skilled	Unskilled	Unskilled to skilled

intensive, i.e., if one person hands the work to the next person. Fixed layout of a construction site requires temporary parking and storage space for operating resources, which usually are not costly. Fixed layout for goods production and for special human services may take more than just parking space; perhaps a well-equipped bay for assembling a missile or for aligning wheels, or a well-equipped operating room. The layout cost can be low if the facilities are mainly general-purpose hand tools, but it can be higher (moderate) if special lighting, holding fixtures, work pits, and so forth, are involved.

Fourth is facility utilization. In process layouts the facilities tend toward low utilization. This is not desirable, but it is typical, because the job mix changes all the time and different jobs use different facilities. High facility utilization—little idleness— is a goal of the product layout. Good line balancing helps achieve the goal. With fixed layouts the tendency is toward moderate facility utilization because the product mix is not very diverse.

The fifth factor is type of production facilities. Process layouts usually hold standard general-purpose machines, hand tools, handling aids, and so forth. Special-purpose machines, handling aids, and other facilities are worth spending money on if the output is large, as it normally is with product or cellular layouts. In fixed layouts, the special products call for some special-purpose facilities, such as an overhead crane or a mounting fixture, but most of the facilities are likely to be general-purpose since production volume is not high.

Sixth is handling equipment. In process layouts variable-path equipment—hand-carry or on wheels—provides needed handling flexibility. Fixed-path handling equipment—conveyors, elevators, chutes, and so on—helps cut handling time in product layouts. Variable-path handling equipment is common in fixed layouts because a variety of resources come to the site from different places.

Seventh is handling distance. There are long distances to traverse in the process layout. That is, distances from one process to another are long. In product and cellular layouts the opposite is true. In fact, a purpose is to cluster the facilities tightly in order to *cut* distance and handling time. Fixed layouts are in between. The product stays put, but the resources do not flow to the product by fixed routes; resources move to the product from various locations over moderate handling distances.

The eighth factor is worker skill level. In process layouts workers tend to be skilled. Stenographers, machinists, plumbers, computer operators, nurses, and accountants fit the category. In industry such workers were historically organized by craft in the American Federation of Labor. If the skill is based on higher education or apprenticeship, the pay tends to be high; if it is based on vocational training, the pay tends to be moderate or low. Workers along product layouts tend to be hired without a particular skill. Such workers may become adept at installing rivets or molding or soldering connections. But they are classed as unskilled because they are easily replaced from a labor market of the unskilled. Historically, they are the type of assembly-line workers that were organized into the Congress of Industrial Organizations (CIO). Their pay may be minimum wage in smaller nonunion shops, although under Walter Reuther's presidency CIO members gained respectable pay levels. In fixed layouts skilled craftsmen, such as carpenters or welders, often work alongside unskilled laborers, such as shovelers or riveters.

While there are many more operating-resource factors that could be discussed, these eight are perhaps enough to show the basic nature of each layout type. Figure 15–8 is not intended as an if-then analysis device. That is, we would not conclude that if workers are skilled, facility utilization is low, and so on, then a process layout should be developed. There are better ways to determine the right kind of layout. We shall consider some of them later.

Layouts for Streamlined Production

Plant and office layout has never been thought of as a strategic factor—until recently. What has changed things is the discovery that some Japanese plants are only one third or one quarter as large as North American plants making the same thing—cars, for instance. They push the equipment together and squeeze out the racks, conveyors, and forklift trucks. The effect is strategic, because when the machines are close together, the products speed through the plant. This means beating the competitor in responding to changes in demand. A great deal of cost—for space, handling gear, and materials—is avoided. Also, the production people are close together, which helps create a spirit of teamwork, dependency, and mutual support.

Knowing these things, our manufacturers are moving work centers close together as a part of a productivity-improvement strategy. Small box furnaces (widely used in electronics plants) may be bought and placed between other pieces of equipment in a production line—rather than a large furnace in a central location. Drill presses may be plucked out of a drill-press area and stuck into a cell making a family of parts. A stamping machine may be pulled out of a stamping-machine area and moved over to where it can make and feed a single part right to a using station on a production line. The photo in Figure 15–9 shows just that: It is a stamping machine that makes junction box brackets at the *point of use* in a General Electric dishwasher plant.

The same concepts can apply in processing documents—and human customers, too, as we shall see later in the chapter. The good old versatile process layout—with the long handling distances and times—is losing favor, because it is inherently inefficient.

U-Shaped Layouts

The main feature of both production lines and cells is that the work stations are close together, which speeds up the flow and cuts stock. Another feature of both *should* be arrangement of stations into a *U.* Much of what is written about cells does call for the *U*-shape. But there is little suggestion in the writings about production lines of any shape other than straight lines—or *L*-shaped if the building is too short

FIGURE 15–9

Point-of-Use Manufacturing

for the line to stay straight. The time for *U*-shaped production lines is here. There are at least five advantages of *U*-shaped cells or lines:

1. Staff flexibility. When volume is low, one person can run all work centers, since walking distance is not great; when demand picks up, add more labor until every station has an operator.

2. Teamwork. Getting all staff into a cluster is necessary if there is to be teamwork and joint problem solving. As we know, a major benefit of just-in-time production is that lack of backup stock forces problem solving and quality improvement. The workers who are starved of parts form a natural team, who must use their heads to solve problems and get production going again. It can't work well if the workers are strung out along long lines or dispersed and separated by walls of inventory.

3. Rework. Separate rework lines at the end have been common practice. Now they are becoming bad form. Rework should go to the original maker so that the maker cannot evade responsibility for product quality. When the line bends around itself, if bad products are found at the end of the line, there is less of a distance to span in sending them back to the right station for rework.

4. Passage. A long straight line interferes with the travel of people and vehicles. We do not like supermarket shelving to be too long. People protest when a superhighway cuts a neighborhood in half. A long straight production line is a similar imposition.

5. Material and tool handling. In labor-intensive cells or production lines the same person who takes away products at the end of one leg of the *U* can bring back parts to load in at the end of the other leg. The principle is, keep the delivery path short for parts and tools. In unmanned cells, put a six-axis robot in the center and assign it to change tools and to load and unload machines. In fully or partly automated production lines making small products, run an automatic guided vehicle around the inside of the loop delivering full tubs of parts and taking away empties.

There are cases when these advantages of the *U*-shape do not apply. For example, where there is a high degree of automation and few parts or tools to be handled, the teamwork and handling benefits mostly are not there. And a line processing wide sheets of steel, aluminum, glass, etc., perhaps should run in a straight line, because transfer between machines is simpler if there are no changes in direction.

Layout Planning

In a complex layout situation hundreds or thousands of small jobs and medium lots may be in progress at any given time. Repetitive, job, and project work may be included, with products and resources delivered to work centers via many routings.

When routes are so diverse, does it matter how work areas are arranged in a building? Yes, it does. Dominant flow patterns are probably there among the apparent jumble of routings. Layout analysis helps find those patterns.

One layout principle is to arrange work areas in the order of dominant flows. A goal is to get production or resources into, through, and out of each work center in minimum time at reasonable cost. The less time products/resources spend in the flow pattern, the less chance they have to collect labor and overhead charges.

Other factors besides flows may be important in a given layout situation. If so, identify the factors and combine them with flow data. The combined data will suggest how close each work area should be to each other one, and a rough layout can be developed. Then determine the space requirements for the rough layout. The last step in layout planning is to fit the rough layout into the available space, that is, a building (the proposed or existing building). Several layout plans may be developed for managers to choose from. These steps in layout planning are reviewed below, along with useful layout-planning tools.

Steps	Possible tools
1. Analyze product (resource) flows.	Flow diagram From-to chart
2. Identify and include nonflow factors, where significant.	Activity-relationship (REL) chart Combined REL chart
3. Assess data and arrange work areas.	Activity-arrangement diagram
4. Determine space-arrangement plan.	Space-relationship diagram
5. Fit space arrangement into available space.	Floor plan Detailed layout models

Layout-Planning Example

The following multipart example demonstrates the layout-planning steps. The method and some of the tools were developed by Muther, who calls the approach **systematic layout planning (SLP)**.[5] SLP is a practical approach that is widely referenced and used.

EXAMPLE 15–2

Layout Planning, Globe County Offices[6]

The main contact that Globe County citizens have with county offices is in registering and licensing vehicles. Many complain because the three county offices involved have not consolidated their services. On busy days there are waiting lines at all three offices. Many vehicle owners must visit all three, and it is not uncommon for a citizen to find out, after shuffling forward for awhile, that it is the wrong line.

The elected officials who run the three offices have decided to jointly undertake consolidation. Mr. Ross, a consultant, has been hired to conduct layout analysis using SLP.

The consultant finds that there are 12 activities to be located in the available space. The 12 activities and their space requirements are listed in Figure 15–10. Ross has found significant product/resource flows among four of the activities, which are starred in the figure. Three of these are the service counters that patrons visit; patrons constitute the "product" flow. The fourth is the copier, which employees from two of the service-counter areas must visit rather often; employees carrying documents to be copied constitute the resource flow. There is negligible product/resource flow between the three county offices.

Product (resource)-flow analysis. Mr. Ross studies in more detail the four work areas in which there are heavy flows. He counts the numbers of people traveling between each pair of activities. He summarizes the data on a simple device called a from-to chart. (It is much like the distance chart found on many road maps.) The from-to chart provides a measure of volume of flow *from* one work area *to* another. (Volume may be measured in natural units like pounds, pallets, gallons, or people. Sometimes it is important to account for distance and transportability as well as volume of flow. Composite measures of these flow factors have been developed but are not discussed.)

The from-to chart for the county offices is given in Figure 15–11. The greatest flow, an average of 250 people per day, is from the motor-vehicle counter in the county clerk's office to the motor-vehicle counter in the county treasurer's office. These are patrons relicensing their vehicles. They may skip the assessor's office since the assessment is mailed to them. The next largest flow is for licensing of newly purchased vehicles, which requires a visit to all three county offices; 100 per day is the average flow. Other

---

[5] Richard R. Muther, *Systematic Layout Planning* (Boston: Cahners, 1973), pp. 3–1 through 3–8 (TS178.M87).

[6] This is an adaptation of a real case. Thanks go to Ross Greathouse of Greathouse-Flanders Associates, Lincoln, Nebraska, for providing original case data.

FIGURE 15–10

Major Work Areas, County Offices

	Activity	Space requirements (square feet)
I.	*County assessor's office*	
	1. Management	600 sq. ft.
	*2. Motor vehicle—counter	300
	3. Motor vehicle—clerical	240
	4. Assessors	960
II.	*County clerk's office*	
	5. Management	840
	6. Recording and filing—counter	240
	7. Recording and filing—clerical	960
	*8. Motor vehicle—counter-clerical	960
III.	*County treasurer's office*	
	9. Management	420
	*10. Motor vehicle—counter-clerical	1,600
IV.	*Support areas*	
	*11. Mail and copier	240
	12. Conference room	160
	Total	7,520 sq. ft.

* Significant flows.

FIGURE 15–11

From-to Chart, County Offices (flow volume in people per day)

To / From	Clerk I	Assessor II	Treasurer III	Copier IV	Totals
Motor-vehicle counter —clerk **I**		A 100	B 250	D 30	380
Motor-vehicle counter —assessor **II**	C 20		A 100	D 10	130
Motor-vehicle counter —treasurer **III**	C 40				40
Copier **IV**	D 30	D 10			40
Totals	90	110	350	40	590

Note: *Types of product flow:*
  A Patrons licensing newly purchased vehicles.
  B Patrons licensing same-owner vehicles.
  C Patrons to wrong office—backtrack to correct office.
  D Round trips to copier.

flows are smaller: backtracking by patrons who are in the wrong office (backtracking is generally indicated by entries below the diagonal dashed line on the from-to chart); and round trips to the office copier by counter employees of the county clerk and the county assessor.

The next step is to simplify the volume-of-flow numbers. The SLP approach is to convert to a rating value designated by one of the five vowels:

A for *a*bnormally high flow.

E for *e*specially high flow.

I for *i*mportant flow.

FIGURE 15–12

Conversion of Flow Volume to Vowel Rating Scale

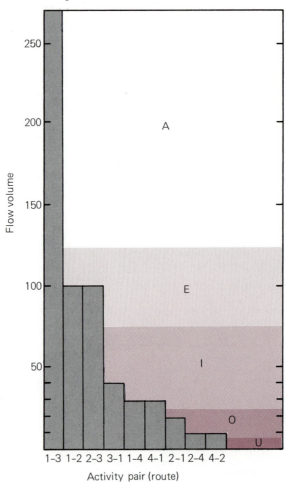

O   for *o*rdinary flow.

U   for *u*nimportant moves of negligible flow volume.

Mr. Ross creates a conversion chart, Figure 15–12, to display the results. Based on examination of the from-to data, he enters each activity pair or route across the bottom of the chart in descending order of flow volume. He plots flow volume for each pair as a vertical bar. Ross then divides the bars at logical breakpoints to form a zone for each vowel. Breakpoints are a matter of judgment, but the "vital few" normally form the *A*-zone, and the "insignificant many" normally form the *U*-zone. In Figure 15–11 one pair, route I–III, seems to Ross to be worthy of the *A* designation. There are two *E*'s, three *I*'s, and three *O*'s. There are many *U*'s, but none were entered on the from-to chart, and therefore none are identified here.

Nonflow factors. Material flows often dominate layout analysis in manufacturing firms. In offices a variety of nonflow factors may be more important. The re-layout of the three Globe County offices is rather more like the typical manufacturing case in that flow (of patrons) is the dominant concern. Still, Ross finds that there are several nonflow factors, mainly in the support areas. In SLP, nonflow factors are combined with flow ratings on an activity-relationship (REL) chart. Ross comes up with the REL chart shown in Figure 15–13.

The chart packs a lot of data into a small space, but it is easy to interpret. The activity on a downsloping line intersects with the activity on an upsloping line at a diamond-shaped box. Each box holds a code. The vowel in the top half indicates how close together activities should be, and the number in the bottom half is coded to reasons why. Vowel and number codes are listed on the figure. Vowel codes are the same in every SLP analysis. Number codes (reasons) depend on the situation.

A few steps leading to the combined REL chart are not included here for the sake of brevity. The omitted steps include separately charting nonflow factors, combining them with flow factors, converting the combined totals to vowel ratings, and finally plotting the vowel ratings on the combined REL chart.[7]

The 66 diamond boxes in Figure 15–13 include one *A,* one *E,* 9 *I*'s, 15 *O*'s, 40 *U*'s, and no *X*'s. The *A* indicates that it is *a*bsolutely necessary for customer-service people in the clerk and treasurer offices to be close together. Reasons why are work flow (1), employee sharing between departments (3), and share counter (4). The same reasons apply to the *E*—for *e*specially important—in the box connecting customer-service people in the clerk and assessor office.

The 9 *I*'s—for *i*mportant—include all five reasons: Several *I*'s are for the sharing of counter space between different types of service in the same office. Several *I*'s are for employees from the same office who need to be close only for supervision (same boss) reasons. A few *I*'s are for facilitating personal communication between counter and clerical people. Work flow and employee sharing also explain a few *I*'s.

The 15 *O*'s call for *o*rdinary closeness. Two are for counter people who

---

[7] See steps in Muther, *Systematic Layout Planning,* appendix 12.

FIGURE 15–13

Combined Activity Relationship (REL) Chart, County Offices

This block shows relation between 1 and 3

Importance of relationship (top)

Reasons in code (below)

"Closeness" rating

Value	Closeness	Number of ratings
A	<u>A</u>bsolutely necessary	
E	<u>E</u>specially important	
I	<u>I</u>mportant	
O	<u>O</u>rdinary closeness OK	
U	<u>U</u>nimportant	
X	<u>X</u>ot desirable	

1	COUNTY ASSESSOR Management
2	Motor vehicle (counter)
3	Motor vehicle (clerical)
4	Real estate (counter)
5	Real estate (clerical)
6	Assessors
7	COUNTY CLERK Management
8	Recording and filing (counter)
9	Recording and filing (clerical)
10	Motor vehicle (counter-clerical)
11	TREASURER Management
12	Motor vehicle (counter-clerical)
13	Real estate, etc. (counter)
14	Real estate, etc. (clerical)
15	SUPPORT Mail and copier
16	Conference room
17	
18	
19	
20	

Reasons behind the "closeness" value

Code	Reason
1	Work flow
2	Supervision
3	Employee sharing (between departments)
4	Share counter
5	Personal communication
6	
7	
8	
9	

Source of REL chart form: Richard Muther and Associates, Kansas City, Missouri. Used with permission.

need to visit the copier room. Three are for personal communication among the three managerial staffs. The rest are for convenience of supervision.

The 40 *U*'s show *u*nimportant relationships between employees in unlike work areas, departments, and so forth.

Activity arrangement. Next Mr. Ross converts the combined REL chart to an activity-arrangement diagram. The diagram shows the arrangement of all activities (circles are used to represent them) without any restrictions on space, shape, utilities, halls, and so on.

Figure 15–14 is Ross's activity-arrangement diagram for the Globe County offices. Lines between circles correspond to relationship codes, as the key on the figure shows. Four lines mean four degrees of closeness for *A*-codes; three lines mean three degrees of closeness for *E*-codes, and so on. Distances between circles are set according to degree of closeness as much as possible. Activities 2 and 8 are in fairly central positions, because each sends out 12 flow lines. Activities 10 and 6 are next at 9 flow lines each. These four; 2, 8, 10, and 6; are all service-counter activities, and earlier ratings placed high importance on having service-counter activities together. Activities 3 and 7 are related clerical-support activities; two lines (important) connect them with counterpart activities in the service-counter cluster. The three sets of double lines at the bottom of the chart connect the conference room (12) to the managers (1, 5, and 9). Most of the single-line (ordinary) links are between managers and activities under their supervision.

Space arrangement.   Mr. Ross converts the activity-arrangement diagram to a space-relationship diagram in two steps:

1. Determine space needs (square feet) for each activity. That is, calculate space needs for each desk, chair, file cabinet, shelf, machine, table, and so on. The organization's own space standards and widely available industry space standards (e.g., 300 square feet per auto in a parking lot) may serve

FIGURE 15–14

Activity-Arrangement Diagram, County Offices

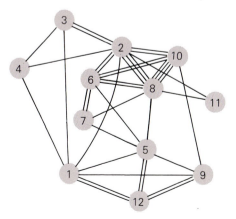

as a guide. Square footage requirements for each of the 12 activities of the Globe County office were given in Figure 15–10.

2. Draw the space-relationship diagram. It should be roughly like the activity-arrangement diagram but with activity blocks sized according to space needed. Space between blocks is unimportant at this point, but it is a good idea to try to end up with a shape similar to that of an existing or proposed building.

Figure 15–15 is the result. It is in the generally rectangular shape of the space into which the activities must fit. All of the service-counter activities are together at the top, where customers may have access. The clerical staff is in the middle band of the chart, which is convenient for the service-counter people at the top and the managers at the bottom.

The space-relationship diagram may be regarded as a rough layout.

Layout into available space. In this step Ross eliminates open spaces on the space-relationship diagram and fits the walls, aisles, utility hookups,

FIGURE 15–15

Space-Relationship Diagram, County Offices

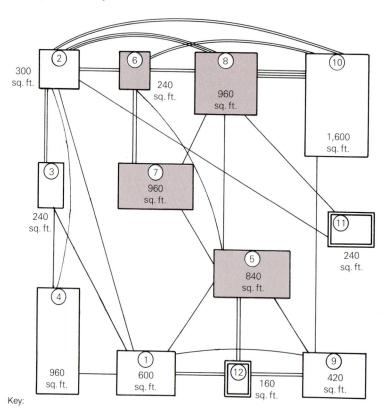

Key:

| Numbers 2, 6, 8, and 10 are service-counter activities. | County assessor activities are 1-4. | County treasurer activities are 9-10. | County clerk activities are shaded. | Shared activities are double-bordered. |

FIGURE 15–16

Possible Final Layout, County Offices

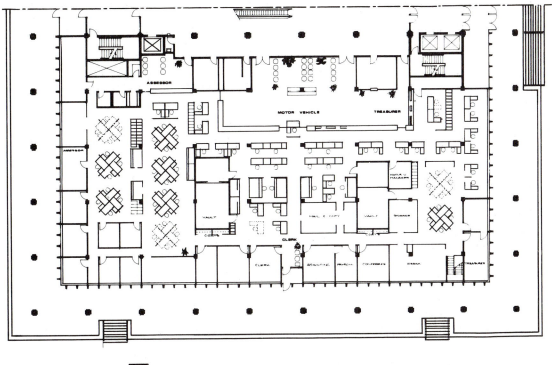

FIRST FLOOR SOUTH PLAN

and so forth into activity areas. Activity areas may be shortened and narrowed, shaped into an L, and so on.

After fitting together the activity areas, Ross lays out facilities and furnishings *within* each area. In a large and complex layout, analysis within activity areas may proceed through the full SLP pattern: *detailed* analysis of material flow, nonflow factors, REL chart, and so on. Templates or two- or three-dimensional models of desks, files, chairs, and so on, are useful in the final stages of detailed layout. These steps are not discussed in this example.

Figure 15–16 is an example of one of Ross's final layouts. The final layout follows the activity arrangement of the space-relationship diagram rather well, but of course activity shapes have been changed to fit the available floor space.[8]

---

[8] While Figure 15–16 is an actual layout of county offices, all the preceding parts of this example were mock designs.

Interior Design

Consultants are often hired to perform or assist in-house staffs in layout planning. One may choose an interior-design consultant, an architectural firm or a firm specializing in layout. Layout specialists are more engineering-oriented and more likely to focus on material-flow factors. Interior-design specialists are more likely to focus on appearance, atmosphere, light and acoustics. It may be best to deal with layout specialists in plant layout, where function rather than appearance tends to be the dominant concern. Interior-design consultants are more important for office layouts, especially offices in which the public is met frequently.[9] Architects are helpful for new construction or major remodeling.

Interior-design consulting for office layout has grown greatly in recent years. A major reason has been the **open-office concept,** which became popular in the 1960s and commonplace in the 1970s. (Fifteen articles with "open office" in the title appeared in *Office* magazine alone from 1975 to 1980.) The open-office idea eliminates many floor-to-ceiling walls and deemphasizes the compartmentalization of people. Open-office layouts are thought to foster communication and to provide flexibility for easy re-layout. Modular office furniture and movable partial-height partitions aid in achieving these goals.

Maintaining a degree of privacy and cutting noise in open offices have been emphasized in recent years. It helps to use wall carpeting, sound-absorbent panels, acoustical screens, fabric-wrapped desk-top risers, and freestanding padded partitions. Office landscaping (the use of plants) is also an important factor in office layout.

The open office is not for all. The Indianapolis office of Peat Marwick Mitchell & Co. (an accounting firm) wanted the feeling of openness but needed privacy for reasons of client confidentiality. Its solution was fixed seven-foot-high partitions with glass extending from there to the ceiling.

Vendors of office equipment often provide interior-design consulting along with product promotion.

Computer Assistance in Layout

Developing the activity-arrangement diagram, the space-relationship diagram, and the layout diagram (see Figures 15–14, 15–15, and 15–16) is not a straightforward process. There are a lot of options for arranging circles, blocks, and activities; trial and error on an erasable surface is common. Where you decide to place a circle on the activity-arrangement diagram tends to limit your choices for placing blocks and activities on the next two diagrams.

Computer programs are available to cut out some of the drudgery and to avoid placement-decision errors in this *search* phase of layout planning. Three prominent programs deserve mention:[10]

---

[9] An architectural firm specializing in interior design developed the layout of Figure 15–16.

[10] Copies of the programs are available as follows: CORELAP from Engineering Management Associates of Boston; ALDEP from IBM; and CRAFT from the IBM Share Library System. Enhanced versions of these programs are announced rather often.

CORELAP (*C*omputerized *R*elationship *L*ayout *P*lanning).

ALDEP (*A*utomated *L*ayout *D*esign *P*rogram).

CRAFT (*C*omputerized *R*elative *L*ocation of *F*acilities *T*echnique).

Each program produces computer-printed layouts.

CORELAP and ALDEP are similar. Both use closeness ratings from the REL chart (see Figure 15–13) as inputs. CORELAP produces a single layout of rectangular-shaped departments; department lengths and widths are set forth in advance. The CORELAP algorithm maximizes common borders for closely related departments. ALDEP produces alternative layouts; each is scored based on the adjacency of departments. A weakness is that irregularly shaped departments tend to emerge.

CRAFT differs from CORELAP and ALDEP in two respects. First, CRAFT requires that an existing layout be input; its job is to improve the layout. Second, CRAFT is based on flow (from-to chart) data but not on nonflow (REL chart) data; the CRAFT algorithm minimizes material handling cost. Generally speaking, CRAFT is suitable mainly for plant layout; because of their flexibility, CORELAP and ALDEP are suitable for either plant or office layout.[11]

LINE BALANCING

After a product or cellular layout has been developed, the task assignments need to be balanced. That is, the tasks must be divided up equally among the workers. Dividing the work is called production-line balancing or assembly-line balancing—or just plain **line balancing.** (Balancing the *machines* assigned to the line also must be done, but that is fairly cut-and-dried: Buy or design machines that all have about the capacity needed; put in two machines instead of one where necessary to get the needed capacity; and so forth.) Some products can be made either in a fixed layout or a product/cellular layout. Of course, line balancing applies only to the latter case. If a personal computer, oscilloscope, or printer is made at a single station **(autonomous production),** then there is no balancing among stations (as there is with **progressive production.)** Also, lines may be balanced for making one product or model—the simple case—or for fixed models.

Line-Balancing Choices

Line balancing is not easily reduced to scientific models or algorithms; there are simply too many choices, given the flexibility and variability of humans. People on the production line can run one machine or several, push a broom or wield a paint brush between machine cycles, handle machine setup and inspection duties or leave those chores for special crews to do, speed up or loaf, stay at their work or wander off, fix broken equipment and suggest improvements or leave it up to the specialists,

---

[11] More complete comparison of the three programs may be found in chapter 3 of Richard L. Francis and John A. White, *Facility Layout and Location* (Englewood Cliffs, N.J.: Prentice-Hall, 1974) (TS178.F7).

move materials or sit around waiting for material handlers to do it. How can balance be designed into the production line with all these uncertainties? The answer is, you can only design a roughly balanced line. Supervisors and the work group itself need to fine tune it.

The designer in charge of rough line balancing is often an industrial engineer. This makes sense, since the IE is the keeper of the time standards and methods-study data. If the production line is to push out a unit of work every 3.5 minutes, then the IE wants to give precisely a 3.5-minute task to each worker or each work station (two or more workers could share the task at a work station). That 3.5 minutes is the **cycle time.** Perhaps time standards show that the total **work-content time** to make one unit is 35 minutes. Then, with each task taking 3.5 minutes, there must be 10 work stations. (A line-balancing survey in 1969 found that 3.5 minutes and 10 stations or workers were the medians for surveyed American firms.)[12]

For a piece having 35 minutes of work content, the **throughput time** is *not* likely to be 35 minutes. Handling between stations and various delays may add time. Also, there may be small buffer stocks between some processes. For example, most high-volume conveyor-driven, or *paced,* production lines making TVs, cameras, videotape players, keyboards, and so forth have one or two units between stations. If there are two idle units between stations for every one being worked on, the throughput time is three times 35 minutes, or 105 minutes. That is, a unit gets 3.5 minutes of work at station 1, then waits for 7 minutes, then gets 3.5 minutes more work at station 2, then 7 minutes' wait time, etc., through 10 stations. Raw material enters every 3.5 minutes and completed units emerge every 3.5 minutes, but each unit spends 105 minutes in the system. This is a **production rate** of 17.14 units per hour.

Cycle time. Production rate. Throughput time. Work content. These concepts can be confusing. Nonetheless they should be understood. If you get your needed production rate, say 17 per hour, with just 35 instead of 105 minutes of throughput time, you are far more efficient: less inventory, less floor space, less time until discovery of errors, faster response to change (design changes, demand changes), closer dependency and better atmosphere for teamwork, and so forth. As a production line ages, a goal should be to *cut throughput time,* as well as cycle time, in order to decrease waste and improve efficiency. Therefore the design of the line should be flexible, and rebalancing or adjusting the balancing should go on continually.

With these points in mind, we may take a look at line-balancing methods used by the IEs in the rough balancing stage. Most begin with a precedence diagram. With data from the diagram, line balancing proceeds by trial and error, heuristics, algorithms, or mathematical models.[13] Computer packages are available for some of the algorithms and models.

---

[12] M. Lehman, "What's Going on in Product Layout?" *Industrial Engineering,* April 1969, pp. 41–45.

[13] A heuristic is a search procedure that may give an optimal (best) solution to a problem but offers no guarantee of doing so. If it can be proven that an exact solution exists, then this becomes an algorithm rather than a heuristic search procedure.

In this chapter we shall look at a manual heuristic line-balancing procedure. Then we consider a fine-tuning method called "watching the lights." The manual heuristic method begins with a precedence diagram.

Precedence Diagram

The precedence diagram charts the work elements and their required sequence. To get the work elements, the whole process is divided into tasks and subtasks. This **division of labor,** as it is called, is carried down to where a task is assignable to a single worker.

One popular type of precedence diagram shows the earliest stage of production where each work element may be done. Production stages are numbered using Roman numerals, and each work element is lined up vertically with one of the Roman numerals. Element durations, numbers, and sometimes descriptions go on the diagram; arrows show what elements must come before what other elements.

The following example demonstrates the precedence diagram. The assembly task is clothing a male doll in a toy factory.[14] All of the work elements for such assembly would probably be done by a single assembler in a real toy factory, because the element times are very short. But for the sake of illustration, we shall assume *progressive assembly* (pass the work from station to station) rather than *autonomous assembly* (all steps done at one station). Precedence diagraming can allow for a variety of special restrictions, but this example is kept simple.

EXAMPLE 15–3

Precedence Diagram for Line Balancing, Doll Assembly

A toy company is coming out with a new male doll. The doll itself and the doll's clothes are parts made off-line. The doll is to be clothed on an assembly line, with different items of clothing put on at different stations along the line. The company wants a balanced assembly line. One step is to prepare a precedence diagram.

Given data:

Methods engineers have performed the division-of-labor step: They have broken up the whole job into 13 separate items of clothing, each of which is a work element. The elements and element times are listed below.

---

[14] Adapted from Theodore O. Prenting and Nicholas T. Thomopoulos, *Humanism and Technology in Assembly Line Systems* (Rochelle Park, N.J.: Spartan Books, 1974), pp. 131–32 (TS178.4.P73).

Element	Element time, t (in 0.01 minute)
1. Put on undershorts	10
2. Put on undershirt	11
3. Put on left sock	9
4. Put on right sock	9
5. Put on slacks	22
6. Put on shirt	42
7. Put on left shoe	26
8. Put on right shoe	26
9. Put on belt	30
10. Insert pocket items (wallet, keys, and handkerchief)	20
11. Put on tie	63
12. Put on coat	32
13. Put on hat	6
Total work-content time, Σt	306

Solution:

The precedence diagram is shown in Figure 15–17.

Work elements are in the circles and element times are beside the circles. Arrows show precedences. The four elements under stage 1 have no predecessors and can be started anytime. No elements can begin until their predecessors have been completed.

In any one column work elements are independent of one another. Three of the elements—left sock, right sock, and hat—have lateral flexibility; that is, they may be moved one column to the right without disturbing precedence restrictions. With these kinds of flexibility, it is clear that a large number of combinations of work-station layout sequences satisfy predecure restrictions.

Precedence diagrams are a bit like the activity-on-node networks used in PERT/CPM (see Chapter 11). A difference is that the precedence diagram does not have a single start and a single end point, as does the PERT/CPM network. The reason is that assembly lines keep running rather than start and end at finite points in time, as projects do. Another difference: The precedence diagram is not a final plan; it just shows sequence limitations (the Roman-numeraled stages in Figure 15–17). The PERT/CPM network is a final sequence plan.

Line-Balancing Analysis

Once the precedence diagram has been completed, the actual line balancing may begin. A perfectly balanced line has zero balance delay, which means no wait time at any work station. Balance delay, d, is:

$$d = \frac{nc - \Sigma t}{nc}$$

FIGURE 15–17

Precedence Diagram, Clothing a Doll

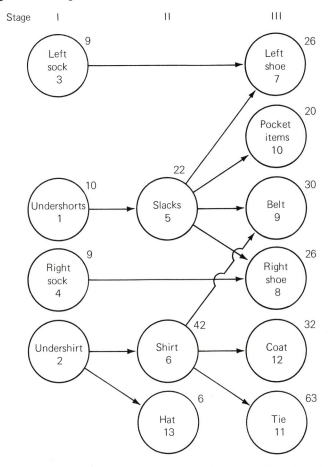

Source: Theodore O. Prenting and Nicholas T. Thomopoulos, *Humanism and Technology in Assembly Line Systems* (Rochelle Park, N.J.: Spartan Books, 1974), p. 132 (TS178.4.P73). Used with permission.

where

$$n = \text{Number of work stations}$$
$$c = \text{Cycle time}$$
$$\Sigma t = \text{Total work-content time for one unit}$$

Manual Heuristic Method. A manual heuristic line-balancing method follows. Doll assembly again serves as the example.

EXAMPLE 15–4

Manual Heuristic Line Balancing, Doll Assembly

Total work content, Σt, for the doll assembly is 306 hundredths of a minute (see given data, Example 15–3). A first step in line-balancing analysis is breaking Σt into its prime numbers. There are five prime numbers:

$$306 = 1 \times 2 \times 3 \times 3 \times 17$$

For the line to be balanced, the cycle time must be equal to the product of some combination of these prime numbers. However, a cycle time shorter than the longest single work element time is not feasible (unless a way can be found to divide the element into two distinct elements). The combinations yield 12 possible cycle times:

$$c_1 = 2 \times 3 \times 3 \times 17 = 306 \qquad c_7 = 17$$
$$c_2 = 3 \times 3 \times 17 = 153 \qquad c_8 = 3 \times 3 = 9$$
$$c_3 = 2 \times 3 \times 17 = 102 \qquad c_9 = 3 \times 2 = 6$$
$$c_4 = 3 \times 17 = 51 \qquad c_{10} = 3$$
$$c_5 = 2 \times 17 = 34 \qquad c_{11} = 2$$
$$c_6 = 2 \times 3 \times 3 = 18 \qquad c_{12} = 1$$

Now we want to see how many work stations, n, we would end up with in a balanced line. To find out, simply divide cycle times into the total work content, 306:

$$n_1 = \frac{\Sigma t}{c_1} = \frac{306}{306} = 1 \text{ station}$$

$$n_2 = \frac{\Sigma t}{c_2} = \frac{306}{153} = 2 \text{ stations}$$

$$n_3 = \frac{\Sigma t}{c_3} = \frac{306}{102} = 3 \text{ stations}$$

$$n_4 = \frac{\Sigma t}{c_4} = \frac{306}{51} = 6 \text{ stations}$$

Note: Six or more stations would be poorly balanced, since the minimum cycle time is 0.63 minutes, which is the time it takes to install the tie on the doll, element 11. So there are just three feasible perfectly balanced options, n_1 through n_3.

The choice of number of stations may be dictated by the production schedule. Assume that the schedule calls for 400 dolls per day, and there is one shift or 400 minutes. Then the cycle time is $400/400 = 1.00$ minutes per doll. The number of stations for this option is $n_3 = 3$ stations.

To develop a plan for a well-balanced line with three stations, we begin by rearranging the precedence diagram, Figure 15–17, into a table, Figure 15–18. Columns A, B, and D in the table are taken directly from the precedence diagram. Column C shows elements that could just as well be performed in a later stage. For example, elements 3 and 4—put on socks—could be done in stage II as well as stage I; and element 13—put on hat—could be done in stage III as well as stage II. Column E sums the element

FIGURE 15–18

Tabular Form of Precedence Relationships in "Assembling Clothes"

(A) Column number in precedence diagram	(B) Element number	(C) Remarks	(D) Element time t	(E) Sum of element times	(F) Cumulative sum of times
I	3	→ II	9	*	
	1		10		
	4	→ II	9		
	2		11	39	39
II	5		22		
	6		42		
	13	→ III	6	70	109
III	7		26		
	10		20		
	9		30		
	8		26		
	12		32		
	11		63	197	306

times for each stage, and Column F cumulatively sums the times for the three stages.

Now inspect Figure 15–18 for ways to achieve a well-balanced line, which must have three stations, each with work content close to 102. We can see from Figure 15–19 that the cumulative sum of stages I and II is close at 109. A way to reduce it closer to 102 presents itself: Move element 13, with a time of 6, from stage II to stage III. This reduces the time for stages I–II to 103, which is very close to the 102 that would give perfect balance.

Moving element 13 to stage III increases the stage III sum from 197 to 203. Now we want to split stage IV into two stations, with cycle times close to 102, the ideal. To find a set of work element times whose sum is close to 102 or 101, it is efficient to begin by adding the larger numbers: Adding elements 11 and 12—63 and 32—gives 95; now add 6, the time for element 13, and you have 101. The remaining four elements—7, 10, 8, and 9—total 102.

Figure 15–19 is the solution. It is nearly perfect: Station 1 has a cycle time of 103; station 2, 102; and station 3, 101. This means that one doll may be clothed every 103 hundredths of a minute, not counting transit time between stations. Station 1's capacity is fully used each cycle; station 2 wastes 0.01 minute per cycle; and station 3 wastes 0.02 minute per cycle. The waste or underuse of capacity for the whole assembly line is the balance

FIGURE 15–19

Improved Line-Balancing Solution for "Assembling Clothes"

(A) Column number in precedence diagram	(B) Element number	(C) Remarks	(D) Element time t	(E) Sum of element times	(F) Cumulative sum of times	
I	3		9			
	1		10			
	4		9			Station 1
	2		11			
II	5		22			
	6		42	103	103	
III	7		26			
	10		20			Station 2
	9		30			
	8		26	102	205	
	13	From stage II	6			
	12		63			Station 3
	11		32	101	306	

delay. It is the time wasted divided by total work time. By the previously given formula, balance delay, d, is:

$$d = \frac{nc - \Sigma t}{nc} = \frac{(3 \times 103) - 306}{3 \times 103}$$

$$= \frac{309 - 306}{309} = \frac{3}{309} \approx 1\%$$

Note that less than three stations is not feasible, since the precedence diagram, Figure 15–17, shows several sequences that include all three stages (for example, 1 to 5 to 7). It is feasible to have four or five stations, but it seems unlikely that either would cut the balance delay below one percent, because the resulting cycle times are not products of primes. Therefore we select n_3 and the analysis ceases.

The heuristic method yields good but not necessarily optimal results. Considerable work has been done on developing algorithms and mathematical models that yield optimal results.

A variety of computer programs are available that incorporate some of the line-balancing algorithms and models. The heuristic programs generally yield good results without taking much computer time. Manual methods, both heuristic and trial-and-error, are used more widely. Computer methods will undoubtedly continue to gain in popularity.

Algorithms have been developed for mixed-model as well as single-model assembly lines. Mixed model means that more than one model of a product is made on the same line. For example, in a mixed-model doll-clothing line male dolls, female dolls, large dolls, small dolls, and so forth, may be clothed in a mixed sequence. Our example above was of a single-model line since there was only one type of male doll. We will consider the mixed-model case next.

Mixed-Model Line-Balancing

Mixed-model line-balancing involves (1) determining the sequence of products (model numbers) moving down the line and (2) balancing the line. Some line-balancing methods allow for various restrictions and special conditions: subassembly lines that feed main lines, distance and direction requirements, safety needs, special groupings of elements, zoning restrictions, maximum and minimum conveyor speeds, and so forth.

The following example illustrates some of the factors involved in mixed-model line-balancing.

EXAMPLE 15–5

Mixed Models, Boring Holes in Pump Housings

Given:

A machine center bores holes in pump housings. It used to take twice as long to set up and run a lot of large pump housings as it did small housings. After a vigorous setup time reduction campaign, the setup times are now nearly zero for either size of housing. With negligible setup times, it seems reasonable to run mixed models down a small hole-boring production line. The schedule calls for 22 large and 88 small pump housings per day. Run times are 12 minutes per large unit, 2 minutes per small unit. What cycle of mixed models will produce the scheduled quantity with balanced production?

Solution:

Model sequence:	L	S	S	S	S	L	S	S	S	S	. . .
Operation time:	12	2	2	2	2	12	2	2	2	2	. . .
			20					20			

This cycle takes 20 minutes and repeats 22 times per day. The production requires 20 × 22 = 440 minutes out of a 480-minute work day, which leaves 40 minutes extra for problem-solving, care of equipment, and so forth.

Fine Tuning

The manual heuristic method seems precise and accurate. It isn't. We know that a good typist can type twice as many words per minute as an average one. Similarly a good welder, solderer, or painter can work twice as fast as an average one. In a line that is balanced based on standard worker pace the fast workers will not have enough to do and the slow ones will have trouble keeping up. Fine tuning is needed. The supervisor will be able to see who the slow workers are and can fine tune by reassigning some work elements from slower to faster workers. A novel method called "watching the lights" serves to make the fine tuning a bit easier.

It is becoming increasingly common for trouble lights to be mounted above production lines to alert troubleshooters and supervisors as to when there is a slowdown or line stoppage. Typically a red light signals shutdown, and a yellow light signals trouble. The production-line workers often have the authority to press the red light button to shut down the line or the yellow light button to summon help. Fine tuning the line balancing is another use of the yellow lights. Here is how it works:

1. When a new production schedule is issued, rough line balancing takes place and the work begins.

2. In the first few hours or first day or two of the new schedule, any worker who has trouble keeping up will, of course, turn on the yellow light frequently. Those who have no trouble keeping up will *not* turn on their yellow lights. The message to the supervisor is clear: Take a few small duties away from those with too much to do and reassign them to those whose lights have not been coming on. When everyone's yellow lights are coming on at about the same frequency, the line is balanced.

3. With the line balanced, yellow lights no longer suggest line imbalance. They indicate trouble. For the remaining days or weeks of the schedule, the problem signaled by a yellow light is recorded so that there is good data for problem solving.

Veterans in industry, when they first hear about this approach, tend to be dubious or full of questions: "But some workers will have much more to do than other workers. Is that fair? Won't the faster workers complain? Or might they not deliberately go slow and push the yellow button in order to avoid getting more tasks to do?"

The first question is not so hard. It is true that the fast workers will end up with more tasks to do, but surely that is *more* fair, not less so. The system should not mask the abilities of the fast workers, nor should it unduly pressure the slower ones. This *does* result in complaints from some of the faster workers. Those complaints may be resolved in two ways.

1. Give the faster workers bonuses, incentive pay, merit wage increases, or promotions.

2. Evolve to a performance appraisal approach in which workers are rewarded for problem solving, quality control, and work improvement. These activities focus on innovativeness, leadership, and communication skills. Make sure that enough labor is available to make it possible to meet the schedule every day and on most days still allow time for problem solving, quality control, and work improvment.

HANDLING

The goals of layout and handling overlap. In layout planning, we are concerned with nonflow as well as flow factors. In handling, flow factors are dominant. Let us take a look at some handling concepts and then at methods for planning the handling system.

Handling Concepts

The best handling system is that which handles least, for handling adds nothing to the product but cost. A well-established practice that is supposed to hold down handling cost is the **unit-load concept.** The simple idea is to avoid moving piece by piece and instead to accumulate enough pieces to move them as a unit load. Common unit loads are truckloads and rail-car loads between plants. Within plants, common unit loads are a loaded pallet, skid, drum, tote box, hand truck, and carton.

While the unit-load idea has dominated our thinking for years, it is now being questioned. The new idea is the opposite: *Avoid* accumulating enough pieces to move them as a unit load; instead try to move them *piece by piece* so that there is *no* extra stock in a state of idleness.

Actually the unit-load and the piece-by-piece viewpoints can converge. If process layouts are broken up and work centers are grouped into production cells or lines, then handling distances collapse. Without distances to span, the economical unit-load size may be pushed downward and approach one piece.

In the last chapter we considered the idea of several small dispersed machines instead of a supermachine. This is a way to cut handling distances since multiple small machines can be located close to where the material comes from and goes to, i.e., in a production line or cell.

Of course, there always will be some distances to span and therefore some handling costs. Good planning can hold down these costs. Apple suggests three approaches to planning for handling: (1) The conventional approach, which concerns point-to-point material flows. (2) The contemporary approach, which is integrated planning for handling materials all over a plant. (3) The progressive approach, which is a broader systems approach that includes incoming raw materials and outgoing finished goods as well as handling between plants.[15]

There seems to be room for a fourth approach. It is Apple's progressive (systems) approach, but applied to *resource* handling, not just material handling. Besides materials, resource handling includes tools, people, and mail. For example, some multibuilding organizations operate a corporate taxi or courier service. At a given time a courier vehicle may carry workers, small parts, tools, and mail. Within a plant one might find an operatorless wire-guided vehicle carrying both materials and tools around a

---

[15] James M. Apple, *Plant Layout and Material Handling,* 3d ed. (New York: Ronald, 1977), pp. 338–39 (TS155.A58).

delivery route. In office areas robot "delivery boys" may carry mail and supplies on a circuit through hallways. A pneumatic-tube system serving plant and offices may move documents, small parts, tools, and funds (and, inevitably, pieces of birthday cake and perhaps an occasional insect or rodent—dispatched by the resident practical joker).

The resource-handling approach has evolved partly because of developments in handling technology, such as operatorless delivery devices and pneumatic tubes.[16] A greater reason is the cost savings of a system in which several resource types may be moved by a single handling device.

Many firms fail to gain these kinds of savings because planning is separate for each type of resource to be moved. The materials-management organization structure (Chapter 8) creates links among all material-oriented activities in the firm. This helps bring about the kind of planning needed to integrate raw-material and finished-goods handling with intraplant handling (Apple's third approach). Broader planning is needed for the resource-handling approach. In one company, the solution was to hold occasional meetings on integrated handling. Representatives came from material handling, warehousing, receiving, shipping, motor pool, courier, mail, the parking coordinator (because employee vehicles were sometimes used for deliveries and employee transportation), and the technical librarian (who sent books and other technical matter to various employees).

Handling Analysis

Handling analysis is done in two basic steps: (1) Analyze resource flows. (2) Prescribe handling methods. If the first step is well done, the second is rather easy.

The **product-quantity (PQ) chart** may also play a role in handling analysis. In Figure 15–20, two sample PQ curves are graphed. Assume that the shallow curve (light) represents all of a plant's material flows. The quantity is low for every one of the products (resources). With such uniform volume a single type of handling (a simple one in this case) may suffice for all products. By contrast, the dark curve is deep. Both high-volume and low-volume products are included. If that curve represented a plant's material flows, there would undoubtedly need to be two types of handling, one for mass handling and another for small quantities.

Data collected about each product or resource may be plotted on a **distance-quantity (DQ) chart**--or, if products/resources are dissimilar, on a **distance-intensity (DI) chart.** *Intensity of flow,* a measure developed by Muther, equals quantity times *transportability.* Transportability is an artificial measure that may include size, density or bulk, shape, risk of damage, condition, and (sometimes) value of the given item.[17]

---

[16] But we are nowhere near a handling technology in which a Captain Kirk might say, "Beam up these ore samples, Scotty. And then beam me up."

[17] A method for determining transportability may be found in Richard Muther, *Systematic Handling Analysis* (Management and Industrial Research Publications, 1969) (TS180.M8).

FIGURE 15-20

PQ Chart Indicating Type of Handling

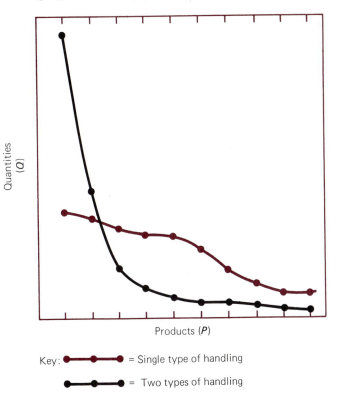

Key: ●——●——● = Single type of handling

●——●——● = Two types of handling

The DQ or DI chart helps show the types of handling methods needed. Figure 15–21 serves as a guide. Four quadrants are shown in the figure. A low-distance, high-volume product would plot in the first quadrant, which suggests *complex handling* equipment, such as conveyors. Low-distance, low-volume calls for *simple handling*, such as hand-carry and the other items in the second quadrant. High-distance, low-volume calls for *simple transport* equipment—any of the types of *vehicles* in the third quadrant. High-distance, high-volume, in the fourth quadrant, suggests poor layout; handling distances are too great. If re-layout is not practical right away, the need is for *complex transport* equipment, such as a railroad.

The solid line cutting through the chart makes another distinction. Above the line are fixed-path types of handling equipment; below the line are variable-path types. It is well to be cautious about investing in the fixed-path variety, because it may be too costly to relocate or modify fixed equipment when needs change. It is common to enter a plant of average age and see unused remnants of an overhead-conveyor or pneumatic-tube system up in the rafters. Automatically guided vehicles and self-guiding order pickers, popularized in the 1960s, were something of a break-through. They have fixed-path advantages, but it is cheap to change their route: Simply paint a new white line on the floor for those that optically follow a line, or embed a new wire in the floor for those that sense a magnetic field generated by a current-carrying wire.

Two of the types of equipment in Figure 15–21 are partly handling devices, partly storage devices: the carousel storage system and the automatic storage/retrieval system (AS/RS). Carousel systems are rotatable racks. They usually hold cartons or trays of small parts out on the shop floor or in a parts receiving area. AS/RS (sometimes called stacker cranes) are rows of racks with automated, perhaps computer-controlled, devices to put away and later select baskets or pallets of stock. Both types of equipment were installed widely in North America in the late 1970s and early 1980s. More recently many companies have been figuring out ways to dismantle some of them, because the racks conflict with the goal of *avoiding* storage.

Forklift trucks seem to be losing favor for about the same reasons. If machines

FIGURE 15–21

DQ or DI Chart Indicating Preferred Handling Methods

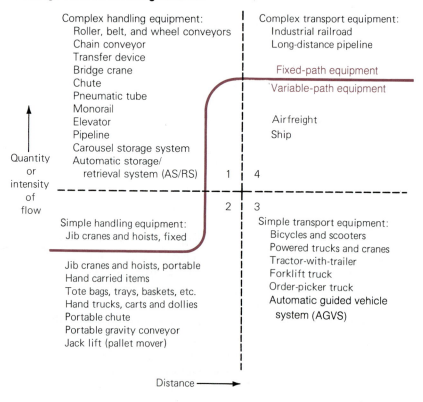

are close together, located in cellular and product layouts, materials may be moved by hand, conveyor, transfer device (transfer between adjacent stations), robot, or chute.

After the analyst has picked out general types of handling equipment, it is time for detailed study. That study should consider cost, reliability, maintainability, and adaptability. Vendors of material handling equipment may help with the detailed design and then are asked to submit bids.

It is worth pointing out that systematic analysis, starting with products and product flows, is by no means the only way to resolve handling problems. The piecemeal way—perhaps starting with the notion that "we ought to acquire a powered-conveyor system"—is common. Piecemeal analysis may include a **feasibility study** in which this question is raised: Is it feasible to acquire the given equipment? The feasibility approach often proceeds from some rather blind presumptions. Still, the approach is quick and cheap, because it requires far less data collection than does systematic analysis. Also, a full-scale systematic analysis involves many organizational units, and it is hard to organize the effort more than perhaps once every five years. Handling problems crop up more often than that, which is why piecemeal analysis is popular.

SUMMARY

Deployment of operating resources includes locating a plant, laying out facilities within the plant, and handling resources among the facilities. Minimizing handling is important in all three levels of deployment.

Location decisions must consider markets, labor, taxes, sources of supply, and a variety of other factors. An emerging strategy for end-product manufacturers is to encourage suppliers to locate a small feeder plant close by. As a result, thousands of parts manufacturing companies may have to rethink the old strategy of building huge plants and shipping vast distances; instead they may disperse to where their customers are located.

Location decisions become more complex when there are several sources of goods (resources) and several destinations. Some of the complexity may be reduced through use of the transportation method of analyzing transportation costs among the plants.

The transportation method is set up as a from-to matrix. Each cell in the matrix contains shipping cost per unit. Quantities supplied (from) and demanded (to) are also shown on the matrix. The method calls for (1) developing an initial feasible solution (the NW-corner method may be used) and (2) improving the initial solution in steps (using the stepping-stone or modified distribution method). The idea is to find a routing pattern that meets supply and demand at minimum transportation cost. When new plantsites are being studied, the optimal transportation-cost routing pattern can be found for each in order to show cost advantages for each site.

Layout is arranging facilities or work activities in order to minimize product/ resource flows and get related activities located close together. A popular layout practice has been to group similar skills, processes, or machines together—the so-called process layout. A weakness is the long flow times and handling between processes. Today those weaknesses are competitive problems. Industry is beginning to break up the process layouts and disperse machines and skills into product and cellular layouts—production lines where work moves short distances between unlike processes. Another kind of layout, the fixed layout, is for the case where the work doesn't move easily, so the resources come to it.

Systematic layout planning (SLP) is a useful layout approach that usually begins with product and quantity analysis. Next comes a from-to chart to show flow volumes for products (or resources) that move in quantity, and an activity-relationship (REL) chart to cover nonflow factors. Data from those charts are used to help arrange work areas on an activity-arrangement diagram, which does not identify the space needed for activities. That diagram converts to a space-relationship diagram, which also shows square footage needs for each activity. Next, develop the activity-area layout to fit an actual floor plan. The three preceding steps may be manual or computer-assisted (as a single step). Finally, the details within each activity area are located on the floor plan, and the layout is complete.

SLP is suitable for office as well as plant layout. But interior design—furnishings, acoustics, light, color, signs, counters, landscaping, and so on—has become important in office layout, and interior designers tend to rely less on systematic analysis and more on art.

In laying out a production line, we try to fully use the capacity of each work station on the line. This is a goal in line balancing. Since labor is flexible and variable, there are many options for trying to give each worker a balanced amount of work. Time standards data are used by industrial engineers to derive a roughly balanced line; fine tuning takes place on the shop floor. It is not enough to just keep the line balanced. Over time, method improvements should cut cycle times, and problem solving should permit removal of buffer stock and handling distance between processes and thereby cut throughput time.

Line balancing often begins with dividing the job into work elements and showing the order of work flow on a precedence diagram. In a manual heuristic method, precedence-diagram data are used to come up with a nearly balanced line. The solution specifies cycle time and number of work stations. A perfectly balanced line is one that has zero balance delay, that is, full utilization of each work station. Computer programs are available for line balancing but are not widely used as yet.

Line balancing is more difficult if mixed models are sequenced down a single production line. In fact sequencing is part of the solution. One model may take longer to make than another, so the solution may call for a cycle to consist of a collection of a few short-cycle-time models along with a long-cycle-time model. The cycle repeats.

One way to fine tune a roughly balanced line is to "watch the lights": A worker who cannot keep up turns on a yellow light. The solution is to take away some of that worker's duties and assign them to a worker whose light is not being turned on.

Handling analysis aims at minimizing handling costs. Unit loads and integrated handling systems that include movement of people, tools, and mail as well as materials may be helpful in achieving that goal. But the ideal is to eliminate the waste of handling altogether. While this ideal is not possible, it may be approached by cutting distance between processes; then move one piece at a time from process to process.

A planning approach called systematic handling analysis proceeds from product-quantity study to distance-quantity study. Distance-quantity (or distance-intensity) data suggest type of handling equipment: simple handling, complex handling, simple transport, or complex transport. Finally, specific equipment is selected. Variable-path handling equipment has the advantage of adaptability. Smaller-scale handling problems may be solved by directly studying the feasibility of a proposed type of equipment, whereas large-scale problems tend to warrant full systematic analysis.

REFERENCES

Books

Apple, James M. *Plant Layout and Material Handling.* 3d ed. New York: Ronald Press, 1977 (TS155.A58).

Burbidge, John L. *The Introduction of Group Technology.* New York: John Wiley & Sons, 1975 (TS155.B7287).

Francis, Richard L., and John A. White. *Facility Layout and Location: An Analytical Approach.* Englewood Cliffs, N.J.: Prentice-Hall, 1974 (TS178.F7).

Muther, Richard. *Systematic Handling Analysis.* Management and Industrial Research Publications, 1969 (TS180.M8).

————. *Systematic Layout Analysis.* 2d ed. Boston: CBI Publishing, 1973 (TS178.M87).

Prenting, Theodore O., and Nicholas T. Thomopoulos. *Humanism and Technology in Assembly Line Systems.* Spartan Books, 1974 (TS178.4.P73).

Sawyer, J. H. F. *Line Balancing.* Machinery Publishing, Brighton, 1970 (TS178.5.S3).

Wild, Ray. *Mass-Production Management: The Design and Operation of Production Flow-Line Systems.* New York: John Wiley & Sons, 1972 (TS178.4.W53).

Periodicals (societies)

Factory Management.

Industrial Engineering (American Institute of Industrial Engineers).

Material Handling Engineering.

Material Management Pacesetter (International Materials Management Society).

Modern Materials Handling.

Office, frequent articles on office layout.

REVIEW QUESTIONS

1. What plant location strategies can be expected in the component parts industries in the near future? Why?

2. What can a community do to attract business or industry?

3. Under what conditions would the transportation method *not* be important in the location decision?

4. What is it that is linear in the transportation method of linear programming?

5. Can a NW-corner solution ever be optimal? Explain.

6. In the transportation method what happens if demand is greater than supply?

7. If data from the transportation method influences you to locate a plant in New Haven, what further use can be made for the data from the method? Explain.

8. In what kinds of industry does the layout plan have far-reaching consequences? Explain.

9. Contrast the product and cellular layouts with the process layout.

10. What kinds of products tend to be produced in fixed layouts, and why?

11. How is handling system related to layout?

12. Why is the *U*-shaped layout well-suited for streamlined production?

13. Where does the data come from that goes on the combined activity-relationship chart? Explain.

14. How are *degrees of closeness* represented on the activity-arrangement diagram? What determines sizes of blocks on the diagram?

15. What has to be done with the space-relationship diagram to convert it to the final layout?

16. What is the *open-office concept?*

17. What problems are involved in cutting throughput time on a production line?

18. How does the precedence diagram differ from the PERT/CPM network?

19. What is a balanced production line?

20. What special problems are there in balancing a mixed-model production line?

21. Which is the computer most useful for, layout planning, line-balancing, or handling analysis? Explain.

22. Is it a good idea to transport in unit loads? Discuss.

23. What are the advantages of *variable*-path handling equipment?

PROBLEMS

1. What are the current location strategies for the following industries?

Carpeting	Petroleum refining
Movie theaters	Boxing and packing materials
Furniture	Electric power generation
Bottling	Plastic molding

2. Find out what you can about the Motor Carrier Deregulation Act of 1980. How has that act affected handling or location strategies (or both) in American industry? Discuss.

3. "Our approach to the labor union is to run from it." That is one auto parts executive's explanation of why they had nonunion plants in small out-of-the-way rural towns around the country. How do you think that strategy will be affected by the automakers' determination to get daily deliveries from their suppliers? Discuss.

4. Recyclation, Inc., has three aluminum-can collection stations located around the metropolitan area. Trucks periodically haul the cans to either of two can-crush facilities; one is referred to as the East facility, the other as the West facility. A third can-crush facility is to be set up, and two alternative sites—a North and a South site—are being considered. The average weekly volume of cans available from the three collection sites is given below, along with the can-crushing capacities of the two present and the two proposed sites. The costs of transportation from each collection site to each can-crush site are also given.

Collection sites	Supply (loads per week)	Routes From	Routes To	Transportation costs per load
1	3	1	E	$8
2	8	1	W	4
3	6	1	N	3
		1	S	7
		2	E	5
Can-crush sites	Capacity (loads per week)	2	W	5
		2	N	7
		2	S	3
East	5	3	E	1
West	7	3	W	3
North	6	3	N	3
South	6	3	S	5

   a. Develop the minimum transportation-cost solution if the new plant is built at the North site. Use NW-corner and stepping-stone.

   b. Develop the minimum transportation-cost solution if the new plant is built at the South site.

   c. Which site is preferable—North or South? Discuss in terms of transportation and also possible nontransportation factors. Do all can-crush sites operate at full capacity? Explain.

5. In a large woodshop tubs of sawdust accumulate in three locations (sawdust is sucked to those three locations via a vacuum system with tubes going to each machine). Several times daily the tubs are grabbed by a fork truck and taken to be dumped at chutes located at two sides of the building. Transportation cost works out to be $1 per 200 feet moved. A third dump chute is to be installed at one of two locations in order to cut move distance. The accompanying floor plan shows the layout with distances. Squares show where sawdust builds up in tubs; solid circles are present chutes; and dashed circles are alternative locations for a new chute.

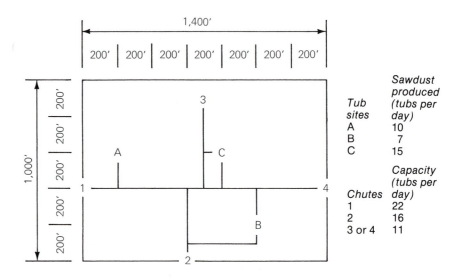

a. Create a transportation matrix for the sawdust-movement problem, assuming that a new chute is installed at site 3.
b. Develop the minimum-cost solution for your matrix from part *a*.
c. Create a transportation matrix for the sawdust-movement problem, assuming that a new chute is installed at site 4.
d. Develop the minimum-cost solution for your matrix from part *c*.
e. Compare the results from parts *b* and *d*. Discuss the need for the chute at either location.

6. American Tractor Company machines engine-block castings in three different plants. The castings come from two of the company's foundries, but the supply of castings has become inadequate. A third foundry, either at Toledo or Rock Island, is to begin casting the tractor engines. Its capacity is to be just enough to make up for the capacity shortage.

   The transportation method is being used to analyze transportation costs for the two sites. Transportation costs, demands, and capacities are given below.

Foundries	Plant	Transportation cost (per casting)	Supply (castings)
A	1	$10	Foundry A— 80/wk.
B	1	3	Foundry B—100/wk.
Toledo	1	5	
Rock Island	1	9	
A	2	7	Demand (castings)
B	2	11	Plant 1— 40/wk.
Toledo	2	6	Plant 2— 90/wk.
Rock Island	2	3	Plant 3—110/wk.
A	3	8	
B	3	5	
Toledo	3	9	
Rock Island	3	7	

   a. Use the transportation method to solve for minimum transportation cost, using Toledo as the foundry site.

   b. Use the transportation method to solve for minimum transportation cost, using Rock Island as the foundry site.

7. Ten thousand TV tubes per month are produced at three different plants; they go to five assembly locations having a total capacity to use 11,000 tubes per month. Set up these data into a transportation matrix, complete with *all* rows and columns that would be needed to work the problem. What other data are needed to work the problem? What decisions would be aided by the solution to the problem?

8. For each of the following types of industry, suggest which types of layout (process, product, cellular, fixed, and mixed) are likely to apply. Some types may have more than one likely type of layout. Explain your choices briefly.

Auto assembly	Military physical exams
Auto repair	Small airplane manufacturing
Shipbuilding	Small airplane overhaul and repair
Machine shop	Large airplane overhaul and repair
Cafeteria	Shoe manufacturing
Restaurant	Shoe repair
Medical clinic	Central processing of insurance forms
Hospital	Packing and crating

9. Draw a layout of a dentists' office (group practice with three dentists). Label the areas as to whether they are process, product, cellular, or fixed, and explain.

10. In a bicycle assembly plant there are five separate shops: (1) Front wheels are built. (2) Rear wheels are built with brake and gear assemblies installed. (3) Tires are mounted on wheels. (4) Sprocket, seat, handlebars, and pedal assembly are mounted on the frame. (5) Wheels are assembled to frame, cables and hand brakes are attached, and the bike is tested and packed. Three sizes of bicycle are made in rotation, with 500 as the average lot size.

   a. What kind of layout does this appear to be? Sketch it.

   b. Now resketch the plant layout to provide a layout for streamlined just-in-time production.

11. Develop an REL chart for a large discount store or department store that you are familiar with. (You may need to visit the store for firsthand information.) Use the store's different departments as activities. Would the REL chart be likely to be helpful in layout or re-layout of such a store? How about a flow diagram or a from-to chart? Explain.

12. Automatic Controls Corp. is building a new plant. Eight departments are involved. As part of a plant-layout analysis, the activity relationships and square-footage needs for the departments are shown on the accompanying combined REL chart (combined flow analysis and nonflow analysis).

Activity	Area (square feet)
1. Shipping and receiving	600
2. Stockroom	1,500
3. Fabrication	800
4. Assembly	700
5. Paint	500
6. Tool crib	300
7. Cafeteria	600
8. Offices	1,200

Total   6,400 square feet

Code	Reasons
1	Personal contact
2	Paperwork contact
3	Product/resource flow
4	Use same equipment/tools
5	Possible fumes

a. Develop an activity-arrangement diagram based on the REL-chart data.
b. Develop a space-relationship diagram for the eight departmental areas.
c. Fit the eight departments into a 100-foot by 80-foot building in as close to an optimal layout as you can. Include aisles between departments on your layout.
d. How necessary is the combined REL chart in this case? If it were not included in the analysis, what would the analysis steps be? Explain. (Hint: Note the pattern of reasons for relationships.)

13. Pharmaco, Inc., manufacturer of a drug line in liquid and tablet forms, is moving to a new building. Layout planning is in process. The data below have been collected on material movements in the drug manufacturing process.

		Unit loads per month	Move distances (feet) in present building
	Raw-material movements:		
	Receiving to raw-material storage		180
1.	Powder in drums	800	
2.	Powder in sacks on pallets	1,100	
3.	Liquid in drums	100	
4.	Controlled substance (heroin) in cans in cartons	10	
5.	Empty bottles in cartons on pallets	8,000	
6.	Water piped into granulating and liquid mixing (gallons)	3,000	
	In-process movements:		
	Raw-material storage to granulating		410
7.	Powder in drums	800	
8.	Powder in sacks	1,000	
9.	Controlled substance in cans	50	
	Raw-material storage to liquid mixing		300
10.	Powder in sacks	100	
11.	Liquid in drums	100	
12.	Controlled substance in cans	10	
13.	Granulating to tableting (granules in drums)	1,500	290
14.	Tableting to fill and pack (tablets in tubs)	6,000	180
15.	Liquid mixing to fill and pack (gallons piped)	4,000	370
16.	Raw-material storage to fill and pack (empty bottles)	8,000	260
17.	Fill and pack to finished storage (cartons of bottles and of tablet packs on pallets)	10,000	320

a. Convert the given flow-volume data to a vowel-rating scale. That is, identify which activity pairs (routes) should be rated A, E, I, O, and U.

b. Develop an activity-arrangement diagram.

c. The layout planners see little need for a from-to chart or an REL chart. Explain why.

d. One option is to call off the move to the new building and update the material handling system in the present building. Develop a DQ chart using data for the present building. From your DQ chart, draw some conclusions about types of handling methods (equipment) that seem suitable for the present building.

14. As a first step in a line-balancing analysis, the following precedence diagram has been developed.

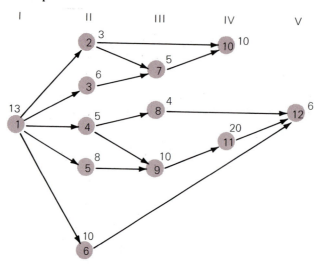

a. Calculate Σt. Now calculate all the possible cycle times and numbers of stations that could be used in a perfectly balanced assembly line.

b. Which of the options developed in part *a* are not worth pursuing further? Why?

c. Balance the line as best you can, and calculate the resulting balance delay.

15. The following precedence diagram has been developed for circuit-breaker assembly.

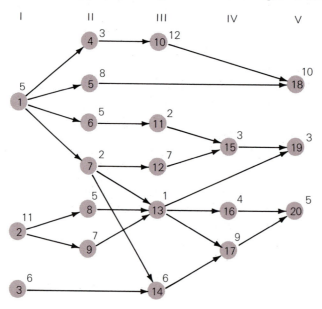

a. Calculate all the possible cycle times and numbers of stations that could be used in a perfectly balanced assembly line.

b. Balance the line as best you can for six stations. Explain. Calculate the resulting balance delay.

16. The processing of workers' compensation claim forms in a state office is being organized as a production line. Work elements have been divided as far as possible and have been organized into the following precedence diagram.

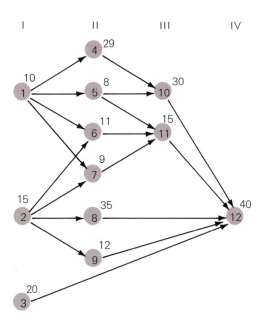

a. Calculate all combinations of cycle time and number of stations that would result in zero balance delay.

b. Which combinations (from part *a*) are not reasonable for further analysis? Explain.

c. Balance the line for five stations, and again for six stations. Which is best? Why?

17. Crow's Eye Foods, Inc., has patent rights to a special type of segmented dish for perfect warming of foods in a microwave oven. The dish permits Crow's to launch a new line of frozen breakfasts. Crow's kitchens are planning for the first breakfast: two strips of bacon, one egg, and two slices of buttered toast.

a. Develop a precedence diagram that could be used in balancing the production line for this breakfast. Make your own (reasonable) assumptions about work elements and element times. Explain your diagram.

b. Determine all sets of cycle time and number of stations that would result in a balanced line.

c. Balance your line.

18. The woodshop building of E-Z Window Co. is undergoing major re-layout in order to reduce backtracking and decrease flow distances. A flow diagram of the frame-manufacturing operation and an REL chart for nonflow factors in the operation are given here.

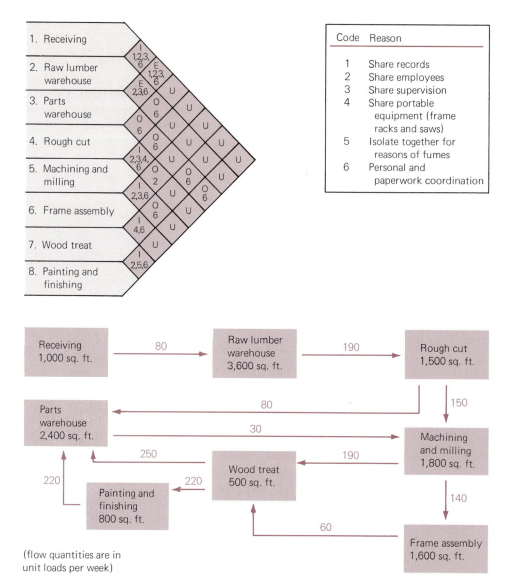

Code	Reason
1	Share records
2	Share employees
3	Share supervision
4	Share portable equipment (frame racks and saws)
5	Isolate together for reasons of fumes
6	Personal and paperwork coordination

(flow quantities are in unit loads per week)

a. Construct a from-to chart based on flow-diagram data. What is the meaning of the notation that quantities are in "unit loads"? Explain by referring to a few examples on the chart.

b. What proportion of total flow on your from-to chart represents backtracking? How does that proportion depend on your chosen order of listing activities on the chart? What does your chosen order of listing activities on the chart imply about the final layout arrangement?

c. Convert the flow-volume data in your from-to chart to a vowel-rating scale. That is, identify which activity pairs (routes) should be rated *A, E, I, O,* and *U.*

d. Combine your vowel-rating data representing flow volumes with the nonflow-factor vowel ratings on the REL chart. Express the result in a new combined REL chart.

e. Convert your combined REL chart into an activity-arrangement diagram.

f. Develop a space-relationship diagram for the eight activity areas.

g. Fit the eight activity areas into a square building without allowances for aisles, etc. Make your layout as nearly optimal as you can.

h. Based on distances between departments in your layout in part g above, develop a DQ chart. From your DQ chart, draw some general conclusions about the type of handling methods (equipment) that seem suitable.

19. A production line assembles two models of hair dryer: standard *(S)* and deluxe *(D)*. Each *S* requires 4 minutes of assembly time, and each *D* takes 12 minutes. Marketing sells twice as many *S*'s as *D*'s. Develop a mixed-model sequence for the two dryers. Make it as well balanced as possible. What is the cycle time, and how many times can it repeat in a 480-minute day?

20. Parts *A* and *B* have to be heat treated. The heat-treat time for part *A* is 5 minutes; for part *B* it is 10 minutes. The schedule calls for 36 *A*'s and 12 *B*'s per day. Develop a balanced mixed-model sequence for the two parts. How many hours will it take to produce the scheduled amount?

21. Acme Corp. has $5 million worth of storage and handling gear: $1 million in pallet racks, $1 million in an operatorless wire-guided vehicle delivery system, $1 million in carousel storage (three carousels), $1 million in an AS/RS, and $1 million in a transporter (moving parts from person to person in production cells and lines).

   Evaluate these five handling/storage systems. Rank them in worst-to-best order for a plant pursuing streamlined just-in-time production. Explain.

MINICASE STUDY: ST. "M'S" HOSPITAL

In 1970 St. "M's" Hospital was built. A unique feature is an automated monorail system to carry linens, food, instruments, medication, and other items all over the hospital from central storage and distribution points. The monorail hauls materials on carts and in baskets. The monorail system, the first of its kind in the world, was justified based on such features as: (1) labor-cost savings, (2) freeing professionals like nurses from various handling tasks, (3) high-quality sterilization of instruments at a site away from operating rooms, and (4) a twin-cart system that provided for one cart to be in loading while its twin was in service. At first the monorail system was feared, ridiculed, misused, and/or ignored by employees. But after about three years, the system realized its potential.

A primary user of the monorail system is the laundry department. Let us follow the flow of laundry from the floor to the basement laundry room. In each patient's room there is a closet having two doors. One leads directly into the room; the other opens into the hall. The closets hold one day's supply of laundry (sheets, towels, etc.) for that room. There are five shelves in each closet. The top two hold the clean laundry while the dirty laundry goes on the three bottom shelves. Every day the laundry crew checks preset lists and restocks shelves. The dirty laundry is sorted into color-coded bags. Then it goes onto charts for transport via the monorail and elevators. The carts are hydraulically raised onto the monorail, and a worker activates a pin code on the cart to direct it to the right laundry area.

Another major user of the monorail is food services, which is run by ARA, a nationwide food service provider. The food service features precooking, freezing, and reheating. The operation is unique in that entrées like steaks are grilled in long production runs, put onto a conveyor, carried through a shrink-wrap process, and moved into blast freeze. Chefs can produce them on an eight-to-five schedule. Later the monorail-elevator system conveys meals from the main kitchen to the patient floors for microwave heating and serving.

By 1980 monorail technology in hospitals had become fairly common. But newer monorail systems used lightweight materials, greaseless moving parts, and computer controls. By contrast, St. M's has a heavy-duty factory-grade monorail—noisy, bulky, mechanically controlled, and very expensive to maintain. Three options are being considered:

1. Maintain present system. The costs include over $20,000 per year for maintenance, including parts. The chain that drives the monorail must be replaced every seven to ten years at $25,000 per replacement. With good preventive maintenance, the system might last 15 to 20 more years.

2. Introduce manual handling. It would cost $15,000 to modify three elevators that are now "injector elevators" and part of the monorail system. The other monorail facilities could be dismantled over a long time period since manual operations would not be hampered much by most of the overhead rails. According to one authority,[1] automated delivery systems do not reduce delivery costs: Manual deliveries take an average of two minutes, whereas unloading/replenishment takes an average of 45 minutes in hospitals around the country. While St. M's was a pioneer in use of the twin-cart system, that system has come into use in hospitals which use manual delivery as well.

3. Replace the monorail. The cost is estimated at $1.2 million, including elevators and computer controls. A part of the cost is for tearing out the old monorail—a considerable task since it is such a heavy-duty system.

DISCUSSION QUESTIONS

1. What kinds of layouts does St. "M's" have for key activities?
2. What should be done about the handling system?

---

[1] Charles E. Housely, "Distributing the Goods the Right Way," *Hospitals,* June 16, 1977, pp. 103–5.

Supplement to Chapter 15
Stepping-Stone Method

The stepping-stone method leads to an optimal solution to a transportation problem. Stepping-stone begins with an initial feasible solution, as the following example (using data from the Hawaiian Islands example from the body of the chapter) demonstrates.

EXAMPLE S15–1

Stepping-Stone Method—Hilo Location

Initial solution—Lihue location. An initial feasible solution using the NW-corner rule is shown in Figure S15–1. The total weekly transportation cost for the NW-corner solution is $965, as calculated below:

Honolulu-Lanai:	$ 7 × 20 =	$140 per week
Honolulu-Molokai:	7 × 5 =	35 per week
Hana-Molokai:	7 × 25 =	175 per week
Hana-Hawaii:	8 × 15 =	120 per week
Lihue-Hawaii:	11 × 45 =	495 per week
Lihue-Dummy:	0 × 5 =	0 per week
Total		$965 per week

NW-corner is subject to improvement. For Lihue, we shall manually improve the NW-corner solution using the stepping-stone method. While computers usually perform these calculations, there are insights to be gained from manual calculations.

Optimal solution—Lihue location. Stepping-stone begins with a degeneracy test. The solution is degenerate if the number of cells in the solution ("filled" cells, that is) is not equal to one less than the number of sources (S) plus destinations (D), or $S + D - 1$. In this case there are six filled cells resulting from the NW-corner method, and $S + D - 1 = 3 + 4 - 1 = 6$. The number of filled cells equals $S + D - 1$, so the initial solution is not degenerate. If it were degenerate, the solution would have to be modified slightly in order to proceed with the stepping-stone method.

Next, we test empty cells. The test determines whether the solution can be improved—that is, whether the total transportation cost can be reduced—by transferring some units into an empty cell. But supply-and-demand restrictions ("rim conditions") must be maintained.

673

FIGURE S15–1

NW-Corner Initial Solution, Lihue Location

The first empty cell to test is Honolulu-Hawaii. Suppose that one pallet-load is transferred to that cell. That added unit creates an imbalance, which requires a series of corrections, as shown in Figure S15–2. The pallet-load can be transferred from Hana in the Hawaii column; this keeps the total in the column at 60, but it drops the total in the Hana row from 40 to 39. The correction is to add one unit to the Hana-Molokai cell, which brings the Hana row back up to 40 but also raises the Molokai column total from 30 to 31. The correction is to subtract one unit from the Honolulu-Molokai cell; this brings Molokai back to 30 and also drops the Honolulu row total back to 25 (recall that one unit was added to Honolulu-Hawaii in the first step, which raised the Honolulu row total to 26). In Figure S15–2A the four steps—adding one, subtracting one, adding one, and subtracting one—are shown connected by arrows. The rectangular circuit of pluses balanced by minuses in affected rows and columns preserves rim values.

The effect on transportation cost is calculated at the right-hand side of Figure S15–2A. Adding one unit in the Honolulu-Hawaii cell increases transportation cost by $10 per week; Hana-Hawaii cuts cost by $8 per week; and so forth. The net change is +$2 per week. This is a higher cost, so the test fails. Honolulu-Hawaii should remain an empty cell; no newspapers should be sent via that route.

The next empty cell is Honolulu-Dummy. The test is shown in Figure S15–2. This test requires pluses and minuses in six rather than four cells:

FIGURE S15–2

Stepping-Stone Revisions, Lihue Location

A. Testing the Honolulu-Hawaii cell

	Lanai	Molokai	Hawaii	Dummy	Supply
Honolulu	7 / 20	7 / 5 / −1	10 / +1	0 /	25
Hana	5 /	7 / 25 / +1	8 / 15 / −1	0 /	40
Lihue	9 /	11 /	11 / 45	0 / 5	50
					115
Demand	20	30	60	5	115

Cell	Units		Rate		Cost change
Honolulu-Hawaii	+1	x	$10	=	+$10 per week
Hana-Hawaii	−1	x	$8	=	−$8 per week
Hana-Molokai	+1	x	$7	=	+$7 per week
Honolulu-Molokai	−1	x	$7	=	−$7 per week
Net change				=	+$2 per week

B. Testing the Honolulu-dummy cell

	Lanai	Molokai	Hawaii	Dummy	Supply
Honolulu	7 / 20	7 / 5 / −1	10 /	0 / +1	25
Hana	5 /	7 / 25 / +1	8 / 15 / −1	0 /	40
Lihue	9 /	11 /	11 / 45 / +1	0 / 5 / −1	50
					115
Demand	20	30	60	5	115

Cell	Units		Rate		Cost change
Honolulu-Dummy	+1	x	$0	=	$0 per week
Lihue-Dummy	−1	x	$0	=	$0 per week
Lihue-Hawaii	+1	x	$11	=	+$11 per week
Hana-Hawaii	−1	x	$8	=	−$8 per week
Hana-Molokai	+1	x	$7	=	+$7 per week
Honolulu-Molokai	−1	x	$7	=	−$7 per week
Net change				=	+$3 per week

a minus offsetting every plus in three rows and three columns. There is no other way to preserve rim values and thus satisfy both supply and demand.

The test starts by adding one unit to the Honolulu-Dummy cell. Next, we subtract one unit from Lihue-Dummy and add one unit to Lihue-Hawaii. Why not add to Lanai or Molokai instead of to Hawaii? A simple reason is that we want to test only one empty cell at a time, and adding Lihue-Lanai or Lihue-Molokai, which are empty, would confound our test of the empty Honolulu-Dummy cell. To conduct a pure test of only one cell

FIGURE S15–2 (continued)

C. Testing the Hana-Lanai cell

	Lanai	Molokai	Hawaii	Dummy	Supply
Honolulu	7 20 −1	7 5 +1	10	0	25
Hana	5 +1	7 25 −1	8 15	0	40
Lihue	9	11	11 45	0 5	50
Demand	20	30	60	5	115 / 115

Cell	Units		Rate		Cost change
Hana-Lanai	+1	x	$5	=	+$5 per week
Honolulu-Lanai	−1	x	$7	=	−$7 per week
Honolulu-Molokai	+1	x	$7	=	+$7 per week
Hana-Molokai	−1	x	$7	=	−$7 per week
Net change				=	−$2 per week

D. Improved transportation solution

	Lanai	Molokai	Hawaii	Dummy	Supply
Honolulu	7	7 25	10	0	25
Hana	5 20	7 5	8 15	0	40
Lihue	9	11	11 45	0 5	50
Demand	20	30	60	5	115 / 115

					New cost
Honolulu-Molokai:	$7	x	25	=	$175 per week
Hana-Lanai:	$5	x	20	=	$100 per week
Hana-Molokai:	$7	x	5	=	$35 per week
Hana-Hawaii:	$8	x	15	=	$120 per week
Lihue-Hawaii:	$11	x	45	=	$495 per week
Lihue-Dummy:	$0	x	5	=	$0 per week
					$925 per week

at a time requires that all other cells involved in the test be already filled.[1]
After adding one unit to the Lihue-Hawaii cell, we subtract one unit
from Hana-Hawaii, add one unit to Hana-Molokai, and subtract one unit

---

[1] Lee offers a picturesque explanation of the rule that only filled cells be used to support the test of an empty cell:

> When we walk into a Japanese garden, we often see a beautiful pond. There are water lilies, goldfish, frogs and dragonflies. Then, no doubt, we will notice a set of stepping-stones going across the pond. We can go across the pond if we carefully step on these stones. [In] the stepping-stone method . . . we evaluate all the empty cells by carefully stepping on the occupied cells. We should always remember that if we step on an empty cell, we shall be in the water, screaming, "help!"

Sang M. Lee, *Linear Optimization for Management* (Princeton, N.J.: Petrocelli-Charter, 1976), p. 261 (HD20.5.L39).

FIGURE S15–2 (continued)

E. Testing the Hana-dummy cell

	Lanai	Molokai	Hawaii	Dummy	Supply
Honolulu	7	7 / 25	10	0	25
Hana	5 / 20	7 / 5	8 / 15 / −1 → +1	0	40
Lihue	9	11	11 / 45 / +1	0 / 5 / −1	50
					115
Demand	20	30	60	5	115

Cell	Units		Rate		Cost change
Hana-Dummy	+1	x	$0	=	$0 per week
Lihue-Dummy	−1	x	$0	=	$0 per week
Lihue-Hawaii	+1	x	$11	=	+$11 per week
Hana-Hawaii	−1	x	$8	=	−$8 per week
Net change				=	+$3 per week

F. Testing the Lihue-Lanai cell

	Lanai	Molokai	Hawaii	Dummy	Supply
Honolulu	7	7 / 25	10	0	25
Hana	5 / 20 / −1	7 / 5	8 / 15 / +1	0	40
Lihue	9 / +1	11	11 / 45 / −1	0 / 5	50
					115
Demand	20	30	60	5	115

Cell	Units		Rate		Cost change
Lihue-Lanai	+1	x	$9	=	+$9 per week
Hana-Lanai	−1	x	$5	=	−$5 per week
Hana-Hawaii	+1	x	$8	=	+$8 per week
Lihue-Hawaii	−1	x	$11	=	−$11 per week
Net change				=	+$1 per week

from Honolulu-Molokai. These steps keep the Lihue row at 50, the Hawaii column at 60, the Hana row at 40, the Molokai column at 30, and the Honolulu row at 25. The net change, calculated at the right-hand side of Figure S15–2B, is +$3 per week; therefore the test fails.

We test the Hana-Lanai cell as shown in Figure S15–2C. Adding a unit to the cell saves $2 per week, so the test passes. If moving one unit into the Hana-Lanai cell saves $2, then moving three units would save $6, moving seven units would save $14, and so forth. (Costs are linearly related to quantities in linear programming.) When an empty-cell test saves any money, you want to move maximum units into that cell to save maximum dollars.

FIGURE S15–2 *(concluded)*

G. Testing the Lihue-Molokai cell

	Lanai	Molokai	Hawaii	Dummy	Supply
Honolulu	7	7 / 25	10	0	25
Hana	5 / 20	7 / -1	5 8 / +1 15	0	40
Lihue	9	11 / +1	11 / -1 45	0 / 5	50
					115
Demand	20	30	60	5	115

Cell	Units		Rate		Cost change
Lihue-Molokai	+1	x	$11	=	+$11 per week
Hana-Molokai	−1	x	$7	=	−$7 per week
Hana-Hawaii	+1	x	$8	=	+$8 per week
Lihue-Hawaii	−1	x	$11	=	−$11 per week
Net change				=	+$1 per week

The maximum here is 20 units, because 20 is the limit that may be subtracted from the "minus" cells without going negative. It is the Honolulu-Lanai cell that so limits the quantity moved: Honolulu-Lanai is at 20 in Figure S15–2C, and it is reduced to zero (emptied) in the improved solution of Figure S15–2D. Each of the other cells tested in Figure S15–2C was also changed by 20 units (up or down).

To the right in Figure S15–2D are cost calculations for the new solution. The new cost is $925 per week. That is $40 less than the NW-corner initial cost of $965—which we would expect, since 20 units were moved at a savings of $2 each.

Whenever units are moved within a matrix, cell testing begins all over again. Conditions have changed, and cells previously tested might test out differently.

Thus, we turn again to the first cell, Honolulu-Lanai. We need not retest the cell, since it was emptied for good reason in the test in Figure S15–2C. We need not retest the Honolulu-Hawaii and Honolulu-Dummy cells either, because inspection shows that testing them would include exactly the same cells and transportation costs that were in the earlier tests of those cells.

Hana-Dummy is the next cell to test. The test result, in Figure S15–2E, is a net change in cost of +$3 per week; the test fails.

The last two tests are Lihue-Lanai and Lihue-Molokai. Both result in $1 greater cost and therefore fail; see Figures S15–2F and S15–2G.

There are no more empty cells to test. The solution in Figure S15–2D, costing $925 per week, is optimal. If the *Island Explorer* builds at Lihue, $925 is the expected transportation cost.

If a nonoptimal solution is degenerate, there are not enough filled cells to be able to test all of the empty ones. The correction is to place a very small quantity into one or more empty cells to eliminate the degeneracy. The small quantity is designated ϵ (the Greek letter *epsilon*). The transportation cost for the cell, times the quantity, ϵ, equals zero because ϵ is so small; therefore ϵ does not alter the cost structure but only helps with the solution. There is no good rule for selecting the proper empty cell in which to place ϵ. You can try a spot and see whether it works out; if not, try another.

The use of ϵ was actually devised for computer-based solutions. Putting ϵ into a degenerate matrix allows the computer to proceed with the normal transportation algorithm. (The computer treats ϵ as equaling the lowest character in the computer's collating sequence.)

Sometimes we want to leave out certain transportation routes. For example, fishermen between Maui and Lanai may object to the noise of a predawn airplane transporting newspapers from Hana. Perhaps one hotheaded fisherman may decide to shoot at the plane. The newspaper may avoid the risk of being hit by excluding Hana as the source of newspapers to Lanai. In the transportation method it is simple to assure that the Hana-Lanai cell ends up empty: Use the value ∞ (symbol for infinity) as the transportation cost in that cell (the symbol M, for *m*aximum cost, is sometimes used).

Chapter 16

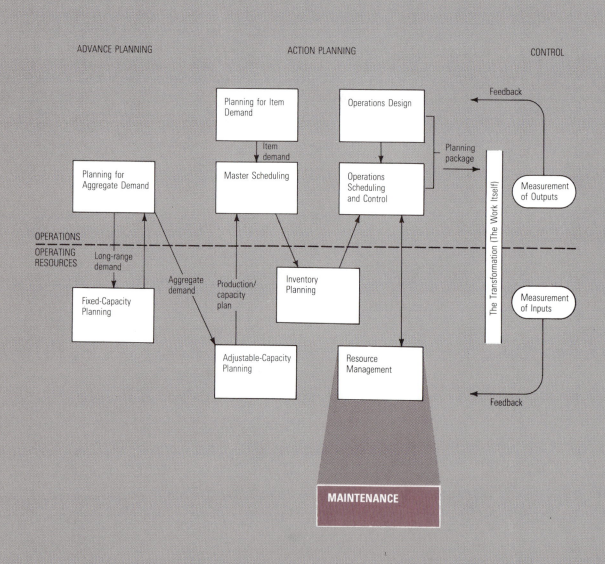

ADVANCE PLANNING   ACTION PLANNING   CONTROL

Planning for Item Demand

Operations Design

Feedback

Item demand

Planning for Aggregate Demand

Master Scheduling

Operations Scheduling and Control

Planning package

Measurement of Outputs

OPERATIONS

OPERATING RESOURCES

Long-range demand

Aggregate demand

Production/ capacity plan

Inventory Planning

The Transformation (The Work Itself)

Measurement of Inputs

Fixed-Capacity Planning

Adjustable-Capacity Planning

Resource Management

Feedback

MAINTENANCE

Maintenance Management

Maintenance is the third of the four stages in the life cycle for operating resources. The stages are diagrammed below.

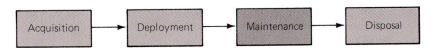

Acquisition → Deployment → Maintenance → Disposal

Maintenance means keeping operating resources in good working order. Plant, equipment, and tools are what usually come to mind, although work force and materials must also be maintained (via training, etc., for people and proper storage of materials). Thus, some of the concepts apply as well to work force and materials. For example, a major problem in managing repair crews is uncertainty about when breakdowns will occur; similarly a major problem in maintaining people's health and well-being—via food services, health services, entertainment services, and so on— is uncertainty about when people "break down" and come in for service. The problems of running a service center with that kind of uncertainty are treated in the next chapter. In this one we stay with traditional maintenance topics, such as preventive maintenance, repairs, group replacement, and standby equipment.

MAINTENANCE RESPONSIBILITY

The first line of defense against equipment failure and an untidy environment is the *person occupying the space*. The maintenance department provides special backup expertise for severe problems.

If this division of maintenance responsibility is not what you have seen, it is because we usually have not followed that prescription. Instead we have given nearly the whole job to the specialists in maintenance. We *thought* it rational to specialize the maintenance function: Save money by hiring low-wage custodians for shop and office cleanup; similarly hire fairly low-wage people to tighten belts, oil machines, and perform other preventive maintenance tasks; and hire a few high-wage people for equipment repair—because the cost to train operators to fix their machines seems prohibitive.

The savings are deceptive. If someone else cares for my equipment and workspace, I become sloppy. My typewriter fills with foreign matter, which causes poor performance, greater maintenance, shorter life. The same goes for desk tops, electronic displays, copiers, milling machines, extruders, furnaces, automobiles, and so on. By relying on outside experts for repairs, I never come to understand my equipment very well. I become incapable even of making simple repairs. When the equipment fails, as it often does with an uncaring operator, I wait for help and may cease being productive while I wait. Furthermore, I do not recognize symptoms of deterioration.

Worker-Centered Maintenance

The case for worker-centered maintenance is strong. It becomes stronger as a plant moves toward just-in-time production, because with JIT, a breakdown at one work center soon causes a work stoppage for lack of parts, clients, documents, etc., at the next work centers. The person running the equipment needs to care for it and to be capable of doing at least some of the repairs, too. Speed is important. Waiting for someone from maintenance may take too long. The operator who feels some kinship with the machine also is more likely to try to get the machine improved so that the same problem does not recur ("foolproof" the machine).

In JIT plants in Japan, machinists wipe the oil off their machines frequently. They watch carefully for oil leaks, which suggest upcoming hydraulic problems. When an oil leak shows, it is fixed. By contrast, our machines are likely to break down before we learn of a leak.

Worker-centered maintenance is sure to become still more common with automation and robotics. Are workers turned out onto the street when machines take over? Some are, but there is a need for a sizable staff to keep the machines running. Hitachi operates a production line producing videotape recorders with about 80 robot and hard-automated work stations. There are several people on hand to maintain the equipment and to fix machines when a red trouble light goes on. They do not work for a maintenance department. They are former assemblers retrained to do equipment maintenance and troubleshooting.[1]

Maintenance Department

Even with a high degree of worker involvement in maintenance, there still is a need for a maintenance department. The department might have not only the pure maintenance functions but also the other three stages in the life cycle of operating resources (i.e., acquisition, deployment, and disposal). The organization structure could look like Figure 16–1.[2] The three major sections shown are *analysis* (planning), on the left; *design* (engineering), in the middle; and *operations*, on the right.

Why are the functions shown in Figure 16–1 grouped together? The common thread is that all the functions share the mission of providing for an *efficient* working environment at *reasonable cost*. Our interest in maintenance management centers mostly on trade-offs among those two goals—efficiency and cost—rather than maintenance operations. But a few points must be made about operations.

Figure 16–1 shows four types of maintenance operations: custodial services, preventive maintenance (PM), repairs, and millwrights and minor construction. The first two, PM and custodial services, fall into the category **periodic maintenance.** Repairs and millwrights/minor construction are **irregular maintenance.** In the maintenance field much of management's attention has been on the proper mix of periodic and irregular maintenance. The sections of this chapter on group replacement and standby equipment include ways to analyze the mix of periodic and irregular maintenance.

The millwright shop employs the tradesmen who move and install machines and other facilities (originally in a mill). But often machines and work centers are not

---

[1] But sometimes education, not just retraining, is necessary. According to one story, robots are "increasing the proportion of males in the Japanese work force—especially males with science and engineering degrees. In the past, new forms of manufacturing technology usually brought more women and part-time workers into the labor force." *The Wall Street Journal,* Friday, September 23, 1983.

[2] A variety of other maintenance facilities organization structures may be found in James A. Murphy, ed., *Plant Engineering Management* (Dearborn Mich.: Society of Manufacturing Engineers, 1971), ch. 2 (TS184 P435x).

FIGURE 16–1

Organization of a Maintenance Department

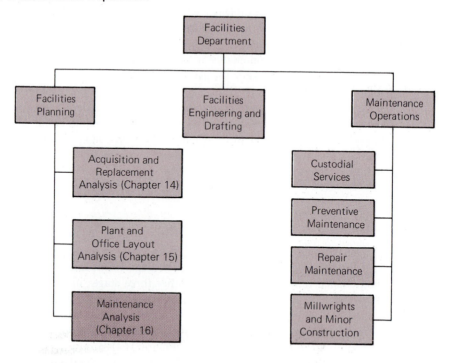

so difficult to move that trained millwrights are needed. Flexible equipment not bolted or dug into the building structure can be a real asset.

Repair workers are skilled, well-paid tradesmen. Repair workers need to know more than how to tighten nuts onto bolts. Their troubleshooter role requires diagnostic skills as well as breadth of technical skills.

In fact, a nice maintenance department career ladder, with increasing skills and wage rates, is from custodianship to preventive maintenance to repairs or to millwright and minor construction. The steps of the ladder are arranged in just that way in Figure 16–1. One irony in maintenance management is this: Lower-paid custodians are easy to keep busy since they do regular, periodic maintenance work; higher-paid repair tradesmen are hard to keep busy since they do irregular breakdown maintenance work.

The maintenance department may be viewed as a minifactory. As such, it has a full operations and operating resources management system. Of course, the minifactory shares many resources with the parent organization. The parent would usually supply the maintenance department with such services as personnel, purchasing, and methods and time standards.

PERIODIC MAINTENANCE

Repair maintenance is usually a necessity, but periodic maintenance is discretionary. Though you may not *have to* do it, periodic maintenance has appeal for at least the following reasons:

1. Periodic maintenance crews may have fairly even schedules; repair crews are busy only when there is something to fix.
2. Periodic maintenance tends to forestall work stoppage; repair crews feed upon adversity: breakdowns and stoppages.
3. Periodic maintenance may often be scheduled to avoid work stoppage; with repair maintenance there is work stoppage not only during repair but also, frequently, while waiting for a repair crew.

Custodial work, one type of periodic maintenance, usually is housed in the maintenance department. The people in the operating departments could do all of the cleaning of their work spaces. They could even share the cleaning of common areas; more likely there will be a permanent custodial crew to at least clean common areas and carry out trash.

Preventive maintenance (PM) is the more issue-laden aspect of periodic maintenance.

There are three types of PM, as follows:

PM based on calendar time.

PM based on time of usage.

PM based on inspection.

PM based on calendar time means doing maintenance at regular intervals. PM based on time of usage is maintenance after a set number of operating hours. PM based on inspection means any maintenance that seems prudent, as revealed by planned inspections.

Among the most ardent believers in the PM concept are aircraft maintenance people. In aircraft maintenance, PM is everything; waiting for a failure is intolerable since, if a failure occurs, there is often nothing left to fix.

Preventive maintenance of aircraft is largely based on time of usage. Flight logs recording hours of usage are the basis for thorough overhauls and replacements.

PM based on inspection is also important. Pilots and ground crews have inspection checklists for routine maintenance. (Japanese workers often have maintenance checklists taped to their machines, and they will not start the machines in the morning until all items have checked out.) Also, critical components are periodically torn down for interior inspections; the U.S. Air Force refers to this as IRAN—*i*nspect and *r*epair *a*s *n*ecessary—maintenance.

There are many shining examples of the success of the PM concept in aircraft. The well-traveled B-52 is one. Even more remarkable is the DC-3, now about 45 years old. (The military version, the C-47, was affectionately known as the "Gooney

Bird.") A few hundred of this venerable aircraft are still logging mileage, thanks to the thoroughness of aircraft PM practices coupled with good design.

Most auto owners do a small amount of PM based on time of usage; examples are oil changes, grease jobs, and tune-ups. The number of recent-model cars in auto graveyards provide mute testimony to the poor job that many of us do in preventively maintaining our cars. In the face of this there is some evidence that applying airplane-style PM to an automobile can yield impressive results: Newspapers a few years ago reported that a taxi owner in Madison, Wisconsin, following a rigorous daily PM regimen, had logged well over 1 million miles on a limousine. This was achieved without body or engine replacement and only one engine overhaul.

The strong commitment to PM for aircraft extends backward to the design of the product. For the military services and private airlines **maintainability** is an important design attribute. Airframe manufacturers try to design maintainability into their aircraft in order to have a chance at government contracts.

A good PM program depends on records. A maintenance history is needed for each piece of equipment. This permits study of breakdown frequency and causes; the findings provide the basis for improving PM procedures. (Lack of a simple maintenance record-keeping system for the auto owner surely contributes to poor auto maintenance. Another factor: Consumers have never made it known to auto manufacturers that they care much about maintainability.)

In some cases a PM program falters because machines are run day and night. The PM people have trouble getting time to check the equipment, tighten, oil, replace components, and so forth. Then machines malfunction and wear out for lack of proper care. A regular daily schedule, such as advanced JIT companies have, can allow regular time periods for PM. This, of course, is especially necessary in a JIT plant in which an equipment breakdown can idle a whole line.

Some companies, Toyota and Ford, for example, go so far as to insert minishifts for preventive maintenance before and after production shifts. Under one such plan there is a four-hour maintenance shift, then an eight-hour production shift, then a four-hour maintenance shift, then an eight-hour production shift, then a four-hour maintenance shift, etc. The companies following this or a similar plan believe they get about the same amount of production in two shifts as they otherwise would in three, because the two production shifts run full blast—no breakdowns. A whole shift of direct labor may be saved; the number of maintenance people may be unchanged, just working different hours.

For all its advantages, PM can be overdone. Preventing all failures is commendable for aircraft, but this is too expensive for most other kinds of equipment; *some* breakdowns must be allowed. Management pays the bills and therefore must make choices as to level of preventive versus repair maintenance. Cost analysis is possible in the case of certain replaceable components: Find the cost of group replacement, which means replacing a whole group of components at periodic intervals, versus the cost to replace as they fail individually. Keeping standby equipment on hand, to be used in case of breakdown of primary equipment, is akin to preventive maintenance. That is, the standby equipment keeps the work going when there is a breakdown. Group-replacement analysis and standby-equipment analysis are considered in the following two sections.

GROUP REPLACEMENT

Replacement (or trade in) of a machine is a capital acquisition problem; the method of analysis (EAC) was discussed in Chapter 14. When to replace machine *components* is a maintenance problem—to be considered here.

For a few kinds of components, replacement is based on wear and tear. Tires are of this type. For most kinds of components, however, sudden failure is a greater problem than wear-out. Examples include electronic components, relays, light bulbs, shoelaces, and to a considerable extent, bearings. Where a number of the same type of component are in use, we should consider group replacement as opposed to replacing individual components as they fail.

Finding the cost of group replacement requires data on the failure pattern for the component.[3] Three examples of a *general* failure probability pattern over component operating life are shown in Figure 16–2. Each represents the failure pattern for a different type of machine or machine system, and a variety of different components of each machine could be the cause of sudden failure.

Three zones are identifiable in the figure. The first is the *infant-mortality zone*. Failure this soon may result from improper assembly or from rough handling or shipping. The probability of infant mortality can sometimes be reduced by preuse or by "burning in" components or the whole machine before shipment. (Our electronics companies often burn in subassemblies for 8, 12, or sometimes 24 hours. A better way is to have the burn in done at the component parts suppliers' plants—"quality at the source." Many electronics companies are beginning to demand this of their suppliers.)

If a component survives the infant-mortality period, the chances of failure tend to be low for a time. Failures occur randomly and for diverse reasons. This is the normal operating period.

After that the component enters the *wear-out zone*. In that zone the probability of failure rises sharply, peaks, and then falls to zero at maximum product life. In both the normal operating period and the wear-out zone, failure probability can sometimes be reduced by operating the product under lower loads or better conditions than it is designed for. This is referred to as "derating" the product—very good practice in a JIT plant where machine failures have chain-reaction effects.

The shape of the curve for a given machine or machine system must be discovered by testing. For a certain component in the machine, a manufacturer or a trade association may do the testing and publish the results. Otherwise the maintenance department may run its own tests. Examples of each source of data follow.

---

[3] Maintenance managers are in need of some understanding of failure patterns but need not know how to calculate failure rates, mean time between failures, and so forth. Those concepts of reliability engineering are important in new-product design.

FIGURE 16–2

Probability of Failure over Operating Life

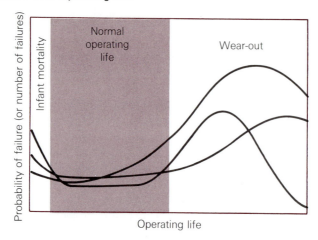

Light-Bulb Example

This example is in two parts. One uses failure data provided by the manufacturer, and the other uses data collected by the firm's maintenance department. In the example we compare two policies on light-bulb replacement. One policy is to allow light bulbs to last as long as they will before replacing them. In this policy a few fail in infant mortality, a few more fail at random for various causes, and the rest (probably the majority) fail in the wear-out zone. The second policy is not to leave bulbs in their sockets long enough for wear-out. Instead, we replace all bulbs at regular intervals (periodic maintenance) when they are part way through their normal life expectancy. It is this second preventive policy, called the group-replacement policy, for which the maintenance manager needs failure-rate data.

EXAMPLE 16–1

Group versus Individual Replacement of Light Bulbs

At present, light bulbs in Building C are replaced as they fail. Whoever notices a failure phones the trouble-call desk, Maintenance Department. The trouble-call dispatcher sends someone to change the light bulb. The average cost: $3.30 per bulb, including labor.

An alternative policy is the preventive one of replacing all Building C bulbs at regular intervals. In the maintenance trade this is known as the group-replacement policy. For Building C the group-replacement policy would cost $1 per bulb, including labor. There are 1,000 light bulbs in Building C. Therefore each group replacement would cost $1,000. What replacement policy is optimal?

Situation A—Failure probabilities known. The operating life for the light bulb is known to have the following probability distribution:

Time until failure	1 mo.	2 mo.	3 mo.	4 mo.	5 mo.
Probability	0.05	0.15	0.20	0.30	0.30

With that probability distribution it is easy to calculate the average life of a light bulb. It is calculated using the expected-value method:

$$\begin{aligned}
\text{Average (expected) life} &= (1 \text{ mo.})(0.05) + (2 \text{ mo.})(0.15) \\
&\quad + (3 \text{ mo.})(0.20) + (4 \text{ mo.})(0.30) \\
&\quad + (5 \text{ mo.})(0.30) \\
&= 0.05 + 0.30 + 0.60 + 1.2 + 1.5 \\
&= 3.65 \text{ months}
\end{aligned}$$

Cost of present policy:

Since there are 1,000 light bulbs in Building C, the number that fail per month is:

$$\frac{1,000 \text{ bulbs}}{3.65 \text{ months average life}} = 274 \text{ bulbs per month}$$

Then the cost of the present replace-as-they-fail policy is:

$$274 \text{ bulbs/mo.} \times \$3.30/\text{bulb} = \$904.20 \text{ per month}$$

Cost of group-replacement policies:

Group replacement every month, every two months, every three months, and so on, are other alternatives. If we replace all 1,000 bulbs as a group at the end of a given period, there are still some failures *during* that period. Those failures must be replaced by the trouble-call process. Thus, the following cost analysis of group-replacement alternatives includes the cost of replacing the bulbs that fail between group-replacement intervals.

If there is a group replacement every month, the costs are:

Group costs: 1,000 bulbs/mo. $\times$ \$1.00/bulb   = \$1,000/mo.
Failure costs: 1,000 bulbs $\times$ 0.05 $\times$ \$3.30/bulb =   165/mo.
                                     Total costs   \$1,165/mo.

If we do a group replacement every two months, the costs are:

Group costs:
  \$1,000 per two months
Failure costs:
  (First month's failures from the original 1,000)(\$3.30)
  + (Second month's failures from the original 1,000)(\$3.30)
  + (Second month's failures from first month's replacements)(\$3.30)
  = [(1,000)(0.05) + (1,000)(0.15) + (1,000)(0.05)][\$3.30]
  = (50 + 150 + 2.5)(\$3.30)
  = (202.5)(\$3.30) = \$668.25 per two months

FIGURE 16–3

Calculating Optimal Group-Replacement Policy for Light Bulbs—Tabular Approach

Replace every . . .	Month: Prob- ability:	Number subject to failure during month					Failures					
		1 0.05	2 0.15	3 0.20	4 0.30	5 0.30	Month	Cumu- lative	Cost @ $3.30	Group cost @ $1	Total cost	Monthly cost
1 month		1,000					50		$ 165	$1,000	$1,165	$1,165
2 months		50	1,000				152	202	667	1,000	1,667	834
3 months		152	50	1,000			215	417	1,376	1,000	2,376	792 ←
4 months		215	152	50	1,000		344	761	2,511	1,000	3,511	878
5 months		344	215	152	50	1,000	395	1,156	3,815	1,000	4,815	963

Total costs:
$1,000 per two months + $668.25 per two months
= $1,668.25 per two months = $834.12 per month

Next, we look at group replacement every three months; then group replacement every four months; and so forth. A table, Figure 16–3, helps simplify the calculations.

Notice that the original quantity, 1,000 bulbs, is entered repeatedly along the diagonal, so that 1,000 appears under each probability; the 50 that fail in month 1 is on the next diagonal; the 152 that fail in month 2 is on the third diagonal; and so forth. Let's examine a sample calculation: In order to find the fourth diagonal value, 215, the calculations are based on failures in the third month: 152(0.05) + 50(0.15) + 1,000(0.20) = 215. Compute the total cost and the monthly cost and then compare the monthly cost with the monthly cost of the previous group-replacement alternative. Stop when the monthly cost bottoms out; it does so for group replacement every three months in this example.

It was shown earlier that the present replace-as-they-fail policy costs $904 per month. Therefore, the optimal policy is group replacement every three months at $792 per month.

Situation B—Failure probabilities unknown. When light-bulb failure data are not given, we need to run an experiment. Place 1,000 sockets in Building C. It is not practical to let the building go dark, so all failures are replaced during the experiment. The following are the experimental results:

Month	1	2	3	4	5	6	7	8	9	10	11	12
Failures during month	46	150	218	360	520	353	387	240	260	330	301	310

It appears that the experiment has been run long enough to achieve a nearly "steady state." That is, all new bulbs put in at the beginning of the year have been replaced, and their replacements have been replaced; the mix of bulbs is now a more uniform mix of ages, and the steady-state failure rate is about 310 per month (a rough average of failures in recent months, e.g., in the last three months). Actually, there is no need to run the experiment long enough to achieve a steady state unless a new type of bulb is being used or the building is new. In an existing building the light-bulb failure rate prior to the experiment would have been steady-state.

Cost of present policy:

The steady-state condition applies to the present replace-as-they-fail policy. Its cost is:

$$310 \text{ bulbs/mo.} \times \$3.30/\text{bulb} = \$1,023 \text{ per month}$$

Cost of group-replacement policy:

The cost of group replacement every month is:

Group cost:	1,000 bulbs × $1.00/bulb = $1,000/mo.
Failure cost:	46 bulbs × $3.30/bulb = 152/mo.
	Total cost $1,152/mo.

The cost of group replacement every two months is:

Group cost:	$1,000/2 mo.
Failure cost:	(46 + 150) × $3.30 = 647/2 mo.
	Total cost $1,647/2 mo.
	= $823/mo.

The cost of group replacement every three months is:

Group cost:	$1,000/3 mo.
Failure cost:	(46 + 150 + 218) × $3.30 = 1,366/3 mo.
	Total cost $2,366/3 mo.
	= $789/mo.

The cost of group replacement every four months is:

Group cost:	$1,000/4 mo.
Failure cost:	(46 + 150 + 218 + 360) × $3.30 = 2,554/4 mo.
	Total cost $3,554/4 mo.
	= $888/mo.

The costs have begun to turn upward; this suggests that we have found the optimum (lowest cost on a U-shaped cost curve). It is $789 per month for group replacement every three months. That beats the $1,023 per month for replacing the bulbs as they fail, so group replacement every three months is the optimum among the policies considered.

The example may suggest that it is better *not* to know the failure probabilities, because the computations are simpler with experimental data collected yourself than when probabilities are provided. The computational advantage is more than offset, however, by the time and cost of collecting experimental data.

Is this all there is to group-replacement analysis? Often not. What about the cost of interruptions for those components that fail? For light bulbs, the cost may be small. If the components were critical, the cost of interruptions would add a new layer of complexity to the problem. Common sense suggests, however, that where failures are costly, group replacement is even more attractive.

Expected-Value Concept

The previous solution method employed the expected-value concept, which deserves further comment. Expected value is a weighted average. It is the sum of all "payoffs" (bulb life was the payoff above) times respective probabilities.[4] The probabilities must add to 1.0, which accounts for all possible payoffs.

The expected-value concept is useful only for probability-distributed input data— and only when records are good enough to yield the probabilities. In maintenance, where breakdowns tend to be probabilistically distributed random events, the expected-value concept is widely applicable. This is especially true since good record keeping on machine failures has become accepted practice in well-run maintenance organizations.[5]

Elsewhere in this book, for the most part, input data are more narrowly distributed, and single-valued estimates (instead of expected values) suffice.[6]

STANDBY EQUIPMENT

Society depends increasingly on technology. We are at the mercy of machines. They break down, and lives are lost, not to mention profits. Sometimes the consequences of breakdowns are severe enough to justify spares. Spares, or standby facilities, provide comforting backup at some price, and they are an alternative to paying for a high level of maintenance in order to reduce the chance of breakdowns.

Machine Failures: The Poisson Distribution

When there are large numbers of identical machines, there is a simplified way to analyze standby policies. The method makes use of our knowledge about patterns

---

[4] Some readers may be aware of an application of the expected-value concept in the behavioral sciences: It is Vroom's expectancy model. In Vroom's model,

$$\text{Motivation} = \Sigma[(\text{Valence})(\text{Expectancy})]$$

One can see that valence is about the same as value or payoff, and expectancy is about the same as probability. Substituting the alternative terms on the right side of the equation, we have $\Sigma[(\text{Payoff})(\text{Probability})]$, which is the general form of the expected-value model.

[5] Thorough discussion of computer automation of this record keeping may be found in J. J. Wilkerson and J. J. Lowe, "A Computerized Maintenance Information System That Works," *Plant Engineering,* March 18, 1971, p. 68.

[6] A point of terminology for those students who have studied decision theory: Use of single-valued estimates is known in decision theory as a condition of assumed certainty; use of probabilistic input data is a condition of assumed risk (or, by some authors, assumed uncertainty).

FIGURE 16–4

Poisson Probability Distribution

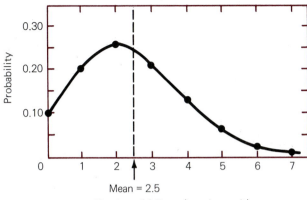

Mean = 2.5

Number of failures (per time unit)

of machine failures. Studies have shown that machine failures per unit of time are random variables that tend to follow the Poisson probability distribution. The shape of the Poisson is based on a mathematical function, and the complete shape can be developed by simply entering the mean number of failures per time unit into the Poisson general formula.

A characteristic shape of the distribution is shown in Figure 16–4. The figure shows that in the Poisson distribution there is some chance of zero failures per time unit (e.g., per day), but of course there can be no chance of negative failure per time unit. Poisson distributions rise to a peak probability and then taper off (are skewed) to the right. There is a 50 percent chance that in the given time period the number of failures will be fewer than the mean (2.5 per time unit in the sketch), and there is also a 50 percent chance that the number of failures will exceed the mean.

Example of Standby-Equipment Analysis

Sometimes the merits of standby equipment may be judged by a cost analysis. The following example illustrates a type of cost analysis that employs the Poisson probability distribution.

EXAMPLE 16–2

Standby "Scopes" and Poisson-Distributed Failures

A large electronics manufacturer does testing with "scopes" at each of 100 assembly and testing stations. When a scope breaks down, testing is halted at one station for one day (the time it takes to get the scope repaired). The company estimates the cost of disruption and idleness at $100 for each day that a scope is down. That cost is $200 if two scopes are down, $300 if three are down, and so forth.

One way to avert the downtime cost is to keep spare scopes on hand. It costs about $50 per day to own and maintain each spare.

If scope breakdowns are random and they average three per day, how many spare scopes should be maintained?

Solution:

The mean number of scope failures is known to be three per day. From that figure, the probabilities of any other number of failures per day can be calculated or can be looked up in a table or graph. The calculations (and the tables and graphs) are based on the Poisson formula.

$$P(n) = \frac{e^{-\lambda}\lambda^{n}}{n!}$$

where

$n =$ Number of failures per time unit
$\lambda =$ Mean number of failures per time period $= 3$ scopes/day
$e = 2.7183$
$P(n) =$ Probability of n failures per time unit

For example, zero scope failures per day has the probability:

$$P(0) = \frac{2.7183^{-3} \times 3^{0}}{0!} = \frac{1}{(1)(2.7183)^{3}} = \frac{1}{(20.086)} = 0.050$$

One scope failure per day has the probability:

$$P(1) = \frac{2.7183^{-3} \times 3^{1}}{1!} = \frac{3}{(1)(20.086)} = 0.150$$

The chapter supplement is an abbreviated table of *cumulative* Poisson probabilities. Find the *individual* probabilities by successive subtraction. For example, in the case of $\lambda = 3$ scopes per day, go to the row where $\lambda = 3.0$. Then, where n = 0, note that P(0) = 0.050. For P(1), find 0.199 in the column where n = 1; subtract 0.050 from 0.199, and get 0.149, which (allowing for rounding error) is the same as the 0.150 that we obtained mathematically. Next, subtract 0.149 from 0.423, and get 0.224, which is P(2); and so forth.

Calculating the optimal number of spare scopes requires a number of steps. The table in Figure 16–5 simplifies the bookkeeping. The calculation procedure in the table follows the expected-value concept. For example, for the first row, zero spares, expected cost of failures is:

$$E_F = \$100(0.150) + \$200(0.224) + \$300(0.224) + \$400(0.168)$$
$$+ \$500(0.101) + \$600(0.050) + \$700(0.022)$$
$$= \$15 + \$44.8 + \$67.2 + \$67.2 + \$50.5 + \$30.0 + \$15.4$$
$$= \$290.10$$

FIGURE 16–5

Calculating Optimal Number of Standby Machines—Tabular Approach

Number of spares	Cost of curtailed scope testing								Daily cost of curtailed testing	Daily cost of spares	Total cost per day
n:	0	1	2	3	4	5	6	7			
P(n):	0.050	0.150	0.224	0.224	0.168	0.101	0.050	0.022			
0	0	$100	$200	$300	$400	$500	$600	$700	$290.10	$ 0	$290.10
1		0	100	200	300	400	500	600	196.20	50	246.20
2			0	100	200	300	400	500	117.30	100	217.30
3				0	100	200	300	400	60.80	150	210.80 ←
4					0	100	200	300	26.70	200	226.70

Calculate each row similarly. Stop when the total cost bottoms out and begins to rise. That identifies the optimal policy; in this case it is to provide three spares at a total cost of $210.80 per day.

The standby method and the group-replacement method have been around for many years, but we should be cautious about their apparent logic. Estimating the cost of downtime is hazardous, and wrong estimates can greatly affect results. Increasingly, companies are simply adopting a principle that downtime is bad. That makes us look more favorably on group replacement and standby equipment.

SUMMARY

Maintenance and cleanliness of work space should be the worker's responsibility to a great extent. If we leave maintenance to outsiders, we get sloppy, never understand our equipment, run it harshly, and have frequent breakdowns. Worker-centered maintenance is especially necessary in a just-in-time plant, where breakdowns are so disruptive. And it is natural to retrain workers to be machine maintainers when robotics and automation are introduced.

A maintenance department usually backs up the worker's efforts. The department may house facilities acquisition, deployment, and disposal as well as maintenance. Maintenance planning centers on choices between periodic and irregular maintenance.

Periodic maintenance ranges from routine custodianship to well-planned preventive maintenance (PM) to group-replacement and standby-equipment policies. Custodianship and PM warrant careful managerial oversight; effective PM also requires good records and time in the schedule to perform it. Group-replacement and standby-equipment decisions usually require cost analysis.

Group replacement may apply to any large group of identical components that fail (rather than wear out). The analyst considers costs of two replacement options. One is replacing components as they fail on a trouble-call basis. The second is replacing all components at periodic intervals, plus trouble-call replacements between periods. Data inputs are: (1) unit costs of each type of replacement and (2) the historical pattern of component lives. The latter may be a failure probability distribution, or actual numbers of failures per time unit as found in a live test may be used.

Standby-equipment analysis also applies to large groups—but groups of machines, not components. Failures of machines (in a group) tend to follow the Poisson probability distribution. If the maintenance manager knows the average number that fail per time period, the probabilities of any other number of failures per time period may be found using Poisson tables or formulas. The probability of any number of out-of-service machines may be multiplied by the cost of lost service. The other cost factor is cost to keep standby machines on hand—to avoid lost service. A minimum-cost standby policy is sought.

REFERENCES

Books

Hildebrand, James K. *Maintenance Turns to the Computer.* Boston: Cahners, 1972 (TS192.H55).

Lewis, Bernard T., and J. P. Marron. *Facilities and Plant Engineering Handbook.* New York: McGraw-Hill, 1973 (TS184.L48).

Mann, Lawrence, Jr. *Maintenance Management.* Lexington, Mass.: Lexington Books, 1976 (TS192.M38).

Murphy, James A., ed. *Plant Engineering Management.* Society of Manufacturing Engineers, 1971 (TS184.P435x).

Periodicals

Plant Engineering, includes plant maintenance.

REVIEW QUESTIONS

1. Who should be responsible for upkeep of machines and work space? Explain.

2. What effect do automation and robotics have on the maintenance function?

3. "If it ain't broke, don't fix it," is a common colloquial phrase. But it is contrary to the PM philosophy. Which is right, and why?

4. What are three keys to a successful PM program?

5. What is the *infant mortality* problem? Do *burn in* or *derating* help with the problem? Explain.

6. Where can you get failure probability data for individual components or products?

7. In group-replacement analysis, group replacement may be every period, every two periods, every three, and so on. Why wouldn't the cost *per period* always be less the longer the interval between replacements?

8. How do you get the average number of failures per day in order to calculate the cost of replacing components as they fail?

9. What are the costs and savings in maintaining standby machines?

10. The Poisson distribution simplifies data analysis in the standby-machine method. Why doesn't Poisson also apply in group-replacement analysis?

PROBLEMS

1. To what extent do commercial semi truck drivers get involved in PM and repairs to their equipment? (You may need to interview someone.) Do you think their involvement is enough?

2. To what extent do copy machine operators get involved in cleaning and maintaining their own machines (clean glass; clean rollers; resupply with fluids, papers, etc.)? in *repairing* their machines? (You may need to interview someone.) Is their involvement adequate?

3. Every maintenance *operation* requires facilities *planning* (see Figure 16–1). A number of maintenance operations are listed below:

> Replace ceramic tiles in a floor.
>
> Mop floors.
>
> Repair power outage.
>
> Change oil and grease equipment.
>
> Change dies—simply unscrew dirty one and screw on clean one—as they randomly clog up (in a factory full of plastics extrusion lines, each with a die to form the plastic).
>
> Replace drive belts, bearings, and so on, as they fail (among large group of various machines on factory floor).
>
> Repaint walls.
>
> Maintain spare motors for bank of spinning machines.
>
> Remodel president's office.
>
> Repair shoes (shoe repair shop).

Your assignment is (1) to name one or more analysis techniques (if there are any) that apply to each maintenance operation and (2) to list the data inputs necessary to conduct the analysis. (Note: Some of the analysis methods were presented in Chapters 14 and 15.) Three completed examples follow:

Maintenance operation	Analysis technique	Data inputs
Rearrange office equipment	Layout analysis (Chapter 15)	Flow data (types and volume) Relationship data
Replace old lathe with new one	Replacement analysis (Chapter 14)	Purchase price O&M cost Salvage (trade-in) value
Prepare platform with utility hookups for new equipment	None	

4. With computers (microprocessors) now in common use as automobile control devices, perhaps the same computers or other computers could serve a preventive maintenance purpose. A dash panel could be used to input into a computer every maintenance operation performed on the car, and mileage data could be entered into the computer automatically. A screen could then recommend preventive maintenance whenever a program determines a need.

   a. How practical do you think this idea is *right now?* What are some obstacles in the way of implementing such a PM system?
   b. What are some important items of historical data that would need to be programmed into the auto's computer? Where would such data come from? Explain.
   c. Large numbers of nearly identical autos are sold, which provides a sizable potential data base for gathering failure and wear-out data. For almost any type of factory machine there is not so large a potential data base, that is, there are far fewer "copies" of the same machine. Yet good factory PM is based on good failure records. How can good records be developed for factory machines?

5. Think of three consumer products that advertisers tout as being especially *maintainable.* Distinguish between the maintainability and the reliability of each of those products.

6. Name two industries in which maintainability is especially important. Especially unimportant. Discuss. What can a maintenance manager do about the maintainability of the facilities in his firm?

7. Diodes in a process control system have the following failure distribution:

Operating hours:	500	1,000	1,500	2,000
Probability of failure:	0.25	0.20	0.20	0.35

The diodes cost $0.10 each, and there are 100 of them. Labor to replace a single diode is $4.90, but it is only $0.90 if all 100 are replaced at one time.

   a. What is the expected operating life of a diode?
   b. For a maintenance policy of replacing the diodes as they fail, what is the replacement cost per 1,000 operating hours?
   c. Calculate the optimal group-replacement policy; assume that any failures between group replacements must be replaced immediately. Is the optimal group-replacement policy superior to the replace-as-they-fail policy?
   d. What important factors have *not* been included in the above analysis?

8. Same as problem 7, except for the following changes: The diodes cost $1.10 each, and there are 50 of them; failures between group replacements need not be replaced.

9. There are 50 filter traps in the cooling system of a nuclear power plant. Monitor lights warn an attendant when a filter clogs up, and the attendant alerts the maintenance department. It costs $100 in labor and downtime to remove plates and clean out the filter. Maintenance can remove plates and clean out all 50 filters at the same time for a labor-and-downtime cost of $800.

    The maintenance department has collected some experimental data on filter-clogging frequencies. The experiment began with 50 clean traps and ran for 6,000 hours. Results are:

Operating hours:	1,000	2,000	3,000	4,000	5,000	6,000
Number of clogged filters replaced during period:	1	3	5	6	6	6

    What is the optimal maintenance policy?

10. A refinery has 50 identical pumps installed in various places. Replacing the seal in the pump motor is a delicate task requiring a visit from a maintenance engineer of the pump company, which is situated in another city. The cost of the trip is $200. The cost of replacing one seal is $20.

    a. The refinery has used the 50 pumps for ten quarters (2½ years), which is the time that the plant has been in service. Pump seals have been replaced as they failed. The following is the failure history for the ten quarters.

Quarter	1	2	3	4	5	6	7	8	9	10
Seal failures	0	1	1	2	3	3	2	4	3	3

    Analyze the merits of a group-replacement policy.

    b. The pump company's engineers estimate the following probability distribution for the operating life of the pump seal.

Time until failure	1 qtr.	2 qtr.	3 qtr.	4 qtr.	5 qtr.	6 qtr.	7 qtr.	8 qtr.	3 yr.	4 yr.	5 yr.
Probability	0.0	0.01	0.02	0.02	0.02	0.04	0.04	0.05	0.25	0.30	0.25

    Analyze the merits of a group-replacement policy, using the probability data.

    c. Which results should be used—those of part *a* or those of part *b*? Or doesn't it make any difference? Explain.

11. Duncan Aviation maintains a fleet of Lear jets. The fleet requires 30 identical jet engines installed in the planes. Spare engines are ready to go at Duncan's hangers in case of malfunction of an engine in one of the planes. The spares cost $500 a week to keep on hand. If a plane is idled for lack of a good engine, the cost (lost net revenue) is about

$2,000 per week. If an average of two engines per week fail, what is the correct number of spares?

12. A refinery has 50 identical pumps installed in various places. When a pump fails, the product flow rate drops, but the refining continues. The estimated average cost of reduced flow rate when a pump is down is $1,000 per day. If a spare pump is on hand when one goes down, the spare can be installed quickly enough so that flow-rate losses are negligible. It costs $60 per day to own and maintain one spare pump. The maintenance manager estimates that one pump per day fails on the average. How many spare pumps should be maintained?

13. Here are three situations where standby-machine analysis *might* be used. Comment on the suitability of standby analysis in each case.

   Case 1. Spare fluorescent tubes in case one burns out in an auditorium.

   Case 2. Spare memory cards (identical ones) in case one fails in one of a large number of microcomputers used in an electronic test equipment center.

   Case 3. Spare pizza ovens in case one (of many) fails in a large take-out/eat-in pizza place.

14. Hewlett-Packard pays its janitors, guards, and food service people the same wage as its product assembly people. Yet the product assembly people have higher status. At one H-P division the division manager intends to begin rotating assembly people into the lower-status positions and vice versa. But he wonders how the assemblers will react when asked to "push a broom."

   From what you have learned about responsibility for maintenance, do you think this rotation plan is a step in the right direction? Explain. What else might be done?

15. Captain Henry Harrison has spent much of his career in Navy shipyards. In the last 10 years he has held three positions of authority over shops building and repairing ships. He has been a firm believer in conducting frequent inspections of shop facilities and is a stickler for having everything neat, clean, and painted. Some people think Captain Harrison spends too much time on this. What do you think?

Supplement to Chapter 16
The Poisson Distribution—Cumulative Probabilities

The Poisson Distribution—Cumulative Probabilities

λ	P										
	0	1	2	3	4	5	6	7	8	9	10
0.02	0.980	1.000									
0.04	0.961	0.999	1.000								
0.06	0.942	0.998	1.000								
0.08	0.923	0.997	1.000								
0.10	0.905	0.995	1.000								
0.15	0.861	0.990	0.999	1.000							
0.20	0.819	0.982	0.999	1.000							
0.25	0.779	0.974	0.998	1.000							
0.30	0.741	0.963	0.996	1.000							
0.35	0.705	0.951	0.994	1.000							
0.40	0.670	0.938	0.992	0.999	1.000						
0.45	0.638	0.925	0.989	0.999	1.000						
0.50	0.607	0.910	0.986	0.998	1.000						

λ	0	1	2	3	4	5	6	7	8	9	10
						P					
0.55	0.577	0.894	0.982	0.998	1.000						
0.60	0.549	0.878	0.977	0.997	1.000						
0.65	0.522	0.861	0.972	0.996	0.999	1.000					
0.70	0.497	0.844	0.966	0.994	0.999	1.000					
0.75	0.472	0.827	0.959	0.993	0.999	1.000					
0.80	0.449	0.809	0.953	0.991	0.999	1.000					
0.85	0.427	0.791	0.945	0.989	0.998	1.000					
0.90	0.407	0.772	0.937	0.987	0.998	1.000					
0.95	0.387	0.754	0.929	0.984	0.997	1.000					
1.00	0.368	0.736	0.920	0.981	0.996	0.999	1.000				
1.1	0.333	0.699	0.900	0.974	0.995	0.999	1.000				
1.2	0.301	0.663	0.879	0.966	0.992	0.998	1.000				
1.3	0.273	0.627	0.857	0.957	0.989	0.998	1.000				
1.4	0.247	0.592	0.833	0.946	0.986	0.997	0.999	1.000			
1.5	0.223	0.558	0.809	0.934	0.981	0.996	0.999	1.000			
1.6	0.202	0.525	0.783	0.921	0.976	0.994	0.999	1.000			
1.7	0.183	0.493	0.757	0.907	0.970	0.992	0.998	1.000			
1.8	0.165	0.463	0.731	0.891	0.964	0.990	0.997	0.999	1.000		
1.9	0.150	0.434	0.704	0.875	0.956	0.987	0.997	0.999	1.000		
2.0	0.135	0.406	0.677	0.857	0.947	0.983	0.995	0.999	1.000		
2.2	0.111	0.355	0.623	0.819	0.928	0.975	0.993	0.998	1.000		
2.4	0.091	0.308	0.570	0.779	0.904	0.964	0.988	0.997	0.999	1.000	
2.6	0.074	0.267	0.518	0.736	0.877	0.951	0.983	0.995	0.999	1.000	
2.8	0.061	0.231	0.469	0.692	0.848	0.935	0.976	0.992	0.998	0.999	1.000
3.0	0.050	0.199	0.423	0.647	0.815	0.916	0.966	0.988	0.996	0.999	1.000
3.2	0.041	0.171	0.380	0.603	0.781	0.895	0.955	0.983	0.994	0.998	1.000
3.4	0.033	0.147	0.340	0.558	0.744	0.871	0.942	0.977	0.992	0.997	0.999
3.6	0.027	0.126	0.303	0.515	0.706	0.844	0.927	0.969	0.988	0.996	0.999
3.8	0.022	0.107	0.269	0.473	0.668	0.816	0.909	0.960	0.984	0.994	0.998
4.0	0.018	0.092	0.238	0.433	0.629	0.785	0.889	0.949	0.979	0.992	0.997
4.2	0.015	0.078	0.210	0.395	0.590	0.753	0.867	0.936	0.972	0.989	0.996
4.4	0.012	0.066	0.185	0.359	0.551	0.720	0.844	0.921	0.964	0.985	0.994
4.6	0.010	0.056	0.163	0.326	0.513	0.686	0.818	0.905	0.955	0.980	0.992
4.8	0.008	0.048	0.143	0.294	0.476	0.651	0.791	0.887	0.944	0.975	0.990
5.0	0.007	0.040	0.125	0.265	0.440	0.616	0.762	0.867	0.932	0.968	9.986
5.2	0.006	0.034	0.109	0.238	0.406	0.581	0.732	0.845	0.918	0.960	0.982
5.4	0.005	0.029	0.095	0.213	0.373	0.546	0.702	0.822	0.903	0.951	0.977
5.6	0.004	0.024	0.082	0.191	0.342	0.512	0.670	0.797	0.886	0.941	0.972
5.8	0.003	0.021	0.072	0.170	0.313	0.478	0.638	0.771	0.867	0.929	0.965
6.0	0.002	0.017	0.062	0.151	0.285	0.446	0.606	0.744	0.847	0.916	0.957
6.2	0.002	0.015	0.054	0.134	0.259	0.414	0.574	0.716	0.826	0.902	0.949
6.4	0.002	0.012	0.046	0.119	0.235	0.384	0.542	0.687	0.803	0.886	0.939
6.6	0.001	0.010	0.040	0.105	0.213	0.355	0.511	0.658	0.780	0.869	0.927
6.8	0.001	0.009	0.034	0.093	0.192	0.327	0.480	0.628	0.755	0.850	0.915
7.0	0.001	0.007	0.030	0.082	0.173	0.301	0.450	0.599	0.729	0.830	0.901
8.0	0.000	0.003	0.014	0.043	0.100	0.192	0.314	0.454	0.594	0.718	0.817
9.0	0.000	0.001	0.006	0.021	0.055	0.116	0.207	0.324	0.456	0.588	0.707
10.0	0.000	0.000	0.002	0.009	0.028	0.066	0.129	0.219	0.332	0.457	0.582

Chapter 17

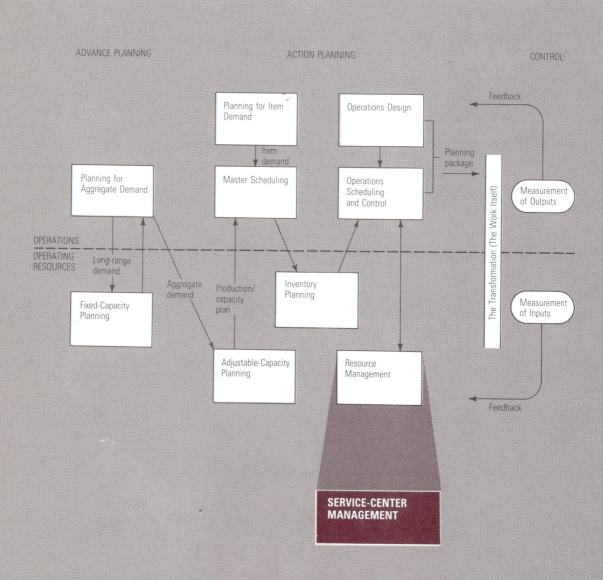

ADVANCE PLANNING   ACTION PLANNING   CONTROL

Planning for Item Demand

Operations Design

Feedback

Planning for Aggregate Demand

Master Scheduling

Operations Scheduling and Control

Planning package

Measurement of Outputs

Item demand

OPERATIONS

OPERATING RESOURCES

Long-range demand

Aggregate demand

Production/ capacity plan

Inventory Planning

The Transformation (The Work Itself)

Measurement of Inputs

Fixed-Capacity Planning

Adjustable-Capacity Planning

Resource Management

Feedback

SERVICE-CENTER MANAGEMENT

Service-Center Management and Waiting Lines

Service centers are everywhere: grocery checkout areas, copying centers, tax-advice offices, highway toll facilities, the college registrar, ticket takers, taxi dispatchers, hotel desks, hospitals. These service centers seem so different. Yet they all have two dominant problems: (1) Waiting lines, (2) Idleness of servers.

A waiting line of customers or documents (e.g., papers awaiting copying) is like raw materials waiting their turn on a machine. They add lead time and carrying charges, and they delay service to the customer. We want to streamline services just as we want to streamline the flow of goods through a factory.

It would be easy to run a service center if the customers arrived at regular intervals. Sometimes we coax the customers into regular-interval arrivals by the appointment system, but running such a system has a cost. Also, appointment systems are imperfect: Customers sometimes miss appointments.

Most services are not offered by appointment. Therefore arrivals are irregular, and we must have enough service-center capacity to keep the lines from gettting too long. Since customers bunch up, it takes a lot of capacity to serve them. Then when customer arrivals slack off, there is the cost of idle servers.

WAITING LINES AND ROLLER-COASTER WORKLOADS

The workload pattern that must be handled in the service center may be likened to a roller coaster. Figure 17–1 graphically indicates how the roller-coaster pattern may

FIGURE 17–1

Roller-Coaster Workloads

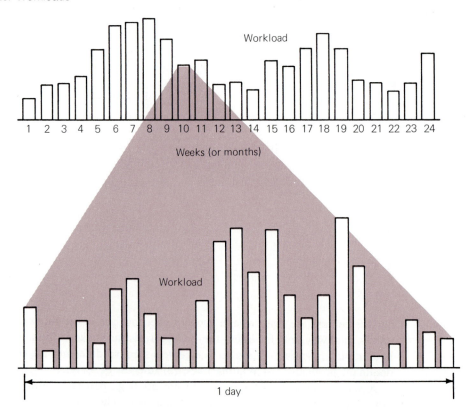

apply from week to week or from month to month (top panel). And on any given day of one of the weeks or months the workload may show a roller-coaster pattern' from hour to hour (or more often).

Waiting Lines

Managing service centers involves all of the usual methods of planning and controlling operating resources. And, as has been noted, the service-center manager also must be greatly concerned about waiting lines. Some basic notions about waiting lines follow.

Channels and Stages.   A waiting line may be simple, involving only one server (or channel) and one stage of service. A single stoplight on the main highway through a very small village acts as such a server (serving to regulate traffic flow). If the village were to grow and install more stoplights on the highway, autos would pass through what is called a multistage waiting line; each light is a stage. Autos may also encounter what is known as multichannel (or multiserver) waiting-line situation: An example is a toll station with several lanes that the driver may choose from. The lanes are channels, each offering the same service (taking tolls). Students registering and paying for classes may pass through a multichannel, multistage waiting line: A student enters one of the registration lines and completes registration; then gets into one of the lines for payment of fees. (On some campuses computer-assisted registration has managed to wipe out some of the queuing.)

These four types of service facilities and waiting-line patterns are sketched in Figure 17–2. The types of waiting lines are: single-channel, single-stage; single-channel, multistage; multichannel, single-stage; and multichannel, multistage. Distinguishing among the four types is necessary in **queuing analysis,** because there are mathematical formulas for each of the four. The analysis begins with determining which type applies so that the right formula is used. The four types are not so important in **simulation** of waiting lines, which can be applied to many combinations of arrival, waiting, and service patterns.

Timing.   In the operation of a service facility customers or jobs arrive, wait in line for a time (a time of zero if the line is empty), receive service, and leave. Two timing factors are the frequency distribution of arrivals and the frequency distribution of service times.

The simplest case is that in which arrivals are evenly spaced and service times are constant. If the evenly spaced arrivals are more frequent than the constant serving rate, the system is unstable. The customer flow must slow down or the service must speed up; otherwise the waiting line grows without limit (instability). If the arrivals are less frequent than the service rate, the system is stable, with zero customer waiting time. The service facility will, however, be idle some of the time: Merely subtract the constant service time from the constant time between arrivals to get the time of idleness per cycle.

FIGURE 17–2

Service Facilities and Waiting-Line Patterns

A. Single channel, single stage

B. Single channel, multistage

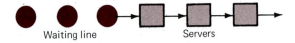

C. Multichannel, single stage

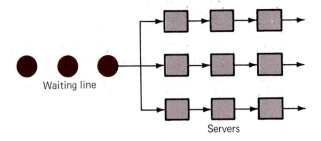

D. Multichannel, multistage

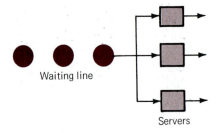

Usually arrivals are not evenly spaced and service times are not constant. In such cases it is no longer so simple to determine customer waiting and service-facility idleness. Mathematical queuing formulas and waiting-line simulation methods have been developed for such problems.

Another timing factor is hours of operation. If the facility operates all of the time, there are no start-up and shutdown conditions to study. The facility moves toward a **steady state.** In a steady-state condition the average waiting line no longer changes (but the waiting line varies around that average).

Some facilities that run for awhile and then shut down never go long enough to achieve steady state. Others do. A production line, for example, may begin the day with all machines empty, but in a short time the factory is humming and waiting lines before each machine have come up to some average state—the steady state.

When human customers rather than production job orders are in the waiting lines, the concept of steady-state operation is more complicated. Arrival rates of customers for food service, copier service, entertainment, and so forth, seem to change all the time. We may divide mealtimes into 15-minute periods and look for a different set of steady-state variables (waiting lines and service-facility idleness) for each of the periods. But it is very costly to collect, analyze, and make and implement decisions for the large number of cases that result from so fine a time division.

A final timing factor is human reaction to waiting lines. Some customers *balk* at entering a waiting line that seems too long, and some *renege* or leave a line that is moving too slowly. The server's reaction to a long line is often to speed up, and the server's reaction to a short or empty line is often to slow down. These tendencies make the study of waiting lines still more difficult.

For all the difficulties, waiting lines must be studied. They are all around us, and if not well managed they are a drain on resources—the customer's waiting time and the service facility's idle time. Mathematical queuing formulas and simulation offer some help in waiting-line analysis. Each is discussed in some depth.

QUEUING FORMULAS

A simple, precise way to run a waiting-line study is to use queuing formulas. The formulas are simple in that most require only two inputs:

1. Mean arrival rate in units arriving per time period; the Greek letter *lambda,* λ, is the symbol.
2. Mean service rate in units served per time period; the Greek letter *mu,* μ, is the symbol.

Queuing formulas have been developed for each of the four queuing patterns shown in Figure 17–2. We examine only the first of the four patterns—single channel, single stage. A few queuing formulas for that pattern are given in Figure 17–3.

Formulas Depending on Means Only

The top two formulas in the figure are for computing the percent of time that the service facility is busy (left formula) and idle (right formula). Percent of time busy, known as **utilization rate,** is the mean arrival rate, λ, divided by the mean service rate, μ. When the server (service facility) is not busy, it is idle. The **idleness rate** is 1 minus the utilization rate, λ/μ. For example, if customers arrive at a mean

FIGURE 17–3

Queuing Formulas for a Single-Channel, Single-Stage Service Facility

Not dependent on probability distributions

Utilization of server: Idleness of server

$$U = \frac{\lambda}{\mu}$$

$$I = 1 - \frac{\lambda}{\mu}$$

Poisson-distributed arrival rate and service rate

Mean waiting time in queue: Mean time in system (in-queue + in-service):

$$T_q = \frac{\lambda}{\mu(\mu - \lambda)}$$

$$T_s = \frac{1}{\mu - \lambda}$$

Mean number in queue: Mean number in system (in-queue + in-service):

$$N_q = \frac{\lambda^2}{\mu(\mu - \lambda)}$$

$$N_s = \frac{\lambda}{\mu - \lambda}$$

Probability of *n* customers in system (in-queue + in-service):

$$P_n = \left(1 - \frac{\lambda}{\mu}\right)\left(\frac{\lambda}{\mu}\right)^n$$

Poisson-distributed arrival rate and constant (c) service rate

Mean waiting time in queue: Mean number in queue:

$$T_q(c) = \frac{\lambda}{2\mu(\mu - \lambda)}$$

$$N_q(c) = \frac{\lambda^2}{2\mu(\mu - \lambda)}$$

λ = Greek letter *lambda,* standing for mean arrival rate in number of arrivals per time unit
μ = Greek letter *mu,* standing for mean service rate in number of customers served per time unit

rate of eight per hour, and the service facility can serve them at a mean rate of ten per hour, utilization rate and idleness rate are:

$$U = \frac{\lambda}{\mu} = \frac{8}{10} = 0.8, \text{ or } 80\%$$

$$I = 1 - \frac{\lambda}{\mu} = 1 - 0.8 = 0.2, \text{ or } 20\%$$

Rate of service, μ, means rate of service *when customers are there.* It is the standard production rate. We are not concerned about whether the rate is based on an engineered or a nonengineered time standard. (See discussion of time standards and their reciprocal, standard production or output rates, in Chapter 13.) But some timing method is necessary to find out what μ is. A simple way is to use a wristwatch to time a few customer-service cycles and average the times; we divide the result, the average time per customer, into 1.0 to yield mean (average) customers per time unit, μ.

For example, suppose that service times for six customers are 5, 7, 5, 6, 4, and 9 minutes. The average is:

$$\frac{5+7+5+6+4+9}{6} = \frac{36}{6} = 6 \text{ minutes per customer}$$

Then, mean service rate is:

$$\mu = \frac{1}{6.0 \text{ min./customer}} \times \frac{60 \text{ min.}}{1 \text{ hr.}} = 10 \text{ customers per hour}$$

Rate of arrivals, λ, is simply a count of number of arrivals divided by the time over which they are counted. For example, suppose that a three-hour study is taken of customer arrivals and that 24 customers are counted. The mean rate of arrivals is:

$$\lambda = \frac{24 \text{ customers}}{3 \text{ hours}} = 8 \text{ customers per hour}$$

Utilization and idleness rates are based only on the means, λ and μ. The pattern of variability distribution around the means makes no difference. The formulas apply for any (or no) variability pattern or distribution. Not so for the formulas discussed next.

Formulas Using Poisson-Distributed Arrival and Service Rates

The second group of queuing formulas in Figure 17–3 is also solved using only λ and μ. But the results are true only if variability patterns about the means form a particular probability distribution: the Poisson distribution.[1]

The first formula in the group shows how to calculate mean queue time, T_q. The second is for mean time in the system, T_s, which includes both queue time and service time. If customers arrive at a mean rate of eight per hour and they can be served at a mean rate of 10 per hour, then

$$T_q = \frac{\lambda}{\mu(\mu-1)} = \frac{8}{10(10-8)} = \frac{8}{(10)(2)} = \frac{8}{20}$$

$$= 0.4 \text{ hour, or 24 minutes waiting time per customer}$$

$$T_s = \frac{1}{\mu-\lambda} = \frac{1}{(10-8)} = \frac{1}{2}$$

$$= 0.5 \text{ hour, or 30 minutes in the system per customer}$$

---

[1] It is usually stated that arrival-*rate* distribution must be Poisson and that service-*time* distribution must be exponential. However, an exponential probability distribution of service times (times to serve customers) transforms into a Poisson probability distribution of service rates (number of customers served per time period—when the facility is busy). Since the queuing formulas use mean rates rather than mean times, the exponential distribution of times need not be discussed here.

The second two formulas in the group are for calculating mean number in the queue, N_q, and mean number in the system, N_s. Again for $\lambda = 8$ and $\mu = 10$,

$$N_q = \frac{\lambda^2}{\mu(\mu - \lambda)} = \frac{8^2}{(10)(10 - 8)} = \frac{64}{(10)(2)} = \frac{64}{20}$$
$$= 3.2 \text{ customers waiting}$$

$$N_s = \frac{\lambda}{\mu - \lambda} = \frac{8}{10 - 8} = \frac{8}{2}$$
$$= 4 \text{ customers in the system}$$

The last formula in the second group is for calculating the probability, P_n, of any given number, n, of customers in the system. For example, the probability of four customers in the system of $\lambda = 8$, $\mu = 10$ is:

$$P_n = \left(1 - \frac{\lambda}{\mu}\right)\left(\frac{\lambda}{\mu}\right)^n$$

$$P_4 = \left(1 - \frac{8}{10}\right)\left(\frac{8}{10}\right)^4 = (1 - 0.8)(0.8)^4 = (0.2)(0.410)$$
$$= 0.082, \text{ or } 8.2\%$$

We know from the earlier calculation of N_s that 4 is the mean number of customers in the system, but the probability that there will be exactly four customers is just 0.082.

Formulas Using Poisson-Distributed Arrival Rates and Constant Service Rates

Two formulas are given in the figure for the case of Poisson arrival rates with constant service rates. The first is for mean waiting time, $T_q(c)$, and the second is for mean number in the queue, $N_q(c)$. Constant service rates are increasingly likely as more services become mechanized in our society. For $\lambda = 8$ and $\mu = 10$,

$$T_q(c) = \frac{\lambda}{2\mu(\mu - \lambda)} = \frac{8}{(2)(10)(10 - 8)} = \frac{8}{(20)(2)} = \frac{8}{40}$$
$$= 0.2 \text{ hour, or 12 minutes per customer}$$

$$N_q(c) = \frac{\lambda^2}{2\mu(\mu - \lambda)} = \frac{8^2}{(2)(10)(10 - 8)} = \frac{64}{40}$$
$$= 1.6 \text{ customers waiting}$$

Imposing a constant service rate makes a big difference. T_q and N_q for Poisson arrival and service rates were calculated earlier as 24 minutes waiting time and 3.2 customers waiting. Those figures are twice as large as $T_q(c)$ and $N_q(c)$. A constant service time reduces waits a great deal (but it does not eliminate them as long as arrivals are variable).

A Queuing Example

The simplicity and power of the queuing formulas, as well as some of their limitations, are brought out in the following example.

EXAMPLE 17–1

Queuing for Plumbing Service

At present the plumbing breakdown crew can easily handle plumbing trouble calls. The logbook shows that trouble calls come in on an average of one call every 100 minutes; thus the mean arrival rate, λ, is 1/100 or 0.01 calls per minute. The dispatcher's logbook also shows that the average plumbing repair takes 33 minutes; that is a mean service rate, μ, of 1/33, or 0.03 repairs per minute. Thus, the service rate, 0.03, is three times as fast as the arrival rate, 0.01.

This is good service, but it means that the crew is busy only one third of the time. That should be obvious, but for those who like formulas, there is one for calculating "busyness" or utilization rate for a service facility—the repair crew in this case.

$$\text{Utilization rate} = \frac{\lambda}{\mu} = \frac{0.01}{0.03} = 0.33, \text{ or } 1/3$$

The plumbing repair crew is really not idle the other 67 percent of the time. It has some shop cleanup and tool upkeep work to do between trouble calls. But should well-paid journeyman plumbers be sweeping floors and honing tools? The maintenance manager does not think so. (Is he right?)

The maintenance manager wants to reduce the plumbing crew size so that things are reversed; that is, his object is to keep the crew busy 67 percent of the time and "idle" only 33 percent of the time. He sees that all he has to do is cut the crew size in half, thereby doubling service time. This halves the wage expense. The manager feels that the change should hardly affect service since mean service rate would still be 50 percent faster than mean arrival rate, which may be proven by using an inversion of the utilization-rate formula.

Since utilization rate, U, $= \lambda/\mu$, then $\mu = \lambda/U$. Since $\lambda = 0.01$ and desired utilization rate, U, $= 0.67$.

$$\mu = \frac{\lambda}{U} = \frac{0.01}{0.67} = 0.015$$

As the manager thought, mean service rate, μ, at 0.015, is 50 percent faster than mean arrival rate, λ, at 0.01.

Is the maintenance manager correct in believing that service would hardly be affected? Further use of queuing formulas may help to answer the question.

Solution:

Service responsiveness to trouble calls may be measured by average trouble-call waiting time, which is the mean time that trouble-call orders sit on the dispatcher's desk waiting, in queue, for a plumbing crew to return from previous trouble-call work. Service also may be measured by the average number of jobs waiting in the queue.

The manager may compute average (mean) time in queue, T_q, and average (mean) number in queue, N_q. The formulas are:

$$T_q = \frac{\lambda}{\mu(\mu - \lambda)} \qquad N_q = \frac{\lambda^2}{\mu(\mu - \lambda)}$$

For the present size of plumbing crew, $\lambda = 0.01$ trouble calls per minute and $\mu = 0.03$ repairs per minute. Therefore,

$$\text{Mean time in queue} = T_q = \frac{\lambda}{\mu(\mu - \lambda)}$$
$$= \frac{0.01}{(0.03)(0.03 - 0.01)}$$
$$= \frac{0.01}{(0.03)(0.02)} = \frac{0.01}{0.0006} = 16.67 \text{ minutes per job}$$

$$\text{Mean number in queue} = N_q = \frac{\lambda^2}{\mu(\mu - \lambda)}$$
$$= \frac{(0.01)^2}{(0.03)(0.03 - 0.01)}$$
$$= \frac{0.0001}{0.0006} = 0.17 \text{ jobs}$$

The manager wants to cut crew size in half, which cuts service rate, μ, from 0.03 to 0.015. Arrival rate, λ, stays at 0.01. For this proposed level of staffing,

$$\text{Mean time in queue} = T_q = \frac{\lambda}{\mu(\mu - \lambda)}$$
$$= \frac{0.01}{(0.015)(0.015 - 0.01)}$$
$$= \frac{0.01}{(0.015)(0.005)}$$
$$= \frac{0.01}{0.000075} = 133.33 \text{ minutes per job}$$

$$\text{Mean number in queue} = N_q = \frac{\lambda^2}{\mu(\mu - \lambda)}$$
$$= \frac{(0.01)^2}{(0.015)(0.015 - 0.01)}$$
$$= \frac{0.0001}{0.000075} = 1.33 \text{ jobs}$$

Now the manager may compare service levels. Cutting the crew size in half increases mean waiting time from $T_q = 16.67$ minutes per job to $T_q = 133.33$ minutes per job. This is an eightfold increase in waiting time, a large deterioration in service. At the same time mean number of plumbing jobs waiting for a crew goes up from $N_q = 0.17$ jobs to $N_q = 1.33$ jobs, which is also an eightfold increase. The maintenance manager believed that cutting crew size in half would have little effect on service. The queuing analysis proves him wrong.

The analysis need not stop here. Even though service worsens when plumbing crews are cut, the wage reduction may justify proceeding with the cut. In some waiting-line problems a cost may be placed on waiting time, and the sum of waiting-time cost and repair-crew wages can be compared for each size of crew. (This type of cost analysis is presented later in a waiting-line simulation example.) The costs of waiting for a plumbing crew are hard to estimate, however. The maintenance manager probably is stuck with the need to weigh service-*time* data and wage-*cost* data, since study results do not condense easily into straight cost data.

Queuing Requirements

The previous problem shows the efficiency of queuing formulas: The casual observer sees a jumble of job arrivals, queue variability, and service-time variability; yet a few trivial calculations reduce it all to easy-to-comprehend responsiveness statistics. And it is not only the calculations that are simple. There are but two items of input data: λ and μ. We may pull sample cases from a dispatcher's logbook to compute the values of λ and μ. These means may be computed based on sample cases from a dispatcher's logbook.

For all this efficiency there are two major requirements or limitations in queuing formulas. One is the Poisson probability distribution requisite; it was mentioned earlier, but it merits further discussion.

Are plumbing trouble calls and service rates sufficiently Poisson for the above solution to be valid? The trouble calls probably are. "Natural" arrival rates, such as "arrival" of breakdowns of mechanical devices, are most likely to follow the idealized Poisson distribution. Anytime people get into the act, their habits and proclivities tend to distort the natural Poisson pattern: *balking* at entering a long queue and *reneging* or leaving a queue that is moving too slowly. But potential trouble spots for plumbing breakdowns are wash basins, sewer systems, water pipes, and so forth. These are mechanical entities; there is little human distortion and so the breakdown frequencies are largely Poisson.

Plumbing service-rate distributions seem more subject to distorting human influences. The natural Poisson shape, shown in Figure 17–4A, has a tail extending (skewed) far to the right. But the plumbers would feel pressure not to allow the tail to go so far. That is, during a very time-consuming plumbing repair a queue of other trouble calls may form. The dispatcher may then put pressure on the plumbers to get done and move on to the next case. Most of us are quite capable of working far faster than we normally do, at least for short spurts of time. That is what the plumbers are likely to do in response to queuing pressure. The distribution is no longer perfect Poisson but is crunched from the left, as in Figure 17–4B.

FIGURE 17–4

Distortions of Service-Rate Distributions

A.

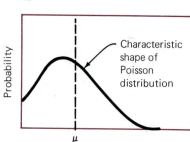

Characteristic shape of Poisson distribution

Probability

μ

Number of repairs completed per time unit

B.

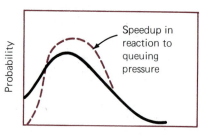

Speedup in reaction to queuing pressure

Probability

Number of repairs completed per time unit

C.

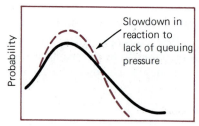

Slowdown in reaction to lack of queuing pressure

Probability

Number of repairs completed per time unit

D.

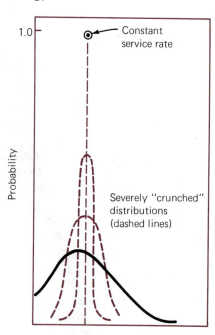

1.0

Constant service rate

Probability

Severely "crunched" distributions (dashed lines)

Number of repairs completed per time unit

There may be an opposite reaction to opposite conditions. Say that the plumbers are on a minor job and know that there are no backlogged trouble calls. Their reaction might be to stretch out the job. (Stretching out work to fill the available time is a phenomenon popularly—or unpopularly—known as Parkinson's Law.) The Poisson curve becomes crunched from the right, as in Figure 17–4C.

Figure 17–4D shows the effect of crunching on both the right and the left. With the stretching out of short jobs and the compressing of long jobs, the distribution narrows and grows taller. The limit is where distribution (variability) disappears and gives way to a constant service rate. That rate is the single circled point, with probability equal to 1.0.

When dealing with humans—customers, servers, or both—queuing formulas clearly will give inaccurate results. Even so, it can be argued that the queuing calculations can be helpful. They show the *limit* on queue length and waiting time.

For example, in a travel agent's office, if customers arrive at a mean of two per hour, and the agent can handle a mean of three per hour, the mean waiting time by queuing formula is:

$$T_q = \lambda/[\mu(\mu - \lambda)] = 2/[3\,(3 - 2)]$$
$$= 0.67 \text{ hours or } 40 \text{ minutes}$$

Of course, some customers will wait for awhile and then renege, or will not wait at all (balk). Therefore, the agent should expect that mean waiting time will be *less than* 40 minutes (probably a good deal less). If the travel agent could speed up the mean serving rate to four per hour—say, by adding a word processor—then the mean waiting-time computation is:

$$T_q = 2/[4\,(4 - 2)] = 0.25 \text{ or } 15 \text{ minutes}$$

Now the agent should expect mean waiting time to be less than 15 minutes—since the calculated time of 15 minutes is an upper limit. This is much better service. While neither 40 minutes nor 15 minutes is accurate, the queuing results show a large improvement in service when the word processor is used. This may be enough to convince the agent to buy the word processor.

A second limitation of queuing formulas is that they be based on a steady-state condition. A repair system may close down at the end of the day without ever having achieved steady state. If so, it is start-up and the **transient state** that are of interest. Queuing formulas do not apply to transient conditions, because λ is changing all the time. In such cases, Monte Carlo simulation, discussed next, is an alternative.

SIMULATION

Simulation means imitation. As a tool in waiting-line analysis, simulation means imitating a waiting line by use of numbers. Simulation differs from mathematical queuing formulas in that queuing formulas do not imitate a waiting line; rather, the formulas simplify a waiting line so that summary waiting-line data can be easily solved for. Simulation of waiting lines also differs from simulation for training or education. Physical simulators help train drivers and pilots. Simulation games (e.g., management games) provide students with realistic experience in making decisions. Since waiting-line simulation applies to *real* situations, its purpose is actual decision making, not education.

Real waiting lines change all the time. Simulation captures these changes with streams of numbers that stand for customers or orders and their progress through a service facility. The numbers can then be examined to find out about maximum, minimum, and average conditions and durations.

One would have to watch real waiting lines for a long time in order to find out the same thing. With the aid of computers, a waiting-line simulation can represent a long time period—hundreds of simulated years if so desired—at rather small expense. The cost is low, at least, in comparison with trial and error on real waiting lines. Even if a simulation is run for a short time, say a few simulated hours or days, a computer may be needed to handle the many numbers necessary to represent the changing flows through the waiting lines and the service facility.

As in queuing analysis, the inputs to simulation are arrival frequencies and service

FIGURE 17–5

Monte Carlo Simulation Analysis

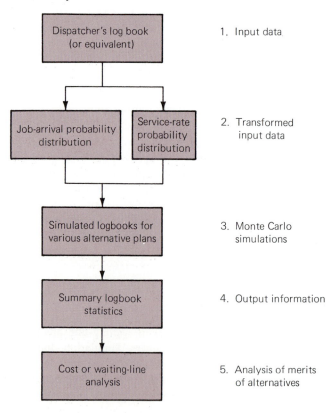

rates. Unlike queuing analysis, simulation can handle any distribution of arrivals and service rates, not just the Poisson probability distribution. We consider the way in which arrivals and service times are simulated next. The method is known as Monte Carlo simulation.

Monte Carlo Simulation

Monte Carlo simulation is not difficult, but it takes time; it is messy compared to the mathematical simplicity of queuing formulas. But Monte Carlo simulation is versatile; it can capture repair-time distributions distorted by repairmen's proclivities, and it can deal with start-up as well as steady-state conditions in a repair system.

Monte Carlo simulation follows the five-step procedure shown in Figure 17–5. The steps are: collect input data on job arrivals and service times, transform the data into probability distributions, perform the simulations, summarize the outputs, and analyze alternatives. The first four steps consist of building the simulation model, the likeness of the real system. Those four are demonstrated in the following simplified example. The fifth step is to test proposed management improvements, and that step is reserved for a more complex example later in the chapter.

EXAMPLE 17–2

Monte Carlo Simulation of a Shoeshine Stand

A shoeshine stand currently has a staff of one. During the peak period, 9:30–11:30 A.M., customers often have to wait, but some are too impatient to do so. The proprietor wonders about the effects of adding staff, using an electric buffer, smoothing the flow of customer arrivals by taking appointments, and so forth. We might find out the answers by a Monte Carlo simulation. We shall set up the simulation model but not simulate management options. Setting up the model requires going through the first four of the five-step Monte Carlo simulation procedure: gather data, transform data, simulate, and extract outputs. Each step is performed below.

Gather arrival and service-time data. We have watched the shoeshine stand for three days from 9:30 A.M. to 11:30 A.M. We have recorded customer arrivals, and we plot them on time charts, Figure 17–6. We must check to see that the three days are mostly alike, and that arrivals are spread out over the 120 minute periods. If the days and minutes have arrival patterns that are not much alike, then it would be best to divide the study into parts, such as first half hour of the day, second half hour, and so forth; then separately simulate for each part. For the data in Figure 17–6A, numbers of customers arriving seem similar enough from minute to minute and day to day to use all of the data in a single simulation.

How long does it take for a shoeshine? Figure 17–6B gives the times. The total number of customers served is only 40, as compared with 50 customers counted as arrivals in Figure 17–6A. The ten-customer difference includes eight customers who refused to wait in line (lost business) and

FIGURE 17–6

Customer-Arrival and Service-Time Data on Time Charts

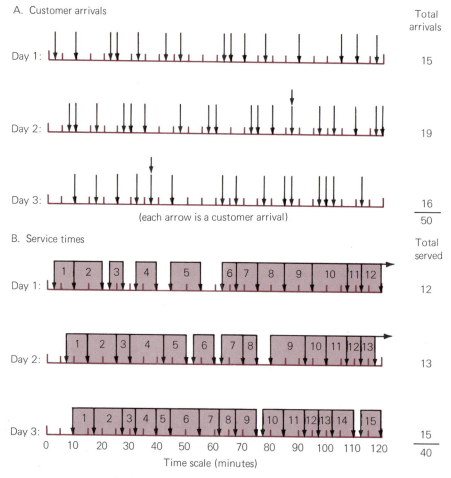

A. Customer arrivals

Day 1:

Day 2:

Day 3:

(each arrow is a customer arrival)

Total arrivals

15

19

16
___
50

B. Service times

Day 1:

Day 2:

Day 3:

Time scale (minutes)

Total served

12

13

15
___
40

(each pair of arrows spans service time for
a customer, each of whom is numbered)

two customers whose shoes were still being shined at the end of the 120-minute periods in days 1 and 2. (We were careful to count even those persons who approached the shoeshine stand but turned away upon seeing a waiting line.)

From Figures 17–6A and 17–6B it is possible to develop summary output data, utilization rate of the server, maximum and average waiting line, and so on. But this is not the purpose of gathering the data. The purpose is to *transform* the data—get it into a form that will permit simulations for present and proposed operating conditions. Transformation of the data follows.

Transform data into probability distributions. Customer arrivals and service times are variable. Figure 17–6 shows us that time between arrivals, or **interarrival time (IAT),** varies from zero (two arrivals at the same time) to 17.5 minutes (which occurs once on day 3, between minute 45 and minute 60.5 in Figure 17–6A). The service time to shine one customer's shoes varies from 5 minutes to 12.5 minutes.

The variability may be captured and condensed into a probability distribution. Set up classification intervals, and count the number of occurrences (frequency) in each interval; the midpoint of each interval is used to represent the whole interval.

Figure 17–7A shows interarrival times transformed into a frequency distribution. (Time between arrivals is easier to measure from the time charts than is its reciprocal, number of customer arrivals per time period.) Four

FIGURE 17–7

Developing an IAT Probability Distribution

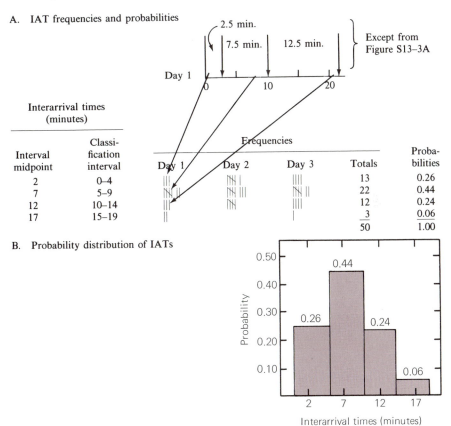

A. IAT frequencies and probabilities

B. Probability distribution of IATs

time intervals are used; the midpoints are 2, 7, 12, and 17. (Division into five or six narrower intervals would work as well.)

Tally marks indicate frequencies. The arrows in the figure show how this is done for the first three arrivals that were entered on the time chart of Figure 17–7A. The first customer arrived 2.5 minutes after the observer began watching, so 2.5 minutes is the first IAT (interarrival time); one tally mark goes in the 0–4 row, since 2.5 minutes falls within that classification interval. The second customer arrived 7.5 minutes after the first. Since 7.5 falls within interval 5–9, a tally goes in the 5–9 row. The third customer arrives 12.5 minutes after the second, and a tally goes in the 10–14 row.

The tallies are shown separately for each day, but then we total them for all three days. Divide the interval totals—13, 22, 12, and 3—by the grand total of 50, and we get the probabilities in the final column in Figure 17–7A.

Figure 17–7B shows the probabilities for each of the four interval midpoints as a bar chart. The bar chart format is not necessary for simulation purposes, but it is a useful visual aid.

We follow the same procedure for service times. The result is the service-time frequency data and probability distribution in Figure 17–8. Since service times may be parts of minutes, the classification intervals allow for decimal parts. By contrast, the intervals for arrivals are in whole numbers only, since there cannot be a part of a customer. The smallest service-time interval is set at 4–6.9, with 5 as the midpoint, since every shoeshine in Figure 17–6B took at least five minutes.

Simulate. The probability distributions in Figures 17–7 and 17–8, plus a table of random numbers, are the inputs needed to conduct Monte Carlo simulation. As a preparatory step we express the probabilities as number ranges, which are sometimes called Monte Carlo number ranges. The number ranges should be the same as the range of the numbers in the table of random numbers—two digits, 00 to 99, for this example. The development of the Monte Carlo number ranges is shown in Figure 17–9A. The size of each number range is 100 times the probability, and the numbers in the ranges increase progressively from 00 to 99. (An alternative is to go from 01 to 00, where 00 stands for 100. Three digits won't work since a two-digit random-number table is to be used.) Thus, the range for IAT 2 has a size of:

$$100 \times 0.26 = 26 \text{ numbers}$$

The 26 numbers go from 00 to 25. The next range begins with 26, and so forth.

Figure 17–9B is a small simulation of the shoeshine stand. The random numbers in columns 2 and 6 come from the second column of the random-number table, Table 17–1. The first random number, 27 (in column 2), is used to represent the IAT for customer number 1. Since 27 falls within Monte Carlo range 26–69 in the IAT table in Figure 17–9A, the IAT is 7. Arrows drawn between Figure 17–9A and Figure 17–9B show these steps. The second random number, 39 (in column 6), is used to represent service time for customer number 1. Since 39 falls within Monte Carlo range 30–74 in the service-time table in Figure 17–9A, the service time is 8 (see arrows).

FIGURE 17–8

Developing a Service-Time Probability Distribution

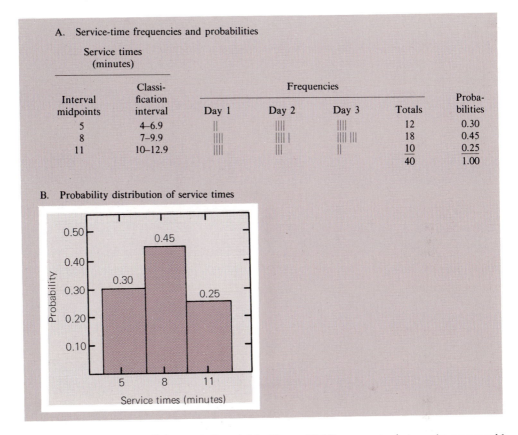

A. Service-time frequencies and probabilities

Service times
(minutes)

Interval midpoints	Classi- fication interval	Frequencies			Totals	Proba- bilities
		Day 1	Day 2	Day 3		
5	4–6.9	||	||||	||||	12	0.30
8	7–9.9	||||	|||| |	|||| |||	18	0.45
11	10–12.9	||||	|||	||	10	0.25
					40	1.00

B. Probability distribution of service times

Columns 4, 5, and 8 in Figure 17–9B represent what an observer would see at the shoeshine stand: Column 4 gives the arrival time for each customer. It is simply the cumulative sum of the IATs in column 3. Column 5 is the time that service starts. Service does not always begin when the customer arrives, because some customers must wait. In this simulation customers 2, 3, 5, 6, 7, 8, 9, and 10 must wait (the waiting time is the difference between the times in columns 4 and 5). Column 8 is the completion time for each shoeshine. It is the start time (column 5) plus the service time (column 7).

To see when the next shine may start, we must look at the time that service ends for earlier customers. For example, the first customer's shine starts at minute 7, takes eight minutes and ends at minute 15. Customer 2 arrives at minute 14 but must wait until customer 1 leaves at minute 15. Therefore, to get a start time in column 5, we must compare the previous end time with the arrival time for the current customer.

Useful summary information may be extracted from the simulation, as is explained next.

FIGURE 17-9

Monte Carlo Simulation of Shoeshine Stand

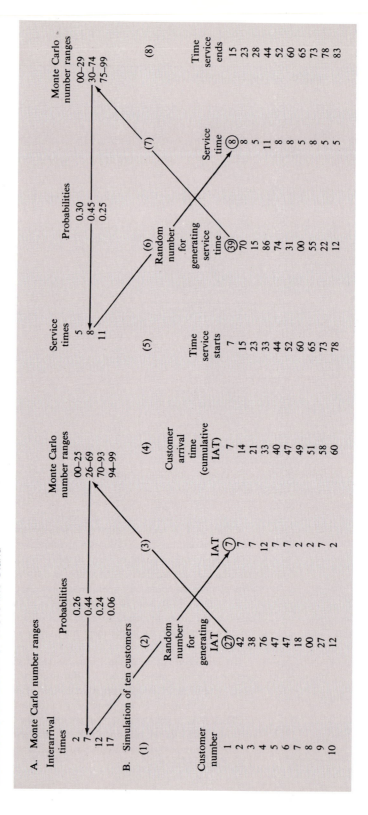

TABLE 17–1

Two-Digit Random Numbers

42	27	11	61	64	20
55	39	37	71	35	78
24	42	25	60	61	78
82	70	68	68	28	08
56	38	62	42	05	47
48	15	21	40	25	78
95	76	15	43	63	18
86	86	96	50	43	17
49	47	10	94	14	22
41	74	33	33	28	76
95	47	92	56	95	95
78	31	27	77	66	63
84	18	88	65	46	81
40	00	61	17	82	53
80	00	85	42	64	44
12	55	13	20	74	16
84	27	50	45	97	19
01	22	40	81	36	10
25	12	07	98	82	74
46	12	83	52	30	42
83	02	73	53	18	07
69	18	16	09	93	65
78	22	36	94	45	32
43	18	05	33	44	45
07	34	46	30	49	10
00	50	31	12	42	88
55	34	73	61	96	44
17	39	51	92	64	44
22	81	84	00	95	32
57	00	21	12	36	96
02	20	12	50	71	82
70	15	52	75	67	60
28	36	84	20	73	23
86	60	52	37	46	79
04	34	33	73	42	91
95	35	13	16	75	03
89	14	24	19	29	82
92	46	72	35	17	81
30	28	74	35	87	67
86	31	84	29	75	89
13	21	48	73	40	73
38	87	98	23	72	43
02	42	81	84	08	38
72	22	79	60	26	26
16	05	14	42	74	74
70	03	63	58	32	12
45	45	96	64	49	83
05	38	40	89	75	32
29	24	05	17	03	53
20	87	26	88	06	18

Extract information. Common information from a Monte Carlo waiting-line simulation includes maximum and average waiting-line length, average waiting time per customer, and percent idleness or utilization of the service facility. All of these statistics come from columns 4, 5, and 8 of the simulation in Figure 17–9B. Those columns, plus three more columns of working figures and summarized information, are given in Figure 17–10.

Columns 5, 6, and 7 in Figure 17–10 show number of customers waiting, customer waiting time, and service-facility idleness. The first customer arrives after the facility has been idle for seven minutes. The second arrives in minute 14 and waits one minute until customer 1 departs in minute 15. Customers 3, 5, and 6 also find a customer ahead of them when they arrive. Customer 7 arrives at minute 49, but customer 5 does not leave until minute 52, so customers 6 and 7 are waiting at the same time. Each of the other calculations follow the same logic.

The summary information below the table tells us that the maximum waiting line is 3 customers; the mean waiting line, 1.5 customers; and the

FIGURE 17–10

Summary Information from Simulation

(1) Customer number	(2) Customer arrival time	(3) Time service starts	(4) Time service ends	(5) Number of customers waiting	(6) Customer waiting time	(7) Time of idleness in service facility
1	7	7	15			7
2	14	15	23	1	1	
3	21	23	28	1	2	
4	33	33	44			5
5	40	44	52	1	4	
6	47	52	60	1	5	
7	49	60	65	2	11	
8	51	65	73	3	14	
9	58	73	78	3	15	
10	60	78	83	3	18	
			Totals	15	70	12

Maximum waiting line =   3 customers

Mean waiting line $= \dfrac{15 \text{ customers waiting}}{10 \text{ customer arrivals}} = 1.5$ customers

Mean waiting time $= \dfrac{70 \text{ minutes waiting}}{10 \text{ customers}} = 7.0$ minutes

Idleness rate $= \dfrac{12 \text{ minutes idle}}{83 \text{ minutes simulated}} = 0.145$, or 14.5% idleness mean waiting time, 7.0 minutes. The idleness rate is found by dividing 12 minutes of idleness by the 83 minutes in the simulation, which equals 14.5 percent idleness.

Assessment. The preceding simulation of a shoeshine stand was simplified for illustrative purposes. A real simulation would usually take longer and generate more and better information:

1. The data-collection phase should perhaps run longer than six hours (three days) and 40–50 customers.

2. With a longer simulation, we get more data. Then we may narrow the classification intervals. The interval midpoints for the IAT and service-time distributions in Figures 17–7 and 17–8 were set rather wide apart (i.e., 2, 7, 12, and 17 for the IAT distribution) because of limited data for narrower intervals.

3. A 10-customer, 83-minute simulation is very short. The simulation period should last 120 minutes, which is the peak period of operation for the shoeshine stand. To have confidence in the final waiting-line and idleness statistics, we should run the simulation for many days. Normally, a Monte Carlo simulation is run on a computer, which permits simulating for hundreds or thousands of days. With many days of simulation, the effects of an unusual selection of random numbers wash out.

4. As was noted at the outset, a purpose of simulation is to test various conditions, such as adding staff. Reruns of the simulation with different IAT or service-time distributions are among the options that we may try. Special computer simulation languages (such as SIMSCRIPT, GPSS, GASP, Q-GERTS, and SLAM) are useful in testing a variety of options, including customer balking and reneging.

Simulation for System Improvement

Having seen how a simulation model is developed, we may now turn to practical uses of the procedure. The following example is long, but even the simplest Monte Carlo simulations always are.

EXAMPLE 17–3

Monte Carlo Simulation of Repair-Crew Sizes

At Echo Engine Co. a serious problem is malfunction and breakdown of the powered conveyor sections that feed various parts to the engine assembly line. Conveyor failure shuts down the given feeder line, idling its work crew. Crew size is nearly the same on each feeder line, and Echo uses a flat $50 per hour as the cost of feeder-line idleness.

A four-hour parts inventory is stockpiled at the end of each feeder line. If any feeder line is idle for more than four hours, the parts stockpile is used up, idling the whole assembly line; the cost of assembly-line idleness is $1,000 per hour. A partial layout sketch of the assembly line and the feeder lines is shown in Figure 17–11.

FIGURE 17–11

Layout Sketch of Echo Engine Plant

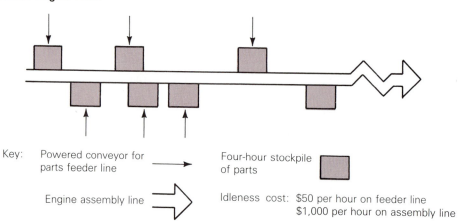

Key: Powered conveyor for
         parts feeder line   ———→   Four-hour stockpile
                                               of parts

         Engine assembly line   ⟹   Idleness cost: $50 per hour on feeder line
                                                            $1,000 per hour on assembly line

Echo's Maintenance Department employs one mechanic whose main job is to repair and adjust conveyors. The mechanic's wage is $10 per hour, time and a half ($15) for overtime. Overtime is scheduled for any maintenance not completed during the eight-hour workday.

Echo operates only one production shift per day, but an evening skeleton crew builds up parts so that the four-hour parts inventories are fully restored by the next morning. That way the regular day-shift production crews are not paid for any overtime.

The question is, Is one mechanic enough?

Solution:

Monte Carlo simulation seems clearly preferable to queuing formulas for the following reasons:

1. Because of distorting human influences, breakdown and service-rate probability distributions are not likely to be Poisson, which is necessary when queuing formulas are used. Monte Carlo simulation is usable with any probability distribution.
2. The system starts fresh each day with empty queues, and average queues grow as the day progresses. Queuing formulas require steady-state queue conditions, but Monte Carlo can capture transient conditions.

Step 1: Input data.   The conveyor repairman acts as his own dispatcher, and his trouble-call logbook is complete and accurate. A page from the logbook is shown in Figure 17–12A. Logbook records on breakdown times and repair start and finish times provide the necessary input data for Monte Carlo simulation.

Step 2: Transformed input data.   The logbook has enough data for computing arrival-time and service-time probability distributions. To the logbook

FIGURE 17–12

Developing IAT and Service-Time Frequency Distributions

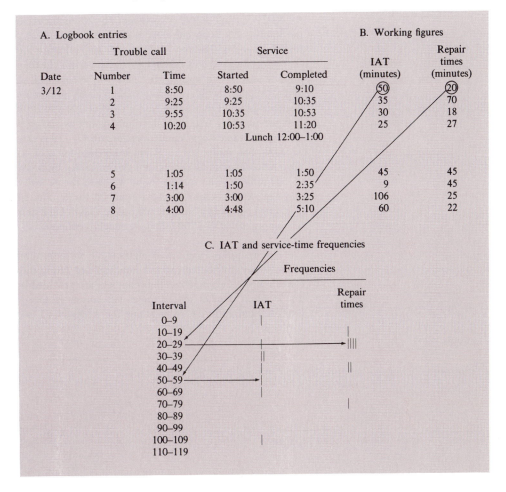

in Figure 17–12A, we add two columns of working figures: an interarrival-time (time-between-arrivals) column and a repair-time column. These working figures are shown in Figure 17–12B, just to the right of the raw data in the repair logbook. Interarrival time (IAT) is determined by successive subtraction of trouble-call times. The first trouble call after the 8:00 A.M. opening time is at 8:50; 8:50 minus 8:00 is 50 minutes, the IAT. The repair time for call number 1 is 9:10 minus 8:50, which is 20 minutes. Each of the other IAT and repair-time working figures is similarly calculated.

Next transform the working figures into frequency distributions. To do this, segment the continuous distributions into intervals; 10-minute intervals will suffice. Then, tally the number of working figures that fall into each interval. This produces the frequency distributions. For the single day's working figures, the tallying is as shown in Figure 17–12C. The arrows in the figure show where the tally marks go for trouble-call number 1. The 50-minute IAT falls within the interval 50–59, so one tally is entered in the 50–59 row under IAT frequencies. The 20-minute repair time falls within the interval 20–29 so one tally is entered in the 20–29 row under repair-time frequencies. The rest of Figure 17–12C is determined similarly.

For only eight trouble calls—one day's worth—the frequency distribution table is sparse. We must gather and tally trouble-call data for a number of days, so that the full range of variability may be captured in the frequency distributions. Let us assume that a total of 100 trouble calls is tallied and that the resulting frequency distributions are as shown in Figure 17–13A.

Step 3: Monte Carlo simulations. Figure 17–13B is extended from Figure 17–13A. The midpoints in B are midpoints for each interval in A; and the probabilities in B are the number of tallies in A divided by the total of 100 tallies in the sample. Now we state the probabilities as ranges of two-digit Monte Carlo numbers from 00 to 99. The sizes of the Monte Carlo number ranges are proportional to the probabilities; for example, 00–03 comprises 4 of the 100 numbers, which is proportional to the probability 0.04.

Now we make a simulated logbook by drawing numbers from a table of uniformly distributed random numbers and fitting them into the Monte Carlo ranges. Two-digit random numbers are provided in Table 17–1. The first random number in the upper left corner of the table is 42; 42 fits into IAT range, 26–48, representing the midpoint 35 (see Figure 17–13B).

FIGURE 17–13

Transformed Trouble-Call and Service-Time Data for Echo Engine Co.

A. Frequency distributions			B. Probabilities and Monte Carlo number ranges				
				IAT		Service Time	
	Distribution						
			Interval midpoints	Proba-bilities	Monte Carlo number ranges	Proba-bilities	Monte Carlo number ranges
Interval	IAT	Service-time					
0–9	IIII	I	5	0.04	00–03	0.01	00
10–19	IIII II	IIII I	15	0.07	04–10	0.06	01–06
20–29	IIII IIII IIII	IIII IIII IIII I	25	0.15	11–25	0.16	07–22
30–39	IIII IIII IIII IIII III	IIII IIII IIII IIII III	35	0.23	26–48	0.23	23–45
40–49	IIII IIII IIII II	IIII IIII IIII IIII III	45	0.17	49–65	0.23	46–68
50–59	IIII IIII III	IIII IIII IIII	55	0.13	66–78	0.15	69–83
60–69	IIII IIII	IIII III	65	0.10	79–88	0.08	84–91
70–79	IIII I	IIII	75	0.06	89–94	0.04	92–95
80–89	III	II	85	0.03	95–97	0.02	96–97
90–99	I	I	95	0.01	98	0.01	98
100–109	I	I	105	0.01	99	0.01	99
	100	100		1.00		1.00	

Therefore, the first trouble call occurs at 00 (beginning of shift) plus 35, that is, the 35th minute. The next lower random number, 55, is used to simulate the service time; the 55 fits into service-time range 46–68, representing 45. Therefore the first simulated trouble call takes 45 minutes to repair.

These numbers go into columns 3, 4, 7, and 8 of Figure 17–14A, which is a simulation of 20 trouble calls with one repairman at Echo Engines. Column 5 contains trouble-call arrival times, which are cumulative interarrival times (from column 4). The IAT for trouble call 2 is 25, which means 25 minutes between call 1 and call 2. Therefore, since call 1 arrived in minute 35, call 2 arrives in 35 + 25 = 60.

Column 9, time service completed, is simply time service started (column 6) plus service time (column 8). For the first call, service time is completed at 35 + 45 = minute 80.

Column 6, time service started, is the same as trouble-call arrival time (column 5) when there is no waiting line of trouble calls. This is the case for call 1. Call 2 arrives in minute 60, but we see from column 9 that call 1 is still in service until minute 80. Thus call 2 has to wait. The wait amounts to 80 − 60 = 20 minutes, which is entered in column 10, feeder-line idleness waiting for repairman.

Column 11, repairman overtime (after 480th minute), may contain entries only at the end of the day—if overtime is needed. In this simulation overtime is not needed in day 1 when there is only one repairman. In day 2, overtime is needed for the last three trouble calls (18, 19, and 20), since all three are completed later than the 480th minute.

Column 12, assembly-line idleness for repair (of feeder line) over 30 minutes, occurs in day 2 for calls 16 through 20. Feeder-line idleness for call 16 is 40 minutes (column 10), which is 10 minutes longer than the 30 minute stockpile of feeder-line parts. When feeder-line parts are gone, the whole assembly line stops.

In Figure 17–14B, the simulation data are applied to two repairmen, but only for the busiest repair day, day 2. The random-number and IAT columns are omitted in Figure 17–14B, and a new column (number 5) is added to show which repairman the job is assigned to.

In Figure 17–14B call 12 is assigned to repairman 2, who leaves at minute 210 and returns at minute 245. Meanwhile, trouble call 13 comes in at minute 225, so it is assigned to repairman 1. Skipping down to call 17, we see that it comes in at minute 335 when both repairmen are out. The first to return is repairman 1 at minute 340, so he gets call 17. Call 17 had to wait 340 − 335 = 5 minutes, which is entered as feeder-line idleness (column 8). Overtime is not needed.

Step 4: Summary logbook statistics. Summary idleness and overtime totals are shown for day 2 in Figures 17–14A and 17–14B. The results are no surprise: Feeder-line idleness while waiting for a repairman is drastically cut from 490 minutes for one repairman to 25 minutes for two repairmen. And, of course, the 70 minutes of feeder-line idleness in day 1 and the 320 minutes assembly-line idleness in day 2 are cut to zero with two repairmen. Overtime is also reduced to zero with two repairmen.

The two-day, 20-call simulation is too short to be precise. Let us assume that the simulation is continued for 100 days, and for one, two, and three

FIGURE 17–14

Simulation of Trouble Calls and Repairs, Echo Engine Co.

A. One repairman

(1) Day	(2) Trouble-call number	(3) Random number for generating IAT	(4) IAT	(5) Trouble-call arrival time (cumulative IAT)	(6) Time service started	(7) Random number for generating service time	(8) Service time	(9) Time service completed	(10) Feeder-line idleness waiting for repairman (minutes)	(11) Repairman overtime (minutes after 480th minute)	(12) Assembly-line idleness for repair over 30 minutes (minutes)
1	1	42	35	35	35	55	45	80			
	2	24	25	60	80	82	55	135	20		
	3	56	45	105	135	48	45	180	30		
	4	95	85	190	190	86	65	255			
	5	49	45	235	255	41	35	290	20		
	6	95	85	320	320	78	55	375			
	7	84	65	385	385	40	35	420			
	8	80	65	450	450	12	25	475			
2	9	84	65	65	65	01	5	70			
	10	25	25	90	90	46	45	135			
	11	83	65	155	155	69	55	210			
	12	78	25	210	210	43	35	245			
	13	07	15	225	245	00	5	250	20		
	14	55	45	270	270	17	25	295			
	15	22	25	295	295	57	45	340			
	16	02	5	300	340	70	55	395	40		10
	17	28	35	335	395	86	65	460	60		30
	18	04	15	350	460	95	75	535	110	55	80
	19	89	75	425	535	92	75	610	110	75	80
	20	30	35	460	610	86	65	675	150	65	120
								Day 2 totals:	490	195	320

B. Two repairmen

(1) Day	(2) Trouble-call number	(3) Trouble-call arrival time	(4) Time service started	(5) Which repairman job is assigned to	(6) Service time	(7) Time service completed	(8) Feeder-line idleness waiting for repairman (minutes)	(9) Repairman overtime (minutes after 480th minute)
2	9	65	65	1	5	70		
	10	90	90	2	45	135		
	11	155	155	1	55	210		
	12	210	210	2	35	245		
	13	225	225	1	5	230		
	14	270	270	2	25	295		
	15	295	295	1	45	340		
	16	300	300	2	55	355		
	17	335	340	1	65	410	5	
	18	350	355	2	75	430	5	
	19	425	425	1	75	500	15	
	20	460	460	2	65	525		
						Day 2 totals	25	0

repairman. Idleness and overtime data for the 100-day simulation may be averaged. Assume that the averaged data are:

One repairman	
Feeder-line idleness	130 min./day
Overtime	110 min./day
Assembly-line idleness	50 min./day
Two repairmen	
Feeder-line idleness	3 min./day
Overtime	0 min./day
Assembly-line idleness	0 min./day
Three repairmen	
Feeder-line idleness	0 min./day
Overtime	0 min./day
Assembly-line idleness	0 min./day

Step 5: Cost analysis of repairman alternatives. The total costs for each repairman alternative are the sum of regular and overtime repairman wages and the cost of feeder-line and assembly-line idleness. Not relevant are the wages of production workers and feeder-line idleness during service; they are constant—not related to number of repairmen. Relevant average daily costs are determined below.

The regular wage rate was given as $10 per hour per repairman. For an eight-hour day, wage costs are:

For one repairman: 1 repairman $\times$ $10/hr. $\times$ 8 hours = $80/day

For two repairmen: 2 repairmen $\times$ $10/hr. $\times$ 8 hours = $160/day

For three repairmen: 3 repairmen $\times$ $10/hr. $\times$ 8 hours = $240/day

Overtime wages are time and a half, or $15 per hour. Simulated overtime per day, from step 4 above, is 110 minutes for one repairman, zero for two repairmen, and zero for three repairmen. Therefore, the daily cost for one repairman is:

$$\frac{110 \text{ min./day}}{60 \text{ min./hr.}} \times \$15/\text{hr.} = \$27.50/\text{day}$$

Feeder-line idleness cost was given as $50 per hour. Simulated feeder-line idleness per day, from step 4 above, is 130 minutes for one repairman, 3 minutes for two repairmen, and 0.0 minute for three repairmen. The daily costs are:

For one repairman:

$$\frac{130 \text{ min./day}}{60 \text{ min./hr.}} \times \$50/\text{hr.} = \$108.33/\text{day}$$

For two repairmen:

$$\frac{3 \text{ min./day}}{60 \text{ min./hr.}} \times \$50/\text{hr.} = \$2.50$$

For three repairmen:

$$\frac{0.0 \text{ min./day}}{60 \text{ min./hr.}} \times \$50/\text{hr.} = \$0.00/\text{day}$$

Assembly-line idleness was given as $1,000 per hour. Simulated assembly-line idleness, from step 4 above, is 50 minutes for one repairman and zero time for two and three repairmen. The daily cost for one repairman is:

$$\frac{50 \text{ min./day}}{60 \text{ min./hr.}} \times \$1,000/\text{hr.} = \$833.33/\text{day}$$

The four types of daily costs are totaled in Figure 17–15 for the three staffing options. Comparing the total costs helps us decide on the best staffing policy.

FIGURE 17–15

Total Costs for Three Staffing Options, Echo Engines Co.

| Number of repairmen | Wages | | Idleness | | Total average daily cost |
	Regular	Overtime	Feeder-line	Assembly-line	
1	$ 80.00	$27.50	$108.33	$833.33	$1,049.16
2	160.00	0.00	2.50	0	162.50
3	240.00	0.00	0.00	0	240.00

In the figure, the total average cost per day for two repairmen is $162.50. This is over $75 per day less than the next lowest cost, $240.00 for three repairmen. The wage cost alone for three repairmen is $240 per day, considerably more than the total daily cost for two repairmen. The $75 per day saving, when extended to a 250-day year, is a saving of $18,750 per year. On the basis of costs alone, two repairmen is clearly the best staffing policy. An additional advantage of two (and three) repairmen over one repairman is that output on the engine line is more predictable and uniform when feeder-line breakdowns can be repaired without waiting time. Of course, the very idea of maintaining a 30-minute buffer stock for each feeder line is questionable. We should try to cut that stock and keep cutting it. A good preventive maintenance program to keep the equipment running justifies cutting the buffer stocks.

When Should You Simulate?

The chief limitation of Monte Carlo simulation is cost. Monte Carlo simulation is as time-consuming—to set up and run—as queuing formulas are time-saving. But Monte Carlo can be as realistic as one cares to make it—and as one cares to pay for.

Despite the time and cost, Monte Carlo simulation can pay large dividends. In the simple case of repairing conveyors, the saving—two repairmen instead of one—amounts to $18,750 per year. The cost to set up and run the simulation is a pittance compared to that. But let us not become overly ecstatic. In some cases the maintenance chief and the production chief together would be able to correctly decide the optimal number of repairmen—*without benefit of simulation,* and without the cost.

The astute manager is able to recognize when a good decision may be based purely on judgment and when simulation or other analysis is called for. What is it that makes a manager who can recognize these things? The answer is, in part, the manager who thoroughly understands waiting-line phenomena. And the best way to understand waiting lines is probably *not* by experience and personal observation; that would provide only limited exposure even in a lifetime. Those who best understand waiting lines are those who have studied many cases—in fairly short periods of time—as students, for example.

It may be true that study is rarely a worthy substitute for the real thing. Let us examine why, in the case of waiting lines, study may well be superior to the real thing.

A valuable lesson for the student of simulation is learning about how waiting lines are affected by different arrival- and service-time distributions. These distributions may be wide or narrow, close together or far apart, in many combinations.

In the Echo Engines example the two distributions look a lot alike. The accompanying sketch shows one superimposed on the other. With the two distributions overlap-

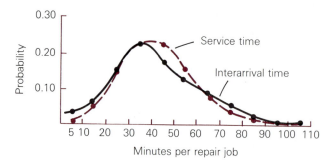

ping so much, we may expect long waiting lines, and long waiting lines are just what happened in the simulation. By making computations based on data from Figure 17–12, we can show that the mean service time is 47.8 and mean interarrival time is 43.4 minutes. When people arrive faster than they can be served, the long-run consequence is waiting lines that grow infinitely long! But Echo Engines prevents this by stopping the arrivals after one eight-hour shift each day. Then the machines awaiting repair are fixed during overtime so that none is waiting the next morning.

With so great a potential for waiting lines, simulation begins to pay for itself. The reason is that it is quite impossible to guess, even if you are experienced, how long the waits will be, how much overtime pay is likely, and how much assembly-line shutdown cost there will be.

Now let's move the distributions apart and draw some conclusions. This sketch is like the previous one, except the IAT distribution has been moved 30 minutes to the right. Now the mean IAT is at 73.4, which means breakdowns occur at 73.4 minute intervals. Time to repair averages 47.8 minutes—much faster. We should surmise, *without simulating,* that long queues of machines waiting for service are unlikely to form. Overtime costs should be very low, perhaps negligible. So stick with one repairman (and be prepared to find other work for that repairman to do in slack periods). And don't bother to conduct a simulation.

Various Arrival- and Service-Time Conditions

Figure 17–16 illustrates the two cases discussed previously: great overlap (case D) and moderate overlap (case C) between interarrival-time and service-time distributions; it also includes three other cases: narrow distributions, no overlap, and "total" overlap with continuous operation.

For case A, narrow distributions, there is no point in simulating. The distributions are too narrow. It is practical to act as if interarrival and service times were not distributed at all. In other words, find the modes of these very narrow distributions, that is, the most frequently occurring interarrival time and service time; then treat the modes as single-valued estimates. That way, decisions on staffing and scheduling are simple—often self-evident.

For case B, the probability distributions are wide but do not overlap. Without overlap, there are no interactions, no chances of waiting lines, and thus there is nothing to simulate. A good management decision may be to cut staff in order to avoid staff idleness and allow a small amount of waiting time.

Case E is nearly total overlap with *continuous* operation; that means no stops at the ends of shifts to allow queues to empty out. The *pattern* of growth could be simulated; this might seem valuable in order to learn about waiting-line behavior in the start-up phase. But it would usually not be worth doing, because the conditions leading to an infinite queue are unstable. Management is likely to quickly intervene to reduce such instability—add staff, for example. The condition would scarcely last long enough to gather data to simulate it.

FIGURE 17–16

Arrival- and Service-Time Conditions and Effects

DISTRIBUTIONS

WAITING-LINE TENDENCIES

A. Narrow distributions

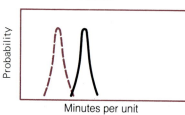

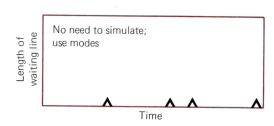

No need to simulate;
use modes

B. No overlap

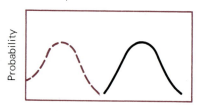

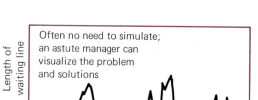

No waiting line, so
no need to simulate

C. Moderate overlap

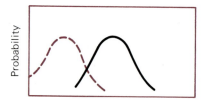

Often no need to simulate;
an astute manager can
visualize the problem
and solutions

D. Great overlap

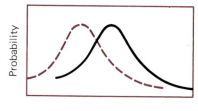

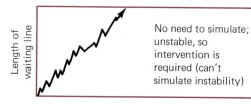

Greatest need to simulate

E. Total overlap with *continuous* operation

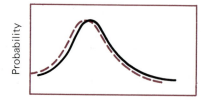

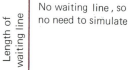

No need to simulate;
unstable, so
intervention is
required (can't
simulate instability)

(dashed lines are service-time
distributions; solid lines
are arrival distributions)

We have seen that four of the five cases in Figure 17–16 do not seem to call for Monte Carlo simulation. Considering the cost of simulation, that is good news!

Managers of service units are not likely to find a lot of uses for Monte Carlo simulation. They should, however, find many uses for a thorough understanding of waiting-line phenomena.

SUMMARY

Service centers are hard to manage, because arrivals of customers or goods for service are irregular, roller-coaster workload patterns. When arrivals bunch up, waiting lines form. The service-center manager tries to match the serving capacity to the arrival rate—no easy task.

A simple waiting line is the single-channel, single-stage line, but other numbers of channels (lines) and stages (servers) also occur. A way to study service centers is to gather arrival and service time data; then create a model of the waiting line patterns for different levels of use of server capacity (often number of servers on hand).

One approach is to use simple queuing formulas to predict average waiting times, number waiting, and utilization of the server. The queuing formulas just require entry of mean arrival rate and mean service rate into the formulas. But the formulas yield valid data only if arrival rates are Poisson-distributed and if service rates are Poisson-distributed or constant. Poisson is the normal pattern. But with *human* customers there are tendencies to balk when the line looks too long, and to leave it if it moves too slowly; these tendencies push the arrival pattern away from Poisson. Similarly Poisson service rates often do not hold up for human servers, because servers tend to speed up when lines are long and slow down when lines are short. These human tendencies cause waiting to decrease and server utilization to be higher. Finally, the queuing formulas do not work out unless average arrival and service rates are stable—what is called the steady state.

For all these limitations, queuing formulas can at least predict an upper limit on average waiting, which can help managers decide on serving capacity. And when the arrivals or the service performed are more mechanical, less human, the formulas can work well indeed.

In studying start-up (nonsteady state) conditions and nonstandard arrival and service-rate patterns, a more difficult waiting-line analysis technique applies: Monte Carlo simulation. It requires keeping records on arrivals and service times, translating them into probability distributions, simulating by matching random numbers against probability distributions, and extracting output information on waiting and on server utilization. Put a price on the waiting times and on the servers, and management can better decide on how to manage the lines and the servers.

Monte Carlo simulation is much more complex and time consuming to do than using queuing formulas. Computers are usually used to generate random numbers and to simulate many time periods so that reliable average statistics emerge. Because of the cost of Monte Carlo simulation, it is not used often. But it can be valuable for a student to run many types of simulation exercises, because these offer insights on what happens to waiting lines under varying combinations of arrival rates and service rates. Actually running a simulation for service-center management purposes is most valuable when the arrival and service rate distributions overlap a lot, creating hard-to-predict waiting patterns.

REFERENCES

Books

Hildebrand, James K. *Maintenance Turns to the Computer.* Boston: Cahners, 1972 (TS192.H55).

Lewis, Bernard T., and J. P. Marron. *Facilities and Plant Engineering Handbook.* New York: McGraw-Hill, 1973 (TS184.L48).

Mann, Lawrence, Jr. *Maintenance Management.* Lexington, Mass.: Lexington Books, 1976 (TS192.M38).

Murphy, James A., ed. *Plant Engineering Management.* Society of Manufacturing Engineers, 1971 (TS184.P435x).

Periodicals

Plant Engineering, includes plant maintenance.

REVIEW QUESTIONS

1. What are two common problems of any service center?

2. What is a waiting-line channel? a waiting-line stage? How many channels and stages are permitted in using the queuing formulas given in this chapter?

3. What is meant by *steady state,* and how does it relate to use of queuing formulas?

4. In using queuing analysis, are the data to be entered into the formulas hard or easy to obtain? Explain.

5. If human servers (who change their work speed all the time) are replaced by mechanical servers, what changes should there be in conducting a queuing analysis?

6. Why does it make a difference to us, in studying a waiting line, whether the customer and server are human or nonhuman?

7. What are some key advantages and disadvantages of queuing formulas?

8. Why are Monte Carlo simulations run over and over again in a single waiting-line study?

9. In using Monte Carlo simulation, are the data to be used in the simulation easy or hard to obtain? Explain.

10. Why do a Monte Carlo simulation? How can the results be used by management?

11. How can a random number represent (simulate) an arrival at a service center or represent the serving time?

12. What happens to the waiting time when the average arrival rate is nearly as great as the average serving rate? Answer the question first of all assuming Poisson distributions, and second assuming a rigid appointment system and a mechanical (constant) server.

13. Under what combinations of arrival-time and service-time distributions is it not very useful to do a Monte Carlo simulation, and why?

14. Why may a *student* of waiting-line analysis perhaps gain a better understanding of waiting lines and server utilization than an experienced service-center manager?

15. If waiting lines are too long, what options are open to the service-center manager?

PROBLEMS

1. At an entry station along the Mexican border, state agents check to see that people on foot are not bringing in fruits, vegetables, etc., that could house undesirable creatures like the Mediterranean fruit fly. It takes an average of 75 seconds to check each person, but there is a good deal of variability around that average. The slow afternoon hours on Tuesday, Wednesday, and Thursday have average arrivals of a person on foot every 95 seconds. The bureau's policy is to have an average of three people waiting to be checked—and to call for another checker whenever that *average* is exceeded (for any appreciable length of time). Can one checker handle the arrivals on Tuesday, Wednesday, and Thursday afternoons? Explain.

2. Metro Pollution Control moves about the city with a mobile unit checking auto emissions. They block the road, stop all cars, and attach an exhaust sampling device. There are two new exhaust sampling devices on the market. One has a fixed test time: one minute. The other has a variable time; the manufacturer claims that the mean test time is 0.85 minutes. If cars arrive at the road block at an average rate of 40 per hour, which is better for minimizing the citizens' total delay for the check? Does your answer change if there are only 10 cars per hour? Explain.

3. Which of the following are queuing situations in which our simple set of queuing formulas—single channel, single server—is *not* adequate (and would require more advanced queuing formulas)? Explain.

Ships entering a busy port and seeking tug boats and then a berth.

Trains coming on different tracks to switch onto the one track going across Royal Gorge.

Airplanes getting into a holding pattern above Chicago's O'Hare field, then seeking a passenger gate.

Long-distance telephone call routing systems that search for open communications channels.

4. Voters arrive at a precinct polling place at a mean rate of 60 per hour during the peak 5:00–8:00 P.M. time period. Their mean voting rate is 61 per hour through just one voting booth.

   a. Though the line is long, there is virtually no balking or reneging on the part of new arrivals. (Those who make the effort to drive to the polls are apparently committed enough to wait through the lines.) What statistical distribution of arrivals seems likely, and why?

   b. The service rates seem to approximate a Poisson distribution. (The distribution is "crunched" on the left just a bit—because voters are hurrying just a bit.) Calculate the mean waiting time in queue and the mean number in queue. Discuss these results.

   c. The precinct captain has the authority to enforce a time limit of under one minute for a voter to finish voting. If the captain were to enforce the time limit, the voting time would be approximately constant at 0.9 minutes, because few voters take much less than that. What, then, would be the mean waiting time in queue and the mean number in queue? Explain your results—as compared with the results in part b.

   d. For part b, draw arrival and service-time distributions on a single graph, as in Figure 17–16. Do the same for part c. Explain your results from parts b and c by referring to the graphs.

5. Plastic parts for medical syringes are manufactured in a completely automated molding plant. It is at present a one-shift (eight-hour-a-day) operation. That is, there are no production workers, only maintenance crews. Maintenance policies need to be reviewed, by type of machine. The review begins with the molding-machine crew.

   a. Molding machines break down at a mean rate of five per day. When a machine breaks down, the molding-machine crew is sent to fix it. The mean repair time is 45 minutes. Refer to the queuing formulas in Figure 17–3 and make use of two that you feel would yield especially useful statistics for setting maintenance policies. Perform the calculations, and explain their value.

   b. Is it reasonable to use queuing rather than Monte Carlo simulation in part a? Explain.

   c. If a preventive maintenance (PM) program is established, molding-machine breakdowns would be expected to decrease from five to four per day. The PM crew would get its budget and staff from decreases in the repair crews; the smaller molding-machine repair crew would then require 60 minutes of mean repair time (instead of 45 minutes as in part a). Is the PM program worthwhile? Base your answer on queuing analysis.

6. An automobile engine plant has four engine assembly lines, lines 1, 2, 3, and 4. On each of the four lines the head is found not to fit properly to the engine block on an average of one engine every 30 minutes. Those that don't fit are reworked at the end of the day by workers on the line where the defect occurred, and the problem is corrected in an average of 25 minutes. Note that the 30 and 25 are just averages within probability distributions. The actual distributions are as follows for the four lines (whole distributions are represented by just a few time values):

Time interval (in minutes) between engine problems		20	25	30	35	40
Probabilities of each time interval on line 1		0.10	0.20	0.40	0.20	0.10
Probabilities of each time interval on line 2		0.05	0.20	0.50	0.20	0.05
Probabilities of each time interval on line 3		0.10	0.20	0.40	0.20	0.10
Probabilities of each time interval on line 4		0.05	0.10	0.70	0.10	0.05
Rework time (in minutes)	15	20	25	30	35	
Probabilities of each rework time value on line 1	0.10	0.20	0.40	0.20	0.10	
Probabilities of each rework time value on line 2	0.10	0.20	0.40	0.20	0.10	
Probabilities of each rework time value on line 3	0.05	0.20	0.50	0.20	0.05	
Probabilities of each rework time value on line 4	0.05	0.10	0.70	0.10	0.05	

You have chosen to use Monte Carlo simulation as an aid in scheduling labor on *one* of the rework lines. Which of the four lines is the best candidate for Monte Carlo simulation, and why? (Hint: Examine the interactions between time interval and rework time for each line.)

7. The figures below summarize the last 100 hours of service-call requests for the typewriter maintenance department, including translation of frequencies into Monte Carlo numbers. Four random numbers are also shown.

Calls per hour	Frequency	Monte Carlo numbers	Random numbers
0	5	00–04	06 80 49 17
1	40	05–44	
2	55	45–99	

Do a Monte Carlo simulation of service calls using the four random numbers. Assume that you have two repair persons to send on calls. What is the total idle time for repair persons, assuming a fixed one-hour service time for each job?

8. A group of similar machines requires servicing. Preventive maintenance is neither feasible nor economical in this case. Therefore, the problem is to hire that number of repairmen which results in minimizing the sum of the costs of machine idle time and the repairmen's wages. Solve the problem, using Monte Carlo simulation; limit your analysis to about 100 simulated hours. Comment on the validity of your simulation.

Data for solution:

Idle machine time is estimated to cost the company $35 per hour.

The daily wage for one repairman is $36.

Historical data on breakdown frequencies and repair times are as follows:

Breakdowns per hour	Frequency	Probability
0	1,025	0.854
1	156	0.130
2	19	0.016
3 or more	0	0.000
	1,200	1.000

Hours spent on repair	Frequency	Probability
2 or less	0	0.000
3	72	0.072
4	178	0.178
5	281	0.281
6	307	0.307
7	115	0.115
8	47	0.047
9 or more	0	0.000
	1,000	1.000

Suggestion: Set up a simulated logbook. Try simulating one repairman; show the resulting waiting-time costs plus wages for a given number of simulated hours. Then try the same thing for two repairmen, and so on, until the optimal hiring policy is apparent. (No two people should get the same results.)

9. The table below shows the results of a Monte Carlo simulation. Time is in hours. (Assume that the simulation began at hour 00 and ended at hour 32.)

Customer number	Arrival time	Service time	Depart time
1	10	3	13
2	13	5	18
3	17	2	20
4	21	6	27
5	25	5	32

a. What is the average amount of waiting time per eight-hour day if there is just one server?

b. What would the total waiting time be if two customers could be served at once?

10. The table below shows the results of a Monte Carlo simulation.

Customer number	Arrival time	Service time	Depart time
1	1		13
2	13		18
3	17		20
4	21		27
5	25		32

If there is one server, what should be the total of the service-time column (which is now empty)? What is the total customer waiting time?

11. The table below shows the results of a Monte Carlo simulation. The simulated time period is 32 hours, or four working days (from hour 00 to hour 32), and there is a single server.

Customer number	Arrival time	Service time	Depart time
1	10	3	13
2	13	5	18
3	15	2	20
4	21	6	27
5	23	5	32

What is the total waiting-time cost for the simulated period, if the cost of customers waiting is $3.00 per hour? What would the cost be if there were two servers instead of one?

12. A factory has two truck docks. Trucks sometimes have to get into a queue to await their turn in one of the docks. There is talk about adding a third dock to hold down this queuing. A Monte Carlo simulation has been done. Results are given below for one 15-truck simulation run.

Truck	Arrival minute	Enters dock	Service time	Leaves dock
1	30	30	35	65
2	32	32	28	60
3	48	60	30	90
4	62	65	41	106
5	64	90	40	130
6	88	106	43	149
7	95	130	75	205
8	110	149	41	190
9	110	190	50	240
10	142	205	37	242
11	170	240	40	280
12	195	242	68	310
13	199	280	52	332
14	208	310	30	240
15	242	332	58	390

The plant manager feels that there should be enough dock space so that the *average* wait for dock space is less than 30 minutes. Should the third dock be built? Prove your answer by applying the same simulation data to a third dock.

13. Global Trade Center, a massive office complex retains its own elevator maintenance staff so that elevator breakdowns may be repaired fast. Problems occur when several elevators break down at the same time. A Monte Carlo simulation of breakdowns and service times is being performed based on logbook data. Simulated breakdowns and repair times are shown below, along with the random numbers used in their generation:

Breakdown number	Random number	Minutes between breakdowns	Random number	Repair minutes
1	29	50	95	60
2	01	10	55	40
3	97	130	80	50
4	54	80	66	40
5	19	40	95	60
6	08	20	12	10
7	27	50	15	20
8	71	90	89	50
9	36	60	58	40
10	17	40	49	30
11	00	10	95	60
12	03	10	21	20
13	92	120	72	40
14	62	80	66	40
15	48	70	64	40

a. Complete the Monte Carlo simulation by setting up a simulated logbook. (The instructor may direct that some of the class base the simulation on the first eight breakdowns, others on the first nine, others on the first ten, and so on.) Assume that the repair crew can work on only one elevator at a time. What is the mean number of elevators that are out of service?

b. Determine the average number of minutes that an out-of-service elevator waits for repair to begin.

c. Determine the percent of utilization (percent of the time busy) for the elevator repair crew.

d. The busy period for Global Trade Center's elevators is the ten-hour period from 7:30 A.M. to 5:30 P.M. Is your simulation of 15 (or fewer) breakdowns adequate to provide statistics good enough for the maintenance manager to make staffing decisions? Explain.

e. To the best of your ability, reconstruct Monte Carlo number ranges and probabilities that fit the breakdown and service-time data for the given 15 simulated breakdowns. Also, estimate mean time between breakdowns and mean time to repair. With the difference in means, how do you explain the average waiting time statistic that you obtained in part *b?*

14. Repeat parts *a, b,* and *c* in problem 13, except assume that two repair crews are available.

15. The maintenance staff of the local office of Aquarius Computers completes trouble-call maintenance at the rate of about three per day, but the exact number of completions varies above and below three. Jobs not completed on one day are delayed until the next. The pattern of variability, taken from maintenance logbooks, is given below:

Daily job completion rate	Probability
1	0.05
2	0.15
3	0.50
4	0.20
5	0.10

The same logbooks also contain enough data to show the frequency of trouble calls per day. This is shown below:

Daily number of trouble calls	Probability
0	0.12
1	0.16
2	0.18
3	0.25
4	0.20
5	0.09
	1.00

  a. Use Monte Carlo simulation to determine the average number of jobs delayed until the next day. Simulate for ten days only. (Each student should get a different answer based on different random numbers.)

  b. What other useful statistics may be obtained from your simulation? Provide two other such statistics, and explain their significance.

  c. Could queuing formulas be used in this problem? Discuss fully.

16. The following are service-center situations where queuing formulas or Monte Carlo simulation *could* be used. For each situation, what value *to management* would there be (if any) in doing a waiting-line study using either method? Explain.

  Light bulbs burn out at random in a large building, and maintenance gets calls to replace them.

  Sears, Roebuck operates small appliance repair centers around the country.

  The San Francisco-Oakland Bay Bridge has a large number of toll booths staffed by humans.

  An attorney's office has 30 attorneys who receive large numbers of clients, all on an appointment basis.

17. Sometimes queuing formulas yield fairly accurate information on average waiting time to receive a service. Other times queuing formulas are not so accurate, and we resort to a more expensive Monte Carlo simulation. Of the following six situations, which would the queuing formulas be reasonable for, and what queuing formula would you use? For which situations would Monte Carlo simulation be preferable? Explain your answers.

  A public health nurse is inoculating large numbers of people for a new strain of Asian flu. There is one helper to make sure sleeves are rolled up, etc.

  Airline passengers returning from a foreign country line up to go through customs.

  Thread breakages occur periodically on any of 500 spinning machines in a fabric mill, and the breakage automatically turns on a flashing light to summon a repair person.

  Students go to make copies on a self-service copier in the dormitory.

  Customers bring telephone sets to the phone center for repairs.

  Season ticket holders arrive at the metropolitan dome for a sports event and line up to have their tickets taken.

18. Human customers line up for services of all kinds in our society. Name *four* actions that can be taken by management to hold down the waiting lines. Explain.

19. The reference librarian at city library is using a log book (below) to keep track of patrons who get help at the reference desk. Her log book entries for two hours are given below. (These hours, 8–10 P.M., are slack periods and are singled out for separate study.) The entries show times when patrons arrive to line up at the desk, when they ask their reference question, and when they leave.

Log book data

Patron number	Patron arrives (minute)	Asks question (minute)	Leaves (minute)		Frequency distributions (tally marks)		
						IAT	Service time
1	8:00	8:00	8:06				
2	8:04	8:06	8:15				
3	8:09	8:15	8:17		0	||	
4	8:18	8:18	8:22		1		||
5	8:21	8:22	8:27		2	|	|||
6	8:27	8:27	8:29		3	||	
7	8:29	8:29	8:35		4	|||	|
8	8:33	8:35	8:40		5	||	||
9	8:33	8:40	8:42		6	||	||
10	8:41	8:42	8:49		7		|
11	8:47	8:49	8:50		8	|	|
12	8:50	8:50	8:58		9	|	|
13	8:55	8:55	8:56		10		
14	8:59	8:59	9:11		11		
15	9:09	9:11	9:14		12		|
16	9:10	9:14	9:15				
17	9:11	9:15	9:17				
18	9:15	9:17	9:20				
19	9:18	9:20	9:24				
20	9:25	9:25	9:26				
21	9:27	9:27	9:32				
22	9:30	9:32	9:38				
23	9:36	9:38	9:39				
24	9:39	9:39	9:46				
25	9:47	9:47	9:48				
26	9:49	9:49	9:53				
27	9:52	9:53	9:59				
28	9:52	9:59	10:05				
29	9:58	10:05	10:07				

The librarian is using the data to create the interarrival (IAT) distribution and the service-time distribution next to the log-book data. But she is only about half done—down through patron 14.

a. Complete the two distributions (i.e., insert the tally marks for patron numbers 15–29). What is the most common interarrival time, and how many cases of it were there in the two-hour period?

b. It was a hot day when the data were collected. In fact many of the reference questions that were answered in only one or two minutes were, "Where's the drinking fountain?"

Do you think more data should be collected in order to do a Monte Carlo simulation? If so, give your suggestions about further data collection?

c. What purpose would a Monte Carlo simulation serve?

20. Students at Southern Quebec University are heading for the Champlain Hall cafeteria for lunch, which is served from 11:00 A.M. to 1:30 P.M. A waiting line study is in progress, and the study leader argues that there is no need to gather arrival data. He says, "Students will arrive and line up for lunch service according to the Poisson distribution." Is the study leader right? Explain.

Chapter 18

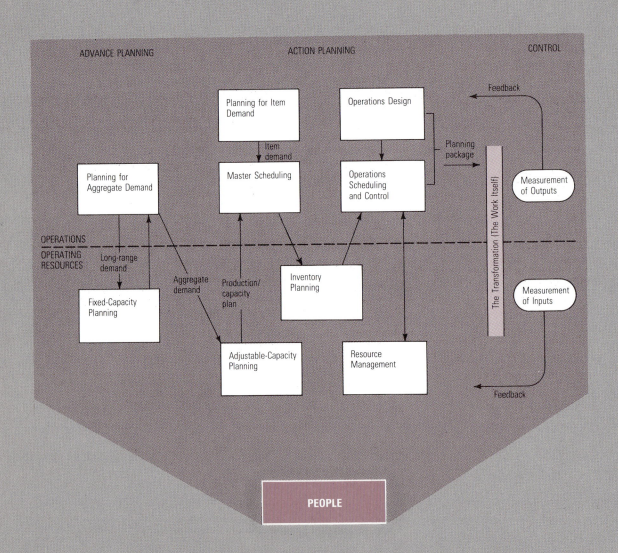

ADVANCE PLANNING   ACTION PLANNING   CONTROL

Feedback

Planning for Item Demand

Operations Design

Planning package

Planning for Aggregate Demand

Item demand

Master Scheduling

Operations Scheduling and Control

Measurement of Outputs

OPERATIONS

OPERATING RESOURCES

Long-range demand

Aggregate demand

Production/ capacity plan

Inventory Planning

The Transformation (The Work Itself)

Measurement of Inputs

Fixed-Capacity Planning

Adjustable-Capacity Planning

Resource Management

Feedback

PEOPLE

Work and People

The optimists among us see signs that we are on the threshold of a new era in managing the human element of operations. The era, if indeed it comes to pass, promises action rather than just lip service to the ideal of an *involved work force*.

What is meant by this term? Ideally, it describes a work force involved in problem solving, innovating, decision making, communicating, and preserving and strengthening the capacity to produce—involved, in short, in *management*.

751

INVOLVEMENT AS AN IDEAL

Involvement hasn't always been recognized as a top-priority ideal. Over the years we have heard more about the need for *motivated* and *respected* workers than involved ones. But we cannot presume that workers who are treated with respect and are motivated to work hard are also going to be involved. If there are already plenty of managers and staff experts to do the innovating, communicating, and so forth, there is that much less for the wage-earner to become involved in.

Overmanagement

Take the typical large company or governmental agency, for example. Inspectors from the quality control department are relied on to improve quality. Buyers from purchasing search for the right materials. Maintenance people from plant engineering keep the facilities in working order. Industrial engineers design the production system and work flow. This goes on and on. Little is left for the people at the work site to do besides crank out Big Macs, widgets, served patrons, or documents.

Reich feels that the recent era of human-social management did little to improve this state of affairs:

> Specialists in organization development swarmed over the workplace, conducting encounter groups and "sensitivity-training" sessions. Industrial psychologists provided group counseling and programs of "job enrichment." Some companies instituted collaborative teams and "quality circles" within which workers could offer ideas for improving productivity—so long as they refrained from challenging the structure of authority in the enterprise. Management consultants espoused "Theory Y" or, better still, "Theory Z." But these factory-tested techniques for making workers feel better simply constructed a facade of workplace collaboration. The distinction between thinkers and doers remained intact.[1]

To make things worse, a central feature of our management approach is to have material control fill empty spaces with stock so that when things go wrong, and many, many things always go wrong, most machines keep humming and most workers keep cranking. Problems are hidden under the excesses. Furthermore, the stocks of materials serve to divide the plant into separate islands of production so that production workers feel little task dependency or need to be concerned with problems other than their own. In that environment, even if enlightened management has nurtured a climate of high motivation and humanity, worker involvement is likely to be slight and the rate of productivity and quality improvement is likely to be modest.

Overspecialization, overplanning, overcontrol, and overmanagement seem to be common characteristics of the recent era. A series of videotapes developed by the Automotive Industry Action Group offers statistics:[2] We have 12 times as many

---

[1] Robert B. Reich, *The New American Frontier* (New York: Times Books, 1983), p. 75 (JK467.R45).

[2] "The Japanese Approach to Productivity," set of four videotapes, Automotive Industry Action Group, Detroit, 1983.

accountants and 10 times as many attorneys per capita as the Japanese do. One of the moderators of the videotape series is Len Ricard, a General Motors vice president. Ricard states that GM has five times as many people in production and materials management staff positions per direct laborer as Toyota does. "They have no expediters," says Ricard. "We have thousands."

Expediters are just one type of specialist. Their job is firefighting, and they have neither time nor responsibility to deal with underlying causes. To some extent, if underlying causes were eliminated, expediters would no longer be needed. That is partly a *dis*incentive to solve problems. And so it is, more or less, with people in data processing, personnel, material handling, customer claims and warranties, inspection, maintenance, and other staff support areas.

With so many staff specialists doing the planning and controlling, there is little left for operating people to become involved in. The operating people are in a position of dependency—like a young child is to its parent. It is little wonder that our workers were rebellious in the 1960s and 1970s, even though Western management massively underwent schooling in the principles of good human relations and the participatory leadership style. We have long *known* that these ideas are sound. But we could not really apply them in the typical environment of excess staff, excess stock, excess space, and decoupled tasks.

New Climate

Conditions are changing. In steel, autos, farm machinery, airlines, appliances, construction, state government, education, and many other industries, work forces have been slashed. In some cases the biggest cuts have been in the staff specialties. In the first half of this decade many plants were closed, and pay cuts of up to 50 percent (for example, Continental Airlines) were imposed on remaining employees.

Besides the staff reductions, pay cuts, and plant closings, three other forces for change have been noticeable:

1. The latest "people" programs and quality-of-work-life programs seem more genuine than similar efforts in the past. There seems to be a real determination, at least in some companies, to break out of the us-against-them relationship between management and labor. Employee stock ownership plans provide glue that helps to bond the interests of the two groups in General Motors, American Airlines, and many other companies. Perhaps both sides, labor and management, are coming together out of fear. Whatever the reason, the change is positive and strong.

2. New deep-seated commitments to quality. Top officials of many of our blue-chip companies have soaked up days worth of education in statistical quality control and related concepts. Most of these are financial and marketing people, who are not at all inclined by education or experience to have an interest in quality assurance. The heart of the message they hear is "quality at the source," which means heavy involvement in quality control by the production employees and process control at the workplace—rather than reliance upon staff experts in a quality department.

3. Large reductions in lot sizes and buffer stocks. These cuts come in small increments, but they add up fast. Each cut means that problems like poor worker training or undependable machines must be addressed.

Demographic Effects

Part of the reason for our unfortunate recent experience with excessive specialization may be traced to demographics. In the 1960s there were too few educated people chasing too many management and professional jobs in an expanding economy. The financially oriented MBAs graduating from the business schools, for example, were snapped up at high salaries and they shot up the promotional ladders with hardly a sideways glance. That is to say, they did not need to stray out of their chosen specialties to learn other sides of the business, such as quality control, marketing, and production.

In the 1970s things changed. The post-World War II baby boom entered the labor market. (The U.S. had a 13-year baby boom; Japan had virtually none.) By the end of the decade these baby-boomers had filled in the cracks in the labor market. Bloated entry-level salaries and quick promotions are no longer the norms. Young people, if they want to advance, have to accept laterals, which means being assigned to different functions at no pay increase. Lateral assignments broaden one's understanding of the business, which is an excellent way for people to gain perspective in order to be able to make decisions for the good of the *whole*. And, of course, it is an ideal way to groom people for upper management. Finally, it helps fashion *generalists,* who should not be so quick to do all of the staff work themselves, but who may be comfortable seeking the involvement of others.

THE INVOLVED WORKER

The office, shop, restaurant, hotel, or clinic employee who is involved may realize a new set of work-related satisfactions. One is the satisfaction of accomplishment. An employee who charts quality and removes special causes of inconsistency surely feels a greater sense of accomplishment than one who has merely met or exceeded a quota. The same goes for the line worker who repairs a machine on the spot, recommends a product design improvement, helps train a new worker, works with an engineer on a machine modification, cuts machine setup time, or develops part of the plans for changing the layout.

A second source of satisfaction is in being the one "doing the telling" instead of the one "being told" all of the time. The line worker in a climate of frugality has to get problems solved quickly, and that often means *summoning* help from a highly paid expert. It's nice to be the one doing the summoning for a change.

A third type of satisfaction comes from seeing that one's employer is using the experience and mental capabilities of its work force to strengthen its competitiveness and provide better job security. Veterans in many North American companies can point to past efforts to involve production workers but with little to show for the efforts. Managers become skeptical of the abilities of labor to contribute, and labor may doubt its own abilities to do so. But the past efforts did not involve squeezing out the excesses. The necessity for involvement was not present, and it is frustrating, not satisfying, for production workers to try to help when the work environment still encourages their helplessness.

When employees become involved, opportunities open up for judging the real worth of people. At Honda every employee is rated annually on such things as problem-solving contributions. This is common enough in Western companies for *salaried* people but rare for shop-floor workers. When the management system fails to involve everyone in problem solving, the company lacks a good basis for rewarding people. It falls back on inadequate measures of worth, such as attendance and output.

Output is inadequate? Yes! Compared with using one's mind—and experience, talent, and initiative—to solve problems, output seems less important. Who is more valuable, the typist who types 30 words per minute and also composes letters, or the one who goes at 50 words per minute but only types? The boss might appreciate the first typist. But the boss must create a climate in which there is the need—and the opportunity—for that typist's letter-writing talents to thrive also. The owners of a bottling plant would similarly value the plant worker who can figure out ways to rapidly change over from one soft drink to another or to modify the equipment to prevent defects like overfilling, underfilling, crooked labels, and broken bottles. But the management system in the bottling plant must encourage, not discourage, these contributions.

Innovativeness is probably not found widely among the populace. But mental and problem-solving activities are not limited to innovations. There may be equal value in communication skills, leadership, enthusiasm, and commitment. In a work group, people with these attributes nicely complement the talents of the innovators. At employee evaluation time a variety of mental traits and talents may be recognized as valuable. The pats, strokes, awards, pay increases, bonuses, and so forth should go to workers who make those kinds of contributions.

EXPERTS ON CALL

"Oh, good! Here comes the efficiency expert. We need him to come up with a way to improve the equipment so that it produces fewer defectives."

Does that sound like what you might hear a production worker say? Hardly. The efficiency expert is as welcome as a popsicle in a blizzard. At least that is the norm in our typical work environment where production employees are expected only to chunk out parts. The efficiency expert just raises the standard of performance.

But in a climate where quality is a top priority, where problems are deliberately exposed via inventory removal and space denial, and where staff specialists are scarce, the efficiency expert—or, more properly, the industrial engineer—may be quite welcome. In a healthy work environment, experts who can fix a machine, make a tool, provide training, analyze a chemical anomaly, and so forth, are equally welcome.

In fact, when workers get fired up to make improvements, they may actively *seek* expert help. In just-in-time plants, when machines are broken down, parts are defective, or other problems cause a work stoppage, the operator may want experts to come on the run.

Being in demand is an unfamiliar role for our staff support people. They are used to "selling" people on the need for their services. Staff people have never enjoyed that role. They always wished that others would appreciate them, welcome them, work with them, and thank them. Thus an environment of involved workers and supervisors enlisting the aid of staff experts can be satisfying for the experts, too.

EXPERIMENTS IN PROCESS IMPROVEMENT

When problems crop up, the people on the floor should be the first to try to solve the problems and should call on experts for the tougher ones. But involvement should go farther than that. Instead of having the workers and supervisors waiting for problems, the management system should induce them to *prevent* problems before they surface and to continually *improve the process.*

Prevention is active rather than passive. A key to operating in the prevention mode is trying things out and seeing what works best. We call this conducting an experiment. It is done in our development labs all of the time. Experiments are also done in the work place, but not very systematically and not often.

We need to make our work places "experimental laboratories," as Hall puts it.[3] The lab people experiment with products; the operating people should experiment with *processes;* and combined product-process experiments are often needed as well. Lab experiments are sometimes elaborate with inferential statistical analysis used to evaluate data. The same kinds of experimental designs sometimes make sense for process analysis. But often a process experiment may be simple. The simplest approach is just to periodically record what is going on, usually in basic terms right in the work place: Plot the production rates and defect rates, perhaps hourly, keep a record or checkoff sheet on preventive maintenance and subsequent machine failures, record the problem each time there is a work stoppage. By observing the trends, the people on the floor can often surmise the cause.

As consumers of human services, we are all familiar with attempts to find out what we think of the way that the service was offered: the form in the restaurant or hotel inviting us to give an opinion about the service; the occasional questionnaire we receive in the mail asking if the telephone installation or the insurance claim service met our expectations; even the question, "Was everything all right?" by the person at the cash register in the restaurant.

These are weak and rather inconclusive ways to test a service procedure, though they are surely better than nothing. A stronger approach is to change something and immediately obtain a proper sample of consumer opinions. Which should the airline flight attendants do first, pour more coffee or pick up the food trays? (Heavy coffee drinkers want more coffee; fast eaters want their trays taken away.) Try it

---

[3] Robert W. Hall, *Zero Inventories* (Homewood, Ill.: Dow Jones-Irwin, 1983), p. 165.

both ways and systematically ask a predetermined sample from each group for their reactions. Should the bank provide a way to channel everyone into a single waiting line, or let patrons form lines at each teller station? Again, try it both ways and ask a predetermined sample for their reactions. And one more example: Suppose that the company mail room sometimes has complaints about special-delivery or express mail not getting to the right person fast. Part of the mail room's problem is that the person may be in a meeting, on a trip, or elsewhere when the delivery attempt is made. As a test, the mail people might leave a one-question survey card, along with the mail, to find out what time the addressee actually received the mail. If the results are not good, then try another way to deliver or to notify.

BROADENED EDUCATION AND RESEARCH

Perhaps it is time for management and professional educators and researchers to join with industry in changing course. Specialism has failed, and our training and education agents must reappraise our system of turning out people whose talents lie in ever-narrowing specialties.

Perhaps it should become rare in business for someone to spend an entire working life as a tax accountant, a machine-shop supervisor, a buyer, a truck dispatcher, or a scheduler. People's capacity to solve problems and make decisions for the good of the whole plant, office, agency, or business depends on growth of their understanding of the *broad effects of local changes*. As business gradually converts itself to this way of thinking, there should be less reliance on staff specialty departments, because plenty of people with breadth of understanding will be sprinkled around the organization. Those people should have the confidence to decide and to act on their own.

This swing toward broader management and professional development matches other movements, especially the quality, just-in-time, and involvement movements. All of these changes in course include shifting responsibilities to the line operators and supervisors, who can take action faster, generally less expensively, and often with superior results.

Generalism in Higher Education

The business and professional schools in North America, for all their faults, have been more responsive to business needs than schools in most other countries. When industry needed marketing people to sell excess capacity in the 1960s, the business schools churned out marketing experts. When the United States felt threatened by the Soviet Union's successful launching of Sputnik in 1957, our colleges helped industry respond by graduating greater numbers of engineers and scientists.

The new challenge for higher education is to produce college graduates who have breadth. Perhaps our graduating electrical and chemical engineers should learn something about manufacturing and data processing; our marketing people should learn something about accounting and operations management; and so forth.

But wait a minute. Aren't our engineering and business schools already requiring sets of core courses to give people some exposure to the other functions? Sure they are. But each course taken is a specialty course. To expect that 5 or 10 specialty courses, each with its own jargon and body of research, will add up to breadth of understanding is wishful thinking. Here is where changes in the course of research enter in.

Integrated Research

Research for business and industry takes many shapes and forms, and there are lots of ways to categorize it. For our purposes, let's slice it into two types: research on the human element and research on the rest.

The rest includes jobs, schedules, strategies, information system, plant, equipment, materials, and tools. An underlying assumption in the research on how to manage these nonhuman factors is that a *planning* approach is good, and a reacting (firefighting) approach is not so good. (For example, expediters are frowned upon in our planning-based theories of production management.) Yet in a sense the highly effective techniques of just-in-time production and total quality control seem to be reactionary: Solve problems in the work place as they occur. This is in contrast to our traditional planning approaches: Plan for permanent countermeasures, such as staffs of inspectors, rework crews, setup crews, maintenance crews, material controllers, operations researchers, and data processors. But the experts who plan the countermeasures get out of touch with reality, and the countermeasures become costly and ineffective. The researchers end up testing one poor planning system against another.

Our prescriptions for managing the human element haven't worked well either. Our behavioral research mostly backs up our natural feelings that treating people well and encouraging worker participation and involvement is the best way. And we have massively trained our managers in these concepts. Yet often they do not seem to heed the advice.

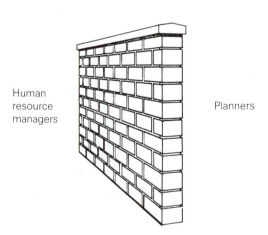

Human
resource
managers

Planners

What has gone wrong? Perhaps the planning research, and therefore our planning systems, have had a planning fixation. That is, in our nonhuman-factor research, we have taken it as a given that planning our way around problems is inherently good. Furthermore, we assume that our planners are capable of developing or finding an effective plan for any situation.

Similarly, our human-factor research has had a human fixation: Experimentally check out worker reactions to supervisory actions, and draw conclusions. The nonhuman factors like materials, product specifications, space, schedules, and accounting systems receive little attention when the research fixes on the human elements. The assumption is that if people can only be motivated, they will do their jobs well; the hope is that that will translate into good management of the nonhuman factors.

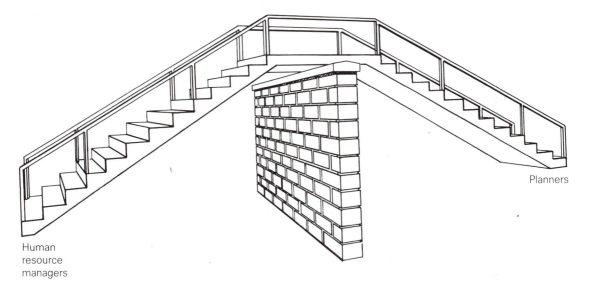

Planners

Human
resource
managers

We need to broaden both classes of research. The human element and the nonhuman elements need to blend together in our research.[4] (It may be hard to do, because it means controlling more factors. But that doesn't negate the need.) Since our colleges teach what the researchers come up with, broader research should broaden *each* of our course offerings. That is, students should hear about effects on workers when they study operations management, engineering, accounting, and so forth—because each of these has considerable effects on people's behaviors. And students studying how people tick should learn about how they behave in a *system* that induces them to take the initiative—to inspect their own work, to summon the experts for assistance, to make in small instead of large lots, etc. Then learn about the very different behaviors

---

[4] There is a class of research called socio-technical research. A few promising experiments in the 1960s at the Tavistock Institute in the United Kingdom helped launch the socio-technical movement. Socio-technical research survives, but it has not lived up to its promise. Perhaps the experiments have used the term, socio-technical, but have in fact separately treated the social and technical factors.

that emerge from a system of excess resources, reliance on experts, complex controls, and low involvement.

The bridge between the planning and the human approaches has always been there. All of us—researchers, teachers, students, practitioners—need to make the commitment to walk across that bridge.

SUMMARY

A new era of worker involvement in management seems to be dawning. More than mere participation, involvement means workers and supervisors solving many problems on the spot. The staff experts then are on call. They help with tough problems instead of trying to plan for all contingencies, handle all problems.

We see signs of the new era in many industries. Quality-of-work-life, total quality-control, and just-in-time programs are catching on widely, and each brings workers into the problem-solving arena.

Overuse of specialists came about in the 1950s and 1960s partly because there were too few college graduates chasing too many jobs in an expanding economy. Now there is a large baby-boom population clogging lower management levels in business and industry. They will have to take laterals and learn the business since promotions upward in narrow specialties no longer are common.

Involvement in problem solving is likely to provide greater satisfaction for workers and supervisors. The staff experts (whose numbers may decrease) may also be more satisfied, because they are responding to need rather than trying to convince people of their worth. In the new era, workers as well as managers and experts, can be evaluated for *mental* contributions.

The new era transforms the workplace into a laboratory for process experiments. Experiments may be as simple as recording problems and output rates and making inferences about causes. There may also be formal experiments based on trying out a new process and observing the effects.

Our education and training approaches need to shift toward developing generalists who will have the confidence to recommend or make decisions for the benefit of the *whole* organization. It is not enough for our colleges to require introductory courses in many specialties. The need is for a broader message in every course. That means that the research backing up each specialty course needs to be broadened. More specifically, our behavioral research should focus on the way the people behave in different systems of managing the nonhuman factors such as materials, schedules, space, and product designs. And our planning research should confront the effects excessive planning has on people.

REFERENCES

Books

Emery, F. E., ed. *Systems Thinking.* New York: Penguin Books, 1969 (includes articles on socio-technical systems).

Reich, Robert B. *The Next American Frontier.* New York: Times Books, 1983 (JK467.R45).

REVIEW QUESTIONS

1. What is an *involved* worker?

2. In what sense have our workers generally been over-managed?

3. What recent forces are leading to increased worker involvement?

4. How have population trends affected the roles of specialists?

5. In the "new era" how will workers feel about their jobs? How will the staff experts feel about theirs?

6. Is it practical to judge line workers on their *mental* contributions? Discuss.

7. While experiments in product improvements are common, experiments in *process* improvement have been rare. Is this a permanent condition? Explain.

8. Explain the need for generalists. Is the need likely to be fulfilled? Why or why not?

9. Is it practical to develop generalists by giving people schooling in each of the specialties? Discuss.

10. What new directions in research and education go along with the worker-involvement movement? Discuss.

PROBLEMS

1. The following are things that might happen in the work life of a production employee. Which are examples of "participation," and which are examples of "involvement"? Explain your choices.

    Your boss asks you for suggestions on vacation policies for the department.

    Meet with a sales representative of a container seller to see if they sell a plastic container that would fit the handling needs in your shop.

    Stop production in order to avoid making a string of bad parts.

    Inform the boss whenever the equipment doesn't sound right.

    You and the rest of your work crew hold meetings to plan the Christmas party.

    You and the rest of your work crew hold a meeting every Friday afternoon to decide who will staff which work station for the next week.

2. There was a shortage of M.D.s and dentists in the 1960s (but now there is an oversupply of dentists and no more overall shortage of M.D.s). Compare these trends with trends in employment of staff specialists in business and industry.

3. Here are five kinds of staff specialists: quality control inspectors, material handlers, industrial engineers, tool makers, and machine oilers. For which *three* of these specialists should there be less need in an environment of worker involvement? Why? Why would the need for the other two kinds continue?

4. Lone Star Manufacturing Co. near Fort Worth, Texas, is a manufacturer of auto air conditioners. One of its assembly areas had been served by 22 inspectors from the quality

assurance (QA) department. In a reorganization, all 22 were moved out of QA and into new positions as assemblers. What do you think the short- and long-term effects of this change will be on (1) the former inspectors? (2) the professionals who remain in the QA department? (3) the quality of the assembled products?

5. At one just-in-time company, shop-floor employees write up one- or two-page descriptions of how they do their jobs, and they handle the training of others in their work group in how to do the same job, so that each employee is multifunctional. Is this consistent with the trend toward worker involvement? What staff specialists are affected, and how?

6. Psychologist B. F. Skinner's reinforcement principle is that a person tends to repeat an act if the person is rewarded soon after the act. Based on that principle, what can we predict about worker behaviors when the system induces workers to be involved in problem solving?

7. Pay and promotion for production employees may be based on hours, output against standard, how much profit the company made, difficulty of the job, and problem-solving activities (to name a few). Which is the *fairest* way? Which is the most *effective* way? Discuss.

8. Labor unions that negotiated contracts calling for rigid work rules in an earlier decade are now accepting relaxation of those rules. Explain how each of the following is related to the work-rules issue.

    State of the economy.

    Competitive needs for better quality.

    Traditional notions of fair pay.

    Just-in-time production.

    Roles of the personnel department.

    Trend toward broader knowledge among staff specialists and managers.

9. Think of each of the following three cases as experimental process laboratories; suggest a simple but effective experiment for *two* of the three.

    Your library.

    Your favorite restaurant.

    The custodial crew in a building that you frequent.

10. All of the classes that you enroll in are experimental process laboratories: The instructor is always trying out instructional ideas to see how they work. What do you think could be done to make such experiments more effective? Restrict your answer to 100 words.

11. What is the fallacy of our planners (and planning researchers) in assuming that they *can* and *will* find a plan that works? What is the fallacy of our human resources managers (and researchers) in assuming that a motivated employee will be an effective one?

Index

This book has been set CAP in 10 and 9 point Times Roman, leaded 2 points. Part and chapter numbers are 36 point Spectra Light. Part and chapter titles are 20 point Spectra. The size of the type page is 36 by 47 picas.